SAS/GRAPH® Software:
Reference
Volume 2

Version 6
First Edition

SAS Institute Inc.
SAS Campus Drive
Cary, NC 27513

The correct bibliographic citation for this manual is as follows: SAS Institute Inc., *SAS/GRAPH® Software: Reference, Version 6, First Edition, Volume 2,* Cary, NC: SAS Institute Inc., 1990. 664 pp.

SAS/GRAPH® Software: Reference, Version 6, First Edition, Volume 2

Contents

Illustrations

Figures

Tables

x

SAS/GRAPH® Procedures

PART *6*

738

CHAPTER 22 The GANNO Procedure

Overview

The GANNO procedure displays the output from Annotate data sets. It ignores all currently defined titles and footnotes and some graphics options. It is used when you want to display only Annotate data set output. The GSLIDE procedure can also display the graphics created by Annotate data sets; however, the GSLIDE procedure includes all footnotes and titles as well as graphics options. Refer to Chapter 37, "The GSLIDE Procedure," for examples of graphics output created with Annotate data sets and displayed with the GSLIDE procedure.

In addition, the GANNO procedure can scale data-dependent output to fit in the graphics output area. This means that if you are using a data coordinate system and the data values are so large that some of the graphics elements do not fit in the graphics output area and are not displayed, you can use the GANNO procedure with the DATASYS option to scale the output to fit the available space. The GSLIDE procedure does not have this capability.

Output 22.1 and Output 22.2 are both generated from the same Annotate data set with the same TITLE definitions and graphics options in effect. However, Output 22.1 was produced by the GANNO procedure so the TITLE statements and the BORDER graphics option are ignored.* Output 22.2 was produced with the GSLIDE procedure and the titles and the border are displayed. The footnote for both of these examples was produced with the Annotate facility. If the information had been specified in a FOOTNOTE statement, it would not have appeared on the GANNO procedure output shown in Output 22.1.

---

* In Output 22.1, the box around the graph denotes the edge of the picture, not a border produced by the GOPTIONS procedure.

Output 22.1 Using the
GANNO Procedure to Display
Annotate Graphics (GR22N01)

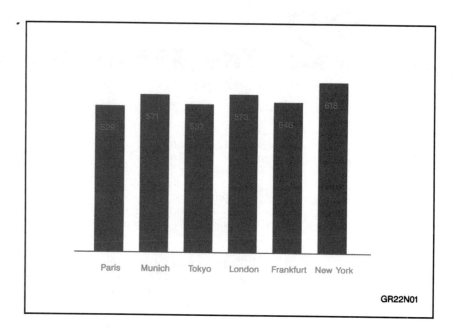

Output 22.2 Using the
GSLIDE Procedure to Display
Annotate Graphics (GR22N02)

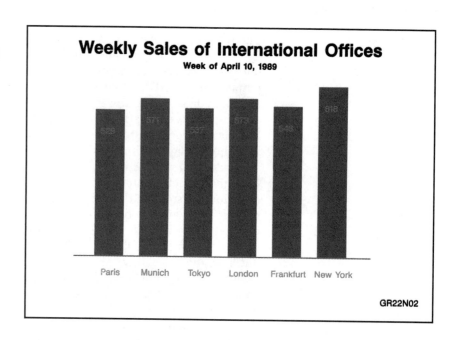

GANNO
Procedure
Syntax

The GANNO procedure uses the following statement:

PROC GANNO ANNOTATE=*Annotate-data-set*
       <DATASYS>
       <DESCRIPTION='*string*'>
       <GOUT=*output-catalog*>
       <NAME='*string*' | *variable-name*>;

Options are fully described in "Options" later in this chapter.

GANNO Procedure Description

You can use the GANNO procedure to display graphs created by Annotate data sets. By default, the GANNO procedure scales graphics output from the data set to fill the entire graphics area. Procedure statement options enable you to

□ scale output that uses absolute or relative data-dependent coordinates

□ produce a graph for each unique value of a specified variable

□ specify a catalog in which to store the output

□ assign a name to identify the graph in the catalog

□ assign a description for the graph in the catalog.

Terminology

The following terms are used in the discussion of the GANNO procedure and are defined in the Glossary:

absolute coordinates

axis

BY variable

coordinate system

coordinates

graphics element

graphics output

graphics output area

procedure output area

relative coordinates

string

Several of these terms are illustrated in Figure 2.3 in Chapter 2, "Running SAS/GRAPH Programs."

PROC GANNO Statement

The PROC GANNO statement starts the procedure and names the Annotate data set to be used as input. It can optionally specify a destination catalog for graphics output, as well as scale the output to accommodate data-dependent coordinate values.

Requirements

The GANNO procedure must specify an input Annotate data set. The ANNOTATE= argument is required.

ANNOTATE=*Annotate-data-set*
ANNO=*Annotate-data-set*
  specifies a data set that includes Annotate variables identifying graphics commands and parameters. See Chapter 18, "The Annotate Data Set," for details.

Options

You can use the following options with the PROC GANNO statement:

DATASYS
  indicates that Annotate data-dependent coordinates occur in the input data set, and scales the coordinates in the data set to fit the graphics output area. It is used only with input data sets that specify the values '1', '2', '7', or '8' with the coordinate system variables XSYS, YSYS, and HSYS.

(DATASYS continued)

You use the DATASYS option when graphics elements that were created with data-dependent variables do not fit in the graphics output area. This happens when the coordinate values generated by the data exceed a range of 0 to 100. When the DATASYS option is used, the GANNO procedure reads the entire input data set before drawing the graph and creates an output environment that is data dependent; that is, the environment is based on the minimum and maximum values contained in the data set. It then scales the data to fit this environment so that all graphics elements can be drawn.

If you do not use the DATASYS option, the GANNO procedure attempts to draw each graphics element according to the data values assigned to it without scaling the values. If the range of data values is too large, some graphics elements are not displayed.

See "Scaling Data-dependent Output with the DATASYS Option" later in this chapter for details.

DESCRIPTION=*'string'*
DES=*'string'*

specifies a descriptive string, up to 40 characters long, that appears in the Description field of the catalog entry for the picture. The description does not appear on the picture. By default, the GANNO procedure assigns the description OUTPUT FROM PROC GANNO.

GOUT=*output-catalog*

specifies the SAS catalog in which to save the graphics output produced by the procedure for later replay. You can use the GREPLAY procedure to view the graphs stored in the catalog. If you do not use the GOUT= option, catalog entries are written to the default catalog WORK.GSEG, which is erased at the end of your session.

NAME=*'string'* | *variable-name*

specifies one of the following:

☐ a string for the name that appears in the catalog entry for the graph

☐ a variable name for each value for which a separate graph is produced.

If the value you assign to the NAME= option is enclosed in quotes, the procedure interprets it as a catalog entry name; if the value is not enclosed in quotes, the procedure interprets it as a variable name.

The value *'string'* specifies a text string of up to eight characters that appears in the Name field of the catalog entry for the picture. The default name is GANNO. If either the name specified or the default name duplicate an existing name in the catalog, then SAS/GRAPH software adds a number to the duplicate name to create a unique name, for example, GANNO2.

If you specify *variable-name*, the GANNO procedure produces a separate graph for each different value of that variable. *Variable-name* must be a valid SAS name. In addition, when you specify NAME=*variable-name*, each value of the variable is used as the name stored in the Name field of the catalog entry for the graph. Consequently, you cannot use NAME=*'string'* at the same time.

Note: Specifying NAME=*variable-name* in the PROC GANNO statement produces results similar to those produced by the BY statement in a procedure that supports BY-group processing. For details, see Chapter 10, "The BY Statement."

Using the GANNO Procedure

The following section explains the effect of the DATASYS option.

Using the DATASYS Option to Scale Graphs

If your Annotate data set specifies a coordinate system that is based on data values (that is, XSYS, YSYS, and HSYS are assigned the values '1', '2', '7', or '8'), your output is drawn using data values to determine the size and location of the graphics elements.

If the procedure that specifies the annotation generates axes (such as GPLOT or GCHART), by default the axes are scaled to accommodate the full range of data values and to fit in the procedure output area. Because all values are included in the axes, all the Annotate output that is dependent on data values is displayed.

However, if the annotation is displayed with the GSLIDE or GANNO procedure, which do not generate axes, the data values may generate coordinate values that exceed the limits of the graphics output area. In this case, you can use the DATASYS option to tell the procedure that the Annotate data set contains data-dependent coordinates and to scale the output accordingly. For an illustration of this process, see "Scaling Data-dependent Output with the DATASYS Option" in "Examples" later in this chapter.

Although the DATASYS option enables you to generate graphs using one of the data-dependent coordinate systems, it requires that the procedure scan the entire data set to determine the minimum and maximum data values. You can save this extra pass of the data set by using data-dependent values only in procedures that generate axes. Annotate coordinate system '5' (percent of the procedure output area) is recommended for use with the GANNO procedure. This coordinate system works equally well with the GSLIDE procedure if you decide to display the annotation with titles and footnotes.

Examples

The following examples illustrate some of the features of the GANNO procedure.

Displaying Annotate Graphics

In this example, the GANNO procedure displays graphics output that is generated by commands in an Annotate data set and stores the output as a catalog entry in an output catalog. The output consists of four colored squares that are displayed as a single graphics output. In this example, the NAME= option specifies the name that is stored with the graphics output in the catalog. The following program statements produce Output 22.3:

```
   /* create Annotate data set */
data squares;
   length function style color $ 8;
   xsys='5'; ysys='5';
   style='solid';

      /* draw first square */
   color='blue';
```

```
                          function='move'; x=10; y=10; output;
                          function='bar';  x=30; y=40; output;

                             /* draw second square */
                          color='gray';
                          function='move'; x=60; y=10; output;
                          function='bar';  x=80; y=40; output;

                             /* draw third square */
                          color='green';
                          function='move'; x=10; y=60; output;
                          function='bar';  x=30; y=90; output;

                             /* draw fourth square */
                          color='red';
                          function='move'; x=60; y=60; output;
                          function='bar';  x=80; y=90; output;

                             /* write out footnote */
                          function='label'; x=92; y=5; style='swissb';
                          position='5'; color=' '; text='GR22N03  ';
                          output;
                       run;

                          /* generate annotated slide */
                       proc ganno annotate=squares
                                name='Squares'
                                gout=ganno2
                                description='Four squares';
                       run;
```

Output 22.3 Annotate
Graphics Displayed with the
GANNO Procedure (GR22N03)

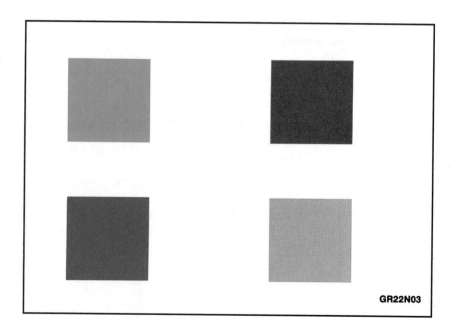

This example illustrates the following features:

□ The variables in the Annotate data set perform the following tasks:

    □ The XSYS and YSYS variables specify that the coordinate system for X and Y is a percent of the procedure output area.

    □ When the STYLE variable is used with the BAR function, it selects the fill pattern for the bar. When it is used with the LABEL function, it selects the font for the text.

    □ The COLOR variable selects the color for each square. For the footnote, the COLOR variable is assigned a null value that defaults to the first color in the colors list.

    □ The FUNCTION variable selects the operation to be performed by the Annotate facility.

    □ The X and Y coordinate values determine the coordinates of the upper-right corner of each square.

    □ The POSITION variable determines where the text is written with respect to X and Y. In this example, the text is centered over the point with coordinates (X,Y).

    □ The TEXT variable specifies the text string to be written.

□ In the PROC GANNO statement, the ANNOTATE= argument specifies the name of the Annotate data set.

□ The NAME= option assigns a name to the catalog entry stored in GANNO2. The name is stored in the catalog directory's Name field.

□ The GOUT= option assigns the catalog in which the graphics output is stored.

□ The DESCRIPTION= option assigns a description to the catalog entry. The description is stored in the catalog directory's Description field.

Using the NAME= Option to Produce Multiple Graphs

In this example, the NAME= option is used to generate multiple graphs from an Annotate data set. Since the NAME= option is assigned the variable name, COLOR, the GANNO procedure produces separate graphics output for each unique value of the COLOR variable. These outputs are stored as separate catalog entries in the output catalog. The catalog entries are named BLUE, GRAY, GREEN, and RED and are stored in GANNO2.

This example uses the same DATA step as the previous example. The following program statements produce Output 22.4 through 22.7:

```
    /* create Annotate data set */
data squares;
   length function style color $ 8;
   xsys='5'; ysys='5';
   style='solid';

      /* draw first square */
   color='blue';
   function='move'; x=10; y=10; output;
   function='bar';  x=30; y=40; output;
```

```
                           /* write out footnote */
            function='label'; x=92; y=5; style='swissb';
            position='5'; text='GR22N04(a)  '; output;

                           /* draw second square */
            color='gray';
            function='move'; x=60; y=10; output;
            function='bar';  x=80; y=40; output;

                           /* write out footnote */
            function='label'; x=92; y=5; style='swissb';
            position='5'; text='GR22N04(b)  '; output;

                           /* draw third square */
            color='green';
            function='move'; x=10; y=60; output;
            function='bar';  x=30; y=90; output;

                           /* write out footnote */
            function='label'; x=92; y=5; style='swissb';
            position='5'; text='GR22N04(c) '; output;

                           /* draw fourth square */
            color='red';
            function='move'; x=60; y=60; output;
            function='bar';  x=80; y=90; output;

                           /* write out footnote */
            function='label'; x=92; y=5; style='swissb';
            position='5'; text='GR22N04(d)  '; output;
      run;

         /* generate annotated slide, separating */
         /* graphs by color                       */
      proc ganno annotate=squares
               name=color
               gout=ganno2
               description='Individual squares';
      run;
```

Output 22.4 *First Unique Value for COLOR Variable (GR22N04(a))*

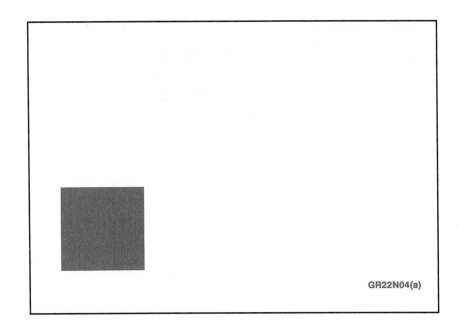

Output 22.5 *Second Unique Value for COLOR Variable (GR22N04(b))*

Output 22.6 *Third Unique Value for COLOR Variable (GR22N04(c))*

GR22N04(c)

Output 22.7 *Fourth Unique Value for COLOR Variable (GR22N04(d))*

GR22N04(d)

Scaling Data-dependent Output with the DATASYS Option

This example illustrates how the DATASYS option is used with the GANNO procedure to scale the data values to fit in the graphics output area. The example generates a vertical bar chart using the Annotate facility. One bar for each site is drawn. The height of the bar is determined by the number of sales for that site. Since the sales for each site cover a wide range of values, the GANNO procedure cannot display all of them in the same output without scaling the output with the DATASYS option.

The following program statements produce Output 22.8:

```
    /* create data set of sales information */
data sales89;
   length sitename $ 10;
   input sitename $ 1-10 mean 12-15;
   cards;
Paris      999
Munich     571
Tokyo      137
London     273
Frankfurt  546
New York   991
;
run;

    /* create Annotate data set */
data anno;
   length function color $ 8;
   retain line 0 xsys ysys '2' hsys '1' x 9 color 'green';
   set sales89 end=end;

    /* position the cursor at the beginning point */
   function='move'; x=x+8; y=20; output;

    /* draw bars representing number of sales */
   function='bar'; y=y+(mean/10); x=x+7;
   style='empty'; color='red'; output;

    /* label the bars with name of site */
   function='label'; y=15; x=x-3; size=3;
   position='5'; style='swissb';
   color='blue'; text=sitename; output;

    /* move pen to point where label should be */
   function='move'; y=y+(mean/10)-2; output;

    /* label the bars */
   function='label'; x=x-1; text=left(put(mean,3.));
   position='5'; style='swissb'; size=3;
   color='green'; output;

    /* at end of data set, output footnote label */
    /* and draw an axis line                     */
   if end=1 then do;
      function='move'; x=12; y=20; output;
      function='draw'; x=90; y=20; line=1;
      size=1; color='green'; output;
      function='label'; x=92; y=5; text='GR22N05  ';
      position='5'; style='swissb'; size=3;
      color=' '; output;
   end;
run;
```

```
                          /* display the annotation, scaling  */
                          /* the data with the DATASYS option */
                   proc ganno annotate=anno datasys;
                   run;
```

Output 22.8 The DATASYS Option Applied to Annotate Data Set Output (GR22N05)

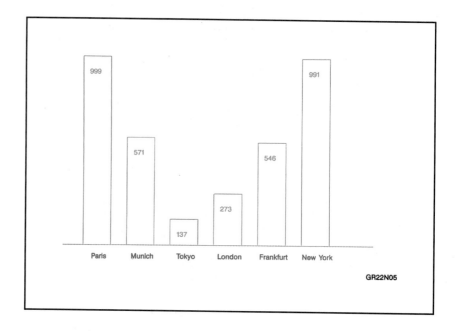

Features not explained in previous examples are described here:

□ The values of the XSYS and YSYS variables specify that the coordinate system used for X and Y is based on data values.

□ The HSYS variable specifies that the coordinate system used for SIZE is data percent.

□ The DATASYS option tells the GANNO procedure to use the maximum and minimum data values in constructing the output environment. As a result, the data values are scaled to fit the environment, and all values of X and Y are displayed.

See Also

Chapter 18, "The Annotate Data Set"
    for information on constructing Annotate data sets

Chapter 19, "Annotate Dictionary"
    for information on Annotate functions and variables

Chapter 37, "The GSLIDE Procedure"
    for information on producing Annotate output with titles, notes, and footnotes

CHAPTER 23 The GCHART Procedure

(continued on next page)

Overview

The GCHART procedure produces vertical and horizontal bar charts, block charts, pie charts, and star charts. These charts graphically represent the value of a statistic calculated for one or more variables in an input SAS data set.

The GCHART procedure can produce graphs based on the following statistics:

☐ frequency counts

☐ cumulative frequency counts

☐ percentages

☐ cumulative percentages

□ sums

□ means.

The GCHART procedure can produce charts for both numeric and character variables.

Output 23.1 through Output 23.5 illustrate the available chart types. All of the charts are generated from the same data, but the specifications are altered to suit the type of chart.

Output 23.1 and Output 23.2 illustrate vertical and horizontal bar charts. Bar charts are used to graphically represent the magnitude of data ranges. The two types of bar charts have essentially the same characteristics, except that horizontal bar charts can include detailed lists of statistic values with the bars, while vertical bar charts can display the values of a single statistic above each bar.

Output 23.1 *Vertical Bar Chart (GR23N01)*

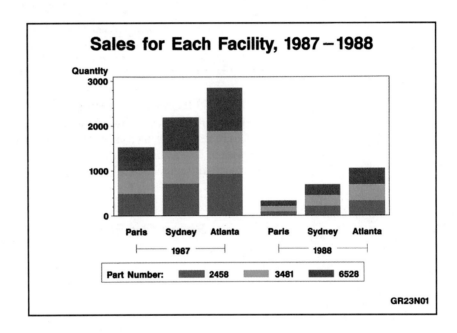

Output 23.2 Horizontal Bar
Chart *(GR23N02)*

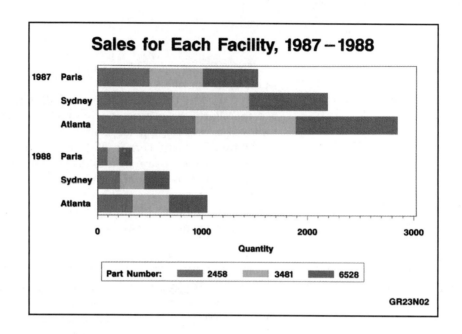

Output 23.3 illustrates a block chart. Like bar charts, block charts are used to represent the magnitude of data graphically. However, because block charts do not use axes, they are most useful when the relative magnitude of the blocks is more significant than the exact magnitude of any particular block.

Output 23.3 Block Chart
(GR23N03)

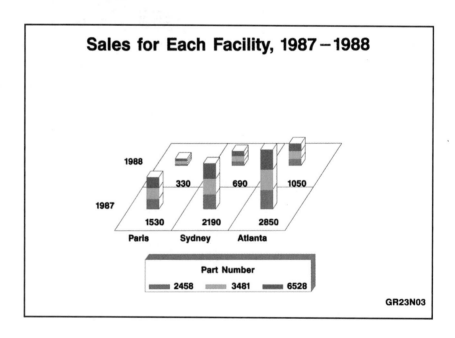

Output 23.4 illustrates a pie chart. Pie charts are ideal for representing the relative contribution of each part to the whole.

Output 23.4 *Pie Chart (GR23N04)*

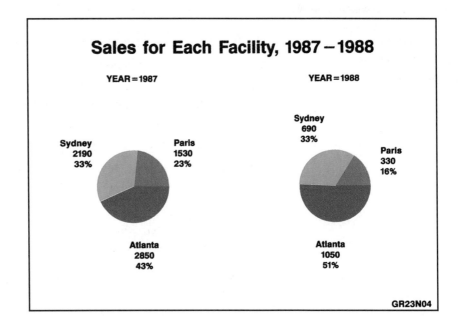

Output 23.5 illustrates a star chart. Star charts are visually similar to pie charts, but the length of the star chart spines or slices represents the magnitude of the chart statistic in much the same way as the bar on a bar chart. The circle surrounding a star chart provides a scale for judging the magnitude of the value represented by each slice or spine.

Output 23.5 *Star Chart (GR23N05)*

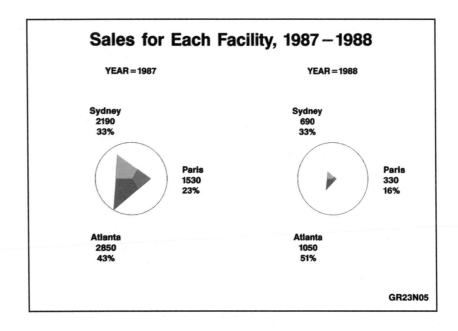

GCHART Procedure Syntax

The GCHART procedure uses the following statements:

□ The PROC GCHART statement is required.

> **PROC GCHART** <DATA=*SAS-data-set*>
> <ANNOTATE=*Annotate-data-set*>
> <GOUT=*output-catalog*>;

□ At least one of the following statements is required:

> **BLOCK** *chart-variable* < . . . *chart-variable-n*>
> </ <ANNOTATE=*Annotate-data-set*>
> <*appearance-options*>
> <*statistic-options*>
> <*midpoint-options*>
> <*description-options*>>;

> **HBAR** *chart-variable* < . . . *chart-variable-n*>
> </ <ANNOTATE=*Annotate-data-set*>
> <*appearance-options*>
> <*statistic-options*>
> <*midpoint-options*>
> <*axes-options*>
> <*description-options*>>;

> **PIE** *chart-variable* < . . . *chart-variable-n*>
> </ <ANNOTATE=*Annotate-data-set*>
> <*appearance-options*>
> <*statistic-options*>
> <*midpoint-options*>
> <*description-options*>>;

> **STAR** *chart-variable* < . . . *chart-variable-n*>
> </ <ANNOTATE=*Annotate-data-set*>
> <*appearance-options*>
> <*statistic-options*>
> <*midpoint-options*>
> <*description-options*>>;

> **VBAR** *chart-variable* < . . . *chart-variable-n*>
> </ <ANNOTATE=*Annotate-data-set*>
> <*appearance-options*>
> <*statistic-options*>
> <*midpoint-options*>
> <*axes-options*>
> <*description-options*>>;

□ The following statements are optional and local:

> **BY** <*options*> *variable*;

> **NOTE** <*options*> <'*text*'>;

□ The following statements are optional and global:

FOOTNOTE<1 . . . 10> <*options*> <'*text*'>;

PATTERN<1 . . . 99> <*options*>;

TITLE<1 . . . 10> <*options*> <'*text*'>;

□ The following statement is optional and global. It can be used only in conjunction with the BLOCK, HBAR, and VBAR statements.

LEGEND<1 . . . 99> <*options*>;

□ The following statement is optional and global. It can be used only in conjunction with the HBAR and VBAR statements.

AXIS<1 . . . 99> <*options*>;

For complete statement syntax, see the section for the appropriate statement.

Statement Descriptions

The purpose of each statement is described here:

AXIS	defines axis characteristics that modify the appearance, position, and content of an axis. See Chapter 9, "The AXIS Statement." Once defined, AXIS definitions are assigned with the GAXIS=, MAXIS=, or RAXIS= option in an HBAR or VBAR statement. The BLOCK, PIE, and STAR statements do not support the AXIS statement.
BLOCK	creates block charts in which the height of the blocks represents the value of the chart statistic for each category of data or midpoint.
BY	specifies the variable or variables by which the data are grouped for processing. A separate graph is produced for each value of the BY variable. See Chapter 10, "The BY Statement."
FOOTNOTE	defines the text and appearance of footnotes. See Chapter 11, "The FOOTNOTE Statement."
HBAR	creates horizontal bar charts in which the length of the bars represents the value of the chart statistic for each category of data or midpoint.
LEGEND	defines legend characteristics that modify the text, appearance, and position of a legend. See Chapter 13, "The LEGEND Statement." Once defined, LEGEND definitions are assigned with the LEGEND= option in a BLOCK, HBAR, or VBAR statement. The PIE and STAR statements do not support the LEGEND statement.
NOTE	defines the text and appearance of notes that appear in the procedure output area. See Chapter 14, "The NOTE Statement."

PIE	creates pie charts in which the size of the pie slices represents the value of the chart statistic for each category of data or midpoint as a percentage of the chart statistic for all categories of data.
PATTERN	defines the color and fill pattern used to fill blocks, bars, and slices. See Chapter 15, "The PATTERN Statement." Once defined, PATTERN definitions are assigned automatically by a BLOCK, HBAR, PIE, STAR, or VBAR statement.
PROC GCHART	starts the procedure and specifies the name of the data set to be used for the chart, as well as any additional input or output options.
STAR	creates star charts in which the length of the spines or center of the slices represents the value of the chart statistic for each category of data or midpoint.
TITLE	defines the text and appearance of titles. See Chapter 17, "The TITLE Statement."
VBAR	creates vertical bar charts in which the height of the bars represents the value of the chart statistic for each category of data or midpoint.

GCHART Procedure Description

The following sections discuss general topics that apply to the GCHART procedure: terminology, data considerations, chart statistics, global statements, and RUN-group processing.

Terminology

The following terms are used in the discussion of the GCHART procedure and are defined in the Glossary. Some of these terms and some additional terms are illustrated in Figure 23.1 and Figure 23.2.

axis	legend
chart statistic	major tick mark
chart variable	midpoint
frame	minor tick mark
group variable	spine
label	subgroup variable

Figure 23.1 *GCHART*
Procedure Terms for Block,
Horizontal Bar, and Vertical
Bar Charts

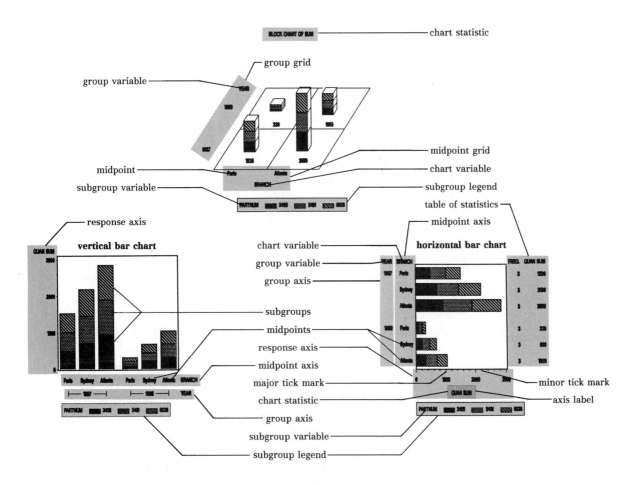

Figure 23.2 *GCHART*
Procedure Terms for Pie and
Star Charts

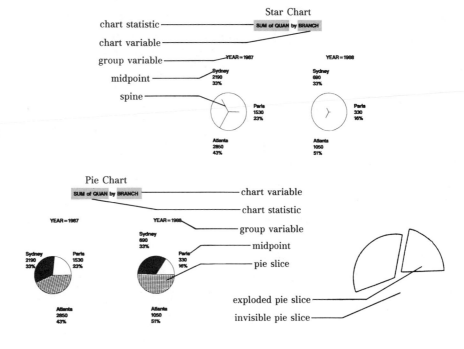

Data Considerations

The following sections discuss special data considerations for the GCHART procedure.

Chart Variables and Midpoint Selection

The GCHART procedure can produce charts for both numeric and character chart variables. Numeric chart variables fall into two categories: discrete and continuous.

Discrete variables contain a finite number of specific numeric values to be represented on the chart. For example, a variable that contains only the values 1989 or 1990 is a discrete variable.

Continuous variables contain a range of numeric values to be represented on the chart. For example, a variable that contains any real value between 0 and 100 is a continuous variable.

Numeric chart variables are always treated as continuous variables unless the DISCRETE option is used in the action statement.

The type of a chart variable affects the way midpoints are selected for the chart. *Midpoints* are the values that identify categories of data on the graph. These categories shown on the graph are based on the values of the chart variable. Based on the type of a chart variable, a midpoint can represent the following:

□ a specific character value. If the chart variable is character type, each unique value of the variable is treated as a midpoint. For example, if the chart variable contains the names of ten cities, each city will be a midpoint, resulting in ten midpoints for the chart.

The following are exceptions to this:

□ The MIDPOINTS= option can be used to choose specific midpoint values. Any chart variable values that do not match one of the specified midpoint values are ignored. For example, if the chart variable contains the names of ten cities and you specify the following, only the observations for `Paris`, `Sydney`, and `London` are included on the chart:

```
midpoints='Paris' 'Sydney' 'London'
```

□ In pie charts, midpoint values with statistic values that compose a small percentage of the total for the chart may be placed in the OTHER slice and will not produce a separate midpoint. For details, see "PIE Statement" later in this chapter.

The character values are truncated to 16 characters.

Figure 23.3 shows bar and pie charts with character midpoints.

Figure 23.3 *Midpoints for Chart Variables with Character Values*

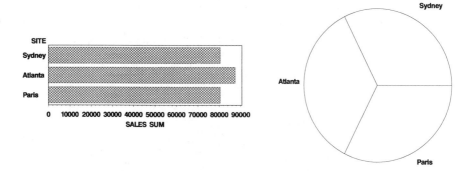

□ a range of numeric values. If the chart variable is numeric, the GCHART procedure uses the algorithm described in Terrell and Scott (1985) to determine the number of midpoints for the chart variable. Each midpoint then represents the median of a range of values.

The following are exceptions to this:

□ The LEVELS= option specifies the number of midpoints to be used on the chart.

□ The DISCRETE option causes the numeric variable to be treated as a discrete variable.

□ The MIDPOINTS= option chooses specific midpoint values that are used as medians of the value ranges.

□ The MIDPOINTS=OLD option chooses default midpoints using the algorithm described in Nelder (1976). This is the algorithm used in Release 82.4 and Version 5 of SAS/GRAPH software.

If the chart variable values are continuous, midpoint intervals are assigned automatically unless you specify otherwise. The midpoints represent a range of values rather than a single value. Figure 23.4 shows bar and pie charts with typical continuous numeric variable midpoints.

Note: The $24,000 midpoint includes observations for values of the chart variable from the minimum value in the data set to $27,000.

Figure 23.4 *Midpoints for Chart Variables with Continuous Numeric Values*

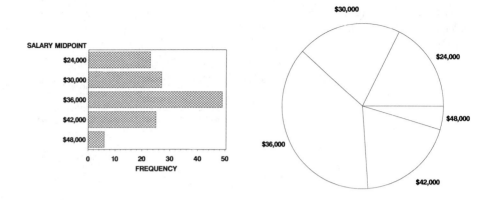

□ a specific numeric value. If the chart variable is numeric and the DISCRETE option is used, it is treated in much the same way as a character chart variable. That is, the GCHART procedure creates a midpoint for each unique value of the chart variable. If the DISCRETE option is used with a numeric chart variable that has an associated format, each formatted value is represented by a block, bar, slice, or spine. Formatted values are truncated to 16 characters.

Figure 23.5 shows bar and pie charts with discrete numeric midpoints. Here the midpoints correspond to the exact chart variable values. The midpoints are listed in the order of the original numeric value.

Figure 23.5 *Midpoints for Chart Variables with Discrete Numeric Values*

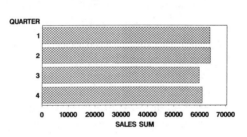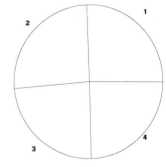

You can change the way midpoints are selected using the DISCRETE, MIDPOINTS=, and LEVELS= options. See the appropriate action statement section later in this chapter for more information.

Missing Values

By default, missing values for the chart variable are ignored. If you specify the MISSING option, missing values are treated as a valid midpoint and are included on the chart. Missing values for the group and subgroup variables are always treated as valid groups and subgroups.

When the value of the variable specified in the FREQ= option is missing, 0, or negative, the observation is excluded from the calculation of the chart statistic.

When the value of the variable specified in the SUMVAR= option is missing, the observation is excluded from the calculation of the chart statistic.

Restricting the Range of Chart Variable Values

You can exclude values from a chart by

□ using the MIDPOINTS= option to select a subset of midpoints for a chart variable that is character type

□ using a WHERE statement in a DATA step to restrict the range of the chart variable.

Note: For a numeric chart variable, you can change the number of midpoints on the chart using the MIDPOINTS= or LEVELS= option. However, while changing the number of midpoints may change the range of values for specific midpoints, it does not change the range of values for the chart as a whole. The range of values for the entire chart remains unchanged.

Chart Statistics

The GCHART procedure can produce charts based on frequency, cumulative frequency, percentage, cumulative percentage, sum, and mean statistics that are calculated from the observations in the input data set. Pie and star charts do not support cumulative frequencies or cumulative percentages. The default chart statistic is frequency.

Frequency Statistic

By default, the frequency statistic is calculated by finding the total number of observations in the data set for each midpoint. For example, if there are seven observations for `Denver` in the input data set, then the frequency for the `Denver` midpoint is 7. Optionally, you can specify a variable that contains frequency information for each observation. You can chart the frequency statistic only when the SUMVAR= option is not used.

Cumulative Frequency Statistic

By default, the cumulative frequency statistic is calculated by adding the frequency for the current midpoint to the frequency of all the preceding midpoints shown on the chart, as shown in the following table:

Midpoint	If the frequency is	then the cumulative frequency is
Denver	7	7
Seattle	9	16
Tokyo	5	21

Optionally, you can specify a variable that contains frequency information for each observation. You can chart the cumulative frequency statistic only when the SUMVAR= option is not used.

Percentage Statistic

The percentage statistic is calculated by dividing the frequency for each midpoint by the total frequency count for all midpoints in the chart or group and multiplying it by 100. For example, if the frequency count for the Denver midpoint is 7 and the total frequency count for the chart is 21, the percentage statistic is 33.3%. You can chart the percentage statistic only when the SUMVAR= option is not used.

Cumulative Percentage Statistic

By default, the cumulative percentage statistic is calculated by adding the percentage for the current midpoint to the percentage for all of the preceding midpoints in the chart or group as shown in this table:

Midpoint	If the percentage is	then the cumulative percentage is
Denver	33.3%	33.3%
Seattle	42.9%	76.2%
Tokyo	23.8%	100.0%

You can chart the cumulative percentage statistic only when the SUMVAR= option is not used.

Sum Statistic

The sum statistic is calculated by finding the total of the values for the SUMVAR= variable for each midpoint. For example, if you specify SUMVAR=SALES and the values of the SALES variable for the seven Denver observations are

8734	4502
982	624
1504	918
3207	

then the sum statistic for the Denver midpoint is 20,471.

Mean Statistic

The mean statistic is calculated by finding the mean, or average, of the values for the SUMVAR= variable for each midpoint. For example, if you specify TYPE=MEAN and SUMVAR=SALES and the values of the SALES variable for the seven Denver observations are

8734	4502
982	624
1504	918
3207	

then the mean statistic for the Denver midpoint is 2924.42.

Using the Chart Statistics

By default, each observation is counted only once in the calculation of the chart statistic. To calculate weighted statistics or statistics in which an observation can be counted more than once, use the FREQ= option to identify a variable used to weight the statistic calculation. For each observation, the value of the variable specified in the FREQ= option is used as a weight or multiplier for the observation in the calculation of the statistic. If you use the SUMVAR= option, then the SUMVAR= variable value for an observation is multiplied by the FREQ= variable value for the observation for use in calculating the chart statistic. The observation is excluded from the calculation if the value of the FREQ= variable is missing, 0, or negative. For example, if you specify FREQ=COUNT in an action statement, then the following is true:

When COUNT is	the observation is counted this many times in the statistic calculation
1	1
5	5
.	0
−3	0

The FREQ= option can be used with all types of chart statistics.

By default, the percentage and cumulative percentage statistics are calculated based on the frequency. If you want to chart a percentage or cumulative percentage based on a sum, you must use the FREQ= option to specify the variable used for the sum calculation. For example, if you want to chart the percentage based on the sum of the variable COUNT, specify the following:

```
freq=count
type=pct
```

When charting the sum or mean statistic, you must use the SUMVAR= option to identify the variable used for calculating the sum and mean for each midpoint.

When charting the frequency, cumulative frequency, percentage, or cumulative percentage, do not use the SUMVAR= option. However, you can use the FREQ= option to identify the variable to be used in calculating these statistics.

For more information on the TYPE=, SUMVAR= and FREQ= options, see the statement option sections for the BLOCK, HBAR, PIE, STAR, and VBAR statements later in this chapter.

Global Statements

All currently defined titles and footnotes are displayed in every graph generated by the GCHART procedure or by a RUN group. The procedure automatically assigns currently defined PATTERN definitions as needed to charts that use patterns. You can assign currently defined AXIS definitions using HBAR or VBAR statement options. You can assign currently defined LEGEND definitions using BLOCK, HBAR, or VBAR statement options.

To display different titles and footnotes on your graphs, define the titles and footnotes at the beginning of a RUN group. Any TITLE or FOOTNOTE statements of a higher level (that is, a lower number) remain in effect and display on the graph.

RUN Groups

The GCHART procedure supports RUN-group processing. The action statements for this procedure are

BLOCK

HBAR

PIE

STAR

VBAR.

For more information on RUN groups, see Chapter 2, "Running SAS/GRAPH Programs."

PROC GCHART Statement

The PROC GCHART statement initiates the procedure and, if necessary, specifies the data set that contains the chart data. In addition, it can optionally specify a data set for annotation and a destination catalog for graphics output. The GCHART procedure ends when a QUIT, DATA, or another PROC statement is encountered, or when the SAS session terminates.

Syntax

The general form of the PROC GCHART statement is

PROC GCHART <DATA=*SAS-data-set*>
        <ANNOTATE=*Annotate-data-set*>
        <GOUT=*output-catalog*>;

Requirements

The GCHART procedure requires an input data set. By default, the procedure uses the most recently created data set as its input data set. You can use the DATA= option to select a specific data set. If no data set has been created in the current SAS session and the DATA= option is not used, an error occurs and the procedure stops.

You must use at least one action statement with the GCHART procedure: BLOCK, HBAR, PIE, STAR, or VBAR.

Options

You can use the following options with the PROC GCHART statement. Options used with a PROC GCHART statement affect all graphs produced by the procedure.

ANNOTATE=*Annotate-data-set*
ANNO=*Annotate-data-set*
> specifies a data set to provide annotation of all graphs produced by the GCHART procedure. (To annotate individual graphs, use the ANNOTATE= option in a BLOCK, HBAR, PIE, STAR, or VBAR statement.) *Annotate-data-set* must contain the appropriate Annotate variables. See Chapter 18, "The Annotate Data Set," for details.

DATA=*SAS-data-set*
> specifies the SAS data set that is the source of variable values for the charts produced by the GCHART procedure. If you do not use the DATA= option and no data set has been created in the current SAS session, an error occurs and the procedure stops.

GOUT=*output-catalog*
> specifies the SAS catalog in which to save the graphics output produced by the GCHART procedure for later replay. You can use the GREPLAY procedure to view the graphs stored in the catalog. By default, catalog entries are written to the default catalog WORK.GSEG, which is erased at the end of your SAS session.

BLOCK Statement

The BLOCK statement creates one or more block charts using the input data set specified in the PROC GCHART statement. The BLOCK statement specifies the chart variable or variables that define the categories of data to be charted. Other variables can be specified to

□ group the blocks

□ subdivide the blocks

□ provide data for the sum and mean statistics.

In addition, options used in the BLOCK statement can select the statistic to be charted and modify the appearance of the chart.

Syntax

The general form of the BLOCK statement is

BLOCK *chart-variable* < . . . *chart-variable-n*>
 </ <ANNOTATE=*Annotate-data-set*>
  <*appearance-options*>
  <*statistic-options*>
  <*midpoint-options*>
  <*description-options*>>;

☐ *chart-variable* specifies a variable in the input data set with categories of data represented on the chart. If you include more than one chart variable in the BLOCK statement, the variable names must be separated with blanks.

☐ *appearance-options* can be one or more of the following:

  ☐ selecting colors

  CAXIS=*grid-color*

  COUTLINE=*block-outline-color*

  CTEXT=*text-color*

  ☐ changing the appearance of the blocks

  BLOCKMAX=*n*

  where *n* is the statistic value of the tallest block

  PATTERNID=BY | GROUP | MIDPOINT | SUBGROUP

  ☐ changing the appearance of the subgroup legend

  LEGEND=LEGEND<1 . . . 99>

  NOLEGEND

  ☐ suppressing the chart heading

  NOHEADING

☐ *statistic-options* can be one or more of the following:

  FREQ=*numeric-variable*

  G100

  SUMVAR=*numeric-variable*

  TYPE=*statistic*

  where *statistic* is one of the following:

  CFREQ

  CPERCENT

  FREQ

  MEAN

  PERCENT

  SUM

☐ *midpoint-options* can be one or more of the following:

☐ manipulating the midpoint values

DISCRETE

LEVELS=*n*

where *n* is the number of midpoints for the numeric chart variable

MIDPOINTS=*value-list*

MIDPOINTS=OLD

MISSING

☐ grouping and subgrouping

GROUP=*variable*

SUBGROUP=*variable*

☐ *description-options* can be either or both of the following:

DESCRIPTION='*string*'

NAME='*string*'

Options are fully described in "Options" later in this section.

Requirements

A BLOCK statement must contain at least one chart variable. A separate chart is drawn for each chart variable.

Options

You can use the following options in the BLOCK statement. Options used in a BLOCK statement affect all graphs produced by that statement. If any of the following options are supplied, they must be separated from the chart variables with a slash (/). If you do not use any options, omit the slash.

ANNOTATE=*Annotate-data-set*
ANNO=*Annotate-data-set*
   specifies a data set to provide annotation of graphs produced by the BLOCK statement. *Annotate-data-set* must contain the appropriate Annotate variables. See Chapter 18 for details.
   Note: Annotate coordinate systems 1, 2, 7, and 8 (data system coordinates) are not valid with block charts.
   If the ANNOTATE= option is also used in the PROC GCHART statement, both sets of annotation are applied. If you specify BY-group processing, the Annotate data set must contain the BY variable. For details, see "Using BY-Group Processing with the Annotate Facility" in Chapter 18 and "Details of BY-Group Processing" in Chapter 10.

BLOCKMAX=*n*
   specifies the chart statistic value of the tallest block on the chart. This option lets you produce a series of block charts using the same scale. All blocks are rescaled as if *n* were the maximum value on the chart.

CAXIS=*grid-color*
> specifies a color for the midpoint grid and for block sides. By default, the grid and block sides display in the first color in the current colors list. Block face colors are controlled by PATTERN definitions.

COUTLINE=*block-outline-color*
> outlines all block faces or block face segments and legend values in the subgroup legend (if it appears) using the specified color. By default, the outline color for block faces is the same as the pattern color.
>
> **Note:** The outline color is the only distinction between empty patterns. Using the COUTLINE= option when VALUE=EMPTY is specified in PATTERN definitions makes the patterns look the same.

CTEXT=*text-color*
> specifies a color for all text on the chart. Text includes the values and labels for the midpoint grid, the subgroup legend, and the descriptive statistic values. If you do not use the CTEXT= option, a color specification is searched for in the following order:
>
> 1. the CTEXT= option in a GOPTIONS statement
>
> 2. the default, the first color in the colors list.
>
> If you use the CTEXT= option, the color specification is overridden in the following situation:
>
> □ If you also use the COLOR= parameter of the LABEL= or VALUE= option in a LEGEND definition assigned to the subgroup legend, that parameter determines the color of the legend label or the color of the legend value descriptions, respectively.

DESCRIPTION='*string*'
DES='*string*'
> specifies a descriptive string, up to 40 characters long, that appears in the Description field of the catalog entry for the chart. The description does not appear on the chart. By default, the GCHART procedure assigns a description of the form BLOCK CHART OF *variable*, where *variable* is the name of the chart variable.

DISCRETE
> treats a numeric chart variable as a discrete variable rather than as a continuous variable. The GCHART procedure creates a separate midpoint and, hence, a separate grid square and block for each unique value of the chart variable. If the chart variable has a format associated with it, each formatted value is treated as a midpoint.
>
> The LEVELS= option is ignored when you use the DISCRETE option. The MIDPOINTS= option overrides the DISCRETE option.

FREQ=*numeric-variable*
> uses the values of *numeric-variable* to weight the contribution of each observation in the computation of the chart statistic. Noninteger values of *numeric-variable* are truncated to integers.
>
> By default, each observation is counted only once in the frequency counts and sums. When you use the FREQ= option, each observation is counted the number of times specified by the value of *numeric-variable* for that observation. Observations for which the value of *numeric-variable* is missing, 0, or negative are not used in the statistic calculation.

Because you cannot use TYPE=PERCENT, TYPE=CPERCENT, TYPE=FREQ, or TYPE=CFREQ when you use the SUMVAR= option, you must use the FREQ= option to calculate percentages, cumulative percentages, frequencies, or cumulative frequencies based on a sum.

G100

calculates the percentage and cumulative percentage statistics separately for each group. The G100 option is ignored unless you also use the GROUP= option. When you use the G100 option, the individual percentages reflect the contribution of the midpoint to the group and total 100 percent for each group.

By default, the individual percentages reflect the contribution of the midpoint to the entire chart and total 100 percent for the entire chart.

GROUP=*variable*

specifies that the data be grouped according to the values of *variable*. *Variable* can be either character or numeric and is always treated as a discrete variable. A group grid is produced, with a separate row for each unique value of *variable*. Missing values for *variable* are treated as a valid group. By default, each group includes all midpoints, even if no observations for the group fall within the midpoint range.

The groups are arranged from front to back in ascending order of the values of *variable*. The corresponding value of *variable* is printed to the left of each row, and the label associated with *variable* is printed at the top of the list of values.

LEGEND=LEGEND<1 . . . 99>

assigns legend characteristics to the subgroup legend. The LEGEND= option is ignored unless you also use the SUBGROUP= option.

▶ *Caution: The LEGEND= option does not generate a legend.*

The option value indicates which LEGEND definition to use. This option is ignored if the specified LEGEND definition is not in effect.

The following options override the LEGEND= option and suppress the subgroup legend:

NOLEGEND

PATTERNID=BY | GROUP | MIDPOINT

LEVELS=*n*

uses the specified number of midpoints for the numeric chart variable. The range for each midpoint is calculated automatically using the algorithm described in Terrell and Scott (1985). This option is ignored if

□ the chart variable is character type

□ the DISCRETE option is used

□ the MIDPOINTS= option is used.

MIDPOINTS=*value-list*

specifies values for midpoints in the block chart. Each midpoint is represented on the chart by a column in the midpoint grid. Blocks representing the value of the chart statistic are drawn in the squares. By default, one of these two methods is used:

□ If the chart variable is numeric type, the GCHART procedure calculates midpoint values.

□ If the chart variable is character type or is numeric type and the DISCRETE option is used, the GCHART procedure creates a midpoint for each unique value.

If *value-list* contains more midpoints than can fit in the available graphics area, an error message is written to the SAS log and no chart is produced. On many devices, this problem can be corrected by increasing the number of cells in your graphics display using the HPOS= and VPOS= graphics options. For details, see Chapter 5, "Graphics Options and Device Parameters Dictionary."

For numeric chart variables, *value-list* can be specified in the following ways:

n n . . . n

n,n, . . . ,n

n TO *n* <BY *increment*> <*n . . . n*> <*n, . . . ,n*>

n n . . . n TO *n* <BY *increment*> <*n . . . n*>

n,n, . . . ,n TO *n* <BY *increment*> <*n, . . . ,n*>

'*SAS-value*'i TO '*SAS-value*'i <BY *interval*>

'*SAS-value*'i '*SAS-value*'i . . . '*SAS-value*'i

If the variable has an associated format, you must specify the unformatted values in *value-list*.

For continuous variables, the midpoints are the medians of the ranges of possible values of the chart variable. A value that falls exactly halfway between two midpoints is placed in the higher range.

For character chart variables, *value-list* must be a list of midpoint values. Values must be enclosed in single quotes and separated by blanks (commas are not allowed as separators), as in this example:

```
midpoints='Paris' 'Sydney' 'Atlanta'
```

The values can be specified in any order, so the *value-list* can be used to order the grid. If the variable has an associated format, you must specify the formatted values in *value-list*. By default, midpoints are arranged left to right in ascending order of the midpoint values. If the character chart variable has an associated format, the values are arranged in order of the formatted values.

You can selectively exclude some chart variable values from the chart, as in this example:

```
midpoints='Paris'
```

Only those observations for which the chart variable exactly matches one of the midpoint values are counted. As a result, observations can be inadvertently excluded if values in the midpoint list are misspelled or if the case does not match exactly.

MIDPOINTS=OLD

tells the GCHART procedure to calculate default midpoints using the algorithm used in Release 82.4 and Version 5 of SAS/GRAPH software. The MIDPOINTS=OLD option is ignored unless the chart variable is numeric type.

MISSING

accepts a missing value as a valid midpoint for the chart variable. By default, observations for which the value of the chart variable is missing are ignored.

Note: Missing values are always valid for the group and subgroup variables.

NAME='*string*'

specifies a string, up to eight characters long, that appears in the Name field of the catalog entry for the chart. *String* must be a valid SAS name. By default, the name assigned is GCHART. If either the name specified or the default name duplicates an existing name in the catalog, SAS/GRAPH software adds a number to the duplicate name to create a unique name, for example, GCHART2.

NOHEADING

suppresses the heading normally printed at the top of each block chart.

NOLEGEND

suppresses the subgroup legend. The NOLEGEND option is ignored unless you also use the SUBGROUP= option.

PATTERNID=BY | GROUP | MIDPOINT | SUBGROUP

specifies the way fill patterns are assigned. By default, PATTERNID=SUBGROUP. The meanings of the option values are as follows:

BY
changes patterns each time the value of the BY variable changes. All blocks use the same pattern if the GCHART procedure does not include a BY statement.

GROUP
changes patterns every time the value of the group variable changes. All blocks in each group use the same pattern, but a different pattern is used for each group.

MIDPOINT
changes patterns every time the midpoint value changes. If the GROUP= option is used, the respective midpoint patterns are repeated for each group.

(PATTERNID= continued)

SUBGROUP   changes patterns every time the value of the subgroup variable changes. Blocks that are divided into subgroups use a different pattern for each subgroup. If the SUBGROUP= option is not used, all block faces have the same pattern.

A warning message is written to the SAS log if the PATTERNID= value is anything other than SUBGROUP when the SUBGROUP= option is used, since this situation may make it impossible to distinguish the subgroups and does not produce a legend.

SUBGROUP=*variable*

divides the blocks into segments according to the values of *variable*. Each block is divided into as many parts as there are different values of *variable* for each midpoint.

By default, a legend appears at the bottom of the chart when you use the SUBGROUP= option. The legend indicates which pattern represents which value of *variable*. The LEGEND= option can be used to assign a LEGEND definition to the subgroup legend.

The following options suppress the subgroup legend:

NOLEGEND

PATTERNID=BY | GROUP | MIDPOINT

SUMVAR=*numeric-variable*

specifies the variable to be used for sum or mean calculations. The GCHART procedure calculates the sum or, if requested, the mean of *numeric-variable* for each midpoint. These statistics then can be represented by the height of the blocks in each square.

When you use the SUMVAR= option, the TYPE= option value must be either SUM or MEAN. By default, TYPE=SUM when the SUMVAR= option is used.

TYPE=*statistic*

specifies the chart statistic for the block chart. *Statistic* can be one of the following when you do not use the SUMVAR= option:

Value of *statistic*	Statistic represented on the chart
FREQ	frequency
CFREQ	cumulative frequency
PERCENT PCT	percentage
CPERCENT CPCT	cumulative percentage

Statistic can be either of the following when you use the SUMVAR= option:

Value of *statistic*	Statistic represented on the chart
SUM	sum
MEAN	mean

By default, TYPE=FREQ when the SUMVAR= option is not used, and TYPE=SUM when SUMVAR= is used.

When you specify TYPE=MEAN and use the SUBGROUP= option, the height of the block represents the mean for the entire midpoint. The subgroup segments are proportional to the subgroup's contribution to the sum for the block.

Because you cannot use TYPE=PERCENT, TYPE=CPERCENT, TYPE=FREQ, or TYPE=CFREQ when you use the SUMVAR= option, you must use the FREQ= option to calculate percentages, cumulative percentages, frequencies, or cumulative frequencies based on a sum.

See "Chart Statistics" earlier in this chapter for a complete description of the types of statistics.

Using the BLOCK Statement

The form of your block chart is governed by the variables you specify and the options you use in the BLOCK statement. A separate block chart is produced for each chart variable specified. For example, the following statement produces two separate block charts:

```
block site year;
```

The height of the blocks represents the magnitude of the chart statistic for the midpoint. The value of the chart statistic is also printed beneath each block. The columns of squares represent the midpoints.

The GCHART procedure automatically scales the response values and calculates midpoint values. However, you can use options to override the defaults and choose the number of midpoints. You also can limit the height of all blocks. The GCHART procedure also can divide the blocks into rows based on the values of a group variable and subdivide the blocks into segments based on the values of a subgroup variable.

The following sections explain how you can change the appearance of your block chart using different BLOCK statement options.

The Chart Variable and the Midpoint Grid

The value of the chart variable determines the midpoint to which each observation in the data set contributes. The way in which midpoints are selected varies depending on the type of the chart variable and the options used. See "Chart Variables and Midpoint Selection" earlier in this chapter for additional information on how midpoints are selected.

Formatted numeric variables are ordered by the unformatted numeric values. If you use the DISCRETE option and the variable is formatted, there is one midpoint for each formatted value.

You can use the MIDPOINTS= and LEVELS= options to change the number of midpoints used for numeric variables. For example, if you specify the following, the GCHART procedure calculates four midpoints for a continuous chart variable:

```
block sales / levels=4;
```

If you specify the following, the GCHART procedure uses 1, 3, and 5 as midpoints for the chart:

```
block x / midpoints=1 3 5;
```

The midpoint value for each block is shown beneath the columns of the midpoint grid. By default, midpoint values are arranged in ascending order from left to right.

If a character chart variable has an associated format, the blocks are ordered according to the formatted values of the character chart variable. You can use the MIDPOINTS= option to change the order of midpoints. For example, the following statement orders the midpoints `Paris Atlanta` instead of the default of `Atlanta Paris`:

```
block branch / midpoints='Paris' 'Atlanta';
```

The midpoint grid includes a label that, by default, indicates the name of the chart variable or the chart variable's label if one has been assigned. The block chart also includes a default heading indicating the chart statistic requested. The heading can be suppressed with the NOHEADING option.

The Chart Statistic and Blocks

The height of each block graphically represents the value of the chart statistic for the corresponding midpoint. These six types of statistics can be charted:

□ frequency

□ cumulative frequency

□ percentage

□ cumulative percentage

□ sum

□ mean.

See "Chart Statistics" earlier in this chapter for more information about these statistics and how they are calculated. Use the TYPE= option to select the chart statistic.

The default chart statistic is frequency. If the SUMVAR= option is used, the default chart statistic is sum. You must use the SUMVAR= option to identify the variable to use for calculating sum or mean statistics. For example, if you want to calculate a sum based on the value of the variable COUNT, specify the following:

```
block branch / sumvar=count;
```

By default, each observation is counted only once in the calculation of the chart statistic. You can use the FREQ= option to identify the variable that indicates the number of times each observation is counted.

The relative block heights in the chart represent the scaled value of the chart statistic value for the midpoint. If the statistic has a value of 0 or, in the case of sum and mean, a negative value, the base of the block is

drawn in the square for the corresponding midpoint. The value
represented by the block is printed at the foot of each block for reference.
Figure 23.6 shows an example of a chart with 0 and negative statistic
values.

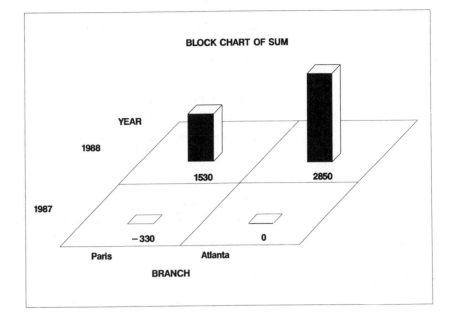

Figure 23.6 *Block Chart
with 0 and Negative Statistic
Values*

The Group Variable

If you want to display your data categorized by both the chart variable
and another variable, you can use the second variable to organize the
blocks into rows or groups. Use the GROUP= option to identify the
second variable as the group variable for your chart. When you use the
GROUP= option, a group grid is created that contains a separate row of
blocks for each unique value of the group variable. Each group contains a
square for each of the midpoints defined for the chart variable. The group
variable is always treated as a discrete variable.

Groups are arranged from front to back in ascending order of the value
of the group variable. The group variable values that distinguish the
groups are listed to the left of the rows. The group grid also includes a
label at the top of the chart that, by default, indicates the name of the
group variable or the label associated with the group variable.

See the description of the GROUP= option in "Options" earlier in this
section for additional details. See "Block Chart Using Groups and
Subgroups" in "BLOCK Statement Examples" later in this section for an
example of grouping in a block chart.

The Subgroup Variable and the Subgroup Legend

If you want to divide each block into segments based on the contribution
of a variable, you can use the variable as a subgroup variable. Use the
SUBGROUP= option to identify the variable as the subgroup variable for
the chart. When you use the SUBGROUP= option, each block contains a
separate segment for every unique value of the subgroup variable for the
block's midpoint. The number of segments in each block depends on the
number of different values of the subgroup variable for the corresponding
midpoint.

Subgrouping is effective only when subgroups can be distinguished by a different color or fill pattern. By default, each segment in the chart is filled with a different pattern. The subgroup legend provides a key to the patterns that identify each subgroup segment. By default, the subgroup legend appears below the midpoint grid and above any footnotes. The subgroup legend also includes a label that, by default, indicates the name or label of the subgroup variable. Figure 23.1 earlier in this chapter shows the subgroup legend on a block chart.

You can create a legend based on the chart midpoints. Simply use the chart variable as the subgroup variable as follows:

```
block city / subgroup=city;
```

You can use the LEGEND= option to assign a LEGEND statement definition to the subgroup legend as shown here:

```
block city / legend=legend3 subgroup=quarter;
```

See the descriptions of the SUBGROUP=, PATTERNID=, and LEGEND= options in "Options" earlier in this section for additional details. See "Block Chart Using Groups and Subgroups" in "BLOCK Statement Examples" later in this section for an example of subgrouping in a block chart.

Selecting Patterns for the Blocks

Block charts can use only bar/block patterns for the block faces. This pattern type uses the following fill patterns:

EMPTY

SOLID

style<density>

    where

style	can be X | L | R.
density	can be 1 . . . 5.

All other fill pattern specifications are ignored. See Chapter 15 for details.

Only the front faces of the blocks can have fill patterns. The block sides and the squares that form the midpoint grid do not use fill patterns. (You can use the CAXIS= option to specify an outline color for block sides and the midpoint grid.) You can use PATTERN statements or the PATTERN window to select specific fills and colors for the blocks or block segments on the chart.

By default, the block fill pattern changes each time the subgroup variable value changes, so a different fill pattern is used for each subgroup segment. The number of different values for the SUBGROUP= variable determines the number of block colors and fill patterns on the chart. If you do not use the SUBGROUP= or PATTERNID= option, all blocks take the same fill pattern and color.

You can use the PATTERNID= option to select which variable determines when fill patterns change. In addition to using a different pattern for each subgroup, the GCHART procedure can change patterns for each midpoint, each group, or each BY group. See the discussion of the PATTERNID= option in "Options" earlier in this section for details.

If you provide fewer valid PATTERN definitions than the chart requires, the GCHART procedure uses the default fill pattern rotation for the blocks or block segments drawn after all defined fill patterns are exhausted. See "Pattern Sequences" in Chapter 15 for details.

You can use the COUTLINE= option to choose an outline color for all block faces or block face segments. By default, the block faces are outlined in the same color as the fill pattern. See "Options" earlier in this section for a discussion of the COUTLINE= option.

Controlling the Chart Text

You can use the FTEXT= and HTEXT= graphics options to control the font and size of text on the chart. See Chapter 5 for more information.

BLOCK Statement Examples

The following examples illustrate major features of the BLOCK statement.

Simple Block Chart

This example uses the BLOCK statement to display the total sales for the three branches of a fictitious company over a one-year period. The sum of the variable SALES is plotted for each value of the variable SITE.

The following program statements produce Output 23.6:

```
      /* set the graphics environment */
goptions reset=global gunit=pct border
         ftext=swissb htitle=6 htext=2.9;

      /* create data set TOTALS */
data totals;
   length dept $ 7 site $ 8;
   input dept site quarter sales;
   cards;
Parts   Sydney  1 7843.97
Parts   Atlanta 1 9225.26
more data lines
Tools   Atlanta 4 3624.19
Tools   Paris   4 6414.25
;
run;

      /* define global statements for chart */
title 'Total Sales';
footnote j=r 'GR23N06  ';
pattern1 value=solid color=green;

      /* generate block chart */
proc gchart data=totals;
   format sales dollar8.;
   block site
         / sumvar=sales;
   label site='00'x;
run;
quit;
```

Output 23.6 *Simple Block Chart (GR23N06)*

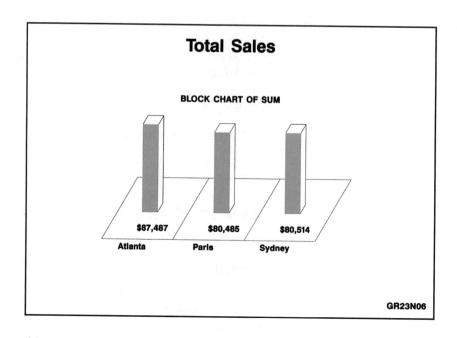

This example illustrates the following features:

☐ The global PATTERN statement defines the pattern and color used for all block faces. (All blocks take the same pattern and color because the default PATTERNID= value is SUBGROUP and the SUBGROUP= option is not used.)

☐ The SUMVAR= option specifies the variable used to calculate chart statistics. Because the TYPE= option is not used, the default statistic is the sum of the SALES variable values for each midpoint.

☐ The LABEL statement for the SITE variable suppresses the label for the horizontal axis by setting the label to an unprintable hexadecimal string.

Block Chart Using Groups and Subgroups

This example uses the BLOCK statement to chart the average sales for two of the branches shown in the first BLOCK statement example. The branches are selected using the MIDPOINTS= option. The average sales are grouped by the DEPT variable and are subgrouped by the QUARTER variable.

The following program statements produce Output 23.7:

```
   /* set the graphics environment */
goptions reset=global gunit=pct border
       ftext=swissb htitle=6 htext=3
       vpos=50 hpos=100;

   /* create data set TOTALS */
data totals;
   length dept $ 7 site $ 8;
   input dept site quarter sales;
   cards;
```

```
Parts   Sydney  1 7843.97
Parts   Atlanta 1 9225.26
more data lines
Tools   Atlanta 4 3624.19
Tools   Paris   4 6414.25
;
run;

    /* define title and footnote for chart */
title 'Average Sales by Department';
footnote j=r 'GR23N07  ';

    /* define pattern characteristics */
pattern1 value=solid color=blue;
pattern2 value=solid color=green;
pattern3 value=solid color=red;

    /* define legend characteristics */
legend frame label=('Quarter:');

    /* generate block chart */
proc gchart data=totals;
   format quarter roman.;
   format sales dollar8.;
   block site
        / type=mean
          sumvar=sales
          midpoints='Sydney' 'Atlanta'
          subgroup=quarter
          legend=legend
          group=dept
          noheading;
   run;
   quit;
```

Note: The chart created by this program is too wide to be displayed on many terminals. If you get a message that the chart is too large, try one of the following:

□ Use the HPOS= and VPOS= graphics options to increase the number of character cells defined for the output device.

□ Use the HTEXT= graphics option to decrease the size of the chart text.

See Chapter 5 for details on these and other graphics options.

Output 23.7 *Block Chart with Grouping and Subgrouping (GR23N07)*

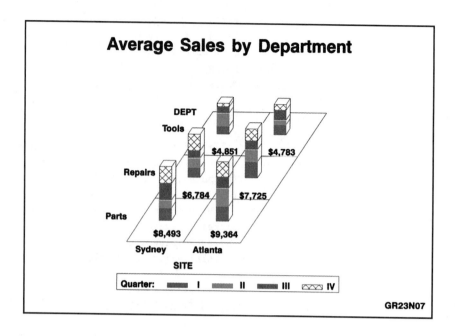

This example illustrates the following features:

☐ Three PATTERN statements define fill patterns for the subgroup categories. The default pattern is used for the fourth subgroup category.

☐ The TYPE= and SUMVAR= options specify the statistic to be charted, the mean of the values of the SALES variable for each midpoint. The statistic values printed beneath each block are formatted because the chart variable has an associated format.

☐ The MIDPOINTS= option selects two branches and specifies the left-to-right order of the branches on the chart.

☐ The SUBGROUP= option divides each block into separate segments for the four sales quarters.

☐ The LEGEND= option assigns the legend characteristics defined in the LEGEND statement to the subgroup legend.

☐ The GROUP= option creates a separate row of blocks for each different value of the DEPT variable.

☐ The NOHEADING option suppresses the default heading that would otherwise appear above the chart.

HBAR Statement

The HBAR statement creates one or more horizontal bar charts using the input data set specified in the PROC GCHART statement. The HBAR statement specifies the chart variable or variables that define the categories of data to be charted. Other variables can be specified to

☐ group the bars

☐ subdivide the bars

☐ provide data for the sum and mean statistics.

In addition, options used in the HBAR statement can select the statistic to be charted, manipulate the axes, and modify the appearance of the bars.

Syntax

The general form of the HBAR statement is

HBAR *chart-variable* < . . . *chart-variable-n*>
  </ <ANNOTATE=*Annotate-data-set*>
    <*appearance-options*>
    <*statistic-options*>
    <*midpoint-options*>
    <*axes-options*>
    <*description-options*>>;

□ *chart-variable* specifies a variable in the input data set with categories of data represented on the bar chart. If you include more than one chart variable in the HBAR statement, the variable names must be separated with blanks.

□ *appearance-options* can be one or more of the following:

  □ selecting colors

    CAXIS=*axis-color*

    COUTLINE=*bar-outline-color*

    CTEXT=*text-color*

  □ changing the appearance of the bars

    GSPACE=*n*

      where *n* is the amount of extra vertical space between groups of bars

    PATTERNID=BY | GROUP | MIDPOINT | SUBGROUP

    SPACE=*n*

      where *n* is the amount of vertical space between individual bars

    WIDTH=*n*

      where *n* is the vertical width of the bars

  □ framing the axis area

    CFRAME=*background-color*

    FRAME

  □ changing the appearance of the subgroup legend

    LEGEND=LEGEND<1 . . . 99>

    NOLEGEND

□ *statistic-options* can be one or more of the following:

  □ specifying statistics represented by the bars

    FREQ=*numeric-variable*

    G100

    SUMVAR=*numeric-variable*

TYPE=*statistic*

where *statistic* is one of the following:

CFREQ

CPERCENT

FREQ

MEAN

PERCENT

SUM

□ displaying statistic values

CFREQ

CPERCENT

FREQ

MEAN

NOSTATS

PERCENT

SUM

□ *midpoint-options* can be one or more of the following:

□ manipulating the midpoint values

DISCRETE

LEVELS=*n*

where *n* is the number of midpoints for the numeric chart variable

MIDPOINTS=*value-list*

MIDPOINTS=OLD

MISSING

□ grouping and subgrouping

GROUP=*variable*

SUBGROUP=*variable*

□ *axes-options* can be one or more of the following:

□ manipulating the axes

GAXIS=AXIS<1 . . . 99>

MAXIS=AXIS<1 . . . 99>

NOAXIS

RAXIS=*value-list* | AXIS<1 . . . 99>

□ setting the number of minor tick marks on the response axis

MINOR=*n*

where *n* is the number of minor tick marks

□ manipulating the midpoint order

ASCENDING

DESCENDING

NOZERO

□ adding and manipulating reference lines

AUTOREF

CLIPREF

NOBASEREF

REF=*value-list*

□ *description-options* can be either or both of the following:

DESCRIPTION='*string*'

NAME='*string*'

Options are fully described in "Options" later in this section.

Requirements

An HBAR statement must contain at least one chart variable. A separate chart is drawn for each chart variable.

Options

You can use the following options in the HBAR statement. Options used in an HBAR statement affect all graphs produced by that statement. If any of the following options are supplied, they must be separated from the chart variables with a slash (/). If you do not use any options, omit the slash.

ANNOTATE=*Annotate-data-set*
ANNO=*Annotate-data-set*

specifies a data set to provide annotation of graphs produced by the HBAR statement. *Annotate-data-set* must contain the appropriate Annotate variables. See Chapter 18 for details.

If the ANNOTATE= option is also used with the PROC GCHART statement, both sets of annotation are applied. If you specify BY-group processing, the Annotate data set must contain the BY variable. For details, see "Using BY-Group Processing with the Annotate Facility" in Chapter 18 and "Details of BY-Group Processing" in Chapter 10.

ASCENDING

arranges the bars in ascending order of the value of the chart statistic. By default, bars are arranged from top to bottom in ascending order of midpoint value, without regard for the lengths of the bars. The ASCENDING option reorders the midpoints so that the shortest bar is at the top and the longest bar is at the bottom. If you use the GROUP= option, the reordering is performed for each group, so the order of midpoint values may be different for each group of bars.

The ASCENDING option overrides any midpoint order specified with the MIDPOINTS= option or specified in the ORDER= option in an AXIS statement assigned to the midpoint axis.

AUTOREF
draws a vertical reference line at each major tick mark on the
response (horizontal) axis. To draw reference lines at specific points
on the response axis, use the REF= option.

AXIS=
See the RAXIS= option later in this section.

CAXIS=*axis-color*
specifies a color for the response and midpoint axis lines and for the
axis area frame if one is used. If you do not use the CAXIS= option,
a color specification is searched for in the following order:

1. the COLOR= option in AXIS definitions

2. the default, the first color in the colors list.

CFRAME=*background-color*
CFR=*background-color*
fills the axis area with the specified color and draws a frame around
the axis area. The FRAME option has no effect when the CFRAME=
option is used. The frame fill color does not affect the frame color,
which is always the same as the midpoint (vertical) axis line color. By
default, the frame area is not filled.

The frame fill color should be different from the colors used for bar
patterns. Bars or bar segments in the frame fill color are invisible
unless the COUTLINE= option is used to outline them in another
color.

CFREQ
prints the value of the cumulative frequency statistic in the table of
statistics. The default statistics are suppressed when you request
specific statistics.

CLIPREF
clips the reference lines at the bars. This makes the reference lines
appear to be behind the bars.

COUTLINE=*bar-outline-color*
outlines all bars or bar segments and legend values in the subgroup
legend (if it appears) using the specified color. By default, the outline
color for bars is the same as the pattern color.

Note: The outline color is the only distinction between empty
patterns. Using the COUTLINE= option when VALUE=EMPTY is
specified in PATTERN definitions makes the patterns look the same.

CPERCENT
CPCT
prints the value of the cumulative percentage statistic in the table of
statistics. The default statistics are suppressed when you request
specific statistics.

CTEXT=*text-color*
specifies the color of all text on the chart that is not otherwise
assigned a color. Text includes axis values and axis labels in the
response, midpoint, and group axes; the subgroup legend; and the
table of statistics. If you do not use the CTEXT= option, a color
specification is searched for in the following order:

1. the CTEXT= option in a GOPTIONS statement

2. the default, the first color in the colors list.

If you use the CTEXT= option, it overrides the color specification for the axis label and the tick mark values in the COLOR= option in an AXIS definition assigned to an axis.

If you use the CTEXT= option, the color specification is overridden by the following conditions:

□ If you also use the COLOR= parameter of a LABEL= or VALUE= option in a LEGEND definition assigned to the subgroup legend, that parameter determines the color of the legend label or the color of the legend value descriptions, respectively.

□ If you also use the COLOR= parameter of a LABEL= or VALUE= option in an AXIS definition assigned to an axis, it determines the color of the axis label or the color of the tick mark values, respectively.

DESCENDING

arranges the bars in descending order of the value of the chart statistic. By default, bars are arranged from top to bottom in ascending order of midpoint value, without regard to the lengths of the bars. The DESCENDING option reorders the midpoints so that the longest bar is at the top and the shortest bar is at the bottom. If you use the GROUP= option, each group is ordered separately, so the order of midpoint values may be different for each group of bars.

The DESCENDING option overrides any midpoint order specified with the MIDPOINTS= option or specified in the ORDER= option in an AXIS statement assigned to the midpoint axis.

DESCRIPTION='*string*'
DES='*string*'

specifies a descriptive string, up to 40 characters long, that appears in the Description field of the catalog entry for the chart. The description does not appear on the chart. By default, the GCHART procedure assigns a description of the form HBAR CHART OF *variable*, where *variable* is the name of the chart variable.

DISCRETE

treats a numeric chart variable as a discrete variable rather than as a continuous variable. The GCHART procedure creates a separate midpoint and, hence, a separate bar for each unique value of the chart variable. If the chart variable has a format associated with it, each formatted value is treated as a midpoint.

The LEVELS= option is ignored when you use the DISCRETE option. The MIDPOINTS= option overrides the DISCRETE option.

FRAME
FR

draws a rectangular frame around the axis area. By default, the frame is drawn in the color of the midpoint axis.

If the FRAME option is used without the CFRAME= option, the frame is empty. If the CFRAME= option is used, the frame is filled with the specified color.

A frame is always drawn when the CFRAME= option is used to fill the axis area, regardless of whether the FRAME option is used.

FREQ

prints the value of the frequency statistic in the table of statistics. The default statistics are suppressed when you request specific statistics.

FREQ=*numeric-variable*

uses the values of *numeric-variable* to weight the contribution of each observation to the statistic being computed. Noninteger values of *numeric-variable* are truncated to integers.

By default, each observation is counted only once in the calculation of the chart statistics. When you use the FREQ= option, each observation is counted the number of times specified by the value of *numeric-variable* for that observation. Observations for which the *numeric-variable* value is missing, 0, or negative are not used in the statistic calculation.

Because you cannot use TYPE=PERCENT, TYPE=CPERCENT, TYPE=FREQ, or TYPE=CFREQ when you use the SUMVAR= option, you must use the FREQ= option to calculate percentages, cumulative percentages, frequencies, or cumulative frequencies based on a sum.

G100

calculates the percentage and cumulative percentage statistics separately for each group. When you use the G100 option, the individual percentages reflect the contribution of the midpoint to the group and total 100 percent for each group. The G100 option is ignored unless you also use the GROUP= option.

By default, the individual percentages reflect the contribution of the midpoint to the entire chart and total 100 percent for the entire chart.

GAXIS=AXIS<1 . . . 99>

assigns axis characteristics to the group axis. This option is meaningful only in conjunction with the GROUP= option. The option value indicates which AXIS definition to use. The GAXIS= option is ignored if the specified definition is not currently in effect.

The AXIS statement options MAJOR= and MINOR= are ignored in AXIS definitions assigned to the group axis because the axis does not use tick marks. A warning message is written to the SAS log if these options appear in the AXIS definition.

You can use the ORDER= option in the AXIS statement to remove groups from the chart.

GROUP=*variable*

specifies that the data be grouped according to values of *variable*. *Variable* can be either character or numeric and is always treated as a discrete variable. A separate group of bars is produced for each unique value of *variable*. Missing values for *variable* are treated as a valid group.

By default, each group includes all midpoints, even if no observations for the group fall within the midpoint range, meaning that no bar is drawn at the midpoint. The NOZERO option suppresses midpoints with no observations.

The group axis appears to the left of the midpoint axis. By default, groups are arranged from top to bottom in ascending order of *variable* values.

The GAXIS= option can be used to assign axis characteristics to the group axis. See the discussion of the GAXIS= option earlier in this section for details.

GSPACE=*n*

specifies the amount of extra vertical space between groups of bars. Units for *n* are character cells. The value does not have to be an integer. For example, you can specify the following:

    hbar site / gspace=1.5;

Use GSPACE=0 to leave no extra space between adjacent groups of bars. In this case, the same space appears between groups of bars as between the bars in the same group.

The GSPACE= option is ignored unless you also use the GROUP= option. By default, the GCHART procedure calculates group spacing based on size of the axis area and the number of bars in the chart.

If the requested spacing results in a chart that is too large to fit in the space available for the midpoint (vertical) axis, an error message is written to the SAS log and no chart is produced.

LEGEND=LEGEND<1 . . . 99>

assigns legend characteristics to the subgroup legend. The LEGEND= option is ignored unless you also use the SUBGROUP= option.

▶ *Caution: The LEGEND= option does not generate a legend.*

The option value indicates which LEGEND definition to use. The LEGEND= option is ignored if the specified LEGEND definition is not currently in effect.

The following options override the LEGEND= option and suppress the subgroup legend:

NOLEGEND

PATTERNID=BY | GROUP | MIDPOINT

LEVELS=*n*

uses the specified number of midpoints for a numeric chart variable. The range for each midpoint is calculated automatically using the algorithm described in Terrell and Scott (1985).

This option is ignored if

□ the chart variable is character type

□ the DISCRETE option is used

□ the MIDPOINTS= option is used.

MAXIS=AXIS<1 . . . 99>

assigns axis characteristics to the midpoint (vertical) axis. The option value indicates which AXIS definition to use. The MAXIS= option is ignored if the specified AXIS definition is not currently in effect.

The AXIS statement options MAJOR= and MINOR= are ignored in AXIS definitions assigned to the midpoint axis because the axis does not use tick marks. A warning message is written to the SAS log if these options appear in the AXIS definition.

MEAN

prints the value of the mean statistic in the table of statistics. The MEAN option is ignored unless you also use the SUMVAR= option. A label is added to the column heading indicating the variable for which the mean is calculated. The default statistics are suppressed when you request specific statistics.

MIDPOINTS=*value-list*

specifies values for midpoints on the midpoint (vertical) axis. By default, one of these two methods is used:

☐ If the chart variable is numeric type, the GCHART procedure calculates midpoint values.

☐ If the chart variable is character type or is numeric type and the DISCRETE option is used, the GCHART procedure creates a midpoint for each unique value of the chart variable.

If *value-list* contains more midpoints than can fit on the midpoint axis, an error message is written to the SAS log and no chart is produced. On many devices, this problem can be corrected by increasing the number of cells in your graphics display using the HPOS= and VPOS= graphics options. See Chapter 5 for details.

The ORDER= option in an AXIS definition assigned to the midpoint axis overrides the order specified in the MIDPOINTS= option. The HBAR statement options ASCENDING and DESCENDING also override both the order specified in the MIDPOINTS= option and the order specified in the ORDER= option in the AXIS statement assigned to the midpoint axis using the MAXIS= option.

For numeric chart variables, *value-list* can be specified in the following ways:

n n . . . n

n,n, . . . ,n

n TO *n* <BY *increment*> <*n . . . n*> <*n, . . . ,n*>

n n . . . n TO *n* <BY *increment*> <*n . . . n*>

n,n, . . . ,n TO *n* <BY *increment*> <*n, . . . ,n*>

'*SAS-value*'*i* TO '*SAS-value*'*i* <BY *interval*>

'*SAS-value*'*i* '*SAS-value*'*i* . . . '*SAS-value*'*i*

If the variable has an associated format, you must specify the unformatted values in *value-list*.

For continuous variables, the midpoints are the medians of the ranges of possible values of the chart variable. A value that falls exactly halfway between two midpoints is placed in the higher range.

For character chart variables, *value-list* must be a list of midpoint values. Values must be enclosed in single quotes and separated by blanks (commas are not allowed as separators), as in this example:

```
midpoints='Paris' 'Sydney' 'Atlanta'
```

The values can be specified in any order, so the *value-list* can be used to order the bars. If the variable has an associated format, you must specify the formatted values in *value-list*. By default, midpoints are arranged top to bottom in ascending order of the midpoint values. If the character chart variable has an associated format, the values are arranged in order of the formatted values.

You can selectively exclude some chart variable values from the chart, as in this example:

```
midpoints='Paris'
```

Only those observations for which the chart variable exactly matches one of the midpoint values are counted. As a result, observations can be inadvertently excluded if values in the midpoint list are misspelled or if the case does not match exactly.

MIDPOINTS=OLD

tells the GCHART procedure to calculate default midpoints using the algorithm used in Release 82.4 and Version 5 of SAS/GRAPH software. The MIDPOINTS=OLD option is ignored unless the chart variable is numeric type.

MINOR=*n*

specifies the number of minor tick marks between each major tick mark on the response (horizontal) axis.

Using the MINOR= option in the HBAR statement overrides the number of minor tick marks specified in the MINOR= option in an AXIS definition assigned to the response axis with the RAXIS= option.

MISSING

accepts a missing value as a valid midpoint for the chart variable. By default, observations for which the value of the chart variable is missing are ignored.

Note: Missing values are always valid for group and subgroup variables.

NAME='*string*'

specifies a string, up to eight characters long, that appears in the Name field of the catalog entry for the chart. *String* must be a valid SAS name. By default, the name assigned is GCHART. If either the name specified or the default name duplicates an existing name in the catalog, SAS/GRAPH software adds a number to the duplicate name to create a unique name, for example, GCHART2.

NOAXIS

suppresses the axes, including axis lines, axis labels, axis values, and all major and minor tick marks. Frames and axis-area fills requested by the FRAME and CFRAME= options are not suppressed. The NOAXIS option overrides the GAXIS=, MAXIS=, and RAXIS= options.

NOBASEREF

suppresses the zero reference line when the SUM or MEAN chart statistic has negative values.

NOLEGEND

suppresses the subgroup legend. The NOLEGEND option is ignored unless you also use the SUBGROUP= option.

NOSTATS

suppresses the descriptive statistic values printed in the table of statistics. The NOSTATS option suppresses both the default statistics and specific statistics requested by the FREQ, CFREQ, PERCENT, CPERCENT, SUM, and MEAN options.

NOZERO

> suppresses any midpoints for which there are no corresponding values of the chart variable and, hence, no bar. The NOZERO option usually is used with the GROUP= option to suppress midpoints when not all values of the chart variable are present for every group or if the chart statistic for the bar is 0.

PATTERNID=BY | GROUP | MIDPOINT | SUBGROUP

> specifies the way fill patterns are assigned. By default, PATTERNID=SUBGROUP. The meanings of the option values are as follows:

> | | |
> |---|---|
> | BY | changes patterns each time the value of the BY variable changes. All bars use the same pattern if the GCHART procedure does not include a BY statement. |
> | GROUP | changes patterns every time the value of the group variable changes. All bars in each group use the same pattern, but a different pattern is used for each group. |
> | MIDPOINT | changes patterns every time the midpoint value changes. If the GROUP= option is used, the respective midpoint patterns are repeated for each group. |
> | SUBGROUP | changes patterns every time the value of the subgroup variable changes. Bars divided into subgroups use a different pattern for each subgroup. If the SUBGROUP= option is not used, all bars have the same pattern. |

> A warning message is written to the SAS log if the PATTERNID= value is anything other than SUBGROUP when the SUBGROUP= option is used, since this situation may make it impossible to distinguish the subgroups and does not produce a legend.

PERCENT
PCT

> prints the value of the percentage statistic in the table of statistics. The default statistics are suppressed when you request specific statistics.

RAXIS=*value-list* | AXIS<1 . . . 99>
AXIS=*value-list* | AXIS<1 . . . 99>

> specify values for the major tick mark divisions on the response (horizontal) axis or assign an AXIS definition to the axis. By default, the GCHART procedure scales the response axis automatically and provides an appropriate number of tick marks.

> *Value-list* can be specified in the following ways:

> *n n . . . n*

> *n,n, . . . ,n*

> *n* TO *n* <BY *increment*> <*n . . . n*> <*n, . . . ,n*>

> *n n . . . n* TO *n* <BY *increment*> <*n . . . n*>

> *n,n, . . . ,n* TO *n* <BY *increment*> <*n, . . . ,n*>

> See the ORDER= option in Chapter 9 for additional information on specifying *value-list*.

Negative values can be specified, but negative values are reasonable only when the TYPE= option value is SUM or MEAN and one or more of the sums or means are less than 0. Frequency and percentage values are never less than 0.

For lists of values, a separate major tick mark is created for each individual value. A warning message is written to the SAS log if the values are not evenly spaced.

If the values represented by the bars are larger than the highest tick mark value, the bars are truncated at the highest tick mark.

To assign an AXIS definition, use a value of the form AXIS<1 . . . 99>. The option is ignored if no AXIS definition is currently in effect. See Chapter 9 for details.

If a BY statement is used with the PROC GCHART statement, the same response axes are produced for each BY group when RAXIS=*value-list* is used or if there is an ORDER= list in the AXIS statement assigned to the response axis.

REF=*value-list*

draws reference lines at the specified points on the response (horizontal) axis. The *value-list* values can be listed in any order. The values should be within the range of values represented by the response axis. A warning is written to the SAS log if any of the points are off the axis, and no reference line is drawn for such points. The AUTOREF option can be used to draw reference lines automatically at all of the major tick marks. The REF= option is ignored if you use the AUTOREF option.

Value-list can be specified in the following ways:

n n . . . n

n,n, . . . ,n

n TO *n* <BY *increment*> <*n . . . n*> <*n, . . . ,n*>

n n . . . n TO *n* <BY *increment*> <*n . . . n*>

n,n, . . . ,n TO *n* <BY *increment*> <*n, . . . ,n*>

See the ORDER= option in Chapter 9 for additional information on specifying *value-list*.

SPACE=*n*

specifies the amount of vertical space between individual bars or between the bars within each group if you also use the GROUP= option. By default, the GCHART procedure calculates spacing based on the size of the axis area and the number of bars on the chart. Units for *n* are character cells. The value does not have to be an integer. For example, you can specify the following:

```
hbar site / space=1.5;
```

Use SPACE=0 to leave no space between adjacent bars.

The SPACE option is ignored if the specified spacing requests a chart that is too large to fit in the space available for the midpoint (vertical) axis, and a warning message is issued.

SUBGROUP=*variable*

divides the bars into segments according to the values of *variable*. Each bar is divided into as many parts as there are discrete values of *variable* for the midpoint.

(SUBGROUP= continued)

By default, a legend appears at the bottom of the graph when you use the SUBGROUP= option. The legend indicates which pattern represents which value of *variable*. The LEGEND= option can be used to assign a LEGEND definition to the subgroup legend.

The following options suppress the subgroup legend:

NOLEGEND

PATTERNID=BY | GROUP | MIDPOINT

SUM

prints the value of the sum statistic in the table of statistics. The SUM option is ignored unless you also use the SUMVAR= option. A label is added to the column heading indicating the variable for which the total is calculated. The default statistics are suppressed when you request specific statistics.

SUMVAR=*numeric-variable*

specifies the variable to be used for sum or mean calculations. The GCHART procedure calculates the sum or, if requested, the mean of *numeric-variable* for each midpoint. These statistics can then be represented by the length of the bars along the response (horizontal) axis.

When you use the SUMVAR= option, the TYPE= option value must be either SUM or MEAN. By default, TYPE=SUM when the SUMVAR= option is used.

TYPE=*statistic*

specifies the chart statistic for the chart. *Statistic* can be one of the following when you do not use the SUMVAR= option:

Value of *statistic*	Statistic represented on the chart
FREQ	frequency
CFREQ	cumulative frequency
PERCENT PCT	percentage
CPERCENT CPCT	cumulative percentage

Statistic can be either of the following when you use the SUMVAR= option:

Value of *statistic*	Statistic represented on the chart
SUM	sum
MEAN	mean

By default, TYPE=FREQ when the SUMVAR= option is not used, and TYPE=SUM when SUMVAR= is used.

When you specify TYPE=MEAN and use the SUBGROUP= option, the length of the bar represents the mean for the entire midpoint. The subgroup segments are proportional to the subgroup's contribution to the sum for the bar.

Because you cannot use TYPE=PERCENT, TYPE=CPERCENT, TYPE=FREQ, or TYPE=CFREQ when you use the SUMVAR= option, you must use the FREQ= option to calculate percentages, cumulative percentages, frequencies, and cumulative frequencies based on a sum.

See "Chart Statistics" earlier in this chapter for a complete description of the types of statistics that can be represented.

WIDTH=*n*

specifies the vertical width of the bars. By default, the GCHART procedure calculates bar width based on the size of the axis area and the number of bars in the chart. Units for *n* are character cells. The value for *n* must be greater than 0, but it does not have to be an integer. For example, you can specify the following:

```
hbar site / width=1.5;
```

The WIDTH= option is ignored if the requested bar width results in a chart that is too large to fit in the space available for the midpoint (vertical) axis.

Using the HBAR Statement

The form of your chart is governed by the variables you specify and the options you use in the HBAR statement. A separate bar chart is produced for each chart variable specified. For example, the following statement produces two separate horizontal bar charts:

```
hbar site year;
```

The values on the midpoint (vertical) axis are the midpoints for ranges of chart variable values. The response (horizontal) axis provides a scale for the values of the chart statistic. A table of statistic values can be displayed to the right of the bars.

The GCHART procedure automatically scales the response axis, determines bar width, and chooses spacing between the bars for display in the procedure output area. However, you can use options to override the defaults and to choose bar intervals and the number and spacing of bars. The procedure also can divide the bars into groups according to the values of a group variable and subdivide the bars into segments according to the values of a subgroup variable.

The following sections explain how you can change the appearance of your horizontal bar chart using different HBAR statement options.

The Chart Variable and the Midpoint Axis

The value of the chart variable determines the bar to which each observation in the data set contributes. The way in which midpoints are selected varies depending on the type of the chart variable and the options used. See "Chart Variables and Midpoint Selection" earlier in this chapter for additional information on how midpoints are determined.

Formatted numeric variables are ordered by the unformatted numeric values. If you use the DISCRETE option and the variable is formatted, there is one bar for each formatted value.

You can use the MIDPOINTS= and LEVELS= options to change the number of midpoints used for numeric variables. For example, if you specify the following, the GCHART procedure calculates four midpoints for a continuous chart variable:

```
hbar sales / levels=4;
```

If you specify the following, the GCHART procedure uses 1, 3, and 5 as the midpoints for the chart:

```
hbar x / midpoints=1 3 5;
```

You can use the ORDER= option in an AXIS definition assigned to the midpoint axis to rearrange the order of the midpoints or to exclude some midpoints from the chart.

Note: The ORDER= option does not change the way chart statistics are calculated. All of the midpoints are included in the calculation of the chart statistic unless you also use the MIDPOINTS= option.

The midpoint value for each bar is shown on the *midpoint (vertical) axis*. By default, midpoint values are arranged in ascending order of the midpoint value down the midpoint axis, starting with the smallest value at the top. If the chart variable is character and has an associated format, the bars are built and ordered according to the formatted values of the chart variable. The midpoint axis also includes a label indicating the chart variable name or label.

You can use the MAXIS= option to assign an AXIS definition to the midpoint axis. You can use the MIDPOINTS= option to change the order of midpoints. For example, the following statement orders the midpoints **Paris Atlanta** instead of the default of **Atlanta Paris**:

```
hbar branch / midpoints='Paris' 'Atlanta';
```

The ASCENDING or DESCENDING option also can be used to modify bar order. For more information on manipulating the midpoint axis, see the discussions of the MIDPOINTS=, MAXIS=, ASCENDING, and DESCENDING options in "Options" earlier in this section.

The Chart Statistic and the Response Axis

The length of each bar graphically represents the value of the chart statistic for the corresponding midpoint. These six types of statistics can be charted:

□ frequency

□ cumulative frequency

□ percentage

□ cumulative percentage

□ sum

□ mean.

See "Chart Statistics" earlier in this chapter for more information.

The default chart statistic is frequency. If the SUMVAR= option is used, the default chart statistic is sum. You can use the TYPE= option to select the chart statistic. You must use the SUMVAR= option to identify the variable to use for calculating sum or mean statistics. For example, if you want to calculate a sum based on the value of the variable COUNT, specify the following in the HBAR statement:

```
hbar branch / sumvar=count;
```

By default, each observation is counted only once in the calculation of the chart statistic. You can use the FREQ= option to identify the variable that indicates the number of times each observation is counted.

The response (horizontal) axis provides a scale for interpreting the magnitude of the chart statistic for each bar. By default, the response axis is divided into evenly spaced intervals identified with tick marks. Major tick marks are labeled with the corresponding statistic value. Minor tick marks are evenly distributed between the major tick marks unless a log axis has been requested. For sum and mean statistics, the major tick marks are labeled with values of the SUMVAR= variable (formatted if the variable has an associated format). The axis also has an overall label indicating the statistic being represented.

You can use the RAXIS= option to change the major tick mark intervals on the response axis or to assign an AXIS definition, which can modify the text, tick mark intervals, or general appearance of the axis.

The Group Variable and the Group Axis

If you want to display your data categorized by both the chart variable and another variable, you can use the second variable to organize the bars into groups. Use the GROUP= option to identify the second variable as the group variable for the chart. When you use the GROUP= option, a separate group of bars is created for each unique value of the group variable. Each group contains all the midpoints defined for the chart variable unless you use the NOZERO option.

The *group axis* identifies the group variable values that distinguish the groups. In horizontal bar charts, the group axis is positioned to the left of the midpoint axis. The group axis provides a list of variable values but does not provide an axis line. The group axis also has a label that, by default, indicates the name or label of the group variable.

By default, the groups are arranged from top to bottom in ascending order of group variable value, starting with the smallest value at the top. You can use the GAXIS= option to assign an AXIS definition to the group axis. The definition can modify the order, text, and appearance of the axis.

See the descriptions of the GROUP= and GAXIS= options in "Options" earlier in this section for details. See "Horizontal Bar Chart Using Groups" in "HBAR Statement Examples" later in this section for an illustration of grouping in a horizontal bar chart.

The Subgroup Variable and the Subgroup Legend

If you want to divide each bar into segments based on the contribution of a variable, you can use the variable as a subgroup variable. Use the SUBGROUP= option to identify the variable as the subgroup variable for the chart. When you use the SUBGROUP= option, each bar contains a separate segment for every unique value of the subgroup variable for the bar's midpoint. The number of segments in each bar depends on the number of different values of the subgroup variable for the corresponding midpoint.

The subgroup legend provides a key to the patterns that identify each subgroup. By default, the subgroup legend appears below the response axis and above any footnotes. The subgroup legend also includes a label that, by default, indicates the name or label of the subgroup variable.

Subgrouping is effective only when subgroups can be distinguished by a different color or fill pattern. Unless you change the PATTERNID= option from its default (SUBGROUP), a different pattern is used for each subgroup within the bar.

You can create a legend based on the chart midpoints. Simply use the chart variable as the subgroup variable as follows:

```
hbar city / subgroup=city;
```

You can use the LEGEND= option to assign a LEGEND statement definition to the subgroup legend as shown here:

```
hbar city / legend=legend3 subgroup=quarter;
```

The subgroup legend is suppressed when the PATTERNID= option value is anything other than SUBGROUP, even if you use the LEGEND= option. In this case, you receive a warning message in the SAS log.

See the descriptions of the SUBGROUP=, PATTERNID=, and LEGEND= options in "Options" earlier in this section for additional details. See "Horizontal Bar Chart Using Subgroups" in "HBAR Statement Examples" later in this section for an illustration of subgrouping in a horizontal bar chart.

The Table of Statistics

In addition to displaying one statistic graphically on the response axis, the HBAR statement can print a table of statistic values to the right of the bars. When TYPE= FREQ, CFREQ, PERCENT, or CPERCENT, the frequency, cumulative frequency, percentage, and cumulative percentage statistic values are all printed next to the bars by default. When TYPE=SUM, the frequency and sum statistic values are printed by default. When TYPE=MEAN, the frequency and mean statistic values are printed by default. For sum and mean, the name of the SUMVAR= variable is added to the heading for the column of values.

You can use the FREQ, PERCENT, CFREQ, CPERCENT, SUM, and MEAN options to select only certain statistics. Regardless of the order in which you use the options, the values are always printed in this order:

1. frequency

2. cumulative frequency

3. percentage

4. cumulative percentage

5. sum

6. mean.

When you do not use the SUMVAR= option, only frequency, cumulative frequency, percentage, and cumulative percentage statistics can be printed. If you use the SUMVAR= option, all six statistics, including the sum and mean, can be printed. You can suppress all statistics with the NOSTATS option. For more information, see "Options" earlier in this section.

You can use the HTEXT= and FTEXT= graphics options to control the font and size of the text in the table of statistics. For more information, see Chapter 5.

Selecting Patterns for the Bars

Horizontal bar charts can use only bar/block patterns. This pattern type uses the following fill patterns:

EMPTY

SOLID

style<*density*>

    where

    style   can be X | L | R.

    density   can be 1 . . . 5.

All other fill pattern specifications are ignored. See Chapter 15 for more information.

By default, the bar pattern changes each time the subgroup variable value changes, so a different fill pattern is used for each subgroup. The number of different values for the SUBGROUP= variable determines the number of bar colors and fill patterns in the chart. If you do not use the SUBGROUP= or PATTERNID= option, all bars take the same fill pattern and color. You can use PATTERN statements or the PATTERN window to define specific fills and colors for the bars or bar segments in the chart.

You can use the PATTERNID= option to select which variable determines when fill patterns change. In addition to using a different fill pattern for each subgroup, the GCHART procedure can change fill patterns for each bar, each group of bars, or each BY group. See the discussion of the PATTERNID= option in "Options" earlier in this section for details.

If you provide fewer valid PATTERN definitions than the chart requires, the GCHART procedure uses the default pattern rotation for the bars or bar segments drawn after all defined patterns are exhausted. See Chapter 15 for details.

You can use the COUTLINE= option to choose an outline color for all bars or bar segments. By default, the bars are outlined in the same color as the fill pattern. See "Options" earlier in this section for a discussion of the COUTLINE= option.

Using Other Global Statements

You can use AXIS and LEGEND definitions to modify the appearance of bar charts produced by the HBAR statement.

You can use axis characteristics defined in AXIS statements or the AXIS window to modify the text and appearance of the axes on the charts. Assign AXIS definitions to the response, midpoint, and group axes using the RAXIS=, MAXIS=, and GAXIS= options, respectively.

Certain restrictions apply; for example, the midpoint and group axes in horizontal bar charts do not have tick marks, so any tick mark options in AXIS statements assigned to those axes are ignored. See the descriptions of the GAXIS=, MAXIS=, and RAXIS= options in "Options" earlier in this section for details of the restrictions for each axis.

You can use legend characteristics defined in LEGEND statements or the LEGEND window to adjust the location, text, and appearance of the subgroup legend on the charts. Legend characteristics are assigned to the subgroup legend using the LEGEND= option.

HBAR Statement Examples

The following examples illustrate major features of the HBAR statement.

Simple Horizontal Bar Chart

This example uses the HBAR statement to display the total sales for the three branches of a fictitious company over a one-year period. The chart statistic and summary information are selected using the SUM and SUMVAR= options.

The following program statements produce Output 23.8:

```
   /* set the graphics environment */
goptions reset=global gunit=pct border
         ftext=swissb htitle=6 htext=3;

   /* create data set TOTALS */
data totals;
   length dept $ 7 site $ 8;
   input dept site quarter sales;
   cards;
Parts   Sydney  1 7843.97
Parts   Atlanta 1 9225.26
more data lines
Tools   Atlanta 4 3624.19
Tools   Paris   4 6414.25
;
run;

   /* define title and footnote for chart */
title 'Total Sales';
footnote j=r 'GR23N08  ';

   /* define axis characteristics */
axis1 label=('Branch') width=3;

   /* define pattern characteristics */
pattern value=solid color=red;
```

```
                          /* generate horizontal bar chart */
                      proc gchart data=totals;
                          format sales dollar8.;
                          hbar site
                              / frame
                                sumvar=sales
                                midpoints='Sydney' 'Atlanta' 'Paris'
                                maxis=axis1
                                sum;
                      run;
                      quit;
```

Output 23.8 *Simple Horizontal Bar Chart (GR23N08)*

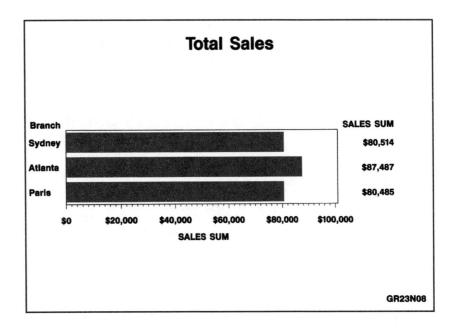

This example illustrates the following features:

□ The global PATTERN statement defines the pattern and color used for all bars. (All bars take the same pattern and color because the default PATTERNID= value is SUBGROUP and the SUBGROUP= option is not used.)

□ The FRAME option draws a rectangular frame around the axis area.

□ The SUMVAR= option specifies the variable used to calculate chart statistics. Because the TYPE= option is not used, the default statistic is the sum of the values of the SALES variable for each midpoint.

□ The MIDPOINTS= option specifies the order of midpoint values on the midpoint axis.

□ The MAXIS= option assigns the axis characteristics defined in the AXIS1 statement to the midpoint axis.

□ The SUM option specifies that only the sum statistic value is printed to the right of the bars.

Horizontal Bar Chart Using Subgroups

This example charts the same data as the first HBAR statement example but adds the SUBGROUP= option to show the contribution of each of the company's three departments to the total for each branch.

The following program statements produce Output 23.9:

```
   /* set the graphics environment */
goptions reset=global gunit=pct border
        ftext=swissb htitle=6 htext=3;

   /* create data set TOTALS */
data totals;
   length dept $ 7 site $ 8;
   input dept site quarter sales;
   cards;
Parts    Sydney  1 7843.97
Parts    Atlanta 1 9225.26
more data lines
Tools    Atlanta 4 3624.19
Tools    Paris   4 6414.25
;
run;

   /* define title and footnote for chart */
title 'Total Sales by Department';
footnote j=r 'GR23N09  ';

   /* define axis characteristics */
axis1 label=('Branch') width=3;

   /* define pattern characteristics */
pattern1 value=solid color=blue;
pattern2 value=solid color=green;
pattern3 value=solid color=red;

   /* define legend characteristics */
legend frame label=('Department:');
```

```
                    /* generate horizontal bar chart */
                proc gchart data=totals;
                    format sales dollar8.;
                    hbar site
                        / frame
                            sumvar=sales
                            maxis=axis1
                            raxis=0 to 90000 by 15000
                            minor=2
                            sum
                            subgroup=dept
                            legend=legend
                            ascending;
                run;
                quit;
```

Output 23.9 *Horizontal Bar Chart with Subgrouping (GR23N09)*

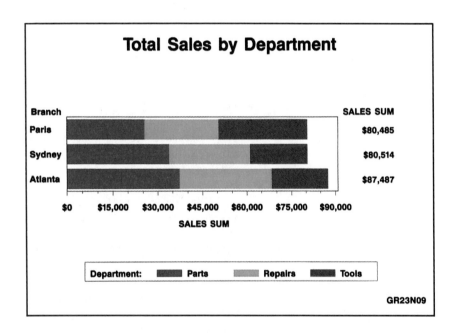

This example illustrates the following features:

□ Three PATTERN statements define the three patterns for the three subgroup categories.

□ The RAXIS= option specifies the range of values on the response (horizontal) axis.

□ The MINOR= option generates two minor tick marks in each interval on the response (horizontal) axis. Given the values specified in the RAXIS= option, each minor tick mark represents $5,000.

□ The SUBGROUP= option specifies the variable used to subgroup the bars.

□ The LEGEND= option assigns the legend characteristics in the LEGEND definition to the subgroup legend.

□ The ASCENDING option specifies that the branches are listed in ascending order by the chart statistic, total sales.

Horizontal Bar Chart Using Groups

This example charts the same data as the first HBAR statement example but adds the GROUP= option to divide the bars into four groups, one for each of the four quarters of sales data in the input data set.

The following program statements produce Output 23.10:

```
     /* set the graphics environment */
goptions reset=global gunit=pct border
         ftext=swissb htitle=6 htext=2.7;

     /* create data set TOTALS */
data totals;
   length dept $ 7 site $ 8;
   input dept site quarter sales;
   cards;
Parts   Sydney  1 7843.97
Parts   Atlanta 1 9225.26
more data lines
Tools   Atlanta 4 3624.19
Tools   Paris   4 6414.25
;
run;

     /* define title and footnote for chart */
title 'Sales by Department';
footnote j=r 'GR23N10  ';

     /* define axis characteristics */
axis1 label=('Branch') width=3;
axis2 label=none width=3;
axis3 label=none order=(0 to 40000 by 5000);

     /* define pattern characteristics */
pattern1 value=solid color=blue;
pattern2 value=solid color=green;
pattern3 value=solid color=red;

     /* define legend characteristics */
legend frame label=('Quarter:');

     /* generate horizontal bar chart */
proc gchart data=totals;
   format quarter roman.;
   format sales dollar8.;
   hbar site
        / frame
          sumvar=sales
          midpoints='Sydney' 'Atlanta' 'Paris'
          maxis=axis1
          raxis=axis3
          minor=1
          nostats
          sum
          subgroup=quarter
```

```
                          legend=legend
                          group=dept
                          gaxis=axis2
                          space=0
                          coutline=gray
                          ref=25000;
            run;
            quit;
```

Output 23.10 *Horizontal Bar Chart with Grouping (GR23N10)*

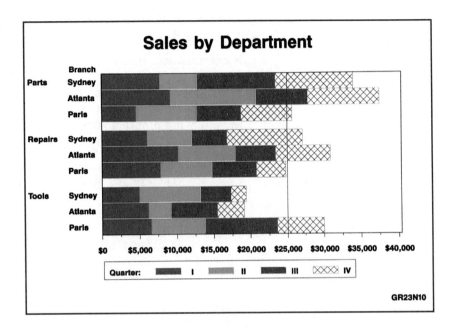

This example illustrates the following features:

□ The global PATTERN statements define the pattern and color used for three of the subgroup categories. The default pattern is used for the fourth category.

□ The RAXIS= option assigns the axis characteristics defined in the AXIS3 statement to the response (horizontal) axis.

□ The MINOR= option generates one minor tick mark in each interval on the response (horizontal) axis. Given the values specified in the ORDER= option in the AXIS3 statement, each minor tick mark represents $2,500.

□ The NOSTATS option suppresses the descriptive statistic values printed to the right of the bars. It also suppresses the statistics requested by the SUM option.

□ The SUBGROUP= option divides each bar into separate segments for the four quarters of sales information.

□ The GROUP= option creates a separate group of bars for each different value of the DEPT variable.

□ The SPACE= option eliminates space between bars within each group, which visually reinforces the effect of grouping.

□ The REF= option draws a vertical reference line at the $25,000 point on the response axis. This reference line highlights which of the branches exceeded that sales amount in any of the departments shown on the chart.

Horizontal Bar Chart with a Continuous Chart Variable

This example uses the HBAR statement to chart the salary distribution for each of five salary classes. Because SALARY is a continuous variable, the GCHART procedure assigns default midpoints. The chart statistic is frequency because the SUMVAR= and TYPE= options are not used.

The following program statements produce Output 23.11:

```
/* set the graphics environment */
goptions reset=global gunit=pct border
         ftext=swissb htitle=6 htext=3;

   /* create data set SALARIES */
data salaries;
   input id class $ salary;
   cards;
101 Z5 41541
102 Z5 40402
more data lines
229 Z1 20475
230 Z1 23450
;
run;

   /* define title and footnote for chart */
title 'Salary Information';
footnote j=r 'GR23N11  ';

   /* define axis characteristics */
axis1 label=('Salary') width=3;
axis2 label=none width=3;

   /* define pattern characteristics */
pattern1 value=solid color=blue;
pattern2 value=solid color=green;
pattern3 value=solid color=red;
pattern4 value=solid color=lib;
pattern5 value=solid color=pink;

   /* define legend characteristics */
legend frame label=('Job Class:');
```

```
                    /* generate horizontal bar chart */
              proc gchart data=salaries;
                 format salary dollar8.;
                 hbar salary
                      / frame
                        maxis=axis1
                        gaxis=axis2
                        subgroup=class
                        space=0
                        coutline=gray
                        legend=legend
                        autoref
                        clipref;
              run;
              quit;
```

Output 23.11 Horizontal Bar Chart with Default Midpoints (GR23N11)

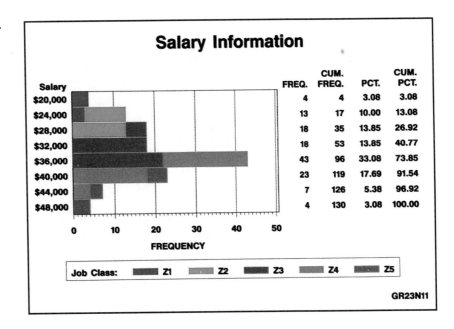

This example illustrates the following features:

□ The global PATTERN statements define the patterns and colors used for the subgroup categories.

□ The AUTOREF option specifies that reference lines should be added to the chart at each major tick mark. The CLIPREF option specifies that the reference lines should appear behind the chart bars.

□ All of the descriptive statistic values are printed to the right of the bars because no specific statistics are requested.

□ Midpoints are selected automatically by the GCHART procedure because the MIDPOINTS= and DISCRETE options are not used.

Horizontal Bar Chart with a Discrete Chart Variable

This example charts the same data as the first HBAR statement example but uses QUARTER as the chart variable. The DISCRETE option is used so that the numeric variable QUARTER is treated as a discrete variable, rather than as a continuous variable.

The following program statements produce Output 23.12:

```
      /* set the graphics environment */
   goptions reset=global gunit=pct border
           ftext=swissb htitle=6 htext=3;

      /* create data set TOTALS */
   data totals;
      length dept $ 7 site $ 8;
      input dept site quarter sales;
      cards;
   Parts   Sydney  1 7843.97
   Parts   Atlanta 1 9225.26
   more data lines
   Tools   Atlanta 4 3624.19
   Tools   Paris   4 6414.25
   ;
   run;

      /* define title and footnote for chart */
   title 'Sales by Department';
   footnote j=r 'GR23N12  ';

      /* define pattern characteristics */
   pattern value=solid color=green;

      /* define axis characteristics */
   axis1 label=('Dept.')
         order=('Repairs' 'Tools' 'Parts') width=3;
   axis2 label=none width=3;
   axis3 label=none order=0 to 30000 by 5000 width=3;

      /* generate horizontal bar chart */
   proc gchart data=totals;
      format quarter roman.;
      format sales dollar8.;
      hbar quarter
           / frame
             sumvar=sales
             maxis=axis2
             raxis=axis3
             minor=0
             nostats
             group=dept
             gaxis=axis1
             discrete;
   run;
   quit;
```

Output 23.12 Horizontal Bar Chart with Discrete Midpoints (GR23N12)

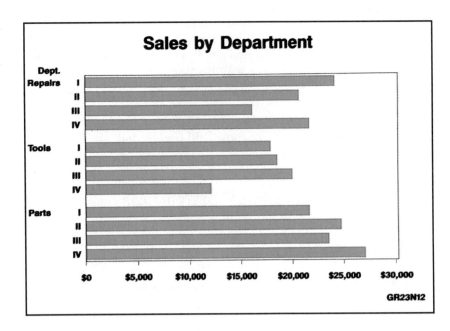

This example illustrates the following features:

□ The FORMAT statements assign formats to the QUARTER and SALES variables.

□ The MINOR= option suppresses minor tick marks for the response (horizontal) axis intervals.

□ The NOSTATS option suppresses the table of statistics.

□ The DISCRETE option specifies that the numeric chart variable QUARTER should be treated as a discrete variable rather than as a continuous variable.

PIE Statement

The PIE statement creates one or more pie charts using the input data set specified in the PROC GCHART statement. The PIE statement specifies the chart variable or variables that define the categories of data to be charted. Other variables can be specified to

□ divide the data into groups of pies

□ provide data for the sum and mean statistics.

In addition, options used in the PIE statement can select the statistic to be charted, determine the ranges of chart variable values for each slice, modify the appearance of the pies, and position the slice labels.

Syntax

The general form of the PIE statement is

PIE *chart-variable* < ... *chart-variable-n*>
    </ <ANNOTATE=*Annotate-data-set*>
        <*appearance-options*>
        <*statistic-options*>
        <*midpoint-options*>
        <*description-options*>>;

□ *chart-variable* specifies a variable in the input data set with categories of data represented on the pie chart. If you include more than one chart variable in the PIE statement, the variable names should be separated with blanks.

□ *appearance-options* can be one or more of the following:

□ selecting colors

CFILL=*fill-color*

COUTLINE=*slice-outline-color*

CTEXT=*text-color*

MATCHCOLOR

□ changing the appearance of the pies

ANGLE=*degrees*

EXPLODE=*value-list*

FILL=SOLID | X

INVISIBLE=*value-list*

□ manipulating the slice labels

PERCENT=ARROW | INSIDE | NONE | OUTSIDE

SLICE=ARROW | INSIDE | NONE | OUTSIDE

VALUE=ARROW | INSIDE | NONE | OUTSIDE

□ suppressing headings

NOGROUPHEADING

NOHEADING

□ *statistic-options* can be one or more of the following:

FREQ=*numeric-variable*

SUMVAR=*numeric-variable*

TYPE=*statistic*

where *statistic* is one of the following:

CFREQ

CPERCENT

FREQ

MEAN

PERCENT

SUM

□ *midpoint-options* can be one or more of the following:

□ manipulating the midpoint values

DISCRETE

LEVELS=*n*

> where *n* is the number of midpoints for the numeric chart variable

MIDPOINTS=*value-list*

MIDPOINTS=OLD

MISSING

OTHER=*n*

> where *n* is the midpoint percentage included in the OTHER slice

□ arranging pies in groups

ACROSS=*n*

> where *n* is the number of pies across the procedure output area

DOWN=*n*

> where *n* is the number of pies down the procedure output area

GROUP=*variable*

□ *description-options* can be either or both of the following:

DESCRIPTION='*string*'

NAME='*string*'

Options are fully described in "Options" later in this section.

Requirements

A PIE statement must contain at least one chart variable. A separate chart is drawn for each chart variable.

Options

You can use the following options in the PIE statement. Options used in a PIE statement affect all graphs produced by that statement. If any of the following options are supplied, they must be separated from the chart variables with a slash (/). If you do not use any options, omit the slash.

ACROSS=*n*

> draws *n* pies across the procedure output area. This option is ignored unless you also use the GROUP= option. By default, ACROSS=1.
>
> If *n* calls for more pies than fit horizontally in the graphics area of the output device, no pies are drawn and an error message is written to the SAS log.
>
> If the DOWN= option also is used, the pies are drawn in left-to-right and top-to-bottom order.

ANGLE=*degrees*

starts the first pie slice at the specified angle. A value of 0 for *degrees* corresponds to the 3 o'clock position. *Degrees* can be either positive or negative. Positive values move the starting position in the counterclockwise direction; negative values move the starting position clockwise. By default, ANGLE=0. Successive pie slices are drawn counterclockwise from the starting slice.

ANNOTATE=*Annotate-data-set*
ANNO=*Annotate-data-set*

specifies a data set to provide annotation of graphs produced by the PIE statement. *Annotate-data-set* must contain the appropriate Annotate variables. See Chapter 18 for details.

Note: Annotate coordinate systems 1, 2, 7, and 8 (data system coordinates) are not valid with pie charts.

If the ANNOTATE= option is also used with the PROC GCHART statement, both sets of annotation are applied. If you specify BY-group processing, the Annotate data set must contain the BY variable. For details, see "Using BY-Group Processing with the Annotate Facility" in Chapter 18 and "Details of BY-Group Processing" in Chapter 10.

CFILL=*fill-color*

specifies a color for all fill patterns in the chart. *Fill-color* overrides any colors specified in PATTERN definitions. If you do not use the CFILL= option, a color specification is searched for in the following order:

1. the COLOR= option used in PATTERN definitions

2. the CPATTERN= option in a GOPTIONS statement

3. the default, the first color in the colors list.

COUTLINE=*slice-outline-color*

outlines all pie slices using the specified color. By default, the outline color for slices is the same as the pattern color or the color specified in the CFILL= option. When adjacent slices use the same color and fill, a contrasting outline color makes the slices easier to distinguish.

Note: The outline color is the only distinction between empty patterns. Using the COUTLINE= option when VALUE=EMPTY is specified in PATTERN definitions makes the patterns look the same.

CTEXT=*text-color*

specifies a color for all text on the chart. Text includes labels for pie slices, the chart heading, and group headings if grouping is used. If you do not use the CTEXT= option, a color specification is searched for in the following order:

1. the CTEXT= option in a GOPTIONS statement

2. the default, the first color in the colors list.

The MATCHCOLOR option overrides the CTEXT= option for pie slice labels.

DESCRIPTION='*string*'
DES='*string*'
>   specifies a descriptive string, up to 40 characters long, that appears in the Description field of the catalog entry for the chart. The description does not appear on the chart. By default, the GCHART procedure assigns a description of the form PIE CHART OF *variable*, where *variable* is the name of the chart variable.

DISCRETE
>   treats a numeric chart variable as a discrete variable rather than as a continuous variable. The GCHART procedure creates a separate midpoint and, hence, a separate pie slice for each unique value of the chart variable. If the chart variable has a format associated with it, each formatted value is treated as a midpoint.
>   The LEVELS= option is ignored when you use the DISCRETE option. The MIDPOINTS= option overrides the DISCRETE option.

DOWN=*n*
>   draws *n* pies vertically in the procedure output area. The DOWN= option is ignored unless you also use the GROUP= option. By default, DOWN=1.
>   If *n* calls for more pies than fit vertically in the graphics area of the output device, no pies are drawn and an error message is written to the SAS log.
>   If the ACROSS= option also is used, the pies are drawn in left-to-right and top-to-bottom order.

EXPLODE=*value-list*
>   pulls the specified slices slightly out from the rest of the pie for added emphasis. *Value-list* is the list of midpoint values for the slices to be exploded. See the MIDPOINTS= option later in this section for details of allowable forms for the list of values.
>   The values in the value list must match the existing midpoints exactly, including the case of character midpoints. Any values in the list that do not correspond to existing midpoints are ignored.
>   When you use the EXPLODE= option, the radius of the pie is reduced to allow room for exploded slices.

FILL=SOLID | X
>   specifies the fill pattern for all pie slices in the chart. By default, pie slices are not filled. The available patterns are

>   SOLID | S   fills each slice with solid color.

>   X   fills each slice with crosshatched lines.

>   The FILL= option overrides any fill specified in PATTERN statements.
>   By default, the fill patterns take the colors from the current colors list in rotation. If any PATTERN statements have been defined, the colors in the PATTERN definitions are used, in order, before the default color rotation.

FREQ=*numeric-variable*
>   uses the values of *numeric-variable* to weight the contribution of each observation in the computation of the chart statistic. Noninteger values of *numeric-variable* are truncated to integers.
>   By default, each observation is counted only once in the frequency counts and sums. When you use the FREQ= option, each observation is counted the number of times specified by the value of *numeric-variable* for that observation. Observations for which the *numeric-variable* value is missing, 0, or negative are not used in the statistic calculation.

(FREQ= continued)

Because you cannot use TYPE=PERCENT or TYPE=FREQ when you use the SUMVAR= option, you must use the FREQ= option to calculate percentages or frequencies based on a sum.

GROUP=*variable*

specifies that multiple pies be produced, grouped according to the values of *variable*. *Variable* can be either character or numeric and is always treated as a discrete variable. Missing values for *variable* are treated as a valid group. By default, each group includes only those midpoints with nonzero chart statistic values.

A separate pie is produced for each unique value of *variable*. By default, each pie is drawn on a separate page or display, so the effect of the GROUP= option is essentially the same as using a BY statement except that the GROUP= option causes the midpoints with the same value to use the same color and fill pattern. This may not be true with a BY statement, depending on how slices are combined into the OTHER slice. Use the ACROSS= and DOWN= options to fit more than one pie on each output page or display.

INVISIBLE=*value-list*

makes the specified slices invisible, as if they had been removed from the pie. Labels are not printed for invisible slices. *Value-list* is the list of midpoint values for the invisible slices. See the MIDPOINTS= option later in this section for details of allowable forms for the list of values.

The values in the value list must match the existing midpoints exactly, including the case of character midpoints. Any values in the list that do not correspond to existing midpoints are ignored.

LEVELS=*n*

uses the specified number of midpoints for the numeric chart variable. The range for each midpoint is calculated automatically using the algorithm described in Terrell and Scott (1985). This option is ignored if

☐ the chart variable is character type

☐ the DISCRETE option is used

☐ the MIDPOINTS= option is used.

MATCHCOLOR

uses the slice pattern color for slice labels and values. The MATCHCOLOR option overrides the color specified in the CTEXT= option.

MIDPOINTS=*value-list*

specifies values for midpoints on the pie chart. By default, one of these two methods is used:

☐ If the chart variable is numeric type, the GCHART procedure calculates midpoint values.

☐ If the chart variable is character type or is numeric type and the DISCRETE option is used, the GCHART procedure creates a midpoint for each unique value of the chart variable.

No slice is created if the chart statistic calculated for the midpoint has a value of 0.

Midpoints that represent small percentages of the pie are collected into a generic midpoint labeled OTHER. See the OTHER= option later in this section for more information on the category.

For numeric chart variables, *value-list* can be specified in the following ways:

n n . . . n

n,n, . . . ,n

n TO *n* <BY *increment*> <*n . . . n*> <*n, . . . ,n*>

n n . . . n TO *n* <BY *increment*> <*n . . . n*>

n,n, . . . ,n TO *n* <BY *increment*> <*n, . . . ,n*>

'SAS-value'i TO *'SAS-value'i* <BY *interval*>

'SAS-value'i 'SAS-value'i . . . 'SAS-value'i

If the variable has an associated format, you must specify the unformatted values in *value-list*.

For continuous variables, the midpoints are the medians of the ranges of possible values of the chart variable. A value that falls exactly halfway between two midpoints is placed in the higher range.

For character chart variables, *value-list* must be a list of midpoint values. Values must be enclosed in single quotes and separated by blanks (commas are not allowed as separators), as in this example:

```
midpoints='Paris' 'Sydney' 'Atlanta'
```

The values can be specified in any order, so the *value-list* can be used to order the slices. If the variable has an associated format, you must specify the formatted values in *value-list*. By default, midpoints are arranged counterclockwise starting at the value specified in the ANGLE= option in ascending order of the midpoint values. If the character chart variable has an associated format, the values are arranged in order of the formatted values.

You can selectively exclude some chart variable values from the chart, as in this example:

```
midpoints='Paris' 'Sydney'
```

Only those observations for which the chart variable exactly matches one of the midpoint values are counted. As a result, observations can be inadvertently excluded if values in the midpoint list are misspelled or if the case does not match exactly.

MIDPOINTS=OLD
tells the GCHART procedure to calculate default midpoints using the algorithm used in Release 82.4 and Version 5 of SAS/GRAPH software. The MIDPOINTS=OLD option is ignored unless the numeric chart variable is numeric type.

MISSING
accepts a missing value as a valid midpoint for the chart variable. By default, observations for which the value of the chart variable is missing are ignored.
Note: Missing values are always valid for the group variable.

NAME='*string*'
specifies a string, up to eight characters long, that appears in the Name field of the catalog entry for the chart. *String* must be a valid SAS name. By default, the name assigned is GCHART. If either the name specified or the default name duplicates an existing name in the catalog, SAS/GRAPH software adds a number to the duplicate name to create a unique name, for example, GCHART2.

NOGROUPHEADING
> suppresses the headings normally printed above each pie when you use the GROUP= option.

NOHEADING
> suppresses the heading normally printed at the top of each page or display of pie chart output.

OTHER=*n*
> collects all midpoints with chart statistic values less than or equal to *n* percentage of the total into a generic midpoint labeled OTHER. The *n* value is a percent from 0 to 100. The default value is 4; by default, any slice that represents 4 percent or less of the pie is put in the OTHER category.
>
> The OTHER slice is the last slice drawn in the pie. (In other words, it is the slice immediately clockwise from the starting slice.) If only one slice falls into the OTHER category, it is positioned as the last slice but is labeled with its midpoint value (that is, it is not labeled as OTHER).
>
> **Note:** Specifying a small value for *n* may cause some small slices not to be labeled. That is, the GCHART procedure may not be able to label all of the small slices.

PERCENT=ARROW | INSIDE | NONE | OUTSIDE
> prints the percentage of the pie represented by each slice using the specified labeling method. See "Slice Labeling Options" later in this section for details of the available methods. By default, PERCENT=NONE.

SLICE=ARROW | INSIDE | NONE | OUTSIDE
> specifies the method for labeling the value of the midpoint associated with each slice. See "Slice Labeling Options" later in this section for details of the available methods. By default, SLICE=OUTSIDE.

SUMVAR=*numeric-variable*
> specifies the variable to be used for sum or mean calculations. The GCHART procedure calculates the sum and, if requested, the mean of *numeric-variable* for each midpoint.
>
> When you use the SUMVAR= option, the TYPE= option value must be either SUM or MEAN. By default, TYPE=SUM when you use the SUMVAR= option.

TYPE=*statistic*
> specifies the chart statistic for the pie chart. *Statistic* can be one of the following when you do not use the SUMVAR= option:

Value of *statistic*	Statistic represented on the chart
FREQ	frequency
PERCENT PCT	percentage

CFREQ and CPERCENT (CPCT) are also allowable values, but for pie charts they are equivalent to FREQ and PERCENT (PCT), respectively.

Statistic can be either of the following when you use the SUMVAR= option:

Value of *statistic*	Statistic represented on the chart
SUM	sum
MEAN	mean

By default, TYPE=FREQ when the SUMVAR= option is not used, and TYPE=SUM when SUMVAR= is used.

Because you cannot use TYPE=PERCENT or TYPE=FREQ when you use the SUMVAR= option, you must use the FREQ= option to calculate percentages or frequencies based on a sum.

See "Chart Statistics" earlier in this chapter for a complete description of the types of statistics that can be represented.

VALUE=ARROW | INSIDE | NONE | OUTSIDE
specifies the method for labeling the value of the chart statistic for each slice. See "Slice Labeling Options" later in this section for details of the available methods. By default, VALUE=OUTSIDE.

Using the PIE Statement

The form of your pie chart is governed by the variables you specify and the options you use in the PIE statement. A separate pie chart or group of pie charts is produced for each chart variable specified. For example, the following statement produces two separate pie charts:

```
pie site year;
```

The slices of the pie represent the midpoints for ranges of chart variable values. The size of each slice represents the contribution of the corresponding midpoint of the chart variable to the statistic being calculated. Descriptive text also can be added to list the exact statistic value and percentage of the pie represented by each slice.

The GCHART procedure determines the number and order of pie slices automatically. However, you can use options to override the defaults and choose the characteristics of the pie. The procedure also can divide the pies into groups according to the values of a group variable.

The following sections explain how you can change the appearance of your pie chart using different PIE statement options.

The Chart Variable and Midpoint Values

The value of the chart variable determines the slice to which each observation in the data set contributes. The way in which midpoints are selected varies depending on the type of the chart variable and the options used. See "Chart Variables and Midpoint Selection" earlier in this chapter for additional information on how midpoints are determined.

Formatted numeric variables are ordered by the unformatted numeric values. If you use the DISCRETE option and the variable is formatted, there is one slice for each formatted value. Slices are drawn for each midpoint for which the value of the chart statistic is not 0.

By default, slices are arranged counterclockwise around the pie in ascending order of midpoint value starting at 0 degrees. If the character chart variable has an associated format, the slices are ordered according to the formatted values of the chart variable. By default, the slice name (the midpoint value for the slice) is printed outside each slice. You can use the MIDPOINTS= option to change the order of slices in the pie.

The Chart Statistic and Pie Slices

The length of the arc of each slice graphically represents the corresponding midpoint's contribution to the total of the chart statistic. These four types of statistics can be charted:

□ frequency

□ percentage

□ sum

□ mean.

See "Chart Statistics" earlier in this chapter for a discussion of these statistics.

The default chart statistic is frequency. If the SUMVAR= option is used, the default chart statistic is sum. You can use the TYPE= option to select other chart statistics. You must use the SUMVAR= option to identify the variable to use for calculating sum or mean statistics. For example, if you want to calculate a sum based on the value of the variable COUNT, specify the following:

```
pie branch / sumvar=count;
```

By default, each observation is counted only once in the calculation of the chart statistic. You can use the FREQ= option to identify the variable that indicates the number of times each observation is counted.

The Group Variable and Pie Groups

If you want to display your data categorized by both the chart variable and another variable, you can use the second variable to organize the pies into groups. Use the GROUP= option to identify the variable as the group variable for the chart.

By default, the pie for each group is placed on a separate page or display of output. The pies are produced in ascending order of group variable value. You can use the ACROSS= and DOWN= options to place more than one pie on a page or display. When you use the ACROSS= and DOWN= options, the pies are arranged from left to right and top to bottom in ascending order of the value of the group variable.

See the description of the GROUP= option in "Options" earlier in this section for additional details. See "Pie Chart Using Groups" in "PIE Statement Examples" later in this section for an illustration of grouping in a pie chart.

Labels and Headings

By default, the midpoint value and the value of the chart statistic for each slice are printed with the slice. You can control the positioning of these labels with the SLICE= and VALUE= options, respectively. You can use the PERCENT= option to have the percentage of the total chart statistic for each slice printed as well. (For the percentage chart statistic, this value is the same as the chart statistic value.) See "Slice Labeling Options" later in this section for details of how these values can be positioned.

A heading is printed at the top of each pie chart indicating the type of statistic charted and the name of the chart variable. You can suppress this heading with the NOHEADING option.

When the GROUP= option is used, a heading is printed above each pie indicating the name of the group variable and its value for the particular pie. You can suppress these headings with the NOGROUPHEADING option.

The AXIS statement is not valid with the PIE statement. However, you can use the FTEXT= and HTEXT= graphics options to control the font and height of labels, respectively. Increasing the value of the HTEXT= graphics option decreases the size of the pie if any slice labels are positioned outside.

Pie charts do not produce legends. You can use the Annotate facility or a FOOTNOTE statement to produce a legend.

Selecting Patterns for the Pies

By default, pie charts do not use fill patterns. Only outlines of the slices are drawn, using the first color in the current colors list. You can use the FILL= option to specify a common fill pattern for all slices, or you can use PATTERN statements to define specific patterns for the slices.

Pie charts can use only pie/star patterns for the slices. This pattern type uses the following fill patterns:

PEMPTY | EMPTY

PSOLID | SOLID

P*density*<*style*<*angle*>>

    where

density	can be 1 . . . 5.
style	can be X	N.
angle	can be 0 . . . 360.

PATTERN statements with other fill patterns are ignored. See Chapter 15 for details.

If you provide fewer valid PATTERN definitions than the chart requires, the GCHART procedure uses the default fill pattern rotation for the slices drawn after all defined patterns are exhausted. See Chapter 15 for details.

You can use the COUTLINE= option to choose an outline color for all slices. By default, the slices are outlined in the same color as the fill color. See "Options" earlier in this section for a discussion of the COUTLINE= option.

Slice Labeling Options

These three text elements can be printed with each slice in a pie chart:

□ the slice name (the value of the midpoint for the slice)

□ the slice value (the value of the chart statistic represented by the slice)

□ the slice percentage (the percentage of the chart statistic total represented by the slice).

By default, only the name and value are printed; the percentage must be specifically requested using the PERCENT= option.

The SLICE=, VALUE=, and PERCENT= options control the placement of the slice name, slice value, and slice percentage elements, respectively. The following four values are valid for these options:

ARROW   places the text outside the slice and connects the text to the slice with a line. The connecting line is the same color as the text. This labeling method reduces the radius of the pie.

INSIDE   places the text inside the slice. The label overlays the slice fill patterns. This labeling method increases the radius of the pie.

NONE   suppresses the text.

OUTSIDE   places the text outside the slice.

Figure 23.7 illustrates the different labeling options.

Figure 23.7 *Slice Labeling Options*

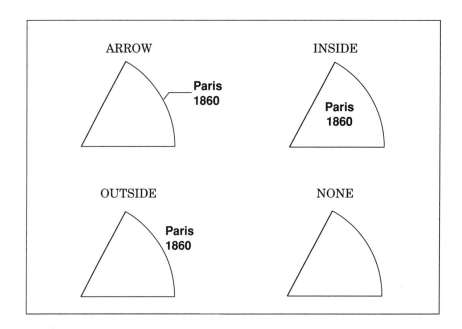

The slice name and slice value elements follow each other by default. That is, if you use the SLICE= option without the VALUE= option or you use VALUE= without SLICE=, then the specified labeling method is used for both elements. If you specify both OUTSIDE and ARROW for different elements in the same PIE statement, the connecting line for the arrow may overlay the text positioned using OUTSIDE. For example, if you specify PERCENT=ARROW and VALUE=OUTSIDE, the line connecting the percentage information to each slice may overlay the value information for the slice.

If your pie has many slices, the GCHART procedure may not be able to label all the slices, particularly if there are several small slices together. If so, a warning is printed in the SAS log with a list of the labels that cannot be displayed on the chart. You may be able to correct this situation by doing one of the following:

□ using the ANGLE= option to change the orientation of the pie.

□ using the MIDPOINTS= option to rearrange slices so that small slices are not together.

□ using the OTHER= option to group more midpoints into the OTHER category.

□ using the HPOS= and VPOS= graphics options to increase the number of cells in your display. See Chapter 5 for details.

See the description of the ANGLE= and OTHER= options in "Options" earlier in this section for details.

PIE Statement Examples

The following examples illustrate major features of the PIE statement.

Simple Pie Chart

This example uses the PIE statement to display the total sales for the three branches of a fictitious company over a one-year period.
The following program statements produce Output 23.13:

```
    /* set the graphics environment */
goptions reset=global gunit=pct border
        ftext=swissb htitle=6 htext=3;

    /* create data set TOTALS */
data totals;
    length dept $ 7 site $ 8;
    input dept site quarter sales;
    cards;
Parts    Sydney  1 7843.97
Parts    Atlanta 1 9225.26
more data lines
Tools    Atlanta 4 3624.19
Tools    Paris   4 6414.25
;
run;

    /* define title and footnote for chart */
title 'Total Sales';
footnote j=r 'GR23N13  ';
```

```
                       /* generate pie chart */
               proc gchart data=totals;
                  format sales dollar8.;
                  pie site
                       / sumvar=sales
                         coutline=gray
                         angle=90
                         percent=inside
                         value=inside
                         slice=outside
                         noheading;
               run;
               quit;
```

Output 23.13 *Simple Pie Chart (GR23N13)*

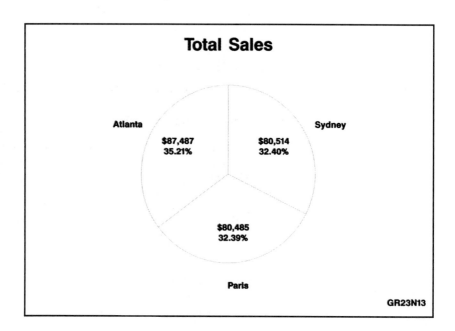

This example illustrates the following features:

□ The FORMAT statement assigns the DOLLAR8. format to the SALES variable and chart statistic.

□ The SUMVAR= option specifies the variable used to calculate chart statistics. Because the TYPE= option is not used, the default statistic is the sum of the values of the SALE variable for each midpoint.

□ The ANGLE= option sets the position of the first slice in the midpoint order.

□ The PERCENT= option prints the percentage statistic inside each slice.

□ The VALUE= option prints the chart statistic value (in this example, the sum) inside each slice.

□ The SLICE= option prints the midpoint value for each slice outside the slice. (If you do not use the SLICE= option, the name follows the value and prints inside the circle.)

□ The NOHEADING option suppresses the default heading that otherwise is printed at the top of the chart.

□ Because no PATTERN definitions are in effect and the FILL= option is not used, the example uses an empty fill pattern (the default).

Pie Chart Using Groups

This example uses the same data set as the first PIE statement example but uses grouping to separate the sales totals by branch.

The following program statements produce Output 23.14:

```
    /* set the graphics environment */
goptions reset=global gunit=pct border
         ftext=swissb htitle=6 htext=3;

    /* create data set TOTALS */
data totals;
   length dept $ 7 site $ 8;
   input dept site quarter sales;
   cards;
Parts   Sydney  1 7843.97
Parts   Atlanta 1 9225.26
more data lines
Tools   Atlanta 4 3624.19
Tools   Paris   4 6414.25
;
run;

    /* define title and footnote for chart */
title 'Total Sales';
footnote j=r 'GR23N14  ';

    /* define pattern characteristics */
pattern1 value=solid color=blue;
pattern2 value=solid color=green;
pattern3 value=solid color=red;

    /* generate pie charts */
proc gchart data=totals;
   format quarter roman.;
   label site='00'x;
   where site='Sydney' or site='Atlanta';
   pie quarter
       / discrete
         sumvar=sales
         coutline=gray
         percent=outside
         slice=outside
         value=none
         group=site
         across=2
         noheading;
   run;
quit;
```

Output 23.14 Pie Chart with
Grouping (GR23N14)

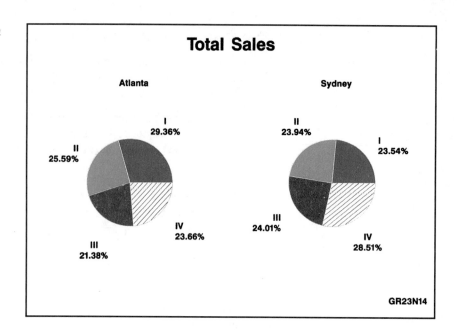

This example illustrates the following features:

□ The global PATTERN statements define three of the colors and patterns used in the chart. The fourth pattern is the default.

□ The WHERE statement subsets the data so that only the observations in which the value of SITE is **Sydney** or **Atlanta** are used for the pie chart.

□ The DISCRETE option specifies that the numeric chart variable QUARTER should be treated as a discrete variable rather than as a continuous variable.

□ The SUMVAR= option specifies the variable used to calculate chart statistics. Because the TYPE= option is not used, the statistic is the sum of the SALES variable values for each midpoint.

□ The VALUE= option is set to NONE and the value of the PERCENT= option is changed to OUTSIDE.

□ The GROUP= option creates a separate pie for each different value of the SITE variable.

□ The ACROSS= option fits the pies for both branches on one page or display.

□ Because the ANGLE= option is not used, the slice for the first midpoint starts at the default angle of 0.

Pie Chart with Exploded Slice

This example charts the same data as the first PIE statement example but emphasizes the sales made at the Sydney branch.

The following program statements produce Output 23.15:

```
/* set the graphics environment */
goptions reset=global gunit=pct border
        ftext=swissb htitle=6 htext=3;
```

```
                              /* create data set TOTALS */
                   data totals;
                      length dept $ 7 site $ 8;
                      input dept site quarter sales;
                      cards;
                   Parts   Sydney  1 7843.97
                   Parts   Atlanta 1 9225.26
                   more data lines
                   Tools   Atlanta 4 3624.19
                   Tools   Paris   4 6414.25
                   ;
                   run;

                              /* define title and footnote for chart */
                   title 'Total Sales';
                   footnote j=r 'GR23N15  ';

                              /* generate pie chart */
                   proc gchart data=totals;
                      format sales dollar8.;
                      pie site
                          / sumvar=sales
                            midpoints='Paris' 'Atlanta' 'Sydney'
                            fill=solid
                            coutline=gray
                            explode='Sydney'
                            noheading
                            matchcolor;
                   run;
                   quit;
```

Output 23.15 *Pie Chart with Exploded Slice (GR23N15)*

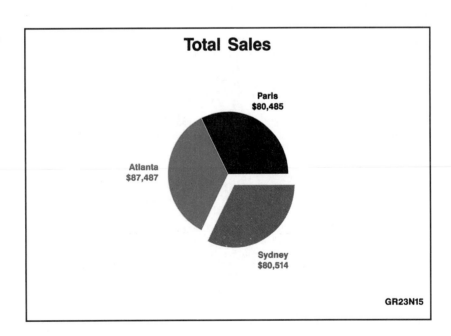

This example illustrates the following features:

□ The MIDPOINTS= option specifies the order of midpoint values for the pie slices.

□ The FILL= option specifies the fill pattern for all pie slices in the chart.

□ The EXPLODE= option pulls the slice for Sydney out from the rest of the pie.

□ The MATCHCOLOR option matches the color of the slice labels to the color of the slice.

Pie Chart with Invisible Slice

This example charts the same data as the first PIE statement example but removes the Paris sales information from the chart.

The following program statements produce Output 23.16:

```
   /* set the graphics environment */
goptions reset=global gunit=pct border
        ftext=swissb htitle=6 htext=3;


   /* create data set TOTALS */
data totals;
   length dept $ 7 site $ 8;
   input dept site quarter sales;
   cards;
Parts    Sydney  1 7843.97
Parts    Atlanta 1 9225.26
more data lines
Tools    Atlanta 4 3624.19
Tools    Paris   4 6414.25
;
run;


   /* define title and footnote for chart */
title 'Total Sales';
footnote j=r 'GR23N16  ';


   /* generate pie chart */
proc gchart data=totals;
   format sales dollar8.;
   pie site
       / sumvar=sales
         midpoints='Sydney' 'Atlanta' 'Paris'
         noheading
         coutline=gray
         fill=solid
         cfill=green
         invisible='Paris';
   run;
   quit;
```

Output 23.16 *Pie Chart with Invisible Slice (GR23N16)*

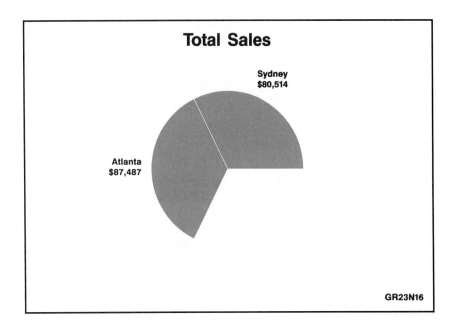

This example illustrates the following feature:

□ The INVISIBLE= option removes the slice for Paris from the pie chart.

STAR Statement

The STAR statement creates one or more star charts using the input data set specified in the PROC GCHART statement. The STAR statement specifies the chart variable or variables that define the categories of data to be charted. Other variables can be specified to

□ divide the data into groups of stars

□ provide data for the sum and mean statistics.

In addition, options used in the STAR statement can select the statistic to be charted, determine the ranges of chart variable values for each slice, and modify the appearance of the stars.

The STAR statement can produce star charts using either spines or slices to represent the value of the chart statistic. For details, see "The Chart Statistic and Star Spines and Slices" later in this section.

Syntax

The general form of the STAR statement is

STAR *chart-variable* < . . . *chart-variable-n*>
    </ <ANNOTATE=*Annotate-data-set*>
        <*appearance-options*>
        <*statistic-options*>
        <*midpoint-options*>
        <*description-options*>>;

□ *chart-variable* specifies a variable in the input data set with categories of data represented on the star chart. If you include more than one chart variable in the STAR statement, the variable names should be separated with blanks.

□ *appearance-options* can be one or more of the following:

    □ selecting colors

        CFILL=*fill-color*

        COUTLINE=*slice-outline-color*

        CTEXT=*text-color*

        MATCHCOLOR

    □ changing the appearance of the spines or slices

        ANGLE=*degrees*

        FILL=SOLID | X

        NOCONNECT

        STARMAX=*n*

            where *n* is the value at the outside of the circle

        STARMIN=*n*

            where *n* is the value at the center of the circle

    □ manipulating slice labels

        PERCENT=ARROW | INSIDE | NONE | OUTSIDE

        SLICE=ARROW | INSIDE | NONE | OUTSIDE

        VALUE=ARROW | INSIDE | NONE | OUTSIDE

    □ suppressing headings

        NOGROUPHEADING

        NOHEADING

□ *statistic-options* can be one or more of the following:

    FREQ=*numeric-variable*

    SUMVAR=*numeric-variable*

    TYPE=*statistic*

        where *statistic* is one of the following:

        CFREQ

        CPERCENT

        FREQ

        MEAN

        PERCENT

        SUM

□ *midpoint-options* can be one or more of the following:

    □ manipulating the midpoint values

        DISCRETE

        LEVELS=*n*

            where *n* is the number of midpoints for the numeric chart variable

MIDPOINTS=*value-list*

MIDPOINTS=OLD

MISSING

□ arranging stars in groups

ACROSS=*n*

where *n* is the number of stars across the procedure output area

DOWN=*n*

where *n* is the number of stars down the procedure output area

GROUP=*variable*

□ *description-options* can be either or both of the following:

DESCRIPTION='*string*'

NAME='*string*'

Options are fully described in "Options" later in this section.

Requirements

A STAR statement must contain at least one chart variable. A separate chart is drawn for each chart variable.

Options

You can use the following options in the STAR statement. Options used in a STAR statement affect all graphs produced by that statement. If any of the following options are supplied, they must be separated from the chart variables with a slash (/). If you do not use any options, omit the slash.

ACROSS=*n*

draws *n* stars across the procedure output area. This option is ignored unless you also use the GROUP= option. If *n* calls for more stars than fit horizontally in the graphics area of the output device, no stars are drawn and an error message is written to the SAS log.

If the DOWN= option also is used, the star charts are drawn in left-to-right and top-to-bottom order.

ANGLE=*degrees*

starts the first star slice at the specified angle. A value of 0 for *degrees* corresponds to the 3 o'clock position. *Degrees* can be either positive or negative. Positive values move the starting position counterclockwise; negative values move the starting position clockwise.

If the star chart uses spines instead of slices, *degrees* specifies the angle of the position halfway between the first spine and the last spine.

The default starting angle is calculated to place the first spine or the center of the first slice of the star at the 0° position. Successive star spines or slices are drawn counterclockwise from the starting position.

ANNOTATE=*Annotate-data-set*
ANNO=*Annotate-data-set*
> specifies a data set to provide annotation of graphs produced by the STAR statement. *Annotate-data-set* must contain the appropriate Annotate variables. See Chapter 18 for details.
>
> **Note:** Annotate coordinate systems 1, 2, 7, and 8 (data system coordinates) are not valid with star charts.
>
> If the ANNOTATE= option is also used with the PROC GCHART statement, both sets of annotation are applied. If you specify BY-group processing, the Annotate data set must contain the BY variable. For details, see "Using BY-Group Processing with the Annotate Facility" in Chapter 18 and "Details of BY-Group Processing" in Chapter 10.

CFILL=*fill-color*
> specifies a color for all fill patterns in the chart. *Fill-color* overrides any colors specified in PATTERN definitions. If the star chart uses spines instead of slices, *fill-color* specifies the color for all spines. If you do not use the CFILL= option, a color specification is searched for in the following order:
>
> 1. the COLOR= option used in PATTERN definitions
>
> 2. the CPATTERN= option in a GOPTIONS statement
>
> 3. the default, the first color in the colors list.

COUTLINE=*slice-outline-color*
> outlines all star slices and draws the circle surrounding the star chart using the specified color. By default, the outline color for slices is the same as the pattern color or the color specified in the CFILL= option. When adjacent slices use the same color and fill, a contrasting outline color makes the slices easier to distinguish.
>
> **Note:** The outline color is the only distinction between empty patterns. Using the COUTLINE= option when VALUE=EMPTY is specified in PATTERN definitions makes the patterns look the same.

CTEXT=*text-color*
> specifies a color for all text on the chart. Text includes labels for star slices, the chart heading, and group headings if grouping is used. If you do not use the CTEXT= option, a color specification is searched for in the following order:
>
> 1. the CTEXT= option in a GOPTIONS statement
>
> 2. the default, the first color in the colors list.
>
> The MATCHCOLOR option overrides the CTEXT= option for star slice labels and values.

DESCRIPTION='*string*'
DES='*string*'
> specifies a descriptive string, up to 40 characters long, that appears in the Description field of the catalog entry for the chart. The description does not appear on the chart. By default, the GCHART procedure assigns a description of the form STAR CHART OF *variable*, where *variable* is the name of the chart variable.

DISCRETE

treats a numeric chart variable as a discrete variable rather than as a continuous variable. The GCHART procedure creates a separate midpoint and, hence, a separate star slice for each unique value of the chart variable. If the variable has a format associated with it, each format value is treated as a separate value.

The LEVELS= option is ignored when you use the DISCRETE option. The MIDPOINTS= option overrides the DISCRETE option.

DOWN=*n*

draws *n* stars vertically in the procedure output area. The DOWN= option is ignored unless you also use the GROUP= option. If *n* calls for more stars than fit vertically in the graphics area of the output device, no stars are drawn and an error message is written to the SAS log.

If the ACROSS= option also is used, the stars are drawn in left-to-right and top-to-bottom order.

FILL=SOLID | X

specifies the fill pattern for all star slices in the chart. By default, the star chart uses spines instead of slices. The available patterns are

SOLID | S   fills each slice with solid color.

X   fills each slice with crosshatched lines.

The FILL= option overrides any fill patterns specified in PATTERN statements.

By default, the fill patterns take the colors from the current colors list in rotation. If any PATTERN statements have been defined, the colors in the PATTERN definitions are used, in order, before the default color rotation.

FREQ=*numeric-variable*

uses the values of *numeric-variable* to weight the contribution of each observation in the computation of the chart statistic. Noninteger values of *numeric-variable* are truncated to integers.

By default, each observation is counted only once in the frequency counts and sums. When you use the FREQ= option, each observation is counted the number of times specified by the value of *numeric-variable* for that observation. Observations for which *numeric-variable* is missing, 0, or negative are not used in the statistic calculation.

Because you cannot use TYPE=PERCENT or TYPE=FREQ when you use the SUMVAR= option, you must use the FREQ= option to calculate percentages or frequencies based on a sum.

GROUP=*variable*

specifies that the data be grouped according to the values of *variable*. *Variable* can be either character or numeric and is always treated as a discrete variable. Missing values for *variable* are treated as a valid group. By default, each group includes only those midpoints with nonzero chart statistic values.

A separate star is produced for each unique value of *variable*. By default, each star is drawn on a separate page or screen, so the effect of the GROUP= option is essentially the same as using a BY statement. The difference between using the GROUP= option and a BY statement is that all of the stars are scaled the same with the GROUP= option. Use the ACROSS= and DOWN= options to fit more than one star on each output page or display.

LEVELS=*n*
> uses the specified number of midpoints for the numeric chart variable. The range for each midpoint is calculated automatically using the algorithm described by Terrell and Scott (1985). This option is ignored if
>
> □ the chart variable is character type
>
> □ the DISCRETE option is used
>
> □ the MIDPOINTS= option is used.

MATCHCOLOR
> uses the color of the slice pattern for the slice midpoint and value label. The MATCHCOLOR option overrides the color specified in the CTEXT= option. If the chart uses spines instead of slices, the spine color is used for the slice label and value text.

MIDPOINTS=*value-list*
> specifies values for midpoints for the star chart. By default, one of these two methods is used:
>
> □ If the chart variable is numeric type, the GCHART procedure calculates midpoint values.
>
> □ If the chart variable is character type or is numeric type and the DISCRETE option is used, the GCHART procedure creates a midpoint for each unique value of the chart variable.
>
> No spine or slice is created if the chart statistic calculated for a midpoint has a value of 0.
>
> **For numeric chart variables,** *value-list* can be specified in the following ways:
>
> *n n . . . n*
>
> *n,n, . . . ,n*
>
> *n* TO *n* <BY *increment*> <*n . . . n*> <*n, . . . ,n*>
>
> *n n . . . n* TO *n* <BY *increment*> <*n . . . n*>
>
> *n,n, . . . ,n* TO *n* <BY *increment*> <*n, . . . ,n*>
>
> '*SAS-value*'i TO '*SAS-value*'i <BY *interval*>
>
> '*SAS-value*'i '*SAS-value*'i . . . '*SAS-value*'i
>
> If the variable has an associated format, you must specify the unformatted values in *value-list*.
>
> For continuous variables, the midpoints are the medians of the ranges of possible values of the chart variable. A value that falls exactly halfway between two midpoints is placed in the higher range.
>
> **For character chart variables,** *value-list* must be a list of midpoint values. Values must be enclosed in single quotes and separated by blanks (commas are not allowed as separators), as in this example:
>
> ```
> midpoints='Paris' 'Sydney' 'Atlanta'
> ```
>
> The values can be specified in any order, so the *value-list* can be used to order the spines or slices. If the variable has an associated format, you must specify the formatted values in *value-list*. By default, midpoints are arranged counterclockwise starting at the ANGLE= value in ascending order of the midpoint values. If the character chart variable has an associated format, the values are arranged in order of the formatted values.

You can selectively exclude some chart variable values from the chart, as in this example:

```
midpoints='Paris' 'Sydney'
```

Only those observations for which the chart variable exactly matches one of the midpoint values are counted. As a result, observations can be inadvertently excluded if values in the midpoint list are misspelled or if the case does not match exactly.

MIDPOINTS=OLD

tells the GCHART procedure to calculate default midpoints using the algorithm used in Release 82.4 and Version 5 of SAS/GRAPH software. The MIDPOINTS=OLD option is ignored unless the chart variable is numeric type.

MISSING

accepts a missing value as a valid midpoint for the chart variable. By default, observations for which the value of the chart variable is missing are ignored.

Note: Missing values are always valid for the group variable.

NAME='*string*'

specifies a string, up to eight characters long, that appears in the Name field of the catalog entry for the chart. *String* must be a valid SAS name. By default, the name assigned is GCHART. If either the name specified or the default name duplicates an existing name in the catalog, SAS/GRAPH software adds a number to the duplicate name to create a unique name, for example, GCHART2.

NOCONNECT

draws only star spines without connecting lines. The NOCONNECT option is ignored if you use the FILL= option or PATTERN definitions.

NOGROUPHEADING

suppresses the headings normally printed above each star when you use the GROUP= option.

NOHEADING

suppresses the heading normally printed at the top of each page or display of star chart output.

PERCENT=ARROW | INSIDE | NONE | OUTSIDE

prints the percentage of the star represented by each spine or slice using the specified labeling method. See "Slice and Spine Labeling Options" later in this section for details of the available methods. By default, PERCENT=NONE.

SLICE=ARROW | INSIDE | NONE | OUTSIDE

specifies the method for labeling the value of the midpoint associated with each spine or slice. See "Slice and Spine Labeling Options" later in this section for detail of the available methods. By default, SLICE=OUTSIDE.

STARMAX=*n*

scales the chart so that the outside (or edge) of the circle represents the value specified by *n*. By default, the value for the STARMAX= option is the maximum chart statistic value.

STARMIN=*n*

    scales the chart so that the center of the circle represents the value specified by *n*. By default, STARMIN=0. If the chart statistic has negative values, by default the value for the STARMIN= option is the minimum chart statistic value.

SUMVAR=*numeric-variable*

    specifies the variable to be used for sum or mean calculations. The GCHART procedure calculates the sum and, if requested, the mean of the value of *numeric-variable* in all observations for each midpoint range.

    When you use the SUMVAR= option, the TYPE= option value must be either SUM or MEAN. By default, TYPE=SUM when you use the SUMVAR= option.

TYPE=*statistic*

    specifies the chart statistic for the star chart. *Statistic* can be either of the following when you do not use the SUMVAR= option:

Value of *statistic*	Statistic represented on the chart
FREQ	frequency
PERCENT PCT	percentage

    CFREQ and CPERCENT (CPCT) are also allowable values, but for star charts they are equivalent to FREQ and PERCENT (PCT), respectively.

    Statistic can be either of the following when you use the SUMVAR= option:

Value of *statistic*	Statistic represented on the chart
SUM	sum
MEAN	mean

    By default, TYPE=FREQ when the SUMVAR= option is not used, and TYPE=SUM when SUMVAR= is used.

    Because you cannot use TYPE=PERCENT or TYPE=FREQ when you use the SUMVAR= option, you must use the FREQ= option to calculate percentages or frequencies based on a sum.

    See "Chart Statistics" earlier in this chapter for a complete description of the types of statistics that can be represented.

VALUE=ARROW | INSIDE | NONE | OUTSIDE

    specifies the method for labeling the chart statistic value of each spine or slice. By default, VALUE=OUTSIDE. See "Slice and Spine Labeling Options" later in this section for details of the available methods.

Using the STAR Statement

The form of your star chart is governed by the variables you specify and the options you use in the STAR statement. A separate star chart or group of star charts is produced for each chart variable specified. For example, the following statement produces two separate star charts:

```
star site year;
```

The spines of the star represent the midpoints for ranges of chart variable values. Slices can be drawn around the spines. The circle surrounding the star provides a scale for the chart. By default, the radius of the circle is the length of the longest spine in the chart. Descriptive text also can be added to list the exact statistic value and percentage of the star represented by each slice.

The GCHART procedure determines the number and order of star slices automatically. However, you can use options to override the defaults and choose the characteristics of the star. The procedure also can divide the stars into groups according to the values of a group variable.

The following sections explain how you can change the appearance of your star chart using different STAR statement options.

The Chart Variable and Midpoint Values

The value of the chart variable determines the slice to which each observation in the data set contributes. The way in which midpoints are selected varies depending on the type of the chart variable and the options used. Slices or spines are drawn for all midpoints where the value of the chart statistic is greater than the value specified in the STARMIN= option. By default, STARMIN=0. See "Chart Variables and Midpoint Selection" earlier in this chapter for additional information on how midpoints are determined.

You can use the MIDPOINTS= and LEVELS= options to change the number of midpoints used for numeric variables. For example, if you specify the following, the GCHART procedure calculates four midpoints for a continuous chart variable:

```
star sales / levels=4;
```

If you specify the following, the GCHART procedure uses 1, 3, and 5 as the midpoints for the chart:

```
star x / midpoints=1 3 5;
```

By default, slices are arranged counterclockwise around the star in ascending order of midpoint value. If the character chart variable has an associated format, the slices are ordered according to the formatted values of the chart variable. By default, the slice name (the midpoint value for the slice) is printed outside each slice. You can use the MIDPOINTS= option to change the order of slices in the star.

The Chart Statistic and Star Spines and Slices

By default, star charts use spines, connected by lines, to graphically represent the magnitude of the chart statistic for the corresponding midpoint. Output 23.17 later in this section shows a star chart using connected spines.

When you use the NOCONNECT option, star charts use unconnected spines to graphically represent the magnitude of the chart statistic for the corresponding midpoint. Output 23.19 later in this section shows a star chart using unconnected spines.

When you use the FILL= option or define PATTERN characteristics, star charts use slices instead of spines. The length of the center of each slice graphically represents the magnitude of the chart statistic for the corresponding midpoint. Output 23.18 later in this section shows a star chart using slices with fill patterns.

These four types of statistics can be charted on star charts:

□ frequency

□ percentage

□ sum

□ mean.

See "Chart Statistics" earlier in this chapter for a discussion of these statistics.

The default chart statistic is frequency. If the SUMVAR= option is used, the default chart statistic is sum. You can use the TYPE= option to select other chart statistics. You must use the SUMVAR= option to identify the variable to use for calculating the sum or mean statistics. For example, if you want to calculate a sum based on the value of the variable COUNT, specify the following:

```
star branch / sumvar=count;
```

By default, each observation is counted only once in the calculation of the chart statistic. You can use the FREQ= option to identify the variable that indicates the number of times each observation is counted.

If all the data to be charted with the STAR statement are positive, the center of the star represents 0 and the outside circle represents the maximum value. If negative values are calculated for the chart statistic, the center represents the minimum value in the data. You can specify other values for the center and outside of the circle with the STARMIN= and STARMAX= options. See "Options" earlier in this section for details.

The Group Variable and Star Groups

If you want to display your data categorized by both the chart variable and another variable, you can use the second variable to organize the stars into groups. Use the GROUP= option to identify the variable as the group variable for the chart.

By default, the star for each group is placed on a separate page or display of output. The stars are produced in ascending order of group variable value. You can use the ACROSS= and DOWN= options to place more than one group star per page or display. When you use the ACROSS= and DOWN= options, the stars are arranged from left to right and top to bottom in ascending order of group variable value.

See the description of the GROUP= option in "Options" earlier in this section for additional details. See "Star Chart Using Groups" in "STAR Statement Examples" later in this section for an illustration of grouping in a star chart.

Labels and Headings

By default, the midpoint value and the value of the chart statistic for each spine or slice are printed with the spine or slice. You can control the positioning of these values with the SLICE= and VALUE= options, respectively. You can use the PERCENT= option to have the percentage of the total chart statistic for each slice printed as well. (For the percentage chart statistic, this value is the same as the chart statistic value.) See "Slice and Spine Labeling Options" later in this section for details of how these values can be positioned.

A heading is printed at the top of each star chart indicating the type of statistic charted and the name of the chart variable. You can suppress this heading with the NOHEADING option.

When you use the GROUP= option, a heading is printed above each star indicating the name of the group variable and its value for the particular star. You can suppress these headings with the NOGROUPHEADING option.

The AXIS statement is not valid with the STAR statement. However, you can use the FTEXT= and HTEXT= graphics options to control the font and height of the labels, respectively.

Selecting Patterns for the Stars

By default, star charts do not use fill patterns. Only connected spines are drawn, using the first color in the current colors list. When you use the FILL= option or establish PATTERN definitions, star charts use slices instead of spines. You can use the FILL= option to specify a common fill for all slices, or you can use PATTERN statements to define specific patterns for the slices.

Star charts can use only pie/star patterns for the star slices. This pattern type uses the following fill patterns:

PEMPTY | EMPTY

PSOLID | SOLID

P*density*<*style*<*angle*>>

where	
density	can be 1 . . . 5.
style	can be X	N.
angle	can be 0 . . . 360.

PATTERN statements with other fill patterns are ignored.

If you provide fewer valid PATTERN definitions than the chart requires, the GCHART procedure uses the default fill pattern rotation for the slices drawn after all defined patterns are exhausted. See Chapter 15 for details.

You can use the COUTLINE= option to choose an outline color for all slices. By default, the slices are outlined in the same color as the fill pattern. See "Options" earlier in this section for a discussion of the COUTLINE= option.

Slice and Spine Labeling Options

These three text elements can be printed with each spine or slice in a star chart:

☐ the name (the value of the midpoint for the spine or slice)

☐ the value (the value of the chart statistic represented by the spine or slice)

☐ the percentage (the percentage of the chart statistic total represented by the spine or slice).

By default, only the name and value are printed; the percentage must be specifically requested.

The SLICE=, VALUE=, and PERCENT= options control the placement of the name, value, and percentage elements, respectively. The following four values are valid for these options:

ARROW   places the text outside the star circle and connects the text to the circle with a line. The line points to the spine or the center of the slice. The connecting line is the same color as the text.

INSIDE   places the text inside the star circle.

NONE   suppresses the text.

OUTSIDE   places the text outside the star circle.

Figure 23.7 earlier in this chapter illustrates the different labeling options.

The name and value elements follow each other by default. That is, if you use the SLICE= option without the VALUE= option or you use VALUE= without SLICE=, then the specified labeling method is used for both elements. If you specify both OUTSIDE and ARROW for different elements in the same STAR statement, the connecting line for the arrow may overlay the text positioned using OUTSIDE. For example, if you specify PERCENT=ARROW and VALUE=OUTSIDE, the line connecting the percentage information to the circle may overlay the value information for each midpoint.

If your star has many spines or slices, the GCHART procedure may not be able to label all of them. If so, a warning is printed in the SAS log with a list of the labels that cannot be displayed on the chart. You may be able to correct this situation by doing one of the following:

☐ using the ANGLE= option to change the orientation of the star.

☐ using the HPOS= and VPOS= graphics options to increase the number of cells in your display. See Chapter 5 for details.

See the description of the ANGLE= option in "Options" earlier in this section for details.

STAR Statement Examples

The following examples illustrate major features of the STAR statement.

Simple Star Charts

In this example, the STAR statements chart the total number of rejected parts for a fictitious company over a one-year period.

The following program statements produce Output 23.17 and Output 23.18:

```
    /* set the graphics environment */
goptions reset=global gunit=pct border
        ftext=swissb htitle=6 htext=3;

    /* create data set MONTHLY */
data monthly;
   informat date date7.;
   input site $ date rejects;
   cards;
Sydney  01JAN89 22
Sydney  01FEB89 26
more data lines
Paris   01NOV89 12
Paris   01DEC89 19
;
run;

    /* define title and footnote for chart */
title 'Rejected Parts';
footnote j=r 'GR23N17(a)  ';

    /* generate star chart */
proc gchart data=monthly;
   format date worddate3.;
   star date
        / freq=rejects
          discrete;
run;

    /* define new footnote for chart */
   footnote j=r 'GR23N17(b)  ';

    /* generate star chart */
   star date
        / freq=rejects
          discrete
          noheading
          fill=solid
          coutline=gray;
run;
quit;
```

Output 23.17 Simple Star
Chart with Spines
(GR23N17(a))

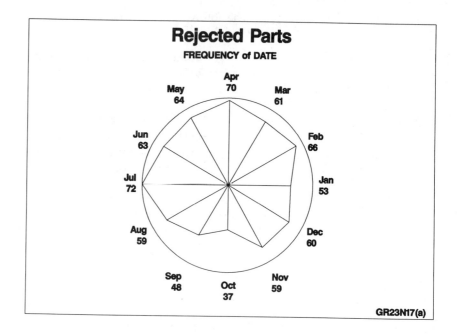

Output 23.18 Simple Star
Chart with Slices
(GR23N17(b))

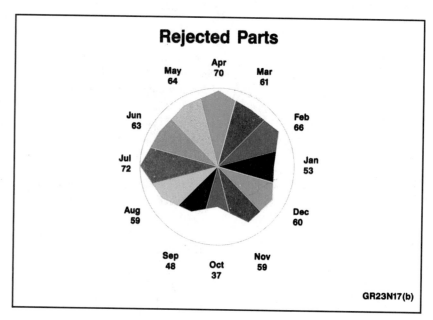

This example illustrates the following features:

□ The first RUN group, which creates Output 23.17, illustrates these
features:

□ The chart statistic defaults to frequency because the SUMVAR=
option and the TYPE= option are not used.

□ The FORMAT statement displays the date using the WORDDATE3.
format.

□ The FREQ= option specifies the variable REJECTS, which contains
a value to use when calculating the frequency statistic.

□ The DISCRETE option specifies that the numeric chart variable, DATE, should be treated as a discrete variable instead of as a continuous variable.

□ By default, the chart uses connected spines.

□ The second RUN group, which creates Output 23.18, illustrates these features:

□ The NOHEADING option suppresses the default heading for the star chart.

□ The FILL= option specifies that the chart should use slices and specifies the pattern used to fill the slices.

□ The COUTLINE= option specifies the color used to outline the star slices and draw the circle.

Star Chart Using Groups

This example charts the same data as the first STAR statement example but creates a separate star chart for each branch and places all three charts in a single picture.

The following program statements produce Output 23.19:

```
      /* set the graphics environment */
goptions reset=global gunit=pct border
         ftext=swissb htitle=6 htext=3;


      /* create data set MONTHLY */
data monthly;
   input site $ date rejects;
   cards;
Sydney  10593 22
Sydney  10625 26
more data lines
Paris   10913 12
Paris   10945 19
;
run;


      /* define title and footnote for chart */
title 'Rejected Parts';
footnote j=r 'GR23N18  ';


      /* generate star chart */
proc gchart data=monthly;
   format date worddate3.;
   label site='00'x;
   star date
        / freq=rejects
          discrete
          noconnect
          value=none
          group=site
          across=3;
   run;
quit;
```

Output 23.19 Star Chart
with Grouping (GR23N18)

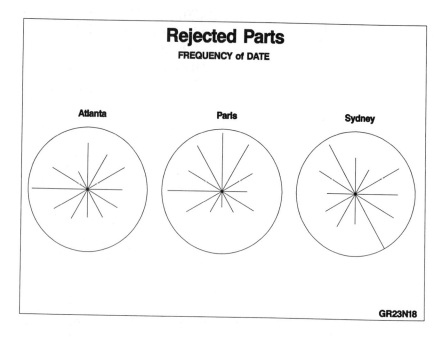

This example illustrates the following features:

□ The LABEL statement suppresses the label for the SITE variable.

□ The NOCONNECT option specifies that unconnected star spines should be drawn.

□ The VALUE= option suppresses the label for the chart statistic value of each spine.

□ The GROUP= option creates a separate star for each different value of the SITE variable.

□ The ACROSS= option fits the stars for all three branches on one page or display.

VBAR Statement

The VBAR statement creates one or more vertical bar charts using the input data set specified in the PROC GCHART statement. The VBAR statement specifies the chart variable or variables that define the categories of data to be charted. Other variables can be specified to

□ group the bars

□ subdivide the bars

□ provide data for the sum and mean statistics.

In addition, options used in the VBAR statement can select the statistic to be charted, manipulate the axes, and modify the appearance of the bars.

Syntax

The general form of the VBAR statement is

VBAR *chart-variable* < . . . *chart-variable-n*>
   </ <ANNOTATE=*Annotate-data-set*>
      <*appearance-options*>
      <*statistic-options*>
      <*midpoint-options*>
      <*axes-options*>
      <*description-options*>>;

□ *chart-variable* specifies a variable in the input data set with categories of data represented on the bar chart. If you include more than one chart variable in the VBAR statement, the variable names must be separated with blanks.

□ *appearance-options* can be one or more of the following:

  □ selecting colors

    CAXIS=*axis-color*

    COUTLINE=*bar-outline-color*

    CTEXT=*text-color*

  □ changing the appearance of the bars

    GSPACE=n

      where *n* is the amount of extra horizontal space between groups of bars

    PATTERNID= BY | GROUP | MIDPOINT | SUBGROUP

    SPACE=n

      where *n* is the amount of horizontal space between individual bars

    WIDTH=n

      where *n* is the horizontal width of the bars

  □ framing the axis area

    CFRAME=*background-color*

    FRAME

  □ changing the appearance of the subgroup legend

    LEGEND=LEGEND<1 . . . 99>

    NOLEGEND

□ *statistic-options* can be one or more of the following:

  □ specifying statistics represented by the bars

    FREQ=*numeric-variable*

    G100

SUMVAR=*numeric-variable*

TYPE=*statistic*

where *statistic* is one of the following:

CFREQ

CPERCENT

FREQ

MEAN

PERCENT

SUM

□ displaying statistic values (only one of the following)

CFREQ

CPERCENT

FREQ

MEAN

PERCENT

SUM

□ *midpoint-options* can be one or more of the following:

□ manipulating the midpoint values

DISCRETE

LEVELS=n

where *n* is the number of midpoints for the numeric chart variable

MIDPOINTS=*value-list*

MIDPOINTS=OLD

MISSING

□ grouping and subgrouping

GROUP=*variable*

SUBGROUP=*variable*

□ *axes-options* can be one or more of the following:

□ manipulating the axes

GAXIS=AXIS<1 . . . 99>

MAXIS=AXIS<1 . . . 99>

NOAXIS

RAXIS=*value-list* | AXIS<1 . . . 99>

□ setting the number of minor tick marks on the response axis

MINOR=*n*

□ manipulating the midpoint order

ASCENDING

DESCENDING

NOZERO

□ adding reference lines

AUTOREF

CLIPREF

NOBASEREF

REF=*value-list*

□ *description-options* can be either or both of the following:

DESCRIPTION='*string*'

NAME='*string*'

Options are fully described in "Options" later in this section.

Requirements

A VBAR statement must contain at least one chart variable. A separate chart is drawn for each chart variable.

Options

You can use the following options in the VBAR statement. Options used in a VBAR statement affect all graphs produced by that statement. If any of the following options are supplied, they must be separated from the chart variables with a slash (/). If you do not use any options, omit the slash.

ANNOTATE=*Annotate-data-set*
ANNO=*Annotate-data-set*

specifies a data set to provide annotation of graphs produced by the VBAR statement. *Annotate-data-set* must contain the appropriate Annotate variables. See Chapter 18 for details.

If the ANNOTATE= option is also used with the PROC GCHART statement, both sets of annotation are applied. If you specify BY-group processing, the Annotate data set must contain the BY variable. For details, see "Using BY-Group Processing with the Annotate Facility" in Chapter 18 and "Details of BY-Group Processing" in Chapter 10.

ASCENDING

arranges the bars in ascending order of the value of the chart statistic. By default, bars are arranged from left to right in ascending order of the value of the midpoint, without regard for the lengths of the bars. The ASCENDING option reorders the midpoints so that the shortest bar is at the left and the longest bar is at the right. If you use the GROUP= option, the reordering is performed for each group, so the order of midpoint values may be different for each group of bars.

The ASCENDING option overrides any midpoint order specified with the MIDPOINTS= option or specified in the ORDER= option in an AXIS statement assigned to the midpoint axis.

AUTOREF

draws a horizontal reference line at each major tick mark on the response (vertical) axis. To draw reference lines only at specific points on the response axis, use the REF= option.

AXIS=

See the RAXIS= option later in this section.

CAXIS=*axis-color*

specifies a color for the response and midpoint axis lines and for the frame around the axis area if one is used. If you do not use the CAXIS= option, a color specification is searched for in the following order:

1. the COLOR= option in AXIS definitions

2. the default, the first color in the colors list.

CFRAME=*background-color*
CFR=*background-color*

fills the axis area enclosed by the frame with the specified color. By default, the frame area is not filled. A frame is also drawn around the filled area, regardless of whether you use the FRAME option. The frame fill color does not affect the frame color, which is the same as the midpoint (horizontal) axis line color by default.

The frame fill color should be different than the colors used for bar patterns. Bars or bar segments in the frame fill color are invisible unless the COUTLINE= option is used to outline them in another color.

CFREQ

prints the value of the cumulative frequency statistic above the bars. The CFREQ option is ignored if the bars are too narrow to avoid overlapping values or if the FREQ option also is used. Only one statistic can be printed on a chart.

CLIPREF

clips the reference lines at the bars. This makes the reference lines appear to be behind the bars.

COUTLINE=*bar-outline-color*

outlines all bars or bar segments and legend values in the subgroup legend (if it appears) using the specified color. By default, the outline color for bars is the same as the pattern color.

Note: The outline color is the only distinction between empty patterns. Using the COUTLINE= option when VALUE=EMPTY is specified in PATTERN definitions makes the patterns look the same.

CPERCENT
CPCT

prints the value of the cumulative percentage statistic above the bars. The CPERCENT option is ignored if the bars are too narrow to avoid overlapping values or if any one of the FREQ, CFREQ, or PERCENT options also is used. Only one statistic can be printed on a chart.

CTEXT=*text-color*

specifies the color of all text on the chart that is not otherwise assigned a color. Text includes axis values and axis labels on the response, midpoint, and group axes; the subgroup legend; and the descriptive statistics. If you do not use the CTEXT= option, a color specification is searched for in the following order:

1. the CTEXT= option in a GOPTIONS statement

2. the default, the first color in the colors list.

If you use the CTEXT= option, it overrides the color specification for the axis label and the tick mark values in the COLOR= option in an AXIS definition assigned to an axis.

If you use the CTEXT= option, the color specification is overridden by the following conditions:

□ If you also use the COLOR= parameter of a LABEL= or VALUE= option in a LEGEND definition assigned to the subgroup legend, that parameter determines the color of the legend label or the color of the legend value descriptions, respectively.

□ If you also use the COLOR= parameter of a LABEL= or VALUE= option in an AXIS definition assigned to an axis, it determines the color of the axis label or the color of the tick mark values, respectively.

DESCENDING

arranges the bars in descending order of the value of the chart statistic. By default, bars are arranged from left to right in ascending order of midpoint value, without regard to the length of the bars. The DESCENDING option reorders the midpoints so that the longest bar is at the left and the shortest bar is at the right. If you use the GROUP= option, each group is ordered separately, so the order of midpoint values may be different for each group of bars. The DESCENDING option overrides any midpoint order specified with the MIDPOINTS= option or specified in the ORDER= option in an AXIS statement assigned to the midpoint axis.

DESCRIPTION='*string*'
DES='*string*'

specifies a descriptive string, up to 40 characters long, that appears in the Description field of the catalog entry for the chart. The description does not appear on the chart. By default, the GCHART procedure assigns a description of the form VBAR CHART OF *variable*, where *variable* is the name of the chart variable.

DISCRETE

treats a numeric chart variable as a discrete variable rather than as a continuous variable. If the chart variable has a format associated with it, each formatted value is treated as a midpoint. The GCHART procedure creates a separate midpoint and, hence, a separate bar for each unique value of the chart variable.

The LEVELS= option is ignored when you use the DISCRETE option. The MIDPOINTS= option overrides the DISCRETE option. The ORDER= option in an AXIS statement assigned to the midpoint axis can rearrange or exclude discrete midpoint values.

FRAME
FR

draws a rectangular frame around the axis area. By default, it is drawn in the color of the midpoint axis.

If the FRAME option is used without the CFRAME= option, the frame is empty. If the CFRAME= option is used, the frame is filled with the specified color.

A frame is always drawn when the CFRAME= option is used to fill the axis area, regardless of whether the FRAME option is used.

FREQ

> prints the value of the frequency statistic above the bars. The FREQ option is ignored if the bars are too narrow to prevent overlapping values. This option overrides the CFREQ, PERCENT, CPERCENT, SUM, and MEAN options. Only one statistic can be printed on a chart.

FREQ=*numeric-variable*

> uses the values of *numeric-variable* to weight the contribution of each observation to the statistic being computed. Noninteger values of *numeric-variable* are truncated to integers.

> By default, each observation is counted only once in the frequency counts and sums. Each observation is counted the number of times specified by the value of *numeric-variable* for that observation. Observations for which *numeric-variable* is missing, 0, or negative are not included in the statistic calculation.

> Because you cannot use TYPE=PERCENT, TYPE=CPERCENT, TYPE=FREQ, or TYPE=CFREQ when you use the SUMVAR= option, you must use the FREQ= option to calculate percentages, cumulative percentages, frequencies, or cumulative frequencies based on a sum.

G100

> calculates the percentage and cumulative percentage statistics for each group. When you use the G100 option, the individual percentages reflect the contribution of the midpoint to the group and total 100 percent for each group. The G100 option is ignored unless you also use the GROUP= option.

> By default, the individual percentages reflect the contribution of the midpoint to the entire chart and total 100 percent for the entire chart.

GAXIS=AXIS<1 . . . 99>

> assigns axis characteristics to the group axis. This option is meaningful only in conjunction with the GROUP= option. The option value indicates which AXIS definition to use. The GAXIS= option is ignored if the specified AXIS definition is not currently in effect.

> The AXIS statement has a special option for the group axis on vertical bar charts. The NOBRACKETS option suppresses the brackets drawn around the values on the group axis.

> The AXIS statement options MAJOR= and MINOR= are ignored in AXIS definitions assigned to the group axis because the axis does not use tick marks. A warning message is written to the SAS log if these options appear in the AXIS definition.

> You can use the ORDER= option in the AXIS statement to remove groups from the chart.

GROUP=*variable*

> specifies that the data be grouped according to values of *variable*. *Variable* can be either character or numeric and is always treated as a discrete variable. A separate group of bars is produced for each unique value of *variable*. Missing values for *variable* are treated as a valid group.

> By default, each group includes all midpoints, even if no observations for the group fall within the midpoint range, meaning that no bar is drawn at the midpoint. The NOZERO option suppresses midpoints with no observations.

In vertical bar charts, the group axis appears below the midpoint axis. By default, groups are arranged from left to right in ascending order of *variable* values. If the axis values for the midpoints within a group are wider than the group axis values, brackets are drawn around the values to emphasize which bars belong to which group.

The GAXIS= option can be used to assign characteristics defined in an AXIS statement to the group axis. See the discussion of the GAXIS= option earlier in this section for details.

GSPACE=*n*

specifies the amount of extra horizontal space between groups of bars. Units for *n* are character cells. The value does not have to be an integer. For example, you can specify the following:

```
vbar site / gspace=1.5;
```

Use GSPACE=0 to leave no extra space between adjacent groups of bars. In this case, the same space appears between groups of bars as between the bars within a group. The GSPACE= option is ignored unless you also use the GROUP= option. By default, the GCHART procedure calculates group spacing based on the size of the axis area and the number of bars in the chart.

If the requested spacing results in a chart that is too large to fit in the space available for the midpoint (vertical) axis, an error message is written to the SAS log and no chart is produced.

LEGEND=LEGEND<1 . . . 99>

assigns legend characteristics to the subgroup legend. The LEGEND= option is ignored unless you also use the SUBGROUP= option.

▶ *Caution: The LEGEND=*
option does not generate a
legend.

The option value indicates which LEGEND definition to use. This option is ignored if the specified LEGEND definition is not currently in effect.

The following options override the LEGEND= option and suppress the subgroup legend:

NOLEGEND

PATTERNID=BY | GROUP | MIDPOINT

LEVELS=*n*

uses the specified number of midpoints for the numeric chart variable. The range is calculated automatically using the algorithm described by Terrell and Scott (1985).

This option is ignored if

□ the chart variable is character type

□ the DISCRETE option is used

□ the MIDPOINTS= option is used.

MAXIS=AXIS<1 . . . 99>

assigns axis characteristics to the midpoint (horizontal) axis. The option value indicates which AXIS definition to use. The MAXIS= option is ignored if the specified AXIS definition is not currently in effect.

The AXIS statement options MAJOR= and MINOR= are ignored in AXIS definitions assigned to the midpoint axis because the axis does not use tick marks. A warning message is written to the SAS log if these options appear in the AXIS definition.

MEAN

prints the value of the mean statistic above the bars. The MEAN option is ignored unless you also use the SUMVAR= option. It also is ignored if the bars are too narrow to prevent overlapping values or if any one of the FREQ, CFREQ, PERCENT, CPERCENT, or SUM options also is used. Only one statistic can be printed on a chart.

MIDPOINTS=*value-list*

specifies values for midpoints on the midpoint (horizontal) axis. By default, one of these methods is used:

□ If the chart variable is numeric type, the GCHART procedure calculates midpoint values.

□ If the chart variable is character type or is numeric type and the DISCRETE option is used, the GCHART procedure creates a midpoint for each unique value of the chart variable.

If *value-list* contains more midpoints than can fit on the midpoint axis, an error message is written to the SAS log and no chart is produced. On many devices, this problem can be corrected by increasing the number of cells in your graphics display using the HPOS= and VPOS= graphics options. See Chapter 5 for details.

The ORDER= option in an AXIS statement assigned to the midpoint axis overrides the order specified in the MIDPOINTS= option but does not affect the way in which chart statistics are calculated. The VBAR statement options ASCENDING and DESCENDING also override both the order specified in the MIDPOINTS= option and the order specified in the ORDER= option in the AXIS statement assigned to the midpoint axis using the MAXIS= option.

For numeric chart variables, *value-list* can be specified in the following ways:

n n . . . n

n,n, . . . ,n

n TO *n* <BY *increment*> <*n . . . n*> <*n, . . . ,n*>

n n . . . n TO *n* <BY *increment*> <*n . . . n*>

n,n, . . . ,n TO *n* <BY *increment*> <*n, . . . ,n*>

'*SAS-value*'*i* TO '*SAS-value*'*i* <BY *interval*>

'*SAS-value*'*i* '*SAS-value*'*i* . . . '*SAS-value*'*i*

If the variable has an associated format, you must specify the unformatted values in *value-list*.

For continuous variables, the midpoints are the medians of the ranges of possible values of the chart variable. A value that falls exactly halfway between two midpoints is placed in the higher range.

For character chart variables, *value-list* must be a list of midpoint values. Values must be enclosed in single quotes and separated by blanks (commas are not allowed as separators), as in this example:

```
midpoints='Paris' 'Sydney' 'Atlanta'
```

The values can be specified in any order, so the *value-list* can be used to order the bars. If the variable has an associated format, you must specify the formatted values in *value-list*. By default, midpoints are arranged left to right in ascending order of the midpoint values. If the character chart variable has an associated format, the values are arranged in order of the formatted values.

You can selectively exclude some chart variable values from the chart as in this example:

```
midpoints='Paris'
```

Only those observations for which the chart variable exactly matches one of the midpoint values are counted. As a result, observations can be inadvertently excluded if values in the midpoint list are misspelled or if the case does not match exactly.

MIDPOINTS=OLD

tells the GCHART procedure to calculate default midpoints using the algorithm used in Release 82.4 and Version 5 of SAS/GRAPH software. The MIDPOINTS=OLD option is ignored unless the chart variable is numeric type.

MINOR=n

specifies the number of minor tick marks between each major tick mark on the response (vertical) axis.

Using the MINOR= option in the VBAR statement overrides the number of minor tick marks specified in the MINOR= option of an AXIS definition assigned to the response axis with the RAXIS= option.

MISSING

accepts a missing value as a valid midpoint for the chart variable. By default, observations for which the value of the chart variable is missing are ignored.

Note: Missing values are always valid for group and subgroup variables.

NAME='*string*'

specifies a string, up to eight characters long, that appears in the Name field of the catalog entry for the chart. *String* must be a valid SAS name. By default, the name assigned is GCHART. If either the name specified or the default name duplicates an existing name in the catalog, SAS/GRAPH software adds a number to the duplicate name to create a unique name, for example, GCHART2.

NOAXIS

suppresses the axes, including axis lines, axis labels, axis values, and all major and minor tick marks. Frames and axis-area fills requested by the FRAME and CFRAME= options are not suppressed. The NOAXIS option overrides the GAXIS=, MAXIS=, and RAXIS= options.

NOBASEREF

suppresses the zero reference line when the SUM or MEAN chart statistic has negative values.

NOLEGEND

suppresses the subgroup legend. The NOLEGEND option is ignored unless you also use the SUBGROUP= option.

NOZERO

suppresses any midpoints for which there are no corresponding values of the chart variable and, hence, no bar. The NOZERO option usually is used with the GROUP= option to suppress midpoints when not all values of the chart variable are present for every group or if the chart statistic for a midpoint is 0.

PATTERNID=BY | GROUP | MIDPOINT | SUBGROUP

specifies the way fill patterns are assigned. By default, PATTERNID=SUBGROUP. The meanings of the option values are as follows:

BY   changes patterns each time the value of the BY variable changes. All bars use the same pattern if the GCHART procedure does not include a BY statement.

GROUP   changes patterns every time the value of the group variable changes. All bars in each group use the same pattern, but a different pattern is used for each group.

MIDPOINT   changes patterns every time the midpoint value changes. If the GROUP= option is used, the respective midpoint patterns are repeated.

SUBGROUP   changes patterns every time the value of the subgroup variable changes. Bars divided into subgroups use a different pattern for each subgroup. If the SUBGROUP= option is not used, all bars have the same pattern.

A warning message is written to the SAS log if the PATTERNID= value is anything other than SUBGROUP when the SUBGROUP= option is used, since this situation may make it impossible to distinguish the subgroups and does not produce a legend.

PERCENT
PCT

prints the value of the percentage statistic above the bars. The PERCENT option is ignored if the bars are too narrow to prevent overlapping values or if either the FREQ or CFREQ option also is used. Only one statistic can be printed on a chart.

RAXIS=*value-list* | AXIS<1 . . . 99>
AXIS=*value-list* | AXIS<1 . . . 99>

specify values for the major tick mark divisions on the response (vertical) axis or assign axis characteristics to the axis. By default, the GCHART procedure scales the response axis automatically and provides an appropriate number of tick marks.

Value-list can be specified in the following ways:

n n . . . n

n,n, . . . ,n

n TO *n* <BY *increment*> <*n . . . n*> <*n, . . . ,n*>

n n . . . n TO *n* <BY *increment*> <*n . . . n*>

n,n, . . . ,n TO *n* <BY *increment*> <*n, . . . ,n*>

See the ORDER= option in Chapter 9 for additional information on specifying *value-list*.

Negative values can be specified, but negative values are reasonable only when the TYPE= option value is SUM or MEAN and one or more of the sums or means are less than 0. Frequency and percentage values are never less than 0.

For lists of values, a separate major tick mark is created for each individual value. A warning message is written to the SAS log if the values are not evenly spaced.

If the values represented by the bars are larger than the highest tick mark value, the bars are truncated at the highest tick mark. No warning is provided, so check for this possibility if one or more bars extend to the top of the axis area.

To assign an AXIS definition, use a value of the form AXIS<1 . . . 99>. The option is ignored if the specified AXIS definition is not currently in effect. See Chapter 9 for details.

If a BY statement is used with the PROC GCHART statement, the same response axes are produced for each BY group when RAXIS=*value-list* is used or if there is an ORDER= list in the AXIS statement assigned to the response axis.

REF=*value-list*

draws horizontal reference lines at the specified points on the response (vertical) axis. The *value-list* values can be listed in any order. The values should be within the range of values represented by the response axis. A warning is written to the SAS log if any of the points are off the axis, and no reference line is drawn for such points. The AUTOREF option can be used to draw reference lines automatically at all of the major tick marks. The REF= option is ignored if you also use the AUTOREF option.

Value-list can be specified in the following ways:

n n . . . n

n,n, . . . ,n

n TO *n* <BY *increment*> <*n . . . n*> <*n, . . . ,n*>

n n . . . n TO *n* <BY *increment*> <*n . . . n*>

n,n, . . . ,n TO *n* <BY *increment*> <*n, . . . ,n*>

See the ORDER= option in Chapter 9 for additional information on specifying *value-list*.

SPACE=*n*

specifies the amount of horizontal space between individual bars or between the bars within each group if you also use the GROUP= option. By default, the GCHART procedure calculates spacing based on the size of the axis area and the number of bars in the chart. Units for the *n* value are character cells. The value does not have to be an integer. For example, you can specify the following:

```
vbar site / space=1.5;
```

Use SPACE=0 to leave no space between adjacent bars.

The SPACE= option is ignored if the specified spacing requests a chart that is too large to fit in the space available for the midpoint (horizontal) axis.

SUBGROUP=*variable*

divides the bars into segments according to the values of *variable*. Each bar is divided into as many parts as there are discrete values of *variable* for the midpoint.

By default, a legend appears at the bottom of the graph when you use the SUBGROUP= option. The legend indicates which pattern represents which value of the variable. The LEGEND= option can be used to assign a LEGEND definition to the subgroup legend.

The following options suppress the subgroup legend:

NOLEGEND

PATTERNID=BY | GROUP | MIDPOINT

SUM

prints the value of the sum statistic above the bars. The SUM option is ignored unless you also use the SUMVAR= option. It also is ignored if the bars are too narrow to prevent overlapping values or if any one of the FREQ, CFREQ, PERCENT, or CPERCENT options is also used. Only one statistic can be printed on a chart.

SUMVAR=*numeric-variable*

specifies the variable to be used for sum and mean calculations. The GCHART procedure calculates the sum and, if requested, the mean of *numeric-variable* for each midpoint. These statistics then can be represented by the length of the bars along the response (vertical) axis.

When you use the SUMVAR= option, the TYPE= option value must be either SUM or MEAN. By default, TYPE=SUM when the SUMVAR= option is used.

TYPE=*statistic*

specifies the chart statistic for the bar chart. *Statistic* can be one of the following when you do not use the SUMVAR= option:

Value of *statistic*	Statistic represented on the chart
FREQ	frequency
CFREQ	cumulative frequency
PERCENT PCT	percentage
CPERCENT CPCT	cumulative percentage

Statistic can be either of the following when you use the SUMVAR=
option:

Value of *statistic*	Statistic represented on the chart
SUM	sum
MEAN	mean

By default, TYPE=FREQ when the SUMVAR= option is not used,
and TYPE=SUM when SUMVAR= is used.

When you specify TYPE=MEAN and use the SUBGROUP= option,
the height of the bar represents the mean for the entire midpoint. The
subgroup segments are proportional to the subgroup's contribution to
the sum for the bar.

Because you cannot use TYPE=PERCENT, TYPE=CPERCENT,
TYPE=FREQ, or TYPE=CFREQ when you use the SUMVAR=
option, you must use the FREQ= option to calculate percentages,
cumulative percentages, frequencies, or cumulative frequencies based
on a sum.

See "Chart Statistics" earlier in this chapter for a complete
description of the types of statistics that can be represented.

WIDTH=*n*

specifies the horizontal width of the bars. By default, the GCHART
procedure calculates bar width based on the size of the axis area and
the number of bars in the chart. Units for *n* are character cells. The
value for *n* must be greater than 0, but it does not have to be an
integer. For example, you can specify the following:

```
hbar site / width=1.5;
```

The WIDTH option is ignored if the requested bar width results in
a chart that is too large to fit in the space available for the midpoint
(horizontal) axis.

Using the VBAR Statement

The form of your chart is governed by the variables you specify and the
options you use in the VBAR statement. A separate bar chart is produced
for each chart variable specified. For example, the following statement
produces two separate vertical bar charts:

```
vbar site year;
```

The values on the midpoint (horizontal) axis are the midpoints for
ranges of chart variable values. The response (vertical) axis provides a
scale for the values of the statistic graphed for the chart variable. The
values of a chart statistic can be printed above the bars if the bars are
wide enough so that the values do not overlap.

The GCHART procedure automatically scales the response axis,
determines bar width, and chooses spacing between the bars. However,
you can use options to override the defaults and to choose bar intervals
and the number and spacing of bars. The procedure also can group the
bars according to the values of a group variable and subdivide the bars
into segments according to the values of a subgroup variable.

The following sections explain how you can change the appearance of your vertical bar chart using different VBAR statement options.

The Chart Variable and the Midpoint Axis

The value of the chart variable determines the bar to which each observation in the data set contributes. The way in which midpoints are selected varies depending on the type of the chart variable and the options used. See "Chart Variables and Midpoint Selection" earlier in this chapter for additional information on how midpoints are determined.

Formatted numeric variables are ordered by the unformatted numeric values. If you use the DISCRETE option and the variable is formatted, there is one bar for each formatted value.

You can use the MIDPOINTS= and LEVELS= options to change the number of midpoints used for numeric variables. For example, if you specify the following, the GCHART procedure calculates four midpoints for a continuous chart variable:

```
vbar sales / levels=4;
```

If you specify the following, then the GCHART procedure uses 1, 3, and 5 as the midpoints for the chart:

```
vbar x / midpoints=1 3 5;
```

You can use the ORDER= option in an AXIS definition assigned to the midpoint axis to rearrange the order of the midpoints or to exclude some midpoints from the chart.

Note: The ORDER= option does not change the way chart statistics are calculated. All of the midpoints are included in the calculation of the chart statistic unless you also use the MIDPOINTS= option.

The midpoint value for each bar is shown on the midpoint (horizontal) axis. By default, midpoint values are arranged on the midpoint axis in ascending order from left to right. If the character chart variable has an associated format, the bars are ordered according to the formatted values of the chart variable. The midpoint axis also includes a label that, by default, indicates the name of the chart variable or variable label.

You can use the MAXIS= option to assign a set of axis characteristics defined in an AXIS statement to the midpoint axis. You can use the MIDPOINTS= option to select and change the order of the midpoints for a character variable. For example, the following statement orders the midpoints **Paris Atlanta** instead of the default of **Atlanta Paris**:

```
vbar branch / midpoints='Paris' 'Atlanta';
```

The ASCENDING or DESCENDING option can also be used to modify bar order. For more information on manipulating the midpoint axis, see the discussions of the MIDPOINTS=, MAXIS=, ASCENDING, and DESCENDING options in "Options" earlier in this section.

The Chart Statistic and the Response Axis

The height of each bar graphically represents the value of the chart statistic for the corresponding midpoint. These six types of statistics can be charted:

□ frequency

□ cumulative frequency

□ percentage

□ cumulative percentage

□ sum

□ mean.

See "Chart Statistics" earlier in this chapter for more information on how these statistics are calculated.

The default chart statistic is frequency. If the SUMVAR= option is used, the default chart statistic is sum. You can use the TYPE= option to select other chart statistics. You must use the SUMVAR= option to identify the variable to use for calculating the sum or mean statistics. For example, if you want to calculate a sum based on the value of the variable COUNT, specify the following:

```
vbar branch / sumvar=count;
```

By default, each observation is counted only once in the calculation of the chart statistic. You can use the FREQ= option to identify the variable that indicates the number of times each observation is counted.

The response (vertical) axis provides a scale for interpreting the magnitude of the chart statistic for each bar. By default, the response axis is divided into evenly spaced intervals identified by tick marks. Major tick marks are labeled with the corresponding statistic value; unlabeled minor tick marks are evenly distributed between the major tick marks. For sums and means, the major tick marks are labeled with values of the SUMVAR= variable (formatted if the variable has an associated format). The axis also has an overall label that, by default, indicates the statistic being represented.

You can use the RAXIS= option to change the major tick mark intervals on the response axis or to assign an AXIS statement definition, which can modify the text, tick mark intervals, or general appearance of the axis. See the description of the RAXIS= option in "Options" earlier in this section for details.

The Group Variable and the Group Axis

If you want to display your data categorized by both the chart variable and another variable, you can use the second variable to organize the bars into groups. Use the GROUP= option to identify the second variable as the group variable for the chart. When you use the GROUP= option, a separate group of bars is created for each unique value of the group variable. Each group contains all the midpoints defined for the chart variable unless you use the NOZERO option.

The group axis identifies the group variable values that distinguish the groups. In vertical bar charts, the group axis is below the midpoint axis. The group axis provides a list of variable values and brackets but does not provide an axis line. If the groups are wider than the axis values, brackets are drawn to emphasize which bars belong in each group. The group axis also has a label that, by default, indicates the name of the group variable or label.

By default, the groups are arranged from left to right in ascending order of group variable value. You can use the GAXIS= option to assign an AXIS statement definition to the group axis. The definition can modify the order, text, and appearance of the axis.

See the descriptions of the GROUP= and GAXIS= options in "Options" earlier in this section for details. See "Vertical Bar Chart Using Groups and Subgroups" in "VBAR Statement Examples" later in this section for an illustration of grouping in a vertical bar chart.

The Subgroup Variable and the Subgroup Legend

If you want to divide each bar into segments based on the contribution of a variable, you can use the variable as a subgroup variable. Use the SUBGROUP= option to identify the variable as the subgroup variable for the chart. When you use the SUBGROUP= option, each bar contains a separate segment for every unique value of the subgroup variable for the bar's midpoint. The number of segments in each bar depends on the number of different values of the subgroup variable for the corresponding midpoint.

The subgroup legend provides a key to the patterns that identify each subgroup. By default, the subgroup legend appears below the midpoint and group axes and above any footnotes. The subgroup legend also includes a label that, by default, indicates the name or label of the subgroup variable.

You can create a legend based on the chart midpoints. Simply use the chart variable as the subgroup variable as follows:

```
vbar city / subgroup=city;
```

You can use the LEGEND= option to assign a LEGEND statement definition to the subgroup legend as shown here:

```
vbar city / legend=legend3 subgroup=quarter;
```

The subgroup legend is suppressed when the PATTERNID= option value is anything other than SUBGROUP, even if you use the LEGEND= option.

See the descriptions of the SUBGROUP=, PATTERNID=, and LEGEND= options in "Options" earlier in this section for additional details. See "Vertical Bar Chart Using Groups and Subgroups" in "VBAR Statement Examples" later in this section for an illustration of subgrouping in a vertical bar chart.

Statistic Values

In addition to displaying one statistic graphically on the response axis, the VBAR statement can print the value of one statistic above the bars, provided the bars are wide enough so that the printed values do not overlap. You can increase the width of the bars using the WIDTH= option. You must specifically request statistic values on vertical bar charts; none are printed by default. No label is provided to indicate which statistic the printed values represent. You can control the size of the text printed using the HTEXT= graphics option.

The FREQ, CFREQ, PERCENT, CPERCENT, SUM, and MEAN options select the corresponding statistics. Since only one value can be printed for each bar, only the highest priority statistic is printed if more than one of the options are used. The priority order, from highest to lowest, is as follows:

1. FREQ
2. CFREQ
3. PERCENT | PCT
4. CPERCENT | CPCT
5. SUM
6. MEAN.

When you do not use the SUMVAR= option, only frequency, cumulative frequency, percentage, or cumulative percentage statistics can be printed. If you use the SUMVAR= option, any of the six statistics can be printed. For more information, see "Options" earlier in this section.

You can mix chart statistics and the type of statistic printed above the bars. For example, you can specify TYPE=SUM and use the MEAN option to produce a chart of the sum of each midpoint with the mean of each midpoint printed above the bars.

Selecting Patterns for the Bars

Vertical bar charts can only use bar/block patterns. This pattern type uses the following fill patterns:

EMPTY

SOLID

style<density>

    where

    style   can be X | L | R.

    density   can be 1 . . . 5.

All other fill pattern specifications are ignored. See Chapter 15 for more information.

By default, the bar fill pattern changes each time the subgroup variable value changes, so a different fill pattern is used for each subgroup. The number of different values for the SUBGROUP= variable determines the number of bar colors and fill patterns in the chart. If you do not use the SUBGROUP= or PATTERNID= option, all bars take the same fill pattern and color. You can use PATTERN statements or the PATTERN window to select specific fill patterns and colors for the bars or bar segments in the chart.

·You can use the PATTERNID= option to select which variable determines when fill patterns change. In addition to using a different fill pattern for each subgroup, the GCHART procedure can change patterns for each bar, each group of bars, or each BY group. See the discussion of the PATTERNID= option in "Options" earlier in this section for details.

If you provide fewer valid PATTERN definitions than the chart requires, the GCHART procedure uses the default fill pattern rotation for the bars or bar segments drawn after all defined patterns are exhausted. See Chapter 15 for details.

You can use the COUTLINE= option to choose an outline color for all bars or bar segments. By default, the bars are outlined in the same color as the fill pattern. See "Options" earlier in this section for a discussion of the COUTLINE= option.

Using Other Global Statements

You can use AXIS and LEGEND definitions to modify the appearance of bar charts produced by the VBAR statement.

You can use axis characteristics in AXIS definitions to modify the text and appearance of the axes on the charts. Assign AXIS definitions to the response, midpoint, and group axes using the RAXIS=, MAXIS=, and GAXIS= options, respectively.

Certain restrictions apply; for example, the midpoint and group axes in vertical bar charts do not have tick marks, so any tick mark options in AXIS statements assigned to those axes are ignored. In addition, if the axis labels do not fit horizontally, they may be drawn vertically or not drawn at all. See the descriptions of the GAXIS=, MAXIS=, and RAXIS= options in "Options" earlier in this section for details on the restrictions for each axis.

You can use legend characteristics in LEGEND definitions to adjust the location, text, and appearance of the subgroup legend on the charts. Legend characteristics are assigned to the subgroup legend using the LEGEND= option.

Using the LEGEND= option does not guarantee that a legend is produced. Subgroup legends appear only when you use the SUBGROUP= option in the VBAR statement and the PATTERNID= option value is SUBGROUP.

VBAR Statement Examples

The following examples illustrate major features of the VBAR statement. The examples in the HBAR statement section earlier in this chapter illustrate other features that also apply to vertical bar charts.

Simple Vertical Bar Chart

This example uses the VBAR statement to chart the total sales for a fictitious company over a one-year period.

The following program statements produce Output 23.20:

```
    /* set the graphics environment */
goptions reset=global gunit=pct border
         ftext=swissb htitle=6 htext=3;

    /* create data set TOTALS */
data totals;
   length dept $ 7 site $ 8;
   input dept site quarter sales;
   cards;
Parts    Sydney  1 7843.97
Parts    Atlanta 1 9225.26
more data lines
Tools    Atlanta 4 3624.19
Tools    Paris   4 6414.25
;
run;
```

```
    /* define title and footnote for chart */
title 'Total Sales';
footnote j=r 'GR23N19 ';

    /* define axis characteristics */
axis label=('Branch') width=3;

    /* define pattern characteristics */
pattern1 value=solid color=blue;
pattern2 value=solid color=green;
pattern3 value=solid color=red;
pattern4 value=solid color=lib;

    /* generate vertical bar chart */
proc gchart data=totals;
    format sales dollar8.;
    vbar site
        / frame
          sumvar=sales
          midpoints='Sydney' 'Atlanta' 'Paris'
          maxis=axis
          raxis=0 to 90000 by 15000
          minor=2
          space=5
          sum
          patternid=midpoint;
run;
quit;
```

Output 23.20 *Simple Vertical Bar Chart (GR23N19)*

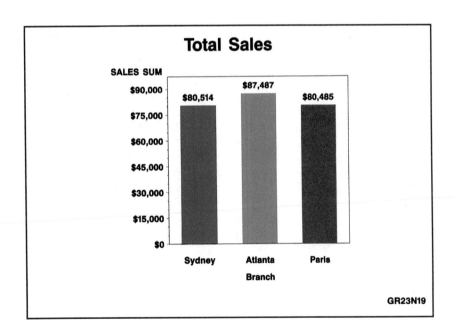

This example illustrates the following features:

□ The global PATTERN statements define the patterns and colors used for all bars. (All bars take a different color and pattern because the PATTERNID= option specifies that the pattern should change for each midpoint value.) The fourth pattern definition is not used.

□ The FRAME option specifies that a rectangular frame be drawn around the axis area.

□ The SUMVAR= option specifies the variable used to calculate the chart statistics. Because the TYPE= option is not used, the default statistic is the sum of the SALES variable values for each midpoint.

□ The MIDPOINTS= option specifies the order of midpoint values on the midpoint axis.

□ The MAXIS= option assigns the axis characteristics defined in the AXIS statement to the midpoint axis.

□ The RAXIS= option specifies the intervals for major tick marks on the response axis. Formatted values are printed at the major tick marks because a format is specified for the SALES variable.

□ The MINOR= option sets the number of minor tick marks between each major tick mark to two. Based on the values specified in the RAXIS= option, each minor tick mark represents $5,000.

□ The SPACE= option increases the space between the bars.

□ The SUM option prints the sum statistic value above the bars.

Vertical Bar Chart Using Groups

This example charts the state sales for each of three regions of a fictitious company. It groups the bars by REGION and suppresses those bars in each region that have a value of 0.

The following program statements produce Output 23.21:

```
     /* set the graphics environment */
  goptions reset=global gunit=pct border
         ftext=swissb htitle=6 htext=3;

     /* create data set REGIONS */
  data regions;
     length region state $ 8;
     format sales dollar8.;
     input region state sales;
     cards;
West    CA   13636
West    OR   18988
more data lines
South   FL   14541
South   GA   19022
  ;
  run;
```

```
    /* define title and footnote for chart */
title 'US Sales Goal:  $15,000';
footnote j=r 'GR23N20  ';

    /* define axis characteristics */
axis width=3;

    /* define pattern characteristics */
pattern1 value=solid color=blue;
pattern2 value=solid color=green;
pattern3 value=solid color=red;

    /* generate vertical bar chart */
proc gchart data=regions;
    vbar state
            / frame
            sumvar=sales
            group=region
            nozero
            ref=15000
            patternid=group
            width=6
            space=0
            gspace=0
            clipref
            gaxis=axis
            raxis=axis
            coutline=gray;
    label sales='Sales';
run;
quit;
```

Output 23.21 *Vertical Bar Chart with Grouping (GR23N20)*

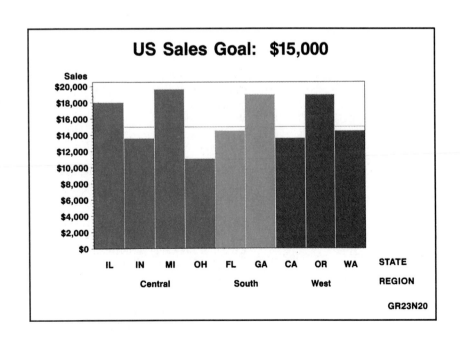

This example illustrates the following features:

☐ The GROUP= option creates a separate group of bars for each different value of the REGION variable.

☐ The NOZERO option suppresses the midpoints with no corresponding values within a group. The NOZERO option prevents a bar from being drawn for every combination of STATE and REGION. If the NOZERO option were not present, there would be midpoint entries for all nine states in each group, whether the state was in the group or not.

☐ The REF= option draws a reference line on the response axis at 15,000.

☐ The PATTERNID= option specifies that the pattern change for each group value. The specified patterns make each group of bars a different color.

☐ The WIDTH= option is used to increase the width of the bars. The SPACE= and GSPACE= options are used to eliminate the space between the bars.

Vertical Bar Chart Subgrouped by Chart Variable

This example charts the same information as the first VBAR statement example but charts the quarterly sales for each branch. The legend identifies the chart midpoints.

The following program statements produce Output 23.22:

```
   /* set the graphics environment */
goptions reset=global gunit=pct border
         ftext=swissb htitle=6 htext=3;

   /* create data set TOTALS */
data totals;
   length dept $ 7 site $ 8;
   input dept site quarter sales;
   cards;
Parts   Sydney  1 7843.97
Parts   Atlanta 1 9225.26
more data lines
Tools   Atlanta 4 3624.19
Tools   Paris   4 6414.25
;
run;

   /* define title and footnote for chart */
title 'Quarterly Site Sales';
footnote j=r 'GR23N21  ';

   /* define axis characteristics */
axis1 value=none label=none;
axis2 width=3;

   /* define pattern characteristics */
pattern1 value=solid color=blue;
pattern2 value=solid color=green;
pattern3 value=solid color=red;
pattern4 value=solid color=lib;
```

```
                /* define legend characteristics */
            legend frame label=none;

                /* generate vertical bar chart */
            proc gchart data=totals;
               format quarter roman.;
               format sales dollar8.;
               vbar site
                     / frame
                       sumvar=sales
                       subgroup=site
                       group=quarter
                       legend=legend
                       maxis=axis1
                       raxis=axis2;
            run;
            quit;
```

Output 23.22 Vertical Bar
Chart Subgrouped by Chart
Variable (GR23N21)

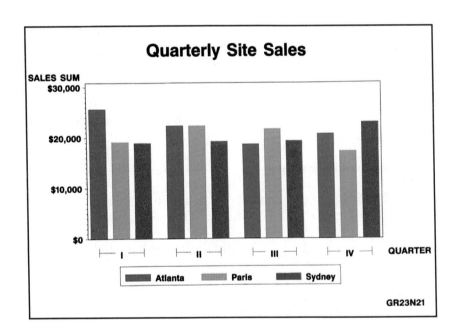

This example illustrates the following features:

□ The SUBGROUP= option divides each bar into sales by SITE. Because
the subgroup variable is the same as the chart variable, each bar
contains information about one branch only and each branch uses a
different pattern.

□ The GROUP= option creates a separate group of bars for each different
value of the QUARTER variable.

□ The midpoint axis label and axis values are suppressed because
identifying information for the midpoints is in the legend.

See Also

Chapter 9, "The AXIS Statement"
for information on

□ specifying an ORDER= option *value-list*

□ specifying axis characteristics that you can define in AXIS statements or in the AXIS window

Chapter 10, "The BY Statement"
for information on BY-group processing

Chapter 13, "The LEGEND Statement"
for information on specifying legend characteristics

Chapter 15, "The PATTERN Statement"
for information on

□ bar/block pattern specifications

□ pie/star pattern specifications

□ default pattern rotation

Chapter 18, "The Annotate Data Set"
for information on using the Annotate facility with the GCHART procedure

SAS Procedures Guide, Version 6, Third Edition
for information on the CHART procedure, which uses simple character graphics to produce charts

References

Nelder, J. A. (1976), "A Simple Algorithm for Scaling Graphs," *Applied Statistics, Volume 25, Number 1,* London: The Royal Statistical Society.

Terrell, G. R. and Scott, D. W. (1985), "Oversmoothed Nonparametric Density Estimates," *Journal of the American Statistical Association,* 80.

CHAPTER *24* The GCONTOUR Procedure

Overview

The GCONTOUR procedure produces plots that represent three-dimensional relationships in two dimensions. Lines or areas in a contour plot represent levels of magnitude z corresponding to a position (x, y) on a plane.

Using the GCONTOUR procedure, you can

□ use lines or patterns to identify contour levels

□ examine trends in your data when they contain too many peaks and valleys to be accurately observed using the G3D procedure

□ examine data in which the levels, not the shape, of the data are important.

Note: The GCONTOUR procedure produces rectangular contour plots, not irregular contour maps.

Output 24.1 illustrates a sample contour plot that maps the bottom of a pond.

Output 24.1 *Sample Contour Plot (GR24N01)*

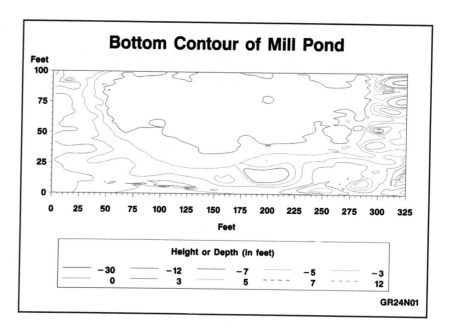

GCONTOUR Procedure Syntax

The GCONTOUR procedure uses the following statements:

□ The GCONTOUR statement is required.

PROC GCONTOUR <DATA=*SAS-data-set*>
   <ANNOTATE=*Annotate-data-set*>
   <GOUT=*output-catalog*>;

□ At least one PLOT statement is required. You can use multiple PLOT statements with a single PROC GCONTOUR statement.

PLOT *y*x=z*
   </ <ANNOTATE=*Annotate-data-set*>
   <*appearance-options*>
   <*axes-options*>
   <*contour-options*>
   <*description-options*>>;

□ The following statements are optional and local:

BY <*options*> *variable* ;

NOTE <*options*> <'*text*'>;

□ The following statements are optional and global:

AXIS<1 . . . 99> <*options*>;

FOOTNOTE<1 . . . 10> <*options*> <'*text*'>;

LEGEND<1 . . . 99> <*options*>;

PATTERN<1 . . . 99> <*options*>;

TITLE<1 . . . 10> <*options*> <'*text*'>;

For complete statement syntax, see the section on the appropriate statement.

Statement Descriptions

The purpose of each statement is described here.

AXIS	defines axis characteristics that modify the appearance, position, and content of an axis. See Chapter 9, "The AXIS Statement." Once defined, AXIS definitions are assigned with the HAXIS= and VAXIS= options in a PLOT statement.
BY	specifies the variable or variables by which the data are grouped for processing. A separate graph is produced for each value of the BY variable. See Chapter 10, "The BY Statement."
FOOTNOTE	defines the text and appearance of footnotes. See Chapter 11, "The FOOTNOTE Statement."
LEGEND	defines legend characteristics that modify the text, appearance, and position of a legend. See Chapter 13, "The LEGEND Statement." Once defined, LEGEND definitions are assigned with the LEGEND= option in the PLOT statement.
NOTE	defines the text and appearance of notes that appear in the procedure output area. See Chapter 14, "The NOTE Statement."
PATTERN	defines the colors and fill patterns that can optionally be used to fill contour areas. See Chapter 15, "The PATTERN Statement."
PLOT	creates contour plots using the data set variables as the source of contour coordinates.
PROC GCONTOUR	starts the procedure and specifies the name of the data set to be used, as well as any additional input or output options.
TITLE	defines the text and appearance of titles. See Chapter 17, "The TITLE Statement."

GCONTOUR Procedure Description

The following sections address issues that pertain to the GCONTOUR procedure as a whole: terminology, special data considerations, and the use of global statements.

Terminology

The following terms are used in the discussion of the GCONTOUR procedure and are defined in the Glossary. Some of these terms and some additional terms are illustrated in Figure 24.1.

axis   major tick mark
contour plot   minor tick mark
label   value

Figure 24.1 *GCONTOUR Procedure Terms*

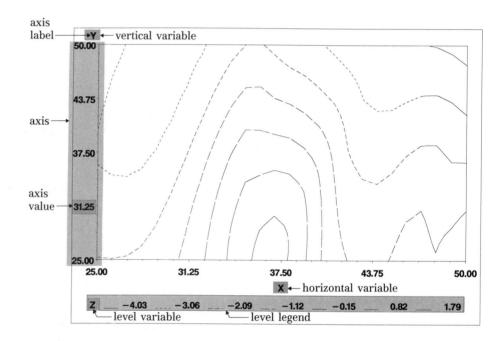

Data Considerations

The GCONTOUR procedure requires data sets that include three numeric variables: x and y for the horizontal and vertical axes, respectively, and z for the contour level. The observations in the input data set should form a rectangular grid of x and y values and exactly one z value for each of these combinations. For example, data containing 5 distinct values of x and 10 distinct values for y should be part of a data set that contains 50 observations with values for x, y, and z. If a single x, y grid location has more than one associated z value, only the last such observation is used.

Data sets often contain so few combinations of x, y, and z values that the GCONTOUR procedure cannot produce a contour plot. The data set must contain nonmissing z values for at least 50 percent of the grid cells in order for the GCONTOUR procedure to produce a satisfactory plot. When the GCONTOUR procedure cannot produce a satisfactory contour plot because of missing z values, SAS/GRAPH software issues an error message and no graph is produced. To correct this problem, you can use the G3GRID procedure to process data sets to be used by the GCONTOUR procedure. The G3GRID procedure interpolates the necessary values to produce a data set with nonmissing z values for every combination of the x and y variables. The G3GRID procedure can also smooth data for use with the GCONTOUR procedure. You use the output data set from the G3GRID procedure as the input data set for the GCONTOUR procedure.

Global Statements

All currently defined titles and footnotes are displayed in every graph generated by the GCONTOUR procedure. Currently defined PATTERN definitions are automatically assigned as needed to contour plots that use patterns. Currently defined AXIS and LEGEND definitions can be assigned by using PLOT statement options.

There are special considerations for using the AXIS statement's ORDER= option with the GCONTOUR procedure. They are described in "Selecting Axis Order" later in this chapter.

PROC GCONTOUR Statement

The PROC GCONTOUR statement initiates the procedure and, if necessary, specifies the input data set. In addition, it can optionally specify a data set for annotation and a destination catalog for graphics output.

Syntax

The general form of the PROC GCONTOUR statement is

PROC GCONTOUR <DATA=*SAS-data-set*>
        <ANNOTATE=*Annotate-data-set*>
        <GOUT=*output-catalog*>;

Requirements

The GCONTOUR procedure must have an input data set. By default, the procedure uses the most recently created data set as its input data set. You can use the DATA= option to select a specific data set. If no data set has been created in the current SAS session and the DATA= option is not supplied, an error occurs and the procedure stops.

Options

You can use the following options with the PROC GCONTOUR statement. Options that you use with the PROC GCONTOUR statement affect all of the plots produced by the procedure.

ANNOTATE=*Annotate-data-set*
ANNO=*Annotate-data-set*
    specifies a data set to provide annotation of all plots produced by the GCONTOUR procedure. (To annotate individual graphs, use the ANNOTATE= option in the PLOT statement.) *Annotate-data-set* must contain the appropriate Annotate variables. See Chapter 18, "The Annotate Data Set," for details.

DATA=*SAS-data-set*
>   specifies the data set that contains the numeric data values to be
>   represented on a contour plot. By default, the procedure uses the most
>   recently created data set.

GOUT=*output-catalog*
>   specifies the SAS catalog in which to save the graphics output
>   produced by the GCONTOUR procedure for later replay. You can use
>   the GREPLAY procedure to view the graphs stored in the catalog. By
>   default, catalog entries are written to the default catalog
>   WORK.GSEG, which is erased at the end of your session.

PLOT Statement

The PLOT statement produces contour plots representing the levels of
magnitude of a variable *z* for a position on a plane given by the values of
two variables *x* and *y*. The GCONTOUR procedure can include multiple
PLOT statements. Contour lines of different colors and line types show
different levels of magnitude of *z* for locations of *x* and *y*. Contour levels
can also be displayed with fill patterns. With PLOT statement options, you
can manipulate plot axes and modify the appearance of plots.

By default, the GCONTOUR procedure plots the values using seven
contour levels of the *z* variable. These levels occur at every 15th
percentile between the 5th and the 95th percentile. You can specify other
values for contour levels with the PLOT statement's LEVELS= option. See
"Selecting Contour Levels" later in this chapter for more information.

Syntax

The general form of the PLOT statement is

PLOT *y*x=z*
>   </ <ANNOTATE=*Annotate-data-set*>
>   <*appearance-options*>
>   <*axes-options*>
>   <*contour-options*>
>   <*description-options*>>;

☐ *PLOT* variables are defined as follows:

> *y*   is a variable whose values are displayed on the vertical (*y*) axis

> *x*   is a variable whose values are displayed on the horizontal (*x*)
>   axis

> *z*   is a variable whose values are displayed as contour lines

☐ *appearance-options* can be one or more of the following:

> COUTLINE=*outline-color*

> CTEXT=*text-color*

□ *axes-options* can affect one or more of the following:

□ horizontal (*x*) axis

CHREF=*reference-line-color*

HAXIS=AXIS<1 . . . 99>

HMINOR=*n*

where *n* is the number of minor tick marks

HREF=*value-list*

where *value-list* specifies points on the horizontal axis

LHREF=*line-type*

where *line-type* can be 0 . . . 46

XTICKNUM=*n*

where *n* is the number of major tick marks

□ vertical (*y*) axis

CVREF=*reference-line-color*

LVREF=*line-type*

where *line-type* can be 0 . . . 46

VAXIS=AXIS<1 . . . 99>

VMINOR=*n*

where *n* is the number of minor tick marks

VREF=*value-list*

where *value-list* specifies points on the vertical axis

YTICKNUM=*n*

where *n* is the number of major tick marks

□ axis appearance

CAXIS=*axis-color*

NOAXIS

NOFRAME

□ *contour-options* can be one or more of the following:

CLEVELS=*color-1* < . . . *color-n*>

where *color-1* < . . . *color-n*> specifies a color for each contour level

JOIN

LEGEND=LEGEND<1 . . . 99>

LEVELS=*value-list*

where *value-list* specifies values of *z* represented by contour lines or patterns

LLEVELS=*line-types*

> where *line-types* specifies the line type (0 . . . 46) for each contour level

NOLEGEND

PATTERN

□ *description-options* can be one or both of the following:

DESCRIPTION=*'string'*

NAME=*'string'*

PLOT statement options are fully described in "Options" later in this section.

Requirements

A PLOT statement must specify exactly one plot request. The plot request specifies a combination of three variables from the input data set. Variables specified in PLOT statements must be numeric variables.

Options

You can use the following options in the PLOT statement. Options used in a PLOT statement affect all graphs produced by that statement. If you use any of the following options, separate them from the plot request with a slash (/). If you do not use any options, omit the slash.

ANNOTATE=*Annotate-data-set*
ANNO=*Annotate-data-set*

> specifies a data set to be used for annotation of graphs produced by the statement. *Annotate-data-set* must contain the appropriate Annotate variables. See Chapter 18 for details.
>
> If the ANNOTATE= option is also used with the PROC GCONTOUR statement, both sets of annotation are applied. If you specify BY-group processing, the Annotate data set must contain the BY variable. For details, see "Using BY-Group Processing with the Annotate Facility" in Chapter 18 and "Details of BY-Group Processing" in Chapter 10.

CAXIS=*axis-color*

> specifies a color for axis lines and all major and minor tick marks. By default, axes are displayed in the second color in the colors list.
>
> If you use the CAXIS= option, it may be overridden by the COLOR= parameter of the MAJOR= or MINOR= option in an AXIS definition assigned to an axis for major and minor tick marks.

CHREF=*reference-line-color*
CH=*reference-line-color*

> specifies the color for reference lines requested by the HREF= option. By default, these lines are displayed in the axis color.

CLEVELS=*color1* < . . . *color-n*>

> specifies a list of colors for plot contour levels. The number of colors specified should correspond to the number of contour levels since one color represents each level of contour. If the number of colors specified does not correspond to the number of levels in the plot, the procedure provides default colors from the current colors list.

By default, the procedure rotates through the current colors list for each line type.

COUTLINE=*outline-color*
> specifies a color for outlining filled areas. This option is ignored unless the PATTERN option is also used. By default, the outline color is the same as the color of the filled area.
>
> **Note:** The outline color is the only distinction between empty patterns. Use of this option when VALUE=EMPTY is specified in PATTERN definitions makes the patterns look the same.

CTEXT=*text-color*
> specifies a color for all text on the axes and legend, including axis labels, tick mark values, legend labels, and legend value descriptions.
>
> If you do not use the CTEXT= option, a color specification is searched for in the following order:
>
> 1. the COLOR= option in the AXIS statement
>
> 2. the CTEXT= option in a GOPTIONS statement
>
> 3. the default, the first color in the colors list.
>
> If you use the CTEXT= option, it overrides the color specification for the axis label and tick mark values in the COLOR= option in an AXIS definition assigned to an axis.
>
> If you use the CTEXT= option, the color specification may be overridden in one or more of the following situations:
>
> □ If you also use the COLOR= parameter of a LABEL= or VALUE= option in a LEGEND definition assigned to the legend, that parameter determines the color of the legend label or the color of the legend value descriptions, respectively.
>
> □ If you also use the COLOR= parameter of a LABEL= or VALUE= option in an AXIS definition assigned to an axis, that parameter determines the color of the axis label or the color of the tick mark values, respectively.
>
> If you use a BY statement in the procedure, the color of the BY variable labels is controlled by the CBY= option in the GOPTIONS statement.

CVREF=*reference-line-color*
CV=*reference-line-color*
> specifies the color for reference lines requested by the VREF= option. By default, these lines are displayed in the axis color.

DESCRIPTION='*string*'
DES='*string*'
> specifies a descriptive string, up to 40 characters long, that appears in the Description field of the catalog entry for the graph. The description does not appear on the graph. By default, the procedure assigns a description of the form PLOT OF $y*x=z$, where $y*x=z$ is the request specified in the PLOT statement.

HAXIS=AXIS<1 ... 99>
> assigns axis characteristics from the corresponding AXIS definition to the horizontal (x) axis. See Chapter 9 for more information.

HMINOR=*n*
HM=*n*
> specifies the number of minor tick marks located between each major tick mark on the horizontal (*x*) axis. No values are displayed for minor tick marks. The HMINOR= option overrides the MINOR= option in an AXIS definition assigned to the horizontal (*x*) axis.

HREF=*value-list*
> specifies one or more reference lines to mark values on the horizontal (*x*) axis.
>
> *Value-list* can be specified in the following ways:
>
> *n n . . . n*
>
> *n,n, . . . ,n*
>
> *n* TO *n* <BY *increment*> <*n . . . n*> <*n, . . . ,n*>
>
> *n n . . . n* TO *n* <BY *increment*> <*n . . . n*>
>
> *n,n, . . . ,n* TO *n* <BY *increment*> <*n, . . . ,n*>
>
> '*SAS-value*'i TO '*SAS-value*'i <BY *interval*>
>
> '*SAS-value*'i '*SAS-value*'i . . . '*SAS-value*'i
>
> For additional information on specifying *value-list*, see the ORDER= option in Chapter 9.

JOIN
> combines adjacent grid cells with the same pattern to form a single area with the same pattern. This option is ignored unless the PATTERN option is also used.
>
> See "Contour Plot Using the JOIN Option" in "PLOT Statement Examples" later in this chapter for an illustration of the JOIN option.

LEGEND=LEGEND<1 . . . 99>
> assigns legend characteristics to the legend. The option value indicates which LEGEND definition to use. The LEGEND= option is ignored if the specified LEGEND definition is not currently in effect. See Chapter 13 for more information.

LEVELS=*value-list*
> specifies values of *z* for plot contour levels. You can specify up to 100 values. By default, the GCONTOUR procedure plots seven contour levels for *z*. These levels occur at every 15th percentile between the 5th and the 95th percentile.
>
> *Value-list* can be specified in the following ways:
>
> *n n . . . n*
>
> *n,n, . . . ,n*
>
> *n* TO *n* <BY *increment*> <*n . . . n*> <*n, . . . ,n*>
>
> *n n . . . n* TO *n* <BY *increment*> <*n . . . n*>
>
> *n,n, . . . ,n* TO *n* <BY *increment*> <*n, . . . ,n*>
>
> '*SAS-value*'i TO '*SAS-value*'i <BY *interval*>
>
> '*SAS-value*'i '*SAS-value*'i . . . '*SAS-value*'i
>
> For additional information on specifying *value-list*, see the ORDER= option in Chapter 9.
>
> By default, the GCONTOUR procedure selects colors and line types for the contour levels by rotating through the colors list for each line

type (1 through 46) until all the levels have been represented. The level lines on the plot represent the intersection of a plane, parallel to the x-y plane, and the surface formed by the data at the z value. See "Selecting Contour Levels" later in this chapter for more information.

You can specify the colors and types of lines for contour levels using the CLEVELS= and LLEVELS= options. Alternatively, you can use the PATTERN option to fill each level with colors and patterns specified in PATTERN statements.

LHREF=*line-type*
LH=*line-type*
> specifies the line type for drawing reference lines requested by the HREF= option. *Line-type* is a number from 1 to 46. By default, LHREF=1, a solid line. See Table 16.5 in Chapter 16, "The Symbol Statement," for available line types.

LLEVELS=*line-types*
> lists numbers for line types for plot contour lines. The number of line types listed should correspond to the number of contour levels, since one line type represents each level of contour. If the number of line types specified does not correspond to the number of levels in the plot, the procedure provides default line types. For a contour plot that uses the default number of levels, you must specify seven line types.

> By default, contour levels rotate through line types 1 through 46, displaying each line type in all of the colors in the colors list before moving to the next line type. See Table 16.5 in Chapter 16 for available line types.

> For colors and lines specified with both the CLEVELS= and LLEVELS= options, the first contour level is displayed in the first color in the CLEVELS= color list and in the first line type specified with the LLEVELS= option. The second level is displayed in the second color and the second line type, and so on.

LVREF=*line-type*
LV=*line-type*
> specifies the line type for drawing reference lines requested by the VREF= option. *Line-type* is a number from 1 to 46. By default, LVREF=1, a solid line. See Table 16.5 in Chapter 16 for available line types.

NAME='*string*'
> specifies a string, up to eight characters long, that appears in the Name field of the catalog entry for the graph. *String* must be a valid SAS name. By default, the name assigned is GCONTOUR. If either the name specified or the default name duplicates an existing name in the catalog, SAS/GRAPH software adds a number to the duplicate name to create a unique name, for example, GCONTOU2.

NOAXIS
NOAXES
> specifies that a plot have no axes, axis values, or axis labels. The frame is displayed around the plot unless you use the NOFRAME option.

NOFRAME
> suppresses the frame that is drawn by default around the plot area.

NOLEGEND

suppresses the plot legend that describes contour levels and their line types or fill patterns and colors.

PATTERN

specifies that plot contour levels be represented by rectangles filled with patterns. The pattern for each rectangle is determined by calculating the mean of the values of the z variable for the four corners of the rectangle and assigning the pattern for the level closest to the mean. See "Selecting Contour Levels" later in this chapter for more information. See "Contour Plot Using Patterns" in "PLOT Statement Examples" later in this chapter for an example of how to use the PATTERN option.

You can define patterns for the levels by creating PATTERN definitions for map/plot patterns. If no PATTERN definitions are created, the procedure uses the default pattern and color rotation. Without the PATTERN option (by default), each contour level is represented by a different line type.

VAXIS=AXIS<1 ... 99>

assigns axis characteristics from the corresponding AXIS definition to the vertical (y) axis. See Chapter 9 for more information.

VMINOR=n
VM=n

specifies the number of minor tick marks located between each major tick mark on the vertical (y) axis. No values are displayed for minor tick marks. The VMINOR= option overrides the MINOR= option in an AXIS definition assigned to the vertical (y) axis.

VREF=*value-list*

specifies one or more reference lines to mark values on the vertical (y) axis.

Value-list can be specified in the following ways:

n n . . . n

n,n, . . . ,n

n TO *n* <BY *increment*> <*n . . . n*> <*n, . . . ,n*>

n n . . . n TO *n* <BY *increment*> <*n . . . n*>

n,n, . . . ,n TO *n* <BY *increment*> <*n, . . . ,n*>

'*SAS-value*'*i* TO '*SAS-value*'*i* <BY *interval*>

'*SAS-value*'*i* '*SAS-value*'*i* . . . '*SAS-value*'*i*

For additional information on specifying *value-list*, see the ORDER= option in Chapter 9.

XTICKNUM=n
YTICKNUM=n

specify the number of major tick marks located on a plot's x or y axis, respectively. The value of n must be 2 or greater. By default, XTICKNUM=5 and YTICKNUM=5.

The MAJOR= or ORDER= option in an AXIS definition assigned to the x axis overrides the XTICKNUM= option. The MAJOR= or ORDER= option in an AXIS definition assigned to the y axis overrides the YTICKNUM= option.

Using the PLOT Statement

You can include any number of PLOT statements within the procedure. For example, the following statements produce two contour plots:

```
plot y*x=z;
plot b*a=c;
```

Note: You cannot produce overlaid contour plots.
You can use PLOT statement options to specify

□ the number of contour levels

□ an Annotate data set for graphic enhancement

□ appearance characteristics

□ axes characteristics

□ descriptive characteristics

□ legend characteristics.

By default, a frame surrounds the plot. You can use the NOFRAME option to display a plot with no frame. The values on the axes are automatically scaled. The x and y axes are labeled, and the contour levels are displayed in the plot's legend.

The default number of contour levels (7) for the plot is automatically chosen by the procedure. You can use the LEVELS= option to specify values for the levels of z and therefore change the number of contour levels. You can use the HREF= and VREF= options to display plots with reference lines perpendicular to plot axes.

Selecting Contour Levels

You can use the LEVELS= option to select the contour levels for your plot. The values specified with LEVELS= are used differently depending on the other options specified in the PLOT statement.

When the PATTERN option is not specified, the levels represent the intersection of a plane (parallel to the x-y plane at the z value) and the surface formed by the data. That is, if you use the data to create a surface plot with the G3D procedure, the contour lines in a GCONTOUR procedure plot represent the intersection of the plane and the surface.

For example, suppose you use the G3D procedure and your data form a surface like the one shown in Figure 24.2a. The same data used with the following PLOT statement in the GCONTOUR procedure produces a contour plot like the one in Figure 24.2b:

```
plot y*x=z / levels=-7.5 to 7.5 by 2.5;
```

Note that the contour lines in Figure 24.2b represent the intersection of the surface in Figure 24.2a with planes parallel to the plane formed by the variables X and Y and located at Z values of -7.5, -5.0, -2.5, and so on.

Figure 24.2 *Line Contour Levels*

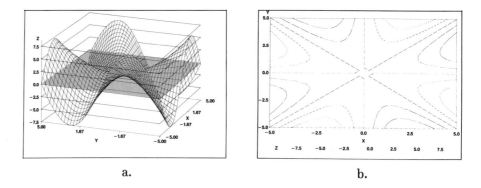

a.   b.

When the PATTERN option is used, contour levels are represented by rectangles filled with patterns. The rectangles are formed by points in the *x-y* grid. The contour pattern of a rectangle, or grid cell, is determined by the mean or average value of the *z* variable for the four corners of the rectangle. The grid cell is assigned the pattern for the level closest to the calculated mean. For example, if you have specified contour levels of 0, 5, and 10, and the plot contains a grid cell with a mean of 100, it is assigned the pattern for the nearest level: 10. A grid cell with a mean of 7.6 will also be assigned the pattern for the 10 level.

Figure 24.3 shows a contour plot with the PATTERN option that uses the same data and contour levels as Figure 24.2b. The pattern for the rectangle is assigned depending on the mean of the grid values at the four corners. As a result, a contour plot using the same contour levels can present your data differently. Note that the contour pattern boundaries do not correspond to the contour lines shown in Figure 24.2b.

Figure 24.3 *Pattern Contour Levels*

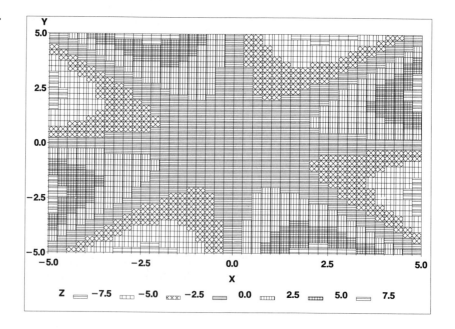

Selecting Axis Order

AXIS definitions, which modify the content and appearance of plot axes, are assigned with the PLOT statement HAXIS= and VAXIS= options. There are special considerations for using the ORDER= option in an AXIS definition used with the GCONTOUR procedure.

A list of variable values specified with the AXIS statement's ORDER= option must contain numbers listed in ascending or descending order. The numbers in an ORDER= list are treated as a continuous data range for an axis. Thus, it is not necessary for the maximum and minimum values of the list to match exactly with the maximum and minimum values of the corresponding x or y variable in order for a contour line or pattern to span the entire specified range. For example, suppose you assign the following AXIS definition to the horizontal (x) axis:

```
axis1 order=-2.5 to 2.5 by .5
```

Suppose also that the horizontal axis variable has the following values: $-5, -4, -3, -2, -1, 0, 1, 2, 3, 4, 5$. Depending on the data, contours could extend through the full range of the ORDER= list rather than from -2 to 2, the specific values of the variable assigned to the horizontal (x) axis.

Internal plotting grid modifications occur according to the following rules, which apply when ORDER= lists cause data clipping:

□ If an ORDER= list causes data clipping on a single axis, linear interpolation generates the z values of the starting and/or ending column of the plotting grid. For example, in the previous example, the value of z is interpolated for -2.5 and 2.5 on the horizontal (x) axis.

□ If ORDER= lists cause data clipping on both axes, the response variable values of the new corners are derived by fitting the new x, y location on a plane formed by three of the original four points of the corresponding grid square.

In addition, if you assign the following AXIS definition to a plot of the same data, the contour levels on the plot will not extend beyond the range of the data:

```
axis1 order=-10 to 10 by 1;
```

Figure 24.4 shows the effects of the ORDER= option when

□ the range of ORDER= values matches the range of values for the variables assigned to the horizontal (x) and vertical (y) axes (Figure 24.4a)

□ the range of ORDER= values is smaller than the range of data values (Figure 24.4b)

□ the range of ORDER= values is larger than the range of data values (Figure 24.4c).

Figure 24.4 *Effects of the AXIS Statement's ORDER= Option*

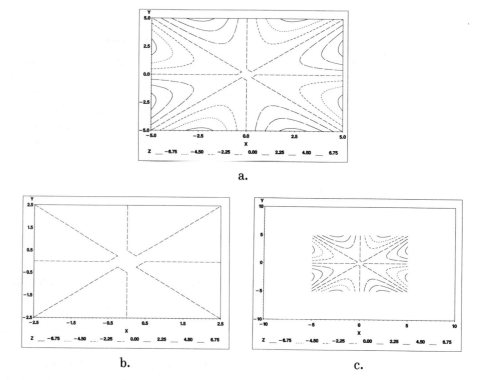

a.

b.

c.

Controlling Plot Appearance

Appearance characteristics include contour plot colors, line types, and whether contour levels are represented by lines or filled areas. Color options specify colors for contour lines, outlining filled contour areas, and plot text. Line-type options specify the line types for representing contour levels and reference lines.

Using Global Statements

You can use axis characteristics defined in AXIS definitions to modify the text and appearance of axes on the plots. AXIS definitions are assigned to the horizontal (*x*) and vertical (*y*) axes using the HAXIS= and VAXIS= options, respectively.

You can use legend characteristics from LEGEND definitions to adjust the location, text, and appearance of the legend on the contour plots. LEGEND definitions are assigned to the legend with the LEGEND= option.

PATTERN definitions describe fill patterns and pattern colors for contour areas. PATTERN definitions are used when you specify the PATTERN option in the PLOT statement.

PLOT Statement Examples

The following examples illustrate major features of the GCONTOUR procedure.

Contour Plot Using Line Types

This example demonstrates the use of line types to distinguish contour levels. The following program statements produce Output 24.2:

```
/* set the graphics environment */
goptions reset=global gunit=pct border
        ftext=swissb htitle=6 htext=3;

/* create data set SWIRL */
data swirl;
   do x=-5 to 5 by 0.25;
      do y=-5 to 5 by 0.25;
         if x+y=0 then z=0;
         else z=(x*y)*((x*x-y*y)/(x*x+y*y));
         output;
      end;
   end;
run;

/* define title and footnote for plot */
title 'Contour Plot of SWIRL Data Set';
footnote j=r 'GR24N02  ';

/* define axis and legend characteristics */
axis width=3;
legend frame;

/* show the contour plot */
proc gcontour data=swirl;
   plot y*x=z
        / levels = -3 -2 -1 1 2 3
          llevels = 41 42 43 5 6 7
          haxis=axis1
          vaxis=axis1
          href=-5 to 5 by 2.5
          vref=-5 to 5 by 2.5
          legend=legend1;
run;
```

Output 24.2 *Contour Plot Using Line Types (GR24N02)*

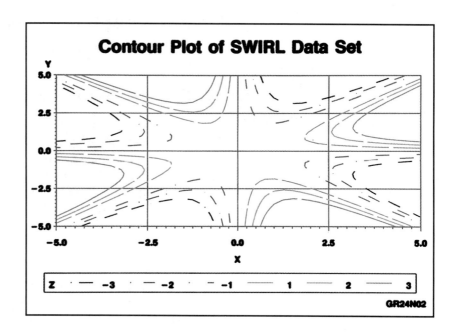

This example illustrates the following features:

□ The PLOT statement specifies the plot request Y*X=Z.

□ The LEVELS= option specifies the values of the contour levels.

□ The LLEVELS= option sets the line types for the contour lines. Dashed lines identify negative contour levels, and broken lines identify positive contour levels.

□ The HAXIS= and VAXIS= options assign AXIS definitions to the horizontal and vertical axes.

□ The HREF= and VREF= options specify reference lines to mark values on the horizontal and vertical axes.

□ The LEGEND= option assigns a LEGEND definition to the legend.

Contour Plot Using Patterns

This example uses patterns to distinguish between contour levels. The following program statements produce Output 24.3:

```
    /* set the graphics environment */
goptions reset=global gunit=pct border
        ftext=swissb htitle=6 htext=3;

    /* create data set SWIRL */
data swirl;
    do x=-5 to 5 by 0.25;
        do y=-5 to 5 by 0.25;
            if x+y=0 then z=0;
            else z=(x*y)*((x*x-y*y)/(x*x+y*y));
            output;
        end;
    end;
run;
```

```
      /* define title and footnote for plot */
   title 'Contour Plot of SWIRL Data Set';
   footnote j=r 'GR24N03 ';

      /* define axis and legend characteristics */
   axis width=3;
   legend frame;

      /* define pattern characteristics */
   pattern value=msolid;

      /* show the contour plot */
   proc gcontour data=swirl;
      plot y*x=z
            / pattern
              ctext=green
              coutline=gray
              haxis=axis1
              vaxis=axis1
              legend=legend1;
   run;
```

Output 24.3 *Contour Plot Using Patterns (GR24N03)*

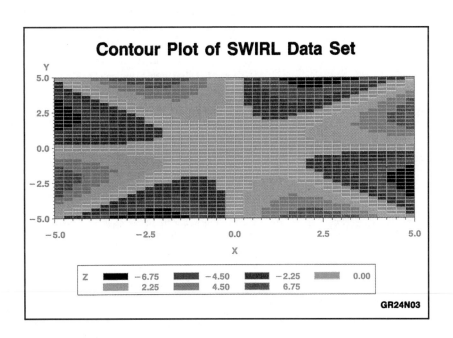

This example illustrates the following features:

□ The PATTERN option fills the contour levels with the patterns defined in the PATTERN statement.

□ The COUTLINE= option names the color used to outline the grid cells.

□ Because the LEVELS= option was not used, the plot uses seven default contour levels.

Contour Plot Using the JOIN Option

This example uses the JOIN option to combine the patterns in grid cells for the same contour level. The following program statements produce Output 24.4:

```
   /* set the graphics environment */
goptions reset=global gunit=pct border
         ftext=swissb htitle=6 htext=3;

   /* create data set SWIRL */
data swirl;
   do x=-5 to 5 by 0.25;
      do y=-5 to 5 by 0.25;
         if x+y=0 then z=0;
         else z=(x*y)*((x*x-y*y)/(x*x+y*y));
         output;
      end;
   end;
run;

   /* define title and footnote for plot */
title 'Contour Plot of SWIRL Data Set';
footnote j=r 'GR24N04   ';

   /* define axis characteristics */
axis1 label=none value=('-5' ' ' '0' ' ' '5') color=red width=3;
axis2 label=none value=('-5' ' ' '0' ' ' '5') color=red width=3;

   /* define legend and pattern characteristics */
legend frame;
pattern value=msolid;

   /* show the contour plot */
proc gcontour data=swirl;
   plot y*x=z
        / pattern
          join
          haxis=axis1
          vaxis=axis2
          legend=legend1;
run;
```

Output 24.4 *Contour Plot Using the PATTERN and JOIN Options (GR24N04)*

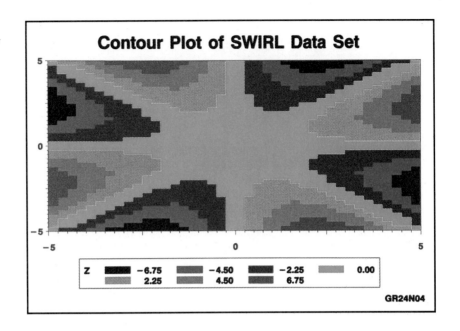

This example illustrates the following feature:

□ The JOIN option combines grid cells for the same contour levels.

See Also

Chapter 9, "The AXIS Statement"
> for information on defining axis characteristics

Chapter 13, "The LEGEND Statement"
> for information on defining legend characteristics

Chapter 15, "The PATTERN Statement"
> for information on defining patterns and pattern rotation

Chapter 18, "The Annotate Data Set"
> for information on using the Annotate facility with the GCONTOUR procedure

Chapter 39, "The G3D Procedure"
> for information on three-dimensional surface, needle, and scatter plots

Chapter 40, "The G3GRID Procedure"
> for information on interpolating or smoothing input data sets for the GCONTOUR procedure

Reference

Snyder, W.V. (1978), "Contour Plotting [J6]," *ACM Transactions on Mathematical Software*, 4, 290–294.

CHAPTER 25 The GDEVICE Procedure

Overview

The GDEVICE procedure is a tool for examining and changing device parameters for graphics devices. With the GDEVICE procedure, you can use full-screen windows or line-mode statements to

□ list the device entries available with your version of SAS/GRAPH software

□ view the parameters for Institute-supplied device entries

□ create and modify new device entries

□ copy device entries

□ rename device entries.

When a SAS/GRAPH procedure produces output, it first checks to see what device driver you have selected. It then looks in the device entry for that driver to find the current parameter settings for the specified output device. The device driver uses a number of parameters to determine how it draws a graph. For example, the parameters indicate how large to draw the graph, what default colors to use, and whether to send the graphics output directly to a device or store it in a file.

You can control the way the device driver produces output for your device by altering parameter values in the device entry. The GDEVICE procedure enables you to review, modify, and create device entries. The modifications made to a device entry are in effect for all SAS sessions.

The new values that you specify for device parameters must be within the device's capabilities. For example, all devices are limited in the size of the output they can display. Some output devices cannot display color. If you try to increase the size of the display past the device's capability or if you specify colors for a device that cannot display them, you will get unpredictable results.

Output 25.1 shows a listing of a device entry that was produced using line-mode statements. The device entry displayed is stored in the Institute-supplied catalog, SASHELP.DEVICES.

Output 25.1 *Listing of the TEK4105 Device Parameters Generated in Line Mode Using the LIST statement*

```
                            GDEVICE procedure
                  Listing from SASHELP.DEVICES - Entry TEK4105

   Orig Driver: TEK4105           Module:   SASGDTK1  Model:      102
   Description: Tektronix 4105 terminal                Type: CRT
   *** Institute-supplied ***
   Lrows:  40  Xmax:   9.500 in    Hsize:   0.000 in  Xpixels:    480
   Lcols:  80  Ymax:   6.875 in    Vsize:   0.000 in  Ypixels:    360
   Prows:   0                      Horigin: 0.000 in
   Pcols:   0                      Vorigin: 0.000 in
   Aspect:    0.000                Rotate:
   Driver query:                   Queued messages: N
   Gprotocol:                      Paperfeed:   0.000 in
   Gaccess:  SASGASTD
   Gsfname:                        Gsfmode:  PORT    Gsflen:      0
   Trantab:                        Devmap:
   Devtype:      GTERM
```

```
 ⌒‿⌒‿‿‿‿‿‿‿‿‿‿‿‿‿‿‿‿‿‿‿‿⌒‿‿‿‿‿‿‿‿
  OPTIONS

  Erase:               Autofeed:              Chartype:   0
  Swap:                Cell:                  Maxcolors:  8
  Autocopy:            Characters:            Repaint:    0
  Handshake:           Circlearc:    N        Gcopies:    0
                       Dash:                  Gsize:      0
  Prompt - startup: X  Fill:                  Speed:      0
         end graph: X  Piefill:      N        Fillinc:    1
         mount pen:    Polyfill:              Maxpoly:    0
         chg paper:    Symbol:                Lfactor:    0
  Promptchars:  '000A010D05000000'X
  UCC:       'D5'X

  Cback:     BLACK              Colortbl:
  Color list:

     WHITE     RED      GREEN    BLUE     CYAN
     MAGENTA   YELLOW
```

You can temporarily override the settings of device parameters by using graphics options in a GOPTIONS statement. Use a GOPTIONS statement to override parameters for one SAS session or in one SAS program. See Chapter 12, "The GOPTIONS Statement," for more information on using a GOPTIONS statement.

GDEVICE Procedure Syntax

The GDEVICE procedure uses the following statements:

□ The PROC GDEVICE statement is required.

PROC GDEVICE⟨CATALOG=*SAS-catalog-name*⟩
    ⟨BROWSE⟩
    ⟨NOFS⟩;

□ If you use the NOFS option in the PROC GDEVICE statement or if you are running the GDEVICE procedure in a non-full-screen or batch environment, you can use the following line-mode statements. You can submit as many of each statement as you want with a single PROC GDEVICE statement.

ADD *entry-name required-parameters* ⟨*optional-parameters*⟩;

COPY *entry-name* ⟨FROM=*SAS-catalog-name*⟩
    ⟨NEWNAME=*new-entry-name*⟩;

DELETE *entry-name*;

END;

FS;

LIST ⟨*entry-name* | _ALL_ | _NEXT_ | _PREV_ | DUMP⟩;

MODIFY *entry-name required-parameters* ⟨*optional-parameters*⟩;

QUIT;

RENAME *entry-name* NEWNAME=*new-entry-name*;

STOP;

GDEVICE Procedure Description

The following sections address issues that pertain to the GDEVICE procedure as a whole, including terminology and procedure requirements and uses.

Terminology

The following terms are used in the discussion of the GDEVICE procedure and are defined in the Glossary:

device driver
device entry
device parameter
graphics option

Summary of Use

The GDEVICE procedure enables you to display and alter device parameters.

Methods of Using the GDEVICE Procedure

You can modify device entries by using the GDEVICE windows or by submitting line-mode statements. By default, if your device supports full-screen mode, the GDEVICE procedure uses the GDEVICE windows. The GDEVICE windows provide you with windows in which to make any modifications to the device entry.

To invoke the GDEVICE windows, submit the PROC GDEVICE statement without the NOFS option, as follows:

```
proc gdevice;
run;
```

SAS/GRAPH software then displays the DIRECTORY window, which contains a list of all device entries in a catalog. By default, the GDEVICE procedure displays the entries in the current catalog in browse mode. (See "Search Order for the Current Catalog to Display" later in this chapter.) You may want to use the CATALOG= option in the PROC GDEVICE statement to modify entries in a catalog. Once you see the DIRECTORY window, you should follow these general steps:

1. Select the device entry you want to view or modify. SAS/GRAPH software then displays the Detail window for that device entry.

2. Make any changes in the Detail window. You can modify device entries only in a catalog for which you have write access.

3. Select other windows to display from the Detail window.

4. Make any changes in the other windows.

If you do not use the GDEVICE windows, you can use line-mode statements to view or modify any of the parameter settings. The GDEVICE procedure automatically uses line mode if you do not have a full-screen device or are running the GDEVICE procedure in a batch environment. To use the GDEVICE procedure in line mode, submit the PROC GDEVICE statement with the NOFS option, as follows:

```
proc gdevice nofs;
run;
```

By default, the GDEVICE procedure displays the current catalog in browse mode. (See "Search Order for the Current Catalog to Display" later in this chapter.) You may want to use the CATALOG= option in the PROC GDEVICE statement to modify entries in a catalog.

Once you enter the PROC GDEVICE statement, you can enter statements and run them without re-entering the PROC GDEVICE statement for each statement. In batch mode, use statements in the same way as in line mode.

You can exit the GDEVICE procedure in line mode in these three ways:

□ Submit the END, QUIT, or STOP statement.

□ Submit another PROC statement or DATA step.

□ Exit your SAS session.

If you are using the GDEVICE procedure in batch mode, you can use line-mode statements to execute commands. The syntax is the same in batch mode as in line mode.

Search Order of Catalogs for a Device Driver

SAS/GRAPH software looks only into catalogs with certain librefs and names to find a device entry for a device driver. SAS/GRAPH software performs a sequential search of these catalogs when locating the device driver you specify.

When you use a procedure that produces graphics output, you must specify a device driver to use (either with the DEVICE= graphics option, in the OPTIONS window, or in the DEVICE prompt window). SAS/GRAPH software searches certain catalogs for the device entry in the following order:

1. If a SAS data library with the libref GDEVICE0 exists, SAS/GRAPH software looks in the library for a catalog named DEVICES. If the GDEVICE0.DEVICES catalog exists, it is checked for the specified device entry. If the device entry is not there, SAS/GRAPH software looks next for a library with the libref GDEVICE1 and for a catalog named DEVICES in that library. The search is repeated for the sequence of librefs through GDEVICE9.

2. If SAS/GRAPH software fails to find the specified device entry in any DEVICES catalog in the libraries GDEVICE0 through GDEVICE9, or if it encounters an undefined libref in that sequence before locating the specified device entry, it searches for the device entry in SASHELP.DEVICES, the catalog that contains device entries. The SASHELP.DEVICES catalog is supplied with SAS/GRAPH software. (SASHELP is one of the standard librefs defined automatically whenever you start your SAS session; you do not need to issue a LIBNAME statement to define it.)

3. If the specified device entry is not found in the SASHELP.DEVICES catalog, you receive an error message.

Since the GDEVICE0.DEVICES catalog is the first place that SAS/GRAPH software looks, you always should assign that libref to the library containing your personal catalog of device entries, if you have one. If for some reason you have personal device catalogs in more than one SAS data library, assign them librefs in the sequence GDEVICE0, GDEVICE1, GDEVICE2, and so on.

Note: The search for entries terminates if there is a break in the sequence; the catalog GDEVICE1.DEVICES is not checked if the libref GDEVICE0 is undefined.

Search Order for the Current Catalog to Display

When the GDEVICE procedure determines which catalog it should use, it searches for the catalog in the following order:

1. the catalog name specified in the CATALOG= option in the PROC GDEVICE statement

2. the catalog associated with the GDEVICE0 catalog, if the libref has been assigned

3. the Institute-supplied catalog, SASHELP.DEVICES. (the SASHELP.DEVICES catalog is usually not updated and is opened in browse mode.)

You can select the current catalog that is used in these two ways:

□ Use the CATALOG= option in the PROC GDEVICE statement.

□ Assign the GDEVICE0 libref to the appropriate catalog.

Requirements

You must have write access to a catalog in order to modify, add, or delete device entries. On multi-user systems, the SAS Software Consultant is usually the person who has write access to the SASHELP.DEVICES catalog and makes any changes.

Each device entry must have values for the following parameters:

MODULE

XMAX

YMAX

XPIXELS

YPIXELS

LCOLS and LROWS

PCOLS and PROWS.

At least one of the LCOLS and LROWS or PCOLS and PROWS pairs must be positive, nonzero values.

When you specify values with line-mode statements, you enter them as follows:

□ Numbers: SPEED=90

□ Literals: ROTATE=LANDSCAPE

□ Strings: GEND='$$'

You must enter hexadecimal strings as strings and include a terminating x, as in this example:

```
gend='04'x
```

If you include more than one parameter in the same statement, separate the parameters with a blank:

```
modify myhp7550 speed=90 rotate=landscape;
```

See Chapter 5, "Graphics Options and Device Parameters Dictionary," for the values each parameter expects.

Global Statements

The GDEVICE procedure ignores all global statements.

PROC GDEVICE Statement

The PROC GDEVICE statement starts the GDEVICE procedure, identifies the catalog to use, and determines how that catalog is opened. If you are using the GDEVICE procedure in line mode, the procedure is ended when a QUIT, STOP, END, DATA, or other PROC statement is encountered. If you are using the GDEVICE windows, the procedure is ended when you exit the windows. (See "Using the GDEVICE Procedure Windows" later in this chapter for details.)

Syntax

The general form of the PROC GDEVICE statement is

PROC GDEVICE⟨CATALOG=*SAS-catalog-name*⟩
⟨BROWSE⟩
⟨NOFS⟩;

Options

You can use the following options with the PROC GDEVICE statement. Options used in the PROC GDEVICE statement affect the way you use the procedure.

BROWSE
> opens a catalog in browse mode. You cannot make changes to a catalog when you open it with the BROWSE option. If you are using line-mode statements, the only statements that are valid when you have specified the BROWSE option are the FS, LIST, QUIT, STOP, and END statements.

CATALOG=*SAS-catalog*
CAT=*SAS-catalog*
C=*SAS-catalog*
> specifies the catalog containing device information. If you do not specify a catalog, the first catalog found in the search order of catalogs is opened in browse mode. You must use the CATALOG= option if you want to edit the device entries in a catalog. See "Search Order for the Current Catalog to Display" earlier in this chapter for an explanation of the search order of the catalog.

NOFS
> specifies that you are using line-mode statements. In full-screen environments, using the GDEVICE windows is the default, but you can switch between the window and line-mode statements while you are running the procedure if you are in a full-screen environment. See the NOFS command in "Window Commands" later in this chapter.

ADD Statement

The ADD statement adds a new device entry to the catalog selected by the CATALOG= option. The device entry is initialized with the default values for your host.

Syntax

The general form of the ADD statement is

ADD *entry-name*
      required-parameters
      ⟨*optional-parameters*⟩;

□ *entry-name* can be any valid entry name for your operating system.

□ *required-parameters* must be the following:

    MODULE=*module-name*

    XMAX=*width* ⟨IN | CM⟩

    YMAX=*height* ⟨IN | CM⟩

    XPIXELS=*width-in-pixels*

    YPIXELS=*height-in-pixels*

At least one of the following pairs of parameters must be positive, nonzero values:

    LCOLS=*landscape-columns*

    LROWS=*landscape-rows*

or

    PCOLS=*portrait-columns*

    PROWS=*portrait-rows*

□ *optional-parameters* can be one or more of the following:

    ASPECT=*scaling-factor*

    AUTOCOPY=Y | N

    AUTOFEED=Y | N

    CBACK=*background-color*

    CELL=Y | N

    CHARACTERS=Y | N

    CHARREC=(*charrec-list*)

    CHARTYPE=*hardware-font-chartype*

    CIRCLEARC=Y | N

    COLORS=(⟨*colors-list*⟩)

    COLORTYPE=NAME | RGB | HLS | GRAY | CMY

    DASH=Y | N

    DASHLINE='*dashed-line-hex-string*'X

    DESCRIPTION='*description-string*'

    DEVMAP=*map-name*

    DEVOPTS='*hardware-capabilities-hex-string*'X

    DEVTYPE=*device-type*

DRVQRY | NODRVQRY

ERASE=Y | N

FILL=Y | N

FILLINC=*fill-increment*

FORMAT=CHARACTER | BINARY

GACCESS='*output-format*'

GCOPIES=*current-number-copies*

GEND='*string*' ⟨ . . . '*string-n*'⟩

GEPILOG='*string*' ⟨ . . . '*string-n*'⟩

GPROLOG='*string*' ⟨ . . . '*string-n*'⟩

GPROTOCOL=*module-name*

GSFLEN=*record-length*

GSFMODE=APPEND | REPLACE | PORT

GSFNAME=*fileref*

GSIZE=*lines*

GSTART='*string*' ⟨ . . . '*string-n*'⟩

HANDSHAKE=SOFTWARE | HARDWARE | XONXOFF | NONE

HEADER='*command*'

HEADERFILE=*fileref*

HORIGIN=*horizontal-offset* ⟨IN | CM⟩

HSIZE=*horizontal-size* ⟨IN | CM⟩

ID='*description*'

INTERACTIVE=USER | GRAPH | PROC

LFACTOR=*line-thickness-factor*

MAXCOLORS=*number-of-colors*

MAXPOLY=*number-of-vertices*

MODEL=*model-number*

NAK='*negative-handshake-response*'X

PAPERFEED=*feed-increment* ⟨IN | CM⟩

PATH=*angle-increment*

PIEFILL=Y | N

POLYGONFILL=Y | N

PROCESS='*command*'

PROCESSINPUT=*fileref*

PROCESSOUTPUT=*fileref*

PROMPT=0 . . . 7

PROMPTCHARS='*prompt-chars-hex-string*'X

QMSG | NOQMSG

RECTFILL='*rectangle-fill-hex-string*'X

REPAINT=*redraw-factor*

ROTATE=LANDSCAPE | PORTRAIT

ROTATION=*angle-increment*

SPEED=*pen-speed*

SWAP=Y | N

SYMBOL=Y | N

SYMBOLS='*hardware-symbols-hex-string*'X

TRAILER='*command*'

TRAILERFILE=*fileref*

TRANTAB=SASGTAB0 | GTABVTAM | GTABTCAM | GTABCMS | *user-defined-nam*

TYPE=CRT | PLOTTER | PRINTER | CAMERA

UCC='*control-characters-hex-string*'X

VORIGIN=*vertical-offset* ⟨IN | CM⟩

VSIZE=*vertical-size* ⟨IN | CM⟩

Options

All options for the ADD statement correspond to device parameters of the same name. Refer to Chapter 5 for details about each parameter.

Requirements

Entry-name must be a one-level name. The ADD statement is not valid if the catalog is opened in BROWSE mode; you must have write access to the current catalog to add a device entry.

   Note: The COLORS= option is not required; the device entry will be created if you do not use it. However, the GDEVICE procedure issues an error message if you do not specify at least one color for the COLORS= option.

COPY Statement

The COPY statement copies a device entry from the current catalog to a different device entry in the same catalog. Device entries also can be copied across catalogs by using the FROM= option in a COPY statement. The catalog is checked to see that a device entry with the new name does not already exist in the catalog. If you are copying device entries across catalogs and you do not specify a new name, the GDEVICE procedure uses the original name for the new device entry.

Syntax

The general form of the COPY statement is

COPY *entry-name*
     ⟨FROM=*SAS-catalog*⟩
     ⟨NEWNAME=*new-entry-name*⟩;

where *entry-name* specifies the device entry to copy.

Options

You must use one of the following options in a COPY statement:

FROM=*SAS-catalog*
    names the catalog from which to copy the original device entry.

NEWNAME=*new-entry-name*
    provides a new name for the created device entry. If the
    NEWNAME= option is not used, the original name is used for the
    new device entry.

Requirements

You must use either the FROM= option or the NEWNAME= option or
both in a COPY statement. If you specify a new name for the device entry
being created, the name must not match the name of any other device
entry in the current catalog. If the new name matches another device
entry, SAS/GRAPH software issues an error message.

    Entry-name must be a one-level name and must exist in the catalog from
which it is being copied. *New-entry-name* must be a valid name for a SAS
catalog entry. The COPY statement is not valid if you used the BROWSE
option in the PROC GDEVICE statement; you must have write access to
the catalog to which the device entry is being copied.

DELETE Statement

The DELETE statement deletes the device entry named in the statement
from the current catalog.
    Note: There is no way to restore a device entry once it has been
deleted. Depending on the environment in which you are using the
GDEVICE procedure, you may be asked to verify that you really want to
delete the entry.

Syntax

The general form of the DELETE statement is

DELETE *entry-name*;

where *entry-name* names the device entry to delete.

Requirements

The device entry specified by *entry-name* must exist in the current catalog.
Entry-name must be a one-level name. The DELETE statement is not valid
if the catalog is opened in browse mode; you must have write access to
the current catalog to delete a device entry from it.

END Statement

The END statement saves all modifications made to device entries during
the procedure and exits the GDEVICE procedure. The END statement
performs the same function as the QUIT and STOP statements.

Syntax

The form of the END statement is

END;

FS Statement

The FS statement switches the GDEVICE procedure from line mode to the GDEVICE windows.

Syntax

The form of the FS statement is

FS;

Requirements

Your device must support full-screen mode to use the FS statement.

LIST Statement

The LIST statement lists all of the parameters of the specified device entry.

Syntax

The general form of the LIST statement is

LIST ⟨*entry-name*⟩
         ⟨_ALL_⟩
         ⟨_NEXT_⟩
         ⟨_PREV_⟩
         ⟨DUMP⟩;

where *entry-name* names the device entry whose contents you want to list.

Options

You can use the following options with the LIST statement:

ALL
    lists only the name, description, and creation date of all device entries in the current catalog. If no entries exist in the catalog, the GDEVICE procedure issues the following message:

        0 entries in the catalog.

NEXT
    lists the contents of the next device entry. The GDEVICE procedure lists the first entry in the catalog if no entries have been previously listed.

PREV
> lists the contents of the previous device entry. If you have not previously listed the contents of a device entry, the GDEVICE procedure issues the following message:
>
> > `No objects preceding current object.`

DUMP
> lists detailed information on *all* device entries in the current catalog. Depending on the number of device entries in the catalog, the DUMP option can create a *large* amount of output.

By default, the LIST statement uses the _ALL_ option.

Requirements

If *entry-name* is specified, it must be a one-level name and must be stored in the current catalog. If *entry-name* is not in the current catalog, the GDEVICE procedure issues this message:

> `(entry-name) is not in the device catalog.`

MODIFY Statement

The MODIFY statement enables you to change the values in a device entry. If you find it necessary to modify a device entry, you should create your own catalog and then copy the device entries you need into it. You can then change your personal copies of the device entries without affecting the original drivers in SASHELP.DEVICES. (Use the COPY statement, the COPY command in the DIRECTORY window, or the CATALOG procedure to copy device entries. See *SAS Procedures Guide, Version 6, Third Edition* for more information about the CATALOG procedure.)

If you try to change a field in an Institute-supplied device entry (either the original device entry in SASHELP.DEVICES or a copy), SAS/GRAPH software asks whether you really want to change the entry. Answer Y to change the entry or N to cancel the operation.

▶ *Caution: Be careful when modifying device entries in line mode.*

In line mode, you cannot use a CANCEL command or statement to cancel any modifications you have just made. To change a value you have modified, you must use another MODIFY statement. (This caution is only for line mode. In the GDEVICE windows, you can use the CANCEL command.)

. . . .

You can reset a character parameter to the default for the device by specifying a null value for it in a MODIFY statement:

> `modify entry-name circlearc=;`

You can reset a numeric parameter to the default for the device by assigning a value of 0 to it in a MODIFY statement:

> `modify entry-name hsize=0;`

See "Examples" for an illustration of how to create your own catalog and copy device entries to it using the GDEVICE windows or line-mode statements.

Syntax

The general form of the MODIFY statement is

MODIFY *entry-name*
    required-parameters
    ⟨*optional-parameters*⟩;

□ *entry-name* can be any valid entry name for your operating system.

□ *required-parameters* must be the following:

    MODULE=*module-name*

    XMAX=*width* ⟨IN | CM⟩

    YMAX=*height* ⟨IN | CM⟩

    XPIXELS=*width-in-pixels*

    YPIXELS=*height-in-pixels*

At least one of the following pairs of parameters must be positive, nonzero values:

    LCOLS=*landscape-columns*

    LROWS=*landscape-rows*

or

    PCOLS=*portrait-columns*

    PROWS=*portrait-rows*

□ *optional-parameters* can be one or more of the following:

    ASPECT=*scaling-factor*

    AUTOCOPY=Y | N

    AUTOFEED=Y | N

    CBACK=*background-color*

    CELL=Y | N

    CHARACTERS=Y | N

    CHARREC=(*charrec-list*)

    CHARTYPE=*hardware-font-chartype*

    CIRCLEARC=Y | N

    COLORS=(⟨*colors-list*⟩)

    COLORTYPE=NAME | RGB | HLS | GRAY | CMY

    DASH=Y | N

    DASHLINE='*dashed-line-hex-string*'X

    DESCRIPTION='*description-string*'

    DEVMAP=*map-name*

    DEVOPTS='*hardware-capabilities-hex-string*'X

    DEVTYPE=*device-type*

    DRVQRY | NODRVQRY

    ERASE=Y | N

    FILL=Y | N

    FILLINC=*fill-increment*

FORMAT=CHARACTER | BINARY

GACCESS='*output-format*'

GCOPIES=*current-number-copies*

GEND='*string*' ⟨ . . . '*string-n*'⟩

GEPILOG='*string*' ⟨ . . . '*string-n*'⟩

GPROLOG='*string*' ⟨ . . . '*string-n*'⟩

GPROTOCOL=*module-name*

GSFLEN=*record-length*

GSFMODE=APPEND | REPLACE | PORT

GSFNAME=*fileref*

GSIZE=*lines*

GSTART='*string*' ⟨ . . . '*string-n*'⟩

HANDSHAKE=SOFTWARE | HARDWARE | XONXOFF | NONE

HEADER=*command*

HEADERFILE=*fileref*

HORIGIN=*horizontal-offset* ⟨IN | CM⟩

HSIZE=*horizontal-size* ⟨IN | CM⟩

ID=*description*

INTERACTIVE=USER | GRAPH | PROC

LFACTOR=*line-thickness-factor*

MAXCOLORS=*number-of-colors*

MAXPOLY=*number-of-vertices*

MODEL=*model-number*

NAK='*negative-handshake-response*'X

PAPERFEED=*feed-increment* ⟨IN | CM⟩

PATH=*angle-increment*

PIEFILL=Y | N

POLYGONFILL=Y | N

PROCESS=*command-name*

PROCESSINPUT=*fileref*

PROCESSOUTPUT=*fileref*

PROMPT=0 . . . 7

PROMPTCHARS='*prompt-chars-hex-string*'X

QMSG | NOQMSG

RECTFILL='*rectangle-fill-hex-string*'X

REPAINT=*redraw-factor*

ROTATE=LANDSCAPE | PORTRAIT

ROTATION=*angle-increment*

SPEED=*pen-speed*

SWAP=Y | N

SYMBOL=Y | N

SYMBOLS='*hardware-symbols-hex-string*'X

TRAILER=*command*

TRAILERFILE=*fileref*

TRANTAB=GTABVTAM | GTABTCAM | GTABCMS

TYPE=CRT | PLOTTER | PRINTER | CAMERA

UCC='*control-characters-hex-string*'X

VORIGIN=*vertical-offset* ⟨IN | CM⟩

VSIZE=*vertical-size* ⟨IN | CM⟩

Options

All options for the MODIFY statement correspond to device parameters of the same name. Refer to Chapter 5 for details about each parameter.

Requirements

Entry-name must be the name of a device entry in the current catalog and must be a one-level name.

The MODIFY statement is not valid if the catalog is opened in browse mode; you must have write access to the current catalog to modify a device entry.

QUIT Statement

The QUIT statement saves any changes and exits the GDEVICE procedure. The QUIT statement performs the same function as the END and STOP statements.

Syntax

The form of the QUIT statement is

QUIT;

RENAME Statement

The RENAME statement changes the name of the device entry to the name specified in the statement. The current catalog is checked first to see that a device entry with the new name does not already exist in the catalog. If it finds the name, the GDEVICE procedure issues an error message stating that it cannot rename that entry.

Syntax

The general form of the RENAME statement is

RENAME *entry-name*
    NEWNAME=*new-entry-name*;

where *entry-name* specifies the name of a device entry in the current catalog.

Requirements

You must use the NEWNAME= option in a RENAME statement. The NEWNAME= option provides the new name for the device entry.

The device entry named by *entry-name* must exist in the current catalog. *Entry-name* must be a one-level name. *New-entry-name* must be a valid entry name and cannot already exist in the current catalog.

The RENAME statement is not valid if the catalog is opened in browse mode; you must have write access to the current catalog to rename a device entry.

STOP Statement

The STOP statement saves any changes and exits the GDEVICE procedure. The STOP statement performs the same function as the QUIT and END statements.

Syntax

The form of the STOP statement is

STOP;

GDEVICE Procedure Windows

If your device is a full-screen device, you can use the GDEVICE windows instead of line-mode statements to create, modify, copy, delete, and view device entries.

The DIRECTORY window is the first window displayed when you use the GDEVICE procedure on a full-screen device without using the NOFS option. It lists all of the entries in the current catalog (either SASHELP.DEVICES or GDEVICE0.DEVICES). From the DIRECTORY window, you can access these subsidiary windows:

□ the Detail window

□ the Parameters window

□ the Gcolors window

□ the Chartype window

□ the Metagraphics window

□ the Gprolog window

□ the Gepilog window

□ the Gstart window

□ the Gend window.

Figure 25.1 shows how you can access the GDEVICE windows. Solid lines indicate the order in which you can access other windows by entering the name of the window on the command line. Broken lines indicate the order in which you access the windows using the NEXTSCR command. See "Window Commands" later in this chapter for an explanation of the commands. See "Moving between Windows" later in this chapter for more information about moving between windows.

Figure 25.1 Accessing
GDEVICE Windows

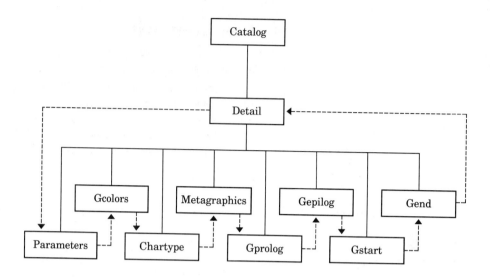

These windows are discussed in detail in order of appearance in the sections following "Window Commands." Most of the windows in this chapter were produced from device entries in the SASHELP.DEVICES catalog. The Gprolog, Gepilog, Gstart, and Gend windows were produced from a modified device entry.

Window Commands

GDEVICE window commands can be entered directly on the command line in a window, selected from the PMENU facility, or programmed as function keys using the KEYS window of the SAS Display Manager System. Table 25.1 describes the commands for the GDEVICE windows. The table names the commands, describes the syntax of the commands, indicates in which windows the commands can be used, and describes the actions performed by the commands. Many other display manager commands can be used in the windows as well. See *SAS Language: Reference, Version 6, First Edition* for an explanation of global window commands.

Table 25.1 *GDEVICE Window Commands*

Command	Used in	Description
BACKWARD ⟨n⟩	all windows	goes backward *n* device entries in the catalog or *n* lines in the window depending on the window from which the command is issued. If *n* is not specified, the BACKWARD command scrolls back an entire page in the window. If you enter the BACKWARD or BACKWARD 1 command in the Detail window, the GDEVICE procedure displays the Detail window of the preceding device entry in the catalog. In all other windows, the BACKWARD *n* command goes backward *n* lines.
BROWSE *entry-name*	DIRECTORY window	shows the contents of the specified device entry, beginning with the Detail window. You cannot change information in the fields while viewing a device entry from a catalog opened with the BROWSE option.
CANCEL	all windows	prevents saving information to the device entry and returns you to the previous window. If you enter the CANCEL command in the DIRECTORY window, the GDEVICE procedure returns you to display manager.
CHARTYPE	Detail window	saves the current information in the Detail window to the device entry and goes to the Chartype window.
COPY *old-name new-name*	DIRECTORY window	copies the information from the device entry specified in *old-name* to a new device entry, using the *new-name* value as the name for the new device entry. If you are copying from another catalog, *old-name* must be in the form *libref.catalog-name.entry-name.type* (that is, fully qualified).
DELETE *entry-name*	DIRECTORY window	deletes the device entry specified in *entry-name*. When you execute the DELETE command, the entry name and description are overwritten with a prompt to verify the deletion. Press ENTER alone to cancel the deletion. You must have write access to the catalog to delete an entry. Be careful when deleting a device entry. There is no way to restore a device entry once it has been deleted. If you are sharing the SASHELP.DEVICES catalog with other users, you should not delete a device entry from the SASHELP.DEVICES catalog. If you are not sharing SASHELP.DEVICES, you may want to delete entries you do not need to save storage space.
DOWN ⟨n⟩	all windows	goes forward *n* device entries in the catalog or *n* lines in the window depending on the window from which the command is issued. If *n* is not specified, the DOWN command scrolls forward an entire page in the window. If you enter the DOWN or DOWN 1 command in the Detail window, the GDEVICE procedure displays the Detail window of the next device entry in the catalog. In all other windows, the DOWN *n* command goes forward *n* lines.

(continued)

Table 25.1 (continued)

Command	Used in	Description
EDIT *entry-name*	DIRECTORY window	shows contents of the device entry specified in *entry-name*, beginning with the Detail window. A new device entry is created if a device entry with the name you specify does not already exist. You must have write access to a catalog to edit a device entry.
END	all windows	saves current information to the device entry and returns you to the previous window. If you enter the END command in the DIRECTORY window, the GDEVICE procedure returns you to display manager.
FORWARD ⟨*n*⟩	all windows	goes forward *n* device entries in the catalog or *n* lines in the window depending on the window from which the command is issued. If *n* is not specified, the FORWARD command scrolls forward an entire page in the window. If you enter the FORWARD or FORWARD 1 command in the Detail window, the GDEVICE procedure displays the Detail window of the next device entry in the catalog. In all other windows, the FORWARD *n* command goes forward *n* lines.
GCOLORS	Detail window	saves the current information in the Detail window to the device entry if in edit mode and goes to the Gcolors window.
GEND	Detail window	saves the current information in the Detail window to the device entry if in edit mode and goes to the Gend window.
GEPILOG	Detail window	saves the current information in the Detail window to the device entry if in edit mode and goes to the Gepilog window.
GPROLOG	Detail window	saves the current information in the Detail window to the device entry if in edit mode and goes to the Gprolog window.
GSTART	Detail window	saves the current information in the Detail window to the device entry if in edit mode and goes to the Gstart window.
META	Detail window	saves the current information in the Detail window to the device entry if in edit mode and goes to the Metagraphics window.
NEXTSCR	all windows except the DIRECTORY window	saves any modified information and goes to the next window. See Figure 25.1 for the order in which the NEXTSCR command displays the windows. The NEXTSCR command is not the same as the NEXT command used in display manager. See *SAS Language: Reference* for details about the NEXT command.

(continued)

Table 25.1 (continued)

Command	Used in	Description
NOFS	all windows	exits the GDEVICE windows and enables you to enter line-mode statements. If you enter the NOFS command in a window, any changes you have made in that window *are not saved*.
PARAMETERS	Detail window	saves the current information in the Detail window and goes to the Parameters window.
RENAME *old-name new-name* ⟨ *'new-description'*⟩	DIRECTORY window	changes the entry name and, optionally, the description of the entry specified in *old-name*. The device entry is given the name specified in *new-name*. If a *new-description* value is also supplied, the value can be up to 40 characters long and replaces the current description field for the device entry. If *new-description* contains blanks, you must enclose the string in quotes; otherwise, the quotes are optional. To change only the description, use the *old-name* value for *new-name*. You must have write access to the current catalog to use the RENAME command.
SAVE	all windows	saves current information to the device entry and remains in the current window.
UP ⟨*n*⟩	all windows	goes backward *n* device entries in the catalog or *n* lines in the window depending on the window from which the command is issued. If *n* is not specified, the UP command scrolls back an entire page in the window. If you enter the UP or UP 1 command in the Detail window, the GDEVICE procedure displays the Detail window of the preceding device entry in the catalog. In all other windows, the UP *n* command goes backward *n* lines.

The DIRECTORY Window

The DIRECTORY window is displayed when you first enter the GDEVICE windows. It lists the device entries in the default catalog or the catalog you specified in the PROC GDEVICE statement. From this window, you can either work with device entries (copy, rename, or delete them) or select a device entry and work with its contents (browse or edit the fields in one device entry).

When you choose a device entry to browse or edit, you are taken automatically to the Detail window. Display 25.1 is an example of the DIRECTORY window.

Display 25.1 *The DIRECTORY Window*

```
┌GDEVICE: DIRECTORY SASHELP.DEVICES (B)──────────────────────┐
│ Command ===>                                               │
│                                                            │
│     Name      Type    Description                 Updated  │
│                                                            │
│  _  HP7475    DEV     HP 7475 plotter--B size paper  11/02/89 │
│  _  HP7475A   DEV     HP 7475 plotter--A size paper  11/02/89 │
│  _  HP7475B   DEV     HP 7475 plotter--B size paper  11/02/89 │
│  _  HP7510    DEV     HP 7510 film recorder          11/02/89 │
│  _  HP7550    DEV     HP 7550 plotter--B size paper  11/02/89 │
│  _  HP7550A   DEV     HP 7550 plotter--A size paper  11/02/89 │
│  _  HP7550B   DEV     HP 7550 plotter--B size paper  11/02/89 │
│  _  HP7570    DEV     HP DraftPro Plotter--C size paper  11/02/89 │
│  _  HP7570C   DEV     HP DraftPro Plotter--C size paper  11/02/89 │
│  _  HP7570D   DEV     HP DraftPro Plotter--D size paper  11/02/89 │
│  _  HP7575    DEV     HP DraftPro DXL Plotter--Arch C paper  11/02/89 │
│  _  HP7576    DEV     HP DraftPro EXL Plotter--Arch D paper  11/02/89 │
│  _  HP7580    DEV     HP 7580 plotter--A size paper  11/02/89 │
│  _  HP7580A   DEV     HP 7580 plotter--A size paper  11/02/89 │
│  _  HP7580B   DEV     HP 7580 plotter--B size paper  11/02/89 │
│  _  HP7580C   DEV     HP 7580 plotter--C size paper  11/02/89 │
│  _  HP7580D   DEV     HP 7580 plotter--D size paper  11/02/89 │
│  _  HP7580E   DEV     HP 7580 plotter--E size paper  11/02/89 │
│                                                         ─R─│
└────────────────────────────────────────────────────────────┘
```

The DIRECTORY window contains two noneditable fields: the Type field and the Updated field. The Type field displays the type of the catalog entry. The Updated field displays the date the entry was last modified. Table 25.2 shows the editable fields in the DIRECTORY window.

Table 25.2 *DIRECTORY Window Fields*

Field	Expected Value	Default	Description
Name	alphanumeric characters	none	provides the name of the device entry; must be a valid name for a SAS catalog entry: must contain only alphanumeric characters, must begin with an alphabetic character, cannot exceed 8 characters, and cannot contain embedded blanks.
Description	alphanumeric characters	none	provides a description of the device entry; can be up to 40 characters of any type.

Selection Field Commands

You can use one-letter commands in the DIRECTORY window's selection fields to execute commands. To use a selection-field command, simply move the cursor to the selection field of the device entry that you want to use. Then type the command letter and press ENTER. These are the selection-field commands for the DIRECTORY window:

B   browses the selected device entry, beginning with the Detail window. You cannot make changes to fields in any window when you use this selection-field command.

D deletes the selected device entry.

▶ *Caution: Be careful when using the D command.*

You cannot restore a device entry once it has been deleted.
....

  When you press ENTER, a message asks you if you really want to delete the device entry. To verify, type V in the selection field and press ENTER. Press ENTER alone to cancel the deletion. You must have write access to the catalog to use the D command.

E edits the selected device entry, beginning with the Detail window. You can make changes to fields in any window while you are in edit mode. You must have write access to the catalog to use the E command.

R renames the device entry. When you press ENTER, the Name and Description fields are highlighted. Just type the new name or description over the old one, delete any extraneous characters, and press ENTER. You must have write access to the catalog to use the R command.

S selects a device entry. This command is the same as the B command if the catalog was opened in browse mode; otherwise, it is equivalent to the E command.

See "Window Commands" earlier in this chapter for a description of the commands you can use in the DIRECTORY window.

The Detail Window

The Detail window appears when you select a device entry from the DIRECTORY window using either the EDIT or BROWSE window commands or the E, B, or S selection field commands. It shows several basic characteristics of the device including the size of the graphics output area, where graphics output is sent by default, and how graphics data are written.

 See "Window Commands" for a description of the commands you can use with this window.

 Display 25.2 shows a Detail window from the HP7475 device entry in the SASHELP.DEVICES catalog. (Some of the values may vary across operating systems.)

Display 25.2 *The Detail Window*

```
┌GDEVICE: DIRECTORY SASHELP.DEVICES (B)──────────────────────────────┐
│┌GDEVICE: Detail─────────────────────────────────────────────────────┐
││ Command ===>                                                       │
││                                                                    │
││ Catalog: SASHELP.DEVICES                              Entry:  HP7475│
││                                                                    │
││ Orig Driver: HP7475          Module: SASGDHPL     Model:    307    │
││ Description: HP 7475 plotter--B size paper        Type:    PLOTTER │
││ Lrows:   40  Xmax:   14.961 IN  Hsize:   0.000 IN  Xpixels: 15200  │
││ Lcols:  100  Ymax:   10.827 IN  Vsize:   0.000 IN  Ypixels: 11000  │
││ Prows:   50                     Horigin: 0.000 IN                  │
││ Pcols:   80                     Vorigin: 0.000 IN                  │
││ Aspect:     0.000               Rotate:  _____                  │
││ Driver query: _             Queued messages: N                    │
││ Gprotocol: _____         Paperfeed:    0.000 IN                │
││ Gaccess: SASGASTD                                                  │
││ Gsfname: _____           Gsfmode: PORT      Gsflen:    0        │
││ Trantab: _____           Devmap:  _____                     │
││ Devtype: GTERM                                                     │
│└────────────────────────────────────────────────────────────────────┘
│  _  HP7580C  DEV    HP 7580 plotter--C size paper         11/02/89  │
│  _  HP7580D  DEV    HP 7580 plotter--D size paper         11/02/89  │
│  _  HP7580E  DEV    HP 7580 plotter--E size paper         11/02/89  │
└───────────────────────────────────────────────────────────────R────┘
```

The Detail window contains three non-editable fields: the Catalog field, the Entry field, and the Orig Driver field. The Catalog field shows the catalog in which the device entry is stored. The Entry field displays the device entry you are currently editing or viewing. The Orig Driver field is used as a documentation aid to track the origin of the device entry. Usually, the Orig Driver field matches the Entry field in the SASHELP.DEVICES catalog. If you copy an entry from SASHELP.DEVICES and change the name, the Orig Driver field retains the original device driver name. If you create your own device driver, Orig Driver contains the value USER.

Table 25.3 shows the editable fields in the Detail window. Fields marked with an asterisk can be overridden by the graphics option of the same name in a GOPTIONS statement. Refer to Chapter 5 for more information about graphics options and the device parameters in this window. Note that in most cases, a default value of 0 or blank for a field indicates that the device driver chooses a value.

Table 25.3 *Detail Window Fields*

Field	Expected Value	Default	Description
Aspect*	numeric	device dependent	aspect ratio for character cells.
Description	character string	none	device description
Devmap*	character; map name	DEFAULT	device map to use
Devtype	literal; device type; GTERM | G3270 | PRINTER | TERMINAL | PIPE	device dependent	device type to use. Usually, you should not modify this field.

(continued)

Table 25.3 (continued)

Field	Expected Value	Default	Description
Driver query	Y | N	device dependent	device can be queried; DRVQRY | NODRVQRY controls parameter when using line-mode statements. Usually, you should not modify this field.
Gaccess*	character; output format	device dependent	format and destination of graphics data
Gprotocol*	character; module name	host dependent	how graphics data generated by the SAS/GRAPH device driver are to be altered for protocol conversion or the GPROTOCOL module to use
Gsflen*	numeric; length	device dependent	length of the records written by the driver to a device, a device port, or a graphics stream file
Gsfmode*	literal; APPEND | REPLACE | PORT	PORT	disposition of records written by the driver to a device, a device port, or a graphics stream file
Gsfname*	character; fileref	none	fileref of the file to which graphics stream data are written
Horigin*	numeric	0.0 IN	horizontal offset from lower-left corner of display area to lower-left corner of graph.
Hsize*	numeric	0.0 IN	horizontal dimension of the graphics output area
Lcols	positive integer; columns	device dependent	number of columns in display when it is in LANDSCAPE mode; the value in the Lcols field is overridden by the HPOS= graphics option
Lrows	positive integer; rows	device dependent	number of rows in display when it is in LANDSCAPE mode; the value in the Lrows field is overridden by the VPOS= graphics option
Model	positive integer; model number	device dependent	model number of output device. Do not modify this field in device entries in SASHELP.DEVICES

(continued)

Table 25.3 *(continued)*

Field	Expected Value	Default	Description
Module	character; module name	device dependent	driver file. Do not modify this field in device entries in SASHELP.DEVICES
Paperfeed*	numeric	0.0 IN	paper eject increment
Pcols	positive integer	device dependent	number of columns in display when it is in PORTRAIT mode; the value in the Pcols field is overridden by the HPOS= graphics option
Prows	positive integer	device dependent	number of rows in display when it is in PORTRAIT mode; the value in the Prows field is overridden by the VPOS= graphics option
Queued messages	Y | N	device dependent	turns message queuing on or off
Rotate*	literal; LANDSCAPE | PORTRAIT	device dependent	graph rotation.
Trantab*	character string	host dependent	translates table. Usually, you should not modify this field in device entries in SASHELP.DEVICES.
Type	literal; CRT | PLOTTER | PRINTER | CAMERA	device dependent	type of output device to which graphics commands are to be sent. Usually, you should not modify this field in device entries in SASHELP.DEVICES.
Vorigin*	numeric	0.0 IN	vertical offset from lower-left corner of the display area to lower-left corner of graph
Vsize*	numeric	0.0 IN	vertical dimension of the graphics output area
Xmax	numeric	device dependent	maximum width of graphics output area
Xpixels	positive integer	device dependent	width of display in pixels
Ymax	numeric	device dependent	maximum height of graphics output area
Ypixels	positive integer	device dependent	height of display in pixels

The Parameters Window

The Parameters window shows additional device parameters that affect the way graphs are drawn. For example, you choose whether certain graphics primitives are drawn by your hardware or by SAS/GRAPH software, whether to feed paper to printers or plotters automatically, and whether to have SAS/GRAPH software prompt you with messages under certain conditions.

See "Window Commands" earlier in this chapter for a list of the commands you can use with this window.

Display 25.3 shows the Parameters window from the HP7475 entry in SASHELP.DEVICES.

Display 25.3 *The Parameters Window*

```
┌GDEVICE: DIRECTORY SASHELP.DEVICES (B)────────────────────────────┐
│┌GDEVICE: Detail──────────────────────────────────────────────────┐
││┌GDEVICE: Parameters───────────────────────────────────────────┐
││ Command ===>
││
││ Catalog: SASHELP.DEVICES                    Entry:     HP7475
││
││ Erase:     _       Autofeed:   _       Chartype:    0
││ Swap:      _       Cell:       _       Maxcolors:   7
││ Autocopy:  _       Characters: _       Repaint:     0
││ Handshake: SOFTWARE   Circlearc: _      Gcopies:     0
││                    Dash:       _       Gsize:       0
││ Prompt:  start up:      X  Fill:     _       Speed:       0
││          end of graph: _  Piefill:  _       Fillinc:    10
││          mount pens:   X  Polyfill: _       Maxpoly:     0
││          change paper: X  Symbol:   _       Lfactor:     0
││ Promptchars: 000A010D05000000       Dashline: _____
││ Rectfill:    _____        Symbols:  _____
││ Devopts:     _____
││ UCC:         _____
││
││
│└────────────────────────────────────────────────────────────────
│ _ HP7580E  DEV    HP7580 with E size paper         06/30/89
└──────────────────────────────────────────────────────────────R──
```

The Parameters window contains two non-editable fields: the Catalog field and the Entry field. The Catalog field shows the catalog in which the device entry is stored. The Entry field displays the device entry you are currently editing or viewing.

Table 25.4 shows the editable fields in the Parameters window. Fields marked with an asterisk can be overridden by the graphics option of the same name in a GOPTIONS statement. Refer to Chapter 5 for more information about graphics options and the device parameters in this window. Note that in most cases, a default value of 0 or blank for a field indicates that the device driver chooses a value.

Table 25.4 *Parameters Window Fields*

Field	Expected Value	Default	Description
Autocopy*	literal; Y | N	N	generates hardcopy automatically on attached devices; not supported by all devices
Autofeed*	literal; Y | N	N	feeds paper automatically; not supported by all devices
Cell*	literal; Y | N	device dependent	specifies to use cell alignment
Chartype*	integer ≥0; a value in the Chartype field in the Chartype window	0	selects number of hardware font to use if device has more than one hardware font
Characters*	literal; Y | N	Y	specifies to use hardware font
Circlearc*	literal; Y | N	device dependent	specifies to use hardware circle-drawing command
Dash*	literal; Y | N	device dependent	specifies to use your device's hardware dashed-line capability
Dashline	hexadecimal string not enclosed in quotes and without a trailing X	device dependent	defines available hardware dashed-line patterns
Devopts	hexadecimal string not enclosed in quotes and without a trailing X	device dependent	specifies hardware capabilities of device
Erase*	literal; Y | N	N	erases the graph after display
Fill*	literal; Y | N	device dependent	specifies to use hardware rectangle-fill capability
Fillinc*	positive integer	device dependent	sets number of pixels between lines in software fill

(continued)

Table 25.4 *(continued)*

Field	Expected Value	Default	Description
Gcopies*	integer	0	specifies number of copies to print; not supported by all devices
Gsize*	positive integer	device dependent	specifies to use number of lines of display for graphics on devices whose displays can be divided into graphics and text areas
Handshake*	literal; SOFTWARE | SOFT | HARDWARE | HARD | XONXOFF | X | NONE	host dependent	specifies type of flow control used to regulate flow of data to hardcopy device
Lfactor*	positive integer	0	specifies default thickness of hardware lines
Maxcolors	positive integer; 2 to 256	device dependent	specifies number of colors that can be displayed at one time
Maxpoly	positive integer	device dependent	sets maximum number of vertices for hardware-drawn polygons. Zero means that there is no limit.
Piefill*	literal; Y | N	device dependent	specifies to use hardware pie-filling capability
Polyfill	literal; Y | N	device dependent	specifies to use hardware polygon-filling capability
Prompt* Action Fields			
start up	literal; X | ''	device dependent	issues a message to turn on the device or the message "PLEASE PRESS RETURN AFTER EACH BELL TO CONTINUE"
end of graph	literal; X | ''	device dependent	signals when the graph is complete

(continued)

Table 25.4 *(continued)*

Field	Expected Value	Default	Description
mount pens	literal; X | ''	device dependent	issues a message to mount pens in a certain order and provide pen-priming strokes for plotters
change paper	literal; X | ''	device dependent	prompts user to change the paper; valid for plotters only
Promptchars*	hexadecimal string not enclosed in quotes and without a trailing X	host dependent	specifies prompt characters and length of records to be used by the device driver
Rectfill	hexadecimal string not enclosed in quotes and without a trailing X	device dependent	identifies available hardware rectangle fills
Repaint*	positive integer	device dependent	redraws graph a specified number of times
Speed*	positive integer	device dependent	specifies pen speed for pen plotters with variable speed selection
Swap*	literal; Y | N	N	reverses BLACK and WHITE foreground colors when graph is displayed
Symbol*	literal; Y | N	device dependent	specifies to use device's hardware symbol-drawing capabilities
Symbols	hexadecimal string not enclosed in quotes and without a trailing X	device dependent	specifies which symbols can be generated by hardware
UCC	hexadecimal string not enclosed in quotes and without a trailing X	none	specifies user-defined control characters for device

The Gcolors Window

The Gcolors window lists the colors that the driver uses by default. When you do not explicitly specify the color of a graphics feature in your program or in a GOPTIONS statement, SAS/GRAPH software uses this list to determine what color to use.

See "Window Commands" earlier in this chapter for a list of the commands you can use with this window.

Display 25.4 shows the Gcolors window from the HP7475 entry in SASHELP.DEVICES.

Display 25.4 The Gcolors Window

```
┌─GDEVICE: Gcolors────────────────────────────────────────────┐
│ Command ===>                                                 │
│                                                              │
│  Catalog: SASHELP.DEVICES                   Entry:   HP7475  │
│                                                              │
│  Cback: WHITE                               Colortbl: _____ │
│  Colors:                                                     │
│                                                              │
│       BLACK         RED         GREEN       BLUE      ORANGE  │
│       LIME          _____       _____       _____     _____  │
│       _____         _____       _____       _____     _____  │
│       _____         _____       _____       _____     _____  │
│       _____         _____       _____       _____     _____  │
│       _____         _____       _____       _____     _____  │
│       _____         _____       _____       _____     _____  │
│       _____         _____       _____       _____     _____  │
│       _____         _____       _____       _____     _____  │
│       _____         _____       _____       _____     _____  │
│       _____         _____       _____       _____     _____  │
│       _____         _____       _____       _____     _____  │
│       _____         _____       _____       _____     _____  │
│       _____         _____       _____       _____     _____  │
│                                                           R  │
└──────────────────────────────────────────────────────────────┘
```

The Gcolors window contains two non-editable fields: the Catalog field and the Entry field. The Catalog field shows the catalog in which the device entry is stored. The Entry field displays the device entry you are currently editing or viewing.

Table 25.5 shows the editable fields in the Gcolors window. Fields marked with an asterick can be overridden by the option of the same name in a GOPTIONS statement.

You can use any color-naming scheme in the Gcolors window. See Chapter 7, "SAS/GRAPH Colors," for details on specifying colors. Refer to Chapter 5 for more information about graphics options and the device parameters in this window.

Table 25.5 Gcolors Window Fields

Field	Expected Value	Default	Description
Cback*	character string or literal	device dependent	specifies background color of display
Colors*	colors list	device's colors list	specifies default colors to use on displays
Colortbl	none	none	not currently implemented

The Chartype Window

The Chartype window lists the hardware fonts that the device can use, along with information about the size of the characters.

The window is used to record the list of hardware fonts available on the device (for those devices that can produce multiple fonts). The Chartype value in the Parameters window corresonds to a Chartype number in this window. When a particular CHARTYPE value is specified in the Parameters window or in a GOPTIONS statement, the Rows field that corresponds to the CHARTYPE value overrides the values of the Lrows and Prows fields in the Detail window, and the Cols field that corresponds to the CHARTYPE value overrides the values of the Lcols and Pcols fields in the Detail window.

See "Window Commands" earlier in this chapter for a description of the commands you can use in this window.

Display 25.5 shows a Chartype window from the HP7475 entry in SASHELP.DEVICES.

Display 25.5 *The Chartype Window*

```
┌┌GDEVICE: Chartype─────────────────────────────────────────────────┐
│ Command ===>                                                       │
│                                                                    │
│ Catalog: SASHELP.DEVICES                      Entry:    HP7475     │
│                                                                    │
│ Chartype  Rows   Cols              Font Name            Scalable   │
│                                                                    │
│        0   40    100    ANSI ASCII                         X       │
│        1   40    100    Hp9825 HPL                         X       │
│        2   40    100    French/German                      X       │
│        3   40    100    Scandinavian                       X       │
│        4   40    100    Spanish                            X       │
│        6   40    100    JIS ASCII                          X       │
│        7   40    100    Roman Extensions                   X       │
│        8   40    100    Katakana                           X       │
│        9   40    100    ISO IRV                            X       │
│       30   40    100    ISO Swedish                        X       │
│       31   40    100    ISO Swedish for Names              X       │
│       32   40    100    ISO Norway Version1                X       │
│       33   40    100    ISO German                         X       │
│       34   40    100    ISO French                         X       │
│       35   40    100    ISO United Kingdom                 X       │
│       36   40    100    ISO Italian                        X       │
│                                                                  R─┘
└────────────────────────────────────────────────────────────────────
```

The Chartype window contains two non-editable fields: the Catalog field and the Entry field. The Catalog field shows the catalog in which the device entry is stored. The Entry field displays the device entry you are currently editing or viewing.

Table 25.6 shows the editable fields in the Chartype window. Refer to Chapter 5 for more information about the device parameters in this window. Note that in most cases, a default value of 0 or blank for a field indicates that the device driver chooses a value.

Table 25.6 *Parameters Window Fields*

Field	Expected Value	Default	Description
Chartype	positive integer; 0 to 9999	0	Chartype number associated with a hardware font
Cols	positive integer	0	number of columns in display when font is used
Font Name	character	none	font name associated with Chartype
Rows	positive integer	0	number of rows in display when font is used
Scalable	literal; X | ' '	device dependent	specifies whether font is scalable; can be used with any values for the Rows and Cols fields

The Metagraphics Window

The Metagraphics window is meaningful only if the device entry is for a Metagraphics (user-written) driver. Such drivers can be created when an Institute-supplied device entry cannot be adapted to support your graphics device.

Do not alter the fields in the Metagraphics window unless you are building a Metagraphics driver. See *SAS/GRAPH Software: Using Graphics, Devices* for your operating system for directions on building and using Metagraphics drivers.

See "Window Commands" earlier in this chapter for a list of the commands you can use with this window.

Display 25.6 shows a Metagraphics window that is from the GXTSLINK entry in the SASHELP.DEVICES catalog.

Display 25.6 *The Metagraphics Window*

```
┌GDEVICE: DIRECTORY SASHELP.DEVICES (B)───────────────────────┐
┌GDEVICE: Detail──────────────────────────────────────────────┐
┌GDEVICE: Metagraphics────────────────────────────────────────┐
 Command ===>

 Catalog: SASHELP.DEVICES                        Entry:   GXTSLINK

 Process: GXTSLINK
 Interactive: PROC
 Processinput: METAFILE     Processoutput: _____
 Header: _____
 Trailer: _____
 Headerfile: _____     Trailerfile: _____
 Rotation:  0             Path:  0      Format: CHARACTER
 Colortype: NAME          Nak: _____
 Id: GXTSLINK

 Trantab: _____           Devmap:  _____
 Devtype: _____

   _  HPPJ180  DEV     HP PaintJet (180 dpi)                   11/02/89
   _  HPPJ180T DEV     HP PaintJet (180 dpi /transparency mode) 11/02/89
   _  HPPJ90   DEV     HP PaintJet (90 dpi)                    11/02/89
                                                            ─R─
```

The Metagraphics window contains two non-editable fields: the Catalog field and the Entry field. The Catalog field shows the catalog in which the device entry is stored. The Entry field displays the device entry you are currently editing or viewing.

Table 25.7 shows the editable fields in the Metagraphics window. Refer to Chapter 5 for more information about the device parameters in this window. Note that in most cases, a default value of 0 or blank for a field indicates that the device driver chooses a value.

Table 25.7 *Parameters Window Fields*

Field	Expected Value	Default	Description
Colortype	literal; NAME | RGB | HLS | GRAY | CMY	NAME	type of color specification
Format	literal; CHARACTER | BINARY	CHARACTER	file format of metafile
Header	command	none	command to create HEADER records for driver
Headerfile	fileref	none	fileref for file from which Institute-supplied portion of Metagraphics driver will read header records
Id	character string	none	description string to be used by Metagraphics driver
Interactive	literal; USER | GRAPH | PROC	USER	when user-written portion of driver is invoked
Nak	hexadecimal string not enclosed in quotes and without a trailing X	none	negative handshake response for software handshaking
Path	integer; between 0 and 360	0	increment for hardware text rotation
Process	command	none	command used to invoke user-written part of driver
Processinput	fileref	none	fileref for file that contains metafile
Processoutput	fileref	none	fileref for file that receives output from user-written or vendor-supplied part of Metagraphics driver
Rotation	integer; between 0 and 360.	0	increment of angle by which device can rotate a letter
Trailer	command	none	command to create TRAILER records for driver
Trailerfile	fileref	none	fileref of file from which Metagraphics driver will read TRAILER records

The Gprolog Window

The Gprolog window enables you to specify a hexadecimal string or hexadecimal strings that are sent to the device just before graphics commands are sent.

See "Window Commands" earlier in this chapter for a description of the commands you can use in this window.

Display 25.7 shows a Gprolog window from a modified device driver.

Display 25.7 *The Gprolog Window*

```
┌GDEVICE: DIRECTORY GDEVICE0.DEVICES (E)────────────────────────┐
│┌GDEVICE: Detail────────────────────────────────────────────┐│
││┌GDEVICE: Gprolog────────────────────────────────────────┐ │
│││ Command ===>                                            │ │
│││                                                         │ │
│││  Catalog: GDEVICE0.DEVICES              Entry:   MYHP   │ │
│││                                                         │ │
│││   7E _____ │ │
│││                                                         │ │
│││      _____ │ │
│││      _____ │ │
│││      _____ │ │
│││      _____ │ │
│││      _____ │ │
│││      _____ │ │
│││      _____ │ │
│││      _____ │ │
│││      _____ │ │
│││      _____ │ │
│││      _____ │ │
│└│      _____ │ │
│ │      _____ │ │
│ │      _____ │ │
│ │      _____ │ │
│ │      _____ │ │
│ │      _____R│ │
└─└─────────────────────────────────────────────────────────┘─┘
```

The Gprolog window contains two non-editable fields: the Catalog field and the Entry field. The Catalog field shows the catalog in which the device entry is stored. The Entry field displays the device entry you are currently editing or viewing.

Table 25.8 shows the editable field in the Gprolog window.

Table 25.8 *Gprolog Window Field*

Field	Expected Value	Default	Description
(no label)	hexadecimal string or strings not enclosed in quotes and without a trailing X.	none	hexadecimal string or strings to be sent to device or file before graphics commands; can be overridden by the GPROLOG= graphics option. See Chapter 5 for details.

You can specify character strings (non-hexadecimal) in line mode on ASCII hosts; however, the only way to specify values that can be used by all hosts for the GPROLOG=, GEPILOG=, GSTART=, and GEND= graphics options or device parameters is to use a hexadecimal string. See "Requirements" in "GDEVICE Procedure Description" earlier this chapter for information on how to specify values.

The Gepilog Window

The Gepilog window enables you to specify a hexadecimal string or hexadecimal strings that are sent to the device just after graphics commands are sent.

See "Window Commands" earlier in this chapter for a description of the commands you can use in this window.

Display 25.8 shows a Gepilog window from a modified device driver.

Display 25.8 *The Gepilog Window*

```
┌GDEVICE: DIRECTORY GDEVICE0.DEVICES (E)─────────────────────────────┐
│ ┌GDEVICE: Detail──────────────────────────────────────────────────┐
│ │ ┌GDEVICE: Gepilog─────────────────────────────────────────────────
│ │ │ Command ===>
│ │ │
│ │ │  Catalog: GDEVICE0.DEVICES                       Entry:    MYHP
│ │ │
│ │ │    7F
│ │ │    _____
│ │ │    _____
│ │ │    _____
│ │ │    _____
│ │ │    _____
│ │ │    _____
│ │ │    _____
│ │ │    _____
│ │ │    _____
│ │ │    _____
│ └ │    _____
│   │    _____
│   │    _____
│   │    _____
│   │    _____
│   │    _____
└───────────────────────────────────────────────────────────────R──┘
```

The Gepilog window contains two non-editable fields: the Catalog field and the Entry field. The Catalog field shows the catalog in which the device entry is stored. The Entry field displays the device entry you are currently editing or viewing.

Table 25.9 shows the editable field in the Gepilog window.

Table 25.9 *Gepilog Window Field*

Field	Expected Value	Default	Description
(no label)	hexadecimal string or strings not enclosed in quotes and without a trailing X.	none	hexadecimal string or strings to be sent to device or file after all graphics commands are sent; can be overridden by the GEPILOG= graphics option. See Chapter 5 for details.

You can specify character strings (non-hexadecimal) in line mode on ASCII hosts; however, the only way to specify values that can be used by all hosts for the GPROLOG=, GEPILOG=, GSTART=, and GEND= graphics options or device parameters is to use a hexadecimal string. See "Requirements" in "GDEVICE Procedure Description" earlier this chapter for information on how to specify values.

The Gstart Window

The Gstart window enables you to specify a hexadecimal string or hexadecimal strings that are placed at the beginning of each record of graphics data.

See "Window Commands" earlier in this chapter for a description of the commands you can use in this window.

Display 25.9 shows a Gstart window from a modified device driver.

Display 25.9 The Gstart Window

```
┌GDEVICE: DIRECTORY GDEVICE0.DEVICES (E)──────────────────────────────────┐
┌GDEVICE: Detail──────────────────────────────────────────────────────────┐
┌GDEVICE: Gstart────────────────────────────────────────────────────────
 Command ===>

 Catalog: GDEVICE0.DEVICES                        Entry:    MYHP

   0D0A_____
   _____
   _____
   _____
   _____
   _____
   _____
   _____
   _____
   _____
   _____
   _____
   _____
   _____
   _____
   _____
                                                              ─R─
└──────────────────────────────────────────────────────────────────────────┘
```

The Gstart window contains two non-editable fields: the Catalog field and the Entry field. The Catalog field shows the catalog in which the device entry is stored. The Entry field displays the device entry you are currently editing or viewing.

Table 25.10 shows the editable field in the Gstart window.

Table 25.10 Gstart Window Field

Field	Expected Value	Default	Description
(no label)	hexadecimal string or strings not enclosed in quotes and without a trailing X.	none	hexadecimal string or strings to prefix every record of graphics data sent to device or file; can be overridden with the GSTART= graphics option. See Chapter 5 for details.

You can specify character strings (non-hexadecimal) in line mode on ASCII hosts; however, the only way to specify values that can be used by all hosts for the GPROLOG=, GEPILOG=, GSTART=, and GEND= graphics options or device parameters is to use a hexadecimal string. See "Requirements" in "GDEVICE Procedure Description" earlier this chapter for information on how to specify values.

The Gend Window

The Gend window enables you to specify a hexadecimal string or hexadecimal strings that are placed at the end of each record of graphics data.

See "Window Commands" earlier in this chapter for a list of the commands you can use with this window.

Display 25.10 shows a Gend window from a modified device driver.

Display 25.10 *The Gend Window*

```
┌GDEVICE: DIRECTORY GDEVICE0.DEVICES (E)──────────────────────────────┐
│┌GDEVICE: Detail──────────────────────────────────────────────────┐ │
││┌GDEVICE: Gend────────────────────────────────────────────────────┐
│││ Command ===>                                                     │
│││                                                                  │
│││  Catalog: GDEVICE0.DEVICES                   Entry:    MYHP      │
│││                                                                  │
│││   0D0A                                                           │
│││                                                                  │
│││  _____ │
│││  _____ │
│││  _____ │
│││  _____ │
│││  _____ │
│││  _____ │
│││  _____ │
│││  _____ │
│││  _____ │
│││  _____ │
│││  _____ │
│││  _____ │
│││  _____ │
│││  _____ │
│└│  _____ │
│ │  _____ │
│ │  _____ │
│ └───────────────────────────────────────────────────────────R────┘
└─────────────────────────────────────────────────────────────────────┘
```

The Gend window contains two non-editable fields: the Catalog field and the Entry field. The Catalog field shows the catalog in which the device entry is stored. The Entry field displays the device entry you are currently editing or viewing.

Table 25.11 shows the editable field in the Gend window.

Table 25.11 *Gend Window Field*

Field	Expected Value	Default	Description
(no label)	hexadecimal string or strings not enclosed in quotes and without a trailing X.	none	hexadecimal string or strings to append to the end of every graphics data record; can be overridden with the GEND= graphics option. See Chapter 5 for details.

You can specify character strings (non-hexadecimal) in line mode on ASCII hosts; however, the only way to specify values that can be used by all hosts for the GPROLOG=, GEPILOG=, GSTART=, and GEND= graphics options or device parameters is to use a hexadecimal string. See "Requirements" in "GDEVICE Procedure Description" earlier this chapter for information on how to specify values.

Using the GDEVICE Procedure Windows

The following sections describe some of the general operations you can perform with the GDEVICE windows. Refer to "Window Commands" earlier in this chapter for more operations that can be performed from the windows.

Opening the GDEVICE Windows

To open the GDEVICE windows, submit the PROC GDEVICE statement without the NOFS option as follows:

```
proc gdevice;
run;
```

These statements open the default catalog (either the SASHELP.DEVICES catalog or the GDEVICE0.DEVICES catalog) in browse mode. If you want to edit a device entry, use the CATALOG= option.

By default, the GDEVICE procedure uses the GDEVICE windows if you are in a full-screen environment. GDEVICE windows can be used only in environments and on devices that support full-screen mode.

Moving between Windows

The first window that appears when you enter the GDEVICE window is the DIRECTORY window. To open other windows, you must select a device entry to browse or modify.

After you have selected a device entry, the Detail window appears. From this window, you can open other windows by entering one of the following on the command line:

□ the NEXTSCR command

□ the name of the window you want to open.

You can return to the previous window from any window by using the following commands:

□ the CANCEL command to cancel any modifications and return to the previous window

□ the END command to save the changes and return to the previous window.

Creating a New Device Entry

From the DIRECTORY window in the GDEVICE procedure, you can create a new device entry with two commands, COPY and EDIT.

The preferred method is to use the COPY command to copy an existing device entry into a new member and modify its parameters. The existing device entry can be from any catalog. (See the COPY command in "Window Commands" earlier in this chapter for the syntax and details of copying a device entry from another catalog.)

The second method is to use the EDIT command. By entering the name of the device entry you want to create, you can force the EDIT command to create a blank device entry. Then you can fill in values for the parameters.

With either method, you must provide values for certain parameters. These parameters are listed in "Requirements" in "GDEVICE Procedure Description" earlier in this chapter. If you use the first method, all of the required parameters will already have values. If you use the EDIT command, the GDEVICE procedure prompts you to fill in the appropriate fields.

Modifying an Existing Device Entry

To customize a device entry, create your own catalog and copy the device entries you need into it from the DIRECTORY window. You can then change the copies of the device entries without affecting the original drivers in the SASHELP.DEVICES catalog. (See "Copying and Modifying Device Entries Using the GDEVICE Windows" in "Examples" later in this chapter for the commands to copy and modify a device entry.)

To change the value of a parameter in a window, move the cursor to the value of the field you want to change and enter the new value. If you try to change a field in a device entry supplied by SAS Institute (either the original entry in the SASHELP.DEVICES catalog or a copy), SAS/GRAPH software asks if you really want to change the entry. Answer Y to save modifications and continue or N to cancel the operation.

You can use the SAVE command on the command line to save any changes without closing the window. See "Window Commands" earlier in this chapter for descriptions of the SAVE command.

Closing a Window

To close a window without saving the changes, enter the CANCEL command on the command line. To save your changes, enter the END command on the command line. See "Window Commands" earlier in this chapter for descriptions of the CANCEL and END commands.

Examples

Listing Catalog Entries with Line-Mode Statements

This example shows how to use the GDEVICE procedure with line-mode statements to list the device entries in the SASHELP.DEVICES catalog. Submit these statements one at a time or together.

The following program statement produces Output 25.2:

```
proc gdevice catalog=sashelp.devices nofs;
    list _all_;
```

Output 25.2 *Listing All Device Entries in Line Mode*

NAME	DESCRIPTION	DATE
AGS1000	AGS 1000 terminal	11/02/89
APLPLUS	Apple Laserwriter Plus (PostScript)	11/02/89
APPLELW	Apple Laserwriter (PostScript)	11/02/89
CAL81	CalComp 81 plotter	11/02/89
CAL84	CalComp 84 plotter	11/02/89
CGM	CGM generator--binary output	11/02/89
CGMC	CGM generator w/colors--binary output	11/02/89
CGMCHAR	CGM generator--character format	11/02/89
CGMCLEAR	CGM generator--Clear text format	11/02/89
CGMCRT	CGM for CRTs--binary format	11/02/89
CGMCRTCH	CGM for CRTs--character format	11/02/89
CGMCRTCL	CGM for CRTs--clear text format	11/02/89
CGMHG	CGM file for Harvard Graphics	11/02/89

```
.
. (more device drivers)
.
X4045C          Xerox 4045 printer--10 x 7.5, 75 DPI        11/02/89
X4045L          Xerox 4045 landscape--10 x 7.5, 300 DPI     11/02/89
X4045P          Xerox 4045 portrait--10 x 7.5, 300 DPI      11/02/89
ZETAVUE         ZETAVUE film recorder                       11/02/89
ZETA1453        ZETA 1453 plotter                           11/02/89
ZETA8           ZETA8 plotter--Kromecote roll               11/02/89
ZETA8F          ZETA8 plotter--film roll                    11/02/89
ZETA8K          ZETA8 plotter--Kromecote roll               11/02/89
ZETA8M          ZETA8 plotter--Mylar roll                   11/02/89
ZETA8T          ZETA8 plotter--translucent roll             11/02/89
ZETA8V          ZETA8 plotter--vellum roll                  11/02/89
ZETA887         ZETA887 plotter--Kromecote roll             11/02/89
ZET1453X        ZETA 1453 plotter--non-error correct        11/02/89
NOTE: 699 entries listed.
```

Note: The number of entries displayed depends on the device entries included with your installation of SAS/GRAPH software.

The following program statement produces Output 25.3:

```
list hp7475;
```

Output 25.3 *Listing One Device Entry in Line Mode*

```
                            GDEVICE procedure
                 Listing from SASHELP.DEVICES - Entry HP7475

Orig Driver: HP7475             Module:  SASGDHPL  Model:     307
Description: HP 7475 plotter--B size paper         Type: PLOTTER
*** Institute-supplied ***
Lrows:  40  Xmax:  14.961 in    Hsize:   0.000 in  Xpixels: 15200
Lcols: 100  Ymax:  10.827 in    Vsize:   0.000 in  Ypixels: 11000
Prows:  50                      Horigin: 0.000 in
Pcols:  80                      Vorigin: 0.000 in
Aspect:  0.000                  Rotate:
Driver query:                   Queued messages: N
Gprotocol:                      Paperfeed:  0.000 in
Gaccess: SASGASTD
Gsfname:                        Gsfmode:  PORT    Gsflen:        0
Trantab:                        Devmap:
Devtype:    GTERM


  OPTIONS

  Erase:                Autofeed:            Chartype:    0
  Swap:                 Cell:                Maxcolors:   7
  Autocopy:             Characters:          Repaint:     0
  Handshake:   SOFTWARE Circlearc:           Gcopies:     0
                        Dash:                Gsize:       0
  Prompt - startup: X   Fill:                Speed:       0
           end graph:   Piefill:             Fillinc:    10
           mount pen: X Polyfill:            Maxpoly:     0
           chg paper: X Symbol:              Lfactor:     0
  Promptchars:   '000A010D05000000'X

  Cback:      WHITE              Colortbl:
  Color list:

    BLACK      RED       GREEN     BLUE      ORANGE
    LIME


  CHARTYPE RECORDS

  Chartype Rows  Cols                  Font Name          Scalable
         0   40   100   ANSI ASCII                           Y
         1   40   100   Hp9825 HPL                           Y
         2   40   100   French/German                        Y
         3   40   100   Scandinavian                         Y
         4   40   100   Spanish                              Y
         6   40   100   JIS ASCII                            Y
         7   40   100   Roman Extensions                     Y
         8   40   100   Katakana                             Y
         9   40   100   ISO IRV                              Y
```

(continued on next page)

```
(continued from previous page)
   30    40    100    ISO Swedish                          Y
   31    40    100    ISO Swedish for Names                Y
   32    40    100    ISO Norway Version1                  Y
   33    40    100    ISO German                           Y
   34    40    100    ISO French                           Y
   35    40    100    ISO United Kingdom                   Y
   36    40    100    ISO Italian                          Y
   37    40    100    ISO Spanish                          Y
   38    40    100    ISO Portuguese                       Y
   39    40    100    ISO Norway Version2                  Y
```

To end the GDEVICE procedure, enter

```
quit;
```

Copying and Modifying Device Entries Using the GDEVICE Windows

This example walks you through the steps of copying device entries into a personal catalog and then altering them using the GDEVICE windows.

1. Assign the libref GDEVICE0 to the library that contains (or will contain) your personal catalog by using the LIBNAME statement as follows:

    ```
    libname gdevice0 'SAS-data-library';
    ```

    The GDEVICE1 through GDEVICE9 librefs can be used under certain circumstances. For this example, GDEVICE0 is used. See "Search Order of Catalogs for a Device Driver" earlier in this chapter for an explanation of the other librefs.

2. Execute the GDEVICE procedure using GDEVICE0.DEVICES as the catalog as follows:

    ```
    proc gdevice catalog=gdevice0.devices;
    ```

3. You are now in the DIRECTORY window. No device entries are listed if you have not yet copied any into your catalog. Copy them now. On the command line, execute the COPY command to get device entries for a graphics terminal and a plotter into the GDEVICE0.DEVICES catalog from the Institute-supplied catalog, SASHELP.DEVICES, as follows:

    ```
    copy sashelp.devices.tek4105.dev
    copy sashelp.devices.hp7550.dev
    ```

4. Now use the R command in the selection field to change the names and descriptions of the device entries. You can change the description to reflect the fact that you have changed the device entries from the way they are listed in the SASHELP.DEVICES catalog. Here is a sample name and description for the plotter device entry:

    ```
    MYHP7550     HP plotter, modified from SASHELP.DEVICES, 6-5-89
    ```

5. Now change a field in the terminal device entry. Enter E in the selection field next to the MYHP7550 device entry name, and press ENTER.

6. You are now in the Detail window. Move the cursor to the Hsize field. Enter 10 IN; then move to the Vsize field. Enter 7.5 IN; then move to the command line.

7. Enter the END command on the command line and press ENTER. You are now in the DIRECTORY window. The modifications are saved. If you wanted to cancel the changes, you could enter the CANCEL command (instead of the END command) and press ENTER. If you wanted to save the changes and remain in the window, you could enter the SAVE command.

8. From the DIRECTORY window, enter the END command on the command line and press ENTER.

9. You are now viewing display manager. The next time you use a SAS/GRAPH procedure, you can use the new device entry name whenever you specify a device driver. Even if the device entry name remains the same as the one in the SASHELP.DEVICES catalog, SAS/GRAPH software uses the one in the GDEVICE0.DEVICES catalog.

Creating a Personal Catalog Using Line-Mode Statements

This example walks you through the steps of copying and altering device drivers using line-mode statements. (This example accomplishes the same task as the previous example.)

1. Assign the libref GDEVICE0 to the library that contains (or will contain) your catalog by using a LIBNAME statement as follows:

```
libname gdevice0 'SAS-data-library';
```

2. Submit PROC GDEVICE using the catalog GDEVICE0.DEVICES. Also use the NOFS option.

```
proc gdevice catalog=gdevice0.devices nofs;
```

3. Submit the COPY statement to get device entries for a graphics terminal and a plotter into the GDEVICE0.DEVICES catalog as follows:

```
copy tek4105 from=sashelp.devices newname=mtek4105;
copy hp7550  from=sashelp.devices newname=myhp7550;
```

The NEWNAME= option in the COPY statement specifies the new name. When you change the names, remember to reference the device entries by their new names whenever you specify a device driver in a SAS/GRAPH procedure.

4. Now submit a MODIFY statement to change the description of the MYHP7550 device entry. You can change the description to reflect that you have changed the device entries from the way they are listed in the SASHELP.DEVICES catalog. Here is a sample description for the plotter device entry:

```
modify myhp7550
       description='hp7550 plotter, modified on 7-14-89';
```

5. List the contents of MYHP7550 by submitting the LIST statement as follows:

```
list myhp7550;
```

Examine the Hsize and Vsize fields (scroll until you find them).

6. Now return to the PROGRAM EDITOR window and change the Hsize and Vsize fields in the MYHP7550 entry. Submit the MODIFY statement as follows:

```
modify myhp7550 hsize=10 in vsize=7.5 in;
```

7. Exit the procedure by submitting the QUIT statement as follows:

```
quit;
```

See Also

Chapter 4, "Device Drivers"
for an overview of how device drivers are used in SAS/GRAPH software

Chapter 5, "Graphics Options and Device Parameters Dictionary"
for complete information about all graphics options and device parameters

Chapter 7, "SAS/GRAPH Colors"
for more information on specifying colors for graphics output

Chapter 12, "The GOPTIONS Statement"
for more information about overriding device parameters with graphics options

SAS Language: Reference, Version 6, First Edition
for an explanation of standards used to name catalog entries and for descriptions of global window commands

CHAPTER 26 The GFONT Procedure

Overview

The GFONT procedure displays new or existing fonts and creates user-generated fonts for use in SAS/GRAPH programs. These fonts can contain standard Roman alphabet characters, foreign language characters, symbols, logos, or figures.

The GFONT procedure

□ displays SAS/GRAPH software fonts

□ displays fonts previously generated with the GFONT procedure (user-generated fonts)

□ displays the character codes or hexadecimal values associated with the characters in a font

□ creates stroked fonts or polygon fonts.

Output 26.1 shows the Swiss font as displayed by the GFONT procedure using the US key map. All available characters are displayed. The associated character codes are not shown.

Output 26.1 *Display of the Swiss Font (GR26N01)*

The SWISS Font

```
©   ®   ■   ™   §   "   ¥   °   ¯   ´   ^       ¦   Œ   Ø   Å   Ä   Ö   Ü

ß   Æ   £   ñ   Ñ   Ç   É   I   ¿   '       ó   â   ê   î   ô   û   à

ç   ë   ï   ÿ   ¤   ¶   Pt  f   æ   œ   ø   å   ä   ö   ü   ì   ò   ù

í   ó   ú   á       ¢   .   <   (   +   &   I   $   *   )   ;   ¬   −

/   ¦   ,   %   _   >   ?   :   #   @   '   =   "   a   b   c   d   e

f   g   h   i   j   k   l   m   n   o   p   q   r   ~   s   t   u   v

w   x   y   z   [   ]   {   A   B   C   D   E   F   G   H   I   }   J

K   L   M   N   O   P   Q   R   \   S   T   U   V   W   X   Y   Z   0

1   2   3   4   5   6   7   8   9
```

GR26N01

Output 26.2 shows the Marker font with character codes displayed. The characters in this font are typical of the kind of symbols or logos you can generate with the GFONT procedure. The program for generating the Marker font is included in sample library member GR26N02. (The Marker font is a SAS/GRAPH software font and can be specified like any other Institute-supplied font.)

Output 26.2 *Display of the Marker Font (GR26N02)*

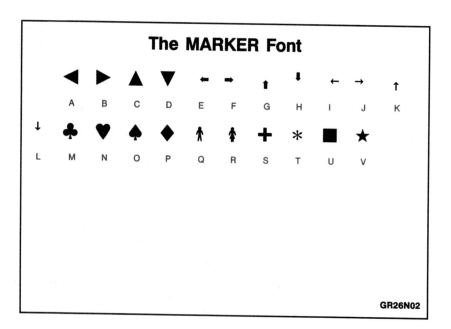

GR26N02

GFONT Procedure Syntax

The GFONT procedure uses the following statements:

□ The PROC GFONT statement is required.

> **PROC GFONT** NAME=*font*
> *mode*
> <*display-options*>
> <*creation-options*>;

□ *mode* must be one of the following:

DATA=*font-data-set*

NOBUILD

□ *display-options* can be one or more of the following:

CTEXT=*text-color*

GOUT=*output-catalog*

HEIGHT=*n*<*units*>

> where *n* is the number of units

NOKEYMAP

NOROMAN

NOROMHEX

REFCOL=*reference-line-color*

REFLINES

ROMCOL=*code-color*

ROMFONT=*font*

ROMHEX

ROMHT=*n*<*units*>

> where *n* is number of units

SHOWALL

SHOWROMAN

□ *creation-options* can be one or more of the following:

BASELINE=*y*

> where *y* is a vertical coordinate

CAPLINE=*y*

> where *y* is a vertical coordinate

CHARSPACETYPE=DATA | FIXED | NONE | UNIFORM

CODELEN=1 | 2

FILLED

KERNDATA=*kern-data-set*

MWIDTH=*n*

> where *n* is the width of the widest character

NODISPLAY

NOKEYMAP

RESOL=1 . . . 4

ROMHEX

SHOWROMAN

SPACEDATA=*space-data-set*

UNIFORM

□ The following statement is optional and local:

NOTE <*options*> <'*text*'>;

□ The following statements are optional and global:

FOOTNOTE<1 . . . 10> <*options*> <'*text*'>;
TITLE<1 . . . 10> <*options*> <'*text*'>;

Options are fully described in "Options" later in this chapter.

Statement Descriptions

The purpose of each statement is described here.

FOOTNOTE	defines the text and appearance of footnotes. FOOTNOTE definitions are used only when the GFONT procedure displays a font. See Chapter 11, "The FOOTNOTE Statement."
NOTE	defines the text and appearance of the notes that appear in the procedure output area. The NOTE statement is used only when the GFONT procedure displays a font. See Chapter 14, "The NOTE Statement."
PROC GFONT	starts the procedure and specifies the name of the font to be displayed or created and the name of the data set to be used if a font is created, as well as any additional input or output options.
TITLE	defines the text and appearance of titles. TITLE definitions are used only when the GFONT procedure displays a font. See Chapter 17, "The TITLE Statement."

GFONT Procedure Description

The GFONT procedure can be used either to display existing software fonts or to create user-generated fonts. Each of these activities has its own requirements, its own process, and its own options (although some options are valid for either process). In this chapter, each topic to which this distinction applies is divided into two sections: "Displaying Fonts" and "Creating Fonts."

Terminology

The following terms are used in the discussion of the GFONT procedure and are defined in the Glossary. Some of these terms are illustrated in Figures 26.1, 26.2, and 26.3.

baseline
capline
font, software
font maximum
font minimum

font units
polygon font
segment
stroked font
type style

Note: The term *uniform font* refers to a font in which all the characters occupy exactly the same amount of space even though the characters themselves are different sizes. Each character in a uniform font is placed in the center of its space, and a fixed amount of space is added between characters. A *proportional font* is a font in which each character occupies a space proportional to its actual width (for example, m occupies more space than i).

Figure 26.1 *GFONT Procedure Terms*

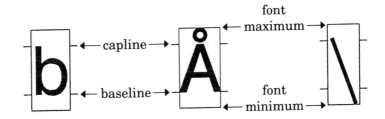

Figure 26.2 illustrates a *stroked font* with several characters from the Simplex font.

Figure 26.2 *Characters from a Stroked Font*

Figure 26.3 illustrates two types of *polygon fonts*: filled and outline. A *filled font* is a polygon font in which the areas between the lines are solid. An *outline font* is a polygon font in which the areas are empty. The fonts illustrated are Century Bold Italic (CENTBI) and Century Bold Italic Empty (CENTBIE).

Figure 26.3 *Filled and Outline Characters from Polygon Fonts*

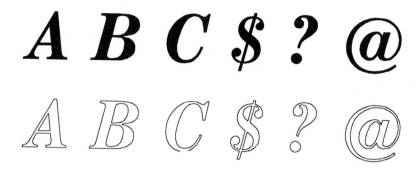

All font characters, regardless of whether they are stroked or polygon, are drawn with line segments. In the GFONT procedure, the term *line segment* means a continuous line that can change direction. For example, the letter C in Figure 26.2 is drawn with one line segment, while the letter A can be drawn with two.

Polygon characters can also be drawn with one or more line segments. In a polygon font, one character can be made up of a single polygon, multiple polygons, or polygons with holes. For example, the letter C in Figure 26.3 is a single polygon with one line segment. The question mark (?) is made up of two polygons, each drawn with a separate line segment. The letter A is one polygon with a hole in it. It is drawn with one line segment that is broken to form the outer boundary of the figure and the boundary of the hole.

Summary of Use

The following sections describe how to use the GFONT procedure to display and create fonts.

Displaying Fonts

Use the GFONT procedure to display a font when you want to do one of the following:

□ review the characters that are available in either Institute-supplied fonts or user-generated fonts

□ see the character codes or the hexadecimal values associated with the characters in a font.

To display a font, you must specify the name of the font with the NAME= argument and include the NOBUILD argument. In addition, you can use options that modify the color and height of displayed font characters, draw reference lines around the characters, or display the associated character codes or hexadecimal values. See "Requirements" and "Options" later in this chapter for details.

For example, to display the Weather font with character codes displayed in the Swiss font, use the following statement:

```
proc gfont name=weather nobuild romfont=swiss;
```

See also "Displaying Fonts Using the SHOWROMAN Option" in "Examples" later in this chapter.

Creating Fonts

You can use the GFONT procedure to create and store fonts of your own design. The GFONT procedure is not limited to creating alphabet fonts. You can use it to create and store any series of figures that you can draw using X and Y coordinates or that you can digitize. The characters or figures in a font can be displayed with any SAS/GRAPH statement or option that allows for font specification and a text string (for example, a TITLE statement). A summary of the procedures and statements that allow you to specify a font is provided in Chapter 6, "SAS/GRAPH Fonts."

To create a font, follow these steps:

1. Create a data set containing font information.

2. Produce the font by invoking the GFONT procedure and specifying the data set that contains the font information. In addition, you can include options to modify the design and appearance of the font.

Creating a font data set   Typically, you use a DATA step to create a SAS data set from which the GFONT procedure generates the font. The data set, which must contain certain variables so it can be used by the GFONT procedure, is referred to as the *font data set* and is specified with the DATA= argument.

Producing the font   After you create the font data set, specify it in the PROC GFONT statement. For example, the following statement uses the data set FONTDATA to generate the font MYLOGO:

```
proc gfont data=fontdata name=mylogo;
```

For a demonstration of the font creation process, see "Creating Figures for a Symbol Font" in "Examples" later in this chapter.

You can modify the appearance of your font in several ways. You can adjust the spacing between characters in the font with the KERNDATA= and SPACEDATA= options. The KERNDATA= option adjusts intercharacter spacing by adding or deleting space between pairs of characters. This is called *kerning*. In addition, the SPACEDATA= option determines the spacing between characters in relation to the height of the font.

Like the DATA= argument, the KERNDATA= and SPACEDATA= options specify SAS data sets that you create and that contain particular variables that affect the spacing of the characters. These data sets are referred to as the *kern data set* and the *space data set*, respectively. The structure and function of the font data set, the kern data set, and the space data set are explained in "Creating Data Sets for the GFONT Procedure" later in this chapter. See also "Creating a Font Using the KERNDATA= Option" and "Creating a Font Using the SPACEDATA= Option" in "Examples" later in this chapter.

Specifying the Libref GFONT0

The GFONT procedure stores user-generated fonts in the location associated with the libref GFONT0. Therefore, before you create a font or display a user-generated font, you must submit a LIBNAME statement that associates the libref GFONT0 with the location where the font is to be stored, as follows:

```
libname gfont0 'SAS-data-library';
```

Since the GFONT0 library is the first place that SAS/GRAPH software looks for fonts, you always should assign that libref to the library containing your personal fonts. If for some reason you have personal fonts in more than one SAS data library, assign them librefs in the sequence GFONT0, GFONT1, GFONT2, and so forth. But remember that the search for entries terminates if there is a break in the sequence; the catalog GFONT1.FONTS is not checked if the libref GFONT0 is undefined.

In addition, if you want to cancel or redefine the libref GFONT*n*, you must submit the following statement:

```
goptions reset=all fcache=0 reset;
```

Note that when you specify RESET, all graphics options are reset to their default values.

Once you have cleared the font cache, you can redefine the libref with a statement with the following form:

```
libname gfont0 'another-SAS-data-library';
```

To cancel a libref use a statement such as the following:

```
libname gfont0;
```

If the libref GFONT0 is not defined, by default SAS/GRAPH software begins searching for fonts in SASHELP.FONTS. For more information on specifying librefs, see Chapter 2, "Running SAS/GRAPH Programs," Chapter 6, and *SAS Language: Reference, Version 6, First Edition.*

Global Statements

All TITLE and FOOTNOTE statements currently in effect are displayed when a font is displayed by the GFONT procedure.

PROC GFONT Statement

The PROC GFONT statement initiates the procedure and names the font to be displayed or created. When the GFONT procedure is used to generate a font, the PROC GFONT statement also specifies the font data set, which provides input to the procedure. When the procedure is used to display a font, it does not require an input data set.

The PROC GFONT statement uses options to modify the design and appearance of the fonts displayed or created and to specify a destination catalog for graphics output.

Requirements

The PROC GFONT statement must name a font to be created or displayed. Additional required arguments depend on whether you are creating or displaying a font.

Displaying Fonts

If you are displaying an existing font, the NAME= and NOBUILD arguments are required.

NAME=*font*
N=*font*
> specifies the font to be displayed. *Font* can be the name of a SAS software font or a font you have previously created. For a complete list of Institute-supplied software fonts, see Chapter 6.

NOBUILD
NB
> specifies that the GFONT procedure is to display an existing font. The NOBUILD argument tells the procedure that no font is being generated and not to look for an input data set.

In order to display a user-generated font, you must submit a LIBNAME statement that associates the libref GFONT0 with the location where the font is stored. See "Specifying the Libref GFONT0" earlier in this chapter for details.

Creating Fonts

If you are creating a font, the NAME= and DATA= arguments are required.

NAME=*font*
N=*font*
> assigns a name to the font you create. *Font* must be a valid SAS name of no more than eight characters. Do not use the name of an Institute-supplied font or NONE for the name of a font. For more information on SAS naming conventions, see *SAS Language: Reference*.

DATA=*font-data-set*
> specifies the SAS data set that the GFONT procedure uses to build the font. The data set must be sorted by the variables CHAR and SEGMENT. If you do not use the DATA= argument, the GFONT procedure uses the most recently created data set as the font data set.

When you create a font, you must submit a LIBNAME statement that associates the libref GFONT0 with the location where the font is to be stored. See "Specifying the Libref GFONT0" earlier in this chapter for details.

> **Note:** If a user-generated font has the same name as an Institute-supplied font and if the libref GFONT0 has been defined, the user-generated font is used because GFONT0 is searched first.

Options

You can use the following options with the PROC GFONT statement. Options for displaying a font are listed first, followed by options for creating a font. Although some options can be used for either font creation or font display, their behavior depends on how they are used. Therefore, these options are described in both sections.

Options for displaying a font can be used when you are creating a font if you also display it (that is, the NODISPLAY option is not used in the PROC GFONT statement). However, none of the display options affect the design and appearance of the stored font except the NOKEYMAP, SHOWROMAN, and ROMHEX options.

Displaying Fonts

You can use the following options with the PROC GFONT statement when you are displaying fonts:

CTEXT=*text-color*
CT=*text-color*
> specifies a color for the body of the characters. If you do not use the CTEXT= option, a color specification is searched for in the following order:
>
> 1. the CTEXT= option in a GOPTIONS statement
> 2. the default, the first color in the colors list.
>
> The CTEXT= value is not stored as part of the font.

GOUT=*output-catalog*
> specifies the SAS catalog in which to save the graphics output generated by the display of the font. The GOUT option is ignored if you use the NODISPLAY option in the PROC GFONT statement. You can use the GREPLAY procedure to view the output stored in the catalog. If you do not use the GOUT= option, catalog entries are written to the default catalog WORK.GSEG, which is erased at the end of your session.

HEIGHT=*n<units>*
H=*n<units>*
> specifies the height of the font characters in number of units, *n*. Height is measured from the minimum font measurement to the capline. By default, HEIGHT=2.
>
> Valid *units* are CELLS (character cells), CM (centimeters), IN (inches), or PCT (percent of graphics output area). If you do not specify *units*, a unit specification is searched for in the following order:
>
> 1. the GUNIT= option in a GOPTIONS statement
> 2. the default unit, CELLS.

NOKEYMAP

specifies that the current key map is ignored when displaying the font and its character codes or hexadecimal values. If you do not use the NOKEYMAP option when you display a font, the current key map remains in effect. If any characters in the font are not available through the current key map, they are not displayed and a warning is issued in the SAS log. This happens when the key map is asymmetrical, that is, not all characters in the font are mapped into the current key map.

Displaying a font using the NOKEYMAP option enables you to see all the characters in the font, including those that are not mapped into your current key map. Note that only those characters that are mapped into your current key map are available (that is, those that are displayed when you display the font without the NOKEYMAP option). For additional information on key maps, see Chapter 6 and Chapter 28, "The GKEYMAP Procedure." See also the NOKEYMAP option description in the next section, "Creating Fonts."

NOROMAN
NR

turns off the automatic display of character codes produced when you use the SHOWROMAN option during font creation.

NOROMHEX
NOHEX

turns off the automatic display of hexadecimal values produced when you use the ROMHEX option during font creation.

REFCOL=*reference-line-color*

specifies a color for reference lines. By default, the first color in the colors list is used.

REFLINES

draws reference lines around each displayed character. Vertical reference lines show the width of the character. Horizontal reference lines show the font maximum and the font minimum, as well as the baseline and the capline. See Figure 26.1 earlier in this chapter for an example of the placement of reference lines.

ROMCOL=*code-color*
RC=*code-color*

specifies the color of the character codes or hexadecimal values displayed with the SHOWROMAN and ROMHEX options. If you do not use the ROMCOL= option, a color specification is searched for in the following order:

1. the CTEXT= option in a GOPTIONS statement

2. the default, the first color in the colors list.

The ROMCOL= value is not stored as part of the font.

ROMFONT=*font*
RF=*font*

> specifies the font for character codes and hexadecimal values displayed by the SHOWROMAN and ROMHEX options. If you do not use the ROMFONT= option, a font specification is searched for in the following order:
>
> 1. the FTEXT= option in a GOPTIONS statement
> 2. the default hardware font, NONE.

ROMHEX
HEX

> displays hexadecimal values below the font characters. If you use both the ROMHEX and SHOWROMAN options, both the character codes and the hexadecimal values are displayed. You also can use the ROMHEX option when creating a font. See the ROMHEX option description in the next section, "Creating Fonts."

ROMHT=*n*<*units* >
RH=*n*<*units* >

> specifies the height of the character codes and the hexadecimal values displayed with the SHOWROMAN and ROMHEX options in number of units, *n*. If you do not use the ROMHT= option, a height specification is searched for in the following order:
>
> 1. the HTEXT= option in a GOPTIONS statement
> 2. the default, ROMHT=1.
>
> Valid *units* are CELLS (character cells), CM (centimeters), IN (inches), and PCT (percentage of the graphics output area). If you do not specify *units*, a unit specification is searched for in the following order:
>
> 1. the GUNIT= option in a GOPTIONS statement
> 2. the default unit, CELLS.

SHOWALL

> displays the font with a space for every possible character position whether or not a font character exists for that position. The characters displayed are those available under your current key map unless you use the NOKEYMAP option. The SHOWALL option usually is used in conjunction with the ROMHEX option, in which case all possible hexadecimal values are displayed. If, under your current key map, a font character is available for a position, it displays above the hexadecimal value. If no character is available for a position, the space above the hexadecimal value is blank. You can use the SHOWALL option to show where undefined character positions fall in the font.

SHOWROMAN
SR

> displays character codes below the font characters even if they are not displayed automatically with the font. If you use both the SHOWROMAN and ROMHEX options, both the character codes and the hexadecimal values are displayed. You also can use the SHOWROMAN option when creating a font. See the SHOWROMAN option description in the next section, "Creating Fonts."

Creating Fonts

You can use the following options with the PROC GFONT statement when you are creating fonts:

BASELINE=*y*
B=*y*

> specifies the vertical coordinate in the font data set that is the baseline of the characters. The baseline is the line upon which the letters rest. If you do not use the BASELINE= option, the GFONT procedure uses the lowest vertical coordinate of the first character in the font data set.

CAPLINE=*y*
C=*y*

> specifies the vertical coordinate in the font data set that is the capline of the characters. The capline is the highest point of normal Roman capitals. If you do not use the CAPLINE= option, the GFONT procedure uses the highest vertical coordinate in the font data set, in which case the capline and the font maximum are the same. See Figure 26.1 earlier in this chapter for an illustration of capline and font maximum.
>
> If you use the CAPLINE= option, then when the GFONT procedure calculates the height of a character, any parts of the character that project above the capline are ignored in the calculation.
>
> You can use this option to prevent an accented capital like Å from being shortened to accommodate the accent. For example, if you do not use the CAPLINE= option, the capline and the font maximum are the same and the A is shortened to make room for the accent below the capline. However, if CAPLINE= is used, the top of the letter A is at the capline, and the accent is drawn above the capline and below the font maximum.

CHARSPACETYPE=DATA | FIXED | NONE | UNIFORM
CSP=DATA | FIXED | NONE | UNIFORM

> specifies the type of intercharacter spacing. The following are valid values:

> DATA
>> specifies that the first observation for each character sets the width of that character. When CHARSPACETYPE=DATA, the PTYPE variable is required, and the observation that specifies the width of the character must have a PTYPE value of W. See "The Font Data Set" later in this chapter for details on the PTYPE variable.
>>
>> Intercharacter spacing is included in the character's width. For example, if the first observation for the letter A specifies a character width of 10 units and the A itself occupies only 8 units, the remaining 2 units serve as intercharacter spacing.
>>
>> **Note:** The character can extend beyond the width specified in the first observation if desired.

> FIXED
>> adds a fixed amount of space between characters based on the font size. The width of the individual character is determined by the data that generate the character.

(CHARSPACETYPE= continued) NONE specifies that no space is added between characters. The width of the individual character is determined by the data that generate the character. This type of spacing is useful for script fonts in which the characters should appear connected.

UNIFORM specifies that the amount of space used for each character is uniform rather than proportional. This means that each character occupies the same amount of space. For example, in uniform spacing m and i occupy the same amount of space, whereas in proportional spacing m occupies more space than i. In uniform spacing, the character is always centered in the space and a fixed space is added between characters.

When UNIFORM is specified, the amount of space used for each character is one of the following:

☐ by default, the width of the widest character in the font.

☐ the width specified by the MWIDTH= option. See the MWIDTH= option description later in this section for details.

Specifying CHARSPACETYPE=UNIFORM is the same as using the UNIFORM option.

By default, CHARSPACETYPE=FIXED.

CODELEN=1 | 2
specifies the length in bytes of the CHAR variable. By default, CODELEN=1. To specify double-byte character sets for languages such as Chinese, Japanese, or Korean, use CODELEN=2. If you specify a double-byte character set, you cannot specify kerning or space adjustment with the KERNDATA= or SPACEDATA= options.

FILLED
F
specifies that the characters in a user-generated polygon font are filled.

KERNDATA=*kern-data-set*
KERN=*kern-data-set*
specifies the SAS data set that contains kerning information. When the KERNDATA= option is used during font creation, the data contained in the kern data set are applied to the font and stored with it. You cannot specify kerning for a double-byte character set created by using the option CODELEN=2.

See "The Kern Data Set" later in this chapter for more information.

MWIDTH=*n*
specifies the width of a character in a uniform font, where *n* is the number of font units. The MWIDTH= option is only valid when uniform spacing is specified by using the UNIFORM option or by specifying CHARSPACETYPE=UNIFORM. If you do not use MWIDTH=, the default is the width of the widest character in the font (usually the letter m).

Typically, you use the MWIDTH= option to tighten the spacing between characters. To do this, specify a smaller value (narrower width) for *n*.

Figure 26.4 shows the effect of decreasing the space allowed for uniformly spaced characters.

Figure 26.4 *Using the MWIDTH= Option to Modify Spacing*

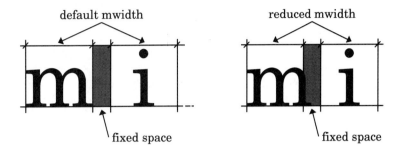

See also the CHARSPACETYPE= option description earlier in this section for more information on intercharacter spacing and uniform fonts. See also the UNIFORM option description later in this section.

NODISPLAY
ND

specifies that the GFONT procedure is not to display the font that it is creating.

NOKEYMAP

specifies that the current key map is ignored when you generate and use the font that is being created, and that the character codes you enter are not mapped in any way before being displayed. As a result, the generated font is *never* affected by any setting of the KEYMAP= graphics option.

▶ *Caution: Fonts generated with the NOKEYMAP option are never affected by any setting of the KEYMAP= graphics option.*

By default, the NOKEYMAP option is *not* used; in which case, when you build a font, the current key map is applied to the values in the CHAR variable. However, your current key map may not be symmetrical; that is, two or more input character codes may be mapped to the same output character. For example, if A is mapped to B, then both A and B map to B, but nothing maps to A. In this case, more than one code in your input data set can map to the same character in the resulting font. For example, if A and B are values of CHAR, both map to B. If this happens, a message indicating the problem characters is displayed in the SAS log. To solve this problem, you can do one of the following:

□ change the character code of one of the characters

□ eliminate one of the characters

□ use the NOKEYMAP option.

Using the NOKEYMAP option means that your font works correctly only if the end user's host or controller encoding is the same as the encoding used to create the input data set.

See also the NOKEYMAP option description in the previous section, "Displaying Fonts."

RESOL=1 . . . 4
R=1 . . . 4

controls the resolution of the fonts by specifying the number of bytes (1 through 4) for storing coordinates in the font. The GFONT procedure provides three resolution levels (RESOL=3 produces the same resolution level as RESOL=4). By default, RESOL=1.

The higher the number, the closer together the points that define the character can be spaced. A high value specifies a denser set of points for each character so that the characters approximate smooth curved lines at very large sizes. RESOL=2 works well for most applications; RESOL=3 or 4 may be too dense to be practical.

The table below shows the resolution number and the maximum number of distinct points that can be defined horizontally or vertically.

Resolution	Number of Distinct Points
1	254
2	32,766
3	2,147,483,646
4	2,147,483,646

ROMHEX
HEX

specifies that hexadecimal values are displayed automatically below the font characters when the font is displayed by the GFONT procedure. See also the SHOWROMAN option description later in this section. If you use the ROMHEX option for a font you create, you can later use the NOROMHEX option to suppress display of the hexadecimal values. See also the descriptions of the ROMHEX and NOROMHEX options in the previous section, "Displaying Fonts."

SHOWROMAN
SR

specifies that character codes are displayed automatically below the font characters when the font is displayed by the GFONT procedure. See also the ROMHEX option description earlier in this section. If you use the SHOWROMAN option for a font you create, you can later use the NOROMAN option to suppress display of the character codes. See also the descriptions of the SHOWROMAN and NOROMAN options in the previous section, "Displaying Fonts."

SPACEDATA=*space-data-set*
SPACE=*space-data-set*

specifies the SAS data set containing font spacing information. When the SPACEDATA= option is used during font creation, the data contained in the space data set are applied to the font and stored with it. You cannot specify space adjustment for a double-byte character set created by using the option CODELEN=2.

See "The Space Data Set" later in this chapter for more information.

UNIFORM

U

> specifies that characters are spaced uniformly rather than
> proportionately. Using the UNIFORM option is the same as specifying
> CHARSPACETYPE=UNIFORM. See the CHARSPACETYPE= option
> description earlier in this section for details. See also the MWIDTH=
> option description for information on controlling the width of the
> characters in a uniform font.

Creating Data Sets for the GFONT Procedure

The GFONT procedure uses three types of data sets: the font data set, the
kern data set, and the space data set. Each type of data set must contain
certain variables and meet certain requirements. The following sections
explain what each data set contains, how it is built, and what the
requirements of the variables are.

The Font Data Set

The font data set consists of a series of observations that include the
horizontal and vertical coordinate values and line segment numbers the
GFONT procedure uses to generate each character. In addition, each
observation must include a character code that is associated with the font
character and is used to specify the font character in a text string. The
font data set also determines whether the font is stroked or polygon.

A font data set that generates a polygon font produces an outline font
by default. You can use the FILLED option with the same data set to
generate a filled font.

The variables in the font data set must be assigned certain names and
types. The following four variables are required:

CHAR

SEGMENT

X

Y.

In addition, the data set can include the following variables:

LP

PTYPE.

Table 26.1 summarizes the characteristics of the font data set variables,
which are described in detail in "Font Data Set Variables" later in this
section.

Table 26.1 *Font Data Set Variables*

Variable	Description	Type	Length	Valid Values	Use in Stroked Fonts	Use in Polygon Fonts
CHAR	the character code associated with the font character	character	1 or 2	keyboard characters or hexadecimal values	required	required
LP	the type of line segment being drawn, either a line or a polygon	character	1	L or P	optional	required
PTYPE	the type of data in the observation	character	1	V or C or W	optional	optional
SEGMENT	the number of the line segment or polygon being drawn	numeric		number	required	required
X	the horizontal coordinate	numeric		number	required	required
Y	the vertical coordinate	numeric		number	required	required

Font Data Set Variables

The following variables are used in font data sets:

CHAR

provides a code for the character or figure being created. CHAR is a character variable with a length of 1 or 2 and is required for all fonts.

▶ ***Caution:*** *Using reserved or undefined hexadecimal codes as CHAR values may require the use of the NOKEYMAP option.*

The CHAR variable takes any character as its value, including characters that you can enter from your keyboard and hexadecimal values from '00'x to 'FF'x. (If you use hexadecimal values as CHAR values, your font may not work correctly under a key map that is different from the one under which the font was created because positions that are not defined in one key map may be defined in another.) When you specify the code character in a text string, the associated font character is drawn.

For example, if you create a Roman alphabet font, typically the characters you specify for CHAR are keyboard characters that match the character in the font. All the observations that build the letter A have a CHAR value of A, and specifying 'A' in a text string produces A in the output.

However, if you build a symbol font, the symbols may not have corresponding keyboard characters. In that case, you select a character or hexadecimal value to represent each symbol in the font and assign it to CHAR. For example, in the Special font, the letter G is assigned as the code for the fleur-de-lis symbol. When the code is specified in a text string, the associated symbol is displayed.

If the CODELEN= option is set to 2, the values for CHAR represent two characters, such as AA, or a four-digit hexadecimal value, such as '00A5'x.

LP

tells the GFONT procedure whether the coordinates of each segment form a line or a polygon. LP is a character variable with a length of 1. It is required for polygon fonts but optional for stroked fonts. The LP variable can be assigned either of the following values:

L   lines

P   polygons.

Every group of line segments with an LP value of P is designated as a polygon; if the observations do not draw a completely closed figure, the program closes the figure automatically.

For example, the following observations do not contain an LP variable. They produce a shape like the one in Figure 26.5.

OBS	CHAR	SEG	X	Y
1	b	1	1	1
2	b	1	1	3
3	b	1	3	3
4	b	1	3	1

Figure 26.5 *Using an LP Value of Line*

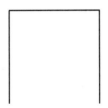

An LP variable with a value of P for all observations added to the data set produces a complete box like the one in Figure 26.6.

OBS	CHAR	SEG	X	Y	LP
1	b	1	1	1	P
2	b	1	1	3	P
3	b	1	3	3	P
4	b	1	3	1	P

(LP continued)

Figure 26.6 *Using an LP Value of Polygon*

The LP variable allows you to mix lines and polygons when creating characters in a font. For example, the following observations produce the single figure composed of a polygon and a line segment shown in Figure 26.7:

OBS	CHAR	SEG	X	Y	LP
1	b	1	1	1	P
2	b	1	1	3	P
3	b	1	3	3	P
4	b	1	3	1	P
5	b	2	0	0	L
6	b	2	2	4	L
7	b	2	4	0	L

Figure 26.7 *Mixing LP Values of Line and Polygon*

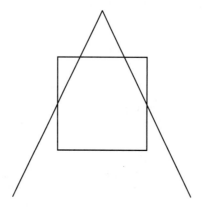

PTYPE
   tells the GFONT procedure what type of data are in the observation. PTYPE is a character variable of length 1 that is optional for both stroked and polygon fonts. For each observation, the PTYPE variable

assigns a characteristic to the point that is determined by the X and Y values. The PTYPE variable can be assigned any of the following values:

V   normal point in the line segment

C   center of a circular arc joining two V points

W   width value for CHARSPACETYPE=DATA.

If the GFONT procedure encounters the sequence V-C-V in consecutive observations, it draws an arc that connects the two V points and has its center at the C point. If a circle cannot be centered at C and pass through both V points, the results are unpredictable. Arcs are limited to 106 degrees or less.

If you specify an observation with a PTYPE value of W, it must always be the first observation for a character. Instead of providing digitizing data to the procedure, the observation gives the minimum and maximum X values for the character. Note that in this case, the Y variable observation actually contains the maximum X value. Usually, these values include a little extra space for intercharacter spacing. Use a PTYPE of W only if you have specified CHARSPACETYPE=DATA; otherwise, the points are ignored. See the CHARSPACETYPE= option description earlier in this chapter for more information on intercharacter spacing.

If you do not specify a PTYPE variable in the font data set, all points are assumed to be V-type points.

The following observations illustrate how the PTYPE variable is used to draw an arc similar to Figure 26.8. (After the figure was generated, a grid was overlaid on it to show the location of the points.) A comment following each observation explains its function.

OBS	CHAR	SEG	X	Y	LP	PTYPE	Comment
1	a	1	40	60	P	W	define width of character as 20 font units, which is the number of units from left margin, 40, to right margin, 60
2	a	1	45	40	P	V	start line segment at position 45,40
3	a	1	45	50	P	V	draw a line to position 45,50, which is start point of arc
4	a	1	45	40	P	C	draw an arc whose center is at 45,40
5	a	1	55	40	P	V	finish drawing the arc at 55,40

(PTYPE continued)

Figure 26.8 *Using the PTYPE Variable to Create an Arc*

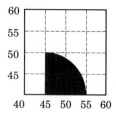

Note the following:

□ Three observations are required to draw the arc: observation 3 and observation 5 denote the start point and endpoint of the arc, respectively, and observation 4 locates the center of the arc.

□ The figure is closed because the line segments have an LP value of P (polygon).

The font containing the figure of the arc was generated with a PROC GFONT statement like the following:

```
proc gfont data=arc name=arcfig charspacetype=data filled;
```

Note that the GFONT procedure uses the CHARSPACETYPE= option with a value of DATA to specify that the first observation sets the width of the character. The FILLED option fills the area of the arc.

SEGMENT

numbers the line segments that compose a character or symbol. SEGMENT is a numeric variable that is required for both polygon and stroked fonts. All the observations for a given line segment have the same segment number. The segment number changes when a new line segment starts.

When the GFONT procedure draws a stroked character with more than one line segment (for example, the letter E), or a polygon character with a hole (for example, the letter A), it needs to know when one line stops and where the next line begins. There are two ways to do this, as follows:

1. Change the segment number when a new line segment starts. If the value of LP is L (line), changing segment numbers tells the GFONT procedure not to connect the last point in line segment 1 and the first point in line segment 2. If the value of LP is P (polygon), changing segment numbers causes both of the following:

   □ The last point in line segment 1 is joined to the first point in line segment 1, thus closing the polygon.

   □ The program starts a new polygon. If the value of CHAR has not changed, the new polygon is part of the same character.

   Use this method for characters that are composed of two polygons, such as a question mark (?). If you are drawing a polygon with a hole in it, such as the letter A, use the second method.

2. Keep the same segment number for all lines, but insert an observation with missing values for X and Y between the observation that marks the end of the first line and the observation

that begins the next line. For example, if you are drawing the letter O, insert an observation with a missing value between the line that draws the outer circle and the beginning of the line that draws the inner circle.

The first method is preferred unless you are creating a polygon character with a hole in it. In this case, you should separate the lines with a missing value and keep the same segment numbers. (Note that if you use separate line segments when you create a polygon with a hole, the results may be unpredictable.) For example, observations such as the following from a data set called BOXES were used to draw the hollow square in Figure 26.9. The data points that form the figure are laid out on a grid shown next to the square.

OBS	CHAR	SEG	X	Y	LP
1	b	1	1	1	P
2	b	1	1	3	P
3	b	1	3	3	P
4	b	1	3	1	P
5	b	1	–	–	P
6	b	1	0	0	P
7	b	1	0	4	P
8	b	1	4	4	P
9	b	1	4	0	P

Note that observation 5, which has missing values for X and Y, separates the observations that draw the inner box from those that draw the outer box and that the segment number is the same for all the observations. Figure 26.9 was generated with a GFONT statement like the following:

```
proc gfont data=boxes name=boxes filled;
```

Note that the FILLED option is included and that only the space between the two squares is filled.

Figure 26.9 *Drawing Nested Polygons*

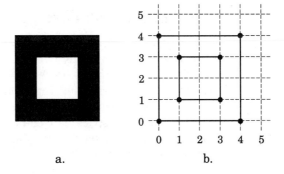

a. b.

See also "Terminology" earlier in this chapter for additional information on line segments.

X
Y

specify the horizontal and vertical coordinates of the points for each character. These variables must be numeric, and they must be named X and Y for the horizontal and vertical coordinates, respectively. Their values describe the position of the points on the character. These values can be in any range you choose, but both variables must describe the character in the same scale or font units. In other words, 10 horizontal units must be the same distance as 10 vertical units. Vertical coordinates for all characters should be defined on the same baseline.

Note: When PTYPE=W is specified, both X and Y contain horizontal coordinate values.

Creating a Font Data Set

You can create a font data set by digitizing the shape of the characters or figures either manually or with special digitizing equipment. To create a font data set by digitizing the characters manually, follow these steps:

1. Determine the coordinate points for each line segment by drawing the characters on a grid.

2. Lay out the observations for each character. Each observation describes a move from one point to another along a line segment. For each line segment, enter the coordinate points in the order in which they are drawn. For a stroked font, when you start a new line segment, change the segment number. For a polygon font, when you start a new polygon, change the line segment number. If the polygon has a hole in it, as in the letter **O**, keep the line segment number and separate the lines with a missing value. Use the same value for CHAR for all the observations that describe one character.

3. Create a SAS data set containing the variables CHAR, SEGMENT, X, and Y, and read in the data for each observation. Include the variables LP and PTYPE if necessary.

4. Sort the data set by CHAR and SEGMENT.

5. Assign the font data set with the DATA= argument.

This process is illustrated in "Creating Figures for a Symbol Font" in "Examples" later in this chapter.

The Kern Data Set

The kern data set consists of observations that specify how much space to add or remove between any two characters when they appear in combination. This process, called kerning, increases or decreases space between the characters. Kerning usually is applied to certain pairs of characters that, because of their shape, have too much space between them. Reducing the space between characters may allow part of one character to extend over the body of the next. Examples of some combinations that should be kerned are AT, AV, AW, TA, VA, and WA.

Kerning is applied to the intercharacter spacing that is specified by the CHARSPACETYPE= option (except for uniform fonts). You can refine the kerning of your characters as little or as much as you like. The kern data set is assigned with the KERNDATA= option.

The kern data set must contain the following variables, which are described in "Kern Data Set Variables" below:

CHAR1

CHAR2

XADJ.

Kern Data Set Variables

The following variables are used in kern data sets:

CHAR1

>   specifies the first character in the pair to be kerned. CHAR1 is a character variable with a length of 1.

CHAR2

>   specifies the second character in the pair to be kerned. CHAR2 is a character variable with a length of 1.

XADJ

>   specifies the amount of space to add or remove between the two characters. XADJ is a numeric variable that uses the same font units as the font data set. The value of XADJ specifies the horizontal adjustment to be applied to CHAR2 whenever CHAR1 is followed immediately by CHAR2. Negative numbers decrease the spacing, and positive numbers increase the spacing.

Creating a Kern Data Set

Each observation in a kern data set names the pair of characters to be kerned and the amount of space to be added or deleted between them. To create a kern data set, follow these steps:

1. Select the pairs of characters to be kerned, and specify the space adjustment (in font units) for each pair as a positive number (more space) or negative number (less space).

2. Create a SAS data set containing the variables CHAR1, CHAR2, and XADJ; produce one observation for each pair of characters and the corresponding space adjustment.

3. Sort the kern data set by CHAR1 and CHAR2.

4. Assign the kern data set with the KERNDATA= option.

This process is illustrated in "Creating a Font Using the KERNDATA= Option" in "Examples" later in this chapter.

The Space Data Set

As the height (point size) of a font increases, less space is required between letters in relation to their height. If the point size decreases, more space may be needed. The space data set tells the GFONT procedure how much to increase or decrease the intercharacter spacing for a given point size. Like kerning, spacing is added to or subtracted from the intercharacter spacing specified by the CHARSPACETYPE= option. However, kerning applies the adjustment to specified pairs of characters, while spacing is applied uniformly to all characters.

Values specified in the space data set are added to the normal intercharacter spacing and any kerning data. Normal intercharacter spacing is determined by the CHARSPACETYPE= option. The space data set must contain the following variables, which are described in "Space Data Set Variables" below:

SIZE

ADJ.

Space Data Set Variables

The following variables are used in space data sets:

SIZE

specifies the point size of the font. SIZE is a numeric variable.

ADJ

specifies the spacing adjustment for the point size in hundredths (1/100) of a point. (A point is equal to 1/72 of an inch.) ADJ is a numeric variable. Positive values for the ADJ variable increase the spacing between characters; negative values reduce the space.

Creating a Space Data Set

Each observation in a space data set specifies a point size (SIZE) and the amount of space (ADJ) to be added or subtracted between characters when a font of that point size is requested. If a point size is specified that is not in the space data set, the adjustment for the next smaller size is used. To create a space data set, follow these steps:

1. Determine the amount of adjustment required for typical point sizes; positive numbers increase spacing, and negative numbers decrease spacing.

2. Create a SAS data set containing the variables SIZE and ADJ; produce one observation for each point size and corresponding space adjustment,

3. Sort the space data set by SIZE.

4. Assign the space data set with the SPACEDATA= option.

This process is illustrated in "Creating a Font Using the SPACEDATA= Option" in "Examples" later in this chapter.

Examples

The following examples illustrate displaying fonts and creating fonts with the GFONT procedure.

Displaying Fonts Using the SHOWROMAN Option

This example illustrates the SHOWROMAN option, which displays the character codes associated with the font characters being displayed. A display such as the one shown in Output 26.3 shows which keyboard character you enter to produce the Greek character you want. In addition, this example shows how to modify the appearance of both the font characters and the character codes when they are displayed.

The following program statements produce Output 26.3:

```
    /* set the graphics environment */
goptions reset=global gunit=pct border
        ftext=swissb htitle=6 htext=3;

    /* define title and footnote */
title 'The GREEK Font with Character Codes';
footnote j=r 'GR26N03 ';

    /* display the GREEK font with character codes */
proc gfont name=greek
        nobuild
        height=3.5
        romcol=red
        romfont=swissl
        romht=2.5
        showroman;
run;
```

Output 26.3 *Display of the Greek Font with Character Codes (GR26N03)*

This example illustrates the following features:

□ The NOBUILD option indicates that the font specified in the NAME= argument is an existing font.

□ The HEIGHT= option specifies the height of the Greek characters.

□ The ROMCOL=, ROMFONT=, and ROMHT= options assign the color, type style, and height of the character codes.

□ The SHOWROMAN option displays the character codes.

Creating Figures for a Symbol Font

This example shows how to create three simple figures. (The code for the first two figures is taken from the program for the Marker font, which is included in sample library member GR26N02.) Each figure is laid out on a grid that is 64 font units square.

The first figure, a right-pointing triangle that is assigned the character code A, is a polygon drawn with three straight lines. Figure 26.10 shows the figure and its coordinate points laid out on a grid.

Figure 26.10 Diagram of
Right-Pointing Triangle Figure

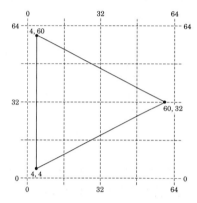

The second figure, a heart that is assigned the character code B, uses the PTYPE variable combination V-C-V to draw the arcs that make up the top of the heart. Each side requires two arcs. Since the arcs are continuous, the observation that marks the end of one arc is also the beginning of the next arc. The heart is drawn beginning at the bottom point and continuing counterclockwise. Figure 26.11 shows the figure and its coordinate points laid out on a grid.

Figure 26.11 Diagram of
Heart Figure

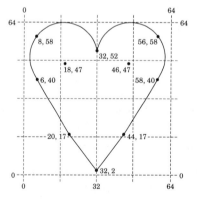

The third figure, a circle with a slash through it that is assigned the character code C, is composed of three polygons: a circle and two empty arcs. An observation with missing values separates the observations defining each of the three polygons. The outer circle is defined by the first group of observations. The empty arcs are drawn with three continuous arcs using the PTYPE variable pattern V-C-V-C-V-C-V. The straight line that closes the arc is drawn automatically by the GFONT procedure in order to complete the polygon. Since all the polygons are part of one character, the continuous space they define is filled. Figure 26.12 shows the figure and some of its coordinate points laid out on a grid.

Figure 26.12 *Diagram of*
Circle with Slash Figure

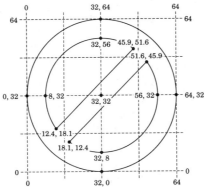

The following program statements produce Output 26.4:

```
      /* assign the libref GFONT0 */
libname gfont0 'SAS-data-library';

      /* set the graphics environment */
goptions reset=global gunit=pct border
         ftext=swissb htitle=6 htext=3;

      /* create the font data set FIGURES              */
      /* for a triangle, a heart, and a circle with slash */
data figures;
   input char $ ptype $ x y segment lp $;
   cards;
A    W    0    64   0    P
A    V    4    4    1    P
A    V    60   32   1    P
A    V    4    60   1    P
A    V    4    4    1    P
B    W    0    64   0    P
B    V    32   2    1    P
B    V    44   17   1    P
B    V    58   40   1    P
B    C    46   47   1    P
B    V    56   58   1    P
B    C    46   47   1    P
B    V    32   52   1    P
B    C    18   47   1    P
B    V    8    58   1    P
B    C    18   47   1    P
B    V    6    40   1    P
B    V    20   17   1    P
B    V    32   2    1    P
C    W    0    64   0    P
C    V    32   64   1    P
C    C    32   32   1    P
C    V    64   32   1    P
C    C    32   32   1    P
C    V    32   0    1    P
C    C    32   32   1    P
C    V    0    32   1    P
```

```
C    C    32    32    1    P
C    V    32    64    1    P
C    V    .     .     1    P
C    V    12.4  18.1  1    P
C    C    32    32    1    P
C    V    8     32    1    P
C    C    32    32    1    P
C    V    32    56    1    P
C    C    32    32    1    P
C    V    45.9  51.6  1    P
C    V    .     .     1    P
C    V    51.6  45.9  1    P
C    C    32    32    1    P
C    V    56    32    1    P
C    C    32    32    1    P
C    V    32    8     1    P
C    C    32    32    1    P
C    V    18.1  12.4  1    P
;
run;


   /* define title and footnote */
title 'A Font of Three Figures';
footnote j=r 'GR26N04  ';


   /* generate and display the font FIGURES */
proc gfont data=figures
           name=figures
           filled
           height=1in
           ctext=red
           showroman
           romht=.5in
           resol=2;
run;
```

Output 26.4 *A Font of Three Figures (GR26N04)*

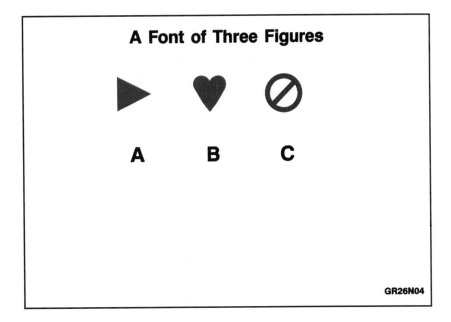

This example illustrates the following features:

□ The LIBNAME statement associates the LIBREF GFONT0 with the SAS data library in which the font catalog is stored.

□ In the PROC GFONT statement, the DATA= argument names the input data set that is used to generate the font and the NAME= argument names the font that the GFONT procedure generates.

□ The FILLED option specifies a filled polygon font.

□ The HEIGHT= and CTEXT= options specify the height and color of the figures in the font display. The height specification and the color specification are not stored with the font.

□ The SHOWROMAN option requests automatic display of the character codes whenever the font is displayed by the GFONT procedure.

□ The ROMHT= option specifies the height of the character codes in the font display. The ROMHT= specification is not stored with the font.

□ The RESOL= option is set to 2 to improve the resolution of the lines.

□ By default, the newly generated font is displayed. (The NODISPLAY option is not used.)

Creating a Font Using the KERNDATA= Option

This example uses the KERNDATA= option to generate a font in which the space between specified pairs of letters is reduced. The font created for this example consists of the letters A, D, and T only. This example has two parts, as follows:

□ The first part creates the data set FONTDATA and generates and displays FONT1.

□ The second part creates the data set KERN1 and the kerned font, FONT2, and compares the spacing between the characters from the two fonts.

Creating FONT1

The following program statements produce Output 26.5:

```
    /* assign the libref GFONT0 */
libname gfont0 'SAS-data-library';

    /* set the graphics environment */
goptions reset=global gunit=pct border
        ftext=swissb htitle=6 htext=3;

    /* create the data set FONTDATA */
data fontdata;
    input char $ x y segment ptype $;
    cards;
A  41  59    1  W
A  50  62    1  V
more data lines
T  43  62    2  V
T  57  62    2  V
;
run;

    /* define title and footnote */
title 'The FONT1 Font';
footnote j=r 'GR26N05(a)  ';

    /* generate and display FONT1 */
proc gfont data=fontdata
        name=font1
        charspacetype=data;
run;
```

Output 26.5 *The FONT1 Font (GR26N05(a))*

This part of the example illustrates the following features:

□ The LIBNAME statement associates the LIBREF GFONT0 with the SAS data library in which the font catalog is stored.

□ In the DATA step, the first observation for each character has a PTYPE variable value of W, which indicates that the observation specifies the width of the character.

□ CHARSPACETYPE=DATA means that the first observation for each character specifies its width. A is 18 font units wide, D is 21, and T is 16.

□ Since none of these three letters extend below the baseline, the BASELINE= option is not used. However, if characters with descenders were added to the font, using the BASELINE= option would provide a constant baseline.

Creating FONT2 and Comparing to FONT1

The following program statements create the font with kerning data and produce Output 26.6:

```
    /* create the kern data set KERN1 */
data kern1;
   input char1 $ char2 $ xadj;
   cards;
A T -4
D A -3
T A -4
;
run;

   /* generate the font containing kerning data */
proc gfont data=fontdata
         name=font2
         charspacetype=data
         kerndata=kern1
         nodisplay;
run;

   /* define title and footnote for the graph */
title 'Unkerned and Kerned Characters';
footnote j=r 'GR26N05(b)  ';

   /* define a title using the unkerned font    */
title3 lspace=6 f=font1 h=10 j=l 'DATA';

   /* define a title using the kerned font */
title4 lspace=4 f=font2 h=10 j=l 'DATA';

   /* display the titles */
proc gslide;
run;
quit;
```

Output 26.6 *Comparison of Kerned and Unkerned Text (GR26N05(b))*

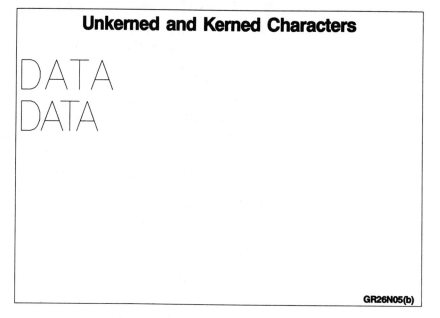

This part of the example illustrates the following features:

□ The variable XADJ specifies the amount of correction to be applied to CHAR2 when it follows CHAR1. Negative values for the XADJ variable bring the two characters closer together.

□ The KERNDATA= option includes the data in KERN1 when FONT2 is created.

□ The NODISPLAY option suppresses display of FONT2 after it is generated.

□ In Output 26.6, the characters A, D, and T are shown as the word DATA. The first line uses the unkerned font, FONT1, and the second line uses the kerned font, FONT2. Note that the characters in FONT2 are spaced more closely than the characters in FONT1.

Creating a Font Using the SPACEDATA= Option

This example shows how to use the SPACEDATA= option with a space data set to generate a font in which intercharacter spacing is adjusted according to the height of the characters. The font created for this example consists of the letters A, D, and T only.

This example does the following:

1. generates FONT1 from the data set FONTDATA. See the previous example in this section for details on creating FONT1.

2. uses the data set SPACE1 to generate FONT3, which is a space adjusted version of FONT1.

3. compares the spacing between the characters from the two fonts.

The following program statements produce Output 26.7:

```
   /* assign the libref GFONT0 */
libname gfont0 'SAS-data-library';

   /* set the graphics environment */
goptions reset=global gunit=pct border
         ftext=swissb htitle=6 htext=3;

   /* create the data set FONTDATA */
data fontdata;
   input char $ x y segment ptype $;
   cards;
A  41  59   1  W
A  50  62   1  V
more data lines
T  43  62   2  V
T  57  62   2  V
;
run;

   /* create the space data set SPACE1 */
data space1;
   input size adj;
   cards;
 6    40
12     0
18   -40
24   -90
30  -150
36  -300
42  -620
;
run;

   /* generate the font containing spacing data */
proc gfont data=fontdata
           name=font3
           charspacetype=data
           spacedata=space1
           nodisplay;
run;

   /* define title and footnote for the graph */
title 'Spacing Adjusted According to Point Size';
footnote j=r 'GR26N06   ';
```

```
              /* compare text with and without spacing adjustments */
           title2;
           title3  f=font3 h=.25in j=1 'DATA';   /* spacing at 18 points */
           title4  f=font1 h=.25in j=1 'DATA';
           title5;
           title6  f=font3 h=.50in j=1 'DATA';   /* spacing at 36 points */
           title7  f=font1 h=.50in j=1 'DATA';
           title8;
           title9  f=font3 h=1.0in j=1 'DATA';   /* spacing at 72 points */
           title10 f=font1 h=1.0in j=1 'DATA';

              /* display the titles */
           proc gslide;
           run;
           quit;
```

Output 26.7 *Comparison of Text with and without Spacing Adjustments (GR26N06)*

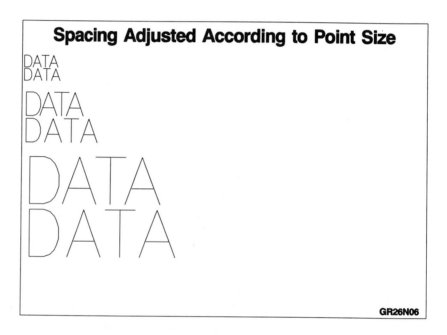

This example illustrates the following features:

□ The LIBNAME statement associates the libref GFONT0 with the SAS data library in which the font catalog is stored.

□ In the data set SPACE1, the variable SIZE specifies the size of the font in points (72 points equal 1 inch), and the variable ADJ specifies the adjustment to the intercharacter spacing in hundredths of a point. Positive values increase the space between characters; negative values decrease the space between characters. The space data set makes the following adjustments:

   □ When the point size is small, spacing increases for better legibility.

   □ As the point size increases, spacing decreases.

   □ Sizes of 42 points or more have an ADJ value of −620.

□ The SPACEDATA= option includes the data in SPACE1 when the font is created. The font does not contain kerning data.

□ The NODISPLAY option suppresses display of FONT3 after it is generated.

□ In Output 26.7, the characters A, D, and T are shown as the word DATA. Each pair of lines displays the word DATA at the same size using first the font with spacing adjustment (FONT3) and then the original font (FONT1). Note that as the size of the characters increases, the space between them decreases.

Height specifications are in inches. Their equivalent point size is as follows:

Inches	Points
.25	18
.50	36
1.00	72

See Also

Chapter 2, "Running SAS/GRAPH Programs"
　for information on specifying librefs

Chapter 5, "Graphics Option and Device Parameters Dictionary"
　for more information on font specification options

Chapter 6, "SAS/GRAPH Fonts"
　for more information on specifying fonts and using special characters, and for lists of available type styles

Chapter 18, "The Annotate Data Set," and Chapter 19, "Annotate Dictionary"
　for information on creating more complicated figures

SAS Technical Report A-107, *Creating Your Own SAS/GRAPH Map Data Sets with a Digitizer*
　for more information on the digitizing process

SAS Technical Report P-170, *Type Styles and Fonts for Use with SAS/GRAPH Software*
　for complete displays of most SAS/GRAPH software fonts and for tables of hexadecimal values for special characters

CHAPTER 27 The GIMPORT Procedure

Overview

The GIMPORT procedure enables you to import graphics output produced with other software applications, graphics output produced by SAS/GRAPH software, or graphics output produced on other machines into SAS/GRAPH software. The GIMPORT procedure takes as its input a computer graphics metafile and produces graphics output that can be displayed in your SAS/GRAPH session and stored in a SAS catalog. This graphics output can be reviewed and played like any other SAS/GRAPH output using the GREPLAY procedure.

A computer graphics metafile (CGM) is a graphics output file created according to a standard (ANSI X3.122). Since many graphics applications, including SAS/GRAPH software, can generate and import CGMs, these files can be read by different applications programs or used on different machines.

You can use the GIMPORT procedure to import CGMs that have been created by

☐ another software application

☐ SAS/GRAPH software.

GIMPORT Procedure Syntax

The GIMPORT procedure uses the following statements.

☐ The PROC GIMPORT statement is required.

PROC GIMPORT FILEREF=*cgm-fileref*
FILETYPE=CGM
FORMAT=BINARY | CHARACTER | CLEARTEXT
<GOUT=*output-catalog*>;

☐ The following statements are optional. Any number of MAP statements can be submitted with a single PROC GIMPORT statement.

MAP '*cgm-font*' TO *SAS-font-name*;

SCALE X=*factor* | Y=*factor* | X=*factor* Y=*factor*;

TRANSLATE X=*offset* | Y=*offset* | X=*offset* Y=*offset*;

For complete statement syntax, see the section for the appropriate statement.

Statement Descriptions

The purpose of each statement is decribed here:

PROC GIMPORT — initiates the procedure, names the input file to be processed, and specifies the file type and format of the input file. It optionally specifies an output catalog.

MAP — specifies a SAS/GRAPH font to substitute for a CGM font.

SCALE — enlarges or reduces the graphics output by increasing or decreasing the values of the *x* and *y* coordinates.

TRANSLATE — moves the graphics output by offsetting it along the *x* or *y* axes.

GIMPORT Procedure Description

The GIMPORT procedure produces SAS/GRAPH graphics output by importing a graphics file that conforms to the CGM standard. As well as displaying the graphics output and creating a catalog entry, the GIMPORT procedure may write the following information to the log:

☐ any elements used in the CGM that the procedure cannot process

☐ color mapping information when a color in a CGM is not available on the destination device

☐ a list of fonts used by the application that produced the CGM.

Terminology

The following terms are used in the discussion of the GIMPORT
procedure and are defined in the Glossary:

colors list	font, hardware
computer graphics metafile	font, software
coordinates	graphics element
device driver	import
device entry	RGB
font	string

Summary of Use

The GIMPORT procedure imports a CGM with which a fileref has been
associated. Using the CGM as input, the procedure displays the graphics
output and creates a catalog entry. The following sections address
assigning the fileref to the external file (CGM) and importing the file.

Specifying a Fileref

You must assign a fileref to the external file (CGM) you want to use as
input so that the GIMPORT procedure can locate it. You can do this with
a FILENAME statement such as the following:

```
filename cgm-fileref 'external-file';
```

Replace *cgm-fileref* with any fileref name you want. Replace *'external-file'*
with the complete filename of the CGM you want to import. You can omit
the FILENAME statement if the fileref has already been defined. You can
also specify a fileref with a host command. For additional information, see
"FILENAME Statements" in Chapter 2, "Running SAS/GRAPH Programs."

Importing the File

The PROC GIMPORT statement reads the input CGM and displays the
graphics output. When the CGM is displayed using only the PROC
GIMPORT statement, the resulting graphics output may not be sized or
positioned correctly for the device on which it is displayed. In these cases,
you can use the SCALE and TRANSLATE statements to adjust the size and
location of the new graphics output.

In addition, if the CGM contains the FONT LIST element, the procedure
lists in the log the fonts used in the CGM. You can change these fonts to
SAS software fonts using the MAP statement. If you do not change these
fonts to SAS software fonts, the GIMPORT procedure uses a default font.

Because it is easier to determine what adjustments the graphics output
needs after it has been displayed, you may want to follow these steps:

1. Import the CGM and display the graphics output using only the PROC
   GIMPORT statement.

2. Decide what adjustments you want to make to the size and position of
   the graphics output.

3. If the procedure lists the fonts used by the CGM, decide what font
   substitutions you want to make.

4. Run the procedure again with the appropriate MAP, SCALE, or
   TRANSLATE statements.

Note: Once you have determined the correct values for the SCALE and TRANSLATE statements for the graphics output produced by a particular CGM, you can use the same values for all other graphics output generated by the same software application.

CGM Elements Not Supported

The GIMPORT procedure does not support certain CGM elements. If the input CGM contains any of the following elements, the GIMPORT procedure writes a message to the log noting that the procedure cannot process them:

□ the CELL ARRAY primitive element

□ the CHARACTER SPACING attribute element

□ the APPLICATION DATA element

□ the ESCAPE element.

These elements are rarely used and their absence should not affect the graphics output produced by the GIMPORT procedure.

Color Mapping

If the CGM specifies colors for the graphics elements it generates, you may or may not be able to map them to the color you want in your SAS/GRAPH output, depending on the way these colors are specified in the CGM.

You cannot change the color mapping if, in the CGM, the COLOUR SELECTION MODE element is set to DIRECT. In this case, the colors are explicitly defined by the CGM and you cannot change them. However, if the CGM was created with a SAS/GRAPH CGM device driver, you can control the colors by specifying the appropriate colors when you create the graphics output or by changing the colors in the CGM device entry and re-creating the CGM. See Chapter 25, "The GDEVICE Procedure," for details. In addition, you can use a color map with the GREPLAY procedure to remap the colors. In the color map, the FROM color must be specified in RGB format, but the TO color can be any valid color name. See Chapter 36, "The GREPLAY Procedure," for details on color maps.

You can change the color mapping if the COLOUR SELECTION MODE element is set to INDEXED and there is no color table defined in the CGM file. In this case, you can map the colors from the CGM to the colors of your choice by using the COLORS= graphics option when you run the GIMPORT procedure. The CGM colors are mapped to match the order of the colors in the colors list. If the procedure cannot reproduce the colors specified in the CGM, the following message is written to the log:

```
WARNING: Invalid color index n encountered. It has been
         mapped to color-name.
```

Note: The color name from the CGM is converted to the RGB format for SAS/GRAPH color names; that is, WHITE is converted to CXFFFFFF, and so on. See Chapter 7, "SAS/GRAPH Colors," for details.

Pattern Mapping

If the CGM contains pattern specifications, you may be able to map them to patterns of your choice using SAS/GRAPH PATTERN definitions.

If the CGM defines a PATTERN TABLE, then the patterns defined by this table are the patterns used and you cannot change them.

If a PATTERN TABLE is not defined in the CGM, under certain conditions you may be able to use SAS/GRAPH PATTERN definitions to control the patterns used. If INTERIOR STYLE is set to PATTERN and if a PATTERN TABLE INDEX has been specified, then the GIMPORT procedure uses the PATTERN TABLE INDEX to look up SAS/GRAPH PATTERN definitions. If patterns are defined, the procedure uses the first available pattern. For example, if the PATTERN TABLE INDEX *n* has been defined, the procedure uses SAS/GRAPH PATTERN definition *n*. If the SAS/GRAPH PATTERN definition is not the correct pattern type, the procedure modifies the pattern as necessary. If no PATTERN definitions are currently in effect, an INVALID PATTERN TABLE INDEX warning is issued and no pattern is used.

Font Mapping

By default, the GIMPORT procedure maps all the fonts in the CGM to the font specified by the FTEXT= graphics option. If the FTEXT= graphics option is not used, the default is the hardware font, NONE. However, you may be able to specify a different font either by mapping the fonts or with a graphics option.

When the CGM is imported, a numbered list of the fonts used in the CGM may be displayed in the LOG window. These are the fonts that were available to the application that originally generated the CGM. Depending on how the fonts are represented in the CGM, you may be able to map these fonts to fonts of your choice.

If the font and text in the imported graphics output are produced with move and draw commands that are included in the CGM, then no font name appears in the LOG window and the font cannot be mapped to a different one.

If the fonts used in the imported graphics output are represented in the CGM as a font name accompanied by a text string, they can be mapped to SAS/GRAPH fonts using the MAP statement. You can use the MAP statement if the message "WARNING: Invalid font index *n*. Font has been mapped to *font-name*" appears in the LOG window after the list of fonts. This means that font *n* in the list could not be reproduced and was mapped to the font specified in the FTEXT= graphics option or to the hardware font. You can map this font to a SAS/GRAPH software font of your choice using the MAP statement. See "MAP Statement" later in this chapter for more information on mapping fonts.

You can also specify a font with the FTEXT= or CHARTYPE= graphics options if both of the following conditions are true:

□ The font has not been mapped with a MAP statement.

□ The CGM font contains a font name and text rather than the move and draw commands that draw the text in the specified font. In the latter case, the font name is not included in FONT LIST.

However, using a graphics option causes all fonts to be mapped to the one specified. See Chapter 6, "SAS/GRAPH Fonts," for details of font specification.

PROC GIMPORT Statement

The PROC GIMPORT statement initiates the procedure. It names the fileref for the input CGM and specifies the type and format of the file. It can optionally specify a destination catalog for graphics output.

Syntax

The general form of the PROC GIMPORT statement is

PROC GIMPORT FILEREF=*cgm-fileref*
    FILETYPE=CGM
    FORMAT=BINARY | CHARACTER | CLEARTEXT
    <GOUT=*output-catalog*>;

Requirements

The following arguments are required with the PROC GIMPORT statement:

FILEREF=*cgm-fileref*
    specifies the fileref that is associated with the external file (CGM) to be used as input for the GIMPORT procedure. *Cgm-fileref* must have been previously defined using a FILENAME statement or host command. For more information on filerefs, see "Specifying a Fileref" earlier in this chapter.

FILETYPE=CGM
    specifies the type of the input file, that is, the graphics standard to which the file conforms. CGM is the only valid value for the FILETYPE= argument. If the FILETYPE= argument is omitted, an error is issued and the procedure stops.

FORMAT=BINARY | CHARACTER | CLEARTEXT
    specifies the format of the input file. CGMs can be encoded in one of the following three formats:

BINARY	specifies binary encoding. It is not printable.
CHARACTER	specifies an encoding suitable for transfer through networks that cannot support binary transfers. It is printable but not readable.
CLEARTEXT	specifies a text format that can be read using a standard text editor.

    Most graphics packages use BINARY format. If you specify the wrong format, an "ERROR: Unable to interpret the CGM file" message is issued and the procedure stops. If this occurs, try a different format.

Option

You can use the following option with the PROC GIMPORT statement:

GOUT=*output-catalog*
    specifies the SAS catalog in which to save the output produced by the GIMPORT procedure. You can use the GREPLAY procedure to view the graphics output stored in the catalog. If you do not use the GOUT= option, catalog entries are written to the default catalog WORK.GSEG, which is erased at the end of your session.

MAP Statement

The MAP statement enables you to substitute SAS/GRAPH software fonts for the fonts in the CGM. Each MAP statement performs one substitution, naming a font from the CGM and a SAS/GRAPH font. You can submit multiple MAP statements with the procedure. The MAP statement has no options. By default, the GIMPORT procedure maps all the CGM fonts to the font specified by the FTEXT= graphics option or, if the FTEXT= graphics option is not used, to the default hardware font, NONE.

Syntax

The general form of the MAP statement is

MAP *'cgm-font'* TO *SAS-font-name*;

Requirements

The name of the font from the CGM and the name of the SAS/GRAPH font must be specified. The following required arguments identify the fonts to be mapped:

'cgm-font'
  specifies the name of a font in the CGM. The name of the font must be enclosed in single quotes and written exactly as it appears in the font list; *cgm-font* is case sensitive. Do not include the font list number in *cgm-font*.

SAS-font-name
  specifies the SAS/GRAPH font to which the CGM font is mapped. You can specify software fonts or hardware fonts for the destination device. Fonts created by the GFONT procedure may also be used.
  Note: Remember to specify the libref GFONT0 with a LIBNAME statement if the font is a user-generated font.

Using the MAP Statement

If the CGM includes the FONT LIST element, the GIMPORT procedure automatically lists the CGM font names in the log. Use this list to select the fonts for mapping. Submit a separate MAP statement for each CGM font that you want to map.

  For example, suppose the font list includes the following entry:

  3. Times Roman

If the LOG window displays the message "WARNING: Invalid font index *n*," you can map the Times Roman font to the SAS/GRAPH font CENTX with the following statement:

```
map 'Times Roman' to centx;
```

SCALE Statement

The SCALE statement enables you to adjust the size of the graphics output imported by the procedure. If the graphics output is too narrow or too wide, you can increase or decrease its width by increasing or decreasing the range of the *x*-coordinate values. If the graphics output is too short or too tall, you can increase or decrease its height by increasing or decreasing the range of the *y*-coordinate values.

The SCALE statement specifies a factor by which to increase or decrease the value of the *x* coordinate or the *y* coordinate or both. The SCALE statement has no options.

Syntax

The general form of the SCALE statement is

SCALE X=*factor* | Y=*factor* | X=*factor* Y=*factor*;

Requirements

At least one of the following arguments is required; both may be used and can be listed in either order:

X=*factor*
> specifies the enlargement or reduction of the values of the *x* coordinates. *Factor*, which cannot be less than or equal to 0, is the number by which these values are multiplied. Values less than 1 reduce the size of the graphics output while values greater than 1 increase the size of the graphics output. There is no limit on the size of *factor*.
>
> For example, if the values of the *x* coordinates range from 5 to 50 and if in the SCALE statement the factor for X= is specified as 2, then the values of all the *x* coordinates are multiplied by 2 and the range of these values increases. The new range is 10 to 100.
> By default, X=1.

Y=*factor*
> specifies the enlargement or reduction of the values of the *y* coordinates. *Factor*, which cannot be less than or equal to 0, is the number by which these values are multiplied. Values less than 1 reduce the size of the graphics output while values greater than 1 increase the size of the graphics output. There is no limit on the size of *factor*.
>
> For example, if the values of the *y* coordinates range from 0 to 25 and if in the SCALE statement the factor for Y= is specified as .5, then the values of all the *y* coordinates are multiplied by .5 and the range of these values decreases. The new range is 0 to 12.5.
> By default, Y=1.

Using the SCALE Statement

The SCALE statement adjusts the size of the graphics output by increasing or decreasing the values of the *x* and *y* coordinates. The value of *factor* for X= or Y= in the SCALE statement is the value times which the *x* or *y* coordinates are increased or decreased. If the shapes in the imported graphics output are too narrow, you can make them wider by increasing the values of the *x* coordinate. To make the elements in the graphics output twice as wide, specify X=2. To make them half as high, specify Y=.5.

You can submit the SCALE statement alone or in conjunction with the TRANSLATE statement. Note that the values specified by the SCALE statement are always processed first.

If you specify a factor that causes the graphics output to exceed the size of the graphics output area, the procedure draws as much of the graphics output as will fit in the available space.

TRANSLATE Statement

The TRANSLATE statement enables you to adjust the location on the display of the graphics output imported by the procedure. If the graphics output is not centered horizontally, you can shift it left or right by offsetting the *x* values. If the graph is not centered vertically, you can shift it up or down by offsetting the *y* values.

The TRANSLATE statement specifies an offset that is applied to the *x* coordinate, the *y* coordinate, or both. The TRANSLATE statement has no options.

Syntax

The general form of the TRANSLATE statement is

TRANSLATE X=*offset* | Y=*offset* | X=*offset* Y=*offset*;

Requirements

At least one of the following arguments is required; both may be used and can be listed in either order:

X=*offset*
> specifies the number of units in percent of the display area to move the graphics output right (positive numbers) or left (negative numbers). The value of *offset* is added to the value of the *x* coordinate.
>
> For example, if the values of the *x* coordinates range from 0 to 50, and if in the TRANSLATE statement the offset for X= is specified as 25, then the values of all the *x* coordinates increase by 25 units. The range of these values becomes 25 to 75, and the graphics output moves right 25% of the display area.
>
> By default, X=0.

Y=*offset*
> specifies the number of units in percent of the display area to move the graphics output up (positive numbers) or down (negative numbers). The value of *offset* is added to the value of the *y* coordinate.
>
> For example, if the values of the *y* coordinates range from 20 to 60 and if in the TRANSLATE statement the offset for Y= is specified as −10, then the values of all the *y* coordinates decrease by 10 units. The range of these values becomes 10 to 50, and the graphics output moves down 10% of the display area.
>
> By default, Y=0.

Using the TRANSLATE Statement

The TRANSLATE statement adjusts the position of the graphics output without changing its size. The amount of the *offset* specified for X= or Y= in the TRANSLATE statement is the amount the graphics output is moved.

For example, suppose your imported graphics output is positioned in the upper-left corner of the display. To move it right 10% and down 5%, use the following statement:

```
translate x=10 y=-5;
```

You can submit the TRANSLATE statement alone or in conjunction with the SCALE statement. Note that the values specified by the SCALE statement are always processed first.

Examples

The following examples illustrate major features of the GIMPORT procedure. For illustration purposes, these examples create a CGM using SAS/GRAPH software and import the resulting CGM using the GIMPORT procedure. Ordinarily, you would use the GIMPORT procedure to import graphics output generated by another software package.

Because these examples use a CGM device driver to produce a graphics stream file, you may need to re-specify a device driver for your output device.

This example uses the HSIZE= and VSIZE= graphics options to set a specific size for the graphics output area for the CGM so that the second example can illustrate the use of the SCALE and TRANSLATE statements. Depending on the output device you are using, you may need to adjust the HSIZE= and VSIZE= values and the values in the SCALE and TRANSLATE statements in the second example.

Importing a CGM

This example creates a CGM in binary format by directing SAS/GRAPH output to a graphics stream file (GSF) and using a CGM device driver. It uses the GIMPORT procedure to import the resulting CGM. The following program statements produce the font list shown in Output 27.1 and the graphics output shown in Output 27.2:

```
/* assign a fileref for a GSF file */
filename gsasfile 'external-file';

/* set the graphics environment, set    */
/* graphics stream file characteristics, */
/* and select CGMCRT device driver for   */
/* binary CGM                            */
goptions reset=global gunit=pct border
        ftext=swissb htitle=6 htext=3
        gaccess=gsasfile gsfmode=replace
        noprompt device=cgmcrt
        hsize=5 in vsize=5 in;

/* define titles and footnote for slide */
title1 f=script 'SCRIPT font';
title2 f=swissbi 'SWISSBI font';
footnote j=r 'GR27N01  ';
```

```
                              /* generate a slide and store the graphics */
                              /* output in the GSF file                  */
                         proc gslide;
                         run;
                         quit;

                              /* reset the graphics environment */
                         goptions reset=goptions gunit=pct border
                                  ftext=swissb htitle=6 htext=3;

                              /* import the GSF file created by the CGMCRT device driver */
                         proc gimport fileref=gsasfile filetype=cgm format=binary;
                         run;
```

Output 27.1 *Font List*

```
    .
    .
    .
NOTE: These fonts are used in this CGM file. You may use the MAP statement
      to map these fonts to SAS/GRAPH fonts.
1. ARABIC
2. BRUSH
3. CENTB
4. CENTBE
5. CENTBI
6. CENTBIE
7. CENTX
8. CENTXE
9. CENTXI
10. CENTXIE
11. GERMAN
12. GITALIC
13. SIMPLEX
14. DUPLEX
15. COMPLEX
16. TRIPLEX
17. TITALIC
18. ITALIC
19. OLDENG
20. SCRIPT
21. CSCRIPT
22. SWISS
23. SWISSE
24. SWISSB
25. SWISSBE
26. SWISSBI
27. SWISSBIE
28. SWISSX
29. SWISSXE
30. SWISSXB
31. SWISSXB
32. SWISSXBE
33. SWISSI
34. SWISSIE
35. SWISSL
36. SWISSLE
37. XSWISS
38. XSWISSE
39. XSWISSB
40. XSWISSBE
41. ZAPF
42. ZAPFE
43. ZAPFB
44. ZAPFBE
45. ZAPFBI
46. ZAPFBIE
47. ZAPFI
48. ZAPFIE
WARNING: Invalid font index 20. Font has been mapped to SWISSB.
WARNING: Invalid font index 26. Font has been mapped to SWISSB.
WARNING: Invalid font index 24. Font has been mapped to SWISSB.
    .
    .
    .
```

Output 27.2 *Imported Graphics Output (GR27N01)*

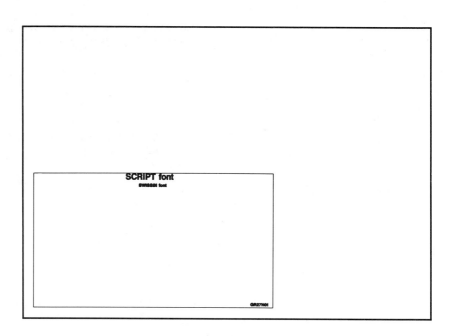

This example illustrates the following features:

□ The GOPTIONS statement specifies a CGM device driver for the graphics stream file.

□ The PROC GSLIDE statement produces graphics output that is written to the graphics stream file.

□ The FILEREF= argument in the PROC GIMPORT statement specifies the fileref where the CGM is located. The fileref was defined using a FILENAME statement.

□ The FILETYPE= argument specifies the type of file to be imported.

□ The FORMAT= argument specifies the format of the CGM being imported.

□ Note the font list shown in the log output. The warning messages following the font list indicate which fonts can be remapped using the MAP statement.

Adjusting the Graphics Output

This example uses the GIMPORT procedure to import a CGM in binary format. It uses the SCALE and TRANSLATE statements to correct the size and position of the imported CGM. The following program statements produce the log output shown in Output 27.3 and the graphics output shown in Output 27.4:

```
     /* assign a fileref for the GSF file */
   filename gsasfile 'external-file';

     /* set the graphics environment, set     */
     /* graphics stream file characteristics, */
     /* and select CGMCRT device driver for   */
     /* binary CGM                            */
   goptions reset=global gunit=pct border
          ftext=swissb htitle=6 htext=3
          gaccess=gsasfile gsfmode=replace
          noprompt device=cgmcrt
```

```
          hsize=5 in vsize=5 in;
  /* define titles and footnote for slide */
title1 f=script 'SCRIPT font';
title2 f=swissbi 'SWISSBI font';
footnote j=r 'GR27N02 ';

  /* generate a slide and store the graphics */
  /* output in the GSF file            */
proc gslide;
run;
quit;

  /* reset the graphics environment */
goptions reset=goptions gunit=pct border
     ftext=swissb htitle=6 htext=3;

  /* import the GSF file created by the CGMCRT device driver */
proc gimport fileref=gsasfile filetype=cgm format=binary;
  scale x=1.5 y=1.8;
  translate x=3.5 y=10;
  map 'SCRIPT' to script;
  map 'SWISSBI' to swissbi;
  map 'SWISSB' to swissb;
run;
```

Output 27.3 *Font List*

```
.
.
.

NOTE: These fonts are used in this CGM file. You may use the MAP statement
      to map these fonts to SAS/GRAPH fonts.
 1. ARABIC
 2. BRUSH
 3. CENTB
 4. CENTBE
 5. CENTBI
 6. CENTBIE
 7. CENTX
 8. CENTXE
 9. CENTXI
10. CENTXIE
11. GERMAN
12. GITALIC
13. SIMPLEX
14. DUPLEX
15. COMPLEX
16. TRIPLEX
17. TITALIC
18. ITALIC
19. OLDENG
20. SCRIPT
21. CSCRIPT
22. SWISS
23. SWISSE
24. SWISSB
25. SWISSBE
26. SWISSBI
27. SWISSBIE
28. SWISSX
29. SWISSXE
30. SWISSXB
31. SWISSXB
32. SWISSXBE
33. SWISSI
34. SWISSIE
35. SWISSL
36. SWISSLE
37. XSWISS
38. XSWISSE
```

(continued on next page)

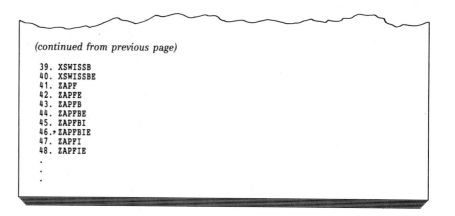

(continued from previous page)

```
39. XSWISSB
40. XSWISSBE
41. ZAPF
42. ZAPFE
43. ZAPFB
44. ZAPFBE
45. ZAPFBI
46. ZAPFBIE
47. ZAPFI
48. ZAPFIE
 .
 .
 .
```

Output 27.4 *Scaled and Translated Graphics Output (GR27N02)*

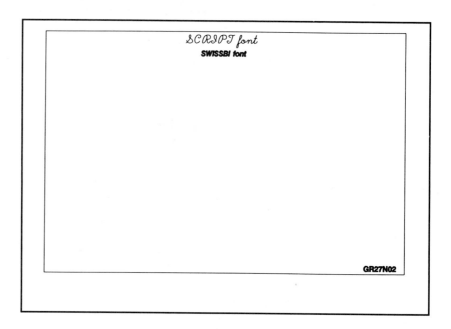

This example illustrates the following features:

□ The SCALE statement specifies the scale factor for the values of the x and y coordinates. The imported graphics output is scaled 1.5 times in the x direction and 1.8 times in the y direction.

□ The TRANSLATE statement specifies the amount that the imported graphics output should be moved horizontally and vertically. It is moved 3.5 units to the right and 10 units up.

□ The MAP statements remap the fonts shown in the first example. Note that no warning messages follow the font list in Output 27.3 because all of the fonts used in the CGM have been remapped.

See Also

Chapter 2, "Running SAS/GRAPH Programs"
  for information on specifying filerefs

Chapter 3, "Graphics Output"
  for additional information on catalog entries and graphics stream files

Chapter 5, "Graphics Options and Device Parameters Dictionary"
  for information on specifying a colors list with the COLORS=
  graphics option and on global text specifications

Chapter 6, "SAS/GRAPH Fonts"
  for a listing of available fonts

Chapter 7, "SAS/GRAPH Colors"
  for information on the selection and use of colors

Chapter 8, "Transporting Graphics"
  for information on using the GIMPORT procedure to transport
  graphics output from Release 6.03

Chapter 36, "The GREPLAY Procedure"
  for more information on color mapping

SAS Language: Reference, Version 6, First Edition
  for additional information on the FILENAME statement

References

ANSI X3.122 –1986 *Computer Graphics Metafile for the Storage and Transfer of Picture Description Information.*

Arnold, D.B. and Bono, P.R. (1988), *CGM and CGI: Metafile Interface Standards for Computer Graphics*, New York: Springer-Verlag.

CHAPTER 28 The GKEYMAP Procedure

Overview

The GKEYMAP procedure creates device maps and key maps that compensate for differences between the way characters are encoded internally by SAS/GRAPH software and the way they are encoded by host systems and output devices.

In addition, the GKEYMAP procedure can create SAS data sets from existing key maps and device maps, either Institute-supplied or user-generated. This capability is useful when you want to make minor alterations in a large key map or device map and do not want to or cannot re-create the original data set with a DATA step.

The Institute supplies key maps for many keyboard configurations. Your SAS Software Consultant should have selected the appropriate key map for your site. If the Institute-supplied device maps and key maps do not meet your needs, you can use this procedure to modify an existing map or create a new one.

This chapter explains how to create and use device maps and key maps as well as how to output them as data sets.

GKEYMAP Procedure Syntax

The GKEYMAP procedure uses the following statement:

PROC GKEYMAP NAME=*map-name*
      data-set-argument
      <DEVICE=*device-name*>
      <KEYMAP | DEVMAP>
      <MULTFONT>
      <TYPE=MAP11 | MAP1N>;

□ *data-set-argument* must be one of the following:

    DATA=*gkeymap-data-set*

    OUT=*SAS-data-set*

GKEYMAP Procedure Description

The GKEYMAP procedure generates new key maps or device maps or outputs existing ones as SAS data sets.

Terminology

The following terms are used in the discussion of the GKEYMAP procedure and are defined in the Glossary.

device map
key map

Summary of Use

The characters A through Z (upper- and lowercase), 0 through 9, and many symbols and national characters are represented by one of two sets of hexadecimal codes (ASCII or EBCDIC). However, a character may be represented by one code for the keyboard, another code for the host, and yet another for the output device. To resolve these differences, SAS/GRAPH software stores all characters using its own internal encoding scheme. This internal character encoding, which is a set of hexadecimal values that are associated with all supported characters, is shown in Table 28.1.

To accommodate differences in the encoding of characters, you must be able to translate the hexadecimal codes generated by your keyboard into the corresponding SAS/GRAPH internal encoding. A key map gives you this ability.

You also must be able to convert the internal encoding used by SAS/GRAPH software to the codes required to produce the corresponding hardware characters on your output device. A device map gives you this ability.

Device maps and key maps are SAS catalog entries. Institute-supplied key maps and device maps are stored in the catalog SASHELP.FONTS. User-generated key maps and device maps are stored in the catalog GFONT0.FONTS. Key maps are stored with the extension KEYMAP (for example, GERMAN.KEYMAP), and device maps are stored with the extension DEVMAP (for example, DEFAULT.DEVMAP).

Table 28.1 *SAS/GRAPH*
Internal Character Encoding

	©	®	■	TM	°	´	´´		Œ	œ	'	'	"	"	¤
00	01	02	03	04	05	06	07	08	09	0A	0B	0C	0D	0E	0F
		↕	«	¶	§	Ø	ø	↑	↓	→	←	»	↔		
10	11	12	13	14	15	16	17	18	19	1A	1B	1C	1D	1E	1F
	!	"	#	$	%	&	'	(	)	*	+	,	—	.	/
20	21	22	23	24	25	26	27	28	29	2A	2B	2C	2D	2E	2F
0	1	2	3	4	5	6	7	8	9	:	;	<	=	>	?
30	31	32	33	34	35	36	37	38	39	3A	3B	3C	3D	3E	3F
@	A	B	C	D	E	F	G	H	I	J	K	L	M	N	O
40	41	42	43	44	45	46	47	48	49	4A	4B	4C	4D	4E	4F
P	Q	R	S	T	U	V	W	X	Y	Z	[	\	]	^	_
50	51	52	53	54	55	56	57	58	59	5A	5B	5C	5D	5E	5F
`	a	b	c	d	e	f	g	h	i	j	k	l	m	n	o
60	61	62	63	64	65	66	67	68	69	6A	6B	6C	6D	6E	6F
p	q	r	s	t	u	v	w	x	y	z	{	|	}	~	
70	71	72	73	74	75	76	77	78	79	7A	7B	7C	7D	7E	7F
Ç	ü	é	â	ä	à	å	ç	ê	ë	è	ï	î	ì	Ä	Å
80	81	82	83	84	85	86	87	88	89	8A	8B	8C	8D	8E	8F
É	æ	Æ	ô	ö	ò	û	ù	ÿ	Ö	Ü	¢	£	¥	Pt	ƒ
90	91	92	93	94	95	96	97	98	99	9A	9B	9C	9D	9E	9F
á	í	ó	ú	ñ	Ñ	ª	º	¿	×	¬	½	¼	¡	‹	›
A0	A1	A2	A3	A4	A5	A6	A7	A8	A9	AA	AB	AC	AD	AE	AF
´	`	¨	~	^	°	˛	¯	ß					†	‡	|
B0	B1	B2	B3	B4	B5	B6	B7	B8	B9	BA	BB	BC	BD	BE	BF
C0	C1	C2	C3	C4	C5	C6	C7	C8	C9	CA	CB	CC	CD	CE	CF
|		´	`	¨	~	^	°	˛	¯						
D0	D1	D2	D3	D4	D5	D6	D7	D8	D9	DA	DB	DC	DD	DE	DF
E0	E1	E2	E3	E4	E5	E6	E7	E8	E9	EA	EB	EC	ED	EE	EF
	±	≥	≤			÷						≠			
F0	F1	F2	F3	F4	F5	F6	F7	F8	F9	FA	FB	FC	FD	FE	FF

Note: Positions 00-1F are reserved.
Note: SAS Institute reserves the right to change, at any time, the character displayed and the hexadecimal code returned for all undefined codes.

Key Maps

A key map changes the code generated by a keyboard key to the value corresponding to the SAS/GRAPH internal character encoding. Otherwise, a different character (or no character) is drawn when the character is requested in a SAS/GRAPH software font. Key maps are required when the code sent to the host does not match the SAS/GRAPH internal encoding for the character corresponding to the key that is pressed.

Key maps are also useful when you want to generate a character that is not available on your keyboard or when the same key on different keyboards sends a different character to the host.

Device Maps

A device map maps the code stored in the SAS/GRAPH internal encoding to the code required to reproduce the character on the output device when a particular hardware character is requested in a SAS/GRAPH program.

Device maps usually are used in these two situations:

☐ reversing the translation performed by key maps. To display the proper hardware character, you must use a device map to convert the SAS/GRAPH internal encoding of the character back to the encoding that the device expects.

☐ accounting for differences between the code that represents a character on the host and the code or codes required to generate the same character as a hardware character on an output device. The problem can be further complicated if you have multiple output devices, each with its own way of generating a particular character using hardware text.

Using Key Maps and Device Maps

You use key maps and device maps by specifying them with the DEVMAP= option or KEYMAP= option in a GOPTIONS statement. You also can specify a device map by filling in the DEVMAP field in the Detail window of the device entry for the device driver you are using.

For example, if you use the GKEYMAP procedure to generate a key map called MYKEYMAP, you can specify it with a statement such as the following:

```
goptions keymap=mykeymap;
```

Once you specify MYKEYMAP as your current key map, whenever you press a key the code it generates is translated by MYKEYMAP into the code specified by the key map.

When you specify a device map with the DEVMAP= graphics option and you use a hardware character set, mapped characters are converted from their SAS/GRAPH internal encoding to the codes required to display the corresponding characters on your device.

Asymmetrical Maps

It is possible, and sometimes necessary, to define a key map or device map that is not symmetrical (that is, two or more input character codes map to the same output character code). For example, if you define a key map to map the keyed character A to the internal encoding for B, the keyed characters A and B both map to the internal encoding for B, but no code maps to A. This situation may make it impossible for you to display certain characters defined in software fonts. To see what characters in a font are available under a key map, do the following:

1. Use the KEYMAP= option in a GOPTIONS statement to specify the key map you are interested in.
2. Use the GFONT procedure with the ROMHEX option to display the font you want to use.

The hexadecimal values and corresponding font characters that are displayed are the ones available under the specified map. If the map is not symmetrical, a warning is issued. See "Special Characters" in Chapter 6, "SAS/GRAPH Fonts" for more information on using hexadecimal values to display special characters. See also Chapter 26, "The GFONT Procedure" for details on displaying fonts.

PROC GKEYMAP Statement

The PROC GKEYMAP statement initiates the procedure and names the key map or device map to be created, or output as a data set. When the GKEYMAP procedure is used to create a map, the PROC GKEYMAP statement also specifies the data set (called the *gkeymap data set*) that provides input to the procedure. When the procedure is used to output a map, the PROC GKEYMAP statement specifies the name of the data set to which the map is written.

The PROC GKEYMAP statement uses options to specify the type of map and details of its creation.

Requirements

The NAME= argument is required, and either the DATA= argument or the OUT= argument is also required.

NAME=*map-name*
    specifies the name of the map to be created or output. Key maps are stored as *map-name*.KEYMAP, and device maps are stored as *map-name*.DEVMAP. The value of the KEYMAP or DEVMAP option determines the type of map and the extension added to *map-name*. It is possible to use the same *map-name* value for both a key map and a device map.

    If you create a key map or device map, the map is stored as an entry in the catalog GFONT0.FONTS and you must use a LIBNAME statement to specify the libref GFONT0. See "Specifying the Libref GFONT0" in Chapter 26 for details.

    If you output an existing key map or device map, SAS/GRAPH software searches for the map using the same search path that it uses to search for fonts. See "Font Locations" in Chapter 6 for details.

DATA=*gkeymap-data-set*

specifies the input data set for the GKEYMAP procedure when you are creating a key map. See "The Gkeymap Data Set" later in this chapter for details on the format and contents of the input data set.

OUT=*SAS-data-set*

specifies the output data set to which the data from a key map or device map are to be written when you output an existing key map or device map as a SAS data set.

Options

You can use the following options with the PROC GKEYMAP statement:

DEVICE=*device-name*

specifies the device driver that a device map is associated with, where *device-name* is the name of an entry in a device catalog. The DEVICE= option is not required when creating a device map, but it can be used if you want to limit the use of the device map to one particular driver. If you do not use the DEVICE= option, the device map can be used with any device. The DEVICE= option is valid only if you are creating a device map.

KEYMAP
DEVMAP

specify whether you are working with a device map or a key map. The default is the KEYMAP option unless you use an option that can be used only with the DEVMAP option. The KEYMAP and DEVMAP options also specify the type of map you are outputting as a data set.

TYPE=MAP11 | MAP1N

specifies whether you are mapping characters one-to-one or one-to-many. If you specify TYPE=MAP11 (the default), each character in a graphics text string is mapped to only one character on the output device. If you specify TYPE=MAP1N, a single character in a graphics text string can be mapped to multiple characters on the output device. For example, if two characters have to be sent to the graphics output device to display a single hardware character, specify TYPE=MAP1N. Specify TYPE=MAP1N only when you are creating a device map.

MULTFONT

specifies that an alternate hardware character set is required to display one or more characters in the device map. Specify the MULTFONT option only when you are creating a device map.

Using the GKEYMAP Procedure

The following sections describe the characteristics of the data set that the GKEYMAP procedure uses as input and that is specified by the DATA= option. In addition, these sections explain briefly how key maps and device maps are created and used.

The Gkeymap Data Set

To generate a key map or device map, you must create a gkeymap data set that contains the mapping information to be used by the GKEYMAP procedure. This data set, which is used as input for the GKEYMAP procedure, should contain one observation for each character or key to be mapped. Any characters not specified in the data set are passed through the map unchanged.

Gkeymap Data Set Variables

The following variables are used to provide information on the mapping to be performed:

CHARTYPE

specifies which hardware character set to use when a device requires that you select an alternate character set in order to display certain characters. CHARTYPE is a numeric variable.

All of the characters in the TO string for a particular FROM value must use the same character set. The CHARTYPE variable is required if you use the MULTFONT option in the PROC GKEYMAP statement; otherwise, it is ignored. (The CHARTYPE variable is always ignored when you are creating a key map.) The CHARTYPE value must match a value listed in the Chartype field in the Chartype window of the device entry for the device to which the map is applied. However, you can set the CHARTYPE variable to a missing value to specify that the character can be drawn in any hardware character set.

FROM

specifies the character you are mapping from. FROM is a character variable. For each observation, the FROM variable should contain a single character value. Any characters after the first are ignored. The data set must be sorted by the FROM variable.

TO

specifies the string that the character in the FROM variable is mapped to. TO is a character variable.

If the TO variable contains more than one character, you must also specify TYPE=MAP1N in the PROC GKEYMAP statement to indicate that a single FROM character is being mapped to multiple TO characters. In addition, you must include the TOLEN variable in your gkeymap data set to specify the length of each TO string.

If you specify TYPE=MAP11 in the PROC GKEYMAP statement or if you do not use the TYPE= option, only the first byte of the TO string is recognized.

TOLEN

specifies the length of the string in the TO variable. TOLEN is a numeric variable. The TOLEN variable is used only with device maps and is required if you specify TYPE=MAP1N in the PROC GKEYMAP statement; otherwise, it is ignored.

Creating a Data Set from an Existing Key Map or Device Map

To generate a data set from an existing key map or device map, follow these steps:

1. Specify the name of the key map or device map with the NAME= argument. If the map is user-generated, the key map or device map name is the one specified with the NAME= argument when the map was created. The map also can be an Institute-supplied map.

2. In the OUT= argument specify the name of the data set to which the data are to be written By default, the data set is written to the temporary catalog WORK.

3. Use the DEVMAP option if a device map is selected.

4. Optionally, use the PRINT procedure to display the newly created data set.

This process is illustrated in "Modifying a Key Map" in "Examples" later in this chapter.

Creating and Using Key Maps and Device Maps

To create and use a key map or device map, follow these steps:

1. Submit a LIBNAME statement that associates the libref GFONT0 with the location where your map is to be stored.

2. Create a gkeymap data set that contains the variables FROM and TO. You can create this data set explicitly using a DATA step, or you can create the data set from an existing key map or device map.

3. Use the GKEYMAP procedure to read the data set and create the key map or device map. The GKEYMAP procedure stores the map in the catalog GFONT0.FONTS.

4. Use the KEYMAP= or DEVMAP= option in a GOPTIONS statement to assign the key map or device map in your SAS session. The specified map is used automatically when you specify fonts in your SAS/GRAPH programs.

    Note: The device map is used only when you use a hardware character set.

This process is illustrated in "Using a Device Map to Change Character Sets" in "Examples" later in this chapter.

Examples

The following examples illustrate the major features of the GKEYMAP procedure.

Modifying a Key Map

This example shows how to change one or more characters in an existing key map. It assumes that you want to be able to type the character ß in text strings, but you do not have a German keyboard. To do this, you must create a key map that translates the code generated when the @ key is pressed into the SAS/GRAPH internal encoding for ß ('B8'x). Whenever the @ character is typed in text that is displayed with a software font, the ß character is drawn instead. Since the example only changes the mapping for one character, the current key map is the basis for your new key map. To produce the key map, follow these steps:

1. Use a LIBNAME statement to associate the libref GFONT0 with the SAS data library where the key maps and device maps that you generate are stored.

2. Use the GOPTIONS procedure to find out the name of your current key map. The SAS log in Display 28.1 shows that the name of the key map is DEFAULT.

3. Use the GKEYMAP procedure to output the key map, DEFAULT, as the data set, TEMP.

4. Modify the TEMP data set to remap the character @ to the character ß.

5. Use the GKEYMAP procedure to create a new key map from the modified data set.

6. Specify the new key map in a GOPTIONS statement.

7. Submit a TITLE statement with the character @ where you want the character ß to print.

   Note: Once you have modified your key map so that @ is mapped to ß, you can no longer generate @ from your keyboard when the key map is in effect.

   The following program creates the key map MYKEYMAP and uses it to produce Output 28.1:

```
/* specify the libref GFONT0 */
libname gfont0 'SAS-data-library';

/* set the graphics environment */
goptions reset=global gunit=pct border
        ftext=swissb htitle=6 htext=3;

/* find the name of the current keymap */
proc goptions;
run;

/* convert the key map DEFAULT to the data set TEMP */
proc gkeymap name=default out=temp;
run;
```

```
                              /* modify the entries in TEMP */
                     data new;
                        from='ə';
                        to='b8'x;
                     run;

                     data temp;
                        update temp new;
                        by from;
                     run;

                        /* create a new key map from the data set TEMP */
                     proc gkeymap name=mykeymap
                                 data=temp
                                 keymap;
                     run;

                        /* specify the key map */
                     goptions keymap=mykeymap;

                        /* print a title with the special character */
                     title 'Kaiserstraəe';
                     footnote j=r 'GR28N01  ';

                     proc gslide;
                     run;
                     quit;
```

Display 28.1 *Partial Log
from GOPTIONS Procedure*

```
┌LOG─────────────────────────────────────────────────────────────────────┐
│ Command ===>                                                            │
│                                                                        │
│ htitle=                      Default height of first TITLE line          │
│ interpol=                    Default symbol interpolation                │
│ keymap=DEFAULT               Input character map for hardware and software│
│                              text                                       │
│ lfactor=                     Hardware line thickness factor              │
│ octext=                      Default outline text color                 │
│ paperfeed=                   Amount of paper to feed on drum plotters    │
│ penmounts=15                 Number of pens/colors to be used            │
│ nopiefill                    Use hardware pie fill generator             │
│ polygonfill                  Use hardware polygon fill generator         │
└─────────────────────────────────────────────────────────────────────────┘
┌PROGRAM EDITOR───────────────────────────────────────────────────────────┐
│ Command ===>                                                            │
│                                                                        │
│ 00001                                                                   │
│ 00002                                                                   │
│ 00003                                                                   │
│ 00004                                                                   │
│ 00005                                                                   │
│ 00006                                                                   │
└─────────────────────────────────────────────────────────────────────────┘
```

Output 28.1 Using a Key
Map to Remap a Character
(GR28N01)

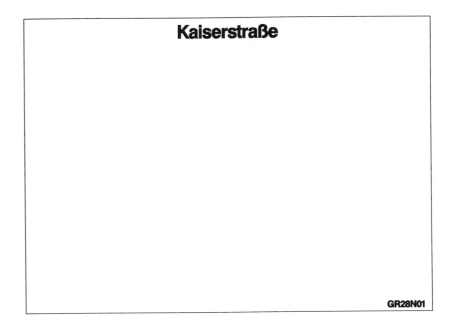

This example illustrates the following features:

□ The LIBNAME statement associates the libref GFONT0 with the location of the SAS data library where you store your device maps and key maps.

□ In the first PROC GKEYMAP statement, the NAME= argument specifies the default key map as input to the procedure.

□ The OUT= argument specifies the data set TEMP, which is created from the specified key map.

□ The first DATA step creates the data set NEW and modifies the entry for the character. The second DATA step updates the data set TEMP.

□ In the second PROC GKEYMAP statement, the NAME= argument assigns the name of the key map, the DATA= argument specifies the data set TEMP as input to the procedure, and the KEYMAP option specifies that the map being generated is a key map (the default).

□ The KEYMAP= option in a GOPTIONS statement specifies the name of the new key map so that when the character @ is specified in a TITLE statement, the character ß is displayed in the output.

Using a Device Map to Change Character Sets

This example shows how you can use a device map to change hardware character sets when one character set does not contain the character required. Suppose you are using an HP 7475 plotter that uses the ANSI Standard character set by default. To display the national characters ü and £, which are not in the plotter's default hardware character set, your device driver must first select an alternate character set and then send a character or characters with appropriate values. The program creates a device map that makes the following translations:

□ When the character ü is specified in a string to be drawn in hardware characters, the driver selects hardware character set 2 and sends the hexadecimal string '757B'x, causing the device to draw the letter u ('75'x), backspace, and draw the umlaut ('7B'x).

□ When a pound sign (#) is specified in a string to be drawn in hardware characters, the driver produces a British sterling sign (£) by selecting hardware character set 2 and sending the code '23'x (corresponding to the £ character in the ANSI Standard character set).

The following program

1. creates a device map that performs these translations
2. specifies the device map in a GOPTIONS statement
3. uses the # character in a TITLE statement to print the £ character on the specified plotter.

Since the output generated by this program is sent to a plotter, it cannot be displayed on your monitor and is not included as output in this book. However, the program is included in the sample library as member GR28N02.

```
     /* specify the libref GFONT0 */
libname gfont0 'SAS-data-library';

     /* create the data set DMAP */
data dmap;

     /* assign variable values for the first translation */
   from='81'x;   /* SAS encoding for u umlaut */
   chartype=2;
   to='757b'x;   /* device encoding for u and for umlaut */
   tolen=2;
   output;

     /* assign variable values for the second translation */
   from='23'x;    /* SAS encoding for # */
   chartype=2;
   to='23'x;       /* device encoding for pound sterling */
   tolen=1;
   output;
run;

     /* create the device map from the data set DMAP */
proc gkeymap name=mydevmap
             data=dmap
             devmap
             device=hp7475
             type=map1n
             multfont;
run;
```

```
                    /* specify the device map and the device */
           goptions device=hp7475
                    devmap=mydevmap;

                    /* print a title with the special character */
           title font=none 'Value is #2000';

           proc gslide;
           run;
           quit;
```

This example illustrates the following features:

□ The LIBNAME statement associates the libref GFONT0 with the location of the SAS data library where you store your device maps and key maps.

□ The DATA step creates the data set DMAP, which contains one observation for each character to be mapped.

□ The values of the FROM variable are hexadecimal codes from the SAS Internal Character Encoding Table.

□ The values of the TO variable are hexadecimal codes for the ANSI Standard character set used by the device.

□ Both observations specify a value of 2 for the CHARTYPE variable since hardware character set 2 is to be selected for both output strings.

□ The TOLEN variable specifies the actual number of bytes to be output for each mapped character.

□ The PROC GKEYMAP statement assigns the name of the device map, MYDEVMAP, using the NAME= argument; uses the data set DMAP as input; and specifies that the map being generated is a device map.

□ The MULTFONT option is required when an alternate hardware character set is used.

□ The TYPE= option specifies that one character, ü, is to be mapped to the two characters represented by the hexadecimal value '757B'x.

□ The DEVMAP= option in a GOPTIONS statement specifies the name of the new device map.

□ The # character used in the TITLE statement is displayed as a £ when the output is sent to the plotter.

See Also

Chapter 5, "Graphics Options and Device Parameters Dictionary"
for more information on the DEVMAP= and KEYMAP= graphics options

Chapter 6, "SAS/GRAPH Fonts"
for more information on hardware fonts, special characters, and the search path for font specifications

Chapter 26, "The GFONT Procedure"
for more information on the libref GFONT0 and on displaying fonts

CHAPTER 29 The GMAP Procedure

(continued on next page)

(continued from previous page)

Overview

The GMAP procedure produces two-dimensional (choropleth) or three-dimensional (block, prism, and surface) color maps that show variations of a variable value with respect to an area. A wide assortment of geographic maps are available with SAS/GRAPH software, and you also can create your own geographic or spatial maps.

The GMAP procedure is used to

□ summarize data that vary by physical area

□ show trends and variations of data between geographic areas

□ highlight regional differences or extremes

□ produce maps.

Output 29.1 through 29.4 illustrate the types of maps that the GMAP procedure can produce.

Output 29.1 *Choropleth Map (GR29N01)*

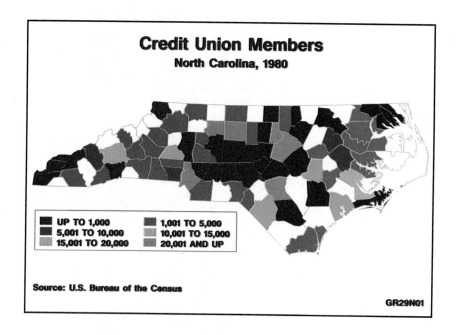

Output 29.2 *Block Map*
(GR29N02)

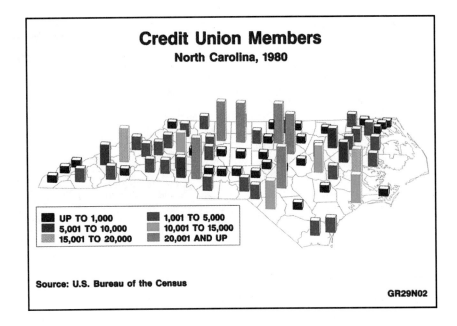

Output 29.3 *Prism Map*
(GR29N03)

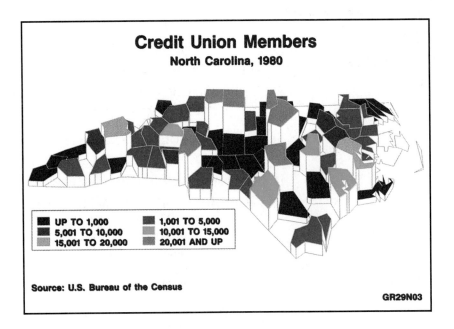

Output 29.4 *Surface Map*
(GR29N04)

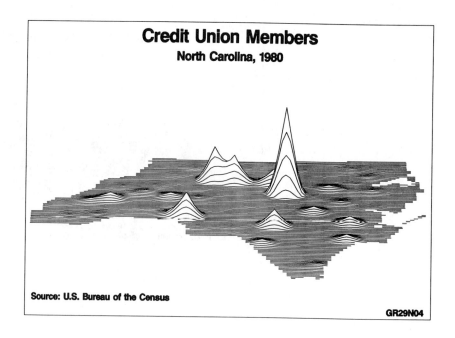

The GMAP procedure uses the following statements:

□ The PROC GMAP statement is required.

> **PROC GMAP** MAP=*map-data-set*
> <DATA=*response-data-set*>
> <ANNOTATE=*Annotate-data-set*>
> <GOUT=*output-catalog*>
> <ALL>;

□ At least one of the following statements is required:

> **CHORO** *response-variable* < . . . *response-variable-n*>
> </ <ANNOTATE=*Annotate-data-set*>
> <*appearance-options*>
> <*mapping-options*>
> <*legend-options*>
> <*description-options*>>;

> **BLOCK** *response-variable* < . . . *response-variable-n*>
> </ <ANNOTATE=*Annotate-data-set*>
> <*appearance-options*>
> <*mapping-options*>
> <*legend-options*>
> <*description-options*>>;

> **PRISM** *response-variable* < . . . *response-variable-n*>
> </ <ANNOTATE=*Annotate-data-set*>
> <*appearance-options*>
> <*mapping-options*>
> <*legend-options*>
> <*description-options*>>;

GMAP Procedure Syntax

> **SURFACE** *response-variable* $< \ldots$ *response-variable-n>*
> $</$ *<*ANNOTATE=*Annotate-data-set>*
> *<appearance-options>*
> *<description-options>>;*

□ An ID statement must accompany each PROC GMAP statement.

> **ID** *variable* $< \ldots$ *variable-n>;*

□ The following statements are optional and local:

> **BY** *<options>* *variable;*

> **NOTE** *<options>* *<'text'>;*

□ The following statements are optional and global:

> **FOOTNOTE**$<1 \ldots 10>$ *<options>* *<'text'>;*

> **LEGEND**$<1 \ldots 99>$ *<options>;*

> **PATTERN**$<1 \ldots 99>$ *<options>;*

> **TITLE**$<1 \ldots 10>$ *<options>* *<'text'>;*

For complete statement syntax, see the section on the appropriate statement.

Statement Descriptions

The purpose of each statement is described here.

BLOCK	creates three-dimensional block maps on which levels of magnitude of the specified response variables are represented by blocks of varying height, fill pattern, and color.
BY	specifies the variable or variables by which data are grouped for processing. A separate map is produced for each value of the BY variable. See Chapter 10, "The BY Statement."
CHORO	creates two-dimensional choropleth maps on which levels of magnitude of the specified response variables are represented by varying fill patterns and colors.
FOOTNOTE	defines the text and appearance of footnotes. See Chapter 11, "The FOOTNOTE Statement."
ID	specifies the variable or variables in the map and response data sets that define unit areas. Any variable identified in the ID statement must be common to both the map data set and the response data set. (The variable should have the same type and length in both data sets, as well as the same name.)

LEGEND	defines legend characteristics that modify the text, appearance, and position of a legend. See Chapter 13, "The LEGEND Statement." Once defined, LEGEND definitions are assigned with the LEGEND= option in BLOCK, CHORO, or PRISM statements.
NOTE	defines the text and appearance of notes that appear in the procedure output area. See Chapter 14, "The NOTE Statement."
PATTERN	defines the color and fill pattern used to fill unit areas and blocks. See Chapter 15, "The PATTERN Statement." Once defined, the PATTERN definitions are assigned automatically by the GMAP procedure.
PRISM	creates three-dimensional prism maps in which levels of magnitude of the specified response variables are represented by polyhedrons (raised polygons) of varying height, fill pattern, and color.
PROC GMAP	starts the procedure and specifies the names of the data sets to be used for the map, as well as any additional input or output options.
SURFACE	creates three-dimensional surface maps in which levels of magnitude of the specified response variables are represented by spikes of varying height.
TITLE	defines the text and appearance of the titles. See Chapter 17, "The TITLE Statement."

GMAP Procedure Description

The following sections address issues that pertain to the GMAP procedure as a whole, including terminology, special data considerations, and the use of global statements and RUN groups.

Terminology

The following terms are used in the discussion of the GMAP procedure and are defined in the Glossary. Some of these terms and some additional terms are illustrated in Figure 29.1.

block map	response variable
boundary	segment
choropleth map	surface map
polygon	unit area
prism map	

Figure 29.1 *GMAP Procedure Terms*

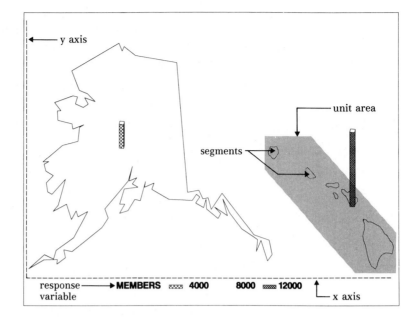

Summary of Use

To use the GMAP procedure, you must do the following:

1. If necessary, issue a LIBNAME statement for the SAS data library containing the map data set you want to display.

2. Determine what processing needs to be done to the map data set before it is displayed. Use the GPROJECT, GREDUCE, and GREMOVE procedures with a DATA step to perform the necessary processing.

3. Issue a LIBNAME statement for the SAS data set containing the response data set, or use a DATA step to create a response data set.

4. Use the PROC GMAP statement to identify the map and response data sets.

5. Use the ID statement to name the identification variable.

6. Use a BLOCK, CHORO, PRISM, or SURFACE statement to display your map.

Data Considerations

The GMAP procedure requires that the map and response data sets have certain characteristics. The procedure stops with an error message if the specified data sets do not meet these requirements.

Map Data Sets

This section discusses topics on creating your own map data sets. If you work only with the map data sets supplied with SAS/GRAPH software, see "SAS/GRAPH Map Data Sets" later in this chapter.

A *map data set* is a SAS data set that defines the boundaries of unit areas, such as states or counties. A map data set must contain the following variables:

□ a numeric variable named X containing the horizontal coordinates of the boundary points.

□ a numeric variable named Y containing the vertical coordinates of the boundary points.

□ one or more variables that uniquely identify the unit areas in the map. Unit area identification variables can be either character or numeric. These variables are indicated in the ID statement.

Optionally, the map data set also can contain a variable named SEGMENT to identify segments of unit areas that are noncontiguous. Each unique value of the SEGMENT variable within a single unit area defines a map *segment*. If the SEGMENT variable is not present, all unit areas in the map are drawn as single closed polygons; that is, all unit areas consist of a single segment.

Any variables in the map data set other than the ones in the list above are ignored for the purposes of determining map boundaries.

The X and Y variable values in the map data set do not have to be in any specific units because they are rescaled by the GMAP procedure based on the minimum and maximum values in the data set. The minimum X and Y values are in the lower-left corner of the map, and the maximum X and Y values are in the upper-right corner.

Map data sets with coordinates in latitude and longitude should be projected before being used with PROC GMAP. See Chapter 33, "The GPROJECT Procedure," for details.

The observations for each segment of a unit area in the map data set must occur in the order in which the points are to be joined. The GMAP procedure forms unit area outlines by connecting the boundary points of each segment in the order they appear in the data set. The first and last points in each segment also are joined.

SAS/GRAPH software includes a number of predefined map data sets. These data sets are described in "SAS/GRAPH Map Data Sets" later in this chapter.

You can also create your own map data sets. For example, the following DATA step creates a SAS data set containing coordinates for a single unit area, a square:

```
data square;
   input id x y;
   cards;
1 0 0
1 0 40
1 40 40
1 40 0
;
```

Unit areas with multiple polygons   A unit area is defined by all of the observations in the map data set that have a single value of the variable that defines unit areas (the variable that is listed in the ID statement). Whether the observations for a unit area compose a single polygon or a collection of polygons depends on the following:

□ the value or values of the SEGMENT variable

□ whether the unit area has separate boundaries for polygons that actually fall outside of the primary polygon.

A unit area will have multiple polygons if one of the following is true:

□ the unit area has more than one value for the SEGMENT variable. For example, the data set created by the following DATA step produces a single unit area containing two segments, as shown in Figure 29.2:

```
data map;
   input id $ 1-8 segment x y;
   cards;
square   1 0 0
square   1 0 4
square   1 4 4
square   1 4 0
square   2 5 5
square   2 5 7
square   2 7 7
square   2 7 5
;
```

Figure 29.2 *Single Unit Area with Two Segments*

SEGMENT=2

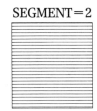

SEGMENT=1

You can use different values of the SEGMENT variable to create separate polygons within a single unit area. For example, in the US map data set supplied with SAS/GRAPH software, the state of Hawaii (a unit area) contains six different values in the SEGMENT variable, one for each island in the state.

□ the unit area consists of a primary polygon plus one or more separate boundaries for polygons that do not fall within the primary polygon boundary. The separate boundaries are separated from the primary polygon boundary by missing values for X and Y. For example, the data set created by the following DATA step produces the map shown in Figure 29.3:

```
data map;
    input id $ 1-8 segment x y;
    cards;
square    1 0 0
square    1 0 4
square    1 4 4
square    1 4 0
square    1 . .
square    1 5 5
square    1 5 7
square    1 7 7
square    1 7 5
;
```

Figure 29.3 *Single Unit Area Containing Two Polygons*

The map data sets supplied with SAS/GRAPH software do not define separate polygons in this manner because this type of unit area is best defined using separate polygon segments by changing the value of the SEGMENT variable.

You also can use separate boundaries to create an enclosed polygon (that is, a polygon that falls within the primary polygon for a single segment). For example, the data set created by the following DATA step produces the map shown in Figure 29.4:

```
data map;
   input id $ 1-8 segment x y;
   cards;
square   1 0 0
square   1 0 4
square   1 4 4
square   1 4 0
square   1 . .
square   1 1 1
square   1 2 2
square   1 3 1
;
```

Figure 29.4 *Single Unit Area with Hole*

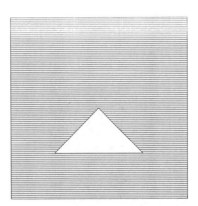

Enclosed polygons are particularly useful for creating holes such as lakes or when a second unit area falls within the unit area. Ordinarily, if one unit area is surrounded by another, the fill pattern of the external unit area is drawn over the fill pattern for the internal one, instead of around it. You can avoid this problem by adding an observation to the map data for the external unit area with missing values for X and Y, followed by the coordinates of the internal unit area, but using the ID values for the external unit area. For example, the data set created by the following DATA step produces the map shown in Figure 29.5:

```
data map;
    input id $ 1-8 segment x y;
    cards;
square   1 0 0
square   1 0 4
square   1 4 4
square   1 4 0
square   1 . .
square   1 1 1
square   1 2 2
square   1 3 1
triangle 1 1 1
triangle 1 2 2
triangle 1 3 1
;
```

Figure 29.5 *Unit Area within a Unit Area*

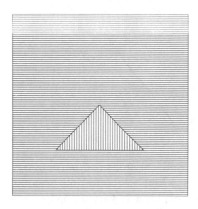

You can use enclosed polygons to create lakes or other empty areas in a map. For example, in the CANADA2 data set supplied with SAS/GRAPH software, the map data for the Northwest Territories (a unit area) use enclosed polygons for two lakes.

Note: A single map segment (a section of a unit area with a single value of the SEGMENT variable) cannot contain multiple polygons without at least one observation with missing values for X and Y. All segments within the map data sets supplied by SAS/GRAPH software contain a single polygon that can have one or more separate boundaries, each separated by an observation with missing values for X and Y.

Response Data Sets

For each unit area, the response data set contains one or more response variables to be represented on the map. The response data set must contain unit area identification variables (the variables specified in the ID statement) of the same name, type, and length as those in the map data set. The GMAP procedure matches the value of the response variables for each unit area in the response data set to the corresponding unit area in the map data set to create the output graphs.

Typically, the response data set includes one observation for each different value of the unit area identification variable or for each unique combination of unit area identification variables if more than one is used. Each observation contains the value of the response variable or variables to categorize the corresponding map unit area.

The values of the unit area identification variables in the response data set determine the unit areas to be included on the map unless you use the ALL option in the PROC GMAP statement. That is, unless you use the ALL option in the PROC GMAP statement, only the unit areas with response values are shown on the map. As a result, you do not need to subset your map data set if you are mapping only a small section of the map. However, if you map the same small section frequently, you should create a subset of the map data set for efficiency.

For choropleth, block, and prism maps, the response variables can be either character or numeric. For surface maps, the response variables must be numeric with only positive values.

Response levels for block, choropleth, and prism maps   The GMAP procedure can produce block, choropleth, and prism maps for both numeric and character response variables. Numeric variables fall into two categories: discrete and continuous.

Discrete variables contain a finite number of specific numeric values to be represented on the map. For example, a variable that contains only the values 1989 or 1990 is a discrete variable.

Continuous variables contain a range of numeric values to be represented on the map. For example, a variable that contains any real value between 0 and 100 is a continuous variable.

Numeric response variables are always treated as continuous variables unless the DISCRETE option is used in the action statement. The type of the response variable affects the way response levels are selected for the map. *Response levels* are the values that identify categories of data on the graph. These categories shown on the graph are based on the values of the response variable. Based on the type of the response variable, a response level can represent the following:

□ a specific character value. If the response variable is character type, the GMAP procedure treats each unique value of the variable as a response level. For example, if the response variable contains the names of ten regions, each region will be a response level, resulting in ten response levels.

The exception to this is that the MIDPOINTS= option chooses specific response level values. Any response variable values that do not match one of the specified response level values are ignored. For example, if the response variable contains the names of ten regions and you specify the following, only the observations for **Midwest**, **Northeast**, and **Northwest** are included on the map:

```
midpoints='Midwest' 'Northeast' 'Northwest'
```

□ a range of numeric values. If the response variable is numeric, the GMAP procedure determines the number of response levels for the response variable. Each response level then represents the median of a range of values.

The following are exceptions to this:

□ The LEVELS= option specifies the number of response levels to be used on the map.

□ The DISCRETE option causes the numeric variable to be treated as a discrete variable.

□ The MIDPOINTS= option chooses specific response level values that are used as medians of the value ranges.

If the response variable values are continuous, the GMAP procedure assigns response level intervals automatically unless you specify otherwise. The response levels represent a range of values rather than a single value.

□ a specific numeric value. If the response variable is numeric and you use the DISCRETE option, the GMAP procedure treats the variable much the same way as it treats a character response variable. That is, the procedure creates a response level for each unique value of the response variable. If the DISCRETE option is used with a numeric response variable that has an associated format, each formatted value is represented by a different response level. Formatted values are truncated to 16 characters.

You can change the way response levels are selected for block, choropleth, and prism maps using the DISCRETE, MIDPOINTS=, and LEVELS= options. See the appropriate action statement section later in this chapter for more information.

Global Statements

All currently defined titles and footnotes are displayed in every map generated by the GMAP procedure or by a RUN group. The procedure automatically assigns currently defined PATTERN definitions as needed to maps that use patterns. You can assign currently defined LEGEND definitions using BLOCK, CHORO, or PRISM statement options.

To display different titles and footnotes on your maps, define the titles and footnotes at the beginning of a RUN group. Any TITLE or FOOTNOTE statements of a higher level (that is, a lower number) remain in effect and display on the graph.

RUN Groups

The GMAP procedure supports RUN-group processing. The action statements for this procedure are

BLOCK

CHORO

PRISM

SURFACE.

For more information on RUN groups, see Chapter 2, "Running SAS/GRAPH Programs."

PROC GMAP Statement

The PROC GMAP statement initiates the procedure and specifies the data sets that contain the map data and the response data. In addition, it can optionally specify a data set for annotation and a destination catalog for graphics output. The GMAP procedure ends when a QUIT, DATA, or another PROC statement is encountered, or when the SAS session terminates.

Syntax

The general form of the GMAP statement is

PROC GMAP MAP=*map-data-set*
      <DATA=*response-data-set*>
      <ANNOTATE=*Annotate-data-set*>
      <GOUT=*output-catalog*>
      <ALL>;

Requirements

The GMAP procedure requires two input SAS data sets: a map data set and a response data set. You must always identify the map data set by including the following required argument with the PROC GMAP statement:

MAP=*map-data-set*
    names a SAS data set containing the Cartesian coordinates for the boundary points of each unit area.

The GMAP procedure also must have an input (response) data set. By default, the procedure uses the most recently created data set as its input data set. You can use the DATA= option to select a specific data set. If no data set has been created in the current SAS session and you do not use the DATA= option, an error occurs and the procedure stops.

The map data set and the response data set must contain one or more common variables that identify the unit areas (for example, counties, states, or provinces) that make up the map. These variables enable the GMAP procedure to relate the information in both data sets and create a map. The PROC GMAP statement must be accompanied by an ID statement that designates the unit area variables. For a more complete description of the map and response data sets, see "Data Considerations" earlier in this chapter.

You must also use at least one CHORO, BLOCK, PRISM, or SURFACE statement to select the type or types of maps to be produced.

Options

You can use the following options with the PROC GMAP statement. Options used with the PROC GMAP statement affect all graphs produced by the procedure.

ALL

specifies that any maps generated should include every unit area from the map data set, even if no observation or response variable value for the unit area is present in the response data set. If you do not use this option, the GMAP procedure does not draw unit areas in the map data set that have no corresponding response values in the response data set.

When you use the ALL option and a BY statement in a RUN group, the maps generated for each BY group include every unit area from the map data set.

ANNOTATE=*Annotate-data-set*
ANNO=*Annotate-data-set*

specifies a data set to provide annotation of all graphs produced by the GMAP procedure. To annotate individual graphs, use the ANNOTATE= option in an action statement.

Note: Annotate coordinate systems 1, 2, 7, and 8 are not valid with block, prism, or surface maps.

Annotate-data-set must contain the appropriate Annotate variables. See Chapter 18, "The Annotate Data Set," for more information.

DATA=*response-data-set*

specifies the name of the input data set that contains the response values evaluated and represented on the map. The data set also must contain the same identification variable or variables as the map data set.

By default, PROC GMAP uses the most recently created SAS data set. If you do not use the DATA= option and no data set has been created in the current SAS session, an error occurs and the procedure stops.

Typically, the response data set contains one observation for each value of the unit area variable and one or more response variables for each observation. For a more complete description of the response data set, see "Response Data Sets" earlier in this chapter.

GOUT=*output-catalog*

specifies the SAS catalog in which to save the graphics output produced by the GMAP procedure for later replay. You can use the GREPLAY procedure to view the graphs stored in the catalog. If you do not use the GOUT= option, catalog entries are written to the default catalog WORK.GSEG, which is erased at the end of your session.

ID Statement

The ID statement lists the variable or variables that identify unit areas in the map data set and the response data set.

Syntax

The general form of the ID statement is

ID *variable* < ... *variable-n*>;

where *variable* is the name of a variable in the input data set that defines unit areas. *Variable* can be either numeric or character.

Requirements

The map and response data sets used with the GMAP procedure must contain all of the variables identified in the ID statement. *Variable* should have the same name, type, and length in both the response and map data sets.

Every variable listed in the ID statement must appear in both the map and response data sets. Furthermore, the values of the unit area identification variable or variables must appear in the same order in both data sets.

BLOCK Statement

The BLOCK statement produces a block map using the map and response data sets specified in the PROC GMAP statement. A block at the approximate center of each unit area conveys information about response variable values. The height of each block represents a response level. The height of the blocks is not directly proportional to the value of the response variable. Instead, the block heights increase in order of the response levels.

You can use options in the BLOCK statement to customize the appearance of the map. For example, you can select the size of the blocks and the colors and fill patterns for both the blocks and the surface of the map areas. You can control the selection of block height for each range of the response variable. You also can specify an Annotate data set used for enhancing the appearance of maps produced by the BLOCK statement.

Syntax

The general form of the BLOCK statement is

BLOCK *response-variable* < ... *response-variable-n*>
    </ <ANNOTATE=*Annotate-data-set*>
        <*appearance-options*>
        <*mapping-options*>
        <*legend-options*>
        <*description-options*>>;

□ *response-variable* is a variable in the response data set that contains response values represented on the map. If more than one response variable is supplied, a separate map is drawn for each.

□ *appearance-options* can be one or more of the following:

BLOCKSIZE=*size*

CBLKOUT=*block-outline-color*

CEMPTY=*empty-unit-outline-color*

COUTLINE=*nonempty-unit-outline-color*

XSIZE=*n* <*units*>

where *n* is the size of the map in the X direction

YSIZE=*n* <*units*>

where *n* is the size of the map in the Y direction

XVIEW=*x*

YVIEW=*y*

ZVIEW=*z*

□ *mapping-options* can be one or more of the following:

AREA=*n*

where *n* indicates which variable in the ID statement determines groups distinguished by surface pattern

DISCRETE

LEVELS=*n*

where *n* specifies the number of response levels

MIDPOINTS=*value-list*

where *value-list* specifies the response levels for a range of response values

MISSING

□ *legend-options* can be one or more of the following:

CTEXT=*text-color*

LEGEND=LEGEND<1 . . . 99>

NOLEGEND

□ *description-options* can be either or both of the following:

DESCRIPTION='*string*'

NAME='*string*'

Options are fully described in "Options" later in this section.

Requirements

The BLOCK statement must specify at least one response variable contained in the response data set. If you specify more than one variable, a map is produced for each response variable. Blocks are not drawn for missing values for the response variable unless you use the MISSING option in the BLOCK statement. The ID statement must be used in conjunction with the BLOCK statement.

Options

You can use the following options in the BLOCK statement. Options used in a BLOCK statement affect all maps produced by that statement. If you use any of the following options, separate them from the response variables with a slash (/). If you do not use any options, omit the slash.

ANNOTATE=*Annotate-data-set*
ANNO=*Annotate-data-set*
> specifies a data set to provide annotation of graphs produced by the BLOCK statement. *Annotate-data-set* must contain the appropriate Annotate variables. See Chapter 18 for details.
>
> **Note:** Annotate coordinate systems 1, 2, 7, and 8 are not valid with block maps.
>
> If the ANNOTATE= option is also used in the PROC GMAP statement, both sets of annotation are applied. If you specify BY-group processing, the Annotate data set must contain the BY variable. For details, see "Using BY-Group Processing with the Annotate Facility" in Chapter 18 and "Details of BY-Group Processing" in Chapter 10.

AREA=*n*
> specifies that a different map/plot pattern be used for the surface of each unit area or group of unit areas on the map, where *n* indicates which variable in the ID statement determines the groups distinguished by surface fill pattern. If your ID statement has only one unit area identification variable, use AREA=1 to indicate that each unit area surface uses a different fill pattern. If you have more than one variable in your ID statement, use *n* to indicate the position of the variable that defines groups that will share a pattern. When you use the AREA= option, the map data set should be sorted in order of the variables in the ID statement.
>
> Only those PATTERN statements with a VALUE= option specifying valid map/plot patterns are used to fill the surface areas in the map. If no appropriate PATTERN definitions have been defined, the GMAP procedure cycles through a default set of fill patterns and colors.
>
> By default, all map unit areas are drawn using the same surface fill pattern.

BLOCKSIZE=*size*
> specifies the width of the blocks. The unit for *size* is the character cell width for the selected output device. By default, BLOCKSIZE=2.

CBLKOUT=*block-outline-color*
> specifies the outline color for all blocks. By default, block outlines are drawn in the same color as the block patterns.

CEMPTY=*empty-unit-outline-color*
> specifies the surface outline color for empty unit areas on the map. This option is ignored unless you use the ALL option in the PROC GMAP statement. If you do not use the ALL option, unit areas without response variable values are not drawn on the graph. If you use the ALL option, unit areas contained in the map data set that are not in the response data set are drawn but left empty.
>
> If you use the ALL option but do not use the CEMPTY= option, PROC GMAP uses the first color in the current colors list to outline

(CEMPTY= continued) unit areas contained in the map data set that are not in the response data set.

COUTLINE=*nonempty-unit-outline-color*

specifies the surface outline color for unit areas that are not empty. By default, the outline color is the same as the surface pattern color for the unit areas.

CTEXT=*text-color*

specifies a color for the text in the legend. If you do not use the CTEXT= option, a color specification is searched for in the following order:

1. the CTEXT= option in a GOPTIONS statement
2. the default, the first color in the colors list.

If you use the CTEXT= option, the color specification is overridden if you also use the COLOR= parameter of a LABEL= or VALUE= option in a LEGEND definition assigned to the map legend. The COLOR= parameter determines the color of the legend label or the color of the legend value descriptions, respectively.

DESCRIPTION='*string*'
DES='*string*'

specifies a descriptive string, up to 40 characters long, that appears in the Description field of the catalog entry for the map. The description does not appear on the map. By default, the GMAP procedure provides a description of the form BLOCK MAP OF *variable*, where *variable* is the name of the variable specified in the BLOCK statement.

DISCRETE

treats a numeric response variable as a discrete variable rather than as a continuous variable. When you use the DISCRETE option, the response variable values are not grouped into ranges; instead, the GMAP procedure uses a separate response level (block height, fill pattern, and color) for each different value of the formatted response variable. The LEVELS= option is ignored when you use the DISCRETE option.

Use this option if your response variable has a user-written format.

LEGEND=LEGEND<1 . . . 99>

assigns legend characteristics to the map legend. The option value indicates which LEGEND definition to use. The LEGEND= option is ignored if the specified LEGEND definition is not currently in effect. See Chapter 13 for more information.

LEVELS=*n*

specifies the number of response levels to be graphed when the response variables are continuous. Each level is assigned a different block height, fill pattern, and color combination.

If neither the LEVELS= option nor the DISCRETE option is used, then the GMAP procedure determines the number of response levels using the formula FLOOR($1+3.3 \log(N)$), where N is the number of unique unit area identification variable values.

The LEVELS= option is ignored when you use the DISCRETE option.

MIDPOINTS=*value-list*
> specifies the response levels for the range of response values represented by each level (block height, fill pattern, and color combination).
>
> **For numeric response variables**, *value-list* can be specified in the following ways:

n n . . . n

n,n, . . . ,n

n TO *n* <BY *increment*> <*n . . . n*> <*n, . . . ,n*>

n n . . . n TO *n* <BY *increment*> <*n . . . n*>

n,n, . . . ,n TO *n* <BY *increment*> <*n, . . . ,n*>

> For discrete numeric values, values can be specified in any order.
>
> **For character response variables**, *value-list* must be a list of response values. Values must be enclosed in single quotes and separated by blanks (commas are not allowed as separators), as shown here:

```
midpoints='Midwest' 'Northeast' 'Northwest'
```

> The values can be specified in any order. You can selectively exclude some response variable values from the map, as shown here:

```
midpoints='Midwest'
```

> Only those observations for which the response variable exactly matches one of the values listed in the MIDPOINTS= option are shown on the map. As a result, observations may be excluded inadvertently if values in the list are misspelled or if the case does not match exactly.

MISSING
> accepts a missing value as a valid level for the response variable.

NAME=*'string'*
> specifies a string, up to eight characters long, that appears in the Name field of the catalog entry for the map. *String* must be a valid SAS name. By default, the name assigned is GMAP. If either the name specified or the default name duplicates an existing name in the catalog, SAS/GRAPH software adds a number to the duplicate name to create a unique name, for example, GMAP2.

NOLEGEND
> suppresses the legend.

XSIZE=*n* <*units*>
YSIZE=*n* <*units*>
> specify the physical dimensions of the map to be drawn, where *n* is the number of units. By default, the map uses the entire procedure output area.
>
> Valid *units* are CM (centimeters), IN (inches), or PCT (percentage of the graphics output area). By default, the unit is character cells.
>
> If you specify values for *n* that are greater than the dimensions of the procedure output area, the map is drawn using the default size.

XVIEW=*x*
YVIEW=*y*
ZVIEW=*z*

specify coordinates of the viewing position in the reference coordinate system. In this system, the four corners of the map lie on the X-Y plane at coordinates (0,0,0), (0,1,0), (1,1,0), and (1,0,0). No axes are actually drawn on the maps produced by PROC GMAP, but imagine that the maps are drawn in an X-Y plane as in Figure 29.1.

Your viewing position cannot coincide with the viewing reference point at coordinates (0.5,0.5,0), the center of the map. The value for *z* cannot be negative.

If you do not use the XVIEW=, YVIEW=, and ZVIEW= options, the default coordinates are (0.5,−2,3). This viewing position is well above and to the south of the center of the map. You can specify one, two, or all three of the view coordinates; any that you do not explicitly specify are assigned the default values.

Figure 29.6 shows the position of the viewing reference point, as well as the default viewing position.

Figure 29.6 *Viewing Position and Viewing Reference Point*

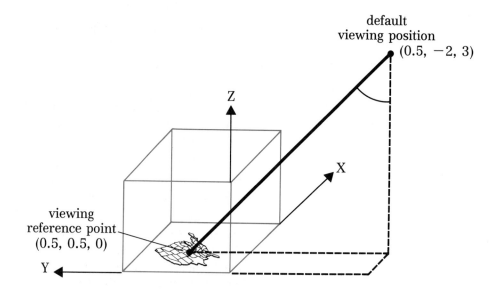

Using the BLOCK Statement

A separate map is produced for each response variable listed in the BLOCK statement. For example, the following statement produces two separate block maps:

```
block resp1 resp2;
```

Response variables can be either numeric or character. Numeric response variables with continuous values are grouped into ranges, or response levels. Each response level is assigned a different block height and a different fill pattern and color combination. Character variables and numeric variables (when you use the DISCRETE option) have a different response level for each unique response variable value. In these cases, the block height can be used to identify discrete values but cannot be used to read a discrete value directly. You must use the legend to determine the exact value of a discrete variable. Numeric variables are treated as continuous unless you use the DISCRETE option.

For numeric response variables with continuous values, you can control the selection of response level ranges using the MIDPOINTS= or LEVELS= option. By default, the GMAP procedure determines the number of levels for the map using the formula FLOOR(1+3.3 log(N)), where N is the number of unique values of the unit area identification variable or variables. If a numeric response variable has an associated format, you should use the DISCRETE option.

For numeric response variables, block heights increase in order of response levels. That is, the lowest blocks correspond to the first level, and the tallest blocks correspond to the last level. For character response variables, the lowest blocks correspond to the first character values, and the tallest blocks correspond to the last character variable.

You can control the width of the blocks in the map using the BLOCKSIZE= option. You can control the surface fill pattern using the AREAS= option.

You can alter the perspective of the map by selecting a viewing position, which represents the point in space from which the map is viewed. See the discussion of the XVIEW=, YVIEW=, and ZVIEW= options in "Options" earlier in this section for details.

Selecting Patterns for the Map

PATTERN definitions can be used to define the fill patterns and colors used to fill block faces and map surfaces. PATTERN definitions that define valid bar/block patterns can be applied to response levels (blocks). These patterns are as follows:

EMPTY

SOLID

style<*density*>

    where

    style   can be X | L | R.

    density   can be 1 . . . 5.

Definitions that define valid map/plot patterns can be applied to map surfaces. These patterns are as follows:

MEMPTY | ME

MSOLID | MS

M*density*<*style*<*angle*>>

    where

    density   can be 1 . . . 5.

    style   can be N | X.

    angle   can be 0 . . . 360.

See Chapter 15 for more information on pattern values and default pattern rotation. See the AREAS= option description in "Options" earlier in this section for more information on surface patterns.

The GMAP procedure chooses default fill patterns and colors if no PATTERN definitions have been defined or if the map uses more patterns than are defined in the PATTERN definitions.

Using Other Global Statements

LEGEND definitions can be used to adjust the location and appearance of the legend that is produced with the map. See Chapter 13 for details on the legend characteristics you can define with the LEGEND statement. You must use the LEGEND= option in the BLOCK statement to apply a LEGEND definition to your map. See "Options" earlier in this section for details of the LEGEND= option.

BLOCK Statement Examples

The following examples illustrate the major features of the BLOCK statement.

The examples use the data set SITES. Each observation in this data set contains a unit area identification variable, STATE, which matches the STATE variable in the SAS/GRAPH map data sets, and a response variable, SITES, which is the number of installed products in the state.

Because the examples use one of the map data sets supplied with SAS/GRAPH software, you may need to replace *SAS-data-library* in the LIBNAME statement with the actual location of the SAS data library containing the Institute-supplied map data sets on your system. Contact your SAS Software Consultant for the location of the map data sets at your site.

If your site automatically assigns the libref MAPS to the SAS data library containing the Institute-supplied map data sets, delete the LIBNAME statement in these examples.

Simple Block Map

This example uses the BLOCK statement to map the number of products installed in each state for a fictitious company.

The following program statements produce Output 29.5:

```
     /* set the graphics environment */
goptions reset=global gunit=pct border
         ftext=swissb htitle=6 htext=3;

     /* assign the libref MAPS */
libname maps 'SAS-data-library';
```

```
        /* create response data set SITES */
data sites;
   length state 2;
   input state sites;
   cards;
 1        80
 2        31
more data lines
55       197
56        59
;
run;


        /* define titles and footnotes for map */
title1 'Products Installed in the USA';
title2 h=4 'XXX Corp.';
footnote1 j=l '  US map data set supplied'
            ' with SAS/GRAPH' '02'x ' Software';
footnote2 j=r 'GR29N05  ';


        /* define pattern characteristics */
pattern1 value=solid;
pattern2 value=mempty;


        /* display the block map */
proc gmap map=maps.us data=sites;
   id state;
   block sites;
run;
quit;
```

Output 29.5 *Simple Block Map (GR29N05)*

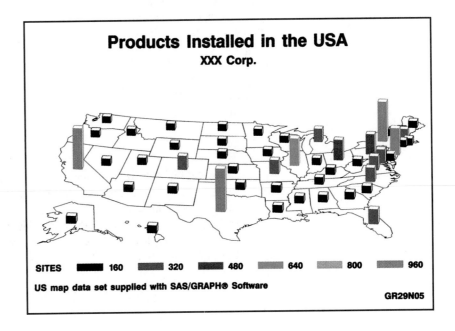

This example illustrates the following features:

☐ The GMAP procedure uses the bar/block pattern defined in the PATTERN1 statement for the block faces. The procedure repeats the pattern for each color in the colors list, as needed for the response levels.

☐ A single pattern, defined in the PATTERN2 statement, is used for all map surfaces.

☐ The ID statement specifies the variable in the map data set and the response data set that defines unit areas.

☐ Since the DISCRETE option is not used, the response variable is assumed to have a continuous range of values. Because neither the LEVELS= nor MIDPOINTS= option is used, the GMAP procedure selects a number of levels based on the number of unit areas and then calculates appropriate response levels.

Enhanced Block Map

This example graphs the same data as the previous example but changes the map viewpoint.

The following program statements produce Output 29.6:

```
    /* set the graphics environment */
goptions reset=global gunit=pct border
         ftext=swissb htitle=6 htext=3;


    /* assign the libref MAPS */
libname maps 'SAS-data-library';


    /* create response data set SITES */
data sites;
   length state 2;
   input state sites;
   cards;
 1        80
 2        31
more data lines
55        197
56        59
;
run;


    /* define titles and footnotes for map */
title1 'Products Installed in the USA';
title2 h=4 'XXX Corp.';
footnote1 j=l '  US map data set supplied'
          ' with SAS/GRAPH' '02'x ' Software';
footnote2 j=r 'GR29N06  ';


    /* define pattern characteristics */
pattern1 value=solid;
pattern2 value=mempty;


    /* define legend characteristics */
legend1 value=(j=l) label=('Sites:') across=4 frame;
```

```
                  /* display the block map */
              proc gmap map=maps.us data=sites;
                 id state;
                 block sites / legend=legend1
                               levels=8
                               xview=0.75
                               zview=5;
              run;
              quit;
```

Output 29.6 *Enhanced Block Map (GR29N06)*

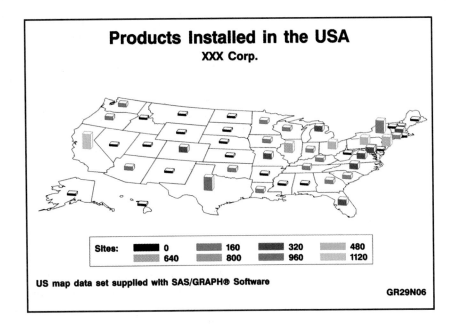

This example illustrates the following features:

□ The PATTERN statements define patterns for both the block faces and the map surface. The GMAP procedure uses bar/block patterns for blocks and map/plot patterns for the map surface, so the PATTERN1 definition is applied to blocks and the PATTERN2 definition is applied to map unit areas. Since no colors are specified, the procedure repeats each pattern for every color in the colors list.

□ The LEGEND= option assigns the legend characteristics defined in the LEGEND1 statement to the map legend.

□ The LEVELS= option specifies the number of response levels for the graph.

□ The XVIEW= option changes the viewpoint for the map so that the map appears to be slightly rotated. The ZVIEW= option raises the height of the viewpoint. Note that the change in viewpoint causes the blocks to appear shorter.

Patterned Block Map

This example graphs the same data as the previous two examples but patterns the surface of the map by unit area.

The following program statements produce Output 29.7 and Output 29.8:

```
    /* set the graphics environment */
goptions reset=global gunit=pct border
        ftext=swissb htitle=6 htext=3;

    /* assign the libref MAPS */
libname maps 'SAS-data-library';

    /* create response data set SITES */
data sites;
   length state 2;
   input state region sites;
   cards;
 1  5     80
 2  1     31
more data lines
55  4    197
56  2     59
;
run;


    /* create map data set STATES1            */
    /* by adding REGION to the US map data set */
data states1;
   set maps.us;
   select;
        /* west */
      when (state=53 or state=41 or state=16 or state=32 or state=06
          or state=02 or state=15) region=1;
        /* north central */
      when (state=30 or state=46 or state=38 or state=31
          or state=20 or state=56 or state=49
          or state=08) region=2;
        /* southwest */
      when (state=04 or state=35 or state=48
          or state=40) region=3;
        /* midwest */
      when (state=27 or state=19 or state=29 or state=55
          or state=17 or state=26 or state=18
          or state=39) region=4;
        /* south */
      when (state=05 or state=22 or state=01 or state=21 or state=47
          or state=28 or state=13 or state=12 or state=45 or state=37
          or state=51 or state=54) region=5;
        /* new england */
      otherwise region=6;
   end;
run;
```

```
    /* sort the new map data set */
proc sort data=states1 out=states;
   by region state;
run;

    /* define titles and footnotes for map */
title1 'Products Installed in the USA';
title2 h=4 'XXX Corp.';
footnote1 j=l '  US map data set supplied'
          ' with SAS/GRAPH' '02'x ' Software';
footnote2 j=r 'GR29N07(a)  ';

    /* define pattern characteristics */
pattern1 value=empty repeat=8;
pattern2 value=msolid repeat=50;

    /* define legend characteristics */
legend1 value=(j=l) label=('Sites:') across=4;

    /* display the block maps */
proc gmap map=states data=sites;
   id region state;
   block sites / legend=legend1
                 levels=8
                 area=1
                 coutline=gray;
run;

      /* define new footnote for map */
   footnote2 j=r 'GR29N07(b)  ';

   block sites / legend=legend1
                 levels=8
                 area=2
                 coutline=gray;
run;
quit;
```

Output 29.7 *Block Map Patterned by REGION (GR29N07(a))*

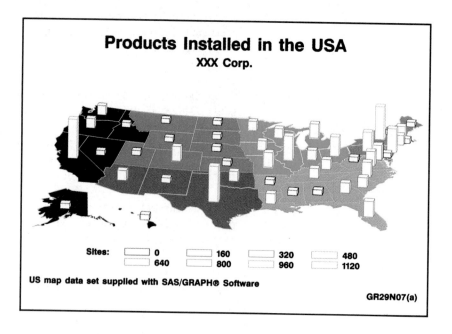

Output 29.8 *Block Map Patterned by STATE (GR29N07(b))*

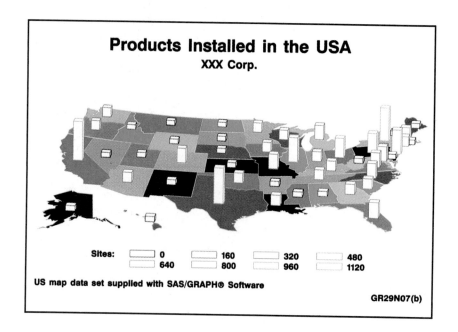

This example illustrates the following features:

□ The PATTERN1 statement defines the fill pattern used for the blocks. The PATTERN2 statement defines the fill patterns used for the map surface.

□ In the first RUN group, which produces Output 29.7, the AREA= option specifies that the map surface should be patterned by the first variable in the ID statement, REGION.

□ In the second RUN group, which produces Output 29.8, the AREA= option specifies that the map surface should be patterned by the second variable in the ID statement, STATE.

CHORO Statement

The CHORO statement produces a choropleth map using the map data set and the response data set specified in the PROC GMAP statement. The colors and fill patterns used to fill each unit area indicate levels of magnitude or response levels of the corresponding response variable.

You can use options in the CHORO statement to customize the appearance of the map. For example, you can select colors and fill patterns used to fill the map areas. You can control the selection of ranges for the response variable. You also can specify an Annotate data set to be used for enhancing the appearance of maps produced by the CHORO statement.

Syntax

The general form of the CHORO statement is

CHORO *response-variable* < . . . *response-variable-n*>
    </<ANNOTATE=*Annotate-data-set*>
        <*appearance-options*>
        <*mapping-options*>
        <*legend-options*>
        <*description-options*>>;

□ *response-variable* is a variable in the response data set that contains response values for unit areas in the map data set.

□ *appearance-options* can be one or more of the following:

    CEMPTY=*empty-unit-outline-color*

    COUTLINE=*nonempty-unit-outline-color*

    XSIZE=*n* <*units*>

    YSIZE=*n* <*units*>

□ *mapping-options* can be one or more of the following:

    DISCRETE

    LEVELS=*n*

        where *n* specifies the number of response levels

    MIDPOINTS=*value-list*

        where *value-list* specifies the response levels for a range of response values

    MISSING

□ *legend-options* can be one or more of the following:

    CTEXT=*color*

    LEGEND=LEGEND<1 . . . 99>

    NOLEGEND

□ *description-options* can be either or both of the following:

    DESCRIPTION='*string*'

    NAME='*string*'

Options are fully described in "Options" later in this section.

Requirements

The CHORO statement must specify at least one response variable contained in the response data set. If you specify more than one variable, a map is produced for each response variable. Missing values for the response variable are not considered valid response values unless you use the MISSING option in the CHORO statement. The ID statement must be used in conjunction with the CHORO statement.

Options

You can use the following options in the CHORO statement. Options used in a CHORO statement affect all maps produced by that statement. If you use any of the following options, separate them from the response variables with a slash (/). If you do not use any options, omit the slash.

ANNOTATE=*Annotate-data-set*
ANNO=*Annotate-data-set*

specifies a data set to provide annotation of graphs produced by the CHORO statement. *Annotate-data-set* must contain the appropriate Annotate variables. See Chapter 18 for details.

If the ANNOTATE= option is also used in the PROC GMAP statement, both sets of annotation are applied. If you specify BY-group processing, the Annotate data set must contain the BY variable. For details, see "Using BY-Group Processing with the Annotate Facility" in Chapter 18 and "Details of BY-Group Processing" in Chapter 10.

CEMPTY=*empty-unit-outline-color*

specifies the outline color for empty unit areas on the map. This option is ignored unless you use the ALL option in the PROC GMAP statement. If you do not use the ALL option, unit areas without response variable values are not included in the map. If you use the ALL option, unit areas contained in the map data set that are not in the response data set are drawn but left empty.

If you use the ALL option but do not use the CEMPTY= option, the GMAP procedure uses the first color in the colors list to outline unit areas contained in the map data set that are not in the response data set.

COUTLINE=*nonempty-unit-outline-color*

specifies the outline color for unit areas that are not empty. By default, the outline color for nonempty unit areas is the same as the fill pattern color for the unit areas.

CTEXT=*text-color*

specifies a color for the text in the legend. If you do not use the CTEXT= option, a color specification is searched for in the following order:

1. the CTEXT= option in a GOPTIONS statement

2. the default, the first color in the colors list.

If you use the CTEXT= option, the color specification is overridden if you also use the COLOR= parameter of a LABEL= or VALUE= option in a LEGEND definition assigned to the map legend. The COLOR= parameter determines the color of the legend label or the color of the legend value descriptions, respectively.

DESCRIPTION='*string*'
DES='*string*'
>   specifies a descriptive string, up to 40 characters long, that appears in the Description field of the catalog entry for the map. The description does not appear on the map. By default, the GMAP procedure provides a description of the form CHOROPLETH MAP OF *variable*, where *variable* is the name of the variable specified in the CHORO statement.

DISCRETE
>   treats a numeric response variable as a discrete variable rather than as a continuous variable. When you use the DISCRETE option, the response variables are not grouped into ranges; instead, the GMAP procedure uses a separate response level (fill pattern and color combination) for each different value of the formatted response variable. The LEVELS= option is ignored when you use the DISCRETE option.
>
>   Use this option if your response variable has a user-written format.

LEGEND=LEGEND<1 . . . 99>
>   assigns legend characteristics to the map legend. The option value indicates which LEGEND definition to use. The LEGEND= option is ignored if the specified LEGEND definition is not currently in effect. See Chapter 13 for more information.

LEVELS=*n*
>   specifies the number of response levels to be graphed when the response variables are continuous. Each level is assigned a different combination of color and fill pattern.
>
>   If neither the LEVELS= option nor the DISCRETE option is used, then the GMAP procedure determines the number of response levels using the formula FLOOR($1 + 3.3 \log(N)$), where N is the number of unique unit area identification variable values.
>
>   The LEVELS= option is ignored when you use the DISCRETE or MIDPOINTS= option.

MIDPOINTS=*value-list*
>   specifies the response levels for the range of response values represented by each level (fill pattern and color combination).
>
>   **For numeric response variables,** *value-list* can be specified in the following ways:
>
>   *n n . . . n*
>
>   *n,n, . . . ,n*
>
>   *n* TO *n* <BY *increment*> <*n . . . n*> <*n, . . . ,n*>
>
>   *n n . . . n* TO *n* <BY *increment*> <*n . . . n*>
>
>   *n,n, . . . ,n* TO *n* <BY *increment*> <*n, . . . ,n*>
>
>   For discrete numeric values, values can be specified in any order.
>
>   **For character response variables,** *value-list* must be a list of response values. Values must be enclosed in single quotes and separated by blanks (commas are not allowed as separators), as shown here:
>
>    ```
>    midpoints='Midwest' 'Northeast' 'Northwest'
>    ```

(MIDPOINTS= continued)   The values can be specified in any order. You can selectively exclude some response variable values from the map, as shown here:

```
midpoints='Midwest'
```

Only those observations for which the response variable exactly matches one of the values listed in the MIDPOINTS= option are shown on the map. As a result, observations may be excluded inadvertently if values in the list are misspelled or if the case does not match exactly.

MISSING
  accepts a missing value as a valid level for the response variable.

NAME='*string*'
  specifies a string, up to eight characters long, that appears in the Name field of the catalog entry for the map. *String* must be a valid SAS name. By default, the name assigned is GMAP. If either the name specified or the default name duplicates an existing name in the catalog, SAS/GRAPH software adds a number to the duplicate name to create a unique name, for example, GMAP2.

NOLEGEND
  suppresses the legend.

XSIZE=*n* <*units*>
YSIZE=*n* <*units*>
  specify the physical dimensions of the map to be drawn, where *n* is the number of units. By default, the map uses the entire procedure output area.
    Valid *units* are CM (centimeters), IN (inches), or PCT (percentage of the graphics output area). By default, the unit is character cells.
    If you specify values for *n* that are greater than the dimensions of the procedure output area, the map is drawn using the default size.
    If you specify either the XSIZE= or YSIZE= option without specifying the other option, the GMAP procedure rescales the dimension for the option that was not specified to retain the original shape of the map.

Using the CHORO Statement

A separate map is produced for each response variable listed in the CHORO statement. For example, the following statement produces two separate maps:

```
choro resp1 resp2;
```

Response variables can be either numeric or character. Numeric response variables with continuous values are grouped into ranges, or response levels. Each response level is assigned a different combination of fill pattern and color. Character variables and numeric variables (when you use the DISCRETE option) have a different response level for each unique response variable value. Numeric variables are treated as continuous unless you use the DISCRETE option.

For numeric response variables with continuous values, you can control the selection of response level ranges using the MIDPOINTS= or LEVELS= option. By default, the GMAP procedure determines the number of levels for the map using the formula FLOOR$(1+3.3 \log(N))$, where N is the number of unique unit area identification variable values.

Selecting Patterns for the Map

PATTERN definitions can be used to define the fill patterns and colors used to fill map areas. Only PATTERN statements that define valid map/plot patterns can be applied to map surfaces. These patterns are as follows:

MEMPTY | ME | EMPTY | E

MSOLID | MS | SOLID | S

M*density*<*style*<*angle*>>

> where
>
> *density*   can be 1 . . . 5.
>
> *style*   can be N | X.
>
> *angle*   can be 0 . . . 360.

See Chapter 15 for more information on fill pattern values and default pattern rotation.

The GMAP procedure chooses default fill patterns and colors if no valid PATTERN definitions have been defined or if the map uses more patterns than are defined in the PATTERN definitions.

Using Other Global Statements

LEGEND definitions can be used to adjust the location and appearance of the legend that is produced with the map. See Chapter 13 for details on the legend characteristics you can define with the LEGEND statement. You must use the LEGEND= option in the CHORO statement to apply a LEGEND definition to your map. See "Options" earlier in this section for details of the LEGEND= option.

CHORO Statement Examples

The following examples illustrate major features of the CHORO statement.

The two examples use the data set SITES. Each observation in the data set contains a unit area identification variable, STATE, which matches the STATE variable in the SAS/GRAPH map data sets, and a response variable, SITES, which is the number of installed products in the state.

Because the examples use one of the map data sets supplied with SAS/GRAPH software, you may need to replace *SAS-data-library* in the LIBNAME statement with the actual location of the SAS data library containing the Institute-supplied map data sets on your system. Contact your SAS Software Consultant for the location of the map data sets at your site.

If your site automatically assigns the libref MAPS to the SAS data library containing the Institute-supplied map data sets, delete the LIBNAME statement in these examples.

Simple Choropleth Map

This example uses the CHORO statement to map the number of products installed in each site for a fictitious company.

The following program statements produce Output 29.9:

```
   /* set the graphics environment */
goptions reset=global gunit=pct border
        ftext=swissb htitle=6 htext=3;


   /* assign the libref MAPS */
libname maps 'SAS-data-library';


   /* create response data set SITES */
data sites;
   length state 2;
   input state sites;
   cards;
 1        80
 2        31
more data lines
55       197
56        59
;
run;


   /* define titles and footnotes for map */
title1 'Products Installed in the USA';
title2 h=4 'XXX Corp.';
footnote1 j=l '  US map data set supplied'
        ' with SAS/GRAPH' '02'x ' Software';
footnote2 j=r 'GR29N08  ';


   /* define pattern characteristics */
pattern value=msolid;


   /* display the choropleth map */
proc gmap map=maps.us data=sites;
   id state;
   choro sites / coutline=gray;
run;
quit;
```

Output 29.9 *Simple Choropleth Map (GR29N08)*

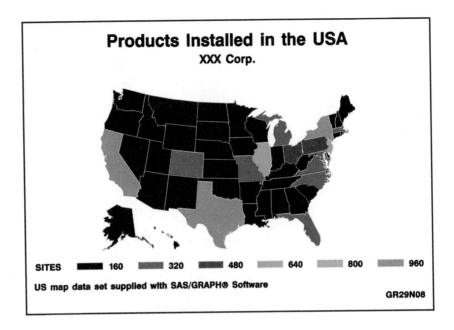

This example illustrates the following features:

□ The GMAP procedure uses the fill pattern defined in the PATTERN statement for the unit areas. The procedure repeats the pattern for every color in the colors list as needed for the map.

□ The ID statement specifies the variable in the map data set and the response data set that defines unit areas.

□ The GMAP procedure selects the response levels.

Choropleth Map with Formatted Numeric Values

This example graphs the same data as the first example but assigns a format to the response variable, which groups the values into ranges. The DISCRETE option is used so that each formatted value is a response level. The following program statements produce Output 29.10:

```
     /* set the graphics environment */
goptions reset=global gunit=pct border
         ftext=swissb htitle=6 htext=3;


     /* assign the libref MAPS */
libname maps 'SAS-data-library';


     /* create response data set SITES */
data sites;
   length state 2;
   input state sites;
   cards;
 1        80
 2        31
more data lines
55       197
56        59
;
run;
```

```
     /* create format SITESFMT */
proc format;
   value sitesfmt low-100='0-100'
                   101-400='101-400'
                   401-700='401-700'
                   701-1000='701-1000'
                   1001-high='over 1000';
run;

   /* define titles and footnotes for map */
title1 'Products Installed in the USA';
title2 h=4 'XXX Corp.';
footnote1 j=l '  US map data set supplied'
          ' with SAS/GRAPH' '02'x ' Software';
footnote2 j=r 'GR29N09  ';

   /* define pattern characteristics */
pattern value=msolid;

   /* define legend characteristics */
legend value=(j=l) frame;

   /* display the choropleth map */
proc gmap map=maps.us data=sites;
   format sites sitesfmt.;
   id state;
   choro sites / discrete legend=legend coutline=gray;
run;
quit;
```

Output 29.10 Enhanced Choropleth Map (GR29N09)

This example illustrates the following features:

☐ The PATTERN statement specifies a fill pattern for the unit areas. Since no colors are specified, the GMAP procedure repeats the pattern for every color in the colors list before moving to the next pattern.

☐ The FORMAT statement applies the SITESFMT. format to the response values. With this format, the response variable has five discrete levels rather than continuous values, so the DISCRETE option is included with the CHORO statement. The discrete formatted values become the response levels for the graph.

☐ The LEGEND= option assigns the LEGEND characteristics defined in the LEGEND statement to the map legend.

PRISM Statement

The PRISM statement produces a prism map using the map data set and the response data set specified in the PROC GMAP statement. Polyhedrons (raised polygons) in the shape of each unit area convey information about response variable values. The height of each polyhedron represents an ordinal level of the response variable.

The PRISM statement does not work well for maps containing intersecting polygons or polygons within polygons, extremely complicated maps, or maps containing line segments that cross. Use the GREDUCE procedure to reduce and simplify the map if necessary.

You can use options in the PRISM statement to customize the appearance of the map.

Syntax

The general form of the PRISM statement is

PRISM *response-variable* < . . . *response-variable-n*>
    </<ANNOTATE=*Annotate-data-set*>
       <*appearance-options*>
       <*mapping-options*>
       <*legend-options*>
       <*description-options*>>;

□ *response-variable* is a variable in the response data set that contains response values for unit areas in the map data set.

□ *appearance-options* can be one or more of the following:

    CEMPTY=*empty-unit-outline-color*

    COUTLINE=*nonempty-unit-outline-color*

    XLIGHT=*x*

    YLIGHT=*y*

    XSIZE=*n* <*units*>

    YSIZE=*n* <*units*>

    XVIEW=*x*

    YVIEW=*y*

    ZVIEW=*z*

□ *mapping-options* can be one or more of the following:

    DISCRETE

    LEVELS=*n*

        where *n* specifies the number of response levels

    MIDPOINTS=*value-list*

        where *value-list* specifies the response levels for a range of response values

    MISSING

□ *legend-options* can be one or more of the following:

    CTEXT=*text-color*

    LEGEND=LEGEND<1 . . . 99>

    NOLEGEND

□ *description-options* can be either or both of the following:

    DESCRIPTION='*string*'

    NAME='*string*'

Options are fully described in "Options" later in this section.

Requirements

The PRISM statement must specify at least one response variable contained in the response data set. If you specify more than one variable, a map is produced for each response variable. Missing values for the response variable are not considered valid unless you use the MISSING option in the PRISM statement. The ID statement must be used in conjunction with the PRISM statement.

Options

You can use the following options in the PRISM statement. Options used in a PRISM statement affect all maps produced by that statement. If you use any of the following options, separate them from the response variables with a slash (/). If you do not use any options, omit the slash.

ANNOTATE=*Annotate-data-set*
ANNO=*Annotate-data-set*
　　specifies a data set to provide annotation of graphs produced by the PRISM statement. *Annotate-data-set* must contain the appropriate Annotate variables. See Chapter 18 for details.

　　Note: Annotate coordinate systems 1, 2, 7, and 8 are not valid with prism maps.

　　If the ANNOTATE= option is also used in the PROC GMAP statement, both sets of annotation are applied. If you specify BY-group processing, the Annotate data set must contain the BY variable. For details, see "Using BY-Group Processing with the Annotate Facility" in Chapter 18 and "Details of BY-Group Processing" in Chapter 10.

CEMPTY=*empty-unit-outline-color*
　　specifies the outline color for empty prisms on the map. This option is ignored unless you use the ALL option in the PROC GMAP statement. If you do not use the ALL option, unit areas without response variable values are not included in the map. If you use the ALL option, unit areas contained in the map data set that are not in the response data set are drawn but left empty.

　　If you use the ALL option but do not use the CEMPTY= option, PROC GMAP uses the first color in the current colors list to outline empty areas. (Empty unit areas are those for which a unit area identification variable value exists in the map data set but not in the response data set.)

COUTLINE=*nonempty-unit-outline-color*
　　specifies the outline color for prisms that are not empty. By default, the outline color for nonempty unit areas is the same as the fill pattern color for the prism surface.

CTEXT=*text-color*
　　specifies a color for the text in the legend. If you do not use the CTEXT= option, a color specification is searched for in the following order:

　　1. the CTEXT= option in a GOPTIONS statement

　　2. the default, the first color in the colors list.

(CTEXT= continued)

If you use the CTEXT= option, the color specification is overridden if you also use the COLOR= parameter of a LABEL= or VALUE= option in a LEGEND definition assigned to the map legend. The COLOR= parameter determines the color of the legend label or the color of the legend value descriptions, respectively.

DESCRIPTION='*string*'
DES='*string*'

specifies a descriptive string, up to 40 characters long, that appears in the Description field of the catalog entry for the map. The description does not appear on the map. By default, the GMAP procedure provides a description of the form PRISM MAP OF *variable*, where *variable* is the name of the variable specified in the PRISM statement.

DISCRETE

treats a numeric response variable as a discrete variable rather than as a continuous variable. When you use the DISCRETE option, the response values are not grouped into ranges; instead, the GMAP procedure uses a separate response level (prism height, color, and surface fill pattern) for each different value of the formatted response variable. The LEVELS= option is ignored when you use the DISCRETE option.

Use this option if your response variable has a user-written format.

LEGEND=LEGEND<1 . . . 99>

assigns legend characteristics to the map legend. The option value indicates which LEGEND definition to use. The LEGEND= option is ignored if the specified LEGEND definition is not currently in effect. See Chapter 13 for more information.

LEVELS=*n*

specifies the number of response levels to be graphed when the response variables are continuous. Each level is assigned a different prism height, surface fill pattern, and color combination.

If neither the LEVELS= option nor the DISCRETE option is used, then the GMAP procedure determines the number of response levels using the formula FLOOR($1+3.3 \log(N)$), where N is the number of unique unit area identification variable values.

The LEVELS= option is ignored when you use the DISCRETE or MIDPOINTS= option.

MIDPOINTS=*value-list*

specifies the response levels for the range of response values represented by each level (prism height, fill pattern, and color combination).

For numeric response variables, *value-list* can be specified in the following ways:

n n . . . n

n,n, . . . ,n

n TO *n* <BY *increment*> <*n . . . n*> <*n, . . . ,n*>

n n . . . n TO *n* <BY *increment*> <*n . . . n*>

n,n, . . . ,n TO *n* <BY *increment*> <*n, . . . ,n*>

For discrete numeric values, values can be specified in any order.

For character response variables, *value-list* must be a list of response values. Values must be enclosed in single quotes and separated by blanks (commas are not allowed as separators), as shown here:

```
midpoints='Midwest' 'Northeast' 'Northwest'
```

The values can be specified in any order. You can selectively exclude some response variable values from the map, as shown here:

```
midpoints='Midwest'
```

Only those observations for which the response variable exactly matches one of the values listed in the MIDPOINTS= option are shown on the map. As a result, observations may be inadvertently excluded if values in the list are misspelled or if the case does not match exactly.

MISSING

accepts a missing value as a valid level for the response variable.

NAME=*'string'*

specifies a string, up to eight characters long, that appears in the Name field of the catalog entry for the map. *String* must be a valid SAS name. By default, the name assigned is GMAP. If either the name specified or the default name duplicates an existing name in the catalog, SAS/GRAPH software adds a number to the duplicate name to create a unique name, for example, GMAP2.

NOLEGEND

suppresses the legend.

XLIGHT=*x*

YLIGHT=*y*

specify the coordinates of the imagined light source in the map coordinate system. The position of the light source affects the way the sides of the map polygons are shaded. Although you can specify any point for the light source using the XLIGHT= and YLIGHT= options, the light source is actually placed in one of only four positions.

Table 29.1 shows how the point you specify is positioned.

Figure 29.7 illustrates the light source positions. Assume that your viewing position, selected by the XVIEW=, YVIEW=, and ZVIEW= options, is point D.

Table 29.1 *Light Source Coordinates*

Specified Light Source	Light Source Position
in quadrants I or II, or on the X or +Y axis	behind the map (point A), and all side polygons are shadowed
on or within approximately 10° of the −Y axis	the viewing position (point D), and none of the side polygons are shadowed
in quadrant III (except within 10° of the Y axis)	to the left of the map (point B), and the right-facing sides of polygons are shadowed
in quadrant IV (except within 10° of the Y axis)	to the right of the map (point C), and the left-facing side polygons are shadowed

(XLIGHT= continued)

By default, the light source position is the same as the viewing position specified by the XVIEW=, YVIEW=, and ZVIEW= options. The light source position cannot coincide with the viewing reference point (0.5,0.5), which corresponds with the position directly above the center of the map. See the XVIEW= option description later in this section and Figure 29.6 earlier in this chapter for additional information on the viewing reference point.

Figure 29.7 *Coordinates of Imagined Light Source in a Map Coordinate System*

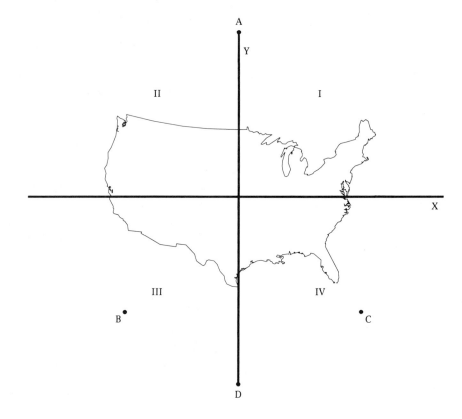

XSIZE=*n* <*units*>
YSIZE=*n* <*units*>

specify the physical dimensions of the map to be drawn, where *n* is the number of units. By default, the map uses the entire procedure output area.

Valid *units* are CM (centimeters), IN (inches), or PCT (percentage of the graphics output area). By default, the unit is character cells.

If you specify values for *n* that are greater than the dimensions of the procedure output area, the map is drawn using the default size.

XVIEW=*x*
YVIEW=*y*
ZVIEW=*z*

specify the viewing position coordinates for the map. In this system, the four corners of the map lie on the X-Y plane at coordinates (0,0,0), (0,1,0), (1,1,0), and (1,0,0). No axes are actually drawn on the maps produced by PROC GMAP, but imagine that the maps are drawn in an X-Y plane as in Figure 29.1.

Your viewing position cannot coincide with the viewing reference point at coordinates (0.5,0.5,0), the center of the map. The value for *z* cannot be negative.

If you omit the XVIEW=, YVIEW=, and ZVIEW= options, the default coordinates are $(0.5, -2, 3)$. This viewing position is well above and to the south of the center of the map. You can specify one, two, or all three of the view coordinates; any that you do not explicitly specify are assigned the default values.

Figure 29.6 earlier in this chapter shows the position of the viewing reference point, as well as the default viewing position.

To ensure that the polygon edges are distinguishable, the angle from vertical must be less than or equal to 45°. If you specify a ZVIEW= value such that this condition cannot be satisfied (that is, a very small value), PROC GMAP increases the ZVIEW= value automatically so that the angle is 45° or less.

Using the PRISM Statement

A separate map is produced for each response variable listed in the PRISM statement. For example, the following statement produces two separate maps:

```
prism resp1 resp2;
```

Response variables can be either numeric or character. Numeric response variables with continuous values are grouped into ranges, or response levels. Each response level is assigned a different prism height and a different fill pattern and color combination. Character variables and numeric variables (when you use the DISCRETE option) have a different response level for each unique response variable value. This means the prism height can be used to identify discrete values but cannot be used to read a discrete value directly. You must use the legend to determine the exact value of a discrete variable. Numeric variables are treated as continuous unless you use the DISCRETE option.

For numeric response variables with continuous values, you can control the selection of response level ranges using the MIDPOINTS= or LEVELS= option. By default, the GMAP procedure determines the number of levels for the map using the formula $FLOOR(1 + 3.3 \log(N))$, where N is the number of unique unit area identification variable values.

Prism heights increase in order of response levels. That is, the lowest prisms correspond to the first level, and the tallest prisms correspond to the last level. The height of the prism is based on ordinal data.

You can alter the perspective of the map by selecting a viewing position, which represents the point in space from which the map is viewed. See the discussion of the XVIEW=, YVIEW=, and ZVIEW= options in "Options" earlier in this section for details. You can select shadowing for the side polygons of the prisms to enhance the illusion of height. See the discussion of the XLIGHT= and YLIGHT= options in "Options" earlier in this section for details.

Selecting Patterns for the Map

PATTERN statements can be used to define the fill patterns and colors used to fill prism surfaces. Only PATTERN statements that define valid map/plot patterns can be applied to map surfaces. These patterns are as follows:

MEMPTY | ME | EMPTY | E

MSOLID | MS | SOLID | S

M*density*<*style*<*angle*>>

  where

density	can be 1 . . . 5.
style	can be N	X.
angle	can be 0 . . . 360.

See Chapter 15 for more information on pattern values and default pattern rotation.

The GMAP procedure chooses default fill patterns and colors if no PATTERN definitions have been defined or if the map uses more patterns than are defined in the PATTERN definitions.

Using Other Global Statements

LEGEND definitions can be used to adjust the location and appearance of the legend that is produced with the map. See Chapter 13 for details of the legend characteristics you can define with the LEGEND statement. You must use the LEGEND= option in the PRISM statement to apply a LEGEND definition to your map. See "Options" earlier in this section for details of the LEGEND= option.

PRISM Statement Examples

The following examples illustrate major features of the PRISM statement.

The examples use the data set SITES. Each observation in the data set contains a unit area identification variable, STATE, which matches the STATE variable in the SAS/GRAPH map data sets, and a response variable, SITES, which is the number of installed products in the state.

Because the examples use one of the map data sets supplied with SAS/GRAPH software, you may need to replace *SAS-data-library* in the LIBNAME statement with the actual location of the SAS data library containing the Institute-supplied map data sets on your system. Contact your SAS Software Consultant for the location of the map data sets at your site.

If your site automatically assigns the libref MAPS to the SAS data library containing the Institute-supplied map data sets, delete the LIBNAME statement in these examples.

Simple Prism Map

This example uses the PRISM statement to map the number of products installed in each state for a fictitious company.

The following program statements produce Output 29.11:

```
/* set the graphics environment */
goptions reset=global gunit=pct border
         ftext=swissb htitle=6 htext=3;
```

```
   /* assign the libref MAPS */
libname maps 'SAS-data-library';

   /* create response data set SITES */
data sites;
  length state 2;
  input state sites;
  cards;
 1    80
 2    31
more data lines
55    197
56    59
;
run;

   /* define titles and footnotes for map */
title1 'Products Installed in the USA';
title2 h=4 'XXX Corp.';
footnote1 j=l ' US map data set supplied'
       ' with SAS/GRAPH' '02'x ' Software';
footnote2 j=r 'GR29N10 ';

   /* define pattern characteristics */
pattern value=msolid;

   /* display the prism map */
proc gmap map=maps.us data=sites;
  id state;
  prism sites / coutline=gray;
run;
quit;
```

Output 29.11 *Prism Map with Default Characteristics (GR29N10)*

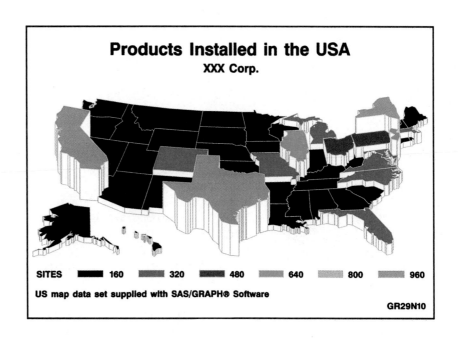

This example illustrates the following features:

□ The ID statement specifies the variable in the map data set and the response data set that defines unit areas.

□ The GMAP procedure uses the pattern defined in the PATTERN statement for the prisms. The procedure repeats the pattern for every color in the colors list as needed for the map.

□ Since the XVIEW=, YVIEW=, and ZVIEW= options are not used, the default viewing position, above and to the east and south of the center of the map, is used.

□ Since the XLIGHT= and YLIGHT= options are not used, none of the side polygons of the prisms are shadowed. The light source is the same as the viewing position.

□ The GMAP procedure selects the response levels.

Enhanced Prism Map

This example graphs the same data as the first example but selects the response level values for the response variable. This example also changes the map viewpoint and light source.

The following program statements produce Output 29.12:

```
/* set the graphics environment */
goptions reset=global gunit=pct border
        ftext=swissb htitle=6 htext=3;

/* assign the libref MAPS */
libname maps 'SAS-data-library';

/* create response data set SITES */
data sites;
   length state 2;
   input state sites;
   cards;
1       80
2       31
more data lines
55      197
56      59
;
run;

/* define titles and footnotes for map */
title1 'Products Installed in the USA';
title2 h=4 'XXX Corp.';
footnote1 j=1 '  US map data set supplied'
        ' with SAS/GRAPH' '02'x ' Software';
footnote2 j=r 'GR29N11  ';

/* define pattern characteristics */
pattern value=msolid;

/* define legend characteristics */
legend value=(j=l) label=('Sites (midpoint of range):') across=3;
```

```
      /* display the prism map */
proc gmap map=maps.us data=sites;
   id state;
   prism sites / legend=legend
                    midpoints=100 300 500 700 900
                    xlight=5
                    xview=.75 zview=5
                    coutline=gray;
run;
quit;
```

Output 29.12 Enhanced
Prism Map (GR29N11)

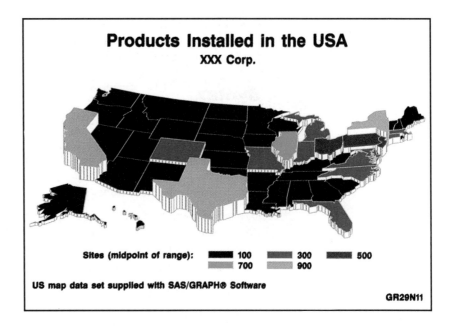

This example illustrates the following features:

□ The PATTERN statement specifies the fill pattern for the unit areas. Since no colors are specified, the GMAP procedure repeats the pattern for every color in the colors list as needed for the map.

□ The MIDPOINTS= option specifies five response levels for the map.

□ The XLIGHT= option moves the light source to the right and adds shadows to the left-side polygons of the prisms.

□ The XVIEW= and ZVIEW= options shift the viewing point to the right and upward, respectively. This reduces the number of prisms that are partially hidden by taller neighbors.

SURFACE Statement

The SURFACE statement produces a surface map using the map data set and the response data set specified in the PROC GMAP statement. A spike at the approximate center of each unit area conveys information about response variable values. The height of the spike corresponds to the relative value of the response variable, not to the actual value of the response variable. Thus, a spike representing a value of 100 may not be exactly 10 times higher than a spike representing a value of 10. Unit area boundaries are not drawn.

You can use options in the SURFACE statement to customize the appearance of the map. For example, you can select the color and number of lines for the representation of the surface area. You can control the selection of spike heights and base widths. You also can specify an Annotate data set to be used for enhancing the appearance of maps produced by the SURFACE statement.

Syntax

The general form of the SURFACE statement is

SURFACE *response-variable* < . . . *response-variable-n*>
   </<ANNOTATE=*Annotate-data-set*>
      <*appearance-options*>
      <*description-options*>>;

☐ *response-variable* is a variable in the response data set that contains response values for unit areas in the map data set. *Response-variable* must be numeric.

☐ *appearance-options* can be one or more of the following:

   CBODY=*surface-map-color*

   CONSTANT=*n*

      where *n* is a denominator to use in the distance decay function

   NLINES=*n*

      where *n* is the number of lines used to draw the surface map

   ROTATE=*degrees*

   TILT=*degrees*

   XSIZE=*n* <*units*>

   YSIZE=*n* <*units*>

☐ *description-options* can be either or both of the following:

   DESCRIPTION='*string*'

   NAME='*string*'

Options are fully described in "Options" later in this section.

Requirements

The SURFACE statement must specify at least one response variable contained in the response data set. If you specify more than one variable, a map is produced for each response variable. Response variables must be numeric and must contain only positive values. The ID statement must be used in conjunction with the SURFACE statement.

Options

You can use the following options in the SURFACE statement. Options used in a SURFACE statement affect all maps produced by that statement. If you use any of the following options, separate them from the response variables by a slash (/). If you do not use any options, omit the slash.

ANNOTATE=*Annotate-data-set*
ANNO=*Annotate-data-set*
> specifies a data set to provide annotation of graphs produced by the SURFACE statement. *Annotate-data-set* must contain the appropriate Annotate variables. See Chapter 18 for details.
>
> **Note:** Annotate coordinate systems 1, 2, 7, and 8 are not valid with surface maps.
>
> If the ANNOTATE= option is also used with the PROC GMAP statement, both sets of annotation are applied. If you specify BY-group processing, the Annotate data set must contain the BY variable. For details, see "Using BY-Group Processing with the Annotate Facility" in Chapter 18 and "Details of BY-Group Processing" in Chapter 10.

CBODY=*surface-map-color*
> specifies the color used to draw the surface map. By default, the first color in the current colors list is used.

CONSTANT=*n*
> specifies a denominator to use in the distance decay function. This function determines the base width of the spike drawn at each unit area center.
>
> By default, CONSTANT=10. Values greater than 10 yield spikes that are wider at the base. Values less than 10 yield spikes that are narrower at the base.
>
> Let x_k and y_k represent the coordinates, and z_k represent the function value at the center of each unit area. The z_k values are scaled from 1 to 11. A square grid of x by y points (where the size of the grid is the NLINES= option value) and the associated function value $f(x,y)$ are generated from the unit area center value using the following formula:

$$f(x,y) = \Sigma_k (1 - 1.5 D_k + .5\ D_k^3)\ \Delta_k z_k$$

where

$$D_k = \sqrt{(((x - x_k)^2 + (y - y_k)^2) / \text{CONSTANT})}$$

and

$$\Delta_k = \begin{cases} 1 \text{ if } D_k < 1 \\ \\ 0 \text{ otherwise.} \end{cases}$$

DESCRIPTION='*string*'
DES='*string*'

> specifies a descriptive string, up to 40 characters long, that appears in the Description field of the catalog entry for the map. The description does not appear on the map. By default, the GMAP procedure provides a description of the form SURFACE MAP OF *variable*, where *variable* is the name of the variable specified in the SURFACE statement.

NAME='*string*'

> specifies a string, up to eight characters long, that appears in the Name field of the catalog entry for the map. *String* must be a valid SAS name. By default, the name assigned is GMAP. If either the name specified or the default name duplicates an existing name in the catalog, SAS/GRAPH software adds a number to the duplicate name to create a unique name, for example, GMAP2.

NLINES=*n*
N=*n*

> specifies the number of lines, *n*, used to draw the surface map. Valid values for *n* are 50 to 100; the higher the value, the more solid the map appears and the more resources used. By default, NLINES=50.

ROTATE=*degrees*

> specifies the degrees of the angle at which to rotate the map about the Z axis in the map coordinate system. *Degrees* can be any angle. Positive values indicate rotation in the counterclockwise direction. By default, ROTATE=70. The ROTATE= option also affects the direction of the lines used to draw the surface map.

TILT=*degrees*

> specifies the degrees of the angle at which to tilt the map about the X axis in the map coordinate system. *Degrees* can be 0 to 90. Increasing values cause the map to tilt backward, making the spikes more prominent. Decreasing values make the map shape more distinguishable and the spikes less prominent. TILT=90 corresponds to viewing the map edge-on, while TILT=0 corresponds to viewing the map from directly overhead. By default, TILT=70.

XSIZE=*n* <*units*>
YSIZE=*n* <*units*>

> specify the physical dimensions of the map to be drawn, where *n* is the number of units. By default, the map uses the entire procedure output area.
>
> Valid *units* are CM (centimeters), IN (inches), or PCT (percentage of the graphics output area). By default, the unit is character cells.
>
> If you specify values for *n* that are greater than the dimensions of the procedure output area, the map is drawn using the default size.

Using the SURFACE Statement

A separate map is produced for each response variable listed in the SURFACE statement. For example, the following statement produces two separate maps:

```
surface resp1 resp2;
```

The response variables must be positive numeric variables. The GMAP procedure scales response variables for presentation on the map. The height of the spikes on the map correspond to the relative value of the response variable, not to the actual value of the response variable. However, after projection and a change in the viewing angle, the spikes may not appear this way. The spikes in the front may appear to be higher than the spikes in the back, which represent greater values.

Unlike the other mapping statements, the SURFACE statement does not draw bounded unit areas within which the response variables are graphed. Instead, it draws a surface of horizontal lines that represents the overall shape of the unit areas. The lines rise to peaks at points that roughly correspond to the centers of the unit areas. The varying height of these peaks, or spikes, represents the relative values of the response values.

Surface maps are somewhat crude in that they provide no clear unit area boundaries and no legend. Thus, surface maps provide a simple way to judge relative trends in the response data but are inappropriate for representing specific response values.

Using Global Statements

Surface maps do not support legends or patterns, so the LEGEND and PATTERN statements have no effect on the maps produced by the SURFACE statement.

SURFACE Statement Examples

The following examples illustrate major features of the SURFACE statement.

The examples use the data set SITES. Each observation in the data set contains a unit area identification variable, STATE, which matches the STATE variable in the SAS/GRAPH map data sets, and a response variable, SITES, which is the number of installed products in the state.

Because the examples use one of the map data sets supplied with SAS/GRAPH software, you may need to replace *SAS-data-library* in the LIBNAME statement with the actual location of the SAS data library containing the Institute-supplied map data sets on your system. Contact your SAS Software Consultant for the location of the map data sets at your site.

If your site automatically assigns the libref MAPS to the SAS data library containing the Institute-supplied map data sets, delete the LIBNAME statement in these examples.

Simple Surface Map

This example uses the SURFACE statement to map the number of products installed in each state for a fictitious company.
The following program statements produce Output 29.13:

```
      /* set the graphics environment */
goptions reset=global gunit=pct border
         ftext=swissb htitle=6 htext=3;

      /* assign the libref MAPS */
libname maps 'SAS-data-library';

      /* create response data set SITES */
data sites;
   length state 2;
   input state sites;
   cards;
 1        80
 2        31
more data lines
55       197
56        59
;
run;

      /* define titles and footnotes for map */
title1 'Products Installed in the USA';
title2 h=4 'XXX Corp.';
footnote1 j=l '  US map data set supplied'
          ' with SAS/GRAPH' '02'x ' Software';
footnote2 j=r 'GR29N12  ';

      /* display the surface map */
proc gmap map=maps.us data=sites;
   id state;
   surface sites;
run;
quit;
```

Output 29.13 *Surface Map with Default Characteristics (GR29N12)*

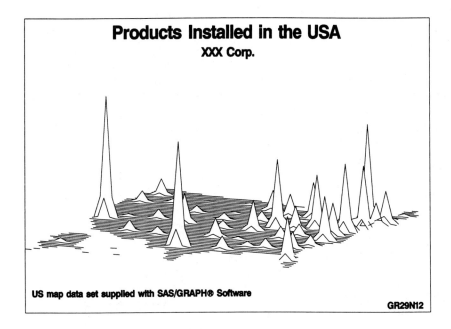

This example illustrates the following features:

□ The ID statement specifies the variable in the map data set and the response data set that defines the unit areas.

□ Since the CONSTANT= and NLINES= options are not used, the GMAP procedure draws a surface consisting of 50 lines and uses the default decay function to calculate spike height and base width.

□ Since the ROTATE= and TILT= options are not used, the map is rotated 70 degrees around the Z axis and tilted 70 degrees with respect to the X axis.

Enhanced Surface Map

This example graphs the same data as the first example but it tilts and rotates the map and uses more lines to draw the surface.

The following program statements produce Output 29.14:

```
    /* set the graphics environment */
goptions reset=global gunit=pct border
         ftext=swissb htitle=6 htext=3;

    /* assign the libref MAPS */
libname maps 'SAS-data-library';

    /* create response data set SITES */
data sites;
   length state 2;
   input state sites;
   cards;
 1        80
 2        31
more data lines
55       197
56        59
;
run;
```

```
                      /* define titles and footnotes for map */
                      title1 'Products Installed in the USA';
                      title2 h=4 'XXX Corp.';
                      footnote1 j=l '  US map data set supplied'
                                ' with SAS/GRAPH' '02'x ' Software';
                      footnote2 j=r 'GR29N13  ';

                      /* display the surface map */
                      proc gmap map=maps.us data=sites;
                         id state;
                         surface sites / constant=4
                                         nlines=100
                                         rotate=40
                                         tilt=60;
                      run;
                      quit;
```

Output 29.14 Enhanced
Surface Map (GR29N13)

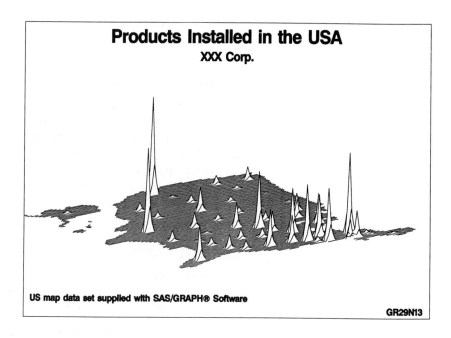

This example illustrates the following features:

□ Since the CONSTANT= value specified is less than the default value, the spikes in this example are narrower at the base than in the first example.

□ The NLINES= option specifies the maximum number of map lines, which gives the best map shape resolution.

□ The ROTATE= and TILT= options adjust the map orientation to make the crowded spikes in the northeast portion of the map easier to distinguish.

SAS/GRAPH Map Data Sets

A collection of map data sets is supplied with SAS/GRAPH software. For a complete description of them, see SAS Technical Report P-196, *SAS/GRAPH Map Data Sets for Release 6.06.*

Note: The map data sets that were previously sold separately as the SAS Data Library Series are now supplied with SAS/GRAPH software. Previously, sites received only maps for their own country or region.

You should contact your SAS Software Consultant to verify the name and location of the SAS data library containing the map data sets at your site before you use the map data sets. Many sites automatically assign a libref of MAPS to the SAS data library containing the Institute-supplied map data sets. However, if you use the map data sets regularly and your site does not automatically assign a libref to the data library containing the map data sets, you can add a LIBNAME statement to your AUTOEXEC file defining the location of the map data set library. If you do this, the libref for the maps is established automatically whenever you begin a SAS session.

Several of the Institute-supplied map data sets have coordinates expressed as longitude and latitude. These data sets must be projected before they can be used as input map data sets for the GMAP procedure.

Map Data Set Descriptions

You can use the CONTENTS or DATASETS procedure to get detailed information on the map data sets supplied with SAS/GRAPH software. For example, the following statements list the map data sets in the SAS data library assigned to the libref MAPS:

```
libname maps 'SAS-data-library';

proc datasets lib=maps;
run;
```

Be sure to replace *SAS-data-library* with the location of the SAS data library containing the map data sets at your site.

The following statements provide detailed information on the map data sets, including the number of observations, the variables in each data set, and a description of each variable:

```
libname maps 'SAS-data-library';

proc contents data=maps._all_;
run;
```

If your site automatically assigns the libref MAPS to the SAS data library containing the Institute-supplied map data sets, you can delete the LIBNAME statement from the preceding examples. See the *SAS Procedures Guide, Version 6, Third Edition* for more information on the CONTENTS and DATASETS procedures.

In display manager, you also can use the DIR window to list the available map data sets or the VAR window to list the variable names and labels in a map data set.

Digitizing Maps

Using a digitizer, you can create your own map data sets from hardcopy maps. See SAS Technical Report A-107, *Creating Your Own SAS/GRAPH Map Data Sets with a Digitizer.*

Using FIPS Codes and Province Codes

The unit area identification variables in some map data sets included with SAS/GRAPH software contain standardized numeric codes. The data sets for the United States contain a variable whose values are FIPS (Federal Information Processing System) codes. The data sets for Canada contain standard province codes or census division codes. When you use the GMAP procedure, the variables that identify unit areas in your response data set must have the same values as the unit area identification variables in the map data set you are using. If the unit area identification variables in your response data set are state or province names or abbreviations, you must convert them to FIPS codes or province codes before using the response data set with one of the Institute-supplied map data sets. Table 29.2 lists the FIPS codes for the United States and the standard codes for Canadian provinces.

Table 29.2 *U.S. FIPS Codes and Canadian Province Codes*

UNITED STATES			
FIPS Code	**State**	**FIPS Code**	**State**
01	Alabama	30	Montana
02	Alaska	31	Nebraska
04	Arizona	32	Nevada
05	Arkansas	33	New Hampshire
06	California	34	New Jersey
08	Colorado	35	New Mexico
09	Connecticut	36	New York
10	Delaware	37	North Carolina
11	District of Columbia	38	North Dakota
12	Florida	39	Ohio
13	Georgia	40	Oklahoma
15	Hawaii	41	Oregon
16	Idaho	42	Pennsylvania
17	Illinois	44	Rhode Island
18	Indiana	45	South Carolina
19	Iowa	46	South Dakota
20	Kansas	47	Tennessee
21	Kentucky	48	Texas
22	Louisiana	49	Utah
23	Maine	50	Vermont
24	Maryland	51	Virginia
25	Massachusetts	53	Washington
26	Michigan	54	West Virginia
27	Minnesota	55	Wisconsin
28	Mississippi	56	Wyoming
29	Missouri	72	Puerto Rico

CANADIAN PROVINCES	
Province Code	**Province**
10	Newfoundland
11	Prince Edward Island
12	Nova Scotia
13	New Brunswick
24	Quebec
35	Ontario
46	Manitoba
47	Saskatchewan
48	Alberta
59	British Columbia
60	Yukon
61	Northwest Territories

The CNTYNAME data set contains a cross-reference of names and FIPS codes for all counties in the United States. The CANCENS data set contains a cross-reference of census district names and codes for Canadian provinces.

Base SAS software provides several functions that convert state names to FIPS codes and vice versa. Table 29.3 lists these functions and a brief description of each function. See *SAS Language: Reference, Version 6, First Edition* for more information.

Table 29.3 FIPS and Postal Code Functions

Function	Description
STFIPS	converts state postal code to FIPS state code
STNAME	converts state postal code to state name in uppercase
STNAMEL	converts state postal code to state name in mixed case
FIPNAME	converts FIPS code to state name in uppercase
FIPNAML	converts FIPS code to state name in mixed case
FIPSTATE	converts FIPS code to state postal code

Using Map Data Sets

Some of the map data sets included with SAS/GRAPH software contain a large number of observations. You can shorten jobs that use only a few states or provinces by excluding the unused portion of the map data set or by using an already reduced data set. The SAS System provides several ways to accomplish this. One is to use the WHERE statement or WHERE= data set option within the GMAP procedure to select only the states or provinces you want.

For example, to use only the observations for Quebec in the CANADA data set, you can begin the GMAP procedure with a statement of this form:

```
proc gmap map=maps.canada(where=(province='24'));
```

Note that if you use the WHERE statement, the WHERE condition applies to both the map data set and the response data sets. The WHERE= data set option applies only to the data set specified in the argument in which the WHERE= option appears.

The WHERE statement and WHERE= data set option are most useful when you are producing a simple map and do not need to make any other changes to the data set.

Another approach is to use a DATA step to create a subset of the larger data set. The following code illustrates another way to extract the observations for Quebec from the CANADA data set:

```
data quebec;
   set maps.canada;
   if province='24';
```

This approach is most useful when you want to create a permanent subset of a map data set or when you need to make additional changes to the map data set.

The unreduced map data sets provided with SAS/GRAPH software have more observations than most graphics output devices can accurately plot.

You can improve performance by plotting fewer observations for each unit area. The unreduced data sets already contain a DENSITY variable like the one calculated by the GREDUCE procedure, so it is not necessary to use the GREDUCE procedure to process these data sets. Values for DENSITY range from 0 through 6 (the lower the density, the coarser the boundary point).

A statement of the following form excludes all but the lowest density points from the map drawn by the GMAP procedure:

```
proc gmap map=maps.states(where=(density<2));
```

The resulting map is much coarser than one drawn using all the observations in the data set, but it is drawn much faster.

Another way to create a reduced map data set is to use a DATA step to exclude observations with larger density values:

```
data states;
   set maps.states;
   if density<2;
```

The unprojected map data sets provided with SAS/GRAPH software must be projected before they are used; the same is true for maps extracted from the unprojected data sets. See Chapter 33 for examples of projecting map data sets.

See Chapter 35, "The GREMOVE Procedure," for an example of using that procedure to create a regional map from one of the data sets supplied with SAS/GRAPH software.

See Also

Chapter 13, "The LEGEND Statement"
 for information on creating LEGEND definitions

Chapter 15, "The PATTERN Statement"
 for information on creating PATTERN definitions

Chapter 18, "The Annotate Data Set"
 for information on annotating GMAP procedure output

Chapter 33, "The GPROJECT Procedure"
 for information on

 □ transforming coordinates stored as longitude and latitude values into horizontal and vertical coordinates on a plane

 □ projecting an Annotate data set along with a map data set

Chapter 34, "The GREDUCE Procedure"
 for information on reducing the number of points needed to draw a map, thus reducing processing time

Chapter 35, "The GREMOVE Procedure"
 for information on

 □ combining groups of unit areas into larger unit areas to create regional maps

 □ removing some of the boundaries in a map and creating a subset of a map that combines the original areas

 □ using the procedure to create a regional map from one of the data sets supplied with SAS/GRAPH software

SAS Language: Reference, Version 6, First Edition
for information on

☐ functions

☐ the LIBNAME statement

☐ the WHERE statement

☐ the WHERE= data set option

SAS Procedures Guide, Version 6, Third Edition
for information on the CONTENTS and DATASETS procedures

CHAPTER 30 The GOPTIONS Procedure

Overview

The GOPTIONS procedure lists the values of graphics options and global statement definitions currently in effect in your session. Using the GOPTIONS procedure, you can

□ list all of the current values of graphics options, either user-defined or the defaults of the device driver

□ list all of the AXIS, FOOTNOTE, LEGEND, PATTERN, SYMBOL, and TITLE definitions currently in effect

□ display the HSIZE=, VSIZE=, HORIGIN=, VORIGIN=, PAPERFEED=, and PAPERLIMIT= graphics options in units of centimeters (CM).

The listings are displayed in the SAS LOG window as shown in Output 30.1.

Output 30.1 *Default Output from the GOPTIONS Procedure*

```
              SAS/GRAPH software options and parameters, version 6.06
    noadmgdf               GDDM driver output an ADMGDF file
    aspect=                Aspect ratio (width/height) for software
                           characters
    noautocopy             Automatic hardcopy after display
    noautofeed             Automatic paper feed after plot
    baud=                  Communications line speed
    noborder               Draw a border around display or plot
    cback=                 Background color
    cby=                   BY line color
    cell                   Hardware characters must be on cell boundaries
    characters             Use hardware characters
    chartype=              Select hardware font
    circlearc              Use hardware circle/arc generator
    colors=()              Default color list
    cpattern=              Default pattern color
    csymbol=               Default symbol color
    ctext=                 Default text color
    ctitle=                Default title, footnote and note color
    dash                   Use hardware dashed line generator
    devaddr=               IBM Device address, qname, or node name
    device=                Default device driver
    devmap=DEFAULT         Output character map for hardware text
    display                Display graph on device
    noerase                Erase graph upon completion

                                          (continued on next page)
```

(continued from previous page)

```
fby=                                BY line font
fcache=3                            Number of software fonts to keep in memory
fill                                Use hardware rectangle fill generator
fillinc=                            Fill increment to use on software polygon
                                    fills.
ftext=                              Default text font
ftitle=                             Default font for first title
gaccess=''                          Output format for graphics stream
gclass=G                            IBM3287 sysout class
gcopies=(0, 20)                     Number of output copies
gddmcopy=FSCOPY                     GDDM driver hardcopy type
gddmnickname=                       GDDM nickname
gddmtoken=                          GDDM token
gdest=LOCAL                         IBM3287 sysout destination
gend=                               Buffer termination string
gepilog=                            Device termination string
gforms=                             IBM3287 sysout forms code
nogopt10                            Miscellaneous
nogopt11                            Miscellaneous
nogopt12                            Miscellaneous
nogopt13                            Miscellaneous
nogopt14                            Miscellaneous
nogopt15                            Miscellaneous
goutmode=APPEND                     GOUT catalog mode: APPEND or REPLACE
gouttype=INDEPENDENT                Graphics segment type
gprolog=                            Device initialization string
gprotocol=                          Graphics protocol converter driver name
gsflen=                             Length of Graphics Stream File records
gsfmode=PORT                        Graphics Stream File access mode
gsfname=                            Graphics Stream File name
gsize=                              Number of lines in graphics display area
gstart=                             Buffer initialization string
gunit=CELLS                         Default text units
gwait=                              Time delay after graphics display
gwriter=SASWTR                      IBM3287 sysout writer name
handshake=                          ASCII device handshake protocol
hby=                                BY line height
horigin=                            Horizontal offset to graph origin
hpos=                               Character cells per line
hsize=                              Horizontal plot size in inches
htext=                              Default text height
htitle=                             Default height of first TITLE line
interpol=                           Default symbol interpolation
keymap=DEFAULT                      Input character map for hardware and software
                                    text
lfactor=                            Hardware line thickness factor
offshadow=(0.0625 IN , -0.0625 IN )
                                    X, Y offset for dropshadows
paperfeed=                          Amount of paper to feed on drum plotters
paperlimit=                         Physical width of the plotting paper
penmounts=                          Number of pens/colors to be used
piefill                             Use hardware pie fill generator
polygonfill                         Use hardware polygon fill generator
prompt                              Allow/disallow user prompting by device driver
promptchars='000A010D05000000'X
                                    Terminal prompt characters
repaint=                            Number of passes made in drawing a graph
NOROTATE                            Rotate plot ninety degrees
simfont=                            Software font to use as simulated hardware
                                    font.
speed=                              Pen speed
noswap                              Substitute BLACK for WHITE
symbol                              Use hardware symbol generator
targetdevice=                       Intended hardcopy device
trantab=SASGTAB0                    Terminal translate table
nov5comp                            Selects maximum version 5 compatibility
vorigin=                            Vertical offset to graph origin
vpos=                               Character cells per column
vsize=                              Vertical plot size in inches
```

Note: With the exception of the NOGOPT10 through NOGOPT15 graphics options, all of the graphics options displayed by the GOPTIONS procedure are described in Chapter 5, "Graphics Options and Device Parameters Dictionary." The NOGOPT10 through NOGOPT15 graphics options are device-specific and set special features for a device. For more information see your SAS Software Consultant.

GOPTIONS Procedure Syntax

The GOPTIONS procedure uses the following statement:

PROC GOPTIONS ⟨*statement-request-options*⟩
⟨*listing-format-options*⟩ ;

□ *statement-request-options* can be one or more of the following:

AXIS
FOOTNOTE
LEGEND
PATTERN
SYMBOL
TITLE

□ *listing-format-options* can be one or more of the following:

CENTIMETERS
NOLIST
NOLOG
SHORT

GOPTIONS Procedure Description

You can use the GOPTIONS procedure to list the current values of graphics options and statement definitions. You also can use it to display some graphics options in units of centimeters. The options used in the PROC GOPTIONS statement determine the information that is displayed.

Note: Do not confuse the GOPTIONS procedure with the GOPTIONS statement. The GOPTIONS procedure lists the values defined in a GOPTIONS statement as well as any other global statement definitions.

Terminology

The following term is used in the discussion of the GOPTIONS procedure and is defined in the Glossary:

graphics option

Global Statements

All global statement definitions affect the information displayed by the GOPTIONS procedure. If you use a GOPTIONS statement, the values specified in the statement are reflected in the output produced by the GOPTIONS procedure (if you do not suppress the display of the values of graphics options). If you use AXIS, FOOTNOTE, LFGEND, PATTERN, SYMBOL, or TITLE statements, the values you specify in these statements are displayed if you use the appropriate options in the PROC GOPTIONS statement. See "Options" for an explanation of the options used with the GOPTIONS procedure.

PROC GOPTIONS Statement

The PROC GOPTIONS statement starts the procedure. By default, if you do not specify any options in the PROC GOPTIONS statement, the graphics options are listed alphabetically in the LOG window. The list includes the names of the graphics options, the current values, and a brief description of each graphics option. You can use options in the PROC GOPTIONS statement to limit the information that is displayed in the SAS LOG window. (See Output 30.1.) See Chapter 12, "The GOPTIONS Statement," for a list of the graphics options you can set with the GOPTIONS statement. Chapter 5 contains a complete description of each graphics option.

Options

You can use the following options with the PROC GOPTIONS statement, individually or in any combination:

AXIS
A

requests a list of all current AXIS definitions. The current values for all graphics options are also listed unless the NOLIST option is used. If no AXIS statements have been used, the GOPTIONS procedure issues the following message:

```
No AXIS statements defined.
```

CENTIMETERS
CM

displays the values of the HSIZE=, VSIZE=, HORIGIN=, VORIGIN=, PAPERFEED=, and PAPERLIMIT= graphics options in units of CM. These graphics options can only use units of IN or CM; PCT and CELLS are not allowed. The values of these graphics options are always stored as inches even if you specified CM as the unit specification. This means that when you use the GOPTIONS procedure, the values of these graphics options also display in inches, by default. If you want to see the values in centimeters, you must use the CENTIMETERS option.

    Note: The CENTIMETERS option affects only the graphics options listed above. These graphics options only use unit specifications of IN and CM. The CENTIMETERS option *does not* affect the graphics options that can use unit specifications of IN, CM, CELLS, and PCT.

FOOTNOTE
F

requests a list of all current FOOTNOTE and TITLE definitions. The current values for all graphics options are also listed unless the NOLIST option is used. If no FOOTNOTE or TITLE statements have been used, the GOPTIONS procedure issues the following messages:

```
No FOOTNOTE statements defined.
No TITLE statements defined.
```

LEGEND

L

> requests a list of all current LEGEND definitions. The current values for all graphics options are also listed unless the NOLIST option is used. If no LEGEND statements have been used, the GOPTIONS procedure issues the following message:

> `No LEGEND statements defined.`

NOLIST

N

> suppresses the display of graphics options. Use the NOLIST option when you want a listing of only the current AXIS, FOOTNOTE, LEGEND, PATTERN, SYMBOL or TITLE definitions. If you use the NOLIST option, you should use at least one of the following options:

AXIS	PATTERN
FOOTNOTE	SYMBOL
LEGEND	TITLE

NOLOG

> causes output to appear in the OUTPUT window instead of in the LOG window.

PATTERN

P

> requests a list of all current PATTERN definitions. The current values for all graphics options are also listed unless the NOLIST option is used. If no PATTERN statements have been used, the GOPTIONS procedure issues the following message:

> `No PATTERN statements defined.`

SHORT

> specifies in paragraph form an alphabetical list of the values of graphics options. When you use the SHORT option, descriptions of the graphics options are not included. By default, each graphics option and a brief description are displayed on a separate line.

SYMBOL

S

> requests a list of all current SYMBOL definitions. The current values for all graphics options are also listed unless the NOLIST option is used. If no SYMBOL statements have been used, the GOPTIONS procedure issues the following message:

> `No SYMBOL statements defined.`

TITLE

T

> requests a list of all current TITLE and FOOTNOTE definitions. The current values for all graphics options are also listed unless the NOLIST option is used. If no FOOTNOTE or TITLE statements have been used, the GOPTIONS procedure issues the following messages:

> `No FOOTNOTE statements defined.`
> `No TITLE statements defined.`

Using the GOPTIONS Procedure

You can use the GOPTIONS procedure at any time during a SAS session. By specifying options in the PROC GOPTIONS statement, you can determine what information is listed and where it is listed. See "Options" earlier in this chapter for details.

Examples

Using the NOLIST Option

This example illustrates how to use the NOLIST option to suppress the listing of graphics options. In this example, NOLIST causes only the current definitions of FOOTNOTE and TITLE statements to display.

The following program statements produce Output 30.2:

```
    /* set the graphics environment */
goptions reset=global gunit=pct;

    /* define titles and footnotes */
title1 h=6 c=blue f=swissb 'Production Quality';
title2 h=4 c=blue f=swissb 'June 1988 - January 1989';
footnote1 h=3 c=green f=swissb
        'Data from SASDATA.QUALITY';
footnote2 h=3 c=green f=swissb '* denotes approximations';

    /* produce the output */
proc goptions nolist footnote;
run;
```

Output 30.2 Information Displayed When Using the NOLIST Option (GR30N01)

```
14      /* set the graphics environment */
15    goptions reset=global gunit=pct;
16
17      /* define titles and footnotes */
18    title1 h=6 c=blue f=swissb 'Production Quality';
19    title2 h=4 c=blue f=swissb 'June 1988 - January 1989';
20    footnote1 h=3 c=green f=swissb
21            'Data from SASDATA.QUALITY';
22    footnote2 h=3 c=green f=swissb '* denotes approximations';
23
24      /* produce the output */
25    proc goptions nolist footnote;
26    run;

TITLE1 Height=6 Color=BLUE Font=SWISSB 'Production Quality' ;

TITLE2 Height=4 Color=BLUE Font=SWISSB 'June 1988 - January 1989' ;

FOOTNOTE1 Height=3 Color=GREEN Font=SWISSB 'Data from SASDATA.QUALITY' ;

FOOTNOTE2 Height=3 Color=GREEN Font=SWISSB '* denotes approximations' ;
```

This example illustrates the following features:

□ The NOLIST option suppresses the listing of the graphics options.

□ The FOOTNOTE option displays the current FOOTNOTE and TITLE definitions.

Specifying the SHORT Option

This example illustrates how to use the SHORT option to show in
paragraph form only the values of graphics options without the
description of each graphics option.

The following program statements produce Output 30.3:

```
          /* set the graphics environment */
   goptions reset=global gunit=pct border
           ftext=swissb htitle=6 htext=3
           ctext=red cpattern=blue ctitle=green
           colors=(blue green red) hby=4;


          /* produce the output */
   proc goptions short;
   run;
```

Output 30.3 *Information
Displayed When Using the
SHORT Option (GR30N02)*

```
5        /* set the graphics environment */
6    goptions reset=global gunit=pct border
7            ftext=swissb htitle=6 htext=3
8            ctext=red cpattern=blue ctitle=green
9            colors=(blue green red) hby=4;
10
11       /* produce the output */
12   proc goptions short;
13   run;

        SAS/GRAPH software options and parameters, version 6.06
noadmgdf aspect= noautocopy noautofeed baud= border cback= cby= cell
characters chartype= circlearc colors=(BLUE GREEN RED ) cpattern=BLUE
csymbol= ctext=RED ctitle=GREEN dash devaddr= device= devmap=DEFAULT
display noerase fby= fcache=3 fill fillinc= ftext=SWISSB ftitle= gaccess=''
gclass=G gcopies=(0, 20) gddmcopy=FSCOPY gddmnickname= gddmtoken=
gdest=LOCAL gend= gepilog= gforms= nogopt10 nogopt11 nogopt12 nogopt13
nogopt14 nogopt15 goutmode=APPEND gouttype=INDEPENDENT gprolog= gprotocol=
gsflen= gsfmode=PORT gsfname= gsize= gstart= gunit=PCT gwait=
gwriter=SASWTR handshake= hby=4 horigin= hpos= hsize= htext=3 htitle=6
interpol= keymap=DEFAULT lfactor= offshadow=(0.0625 IN , -0.0625 IN )
paperfeed= paperlimit= penmounts= piefill polygonfill prompt
promptchars='000A010D05000000'X repaint= NOROTATE simfont= speed= noswap
symbol targetdevice= trantab=SASGTAB0 nov5comp vorigin= vpos= vsize=
```

This example illustrates the following feature:

□ The SHORT option suppresses the display of the description of each
graphics option.

Using the CENTIMETERS Option

This example illustrates how the CENTIMETERS option changes units in
inches to centimeters. Notice that only those graphics options that use
only IN and CM as the units (the HSIZE=, VSIZE=, HORIGIN=,
VORIGIN=, PAPERFEED=, and PAPERLIMIT= graphics options) are
affected.

The following program statements produce Output 30.4:

```
        /* set the graphics environment */
goptions reset=global gunit=pct border
        ftext=swissb htitle=6 in htext=3 cells
        hsize=10 in vsize=7 in
        paperfeed=8.5 in
        horigin=.5 in vorigin=.5 in;

        /* produce the output using     */
        /* the CENTIMETERS option       */
proc goptions centimeters short;
run;
```

Output 30.4 *Information Displayed When Using the CENTIMETERS Option (GR30N03)*

```
30       /* set the graphics environment */
31  goptions reset=global gunit=pct border
32           ftext=swissb htitle=6 in htext=3 cells
33           hsize=10 in vsize=7 in
34           paperfeed=8.5 in
35           horigin=.5 in vorigin=.5 in;
36
37       /* produce the output using     */
38       /* the CENTIMETERS option       */
39  proc goptions centimeters short;
40  run;

        SAS/GRAPH software options and parameters, version 6.06
noadmgdf aspect= noautocopy noautofeed baud= border cback= cby= cell
characters chartype= circlearc colors=() cpattern= csymbol= ctext= ctitle=
dash devaddr= device= devmap=DEFAULT display noerase fby= fcache=3 fill
fillinc= ftext=SWISSB ftitle= gaccess='' gclass=G gcopies=(0, 20)
gddmcopy=FSCOPY gddmnickname= gddmtoken= gdest=LOCAL gend=
gepilog= gforms= nogopt10 nogopt11 nogopt12 nogopt13 nogopt14 nogopt15
goutmode=APPEND gouttype=INDEPENDENT gprolog= gprotocol= gsflen=
gsfmode=PORT gsfname= gsize= gstart= gunit=PCT gwait= gwriter=SASWTR
handshake= hby= horigin=1.27 CM hpos= hsize=25.4 CM htext=3 CELLS htitle=6
IN interpol= keymap=DEFAULT lfactor= offshadow=(0.0625 IN , -0.0625 IN )
paperfeed=21.59 CM paperlimit= penmounts= piefill polygonfill prompt
promptchars='000A010D05000000'X repaint= NOROTATE simfont= speed= noswap
symbol targetdevice= trantab=SASGTAB0 nov5comp vorigin=1.27 CM vpos= vsize=
17.78 CM
```

This example illustrates the following feature:

□ The CENTIMETERS option displays the values of graphics options defined in inches as units of centimeters. It affects only the HSIZE=, HORIGIN=, PAPERFEED=, PAPERLIMIT=, VSIZE=, and VORIGIN= graphics options. Notice that the value of the HTEXT= graphics option is still in units of CELLS. The HTEXT= graphics option uses units of IN, CM, PCT, and CELLS.

See Also

Chapter 5, "Graphics Options and Device Parameters Dictionary"
for details on each graphics option and device parameter

Chapter 9, "The AXIS Statement"
for information on how to specify an AXIS definition

Chapter 11, "The FOOTNOTE Statement"
for information on how to specify a FOOTNOTE definition

Chapter 12, "The GOPTIONS Statement"
    for details on how to set graphics options

Chapter 13, "The LEGEND Statement"
    for information on how to specify a LEGEND definition

Chapter 15, "The PATTERN Statement"
    for information on how to specify a PATTERN definition

Chapter 16, "The SYMBOL Statement"
    for information on how to specify a SYMBOL definition

Chapter 17, "The TITLE Statement"
    for information on how to specify a TITLE definition

CHAPTER *31* The GPLOT Procedure

Overview

The GPLOT procedure produces two-dimensional graphs that plot one variable against another within a set of coordinate axes. The coordinates of each point on the plot correspond to two variable values in an observation of the input data set. You can plot character variables (of length 16 or less) as well as numeric variables. Graphs are automatically scaled to the values of your data, although you can control scaling with options or with associated AXIS statements.

The GPLOT procedure can be used when you want to

□ display long series of data, showing trends and patterns

□ interpolate between data points

□ extrapolate beyond existing data, using regression and confidence limits.

The GPLOT procedure can produce several kinds of graphs:

□ overlay plots

□ plots against one or two vertical axes

□ bubble plots in which circles of varying proportions representing the values of a third variable are plotted on the vertical and horizontal axes

□ plots with a legend

□ scatter graphs, needle plots, and plots with simple or spline-interpolated lines (controlled by the SYMBOL statement)

□ logarithmic plots (controlled by the AXIS statement).

You can also produce combinations of these types of graphs. Output 31.1 through Output 31.4 illustrate a few of the types of plots the GPLOT procedure can produce.

Output 31.1 illustrates a scatter plot with a nonlinear regression line fitted to the points. A PLOT statement generates the scatter plot, and the INTERPOL= option in a SYMBOL statement specifies the regression line. The variable HEIGHT is plotted against the variable WEIGHT in a plot request of the type *vertical*horizontal*.

Output 31.1 Scatter Plot
with Regression Line
(GR31N01)

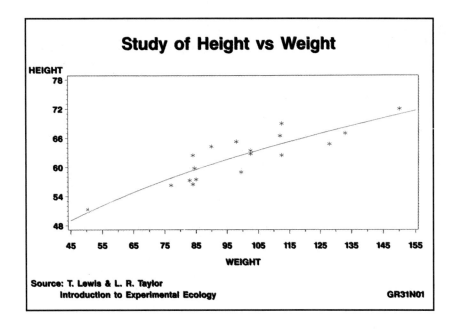

Output 31.2 illustrates a plot request of the form
vertical*horizontal=third-variable, which produces multiple plots on a
single graph and automatically generates a legend. (Only a plot request of
this type generates a legend.) This graph compares the trends of yearly
total sales for three sites. The legend explains the values of the third
variable, SITE.

Output 31.2 Plot of Three
Variables with Legend
(GR31N02)

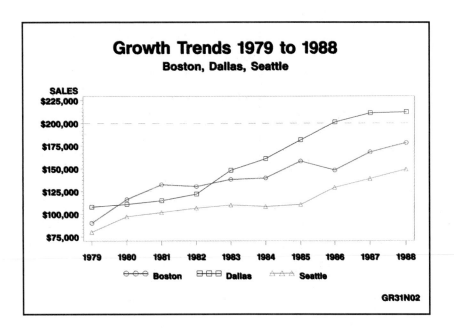

Output 31.3 illustrates a plot with a second vertical axis. In this
example the left axis, generated by a PLOT statement, represents the
number of units produced; and the right axis, generated by a PLOT2
statement, represents the cost per unit in dollars. Both plots automatically
display on the same graph.

Output 31.3 *Plot with a*
Second Vertical Axis
(GR31N03)

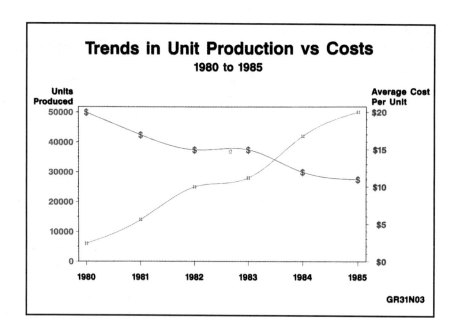

Output 31.4 illustrates a bubble plot in which each bubble represents a
product. The location of the bubble is determined by the product's rate of
change (plotted on the vertical axis) and percent of the market (plotted on
the horizontal axis). The size of each bubble represents the relative
amount of the product's sales.

Output 31.4 *Bubble Plot of*
Market Share Analysis
(GR31N04)

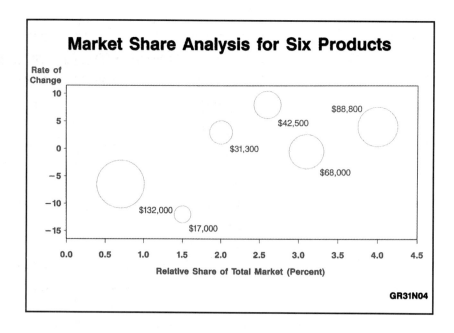

GPLOT Procedure Syntax

The GPLOT procedure uses the following statements:

□ The PROC GPLOT statement is required.

　PROC GPLOT<DATA=*SAS-data-set*>
　　　<ANNOTATE=*Annotate-data-set*>
　　　<GOUT=*output-catalog*>
　　　<UNIFORM>;

□ At least one of the following statements is required:

　BUBBLE *request* < . . . *request-n*>
　　</ <ANNOTATE=*Annotate-data-set*>
　　　<*bubble-appearance-options*>
　　　<*axes-options*>
　　　<*description-options*>>;

　PLOT *request* < . . . *request-n*>
　　</ <ANNOTATE=*Annotate-data-set*>
　　　<*appearance-options*>
　　　<*axes-options*>
　　　<*description-options*>>;

□ The following statements are optional. You can only use them with a PLOT or BUBBLE statement.

　BUBBLE2 *request* < . . . *request-n*>
　　</ <ANNOTATE=*Annotate-data-set*>
　　　<*bubble-appearance-options*>
　　　<*axes-options*>>;

　PLOT2 *request* < . . . *request-n*>
　　</ <ANNOTATE=*Annotate-data-set*>
　　　<*appearance-options*>
　　　<*axes-options*>>;

□ The following statements are optional and local:

　BY <*options*> *variable*;

　NOTE <*options*> <'*text*'>;

□ The following statements are optional and global:

　AXIS<1 . . . 99> <*options*>;

　FOOTNOTE<1 . . . 10> <*options*> <'*text*'>;

　LEGEND<1 . . . 99> <*options*>;

　PATTERN<1 . . . 99> <*options*>;

　SYMBOL<1 . . . 99> <*options*>;

　TITLE<1 . . . 10> <*options*> <'*text*'>;

For complete statement syntax, see the section on the appropriate statement.

Statement Descriptions

The purpose of each statement is described here.

AXIS defines axis characteristics that modify the appearance, position, and content of an axis. See Chapter 9, "The AXIS Statement." Once defined, axis specifications are assigned with the HAXIS= or VAXIS= options in a PLOT, BUBBLE, PLOT2, or BUBBLE2 statement.

BUBBLE creates bubble plots in which a third variable is plotted against two variables represented by the horizontal and vertical axes; the value of the third variable controls the size of the bubble.

BUBBLE2 generates a second vertical axis on the right side of the graph against which a second dependent variable can be plotted. It can also produce overlaid plots on one set of axes. The BUBBLE2 statement must be used with a BUBBLE or PLOT statement.

BY specifies the variable or variables by which the data are grouped for processing. The procedure produces a separate graph for each value of the BY variable. See Chapter 10, "The BY Statement."

FOOTNOTE defines the text and appearance of the footnotes. See Chapter 11, "The FOOTNOTE Statement."

LEGEND defines legend characteristics that modify the text, appearance, and position of a legend. See Chapter 13, "The LEGEND Statement." Once defined, legend specifications are assigned with the LEGEND= option in a PLOT or PLOT2 statement.

NOTE defines the text and appearance of notes that appear in the procedure output area. See Chapter 14, "The NOTE Statement."

PATTERN defines the color and fill pattern used to fill the area below the plot lines. See Chapter 15, "The PATTERN Statement." A PATTERN definition is automatically assigned and used only when the AREAS= option is specified in the PLOT or PLOT2 statement.

PLOT creates plots in which an independent variable is plotted on the horizontal axis and a dependent variable is plotted on the left vertical axis. It can also produce overlaid plots on one set of axes or generate multiple overlaid plots from the values of a third variable.

PLOT2 generates a second vertical axis on the right side of the graph against which a second dependent variable can be plotted. It can also produce overlaid plots on one set of axes or generate multiple overlaid plots from the values of a third variable. PLOT2 must be used with a PLOT or BUBBLE statement.

PROC GPLOT starts the procedure and specifies the name of the data set to be used for the graph, as well as additional input or output options.

SYMBOL	defines the appearance of the plotting symbol and plot lines, as well as specifying interpolation methods. See Chapter 16, "The SYMBOL Statement."
TITLE	defines the text and appearance of the titles. See Chapter 17, "The TITLE Statement."

GPLOT Procedure Description

The following sections address issues that pertain to the GPLOT procedure as a whole: terminology, special data considerations, and the use of global statements and RUN groups.

Terminology

The following terms are used in the discussion of the GPLOT procedure and are defined in the Glossary:

axis	label
axis area	legend
coordinates	major tick mark
dependent variable	minor tick mark
frame	offset
graph	plot
independent variable	plot line
interpolate	value

Some of these terms and some additional terms are illustrated in Figures 31.1 and 31.2.

Figure 31.1 *GPLOT*
Procedure Terms

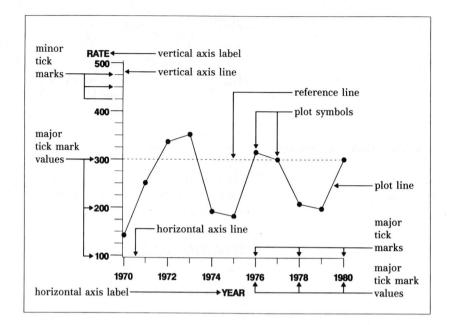

Figure 31.2 *Additional*
GPLOT Procedure Terms

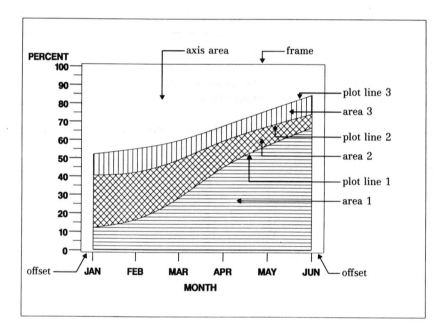

Data Considerations

Missing Values

If either of the plot variables is missing, the GPLOT procedure does not
include the observation in the plot. If you specify interpolation with a
SYMBOL definition, the plot is not broken at the missing value. To break
the plot line or area fill at the missing value, use the SKIPMISS option.

Values Out of Range

You can exclude data values from a graph by restricting the range of axis values with the VAXIS= or HAXIS= options or with the ORDER= option in an AXIS statement. When an observation is encountered with values outside the specified axis range, the GPLOT procedure issues a message to the log and excludes the observation from the plot.

If you specify interpolation with a SYMBOL definition, by default values outside the axis range are excluded from interpolation calculations and as a result may change interpolated values for the plot. Omitting values from interpolation calculations has a particularly noticeable effect on the high-low interpolation methods: HILO, STD, and BOX. In addition, regression lines and confidence limits will represent only part of the original data.

However, you can specify that the omitted values be included in the interpolation calculations by using the MODE= option in a SYMBOL statement. When MODE=INCLUDE, values that fall outside the axis range are included in interpolation calculations but excluded from the plot. The default (MODE=EXCLUDE) omits observations outside the axis range from interpolation calculations. See the MODE= option in Chapter 16 for details.

Sorting Data

Data points are plotted in the order in which the observations are read from the data set. Therefore, if you use any type of interpolation that generates a line, you should sort your data by the horizontal axis variable.

Global Statements

All currently defined titles and footnotes display in every graph generated by the GPLOT procedure or by a RUN group. The procedure automatically assigns currently defined SYMBOL and PATTERN statements as needed to plots that use symbols or patterns. You can assign currently defined AXIS statements using BUBBLE, BUBBLE2, PLOT, or PLOT2 statement options. You can assign currently defined LEGEND statements to plots that automatically generate a legend using PLOT or PLOT2 statement options.

To display different titles or footnotes on your graphs, define the titles at the beginning of a RUN group. Any TITLE statements of a higher level (that is, a lower number) remain in effect and display on the graph.

RUN Groups

The GPLOT procedure supports RUN-group processing. The action statements for this procedure are

BUBBLE

BUBBLE2

PLOT

PLOT2.

For more information on using RUN groups, see Chapter 2, "Running SAS/GRAPH Programs."

PROC GPLOT Statement

The PROC GPLOT statement initiates the procedure and, if necessary, specifies the data set that contains the plot data. In addition, it can optionally specify a data set for annotation and a destination catalog for graphics output, as well as uniform scaling for all graphs. The procedure ends when a QUIT, DATA, or another PROC statement is encountered, or when the SAS session terminates.

Syntax

The general form of the PROC GPLOT statement is

PROC GPLOT <DATA=*SAS-data-set*>
     <ANNOTATE=*Annotate-data-set*>
     <GOUT=*output-catalog*>
     <UNIFORM>;

Requirements

The GPLOT procedure requires an input data set. The procedure uses the data set specified by the DATA= option, or if the DATA= option is omitted, the procedure uses the most recently created SAS data set (the one specified in the _LAST_= system option).

You must use either a PLOT statement or a BUBBLE statement within the GPLOT procedure.

Options

You can use the following options with the PROC GPLOT statement. Options used with this statement affect all the graphs produced by the procedure.

ANNOTATE=*Annotate-data-set*
ANNO=*Annotate-data-set*
    specifies a data set to provide annotation for all the graphs produced by the GPLOT procedure. (To annotate individual graphs, use the ANNOTATE= option in an action statement.) *Annotate-data-set* must contain the appropriate Annotate variables. See Chapter 18, "The Annotate Data Set," for details.

DATA=*SAS-data-set*
    specifies the SAS data set to be used by the procedure. If you do not use the DATA= option and if no data set has been created in the current SAS session, an error occurs and the procedure stops.

GOUT=*output-catalog*
    specifies the SAS catalog in which to save the graphics output produced by the GPLOT procedure for later replay. You can use the GREPLAY procedure to view the graphs stored in the catalog. If you do not use the GOUT= option, catalog entries are written to the default catalog WORK.GSEG, which is erased at the end of your session.

UNIFORM
    specifies that the same axis scaling is to be used for all graphs produced by the procedure. By default, the range of axis values for each axis is based on the minimum and maximum values in the data

and therefore may vary from graph to graph and among BY groups. Using the UNIFORM option forces the value range for each axis to be the same for all graphs. That is, if the procedure produces multiple graphs with both left and right vertical axes, the UNIFORM option scales all the left axes the same and all the right axes the same.

BUBBLE Statement

The BUBBLE statement creates one or more bubble plots using the data set specified in the PROC GPLOT statement. A bubble request specifies which variables to plot on the vertical and horizontal axes and which variable determines the size of the bubble.

The BUBBLE statement produces graphs in which the values of a third variable are shown as circles of varying size. The center of each circle is located at a data point determined by the values of the vertical and horizontal variables.

By default, the procedure automatically scales the axes to include the maximum and minimum data values. It labels each axis with the name of its variable or an associated label and displays each major tick mark value. The BUBBLE statement draws circles for values located within the axes. Bubbles are not drawn for values that lie outside the axis range. If a bubble size value causes a bubble to overlap the axis, the bubble is clipped against the axis line.

You can specify options in your BUBBLE statement to manipulate the axes, modify the appearance of the graph, modify the appearance of the bubbles, and describe catalog entries. To generate a bubble plot with a second vertical axis, use a BUBBLE2 or a PLOT2 statement with the BUBBLE statement.

Syntax

The general form of the BUBBLE statement is

BUBBLE *request* < . . . *request-n*>
    </ <ANNOTATE=*Annotate-data-set*>
       <*bubble-appearance-options*>
       <*axes-options*>
       <*description-options*>>;

□ *request* is

    vertical*horizontal=bubble-size

      where

vertical	specifies the variable plotted on the left vertical axis
horizontal	specifies the variable plotted on the horizontal axis
bubble-size	specifies the third variable, which dictates the size of the bubbles

□ *bubble-appearance-options* can be one or more of the following:

BCOLOR=*bubble-color*

BFONT=*font*

BLABEL

BSCALE=AREA | RADIUS

BSIZE=*multiplier*

    where *multiplier* is a multiplication factor applied to all bubbles

□ *axes-options* can be one or more of the following:

  □ reference lines

    AUTOHREF

    AUTOVREF

    CHREF=*reference-line-color*

    CVREF=*reference-line-color*

    GRID

    HREF=*value-list*

        where *value-list* specifies points on the horizontal axis

    LHREF=*line-type*

        where *line-type* can be 1 . . . 46

    LVREF=*line-type*

        where *line-type* can be 1 . . . 46

    VREF=*value-list*

        where *value-list* specifies points on the vertical axis

  □ horizontal axis

    HAXIS=*value-list* | AXIS<1 . . . 99>

        where *value-list* specifies major tick marks

    HMINOR=*n*

        where *n* is the number of minor tick marks

    HZERO

  □ vertical axis

    VAXIS=*value-list* | AXIS<1 . . . 99>

        where *value-list* specifies major tick marks

    VMINOR=*n*

        where *n* is the number of minor tick marks

    VREVERSE

    VZERO

  □ axes appearance

    CAXIS=*axis-color*

    CFRAME=*background-color*

    CTEXT=*text-color*

    FRAME

    NOAXIS

□ *description-options* can be either or both of the following:

DESCRIPTION='*string*'

NAME='*string*'

See "Options" for the BUBBLE statement for more information.

Requirements

A BUBBLE statement must include at least one bubble request of the form *vertical*horizontal=bubble-size*. Only bubble requests of this form are valid. The variable *bubble-size* must be numeric. You can submit multiple bubble requests in one BUBBLE statement, and you can include any number of BUBBLE statements within the procedure. You must use either a BUBBLE statement or a PLOT statement with the PROC GPLOT statement.

Options

You can use the following options in the BUBBLE statement. Options used in a BUBBLE statement affect all graphs produced by that statement. If you use any of the following options, separate them from the bubble requests with a slash (/). If you do not use any options, omit the slash.

ANNOTATE=*Annotate-data-set*
ANNO=*Annotate-data-set*
    specifies a data set to be used for annotation of graphs produced by the statement. *Annotate-data-set* must contain the appropriate Annotate variables. See Chapter 18 for details.

      If the ANNOTATE= option is also used in the PROC GPLOT statement, both sets of annotation are applied. If you specify BY-group processing, the Annotate data set must contain the BY variable. For details, see "Using BY-Group Processing with the Annotate Facility" in Chapter 18 and "Details of BY-Group Processing" in Chapter 10.

AUTOHREF
    draws reference lines at all major tick marks on the horizontal axis.

AUTOVREF
    draws reference lines at all major tick marks on the vertical axis.

BCOLOR=*bubble-color*
    specifies the color for the bubbles. If you do not use the BCOLOR= option, a color specification is searched for in the following order:

    1. the CAXIS= option in the BUBBLE statement

    2. the default, the first color in the colors list.

BFONT=*font*
    specifies the font to use for bubble labels. If you do not use the BFONT= option, a font specification is searched for in the following order:

    1. the FTEXT= option in a GOPTIONS statement

    2. the default hardware font.

    (See the description of the BLABEL option for information on the location and color of labels.)

BLABEL

labels the bubbles with the values of the third variable. If the variable has a format, the formatted value is used. By default, bubbles are not labeled.

The procedure normally places labels directly outside the circle at 315 degrees rotation. If a label in this position does not fit in the axis area, other 45-degree placements (that is, 45, 135, and 225 degrees) are attempted. If the label cannot be placed at any of the positions (45, 135, 225, or 315 degrees) without being clipped, the label is omitted. However, labels may collide with other bubbles or previously placed labels.

Labels display in the color specified by the CTEXT= option. If you do not use the CTEXT= option, the default is the first color in the colors list.

BSCALE=AREA | RADIUS

specifies whether the bubble-scaling proportion is based on the area of the circles or the radius measure. By default, BSCALE=AREA.

The value assigned to the BSCALE= option affects how large the bubbles appear in relation to each other. For example, suppose the third variable value is twice as big for one bubble as it is for another. If BSCALE=AREA, the area of the larger bubble will be twice the area of the smaller bubble. If BSCALE=RADIUS, the radius of the larger bubble will be twice the radius of the smaller bubble and the larger bubble will have more than twice the area of the smaller bubble.

BSIZE=*multiplier*

specifies an overall scaling factor for the bubbles so that you can increase or decrease the size of all bubbles by this factor. By default, BSIZE=5.

CAXIS=*axis-color*

CA=*axis-color*

specifies the color for the axis line and all major and minor tick marks. By default, the procedure uses the first color in the colors list.

If you use the CAXIS= option, it may be overridden by

1. the COLOR= option in an AXIS definition, which in turn is overridden by

2. the COLOR= parameter of the MAJOR= or MINOR= option in an AXIS definition.

CFRAME=*background-color*

CFR=*background-color*

fills the axis area with the specified color and automatically draws a frame around the axis area. The procedure determines the color of the frame according to the precedence list given later in the FRAME option description.

CHREF=*reference-line-color*

CH=*reference-line-color*

specifies the color for reference lines requested by the HREF= and AUTOHREF options. By default, these reference lines display in the color of the horizontal axis.

CTEXT=*text-color*
C=*text-color*
> specifies the color for all text on the axes, including tick mark values, axis labels, and bubble labels.
>
> If you do not use the CTEXT= option, a color specification is searched for in the following order:
>
> 1. the CTEXT= option in a GOPTIONS statement
>
> 2. the default, the first color in the colors list.
>
> If you use the CTEXT= option, it overrides the color specification for the axis label and the tick mark values in the COLOR= option in an AXIS definition assigned to the axis.
>
> If you use the CTEXT= option, the color specification is overridden in the following situation: if you also use the COLOR= parameter of a LABEL= or VALUE= option in an AXIS definition assigned to the axis, that parameter determines the color of the axis label or the color of the tick mark values, respectively.

CVREF=*reference-line-color*
CV=*reference-line-color*
> specifies the color for reference lines requested by the VREF= and AUTOVREF options. By default, these reference lines display in the color of the vertical axis.

DESCRIPTION=*'string'*
DES=*'string'*
> specifies a descriptive string, up to 40 characters long, that appears in the Description field of the catalog entry for the graph. The description does not appear on the graph. By default, the procedure assigns a description of the form BUBBLE OF *variable*variable*= *variable*.

FRAME
FR
> draws a frame around the axis area. A specification for the color of the frame is searched for in the following order:
>
> 1. the CAXIS= option
>
> 2. the COLOR= option in the AXIS definition assigned to the vertical axis
>
> 3. the COLOR= option in the AXIS definition assigned to the horizontal axis
>
> 4. the default, the first color in the colors list.
>
> The axis area is not outlined unless you use the FRAME option. To outline the axis area *and* fill it with a background color, use the CFRAME= option.

GRID
> draws reference lines at all major tick marks on both axes. You get the same result when you use all the following options in a BUBBLE statement: AUTOHREF, AUTOVREF, FRAME, LVREF=34, and LHREF=34. The line type for GRID is 34. The line color is the color of the axis.

HAXIS=*value-list* | AXIS<1 . . . 99>

    specifies major tick mark values for the horizontal axis or assigns an axis definition to the axis. By default, the procedure scales the axis automatically and provides an appropriate number of tick marks.

    When the horizontal axis variable is numeric, *value-list* can be specified in the following ways:

n n . . . n

n,n, . . . ,n

n TO *n* <BY *increment*> <*n . . . n*> <*n, . . . ,n*>

n n . . . n TO *n* <BY *increment*> <*n . . . n*>

n,n, . . . ,n TO *n* <BY *increment*> <*n, . . . ,n*>

'*SAS-value*'i TO '*SAS-value*'i <BY *interval*>

'*SAS-value*'i '*SAS-value*'i . . . '*SAS-value*'i

    The values must be in either ascending or descending order. By default, the increment value is 1. You can use a negative value for *increment* to specify a value list in descending order. The specified values are spaced evenly along the horizontal axis even if the values are not uniformly distributed. A warning message is written to the SAS log if the values are not evenly distributed. For additional information on specifying a value list, see the discussion of the ORDER= option in Chapter 9.

    When the horizontal axis variable is character, values are enclosed in single quotes and can be listed in any order, as in this example:

```
haxis= 'item-one' 'item-two' 'item-three'
```

Character strings in a value list are case-sensitive.

    To assign an AXIS definition, use a value of the form AXIS<1 . . . 99>. The option is ignored if no AXIS definition is currently in effect. See Chapter 9 for details.

    Note: If data values fall outside the range specified by the HAXIS= option, then by default the outlying data values are not used in interpolation calculations. See "Data Considerations" earlier in this chapter for more information on values out of range.

HMINOR=*n*
HM=*n*

    specifies the number of minor tick marks drawn between each major tick mark on the horizontal axis. Minor tick marks are not labeled. The HMINOR= option overrides the NUMBER= parameter of the VALUE= option in an AXIS definition.

HREF=*value-list*

    draws one or more reference lines perpendicular to the horizontal axis at points specified by *value-list*. For a description of how you can specify *value-list*, see the HAXIS= option. For a description of color specifications for reference lines, see the CHREF= option.

HZERO

    specifies that tick marks on the horizontal axis begin in the first position with a value of zero. The HZERO request is ignored if negative values are present for the horizontal variable or if the horizontal axis has been specified with the HAXIS= option.

LHREF=*line-type*

LH=*line-type*

> specifies the line type for drawing reference lines requested by the AUTOHREF or HREF= option. *Line-type* can be 1 through 46. By default, LHREF=1, a solid line. See Table 16.5 in Chapter 16 for examples of available line types.

LVREF=*line-type*

LV=*line-type*

> specifies the line type for drawing reference lines requested by the AUTOVREF or VREF= option. *Line-type* can be 1 through 46. By default, LVREF=1, a solid line. See Table 16.5 in Chapter 16 for examples of available line types.

NAME='*string*'

> specifies a string of up to eight characters that appears in the Name field of the catalog entry for the graph. The default name is GPLOT. If either the name specified or the default name duplicates an existing name in the catalog, then SAS/GRAPH software adds a number to the duplicate name to create a unique name, for example, GPLOT2.

NOAXIS

NOAXES

> suppresses the axes, including axis lines, axis labels, all major and minor tick marks, and tick mark values.

VAXIS=*value-list* | AXIS<1 . . . 99>

> specifies the major tick mark values for the vertical axis or assigns an AXIS definition to the axis. For a description of *value-list*, see the HAXIS= option.
>
> To assign an AXIS definition use a value of the form AXIS<1 . . . 99>. The option is ignored if the definition has not been previously established. See Chapter 9 for details.

VMINOR=*n*

VM=*n*

> specifies the number of minor tick marks drawn between each major tick mark on the vertical axis. Minor tick marks are not labeled. The VMINOR= option overrides the NUMBER= parameter of the VALUE= option in an AXIS definition.

VREF=*value-list*

> draws one or more reference lines perpendicular to the vertical axis at points specified by *value-list*. For a description of how you can specify *value-list*, see the HAXIS= option. For a description of color specifications for reference lines, see the CVREF= option.

VREVERSE

> specifies that the order of the values on the vertical axis be reversed.

VZERO

> specifies that tick marks on the vertical axis begin in the first position with a zero. The VZERO request is ignored if negative values are present for the vertical variable or if the vertical axis has been specified with the VAXIS= option.

Using the BUBBLE Statement

Bubble requests must follow the form *vertical*horizontal=bubble-size*, as in this example,

```
bubble y*x=s;
```

This statement produces a bubble plot like the diagram in Figure 31.3 in which the Y values are plotted on the vertical axis, the X values are plotted on the horizontal axis, and the S values determine the size of the bubble. If the S value is positive, bubbles are drawn with a solid line; if the S value is negative, bubbles are drawn with a dashed line.

Figure 31.3 *Diagram of a Bubble Plot*

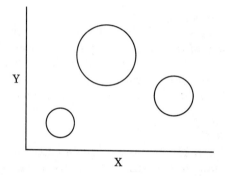

If any part of a bubble extends over an axis, the bubble is clipped against the axis line. The bubbles for the highest value and lowest value may be clipped unless you modify the axes by offsetting the first and last values or by adding values to the range represented by the axis.

Observations with values that lie outside the axis area are not plotted. You can specify the range of values on an axis with the HAXIS= or VAXIS= option, or with AXIS definitions.

You can include two or more bubble requests in one BUBBLE statement. Separate the bubble requests by blanks. The following statement has two bubble requests and produces two graphs:

```
bubble b*a=c s*r=t;
```

The first graph has vertical axis values of B, horizontal axis values of A, and bubble size values of C; the second graph has vertical axis values of S, horizontal axis values of R, and bubble size values of T.

Using Global Statements

AXIS definitions can be assigned with BUBBLE statement options. LEGEND, SYMBOL, and PATTERN statements are not used since BUBBLE statements do not create legends, plot data points, or support the AREAS= option.

BUBBLE Statement Example

The following example illustrates the major features of the BUBBLE statement.

Bubble Plot

This example shows a bubble plot in which each bubble represents a category of engineer (variable ENG). The size of the bubble indicates the relative number of members (variable NUM) for that category, while the label for the bubble displays the actual value of NUM. The location of the bubbles in relation to the vertical axis represents the average salary (variable DOLLARS). In addition, this example shows how BUBBLE statement options control the appearance of the bubbles and their labels.

The following program statements produce Output 31.5:

```
    /* set the graphics environment */
goptions reset=global gunit=pct border
        ftext=swissb htitle=6 htext=3;

    /* create the data set JOBS */
data jobs;
    input eng dollars num;
    cards;
1 27308 73273
2 29844 70192
3 22920 89382
4 32816 19601
5 28116 25541
6 18444 34833
;
run;

    /* define titles and footnote */
title1 '1988 Member Profile';
title2 h=4 'Salaries and Number of Member Engineers';
footnote j=r 'GR31N05  ';

    /* define axis characteristics */
axis1 order=(1 to 6)
      label=none
      value=('Civil' 'Aero.' 'Elec.' 'Mech.' 'Chem.' 'Petro.')
      offset=(5,5)
      width=3;
axis2 order=(0 to 40000 by 10000)
      label=none
      major=(height=1.5)
      minor=(number=1 height=1)
      width=3;
```

```
                          /* generate bubble plot */
                proc gplot data=jobs;
                   format dollars dollar9.;
                   format num comma7.0;
                   bubble dollars*eng=num / haxis=axis1
                                            vaxis=axis2
                                            hminor=0
                                            bcolor=red
                                            bfont=swissi
                                            blabel
                                            bscale=area
                                            bsize=12
                                            caxis=blue
                                            frame;
                run;
                quit;
```

Output 31.5 *Bubble Plot Modified with BUBBLE Statement Options (GR31N05)*

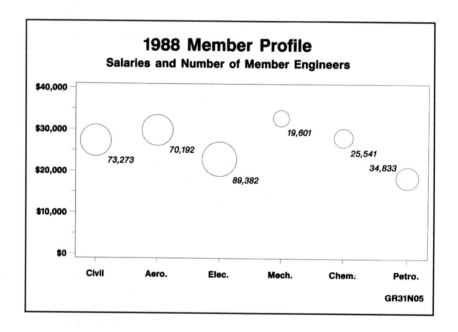

Some of the features of this example are described here.

□ The HAXIS= option specifies the AXIS1 definition, which suppresses major tick marks and uses the OFFSET= option to move the first and last major tick mark values away from the vertical axes so that the axis does not clip the bubbles.

□ The VAXIS= option specifies the AXIS2 definition, which uses the ORDER= option to set major tick marks at 10000 dollar intervals beginning with 0 and ending with 40000.

☐ The BCOLOR= option colors the bubbles.

☐ The BFONT= option specifies the font for the text that labels the bubbles.

☐ The BLABEL option labels each bubble with the value of the variable NUM.

☐ BSCALE=AREA specifies that the relative size of the bubbles is based on their area. AREA is the default value.

☐ The BSIZE= option increases the size of the bubbles by increasing the size of the scaling factor to 12.

☐ The CAXIS= option colors the axis lines and all major and minor tick marks.

☐ The FRAME option draws a frame around the axis area.

BUBBLE2 Statement

The BUBBLE2 statement generates a second vertical axis on the right side of a graph produced by an accompanying BUBBLE or PLOT statement. The BUBBLE2 statement uses the data set specified in the GPLOT statement. Use the BUBBLE2 statement to generate a right axis when you want

☐ to provide a second scale of values for a variable, for example, displaying cost in francs on the left axis and cost in deutsche marks on the right axis

☐ to plot different data on each vertical axis, for example, sales on the left axis and quantities on the right axis

☐ to display the same scale of values on both left and right axes.

With a BUBBLE2 statement you can produce the equivalent of an overlaid plot by generating a second set of bubbles with different values for the right axis or the bubble size or both.

Typically, in a BUBBLE2 plot request, you specify the same independent variable for the horizontal axis as in the BUBBLE or PLOT statement, and a different dependent variable for the right vertical axis. However, you can specify the same values for both the left and right axes and a different set of values for the bubble size.

By default, the procedure automatically scales the axes to include the maximum and minimum data values. It labels each axis with the name of its variable or an associated label and displays each major tick mark value. The BUBBLE2 statement draws circles for values located within the axes. Bubbles are not drawn for values that lie outside the axis range. If a bubble size value causes a bubble to overlap the axis, the bubble is clipped against the axis line.

You can specify options in your BUBBLE2 statement to manipulate the axes, modify the appearance of the graph, and modify the appearance of the bubbles.

Syntax

The general form of the BUBBLE2 statement is

BUBBLE2 *request* < . . . *request-n*>
   </ <ANNOTATE=*Annotate-data-set*>
     <*bubble-appearance-options*>
     <*axes-options*>>;

□ *request* is

   *vertical*horizontal*=*bubble-size*

     where

vertical	specifies the variable plotted on the right vertical axis
horizontal	specifies the variable plotted on the horizontal axis
bubble-size	specifies a third variable that dictates the size of the bubbles

□ *bubble-appearance-options* can be one or more of the following:

   BCOLOR=*bubble-color*

   BFONT=*font*

   BLABEL

   BSCALE=AREA | RADIUS

   BSIZE=*multiplier*

     where *multiplier* is a multiplication factor applied to all bubbles

□ *axes-options* can be one or more of the following:

   □ reference lines

     AUTOVREF

     CVREF=*reference-line-color*

     GRID

     LVREF=*line-type*

       where *line-type* can be 1 . . . 46

     VREF=*value-list*

       where *value-list* specifies points on the vertical axis

   □ vertical axis

     VAXIS=*value-list* | AXIS<1 . . . 99>

       where *value-list* specifies major tick marks

     VMINOR=*n*

       where *n* is the number of minor tick marks

     VREVERSE

     VZERO

□ axes appearance

      CAXIS=*axis-color*

      CFRAME=*background-color*

      CTEXT=*text-color*

      FRAME

      NOAXIS

See "Options" for the BUBBLE2 statement for more information.

Requirements

A BUBBLE2 statement can only be used with a BUBBLE or PLOT statement. A BUBBLE2 statement must include at least one bubble request of the form *vertical*horizontal=bubble-size*. Only bubble requests of this form are valid. You can submit multiple bubble requests in one BUBBLE2 statement.

When you use a BUBBLE2 statement, the GPLOT procedure assumes that the horizontal axis specified in the BUBBLE2 statement is identical to the horizontal axis specified in the BUBBLE or PLOT statement. If the two horizontal axes specifications are different, the BUBBLE2 axis specification is ignored.

The bubble requests on both statements must be evenly matched, as in the following example:

```
bubble  y*x=s  b*a=c;
bubble2 y2*x=s b2*a=c2;
```

These statements produce two graphs each with two vertical axes. The first pair of bubble requests (Y*X=S and Y2*X=S) produce one graph in which the variable X is plotted on the horizontal axis, the variable Y is plotted on the left axis, and the variable Y2 is plotted on the right axis. In this pair, the value of S is the same for both requests. The second pair of bubble requests (B*A=C and B2*A=C2) produce another graph in which the variable A is plotted on the horizontal axis, the variable B is plotted on the left axis, and the variable B2 is plotted on the right axis.

If the scale of values for the left and right vertical axes is the same and you want both axes to represent the same range of values, you can specify the range with a VAXIS= option in both the BUBBLE and BUBBLE2 statements.

Options

Options for the BUBBLE2 statement are identical to those for the BUBBLE statement except for the following, which are ignored if specified:

AUTOHREF

CHREF=

DESCRIPTION=

HAXIS=

HMINOR=

HREF=

HZERO=

LHREF=

NAME=.

See "Options" in "BUBBLE Statement" earlier in this chapter for complete descriptions of options used with the BUBBLE2 statement.

Using the BUBBLE2 Statement

Like the BUBBLE statement, the BUBBLE2 statement plot request must follow the form *vertical*horizontal=bubble-size*, but a BUBBLE2 statement always plots the values of the dependent variable on the right vertical axis.

In the BUBBLE2 statement either of the variables *vertical* or *bubble-size* or both may be different from the variables *vertical* or *bubble-size* in the BUBBLE statement. The variable *horizontal* must stay the same. If the values of *vertical* are different in the BUBBLE and BUBBLE2 statements, the right axis is different from the left and the location of the second set of bubbles varies accordingly. If the values of *vertical* in the two statements are the same, the right axis is identical to the left axis. Similarly, the values of *bubble-size* determine whether or not the size of the bubbles in the two plots is the same or different. Different types of bubble plots are generated according to how *vertical* and *bubble-size* are specified in the BUBBLE2 statement.

There are three possible combinations of BUBBLE and BUBBLE2 statement pairs. The general form of each combination is as follows:

□ When the vertical axis variables are different, the statement pair has the following form:

```
bubble y*x=s;
bubble2 y2*x=s;
```

In this pair, Y2 in the BUBBLE2 statement is different from Y in the accompanying BUBBLE statement, but S is the same in both. This form generates a plot in which both sets of bubbles have the same value but different locations on the graph.

□ When the bubble size variables are different, the statement pair has the following form:

```
bubble y*x=s;
bubble2 y*x=s2;
```

In this pair, X and Y are the same in both statements, but the S and S2 are different. The resulting plot has two identical vertical axes and two sets of concentric bubbles with different values.

□ When both the vertical axis variables and the bubble size variables are different, the statement pair has the following form:

```
bubble y*x=s;
bubble2 y2*x=s2;
```

In this pair, Y2 and S2 in the BUBBLE2 statement are both different from Y and S in the BUBBLE statement. This combination produces the equivalent of an overlaid plot in which both bubble location and bubble size are different.

Using Global Statements

AXIS definitions that modify the vertical axis can be assigned with BUBBLE2 statement options. LEGEND, SYMBOL, and PATTERN definitions are not used since BUBBLE2 statements do not create legends, plot data points, or support the AREAS= option.

BUBBLE2 Statement Example

The following example illustrates the major features of the BUBBLE2 statement.

Bubble Plot with Second Vertical Axis

This example shows how a BUBBLE2 statement generates a right vertical axis that displays the values of the vertical coordinates in a different scale from the scale used for the left vertical axis.

The example produces a bubble plot in which each bubble represents a category of engineer (variable ENG). The size of the bubble indicates the relative number of members (variable NUM) for that category, while the label for the bubble displays the actual value of NUM. The location of the bubbles in relation to the vertical axes represents average salary. Salary values are scaled by dollars on the left vertical axis and by yen on the right vertical axis.

BUBBLE and BUBBLE2 statement options control the size and appearance of the bubbles and their labels. AXIS definitions calibrate the axes so that the data points are identical and only one set of bubbles appears. (If the data points are not identical, two sets of bubbles are displayed.)

The following program statements produce Output 31.6:

```
    /* set the graphics environment */
goptions reset=global gunit=pct border
        ftext=swissb htitle=6 htext=3;
```

```
                /* create the data set JOBS */
                /* calculate variable YEN    */
           data jobs;
              input eng dollars num;
              yen=dollars*125;
              cards;
           1 27308 73273
           2 29844 70192
           3 22920 89382
           4 32816 19601
           5 28116 25541
           6 18444 34833
           ;
           run;

                /* define titles and footnote */
           title1 '1988 Member Profile';
           title2 h=4 'Salaries and Number of Member Engineers';
           footnote j=r 'GR31N06  ';

                /* define axis characteristics */
           axis1 order=(1 to 6)
                 value=('Civil' 'Aero.' 'Elec.' 'Mech.' 'Chem.' 'Petro.')
                 offset=(5,5)
                 label=none
                 width=3;
           axis2 minor=(number=1 height=1)
                 major=(height=1.5)
                 order=(10000 to 40000 by 10000)
                 width=3;
           axis3 minor=(number=1 height=1)
                 major=(height=1.5)
                 order=(1250000 to 5000000 by 1250000)
                 width=3;

                /* generate bubble plot with second vertical axis */
           proc gplot data=jobs;
              format dollars dollar7.;
              format num comma7.0;
              format yen comma9.0;
              bubble dollars*eng=num / haxis=axis1
                                       vaxis=axis2
                                       hminor=0
                                       bcolor=red
                                       bfont=swissi
                                       blabel
                                       bscale=area
                                       bsize=12
                                       caxis=blue
                                       frame;
```

```
bubble2 yen*eng=num / vaxis=axis3
                      bcolor=red
                      bscale=area
                      bsize=12
                      caxis=blue;
run;
quit;
```

Output 31.6 *BUBBLE2 Plot (GR31N06)*

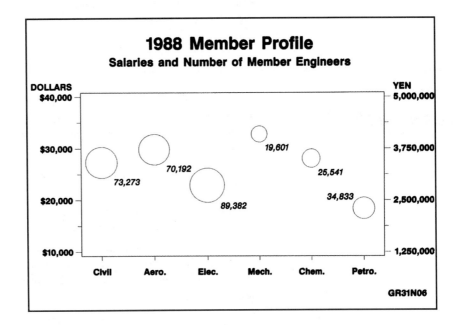

Some of the features of this example are described here.

□ The HAXIS= option in the BUBBLE statement specifies the AXIS1 definition.

□ The VAXIS= option specifies AXIS2 and AXIS3 definitions in the BUBBLE and BUBBLE2 statements, respectively. In the AXIS2 and AXIS3 definitions, the ORDER= option controls the scaling of the axes. Both axes represent exactly the same range of monetary value.

□ The following options are used in both the BUBBLE and BUBBLE2 statements so that the bubbles generated by each statement are identical:

  □ The BCOLOR= option colors the bubbles.

  □ BSCALE=AREA specifies that the relative size of the bubbles is based on their area. AREA is the default value.

  □ The BSIZE= option increases the size of the bubble by increasing the size of the scaling factor to 12.

□ The BLABEL option labels each bubble with the value of the variable NUM.

□ The BFONT= option specifies the font for the text that labels the bubbles.

□ The FRAME option draws a frame around the axis area.

□ The CAXIS= option, which is used in both the BUBBLE and BUBBLE2 statements, colors the axis lines and all major and minor tick marks. Axis labels and major tick mark values use the default color, which is the first color in the colors list.

PLOT Statement

The PLOT statement creates one or more plots using the data set specified in the PROC GPLOT statement. It uses plot requests to name the variables to be plotted and to determine the type of plot. The PLOT statement can produce

□ simple plots of two variables against one horizontal axis and one vertical axis

□ overlay plots in which multiple sets of data points are displayed on one graph but no legend is generated

□ plots in which two variables are plotted according to the values of a third variable producing multiple plots on one set of axes and automatically generating a legend. (Only plot requests of three variables generate legends.)

By default, the PLOT statement plots data points within the axes. The procedure automatically scales the axes to include the maximum and minimum data values. It labels each axis with the name of its variable and displays each major tick mark value.

You can specify options in your PLOT statement to manipulate the axes, modify the appearance of your graph, and describe catalog entries. In addition you can use SYMBOL definitions to assign plot symbols for the data points, to join data points, to draw regression lines, or to plot confidence limits.

To generate a plot with a second vertical axis, use a PLOT2 or a BUBBLE2 statement with the PLOT statement.

Syntax

The general form of the PLOT statement is

PLOT *request* < . . . *request-n*>
    </ <ANNOTATE=*Annotate-data-set*>
       <*appearance-options*>
       <*axes-options*>
       <*description-options*>>;

□ *request* can be any of the following:

> *vertical*horizontal*
>
> *(vertical* < . . . *vertical-n*>*)*(horizontal* < . . . *horizontal-n*>*)*
>
> *vertical*horizontal=third-variable*
>
> *vertical*horizontal=number*

> > where

vertical	specifies the variable plotted on the left vertical axis
horizontal	specifies the variable plotted on the horizontal axis
third-variable	specifies a third (classification) variable against which *vertical* and *horizontal* are plotted; *third-variable* values appear in a legend
n	specifies the *n*th generated SYMBOL definition

□ *appearance-options* can be one or more of the following:

> AREAS=*n*
>
> LEGEND=LEGEND<1 . . . 99>
>
> NOLEGEND
>
> OVERLAY
>
> SKIPMISS

□ *axes-options* can be one or more of the following:

> □ reference lines

> > AUTOHREF
> >
> > AUTOVREF
> >
> > CHREF=*reference-line-color*
> >
> > CVREF=*reference-line-color*
> >
> > GRID
> >
> > HREF=*value-list*
> >
> > > where *value-list* specifies points on the horizontal axis
> >
> > LHREF=*line-type*
> >
> > > where *line-type* can be 1 . . . 46
> >
> > LVREF=*line-type*
> >
> > > where *line-type* can be 1 . . . 46
> >
> > VREF=*value-list*
> >
> > > where *value-list* specifies points on the vertical axis

> □ horizontal axis

> > HAXIS=*value-list* | AXIS<1 . . . 99>
> >
> > > where *value-list* specifies major tick marks
> >
> > HMINOR=*n*
> >
> > > where *n* is number of minor tick marks
> >
> > HZERO

☐ vertical axis

VAXIS=*value-list* | AXIS<1 . . . 99>

where *value-list* specifies major tick marks

VMINOR=*n*

where *n* is the number of minor tick marks

VREVERSE

VZERO

☐ axes appearance

CAXIS=*axis-color*

CFRAME=*background-color*

CTEXT=*text-color*

FRAME

NOAXIS

☐ *description-options* can be either or both of the following:

DESCRIPTION='*string*'

NAME='*string*'

See "Options" for the PLOT statement for more information.

Requirements

A PLOT statement must contain at least one plot request, but you can submit multiple plot requests in one PLOT statement, and you can include any number of PLOT statements within the procedure. You must use either a PLOT statement or a BUBBLE statement with the PROC GPLOT statement.

Options

You can use the following options in the PLOT statement. Options used in a PLOT statement affect all the graphs produced by that statement. If you use any of the following options, separate them from the plot requests with a slash (/). If you do not use any options, omit the slash.

ANNOTATE=*Annotate-data-set*
ANNO=*Annotate-data-set*

specifies a data set to be used for annotation of graphs produced by the statement. *Annotate-data-set* must contain the appropriate Annotate variables. See Chapter 18 for details.

If the ANNOTATE= option is also used with the PROC GPLOT statement, both sets of annotation are applied. If you specify BY-group processing, the Annotate data set must contain the BY variable. For details, see "Using BY-Group Processing with the Annotate Facility" in Chapter 18 and "Details of BY-Group Processing" in Chapter 10.

AREAS=*n*

fills all the areas below plot line *n* with a pattern. Before an area can be filled, the data points that border the area must be joined by a line. Use a SYMBOL statement with one of the following interpolation methods to join the data points:

INTERPOL=JOIN

INTERPOL=STEP

INTERPOL=R*series*

INTERPOL=SPLINE | SM | L

See Chapter 16 for details on interpolation methods.

PATTERN definitions are assigned to the areas below the plot lines in the order the plots are drawn. The first area is that between the horizontal axis and the plot line that is drawn first. The second area is that above the first plot line and below the plot line that is drawn second, and so forth. If the line that is drawn second lies below the line that is drawn first, the second area is hidden when the first is filled. The plots with the lower line values must be drawn first to prevent one area fill from overlaying another.

Therefore, if you produce multiple plots by submitting multiple plot requests and using the OVERLAY option, the plot requests must be ordered in the PLOT statement so that the plot request that produces the lowest line values is the first (leftmost) plot request, the plot request that produces the next lowest line values is the second plot request, and so on.

If you produce multiple plots with a *vertical*horizontal*= *third-variable* plot request, the lines are plotted in order of increasing third variable values. Therefore the data must be sorted by the third variable so that the plot lines are drawn in order from the lowest value of third variable to the highest.

The AREAS= option works only if all plot lines are generated by the same PLOT or PLOT2 statement.

The value of *n* specifies which areas to fill:

□ AREAS=1 fills the first area.

□ AREAS=2 fills both the first and second areas, and so forth.

If you specify a value for the AREAS= option that is greater than the number of bounded areas in the chart, the area between the top plot line and the axis frame is filled.

You can specify the type of pattern for the area fill with a PATTERN definition that specifies a map and plot pattern type. The patterns are drawn with the lowest numbered PATTERN statement first. If no valid PATTERN definition exists, the procedure uses the first default map and plot pattern, which is INTERPOL=M2N0. See Chapter 15 for details on specifying map and plot patterns.

If you use the VALUE= option in the SYMBOL statement, some symbols may be hidden. If reference lines are also specified with the AREAS= option, they are drawn behind the pattern fill.

See "Using the AREAS= Option with Overlaid Plots" in "Plot Statement Examples" later in this section.

AUTOHREF
> draws reference lines at all major tick marks on the horizontal axis.

AUTOVREF
> draws reference lines at all major tick marks on the vertical axis.

CAXIS=*axis-color*
CA=*axis-color*
> specifies the color for the axis line and all major and minor tick
> marks. By default, the procedure uses the first color in the colors list.
> If you use the CAXIS= option, it may be overridden by
>
> 1. the COLOR= option in an AXIS definition, which in turn is
>   overridden by
>
> 2. the COLOR= parameter of the MAJOR= or MINOR= option in
>   an AXIS definition for major and minor tick marks.

CFRAME=*background-color*
CFR=*background-color*
> fills the axis area with the specified color and automatically draws a
> frame around the axis area. The procedure determines the color of
> the frame according to the precedence list given later in the FRAME
> option description.

CHREF=*reference-line-color*
CH=*reference-line-color*
> specifies the color for reference lines requested by the HREF= and
> AUTOHREF options. By default, these reference lines display in the
> color of the horizontal axis.

CTEXT=*text-color*
C=*text-color*
> specifies the color for all text on the axes, including tick mark values
> and axis labels. If the PLOT request generates a legend, the CTEXT=
> option also colors the legend label and the value descriptions.
>
> If you do not use the CTEXT= option, a color specification is
> searched for in the following order:
>
> 1. the CTEXT= option in a GOPTIONS statement
>
> 2. the default, the first color in the colors list.
>
> If you use the CTEXT= option, it overrides the color specification for
> the axis label and the tick mark values in the COLOR= option in an
> AXIS definition assigned to the axis.
>
> If you use the CTEXT= option, the color specification is overridden
> in one or more of the following situations:
>
> □ If you also use the COLOR= parameter of a LABEL= or VALUE=
> option in a AXIS definition assigned to the axis, that parameter
> determines the color of the axis label or the color of the tick mark
> values, respectively.
>
> □ If you also use the COLOR= parameter of a LABEL= or VALUE=
> option in a LEGEND definition assigned to the legend, it determines
> the color of the legend label or the color of the legend value
> descriptions, respectively.

CVREF=*reference-line-color*
CV=*reference-line-color*
> specifies the color for reference lines requested by the VREF= and AUTOVREF options. By default, these reference lines display in the color of the vertical axis.

DESCRIPTION='*string*'
DES='*string*'
> specifies a descriptive string, up to 40 characters long, that appears in the Description field of the catalog entry for the graph. The description does not appear on the graph. By default, the procedure assigns a description of the form PLOT OF *vertical** *horizontal*, where *vertical* and *horizontal* are the names of the plot variables.

FRAME
FR
> draws a frame around the axis area. A specification for the color of the frame is searched for in the following order:
>
> 1. the CAXIS= option
>
> 2. the COLOR= option in the AXIS definition assigned to the vertical axis
>
> 3. the COLOR= option in the AXIS definition assigned to the horizontal axis
>
> 4. the default, the first color in the colors list.
>
> The axis area is not outlined unless you use the FRAME option. To outline the axis area *and* fill it with a background color, use the CFRAME= option.

GRID
> draws reference lines at all major tick marks on both axes. You get the same result when you use all the following options in a PLOT statement: AUTOHREF, AUTOVREF, FRAME, LVREF=34, and LHREF=34. The line type for GRID is 34. The line color is the color of the axis.

HAXIS=*value-list* | AXIS<1 . . . 99>
> specifies major tick mark values for the horizontal axis or assigns an axis definition to the axis. By default, the procedure scales the axis automatically and provides an appropriate number of tick marks.
>
> When the horizontal axis variable is numeric, *value-list* can be specified in the following ways:
>
> *n n . . . n*
>
> *n,n, . . . ,n*
>
> *n* TO *n* <BY *increment*> <*n . . . n*> <*n, . . . ,n*>
>
> *n n . . . n* TO *n* <BY *increment*> <*n . . . n*>
>
> *n,n, . . . ,n* TO *n* <BY *increment*> <*n, . . . ,n*>
>
> '*SAS-value*'i TO '*SAS-value*'i <BY *interval*>
>
> '*SAS-value*'i '*SAS-value*'i . . . '*SAS-value*'i

(HAXIS= continued)

The values must be in either ascending or descending order. By default, the increment value is 1. You can use a negative value for *increment* to specify a value list in descending order. The specified values are spaced evenly along the horizontal axis even if the values are not uniformly distributed. A warning message is written to the SAS log if the values are not evenly distributed. For additional information on specifying a value list, see the discussion of the ORDER= option in Chapter 9.

When the horizontal axis variable is character, values are enclosed in single quotes and can be listed in any order, as in this example:

```
haxis= 'item-one' 'item-two' 'item-three'
```

Character strings in a value list are case-sensitive.

To assign an AXIS definition, use a value of the form AXIS<1 . . . 99>. The option is ignored if no AXIS definition is currently in effect. See Chapter 9 for details.

Note: If data values fall outside the range specified by the HAXIS= option, then by default the outlying data values are not used in interpolation calculations. See "Data Considerations" earlier in this chapter for more information on values out of range.

HMINOR=*n*
HM=*n*

specifies the number of minor tick marks drawn between each major tick mark on the horizontal axis. Minor tick marks are not labeled. The HMINOR= option overrides the NUMBER= parameter of the VALUE= option in an AXIS definition.

HREF=*value-list*

draws one or more reference lines perpendicular to the horizontal axis at points specified by *value-list*. For a description of how you can specify *value-list*, see the HAXIS= option. For a description of color specifications for reference lines, see the CHREF= option.

HZERO

specifies that tick marks on the horizontal axis begin in the first position with a value of zero. The HZERO request is ignored if the horizontal variable either contains negative values or has been ordered with the HAXIS= option or the ORDER= option in an AXIS statement.

▶ *Caution: The LEGEND= option does not generate a legend.*

LEGEND=**LEGEND**<1 . . . 99>

assigns a legend definition to a legend. This option is meaningful *only* if you request a graph of the type *vertical*horizontal=third-variable* and specify a LEGEND definition. Simply using the LEGEND= option in the PLOT statement does not generate a legend. See Chapter 13 for details on specifying legend characteristics.

See also "Plots of Three Variables with a Legend" in "PLOT Statement Examples" later in this section.

LHREF=*line-type*
LH=*line-type*

specifies the line type for drawing reference lines requested by the AUTOHREF or HREF= option. *Line-type* can be 1 through 46. By default, LHREF=1, a solid line. See Table 16.5 in Chapter 16 for examples of available line types.

LVREF=*line-type*
LV=*line-type*
>   specifies the line type for drawing reference lines requested by the AUTOVREF or VREF= option. *Line-type* can be 1 through 46. By default, LVREF=1, a solid line. See Table 16.5 in Chapter 16 for examples of available line types.

NAME= *'string'*
>   specifies a string of up to eight characters that appears in the Name field of the catalog entry for the graph. The default name is GPLOT. If either the name specified or the default name duplicates an existing name in the catalog, then SAS/GRAPH software adds a number to the duplicate name to create a unique name, for example, GPLOT2.

NOAXIS
NOAXES
>   suppresses the axes, including axis lines, axis labels, all major and minor tick marks, and tick mark values.

NOLEGEND
>   suppresses the legend generated by a plot request of the type *vertical*horizontal=third-variable*.

OVERLAY
>   places all the plots requested by the PLOT statement on one set of axes. The axes are scaled to fit all the variables, and the variable names or labels associated with the first pair of variables are drawn next to the axes.

▶ *Caution: The OVERLAY option does not generate a legend.*

>   The OVERLAY option does not produce a legend, nor can you use OVERLAY with plots of the type *vertical*horizontal=third-variable*.
>   You can create special effects by overlaying the same plot line with different symbols, colors, and so on. See "Overlaid Plots with Simulated Legend" in "PLOT Statement Examples" later in this section.

SKIPMISS
>   breaks a plot line or an area fill at occurrences of missing values. By default, plot lines and area fills are not broken at missing values. If SKIPMISS is used, observations should be sorted by the independent (horizontal axis) variable. If the plot request is *vertical*horizontal= third-variable*, observations should also be sorted by the values of the third variable. See also "Data Considerations" earlier in this chapter.

VAXIS=*value-list* | AXIS<1 ... 99>
>   specifies the major tick mark values for the vertical axis or assigns an AXIS definition to the axis. For a description of *value-list*, see the HAXIS= option.
>   To assign an AXIS definition use a value of the form AXIS<1 ... 99>. The option is ignored if the definition has not been previously established. See Chapter 9 for details.

VMINOR=*n*
VM=*n*
>   specifies the number of minor tick marks drawn between each major tick mark on the vertical axis. Minor tick marks are not labeled. The VMINOR= option overrides the NUMBER= parameter of the VALUE= option in an AXIS definition.

VREF=*value-list*

> draws one or more reference lines perpendicular to the vertical axis at points specified by *value-list* . For a description of how you can specify *value-list*, see the HAXIS= option. For a description of color specifications for reference lines, see the CVREF= option.

VREVERSE

> specifies that the order of the values on the vertical axis be reversed.

VZERO

> specifies that tick marks on the vertical axis begin in the first position with a zero. The VZERO request is ignored if the vertical variable either contains negative values or has been ordered with the VAXIS= option or the ORDER= option in an AXIS statement.

Using the PLOT Statement

You can request plots in several different ways. The type of plot request affects the number of graphs produced by the procedure, the number of variables plotted on each graph, and which SYMBOL definitions affect the data points and lines. You can submit multiple plot requests in one PLOT statement, and you can combine different types of plot requests in one PLOT statement. You can include any number of PLOT statements within the procedure.

The following sections explain the different types of plot requests.

Requesting Plots of Two Variables

Plot requests with two variables follow the form *vertical*horizontal*. For example, the statement

```
plot y*x;
```

produces a plot like the diagram in Figure 31.4 in which the Y values are plotted on the vertical axis and the X values on the horizontal axis.

Figure 31.4 *Diagram of Plot with Two Variables*

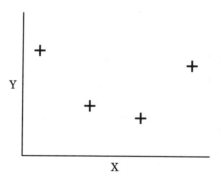

You can include two or more plot requests in one PLOT statement. Separate the plot requests by blanks. The following statement has two plot requests and produces two separate graphs: one with vertical axis values of B and horizontal axis values of A, the second with vertical axis values of S and horizontal axis values of R.

```
plot b*a s*r;
```

You can request plots for combinations of several variables by enclosing each set of variables in parentheses and separating the sets with an asterisk (*). This plot request follows the form *(vertical < ... vertical-n>)*(horizontal < ... horizontal-n>)*. The following statement produces four separate graphs like the diagrams shown in Figure 31.5:

```
plot (y b)*(x a);
```

Figure 31.5 *Diagram of Graphs Generated by Multiple Plot Requests*

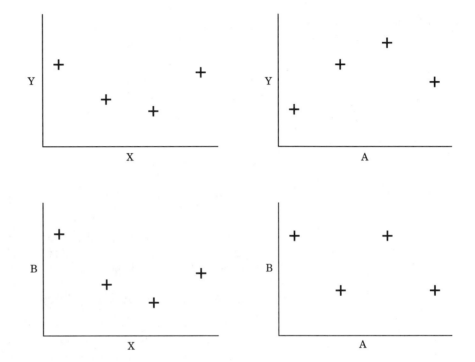

You can use the OVERLAY option with plot requests of two variables to draw multiple plots on a single set of axes. For example, the following statement generates one plot for the values of Y and another for the values of W:

```
plot y*x w*x / overlay;
```

When you use the OVERLAY option, the range of values on the axes is expanded automatically to include the minimum and maximum values of all the plot requests.

Note: Plot requests with two variables *never* generate a legend.

Requesting Plots of Three Variables with a Legend

Plot requests with three variables follow the form *vertical*horizontal= third-variable*. Use this type of plot request when you want to create a plot for every formatted value of *third-variable*. *Third-variable* values should be discrete rather than continuous and may be character. They need not be in sorted order, but they cannot exceed a length of 16. Character values longer than 16 are truncated.

In this type of request, all the plots are drawn on the same graph, and a legend is automatically produced explaining the values of *third-variable*. For example, the following PLOT statement produces a single graph with a plot for each value of *third-variable*:

```
plot y*x=z;
```

If *third-variable* has three values and if the data points are joined, the graph will have three plot lines like the diagram in Figure 31.6.

Figure 31.6 *Diagram of Plot with Three Variables*

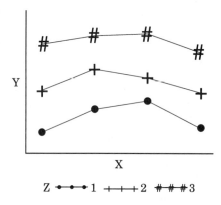

Note: Only plot requests of the form *vertical*horizontal=third-variable* generate a legend. See "Plot of Three Variables with a Legend" in "Examples" later in this section.

Requesting Plots That Assign a SYMBOL Definition

Plot requests that explicitly assign a SYMBOL definition to a plot follow the form *vertical*horizontal=n*. The procedure assigns the SYMBOL definition designated by *n* to the plot produced by *vertical*horizontal*. Plot requests of this type are useful when you use the OVERLAY option to produce multiple plots on one graph and you want to assign a particular SYMBOL definition to each plot.

▶ *Caution: The nth generated SYMBOL definition is not necessarily the same as the nth SYMBOL statement.*

When you use this type of plot request, it is important to remember that the SYMBOL definition designated by *n* is not necessarily the same as the SYMBOL statement of the same number; that is, the third SYMBOL definition is not necessarily the same as the SYMBOL3 statement. For example, if a color specification is omitted from SYMBOL1, the procedure uses SYMBOL1 to generate a sequence of definitions by cycling the SYMBOL1 statement through each color in the colors list. For more information, see "Assigning SYMBOL Definitions."

Using SYMBOL Definitions

PLOT statements use SYMBOL definitions to

□ specify the shape of the plot symbols used to mark the data points, as well as their size and color

□ specify one of the following interpolation methods for plotting data. You can

   □ connect the data points with straight lines

   □ use regression analysis to fit a line to the points and, optionally, display lines for confidence limits

□ connect the data points to the zero line on the vertical axis

□ display the minimum and maximum values of Y at each X value and mark the mean value; also, calculate standard deviation, connect the data points with lines or bars, generate box plots, or plot high-low-close stock market data

□ fill a figure defined by the data points with a pattern

□ smooth plot lines with spline interpolation

□ use a step function to connect the data points

□ cancel an interpolation method and return to the default scatter plot

□ specify line style, color, and width

□ determine how missing values are treated in interpolation calculations.

See Chapter 16 for a complete discussion of the features of the SYMBOL statement.

Assigning SYMBOL Definitions

SYMBOL definitions are assigned either by default by the GPLOT procedure or explicitly with a plot request.

If no SYMBOL definition is currently in effect, the GPLOT procedure produces a scatter plot of the data points using the default plot symbol, the plus sign (+). If more than one SYMBOL definition is needed, the procedure cycles through the current colors list to produce symbols of different colors. If the current colors list contains only one color, additional plot symbols are used.

If SYMBOL definitions have been defined but not explicitly assigned by a plot request of the form *vertical*horizontal*=n, the procedure assigns them in the order in which they are generated. For example, the following statement creates three plots:

```
plot y*x b*a s*r;
```

The procedure assigns the first generated SYMBOL definition to Y*X, the second generated SYMBOL definition to B*A, and the third generated SYMBOL definition to S*R. If more SYMBOL definitions are needed than have been defined, the procedure uses the default definitions for the remaining plots.

You can assign SYMBOL definitions explicitly with a PLOT request of the form *vertical*horizontal*=n, which assigns the nth generated SYMBOL definition to the plot. Whether this SYMBOL definition is the same as SYMBOLn depends on whether specifications for color or repetition or both are included in the SYMBOL definition and whether the statements are numbered sequentially. By default, a SYMBOL definition that specifies a color is generated one time. A SYMBOL definition that does not specify a color is generated once if you use the CSYMBOL= option in a GOPTIONS statement, or once for each color in the colors list. If the SYMBOL definition specifies a color and if the REPEAT= option is used, then the definition is used the number of times specified by REPEAT=. See "Symbol Sequences" in Chapter 16 for a complete explanation of this process.

Using Global Statements

AXIS, LEGEND, and PATTERN definitions can also be used with the PLOT statement.

AXIS definitions, which modify the content and appearance of the axes, are assigned with the HAXIS= and VAXIS= options.

LEGEND definitions can adjust the location and appearance of the legend that is automatically produced with a plot request of the type *vertical*horizontal=third-variable*. The LEGEND= option assigns LEGEND definitions. LEGEND statements themselves do not create legends.

PATTERN statements define the fill pattern and color that are used by the AREAS= option. Only PATTERN definitions that specify map and plot patterns are used. A separate PATTERN definition is needed for each area specified; however, additional PATTERN definitions are generated if necessary. See the AREAS= option in "Options" earlier in this section and Chapter 15 for details.

SYMBOL statements are used with PLOT statements to define the interpolation methods and the appearance of the symbols used in plots. See "Using SYMBOL Definitions" for details.

PLOT Statement Examples

The following examples illustrate the major features of the PLOT statement.

Plot of Two Variables

In this example the PLOT statement uses a plot request of the type *vertical*horizontal* to plot the variable HIGH against the variable YEAR to show the annual highs of the Dow Jones Industrial Average over a 34-year period. In addition, this example shows how PLOT statement options can modify axes; AXIS statements are not used.

The following program statements produce Output 31.7:

```
    /* set the graphics environment */
goptions reset=global gunit=pct border
        ftext=swissb htitle=6 htext=3;

    /* create the data set STOCKS */
data stocks;
   input year @15 high;
   cards;
1954   31DEC54   404.39   11JAN54   279.87
1955   30DEC55   488.40   17JAN55   388.20
   more data lines
1986   02DEC86 1955.57   22JAN86 1502.29
1987   25AUG87 2722.42   19OCT87 1738.74
;
run;
```

```
   /* define titles and footnote */
title1 'Dow Jones Industrial Average Highs';
title2 h=4 '1954 to 1987';
footnote j=l ' Source: 1988 World Almanac'
         j=r 'GR31N07 ';

   /* define symbol characteristics */
symbol1 color=red interpol=join value=dot height=2;

   /* generate plot of two variables */
proc gplot data=stocks;
   plot high*year / haxis=1952 to 1988 by 4
                    vaxis=200 to 2800 by 200
                    hminor=3
                    vminor=1
                    vref=1000
                    lvref=2
                    cvref=blue
                    caxis=blue
                    ctext=red;
run;
quit;
```

Output 31.7 *Using PLOT Statement Options to Modify Axes (GR31N07)*

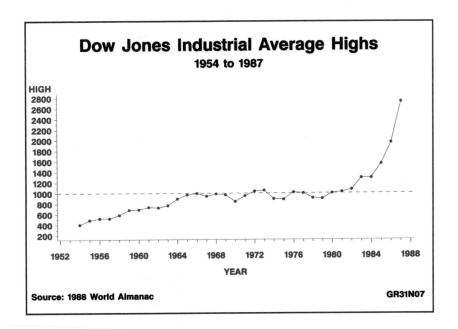

Some of the features of this example are described here.

□ The SYMBOL statement defines the symbol used to mark the data points and specifies its height and color. INTERPOL=JOIN specifies that straight lines join the data points.

□ The HAXIS= option sets major tick marks for the horizontal axis at four-year intervals. The HMINOR= option specifies the number of minor tick marks between major tick marks.

☐ The VAXIS= option sets major tick marks for the vertical axis at 200-point intervals beginning with 200 and ending with 2800. The VMINOR= option specifies one minor tick mark between major tick marks.

☐ The VREF= option draws a horizontal reference line on the vertical axis at the 1000 mark. The LVREF= option specifies the line type of the reference line; the CVREF= option specifies the color.

☐ The CAXIS= option colors the axis lines and all major and minor tick marks. The CTEXT= option colors all text associated with the plot, including axis labels and major tick mark values.

Overlaid Plots with Simulated Legend

In this example, one PLOT statement plots both the HIGH and LOW variables against the variable YEAR using two plot requests and the OVERLAY option. Two plot lines appear on the graph. When two plots are generated in this way, no legend is produced. This example uses FOOTNOTE statements to simulate a legend. In addition, it uses AXIS statements to define the horizontal and vertical axes.

Note: If the OVERLAY option were not specified, each plot request would generate a separate graph.

The following program statements produce Output 31.8:

```
   /* set the graphics environment */
goptions reset=global gunit=pct border
        ftext=swissb htitle=6 htext=3;

   /* create the data set STOCKS */
data stocks;
   input year @15 high @32 low;
   cards;
1954   31DEC54   404.39   11JAN54   279.87
1955   30DEC55   488.40   17JAN55   388.20
   more data lines
1986   02DEC86 1955.57   22JAN86 1502.29
1987   25AUG87 2722.42   19OCT87 1738.74
;
run;

   /* define titles and footnotes */
title1 'Dow Jones Industrial Average';
title2 height=4 'Highs and Lows From 1954 to 1987';
footnote1 c=red f=special h=6 'J J J'
          f=swissb h=3 '   High'
          c=blue f=special h=4 '   D D D'
          f=swissb h=3 '   Low';
footnote2 j=1 ' Source: 1988 World Almanac'
          j=r 'GR31N08  ';

   /* define symbol characteristics */
symbol1 color=red interpol=join value=dot height=2;
symbol2 color=blue interpol=join value=diamond height=3;
```

```
    /* define axis characteristics */
axis1 order=(1952 to 1988 by 4)
      label=none
      major=(height=2)
      minor=(number=3 height=1)
      offset=(2)
      width=3;
axis2 order=(200 to 2800 by 200)
      label=none
      major=(height=2)
      minor=(number=1 height=1)
      width=3;

    /* generate two plots */
proc gplot data=stocks;
   plot high*year low*year / overlay
                             caxis=blue
                             haxis=axis1
                             vaxis=axis2;
run;
quit;
```

Output 31.8 *Plots of Two Variables Using the OVERLAY Option (GR31N08)*

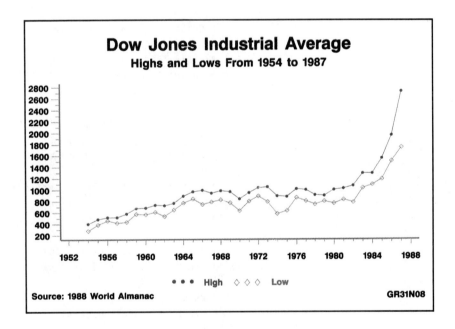

Features not explained in the previous PLOT statement example are described here.

□ The first plot, HIGH*YEAR, uses the first SYMBOL definition; and the second plot request, LOW*YEAR, uses the second SYMBOL definition.

□ The first FOOTNOTE statement uses text, color, and symbols from the SPECIAL font to provide a legend for the plots.

    Note: These symbols are not the same as the special symbols that are used in SYMBOL definitions and are illustrated in Table 16.1.

□ The HAXIS= and VAXIS= options specify AXIS definitions, which set the major tick marks with the ORDER= option. The AXIS definitions also specify the minor tick marks and suppress both axis labels.

Using the AREAS= Option with Overlaid Plots

This example uses the AREAS= and FRAME options to fill areas under plot lines and draw a frame around the axis area. As in the previous example, two plots are overlaid on the same graph.

The following program statements produce Output 31.9:

```
     /* set the graphics environment */
goptions reset=global gunit=pct border
         ftext=swissb htitle=6 htext=3;

     /* create the data set STOCKS */
data stocks;
   input year a15 high a32 low;
   cards;
1954  31DEC54  404.39  11JAN54  279.87
1955  30DEC55  488.40  17JAN55  388.20
   more data lines
1986  02DEC86 1955.57  22JAN86 1502.29
1987  25AUG87 2722.42  19OCT87 1738.74
;
run;

     /* define title and footnote */
title1 'Dow Jones Industrial Average';
title2  h=4 'Highs and Lows From 1954 to 1987';
footnote j=l ' Source: 1988 World Almanac'
         j=r 'GR31N09  ';

     /* define symbol characteristics */
symbol1 interpol=join value=none;
symbol2 interpol=join value=none;

     /* define pattern characteristics for area fill */
pattern1 value=msolid color=blue;
pattern2 value=msolid color=red;

     /* define axis characteristics */
axis1 order=(1952 to 1988 by 4)
      label=none
      major=(height=2)
      minor=(number=3 height=1)
      width=3;
axis2 order=(200 to 2800 by 200)
      label=none
      major=(height=2)
      minor=(number=1 height=1)
      width=3;
```

```
              /* generate plot */
          proc gplot data=stocks;
              plot low*year high*year / overlay
                                        haxis=axis1
                                        vaxis=axis2
                                        areas=2
                                        frame;
          run;
          quit;
```

Output 31.9 *Overlay Plots Using the AREAS= Option (GR31N09)*

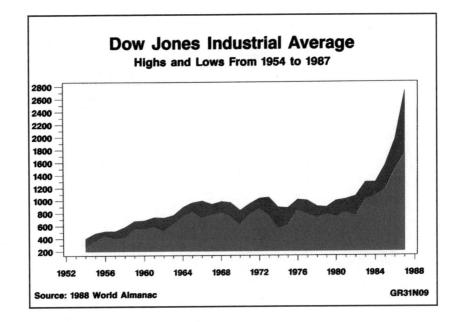

Features not explained in previous PLOT statement examples are described here.

□ The INTERPOL= option must specify a line that joins the data points. In this case JOIN is specified. The line creates the fill boundary; without it, you cannot fill areas. VALUE=NONE suppresses the plot symbol. Specifications for colors and plotting symbols are omitted.

□ The plot requests are ordered to draw the lowest plot first. As a result, area 1 occupies the space between the lowest (first) plot line and the horizontal axis, and area 2 is below the highest (second) plot line. This arrangement prevents the pattern for area 1 from overlaying the pattern for area 2.

□ AREAS=2 fills all the areas below the second plot line.

□ PATTERN statements specify the colors and map/plot pattern used by the AREAS= option.

□ FRAME draws a frame around the axis area.

Plots of Three Variables with a Legend

This example shows how a plot request of the form *vertical*horizontal=third-variable* automatically generates a legend.

In order to use this type of plot request, the data must be structured so that one variable contains the values that generate the individual plots. The DATA step in this example creates the variable CITY, which is *third-variable* in the plot request. Each separate value of CITY generates a plot line and an entry in the legend. The example illustrates the default legend. Since no LEGEND definition is specified, the LEGEND= option is omitted.

Note: The original data (without restructuring) used with multiple plot requests and the OVERLAY option produce the same plot without the legend.

The following program statements produce Output 31.10:

```
      /* set the graphics environment */
goptions reset=global gunit=pct border
         ftext=swissb htitle=6 htext=3;


      /* create the data set CITYTEMP */
data citytemp;
    input  date  date7.
           month
           season
           f1      /* Raleigh, North Carolina */
           f2      /* Minneapolis, Minnesota  */
           f3;     /* Phoenix, Arizona        */


      /* restructure data so that there is */
      /* one observation for each city     */
    drop date season f1-f3;
    faren=f1; city='Raleigh'; output;
    faren=f2; city='Minn'; output;
    faren=f3; city='Phoenix'; output;
    cards;
01JAN83  1    1    40.5  12.2  52.1
01FEB83  2    1    42.2  16.5  55.1
    more data lines
01NOV83  11   4    50.0  32.4  59.8
01DEC83  12   1    41.2  18.6  52.5
;
run;


      /* define titles and footnotes */
title1 'Average Monthly Temperature';
title2 h=4  'Minneapolis, Phoenix, and Raleigh';
footnote1 j=1 ' Source: 1984 American Express';
footnote2 j=1 '          Appointment Book'
          j=r 'GR31N10  ';
```

```
          /* define symbol characteristics */
   symbol1 color=green interpol=spline width=2 value=triangle
           height=3;
   symbol2 color=blue interpol=spline width=2 value=circle
           height=3;
   symbol3 color=red interpol=spline width=2 value=square
           height=3;

          /* define axis characteristics */
   axis1 label=none
         value=('JAN' 'FEB' 'MAR' 'APR' 'MAY' 'JUN'
                'JUL' 'AUG' 'SEP' 'OCT' 'NOV' 'DEC')
         offset=(2)
         width=3;
   axis2 label=('Degrees' justify=right 'Fahrenheit')
         order=(0 to 100 by 10)
         width=3;

          /* generate a plot of three variables */
          /* that produces a legend              */
   proc gplot data=citytemp;
      plot faren*month=city / haxis=axis1
                              vaxis=axis2
                              hminor=0
                              vminor=1
                              caxis=red
                              frame;
   run;
   quit;
```

Output 31.10 *Plots of Three Variables with a Legend (GR31N10)*

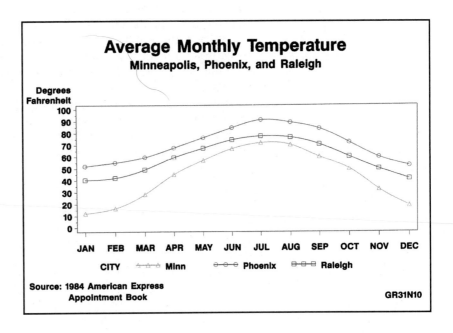

Features not explained in previous PLOT statement examples are
described here.

☐ The PLOT request FAREN*MONTH=CITY draws one plot on the graph
for each value of CITY and produces a legend defining the values of
CITY.

☐ The default legend uses the variable name CITY for the legend label and
the variable values for the legend value descriptions. Since no LEGEND
definition is used in this example, the font and height of the legend
label and the legend value descriptions are set by the graphics options
FTEXT= and HTEXT=. Height specifications in the SYMBOL statement
do not affect the size of the symbols in the legend values.

☐ SYMBOL statements are assigned to the values of CITY in alphabetical
order. For example, the value `Minn` is assigned SYMBOL1.

PLOT2 Statement

The PLOT2 statement generates a second vertical axis on the right side of
a graph produced by an accompanying PLOT or BUBBLE statement. Use
the PLOT2 statement to generate a right axis when you want to

☐ display a second scale of values for a variable (for example, show height
in inches on the left axis and height in centimeters on the right axis)

☐ plot different data on each vertical axis (for example, height on the left
axis and weight on the right axis)

☐ display the same scale of values on both left and right axes.

In a PLOT2 plot request, you specify the same independent variable for
the horizontal axis as in the accompanying PLOT or BUBBLE statement
and a different dependent variable for the right vertical axis. The PLOT2
statement uses the data set specified in the GPLOT statement.

By default, the PLOT2 statement plots data points within the axes. The
procedure automatically scales the axes to include the maximum and
minimum data values. It labels each axis with the name of its variable and
displays each major tick mark value.

You can specify options in your PLOT2 statement to manipulate the
axes and modify the appearance of your graph. In addition you can use
SYMBOL definitions to assign plotting symbols for the data points, to join
data points, to draw regression lines, or to plot confidence limits.

Syntax

The general form of the PLOT2 statement is

PLOT2 *request* < . . . *request-n*>
    </ <ANNOTATE=*Annotate-data-set*>
    <*appearance-options*>
    <*axes-options*>>;

□ *request* can be any of the following:

  vertical*horizontal

  (*vertical* < . . . *vertical-n*>)*(*horizontal*< . . . *horizontal-n*>)

  vertical*horizontal=*third-variable*

  vertical*horizontal=*n*

    where

vertical	specifies the variable plotted on the right vertical axis
horizontal	specifies the variable plotted on the horizontal axis
third-variable	specifies a third (classification) variable against which *vertical* and *horizontal* are plotted; *third-variable* values appear in a legend
n	specifies the *n*th generated SYMBOL definition

□ *appearance-options* can be one or more of the following:

  AREAS=*n*

  LEGEND=LEGEND<1 . . . 99>

  NOLEGEND

  OVERLAY

  SKIPMISS

□ *axes-options* can be one or more of the following:

  □ reference lines

    AUTOVREF

    CVREF=*reference-line-color*

    GRID

    LVREF=*line-type*

      where *line-type* can be 0 . . . 46

    VREF=*value-list*

      where *value-list* specifies points on the vertical axis

  □ vertical axis

    VAXIS=*value-list* | AXIS<1 . . . 99>

      where *value-list* specifies major tick marks

    VMINOR=*n*

      where *n* is the number of minor tick marks

VREVERSE

VZERO

□ axes appearance

CAXIS=*axis-color*

CFRAME=*background-color*

CTEXT=*text-color*

FRAME

NOAXIS

See "Options" for the PLOT2 statement for more information.

Requirements

A PLOT2 statement can only be used if a PLOT or BUBBLE statement is also used. When you use a PLOT2 statement, the GPLOT procedure assumes that the horizontal axis specified in the PLOT2 statement is identical to the horizontal axis specified in the PLOT or BUBBLE statement. If the two horizontal axes specifications are different, the PLOT2 axis specification is ignored.

The plot requests in both statements must be evenly matched as in the following example:

```
plot  y*x  b*a;
plot2 y2*x b2*a;
```

These statements produce two graphs each with two vertical axes. The first pair of plot requests (Y*X and Y2*X) produce one graph in which X is plotted on the horizontal axis, Y is plotted on the left axis, and Y2 is plotted on the right axis. The second pair of plot requests (B*A and B2*A) produce another graph in which A is plotted on the horizontal axis, B is plotted on the left axis, and B2 is plotted on the right axis.

Options

Options for the PLOT2 statement are identical to those for the PLOT statement except for the following, which are ignored if specified:

AUTOHREF

CHREF=

DESCRIPTION=

HAXIS=

HMINOR=

HREF=

HZERO=

LHREF=

NAME=.

See "Options" in "PLOT Statement" earlier in this chapter for complete descriptions of options used with the PLOT2 statement.

Using the PLOT2 Statement

You can use the same types of plot requests with a PLOT2 statement that you can with a PLOT statement, but a PLOT2 statement always plots the values of the dependent variable on the right vertical axis. The type of plot request used by the PLOT2 statement and its accompanying PLOT or BUBBLE statement affects the number of graphs produced by the procedure, the number of variables plotted on each graph, and the assignment of SYMBOL definitions.

The following sections explain how the values displayed on the right axis relate to values displayed on the left axis, how to produce multiple graphs and graphs with legends, and how to assign SYMBOL definitions. For additional information on plot requests of two and three variables, see "Using the PLOT Statement" earlier in this chapter.

Displaying Values on the Right Axis with Plot Requests of Two Variables

Depending on the data, the values and scale of values displayed on the left and right axes may be the same or they may be different. The values displayed on the right axis depend on the type of data you are plotting.

Same values, different scale   If your data contain the same variable values in two different scales, such as height in inches and height in centimeters, you can display one scale of values on the left axis and the other scale of values on the right axis. If both vertical axes are calibrated so that they represent the same range of values, then for each observation of X the data points for Y and Y2 are the same.

For example, if Y is height in inches and Y2 is height in centimeters and if the Y axis values range from 0 to 84 inches and the Y2 axis values range from 0 to 213.36 centimeters, the plot will be like the diagram shown in Figure 31.7.

Figure 31.7 *Diagram of Right Axis with Different Scale of Values*

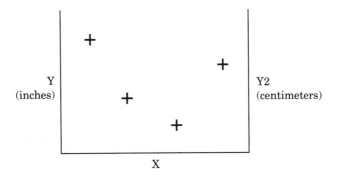

In such cases where there is one set of data but two axes, the PLOT2 statement should use a SYMBOL statement that specifies INTERPOL=NONE and VALUE=NONE.

Different values, different scale If your data contain variables with different data values (such as height and weight), you can display one type of data on the left axis and another type of data on the right axis. Since the Y variable and the Y2 variable contain different data, two sets of data points are displayed on the graph. For example, if Y is height and Y2 is weight, the plot will be like the diagram in Figure 31.8.

Figure 31.8 Diagram of
Right Axis with Different
Values and Different Scale

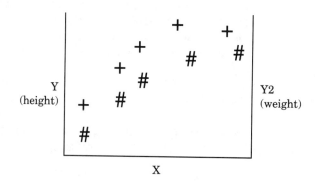

Different values, same scale If your data contain two sets of values for the same type of data, you can use the PLOT2 statement to generate a right axis that is calibrated the same as the left axis so that the data points on the right of the graph are easier to read. For example, if Y is high temperatures and Y2 is low temperatures, you can create a graph like the diagram in Figure 31.9.

Figure 31.9 Diagram of
Right Axis with Same Scale of
Values

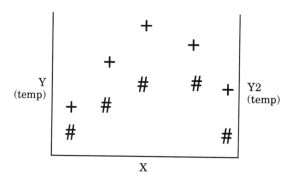

To force both axes to represent the same range of values, you can specify the same values with the VAXIS= option in both the PLOT and PLOT2 statements or you can use AXIS definitions.

Producing Multiple Graphs with Plot Requests of Two Variables

Using plot requests of the form
(vertical < ... vertical-n>)*(horizontal < ... horizontal-n>) in both the
PLOT and PLOT2 statements generates multiple graphs. The following
statements produce graphs like the ones diagrammed in Figure 31.10:

```
plot (y b)*(x a);
plot2 (y2 b2)*(x a);
```

Figure 31.10 *Diagram of Graphs Produced by Multiple Plot Requests in PLOT and PLOT2 Statements*

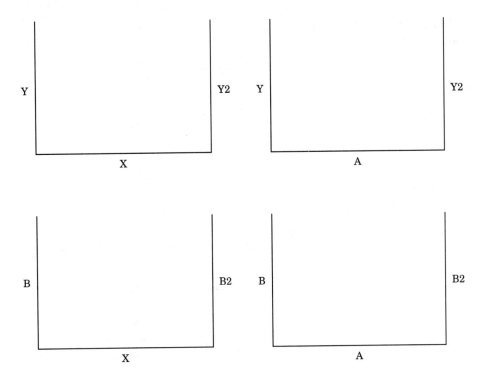

Requesting Plots of Three Variables with a Legend

You can specify plot requests of the type *vertical*horizontal=third-variable* in both the PLOT and PLOT2 statements to produce multiple plots on one graph. The PLOT and PLOT2 statements generate separate legends. If the third variable has two values, the following statements produce one graph with four sets of data points as shown in Figure 31.11:

```
plot y*x=z;
plot2 y2*x=z;
```

Figure 31.11 *Diagram of Multiple Plots on One Graph*

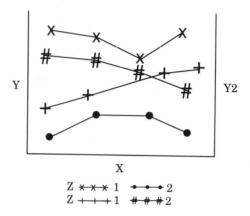

Requesting Plots That Assign a SYMBOL Definition

Plot requests that explicitly assign a SYMBOL definition to a plot follow the form *vertical*horizontal=n*. The procedure assigns the SYMBOL definition designated by *n* to the plot produced by *vertical*horizontal*. Plot requests of this type are useful when you want to assign a particular SYMBOL definition to each plot.

The PLOT2 statement uses SYMBOL definitions in the same way the PLOT statement does. For details, see "Using SYMBOL Definitions" earlier in this chapter.

Using Global Statements

AXIS, LEGEND, PATTERN, and SYMBOL definitions can be used with the PLOT2 statement in the same way that they are used with the PLOT statement. The PLOT2 statement uses PATTERN and SYMBOL definitions not previously used in the PLOT statement. For details, see "Using the PLOT Statement" earlier in this chapter.

PLOT2 Statement Example

The following examples illustrate the major features of the PLOT2 statement.

Plot with Second Vertical Axis

This example shows how a PLOT2 statement generates a right axis that displays the values of the vertical coordinates in a different scale from the scale used for the left axis.

In this plot of the average monthly temperature for Minneapolis, temperature variables representing degrees centigrade (displayed on the left axis) and degrees fahrenheit (displayed on the right axis) are plotted against the variable MONTH.

Although the procedure produces two sets of data points, it calibrates the axes so that the data points are identical and displays only one plot.

The following program statements produce Output 31.11:

```
    /* set the graphics environment */
goptions reset=global gunit=pct border
        ftext=swissb htitle=6 htext=3;


    /* create the data set MINNTEMP */
data minntemp;
    input a10 month
            a23 f2;    /* fahrenheit temperature for Minneapolis */


        /* calculate centigrade temperature */
        /* for Minneapolis                   */
    c2=(f2-32)/1.8;
    output;
    cards;
01JAN83  1    1    40.5  12.2  52.1
01FEB83  2    1    42.2  16.5  55.1
    more data lines
01NOV83  11   4    50.0  32.4  59.8
01DEC83  12   1    41.2  18.6  52.5
;
run;


    /* define title and footnote */
title1 'Average Monthly Temperature for Minneapolis';
footnote1 j=l ' Source: 1984 American Express';
footnote2 j=l '            Appointment Book'
            j=r 'GR31N11  ';


    /* define symbol characteristics */
symbol1 interpol=needle ci=blue cv=red width=3 value=star
        height=3;
symbol2 interpol=none value=none;
```

```
                              /* define axis characteristics */
                    axis1 label=none
                         value=('JAN' 'FEB' 'MAR' 'APR' 'MAY' 'JUN'
                                'JUL' 'AUG' 'SEP' 'OCT' 'NOV' 'DEC')
                         offset=(2)
                         width=3;
                    axis2 label=('Degrees' justify=right ' Centigrade')
                         order=(-20 to 30 by 10)
                         width=3;
                    axis3 label=('Degrees' justify=left 'Fahrenheit')
                         order=(-4 to 86 by 18)
                         width=3;

                       /* generate a plot with a second vertical axis */
                    proc gplot data=minntemp;
                       plot c2*month / frame
                                       caxis=red
                                       haxis=axis1
                                       vaxis=axis2
                                       hminor=0
                                       vminor=1;
                       plot2 f2*month / caxis=red
                                        vaxis=axis3
                                        vminor=1;
                    run;
                    quit;
```

Output 31.11 *Plot with Second Vertical Axis (GR31N11)*

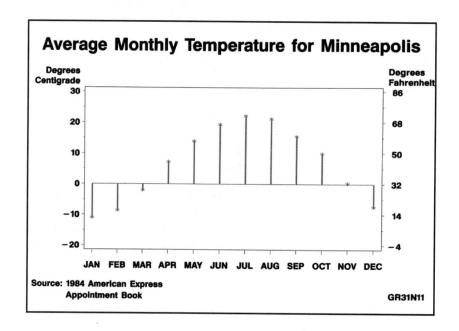

Some of the features of this example are described here.

□ The SYMBOL1 statement defines the characteristics of the lines and symbols displayed on the graph. INTERPOL=NEEDLE generates a horizontal reference line at zero on the left axis and draws vertical lines from the data points to the reference line. The CI= option specifies the color of the interpolation line and the CV= option specifies the color of the plot symbol.

□ The SYMBOL2 statement specifies null values for the data points. However, if SYMBOL2 specifies interpolation lines or plotting symbols, they will overlay the lines or symbols displayed by SYMBOL1.

□ The HAXIS= option in the PLOT statement specifies the AXIS1 definition.

□ The VAXIS= option specifies AXIS2 and AXIS3 definitions in the PLOT and PLOT2 statements, respectively. In the AXIS2 and AXIS3 statements, the ORDER= option controls the scaling of the axes. Both axes represent exactly the same range of temperature, and the distance between the major tick marks on both axes represent an equivalent quantity of degrees (10 for centigrade and 18 for Fahrenheit).

□ The CAXIS= option colors the axis lines and all major and minor tick marks. Axis labels and major tick mark values use the default color.

□ The VMINOR= option specifies the number of minor tick marks for each axis.

See Also

Chapter 2, "Running SAS/GRAPH Programs"
for information on using RUN groups and action statements

Chapter 3, "Graphics Output"
for information on creating graphics catalogs

Chapter 6, "SAS/GRAPH Fonts"
for more information on font specifications and a listing of available fonts

Chapter 7, "SAS/GRAPH Colors"
for information on the selection and use of colors

Chapter 9, "The AXIS Statement"
for more information on

□ creating axis definitions

□ defining a value list

Chapter 13, "The LEGEND Statement"
for more information on creating legend definitions

Chapter 15, "The PATTERN Statement"
for more information on defining map and plot patterns for the AREAS= option

Chapter 16, "The SYMBOL Statement"
for more information on

□ creating SYMBOL definitions

□ specifying interpolation methods

□ specifying line types

Chapter 18, "The Annotate Data Set"
for more information on creating an Annotate data set

Chapter 36, "The GREPLAY Procedure"
for more information on names and descriptions of catalog entries

CHAPTER

32 The GPRINT Procedure

Overview

The GPRINT procedure enables you to convert a text file into graphics output. You can enhance the output with TITLE, NOTE, and FOOTNOTE definitions or include Annotate graphics, or both. GPRINT procedure output is a graph composed of the contents of the text file that is used as input to the procedure, plus the enhancements you specify. Output generated by the GPRINT procedure is just like any other SAS/GRAPH output and can be stored in catalogs and replayed with the GREPLAY procedure.

The GPRINT procedure can be used when you want to create graphics output from tabular material, reports, or any external text file produced by the SAS System or other software application. To display text and graphics generated by SAS/GRAPH software, use the GSLIDE procedure.

Output 32.1 shows a graphics output generated by the GPRINT procedure from SAS output generated by the MEANS procedure. Titles and footnotes have been added, and the Swiss font has been assigned to the procedure output text.

Output 32.1 *Graph Generated with the GPRINT Procedure(GR32N01)*

Regional Sales Report

Region	Staff	Total Sales	Total Sales/Staff
NE	4	$715,607	$178,902
NW	3	$486,125	$162,042
SE	2	$665,748	$332,874
SW	4	$620,941	$155,235

GR32N01

GPRINT Procedure Syntax

The GPRINT procedure uses the following statements:

□ The PROC GPRINT statement is required.

> **PROC GPRINT** FILEREF=*fileref*
>   <ANNOTATE=*Annotate-data-set*>
>   <GOUT=*output-catalog*>
>   <*text-options*>
>   <*description-options*>;

   □ *text-options* can be one or more of the following:

      CTEXT=*text-color*

      NOCC

      O

   □ *description-options* can be one or more of the following:

      DESCRIPTION='*string*'

      NAME='*string*'

□ The following statement is optional and local:

   NOTE <*options*> <'*text*'>;

□ The following statements are optional and global:

   FOOTNOTE<1 ... 10> <*options*> <'*text*'>;

   TITLE<1 ... 10> <*options*> <'*text*'>;

Statement Descriptions

The purpose of each statement is described here:

FOOTNOTE — defines the text and appearance of footnotes. (See Chapter 11, "The FOOTNOTE Statement.")

NOTE — defines the text and appearance of notes that appear in the procedure output area. (See Chapter 14, "The NOTE Statement.")

PROC GPRINT — starts the procedure and specifies the fileref of the file to be converted, as well as any additional input and output options.

TITLE — defines the text and appearance of titles. (See Chapter 17, "The TITLE Statement.")

GPRINT Procedure Description

The GPRINT procedure is used to convert external text files to graphics output that can be displayed or printed on a graphics device. Unlike most SAS/GRAPH procedures, the GPRINT procedure does not get its input from a SAS data set. The GPRINT procedure takes an external text file as input and displays it as graphics output.

Terminology

The following terms are used in the discussion of the GPRINT procedure and are defined in the Glossary:

aspect ratio	graphics device
cell	graphics output
device entry	graphics output area
device parameter	procedure output area

Several of these terms are illustrated in Figure 2.3 in Chapter 2, "Running SAS/GRAPH Programs."

Summary of Use

Several steps are involved in producing graphics output with the GPRINT procedure. They are outlined in the following list. For details, see "Using the GPRINT Procedure" later in this chapter.

1. Create an external text file using SAS software or another software application, such as a text editor.

2. Determine if the external text file contains carriage-control characters. If not, use the NOCC option. See the NOCC option in "Options" later in this chapter for details.

3. Determine if adjustments need to be made either to the page size of the external text file or to the size of the graphics output area. If the external file is created with SAS software, you can change the width of the line or the number of lines per page by using the LINESIZE= and PAGESIZE= options in an OPTIONS statement when you generate the SAS output. You can change the size of the text displayed as graphics

output by adjusting the number of columns and rows in the graphics output area with the HPOS= and VPOS= graphics options in a GOPTIONS statement when you run the GPRINT procedure. See "Adjusting SAS Output and Graphics Output" later in this chapter for details.

4. Use the FILENAME statement or a host command to specify a fileref that points to the location of the external text file you want to print. This external file serves as the input file for the procedure. See the next section, "Specifying a Fileref," for details.

5. Run the GPRINT procedure.

Specifying a Fileref

You must assign a fileref to the external text file you want to use as input so that the GPRINT procedure can locate it. You can do this with a FILENAME statement like the following:

```
filename fileref 'external-file';
```

Replace *fileref* with any valid SAS name. Replace *'external-file'* with the complete filename of the file you want to use. You can omit the FILENAME statement if the fileref has already been defined. You can also specify a fileref with a host command. For additional information, see "FILENAME Statements" in Chapter 2, "Running SAS/GRAPH Programs."

   Note: If you are using the GPRINT procedure in the same session in which you produced SAS output, you can use the same fileref that you used to send the SAS output to the external text file.

Global Statements

All TITLE and FOOTNOTE statements currently in effect are displayed by the GPRINT procedure.

PROC GPRINT Statement

The PROC GPRINT statement initiates the procedure and names the external file to be converted by the procedure. The PROC GPRINT statement uses options to modify the appearance of the graphics output, to specify a destination catalog for graphics output, and to specify an Annotate data set to use as input.

Requirements

The FILEREF= argument is required.

FILEREF=*fileref*
   specifies the fileref that is associated with the external file to be used as input to the GPRINT procedure. *Fileref* must have been previously defined in a FILENAME statement or host command. For more information, see "Specifying a Fileref" earlier in this chapter.

Options

You can use the following options with the PROC GPRINT statement:

ANNOTATE=*Annotate-data-set*
ANNO=*Annotate-data-set*
> specifies a data set to provide annotation. *Annotate-data-set* must contain the appropriate Annotate variables. See Chapter 18, "The Annotate Data Set," for details.

CTEXT=*text-color*
> specifies the color in which the procedure displays the text from the input file. If you do not use the CTEXT= option, a color specification is searched for in the following order:
>
> 1. the CTEXT= option in a GOPTIONS statement
>
> 2. the default, the first color in the colors list.
>
> The CTEXT= option in the PROC GPRINT statement does not affect titles and footnotes generated by TITLE and FOOTNOTE definitions.

DESCRIPTION=*'string'*
DES=*'string'*
> specifies a descriptive string, up to 40 characters long, that appears in the Description field of the catalog entry for the output. The description does not appear on the output. By default, the GPRINT procedure assigns the description OUTPUT FROM PROC GPRINT.

GOUT=*output-catalog*
> specifies the SAS catalog in which to save the output produced by the GPRINT procedure. By default, catalog entries are written to the default catalog WORK.GSEG, which is erased at the end of your session. See Chapter 36, "The GREPLAY Procedure," for details.

NAME=*'string'*
> specifies a string of up to eight characters that appears in the Name field of the catalog entry for the output. By default, the name assigned is GPRINT. If either the name specified or the default name duplicates an existing name in the catalog, then SAS/GRAPH software adds a number to the duplicate name to create a unique name, for example, GPRINT2.

NOCC
> tells the procedure that the external text file does not contain carriage-control characters. If you include the NOCC option, the procedure assumes the first character on each line of the input file is a text character and not a carriage-control character. If you omit the NOCC option, the characters in column one are read as carriage-control characters. If they are valid carriage-control characters, the GPRINT procedure recognizes and executes them. If they are not valid carriage-control characters, the GPRINT procedure issues an error message.

O
> causes a 0 (numeric zero) to be converted to the letter O in the output. This option circumvents the use of a numeric zero with an interior slash that is present on some devices.

Using the GPRINT Procedure

Creating External Text Files

External text files used with the GPRINT procedure can be generated in several ways. Three common methods are described here; the first two produce SAS output.

□ Save the contents of the OUTPUT window or the LOG window to an external file with the FILE command.

□ Direct the output from SAS procedures to an external file using the PRINTTO procedure or a FILE statement.

□ Create a text file from another software application such as a text editor or a spreadsheet program.

Note: Depending on the operating system and the method used to generate the file, external text files may contain carriage-control characters. For more information on carriage-control characters, see the NOCC option in "Options" earlier in this chapter.

Adjusting SAS Output and Graphics Output

The size of SAS output (or other text) in columns and rows and the size of graphics output are independently controlled. Depending on the result you want, you can do either of the following:

□ You can adjust the size of your SAS output (or other text) to fit the available space on your graph.

□ You can adjust the dimensions of the graphics output area and the size of the cells within the graphics output area to control the size of the characters that are displayed as graphics output by the GPRINT procedure.

You can adjust the size (columns and rows) of any other external text file that you use as input to the GPRINT procedure. Although the following sections explain how to adjust the size of SAS output, the general process can be applied to any text file.

SAS Output Size

SAS output is printed in pages. The length (in number of rows) and the width (in number of columns) of the page are determined by the PAGESIZE= and LINESIZE= options, respectively. Each character of SAS output occupies one column of space in a row (one cell) as shown in Figure 32.1.

Figure 32.1 *SAS Output Size*

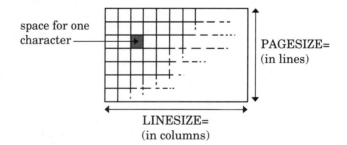

Graphics Output Size

Graphics output is drawn in the graphics output area, which is also divided into cells. The overall dimensions of the graphics output area (width and height) are determined by the values of the device parameters XMAX and YMAX. These values, which determine the aspect ratio of the graphics output area, can be temporarily reduced with the HSIZE= and VSIZE= graphics options.

The number of columns and rows that fill the area is determined by the values of the LCOLS or PCOLS and LROWS or PROWS device parameters. These values, which determine the size and aspect ratio of a cell, can be temporarily altered with the HPOS= and VPOS= graphics options. The more columns and rows there are in a given area, the smaller the cells are. Therefore, using HPOS= and VPOS= to change the number of columns and rows also changes the size of the cells and may change the size of the characters. However, it does not affect the overall dimensions of the graph. For details, see "Maintaining the aspect ratio of cells" in the next section.

For a complete description of the graphics output area, see "Defining the Graphics Output Area" in Chapter 2, "Running SAS/GRAPH Programs." For more information on device parameters and graphics options, see Chapter 5 "Graphics Options and Device Parameters Dictionary."

Matching Sizes

When you use the GPRINT procedure to convert SAS output to graphics output, you may need to manipulate the dimensions of either or both to get the proper size characters in the graphics output and to avoid truncating lines. Adjustment may be necessary in the following situations:

□ If the number of rows per page in the SAS output (PAGESIZE=) exceeds the number of rows in the graphics output area (LROWS or PROWS), then the GPRINT procedure produces additional pages of graphics output.

□ If the number of rows per page in the SAS output (PAGESIZE=) is much less than the number of rows in the graphics output area (LROWS or PROWS), then the output does not fill the graphics output area.

□ If the width of a line of SAS output (LINESIZE=) exceeds the number of columns in the graphics output area (LCOLS or PCOLS), then the GPRINT procedure truncates the line.

□ If the width of SAS output (LINESIZE=) is much less than the number of columns in the graphics output area (LCOLS or PCOLS), then the output does not fill the graphics output area.

You can adjust the size of the SAS output or the size of the graphics output, or both.

Adjusting the size of the SAS output   The following steps use the PAGESIZE= and LINESIZE= options to adjust the page size of the SAS output to fit the size of the graphics output area.

1. Use the GDEVICE procedure to determine the number of rows (LROWS or PROWS) and the number of columns (LCOLS or PCOLS) on the graphics device you intend to use. For details, see Chapter 25, "The GDEVICE Procedure."

2. Determine the number of columns and rows that you are going to use for SAS/GRAPH titles and footnotes. (If you specify height in units of CELLS, each unit of height equals one row.)

3. Use the OPTIONS statement to set the PAGESIZE= option equal to the number of rows on the device minus the number of positions to be used by TITLE and FOOTNOTE definitions. Set the LINESIZE= option equal to the number of columns on the device minus the number of positions used by titles and footnotes if the titles and footnotes are positioned vertically.

4. Produce the SAS output.

Adjusting the size of the graphics output   The following steps show you how to use the HPOS= and VPOS= graphics options to adjust the number of columns and rows in the graphics output area on the output device so it can accommodate the page size of your SAS output.

1. Determine the number of columns (LINESIZE=) and rows (PAGESIZE=) in the SAS output.

2. Use the GOPTIONS statement to set the VPOS= graphics option equal to the number of rows in the SAS output plus the number of rows to be used by TITLE and FOOTNOTE definitions. Set the HPOS= graphics option equal to the number of columns in the SAS output plus the number of columns to be used by titles and footnotes if the titles and footnotes are positioned vertically.

3. Produce the GPRINT output.

Similarly, adjusting the overall dimensions of the graphics output area with the HSIZE= and VSIZE= graphics options may affect the size and possibly the aspect ratio of the cells.

  Note: Changing the values of the HPOS= and VPOS= graphics options changes the size of the cells and consequently of characters in the output. On devices with nonscalable hardware fonts, changing the aspect ratio with HPOS= and VPOS= causes the Simulate font to be used instead of hardware characters. However, if you specify software fonts, the change in aspect ratio may be ignored. (See "Using Fonts" later in this chapter and "Hardware Fonts" in Chapter 6, "SAS/GRAPH Fonts."

Maintaining the aspect ratio of cells   If you change the values of the HPOS= and VPOS= graphics options to control the size of characters or to match the rows and columns of the external text file, you should try to maintain the same ratio of columns to rows as the original values of the device parameters. For example, suppose you have SAS output with 50 columns and 10 rows, and a graphics device that has 80 columns and 32 rows. The aspect ratio of the device is 5:2. If you print 10 rows of output on a device with 32 rows, you will have 22 blank lines. You can reduce the number of blank lines and increase the size of the characters by reducing the number of rows in the graphics output area with VPOS=. If, in addition to the 10 rows of output, you allow 4 lines of space for titles and 2 lines of space for a footnote, you need a total of 16 rows. Therefore, assigning a value of 20 to VPOS= should produce readable text and plenty of space. If VPOS=20, setting HPOS= to 50 retains the original aspect ratio of the device (80:32 or 5:2).

Note that this method allows space for titles and footnotes in terms of rows; the actual size of the titles and footnotes depends on the height specification you use. Using the unit CELLS to define the height of titles and footnotes makes it easier to calculate precisely how much space is available.

Using Fonts

By default, the GPRINT procedure uses the default hardware font with a height of 1 cell to display the text from the external file. However, if a nonscalable hardware font is specified, SAS/GRAPH may use the Simulate font instead. (For details, see "Default Fonts and the SIMULATE Font" in Chapter 6, "SAS/GRAPH Fonts.")

Font and height specifications for titles and footnotes are determined by the TITLE and FOOTNOTE definitions. (See Chapter 17 and Chapter 11, respectively, for details.)

To specify a font and height for the text, use the FTEXT= and HTEXT= graphics options. If you specify a software font, it is best to use a uniform font such as Swiss Uniform so that your text will be evenly spaced.

▶ *Caution: Changes in the aspect ratio of cells made with the HPOS= and VPOS= graphics options are ignored if software fonts are specified. Change the aspect ratio in the device entry if you want the software characters proportioned to fit the new aspect ratio.*

If you specify a software font and change the aspect ratio of the cells with the HPOS= and VPOS= graphics options, the change in aspect ratio is ignored and the procedure continues to draw the font in the original proportions. As a result, your text may not fit the graphics output area.

However, if you want the software characters to reflect a change in aspect ratio or you want the characters to fit the new aspect ratio even if they are distorted, use the LCOLS or PCOLS and LROWS or PROWS device parameters in the device entry to change the aspect ratio of the cells. Using the device entry to specify a change in the aspect ratio enables you to distort the characters. For more information on changing device parameters, see Chapter 25, "The GDEVICE Procedure."

Examples

The following examples illustrate some of the features of the GPRINT procedure.

Adjusting the Size of Characters

This example creates a graph from a text file containing SAS output. It shows how you can use the HPOS= and VPOS= graphics options to change the size of the characters. This example also uses the PRINTTO procedure to direct the SAS output to the external file that the GPRINT procedure subsequently uses as input. This example has two parts.

Creating GPRINT Output with Default Settings

In the first part of this example, the text file created by the PRINT procedure sets the LINESIZE= option (columns) to 76 and the

PAGESIZE= option (rows) to 20. Therefore, the 16 observations in the SAS output fit on one 20-line page. Since the output device on which the graph was generated uses 142 columns and 68 rows, a single page of SAS output occupies only 20 rows of the 68 rows available. (A GOPTIONS statement specifying the rows and columns for the output device has been included so that the example can be reproduced on another device.) Note that the SAS output occupies only a small portion of the graphics output area and the characters are very small.

The following code produces Output 32.2:

```
      /* suppress the date line and page numbers */
      /* set linesize and pagesize               */
options nodate nonumber linesize=76 pagesize=20;

      /* set the graphics environment */
goptions reset=global border
         ftitle=swissb htitle=6 pct
         hsize=10 in vsize=7 in
         hpos=142 vpos=68 ftext=none;

      /* assign the fileref DOW to the external file */
filename dow 'external-file';

      /* create the data set DOWDATA */
data dowdata;
   input date date7. volume high low close;
   format date date7.;
   cards;
07AUG81 3884.3  954.15  938.45  942.54
10AUG81 2937.7  948.82  935.88  943.68
more data lines
27AUG81 3676.1  900.49  883.66  889.08
28AUG81 3024.2  898.78  884.80  892.22
;
run;

      /* specify the destination for all */
      /* subsequent procedure output     */
proc printto print=dow new;
run;

      /* send the output to the destination file */
proc print;
run;

      /* reset destination for printed output to the default */
proc printto;
run;

      /* define title and footnote */
title 'Dow-Jones Averages';
footnote h=3 pct f=swissb j=r 'GR32N02(a)  ';

      /* generate graph from the external file */
proc gprint fileref=dow;
run;
```

Output 32.2 GPRINT
*Procedure Output with No
Adjustments (GR32N02(a))*

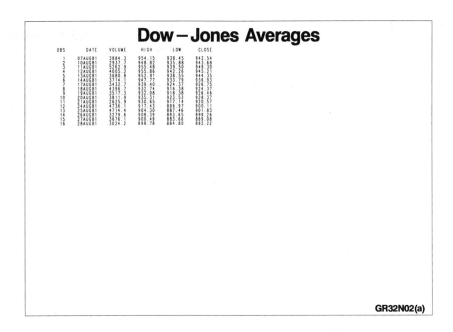

Note the following features of this program:

□ The FTEXT= graphics option specifies the default hardware font. (This is the default setting.)

□ The FILENAME statement associates the fileref DOW with the external file where the output from PROC PRINT is stored.

□ The DATA step creates the data set DOWDATA.

□ The PRINTTO procedure directs all printed procedure output to the file referenced by the fileref. The NEW option causes the output file to be replaced each time the program is run.

□ The PRINT procedure generates the text and sends it to the external file specified by PROC PRINTTO.

□ The destination for printed output is reset to the default by resubmitting PROC PRINTTO with no options.

□ In the PROC GPRINT statement, the NOCC option is omitted because the input text file contains carriage-control characters.

Adjusting the Size of the Graphics Output

In the second part of this example, the number of columns and rows in the graphics output area is reduced, increasing the size of the characters in the graph. The number of columns and rows is specified with the HPOS= and VPOS= graphics options. The following code produces Output 32.3:

```
    /* reduce HPOS= and VPOS= to increase cell size */
goptions hpos=75 vpos=30;

    /* define footnote */
footnote h=3 pct f=swissb j=r 'GR32N02(b)  ';

    /* generate adjusted graph */
proc gprint fileref=dow;
run;
```

Output 32.3 GPRINT
Procedure Output with
Adjusted Sizing (GR32N02(b))

Dow — Jones Averages

OBS	DATE	VOLUME	HIGH	LOW	CLOSE
1	07AUG81	3884.3	954.15	938.45	942.54
2	10AUG81	2937.7	948.82	935.88	943.68
3	11AUG81	5262.9	955.48	939.50	949.30
4	12AUG81	4005.2	955.86	942.26	945.21
5	13AUG81	3680.8	952.91	938.55	944.35
6	14AUG81	3714.1	947.77	933.79	936.93
7	17AUG81	3432.7	939.40	924.37	926.75
8	18AUG81	4396.7	932.74	916.38	924.37
9	19AUG81	3517.3	932.08	918.38	926.46
10	20AUG81	3811.9	935.31	923.52	928.37
11	21AUG81	2625.9	930.65	917.14	920.57
12	24AUG81	4736.1	917.43	896.97	900.11
13	25AUG81	4714.4	904.30	887.46	901.83
14	26AUG81	3279.6	908.39	893.65	899.26
15	27AUG81	3676.1	900.49	883.66	889.08
16	28AUG81	3024.2	898.78	884.80	892.22

GR32N02(b)

Specifying a Software Font and Color for the Input Text

This example generates a graph from output produced by the TIMEPLOT procedure using the data set DOWDATA. The TIMEPLOT procedure is not a graphics procedure and produces text output only. (For details, see Chapter 40, "The TIMEPLOT Procedure" in *SAS Procedures Guide, Version 6, Third Edition*.)

In this example, the text generated by the TIMEPLOT procedure is displayed in a software font and in a color. (A GOPTIONS statement specifying a target device has been included so that the aspect ratio of the output remains the same regardless of the device you use to display the example.)

The following code produces Output 32.4, which shows the SAS output produced by the TIMEPLOT procedure, and Output 32.5, which shows the TIMEPLOT procedure output after it has been converted to a graph by the GPRINT procedure.

```
/* suppress the date line and page numbers */
/* set linesize and pagesize             */
options nodate nonumber linesize=80 pagesize=60;

/* set the graphics environment */
goptions reset=global border
        ftitle=swissb htitle=6 pct
        htext=1 cells ftext=xswissu
        targetdevice=ps rotate=landscape
        hsize=10 in vsize=7 in;

/* assign the fileref OUT to the external file */
filename dow 'external-file';
```

```
                                /* create the data set DOWDATA */
                        data dowdata;
                           input date date7. volume high low close;
                           format date date7.;
                           cards;
                        07AUG81 3884.3 954.15 938.45 942.54
                        10AUG81 2937.7 948.82 935.88 943.68
                        more data lines
                        27AUG81 3676.1 900.49 883.66 889.08
                        28AUG81 3024.2 898.78 884.80 892.22
                        ;
                        run;


                                /* specify the destination for all */
                                /* subsequent procedure output     */
                        proc printto print=out new;
                        run;


                                /* generate TIMEPLOT graph         */
                                /* output is sent to external file */
                        proc timeplot data=dowdata;
                           plot low close high / overlay
                                                 hiloc
                                                 ref=mean(low)
                                                 npp
                                                 axis=880 to 966 by 2;
                           id date volume;
                           format volume 6.0 high low close 6.0;
                        run;


                                /* reset destination for printed output to default */
                        proc printto;
                        run;
```

Output 32.4 *SAS Output from the TIMEPLOT Procedure*

```
     DATE      VOLUME    min                                    max
                         880                                    966
                         *-------------------------------------------*
   07AUG81      3884     |                  |          L-C-----H     |
   10AUG81      2938     |                  |          L---C--H      |
   11AUG81      5263     |                  |          L----C--H     |
   12AUG81      4005     |                  |           LC----H      |
   13AUG81      3681     |                  |         L--C---H       |
   14AUG81      3714     |                  |       L-C----H         |
   17AUG81      3433     |                  |  LC-----H              |
   18AUG81      4397     |              L---C---H                    |
   19AUG81      3517     |             |L---C-H                      |
   20AUG81      3812     |                 | L--C--H                 |
   21AUG81      2626     |                 L-C----H                  |
   24AUG81      4736     |           L-C-------H                     |
   25AUG81      4714     |   L------C-H     |                        |
   26AUG81      3280     |        L--C----H |                        |
   27AUG81      3676     | L--C-----H       |                        |
   28AUG81      3024     |  L---C--H        |                        |
                         *-------------------------------------------*
```

```
        /* define title and footnote */
        /* and leave blank line      */
title 'TIMEPLOT of Dow-Jones Averages';
title2 h=6 ' ';
footnote h=3 pct f=swissb
        j=l ' L=Low' ' C=Close' ' H=High'
        j=r 'GR32N03 ';

    /* generate graph from the external file */
    /* specify text color                    */
proc gprint fileref=out ctext=red;
run;
```

Output 32.5 GPRINT
Procedure Output with
Enhanced Text (GR32N03)

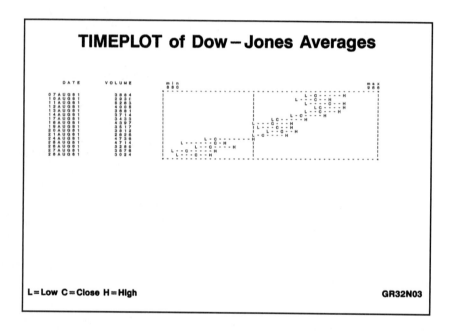

Features not described in the previous example are described here.

□ The TIMEPLOT procedure generates text output that is sent to the external file.

□ The FTEXT= and HTEXT= graphics options in the GOPTIONS statement assign the font and height in cells for the text.

□ The TARGETDEVICE= option in the GOPTIONS statement specifies a PostScript printer. This causes the graphics output area to have the same aspect ratio as the printer. The ROTATE= option sets the orientation of the display to landscape.

□ The CTEXT= option assigns a color to the text produced by the GPRINT procedure.

□ A blank TITLE2 statement leaves a blank line below the title.

See Also

Chapter 2, "Running SAS/GRAPH Programs"
for additional information on the graphics output area and procedure output area and for information on specifying filerefs

Chapter 5, "Graphics Options and Device Parameters Dictionary"
for additional information on the HTEXT=, FTEXT=, HPOS=, VPOS=, HSIZE=, and VSIZE= graphics options.

Chapter 6, "SAS/GRAPH Fonts"
for more information on font specifications and a listing of available fonts

Chapter 11, "The FOOTNOTE Statement"
for details on putting footnotes on graphs

Chapter 14, "The NOTE Statement"
for details on putting other text on graphs

Chapter 17, "The TITLE Statement"
for details on putting titles on graphs

Chapter 18, "The Annotate Data Set"
for information on constructing Annotate data sets

Chapter 25, "The GDEVICE Procedure"
for determining default values for device entry

Chapter 36, "The GREPLAY Procedure"
for more information on names and descriptions of catalog entries

Chapter 9, "SAS Language Statements," in *SAS Language: Reference, Version 6, First Edition*
for additional information on the FILENAME statement and the LINESIZE= and PAGESIZE= options in the OPTIONS statement

Chapter 28, "The PRINTTO Procedure" in *SAS Procedures Guide, Version 6, Third Edition*
for details on the PRINTTO procedure

Chapter 40, "The TIMEPLOT Procedure" in *SAS Procedures Guide, Version 6, Third Edition*
for details on the TIMEPLOT procedure

CHAPTER 33 The GPROJECT Procedure

Overview

The GPROJECT procedure processes map coordinate data in map data sets to convert spherical coordinates (longitude and latitude) into Cartesian coordinates for use by the GMAP procedure. In many of the geographic map data sets available for use with SAS/GRAPH software, the observation values are stored as latitude and longitude coordinates on a sphere. When these observations are plotted by the GMAP procedure, which is designed to plot points on a two-dimensional plane, the resulting map is often reversed and elongated as a result of forcing the curved map surface onto a flat plane.

The GPROJECT procedure enables you to use one of several map projection techniques to project the coordinates onto a plane while attempting to minimize the distortion of area, distance, direction, and shape properties of the original sphere. (The earth is not precisely spherical, but the GPROJECT procedure does not attempt to correct this small distortion.) The output data set produced by the procedure contains coordinate variable values expressed in Cartesian coordinates that can be displayed correctly using the GMAP procedure.

The GPROJECT procedure also can create a rectangular subset of the input data set by excluding all points with longitude and latitude values that fall outside a specified range. This provides a handy way to reduce the size of the map data set if you need only a portion of a larger map.

Note: The GPROJECT procedure does not produce any graphics output. The output data set from the GPROJECT procedure typically is used as the MAP= data set in the GMAP procedure.

Output 33.1 and Output 33.2 illustrate the effect of projecting a typical map data set with coordinates stored as longitude and latitude.

Output 33.1 Map before Projection (GR33N01(a))

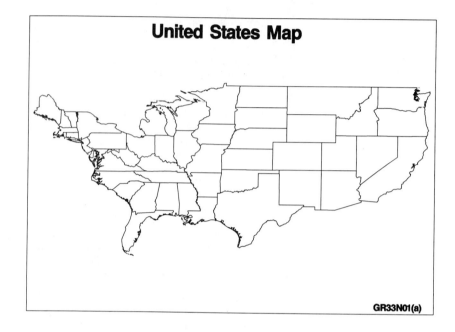

Output 33.2 Map after Projection (GR33N01(b))

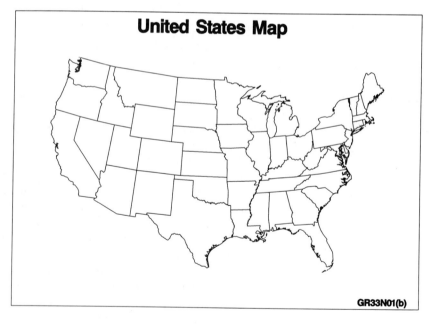

GPROJECT Procedure Syntax

The GPROJECT procedure uses the following statements:

□ The PROC GPROJECT statement is required.

> **PROC GPROJECT** <DATA=*input-data-set*>
>   <OUT=*output-data-set*>
>   <*projection-options*>
>   <*coordinate-options*>
>   <*clipping-options*>;

□ The ID statement also is required.

> **ID** *variable* < . . . *variable-n*>;

For complete statement syntax, see the section on the appropriate statement.

Statement Descriptions

The purpose of each statement is described here.

ID   specifies the variable or variables in the input data set that define unit areas.

PROC GPROJECT   starts the procedure and specifies the name of the input data set and any additional input or output options.

GPROJECT Procedure Description

The following sections address issues that pertain to the GPROJECT procedure as a whole, including terminology and special data considerations.

Terminology

The following terms are used in the discussion of the GPROJECT procedure and are defined in the Glossary:

latitude	projection
longitude	segment
meridian	unit area
parallel	

Summary of Use

To use the GPROJECT procedure, you must do the following:

1. If necessary, issue a LIBNAME statement for the SAS data library containing the map data set you want to project.

2. If you do not want to use the default projection criteria, select the projection method and projection criteria to use for the map data set.

3. Use the PROC GPROJECT statement to identify the input and output data sets and to specify the projection method and other projection criteria.

4. Use the ID statement to identify the variable or variables in the input data set that identify the unit areas.

You can display the output data set using the GMAP procedure or save it for later use.

Data Considerations

The input data set must contain the following variables:

☐ a numeric variable named X containing the longitude coordinates of the map boundary points.

☐ a numeric variable named Y containing the latitude coordinates of the map boundary points.

☐ one or more variables that uniquely identify the unit areas in the map. Unit area identification variables can be either character or numeric. These variables are indicated in the ID statement.

You also can include the optional variable SEGMENT, which identifies nonconterminous segments of the unit areas.

If the input data set contains the DENSITY variable, the value of the DENSITY variable affects the output from the GPROJECT procedure. See "Clipping Map Data Sets" later in this chapter for more information. Any other variables in the input data set do not affect the GPROJECT procedure.

The X and Y variables contain the values to be projected. Projection is only appropriate for map data sets in which the X and Y variable values represent longitude and latitude. Some of the map data sets supplied with SAS/GRAPH software have already been projected; such data sets should not be projected again. If you want to take advantage of the clipping features of the GPROJECT procedure to create a subset of a previously projected map, be sure to use the PROJECT=NONE option with the PROC GPROJECT statement. Some of the other SAS/GRAPH map data sets may require projection before they are used. See SAS Technical Report P-196, *SAS/GRAPH Map Data Sets for Release 6.06* for more information on the map data sets supplied with SAS/GRAPH software.

Figure 33.1 shows the standard coordinate system for map data sets with coordinates in longitude and latitude. For the longitude and latitude values (below and to the right of the figure, respectively) the upper value is expressed in degrees and the lower is expressed in radians. A radian is approximately 57.3 degrees.

Figure 33.1 *Longitude and Latitude Coordinates*

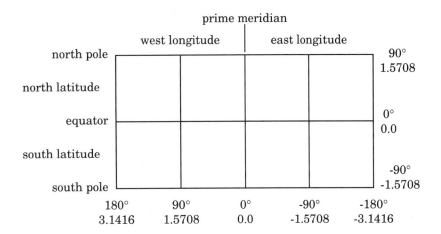

By default, the GPROJECT procedure assumes that the units for the input coordinate values are radians and that values for the horizontal coordinate increase from east to west across the map. If your map coordinates are stored as degrees of arc, you must use the DEGREE option in the PROC GPROJECT statement. If the horizontal coordinate values in the map increase west-to-east rather than east-to-west, you must use the EASTLONG option in the PROC GPROJECT statement. See "Options" later in this chapter for details of the DEGREE and EASTLONG options.

The unprojected map data sets provided with SAS/GRAPH software can be projected using the default procedure characteristics: coordinate units in the data sets are radians, and horizontal values increase east-to-west.

For additional information on map data sets, see Chapter 29, "The GMAP Procedure."

PROC GPROJECT Statement

The PROC GPROJECT statement initiates the procedure and, optionally, identifies the type of projection to be performed and specifies criteria for clipping and projection.

Syntax

The general form of the GPROJECT statement is

PROC GPROJECT <DATA=*input-data-set*>
      <OUT=*output-data-set*>
      <*projection-options*>
      <*coordinate-options*>
      <*clipping-options*>;

☐ *projection-options* can be one or more of the following:

PARADIV=*n*

where *n* is the divisor used to compute the values for standard parallels

PARALEL1=*latitude*

PARALEL2=*latitude*

POLELAT=*latitude*

POLELONG=*longitude*

PROJECT=ALBERS | LAMBERT | GNOMON | NONE

☐ *coordinate-options* can be one or more of the following:

ASIS

DEGREE

DUPOK

EASTLONG

☐ *clipping-options* can be one or more of the following:

LATMIN=*minimum-latitude*

LATMAX=*maximum-latitude*

LONGMIN=*minimum-longitude*

LONGMAX=*maximum-longitude*

Options are fully described in "Options" later in this section.

Requirements

The GPROJECT procedure requires an input data set. By default, the procedure uses the most recently created data set as its input data set. You can use the DATA= option to select a specific data set. If no data set has been created in the current SAS session and you do not use the DATA= option, an error occurs and the procedure stops.

The PROC GPROJECT statement must be accompanied by an ID statement to indicate which variable or variables in the input data set define unit areas.

For the Albers' and Lambert's projections, the two standard parallels must both lie on the same side of the equator. The GPROJECT procedure stops with an error message if this condition is not met, regardless of whether you explicitly specify parallel values or let the procedure calculate default values. See the descriptions of the PARALEL1= and PARALEL2= options in "Options" later in this section for more information on specifying the two standard parallels.

See "Data Considerations" earlier in this chapter for information on input data set requirements.

Options

You can use the following options with the PROC GPROJECT statement:

ASIS
DUPOK

> specify that observations for which the projected values for the X and Y variables are identical to those in the previous observation should be retained. By default, successive identical observations are deleted.

DATA=*SAS-data-set*

> specifies the name of the input map data set to be processed by PROC GPROJECT.
>
> By default, PROC GPROJECT uses the most recently created SAS data set as the input map data set. If you do not use the DATA= option and no data set has been created in the current SAS session, an error occurs and the procedure stops.

DEGREE
DEG

> specifies that the units for the longitude (X variable) and latitude (Y variable) coordinates are degrees of arc. By default, coordinate units are considered to be radians.

EASTLONG
EAST

> specifies that the longitude (X variable) values in the input data set increase to the east. By default, longitude values increase to the west.

LATMAX=*max-latitude*
LATMIN=*min-latitude*

> specify the maximum and minimum latitudes, respectively, to be included in the projection. Any unit areas that cross the selected latitudes are clipped and closed along the specified parallels. These options do not have to be paired; you can specify a maximum latitude without specifying a minimum, and vice versa.
>
> When PROJECT=ALBERS, LAMBERT, or GNOMON, the GPROJECT procedure treats the values of *max-latitude* and *min-latitude* as degrees. When PROJECT=NONE, the procedure treats the values as Cartesian coordinates.

LONGMAX=*max-longitude*
LONGMIN=*min-longitude*

> specify the maximum and minimum longitudes, respectively, to be included in the projection. Any unit areas that cross the selected longitudes are clipped and closed along the specified meridians. These options do not have to be paired; you can specify a maximum longitude without specifying a minimum, and vice versa.
>
> When PROJECT=ALBERS, LAMBERT, or GNOMON, the GPROJECT procedure treats the values of *max-longitude* and *min-longitude* as degrees. When PROJECT=NONE, the procedure treats the values as Cartesian coordinates.

OUT=*SAS-data-set*

> names the new map data set to contain the coordinates of the new unit areas created by the GPROJECT procedure.

(OUT= continued)

By default, PROC GPROJECT names the new data set using the DATA*n* naming convention. That is, the procedure uses the name WORK.DATA*n*, where *n* is the next unused number in sequence. Thus, the first automatically named data set is DATA1, the second is DATA2, and so on.

PARADIV=*n*

specifies the divisor used to compute the values used for standard parallels for the Albers' or Lambert's projections when explicit values are not provided. By default PARADIV=4, which causes standard parallels to be set at 1/4 and 3/4 of the range of latitude values in the input map data set. See the discussion of the PARALEL1= and PARALEL2= options for details of the formula used to calculate the default standard parallel values.

PARALEL1=*latitude*
PARALEL2=*latitude*

specify values for the standard parallels used in the Albers' or Lambert's projection. *Latitude* must be in degrees. Positive values indicate north of the equator, and negative values indicate south of the equator. These options are ignored for the gnomonic projection.

By default, the GPROJECT procedure calculates values for the standard parallels. The defaults are chosen to minimize the distortion inherent in the projection process. The algorithm used is

$$\text{PARALEL1} = \text{minlat} + R / P_D$$

$$\text{PARALEL2} = \text{maxlat} - R / P_D$$

where

R   is the range of latitude values in the input map data set.

P_D is the PARADIV= value (see the discussion of the PARADIV= option in this section).

minlat   is the minimum latitude value in the input map data set.

maxlat   is the maximum latitude value in the input map data set.

If you do not use the PARALEL1= option or the PARALEL2= option, or you do not use either option, the GPROJECT procedure uses the calculated value for the missing parameter.

The standard parallels, whether explicitly specified or supplied by the procedure, must lie on the same side of the equator. If they do not, the GPROJECT procedure prints an error message and stops. (The procedure may calculate standard parallels that lie on opposite sides of the equator.) When projecting a map data set containing unit areas that cross the equator, you may have to explicitly specify standard parallels that both lie on the same side of the equator. If this causes excessive distortion of the map, you may be able to use the gnomonic projection instead of the Albers' or Lambert's projection since the gnomonic technique has no such limitations at the equator.

POLELAT=*latitude*
POLELONG=*longitude*

specify a projection pole to use for the gnomonic projection. The projection pole is the point at which the surface of the sphere touches the surface of the imaginary plane onto which the map is projected. The POLELAT= option specifies the latitude of the projection point.

Units for *latitude* are degrees; positive values indicate north of the equator, and negative values indicate south of the equator. The POLELONG= option gives the longitude for the projection point. Units for *longitude* are degrees; positive values indicate west of the prime meridian, and negative values indicate east of the prime meridian (unless the EASTLONG option also has been used in the PROC GPROJECT statement.)

If you do not use the POLELAT= option or the POLELONG= option, or you do not use either option, the GPROJECT procedure uses values for the position of the center of the unit areas defined by the DATA= data set for the missing parameter.

Note: The map defined by the input data set should not contain points more than 85 degrees (1.48353 radians) from the projection pole; all points that exceed this value are deleted from the output data set.

PROJECT=ALBERS | LAMBERT | GNOMON | NONE
specifies the projection method to be applied to the map data set. You can specify the following values in the PROJECT= option:

ALBERS   specifies Albers' equal-area projection with two standard parallels.

LAMBERT   specifies Lambert's conformal projection with two standard parallels.

GNOMON   specifies the gnomonic projection, which is an azimuthal projection.

NONE   specifies that no projection should be performed. You can use this option in conjunction with the LATMIN=, LATMAX=, LONGMIN=, and LONGMAX= options to perform clipping without projection (for example, on map data sets that have already been projected).

By default, PROJECT=ALBERS. See "Map Projection Technique Descriptions" later in this chapter for details of the projection methods.

ID Statement

The ID statement specifies which variable or variables in the input data set define unit areas. Each group of observations with a different ID variable value is evaluated as a separate unit area. The ID statement is required with the GPROJECT procedure.

Syntax

The general form of the ID statement is

ID *variable* < ... *variable-n*>;

where *variable* is the name of a variable in the input data set that defines unit areas. *Variable* can be either numeric or character.

Requirements

The input data set to the GPROJECT procedure must contain all of the variables identified in the ID statement.

Using the GPROJECT Procedure

The GPROJECT procedure uses a default projection method and default projection criteria for projecting your map data set. If you do not want to use these defaults, you can use PROC GPROJECT statement options to

□ select the map projection method

□ specify the map projection criteria

□ create a rectangular subset of the input data set.

The following sections describe how you can use PROC GPROJECT statement options to select your own projection method and projection criteria.

Map Projection Method Descriptions

The GPROJECT procedure can perform three different types of projection: Albers' equal-area projection with two standard parallels (the default method), Lambert's conformal projection with two standard parallels, or the gnomonic projection (an azimuthal equidistant projection). Except when projecting map data sets that cover large areas, all three types of projections produce relatively similar results when default projection criteria are used, so you usually do not need to be concerned about which projection method to use when producing maps solely for graphics output.

However, the default projection criteria may be unsuitable in some circumstances. In particular, the default specifications fail when the map being projected extends on both sides of the equator. On other occasions, you may want to select a projection method to achieve a particular effect.

Output 33.3 shows an unprojected map of the northern hemisphere.

Output 33.3 Unprojected Map (GR33N02)

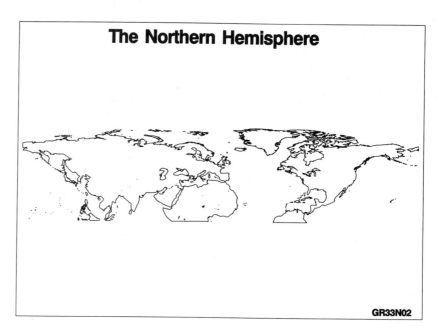

The Northern Hemisphere

GR33N02

The following sections describe the basic theory of each projection method.

Albers' Equal-Area Projection

The Albers' projection is a conic projection from the surface of the sphere to a cone secant to the sphere, cutting it at two standard parallels of latitude. The axis of the cone coincides with an extension of the polar axis of the sphere. Each section of the resulting map bears a constant ratio to the area of the sphere. In general, distortion in shape tends to increase toward the poles in latitudes outside of the two standard parallels.

The Albers' projection is well suited to portray areas of large and small east-to-west extent. It is the default method for the GPROJECT procedure and produces satisfactory results in most cases. However, both standard parallels must lie on the same side of the equator, so this method may not be suitable for map data sets of large north-to-south extent that span the equator. For these map data sets, use the gnomonic projection method.

Output 33.4 illustrates an Albers' equal-area projection of the northern hemisphere.

Output 33.4 *Albers' Projection (GR33N03)*

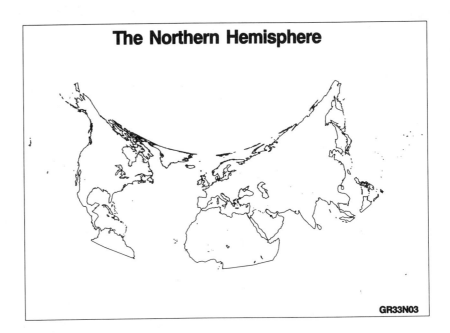

The Albers' projection is the default projection method for the GPROJECT procedure.

Lambert's Conformal Projection

The Lambert's projection is obtained from a secant cone in the same manner as Albers' projection. In the Lambert's projection, meridians of longitude are straight lines radiating from the apex of the cone, while parallels of latitude are concentric circles. The Lambert's projection is somewhat better than the Albers' projection at representing the original shape of projected unit areas, while the Albers' projection is somewhat better at representing relative sizes of projected unit areas.

The Lambert's projection is ideal for navigational charts and maps of relatively small east-to-west extent. However, as in the Albers' projection, both standard parallels must lie on the same side of the equator, so this method may not be suitable for map data sets that span the equator. For these map data sets, use the gnomonic projection method.

Output 33.5 illustrates a Lambert's conformal projection of the northern hemisphere.

Output 33.5 Lambert's Projection (GR33N04)

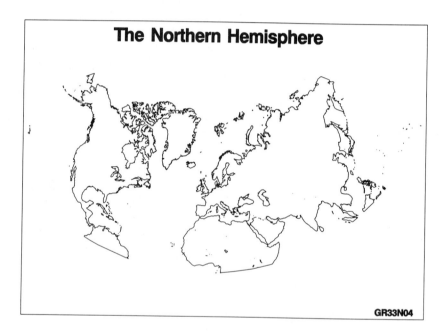

Select the Lambert's projection by specifying PROJECT=LAMBERT in the PROC GPROJECT statement.

Gnomonic Projection

The gnomonic projection is a planar projection from the surface of the sphere directly onto an imaginary plane tangent to the sphere at the map projection pole. By default, the projection pole is placed at the center of the map data set to be projected, but you can specify the projection pole to be anywhere on the surface of the sphere. (See the discussion of the POLELONG= and POLELAT= options in "Options" earlier in this chapter.)

In the gnomonic projection, distortion increases as the distance from the map pole increases. Because of this distortion, the GPROJECT procedure deletes all observations that lie more than 85 degrees from the map pole.

The gnomonic projection is best suited for mapping areas of small east-to-west extent.

Output 33.6 illustrates a gnomonic projection of the northern hemisphere.

Output 33.6 Gnomonic Projection (GR33N05)

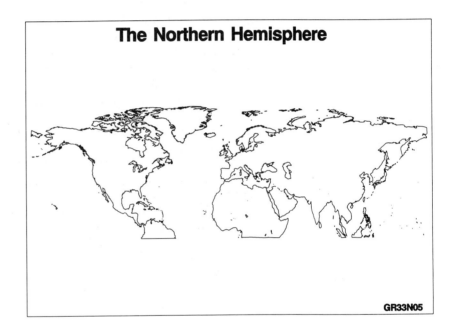

Select the gnomonic projection by specifying PROJECT=GNOMON in the PROC GPROJECT statement.

Controlling Projection Criteria

For both the Albers' and Lambert's projections, the GPROJECT procedure calculates appropriate standard parallels. You can override either or both of these selections by explicitly specifying values for the PARALEL1= or PARALEL2= option. You also can influence the selection of default parallels using the PARADIV= option. See "Options" earlier in this chapter for more information on these options.

For the gnomonic projection, the GPROJECT procedure determines the longitude and latitude of the approximate center of the input data set area. You can override either or both of these selections by explicitly specifying values for the POLELAT= or POLELONG= option. See "Options" earlier in this chapter for more information.

The clipping options, discussed in "Clipping Map Data Sets" later in this section, also can influence the calculations of the default standard parallels by changing the minimum and maximum coordinate values.

Clipping Map Data Sets

The GPROJECT procedure can create rectangular subsets of the map data set being projected. This capability provides a way to extract a portion of a larger map if you do not need all the original unit areas for your graph. The procedure enables you to clip unit area boundaries at specified parallels of latitude or meridians of longitude or both. Unit areas that fall completely outside the specified clipping limits are excluded from the output data set. Unit areas bisected by the clipping limits are closed along the clipping parallels and meridians, and all points outside the clipping limits are excluded.

If the input data set contains the DENSITY variable, any new vertex points and corners created by the GPROJECT procedure are assigned a DENSITY value of 0 in the output data set. This enables you to use a subset of the clipped map without using the GREDUCE procedure to assign new DENSITY values.

You specify the minimum latitude to be retained in the output data set with the LATMIN= option and the maximum latitude with the LATMAX= option. Minimum and maximum longitude values are specified with the LONGMIN= and LONGMAX= options, respectively. See "Options" earlier in this chapter for more details on these options.

The GPROJECT procedure has two ways to interpret the clipping longitude and latitude values you supply, as follows:

□ If you are only clipping the map (that is, if PROJECT=NONE is also specified in the PROC GPROJECT statement), then the clipping longitude and latitude values are assumed to be Cartesian coordinates. You must be familiar with the range of values in the X and Y variables in order to select appropriate clipping limits. In this case, the LATMAX= and LATMIN= options specify the top and bottom edges, respectively, of the area to be extracted, and the LONGMAX= and LONGMIN= options specify right and left edges, respectively.

You can use the MEANS or SUMMARY procedure in base SAS software to determine the range of values in X and Y. See the *SAS Procedures Guide, Version 6, Third Edition* for more information.

□ If PROJECT=ALBERS, LAMBERT, or GNOMON, the values are treated as degrees.

Note: Depending on the size and position of the clipped area and the type of projection being performed, the resulting map may not be exactly rectangular. The GPROJECT procedure performs clipping before projection, so the clipped area may be distorted by the projection process.

To produce a clipped area with a rectangular shape, you must use the GPROJECT procedure in two steps:

1. Project the map using the appropriate projection method and projection criteria.

2. Project the map using PROJECT=NONE, and use the LATMIN=, LATMAX=, LONGMIN=, and LONGMAX= options to clip the map.

See "Clipping an Area from the Map" in "Examples" later in this chapter for an example of clipping an area from a map data set.

Examples

The following examples illustrate major features of the GPROJECT procedure.

Because the examples use one of the map data sets supplied with SAS/GRAPH software, you may need to replace *SAS-data-library* in the LIBNAME statement with the actual location of the SAS data library containing the Institute-supplied map data sets on your system. Contact your SAS Software Consultant for the location of the map data sets at your site.

If your site automatically assigns the libref MAPS to the SAS data library containing the Institute-supplied map data sets, delete the LIBNAME statement in these examples.

Using Default Projection Criteria

This example demonstrates the effect of using the GPROJECT procedure on an unprojected map data set without specifying any options.

The following program statements produce Output 33.1 and Output 33.2 at the beginning of this chapter:

```
/* set the graphics environment */
goptions reset=global gunit=pct border
        ftext=swissb htitle=6 htext=3;


/* assign the libref MAPS */
libname maps 'SAS-data-library';


/* create reduced continental U.S. map data set */
/* and remove Alaska, Hawaii, and Puerto Rico   */
data us48;
   set maps.states;
   if state ne 2 and state ne 15 and state ne 72;
   if density<4;
run;


/* define title and footnote for unprojected map */
title 'United States Map';
footnote j=r 'GR33N01(a)  ';
```

```
      /* define pattern characteristics */
   pattern value=mempty repeat=50 color=blue;

      /* show unprojected map */
   proc gmap map=us48 data=us48 all;
      id state;
      choro state / nolegend;
   run;

      /* project map data set using all default criteria */
   proc gproject data=us48 out=us48proj;
      id state;
   run;

      /* define footnote for projected map */
   footnote j=r 'GR33N01(b)  ';

      /* show projected map */
   proc gmap map=us48proj data=us48proj all;
      id state;
      choro state / nolegend;
   run;
   quit;
```

This example illustrates the following features:

□ Because the PROJECT= option is not used in the PROC GPROJECT statement, the Albers' equal-area projection method is used by default. The GPROJECT procedure supplies default values for the standard parallels that minimize distortion of the projected map areas.

□ The ID statement in the GPROJECT procedure step identifies the variable in the input data set that defines unit areas.

Using Gnomonic Projection

This example uses the gnomonic projection method to create a map in which the east coast of the United States appears disproportionately large compared to the west coast.

The following program statements produce Output 33.7:

```
      /* set the graphics environment */
   goptions reset=global gunit=pct border
            ftext=swissb htitle=6 htext=3;

      /* assign the libref MAPS */
   libname maps 'SAS-data-library';

      /* create reduced continental U.S. map data set */
      /* and remove Alaska, Hawaii, and Puerto Rico   */
   data us48;
      set maps.states;
      if state ne 2 and state ne 15 and state ne 72;
      if density<4;
   run;
```

```
                          /* project map onto plane centered in the Pacific */
               proc gproject data=us48
                              out=skew
                              project=gnomon
                              polelong=160
                              polelat=45;
                   id state;
               run;

                          /* define title and footnote for map */
               title 'United States Map';
               footnote j=r 'GR33N06  ';

                          /* define pattern characteristics */
               pattern value=mempty repeat=49 color=blue;

                          /* show projected map */
               proc gmap map=skew data=skew all;
                   id state;
                   choro state / nolegend;
               run;
               quit;
```

Output 33.7 *Emphasizing Map Areas with Gnomonic Projection (GR33N06)*

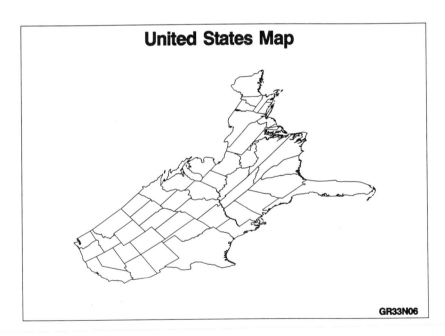

This example illustrates the following features:

□ The PROJECT= option specifies the projection method for the map data set.

□ The POLELONG= and POLELAT= options specify a projection pole for the gnomonic projection. In this example, the pole is positioned in the Pacific Ocean.

Clipping an Area from the Map

This example uses the clipping capabilities of the GPROJECT procedure to create a map of the states in the United States that border the Gulf of Mexico.

The following program statements produce Output 33.8:

```
/* set the graphics environment */
goptions reset=global gunit=pct border
        ftext=swissb htitle=6 htext=3;

/* assign the libref MAPS */
libname maps 'SAS-data-library';

/* clip and project rectangular subset of the map */
proc gproject data=maps.states
            out=gulf
            longmin=81
            longmax=98
            latmin=25
            latmax=33;
    where density<5;
    id state;
run;

/* define title and footnote for map */
title 'Northern Gulf Coast';
footnote j=r 'GR33N07  ';

/* define pattern characteristics */
pattern value=mempty repeat=7 color=blue;

/* show clipped map */
proc gmap map=gulf data=gulf all;
    id state;
    choro state / nolegend;
run;
quit;
```

Output 33.8 *Clipping a Map (GR33N07)*

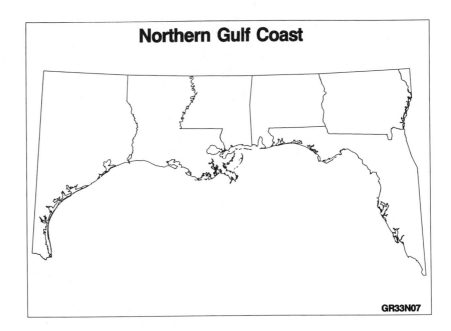

This example illustrates the following features:

□ The LONGMIN= and LONGMAX= options specify the minimum and maximum longitudes to be included in the map projection.

□ The LATMIN= and LATMAX= options specify the minimum and maximum latitudes to be included in the map projection.

□ Because the PROJECT= option is not used, the Albers' equal-area projection method is used by default.

Projecting an Annotate Data Set

This example illustrates how to project an Annotate data set for use with a map data set.

The example labels the locations of Miami, Boston, and Bangor on the map shown in the second example. Because the X and Y variables in the USCITY data set already have been projected to match the US data set, they cannot be used with the map produced by the second example. To properly label the projected map, the example uses the same projection method for the city coordinates as that used for the map coordinates. To use the same projection method for both data sets, this example does the following:

1. creates the Annotate data set CITIES from the USCITY data set. The unprojected LONG and LAT variable values are converted to radians and substituted for the projected X and Y variable values. LONG and LAT are converted by multiplying them by the arccosine of −1 and dividing that amount by 180. The cities are each assigned a value for the STATE variable, sequentially beginning at 100.

2. creates the map data set US48, a subset of the STATES data set.

3. combines the US48 data set and the CITIES data set into a single data set, ALL.

4. projects the ALL data set using the GPROJECT procedure to create the ALLP data set.

5. separates the ALLP projected data set into a projected map data set and a projected Annotate data set.

The following program statements produce Output 33.9:

```
     /* set the graphics environment */
goptions reset=global gunit=pct border
         ftext=swissb htitle=6 htext=3;

     /* assign the libref MAPS */
libname maps 'SAS-data-library';

     /* create Annotate data set CITIES */
data cities;
   set maps.uscity(drop=state);
   length function style color $ 8 position $ 1 text $ 20;
   retain function 'label' xsys ysys '2'
          hsys '1' when 'b' state 100;
   if city='Miami' | city='Boston' | city='Bangor';
   state+1;
   color='blue';
   size=10;
   text='T';
   position='5';
   style='marker';
   x=long*arcos(-1)/180;
   y=lat*arcos(-1)/180;
   output;
   color='blue';
   state+1;
   size=4;
   text='     '||city;
   position='6';
   style='swissb';
   output;
run;


     /* create reduced continental U.S. map data set */
     /* and remove Alaska, Hawaii, and Puerto Rico   */
data us48;
   set maps.states;
   if state ne 2 and state ne 15 and state ne 72;
   if density<4;
run;

     /* create data set ALL by combining data set */
     /* US48 and data set CITIES                  */
data all;
   set us48 cities;
run;
```

```
         /* project the ALL data set */
proc gproject data=all
              out=allp
              project=gnomon
              polelong=160
              polelat=45;
   id state;
run;

   /* separate the projected data set into */
   /* the CITIESP Annotate data set and    */
   /* the US49P map data set               */
data citiesp us48p;
   set allp;
   if state>100 then output citiesp;
   else output us48p;
run;

   /* define title and footnote for map */
title1 'Distribution Center Locations';
title2 'East Coast';
footnote j=r 'GR33N08  ';

   /* define pattern characteristics */
pattern value=mempty repeat=49 color=blue;

   /* show the annotated map */
proc gmap data=us48p map=us48p all;
   id state;
   choro state
         / nolegend
           annotate=citiesp;
run;
quit;
```

Output 33.9 Projected
Annotate Data Set (GR33N08)

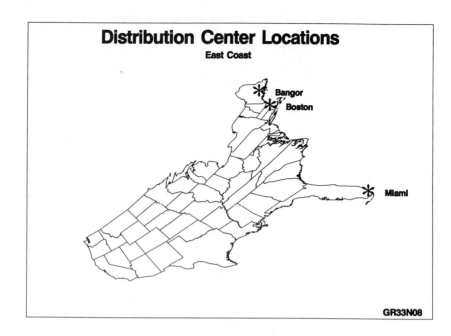

This example illustrates the following features:

☐ The ID statement in the GPROJECT procedure step identifies the variable in the input data set that defines unit areas.

☐ The CHORO statement in the GMAP procedure displays the projected map and annotates it using the projected Annotate data set.

See Also

Chapter 29, "The GMAP Procedure"
for information on map data sets

Chapter 34, "The GREDUCE Procedure"
for information on reducing the number of points needed to draw a map, thus reducing processing time

Chapter 35, "The GREMOVE Procedure"
for information on

☐ combining groups of unit areas into larger unit areas to create regional maps

☐ removing some of the boundaries in a map and creating a subset of a map that combines the original areas

References

Pearson, F., II (1977), "Map Projection Equations," Report Number TR-3624, Naval Surface Weapons Center, Dahlgren Laboratory, March, 1977.

Richardus, P. and Adler, R.K. (1972), *Map Projections*, Amsterdam: North-Holland Publishing Company; New York: American Elsevier Publishing Company.

Robinson, A.H. (1978), *Elements of Cartography*, New York: John Wiley & Sons, Inc.

34 The **GREDUCE** Procedure

Overview

The GREDUCE procedure enables you to process map coordinate data in map data sets to provide information that can be used to reduce the number of points needed to draw a map. It creates an output map data set containing all the variables in the input map data set plus a new variable named DENSITY. For each observation in the input map data set, the procedure determines the significance of that point for maintaining a semblance of the original shape and gives the observation a corresponding DENSITY value.

You can use the value of the DENSITY variable to create a subset of the original map data set. The observations in the subset can be used to draw a map that retains the overall appearance of the original map but contains fewer points, requires considerably less storage space, and can be drawn much more quickly.

The GREDUCE procedure does not produce any graphics output. Instead, the output data set generated by the GREDUCE procedure is used as

□ the MAP= data set for the GMAP procedure

□ the input data set for a DATA step to remove points from the map.

Output 34.1 and Output 34.2 illustrate the effect of reduction on a typical map data set. Output 34.1 is produced by using observations with any DENSITY values as input to the GMAP procedure.

Output 34.1 Map before
Reduction (GR34N01(a))

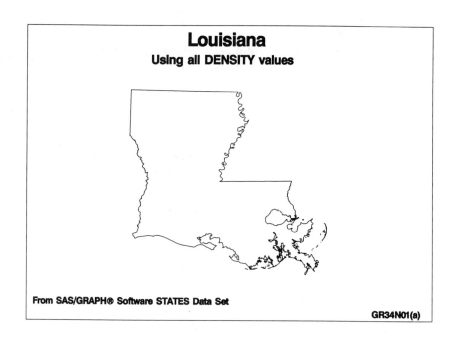

Output 34.2 is produced by using only those observations with a
DENSITY value of 0 or 1 as input to the GMAP procedure.

Output 34.2 Map after
Reduction (GR34N01(b))

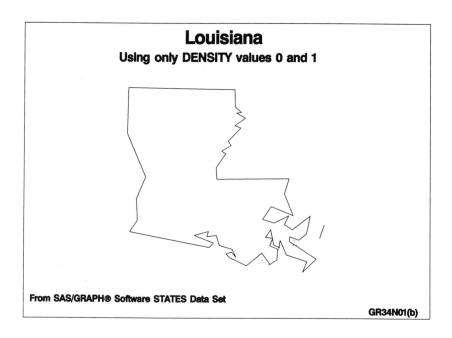

The reduced map shown in Output 34.2 retains the overall shape of the
original but requires only 166 observations compared to the 2834
observations needed to produce the map in Output 34.1.

Note: Many of the map data sets supplied by SAS Institute already
have been processed by the GREDUCE procedure. If the map data set
contains a DENSITY variable, you do not need to process the data set
using the GREDUCE procedure. See SAS Technical Report P-196,
SAS/GRAPH Map Data Sets for Release 6.06 for more information on the
map data sets supplied with SAS/GRAPH software.

GREDUCE Procedure Syntax

The GREDUCE procedure uses the following statements:

□ The PROC GREDUCE statement is required.

> **PROC GREDUCE** <DATA=*input-data-set*>
> <OUT=*output-data-set*>
> <*level-options*>;

□ The ID statement is also required.

> **ID** *variable* <... *variable-n*>;

□ The following statement is optional and local:

> **BY** <*options*> *variable*;

For complete statement syntax, see the section on the appropriate statement.

Statement Descriptions

The purpose of each statement is described here.

BY
: specifies the variable or variables by which the data are grouped for processing. Processing is performed for each value of the BY variable. See Chapter 10, "The BY Statement."

ID
: specifies the variable or variables in the input data set that define unit areas.

PROC GREDUCE
: starts the procedure and, optionally, specifies the names of the input and output data sets and the reduction criteria.

GREDUCE Procedure Description

The following sections address issues that pertain to the GREDUCE procedure as a whole, including terminology and special data considerations.

Terminology

The following terms are used in the discussion of the GREDUCE procedure and are defined in the Glossary:

density   unit area
segment

Summary of Use

To use the GREDUCE procedure, you must do the following:

1. If necessary, issue a LIBNAME statement for the SAS data library containing the map data set you want to process.

2. If you do not want to use the default reduction criteria, determine the necessary reduction criteria.

3. Use the PROC GREDUCE statement to identify the input and output data sets and to specify the reduction criteria.

4. Use the ID statement to identify the variable or variables in the input data set that identify the unit areas.

You can display the output data set using the GMAP procedure or save it for later use.

Data Considerations

The input data set must contain the following variables:

□ a numeric variable named X containing the horizontal coordinates of the map boundary points.

□ a numeric variable named Y containing the vertical coordinates of the map boundary points.

□ one or more variables that uniquely identify the unit areas in the map. Unit area identification variables can be either character or numeric. These variables are indicated in the ID statement.

The input data set also can contain the following optional variables:

□ one or more variables that identify groups of unit areas (for BY-group processing)

□ SEGMENT, which is used to distinguish nonconterminous segments of the unit areas.

Any other variables in the input data set do not affect the GREDUCE procedure.

If your input data set contains a variable named DENSITY, the GREDUCE procedure replaces the contents of the variable in the output data set. The original values of the DENSITY variable from the input data set are not included in the output data set.

If you are using map data sets in which area boundaries do not match precisely (for example, if the boundaries were digitized with a different set of points), PROC GREDUCE will not be able to identify common boundaries properly, resulting in abnormalities in your maps. These abnormalities include mismatched borders, missing vertex points, stray lines, gaps, and distorted polygons.

If the points in the area boundaries match up except for precision differences, round each X and Y value in your map data set accordingly, using the DATA step function ROUND before using PROC GREDUCE. (See Chapter 11, "SAS Functions," in *SAS Language: Reference, Version 6, First Edition* for information on the ROUND function.)

For example, if you have a map data set named APPROX in which the horizontal and vertical coordinate values for interior boundaries of unit areas are exactly equal only to three decimal places, then the following DATA step creates a new map data set, EXACT, that will be better suited for use with PROC GREDUCE:

```
data exact;
   set approx;
   if x ne . then x=round(x,.001);
   if y ne . then y=round(y,.001);
run;
```

For additional information on map data sets, see Chapter 29, "The GMAP Procedure."

PROC GREDUCE Statement

The PROC GREDUCE statement initiates the procedure, identifies the input and output data sets, and, optionally, specifies constraints for the reduction.

Syntax

The general form of the PROC GREDUCE statement is

PROC GREDUCE <DATA=*input-data-set*>
    <OUT=*output-data-set*>
    <*level-options*>;

□ *level-options* can be one or more of the following:

    E1=*min-distance*

    E2=*min-distance*

    E3=*min-distance*

    E4=*min-distance*

    E5=*min-distance*

    where *min-distance* is the minimum distance a point must lie from a straight line segment to be included in the corresponding density level

    N1=*max-points*

    N2=*max-points*

    N3=*max-points*

    N4=*max-points*

    N5=*max-points*

    where *max-points* is the maximum number of points in a unit area boundary for the corresponding density level

Options are fully described in "Options" later in this section.

Requirements

The GREDUCE procedure requires an input data set. By default, the procedure uses the most recently created data set as its input data set. You can use the DATA= option to select a specific data set. If no data set has been created in the current SAS session and you do not use the DATA= option, an error occurs and the procedure stops. There is no default input data set.

The PROC GREDUCE statement must be accompanied by an ID statement to indicate which variable or variables in the input data set define unit areas.

See "Data Considerations" earlier in this chapter for information on input data set requirements.

Options

You can use the following options with the PROC GREDUCE statement:

DATA=*SAS-data-set*
> specifies the name of the input map data set to be processed by the GREDUCE procedure.
>
> By default, the GREDUCE procedure uses the most recently created SAS data set as the input map data set. If you do not use the DATA= option and no data set has been created in the current SAS session, an error occurs and the procedure stops.

E1=*min-distance*
E2=*min-distance*
E3=*min-distance*
E4=*min-distance*
E5=*min-distance*
> specify the minimum distance that a point must lie from a straight line segment to be included at density level 1, 2, 3, 4, or 5, respectively. That is, in a reduced curve of three points, the middle point is at least a distance that is *min-distance* from a straight line between the two outside points.
>
> *Min-distance* values should be expressed in the units for the coordinate system of the input data set. For example, if the input data set contains coordinates expressed in radians, the *min-distance* values should be expressed in radians.
>
> The En= values should be specified in decreasing order. For example, the E2= value should be less than the E1= value and so on.

N1=*max-points*
N2=*max-points*
N3=*max-points*
N4=*max-points*
N5=*max-points*
> specify that for density level 1, 2, 3, 4, or 5, the boundary of a unit area should contain no more than *max-points* points.
>
> The Nn= values should be specified in increasing order. For example, the N2= value should be greater than or equal to the N1= value and so on.
>
> By default, if you omit the Nn= and En= options, the GREDUCE procedure calculates values for the five Nn= parameters using the following formula:
>
> $$N_n = n^2 \times N_{max} / 36$$
>
> Here N_{max} is the maximum number of points in any unit area in the input data set. However, the restriction that the number of points for any level cannot be less than the number of points in level 0 still applies.

OUT=*SAS-data-set*
> names the output map data set, which contains all the observations and variables in the original map data set plus the new DENSITY variable. If the input data set contains a variable named DENSITY, the GREDUCE procedure replaces the values of the variable in the output data set.

By default, PROC GREDUCE names the new data set using the
DATA*n* naming convention. That is, the procedure uses the name
WORK.DATA*n*, where *n* is the next unused number in sequence.
Thus, the first automatically named data set is DATA1, the second is
DATA2, and so on.

ID Statement

The ID statement lists the variable or variables that identify unit areas in
the map. Each group of observations with a different ID variable value is
evaluated as a separate unit area. The ID statement is required with the
GREDUCE procedure.

Syntax

The general form of the ID statement is

ID *variable* < . . . *variable-n*>;

where *variable* is the name of the variable in the input data set that
defines unit areas. *Variable* can be either numeric or character.

Requirements

The input data set to the GREDUCE procedure must contain all of the
variables identified in the ID statement.

Using the GREDUCE Procedure

The GREDUCE procedure uses default criteria for determining the
appropriate DENSITY variable value for each observation in the input
data set. If you do not want to use the default criteria, you can use PROC
GREDUCE statement options to select the following:

□ the maximum number of observations for each DENSITY level

□ the minimum distance an intermediate point must lie from a line
between two end points to be included in the level.

If you do not explicitly specify criteria, the procedure computes and uses
default values.

The GREDUCE procedure creates seven density levels, numbered 0
through 6. You can specify criteria for density levels 1 through 5. You
cannot define criteria for level 0, which is reserved for map vertex points,
such as common corners of unit areas. You also cannot define criteria for
level 6, which is assigned to those points that do not meet the criteria for
any lower level.

You specify the maximum number of observations per density level
using the N*n*= options in the PROC GREDUCE statement, and you specify
the minimum point distance using the E*n*= options. You must have
knowledge of the X and Y variable values in the particular input data set
to determine appropriate values for the E*n*= options. See "Options"
earlier in this chapter for details of the N*n*= and E*n*= options.

Figure 34.1 illustrates how the minimum distance parameter is used to
determine which points belong in a particular density level. At density
level *n*, only point C lies at a distance greater than the E*n*= value (70)

from a line between points A and B. Thus, after reduction only point C remains between points A and B at density level *n*, and the resulting reduced boundary is shown in Figure 34.2. See Douglas and Peucker (1973) for details of the algorithm used.

Figure 34.1 *Points in Data Set before Reduction*

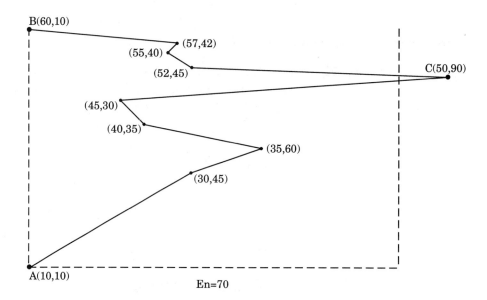

Figure 34.2 *Points in Data Set at Density n after Reduction*

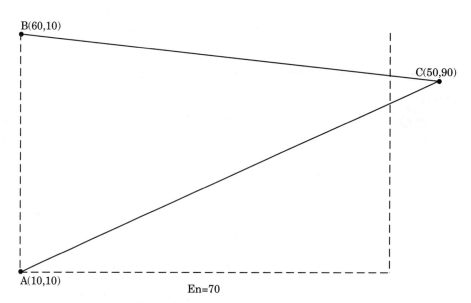

The GREDUCE procedure uses the usual Euclidean distance formula to determine the distance between points. For example, the distance *d* between the points (x_0, y_0) and (x_1, y_1) is

$$d = \sqrt{(x_1 - x_0)^2 + (y_1 - y_0)^2} \quad .$$

If this distance function is not suitable for the coordinate system in your input data set, you should transform the X and Y values to an appropriate coordinate system before using the GREDUCE procedure. An example of inappropriate coordinates is latitude and longitude values around one of the poles. In this case, the data values should be projected before they are reduced. See Chapter 33, "The GPROJECT Procedure," for more information on map projection.

If you specify both N*n*= and E*n*= values for a density level, the GREDUCE procedure attempts to satisfy both criteria. However, the number of points for any level is never reduced below the number of points in density level 0. If you specify a combination of N*n*= or E*n*= values such that the resulting DENSITY values are not in order of increasing density, a note is printed in the SAS log, and the DENSITY values are calculated in increasing order of density.

Producing a Subset of a Map Data Set

A map data set processed by the GREDUCE procedure does not result automatically in a map that uses fewer points. By default, the GMAP procedure produces a map using all of the points in the map data set, even if the data set has been processed by the GREDUCE procedure. In order to decrease the number of points used to produce the map, you must create a subset of the original data set using a DATA step or the WHERE= data set option. For example, to create a subset of a map using only the DENSITY values 0, 1, and 2, use the following DATA step:

```
data smallmap;
   set map;
   if density <= 2;
run;
```

Alternatively, you can use the WHERE= data set option in the PROC GMAP statement as follows:

```
proc gmap map=map(where=(density<=2)) data=response;
```

Note: The GREDUCE procedure does not reduce the size of the output data set compared to the input data set. In fact, the output data set from PROC GREDUCE may be larger than the input data set since it contains all the variables and observations from the original data set, with the addition of the DENSITY variable if it was not present in the original data set.

Example

The following example illustrates major features of the GREDUCE procedure. In this example, the GREDUCE procedure creates the DENSITY variable for the CANADA2 data set provided with SAS/GRAPH software. The map is displayed at its original density and at two levels of reduced density using the GMAP procedure.

Because the example uses one of the map data sets supplied with SAS/GRAPH software, you may need to replace *SAS-data-library* in the LIBNAME statement with the actual location of the SAS data library containing the Institute-supplied map data sets on your system. Contact your SAS Software Consultant for the location of the map data sets at your site.

If your site automatically assigns the libref MAPS to the SAS data library containing the Institute-supplied map data sets, delete the LIBNAME statement in this example.

The following program statements produce Output 34.3, Output 34.4, and Output 34.5:

```
/* set the graphics environment */
goptions reset=global gunit=pct border
        ftext=swissb htitle=6 htext=3;

/* assign the libref MAPS */
libname maps 'SAS-data-library';

/* define the titles and footnotes for the first map */
title1 'Canada';
title2 h=4 'Using all DENSITY values';
footnote1 j=1 ' From SAS/GRAPH' '02'x ' Software CANADA2 Data Set';
footnote2 j=r 'GR34N02(a)   ';

/* define pattern characteristics */
pattern value=mempty repeat=12 color=blue;

/* show the unreduced map */
proc gmap map=maps.canada2 data=maps.canada2 all;
  id province;
  choro province / nolegend;
run;

/* create the map data set CAN2 using */
/* the GREDUCE procedure             */
proc greduce data=maps.canada2 out=can2;
  id province;
run;

/* define new title and footnote for the second map */
title2 h=4 'Using only DENSITY values 0 to 3';
footnote2 j=r 'GR34N02(b)   ';

/* show reduced map with density levels 0-3 */
proc gmap map=can2(where=(density<4)) data=can2 all;
  id province;
  choro province / nolegend;
run;

/* define new title and footnote for the third map */
title2 h=4 'Using only DENSITY values 0 to 2';
footnote2 j=r 'GR34N02(c)   ';

/* show reduced map with density levels 0-2 */
proc gmap map=can2(where=(density<3)) data=can2 all;
  id province;
  choro province / nolegend;
run;
quit;
```

Output 34.3 *CANADA2 Map at Full Density (GR34N02(a))*

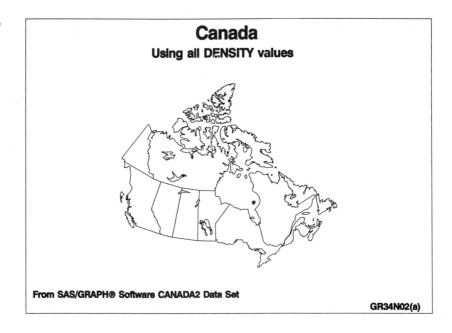

Output 34.4 *CANADA2 Map Using Density Values 0 to 3 (GR34N02(b))*

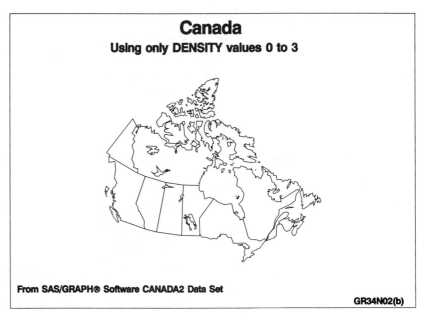

Output 34.5 *CANADA2 Map Using Density Values 0 to 2 (GR34N02(c))*

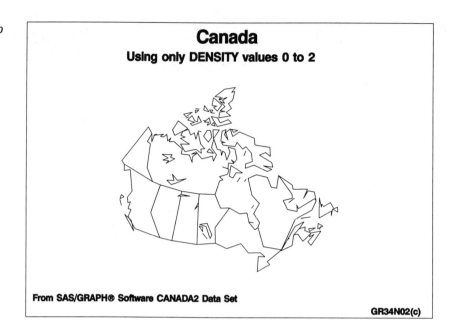

This example illustrates the following features:

□ The ID statements in the GREDUCE and GMAP procedure steps specify the variable in the map data set that defines unit areas.

□ In the second and third PROC GMAP statements, the WHERE= data set option selects map coordinates with the appropriate DENSITY values.

See Also

Chapter 29, "The GMAP Procedure"
   for information on map data sets

Chapter 33, "The GPROJECT Procedure"
   for information on

   □ transforming coordinates stored as longitude and latitude values into horizontal and vertical coordinates on a plane

   □ projecting an Annotate data set along with a map data set

Chapter 35, "The GREMOVE Procedure"
   for information on

   □ combining groups of unit areas into larger unit areas to create regional maps

   □ removing some of the boundaries in a map and creating a subset of a map that combines the original areas

Reference

Douglas, D.H. and Peucker, T.K. (1973), "Algorithms for the Reduction of the Number of Points Required to Represent a Digitized Line or Its Caricature," *The Canadian Cartographer*, 10, 112–122.

CHAPTER *35* The GREMOVE Procedure

Overview

The GREMOVE procedure enables you to combine unit areas defined in a map data set into larger unit areas by removing shared borders between the original unit areas. For example, the procedure is useful for producing regional maps from data sets containing state boundaries.

Note: The GREMOVE procedure does not produce any graphics output. Instead, the output data set generated by the GREMOVE procedure usually is used as input to the GMAP procedure.

Output 35.1 and Output 35.2 illustrate the effect of combining unit areas in a typical map data set. The statements used to produce Output 35.1 and Output 35.2 are discussed in "Example" later in this chapter.

Output 35.1 *Map before Removing Borders (GR35N01(a))*

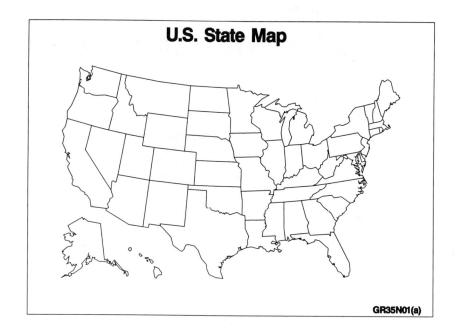

Output 35.2 *Map after Removing Borders (GR35N01(b))*

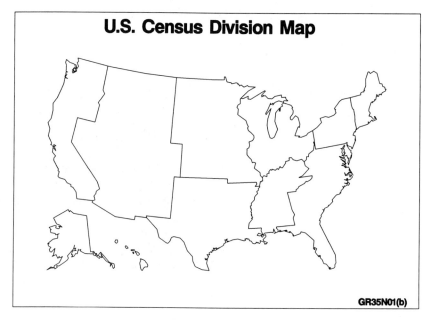

GREMOVE Procedure Syntax

The GREMOVE procedure uses the following statements:

□ The PROC GREMOVE statement is required.

> **PROC GREMOVE** <DATA=*input-data-set*>
> <OUT=*output-data-set*>;

□ The BY and ID statements also are required.

> **BY** <DESCENDING> *variable*
> < . . . <DESCENDING> *variable-n*>
> <NOTSORTED>;

> **ID** *variable* < . . . *variable-n*>;

For complete statement syntax, see the section on the appropriate statement.

Statement Descriptions

The purpose of each statement is described here.

BY	specifies the variable or variables in the input data set that identify the new unit areas.
ID	specifies the variable or variables in the input data set that define the current unit areas.
PROC GREMOVE	starts the procedure and, optionally, specifies the names of the input and output data sets.

GREMOVE Procedure Description

The following sections address issues that pertain to the GREMOVE procedure as a whole, including terminology and special data considerations.

Terminology

The following terms are used in the discussion of the GREMOVE procedure and are defined in the Glossary:

segment
unit area

Summary of Use

To use the GREMOVE procedure, you must do the following:

1. If necessary, issue a LIBNAME statement for the SAS data library containing the map data you want to process.

2. If necessary, use a DATA step to add the variable that defines the new unit areas to the map data set.

3. Use the PROC GREMOVE statement to identify the input and output data sets.

4. Use the ID statement to identify the variable or variables in the input data set that define the current unit areas.

5. Use the BY statement to identify the variable or variables in the input data set that define the new unit areas.

You can display the output data set using the GMAP procedure or save it for later use.

Data Considerations

The input data set must contain the following variables:

□ a numeric variable named X containing the horizontal coordinates of the map boundary points.

□ a numeric variable named Y containing the vertical coordinates of the map boundary points.

□ one or more variables that uniquely identify the current unit areas in the map. Unit area identification variables can be either character or numeric. These variables are indicated in the ID statement.

□ one or more variables that identify the new unit areas to be created in the output data set. These variables are indicated in the BY statement.

The optional variable SEGMENT can be used to distinguish nonconterminous segments of the current unit areas. Any other variables in the input data set do not affect the GREMOVE procedure.

The new unit areas in the output data set have all interior line segments removed. All variables in the input data set except X, Y, SEGMENT, and the variables listed in the BY statement are omitted from the output data set.

The output data set may contain missing X, Y coordinates to construct any polygons that have enclosed boundaries (like lakes or combined regions that have one or more hollow interior regions).

The SEGMENT variable in the output data set is ordered according to the size of the bounding box around the polygon it describes. A SEGMENT value of 1 describes the polygon whose bounding box is the largest in the unit area and so on. This information is useful for removing small polygons that clutter up maps.

If you are using map data sets in which area boundaries do not match precisely (for example, if the boundaries were digitized with a different set of points), PROC GREMOVE will not be able to identify common boundaries properly, resulting in abnormalities in your output data set.

If the points in the area boundaries match up except for precision differences, before using PROC GREMOVE you should round each X and Y value in your map data set accordingly, using the DATA step function ROUND. See Chapter 11, "SAS Functions," in *SAS Language: Reference, Version 6, First Edition* for information on the ROUND function.

For example, if you have a map data set named APPROX in which the horizontal and vertical coordinate values for interior boundaries of unit areas are exactly equal only to three decimal places, the following DATA step creates a new map data set, EXACT, that is better suited for use with the GREMOVE procedure:

```
data exact;
   set approx;
   if x ne . then x=round(x,.001);
   if y ne . then y=round(y,.001);
run;
```

For additional information on map data sets, see Chapter 29, "The GMAP Procedure."

PROC GREMOVE Statement

The PROC GREMOVE statement initiates the procedure to remove interior map boundaries and, optionally, identifies the input and output data sets.

Syntax

The general form of the PROC GREMOVE statement is

PROC GREMOVE <DATA=*input-data-set*>
   <OUT=*output-data-set*>;

Options are fully described in "Options" later in this section.

Requirements

The GREMOVE procedure requires an input data set. By default, the procedure uses the most recently created data set as its input data set. You can use the DATA= option to select a specific data set. If no data set has been created in the current SAS session and you do not use the DATA= option, an error occurs and the procedure stops.

The PROC GREMOVE statement must be accompanied by both of the following:

□ an ID statement to indicate which variable or variables in the input data set identify current unit areas to be combined

□ a BY statement to indicate which variable or variables in the input data set identify the new unit areas to be created.

See "Data Considerations" earlier in this chapter for information on input data set requirements.

Options

You can use the following options with the PROC GREMOVE statement:

DATA=*SAS-data-set*
    specifies the name of the input map data set to be processed by the GREMOVE procedure.

    By default, the GREMOVE procedure uses the most recently created SAS data set as the input map data set. If you do not use the DATA= option and no data set has been created in the current SAS session, an error occurs and the procedure stops.

OUT=*SAS-data-set*
    names the new map data set containing coordinates of the new unit areas created by the GREMOVE procedure.

    By default, the GREMOVE procedure names the new data set using the DATA*n* naming convention. That is, the procedure uses the name WORK.DATA*n*, where *n* is the next unused number in sequence. Thus, the first automatically named data set is DATA1, the second is DATA2, and so forth.

BY Statement

When used with the GMAP procedure, the BY statement specifies the variable or variables in the input data set that identify the new unit areas in the output data set. The BY variables in the input map data set become the ID variables for the output map data set. The BY statement is required with the GREMOVE procedure.

Syntax

The general form of the BY statement is

BY <DESCENDING> *variable*
        < . . . <DESCENDING> *variable-n*>
        <NOTSORTED>;

where *variable* is the name of the variable in the input data set that identifies the new unit areas. *Variable* can be either numeric or character.

Requirements

By default, the GREMOVE procedure expects the observations in the input data set to be sorted in ascending order of the BY-variable values. This applies regardless of whether the BY variables are character or numeric. You must use the DESCENDING option if the values of the BY variable appear in descending order.

Note: The GREMOVE procedure stops with an error message if an observation is encountered for which the BY-variable value is out of the proper order. You can use the SORT procedure in base SAS software to sort the input data set in the desired order. Use the same BY statement in the SORT procedure as in the GREMOVE procedure, as illustrated in this example:

```
    /* arrange the observations in the desired order */
proc sort data=tempdata out=tempsort;
   by state;
run;

    /* remove the county boundaries                 */
proc gremove data=tempsort out=newmap;
   by state;
   id county;
run;
```

See the *SAS Procedures Guide, Version 6, Third Edition* for further information on the SORT procedure.

If the observations in the input data set are not in ascending or descending order and you want them to be processed in the order in which they appear, you must use the NOTSORTED option to avoid the error condition.

Options

The following options can be used with the BY statement:

DESCENDING
> indicates that the input data set is sorted in descending order. By default, the GREMOVE procedure expects all BY-variable values to appear in ascending order.
>
> This option affects only the variable specified immediately following the option.

NOTSORTED
> indicates that observations with the same BY-variable values are to be grouped as they are encountered without regard for whether the values are in alphabetical or numerical order. The NOTSORTED option can appear anywhere in the BY statement. It affects all variables specified in the statement. The NOTSORTED option overrides the DESCENDING option if both appear in the same BY statement.

ID Statement

The ID statement specifies which variable or variables in the input data set define current unit areas. Each group of observations with a different ID variable value is evaluated as a separate unit area. The ID statement is required with the GREMOVE procedure.

All current unit areas with a common BY-variable value are combined into a single unit area in the output data set. The new unit area contains

□ all boundaries that are not shared, such as islands and lakes

□ all boundaries that are shared by two different BY groups.

Variables specified in the ID statement do not appear in the output map data set.

Syntax

The general form of the ID statement is

ID *variable* < . . . *variable-n*>;

where *variable* is the name of the variable in the input data set that defines the current unit areas. *Variable* can be either numeric or character.

Requirements

The input data set to the GREMOVE procedure must contain all of the variables identified in the ID statement.

Example

The following example illustrates major features of the GREMOVE procedure. This example processes the US map data set, supplied with SAS/GRAPH software, to produce a new map data set containing boundaries for the U.S. Bureau of the Census divisions.

Because the US map data set does not contain a variable to identify any unit area other than states, this example creates a map data set that contains the census divisions and that can be processed with the GREMOVE procedure. This new map data set is created by the following steps:

1. generating a new data set, CBSTATES, that includes a variable, DIVISION, that contains the number of the U.S. Bureau of the Census division for the state.

2. sorting the CBSTATES data set into FIPS-code order to create the CBSORT data set. CBSORT can be properly match-merged with the US map data set supplied with SAS/GRAPH software. Note that the US map data set is already sorted in FIPS-code order.

3. merging the CBSORT data set with the US map data set supplied with SAS/GRAPH software. This step creates a new map data set, USCB, containing all the state boundary coordinates from the US data set plus the added variable DIVISION.

4. sorting USCB by the DIVISION variable to create the DIVSTATE data set. The DIVSTATE data set can be properly processed by the GREMOVE procedure.

Because the example uses one of the map data sets supplied with SAS/GRAPH software, you may need to replace *SAS-data-library* in the LIBNAME statement with the actual location of the SAS data library containing the Institute-supplied map data sets on your system. Contact your SAS Software Consultant for the locations of the map data sets at your site.

If your site automatically assigns the libref MAPS to the SAS data library containing the Institute-supplied map data sets, delete the LIBNAME statement in this example.

The following program statements produce Output 35.1 and Output 35.2 at the beginning of this chapter:

```
    /* set the graphics environment */
goptions reset=global gunit=pct border
        ftext=swissb htitle=6 htext=3;

    /* assign the libref MAPS */
libname maps 'SAS-data-library';

    /* create data set CBSTATES */
data cbstates;
   length state 8 stcode $ 2 division 4;
   input stcode division;
   state=stfips(stcode);
   drop stcode;
   cards;
CT 1
MA 1
more data lines
OR 9
WA 9
;
run;

    /* sort data set in FIPS-code order */
proc sort data=cbstates out=cbsort;
   by state;
run;

    /* merge DIVISION variable into map data set */
data uscb;
   merge cbsort maps.us;
   by state;
run;

    /* sort data set in DIVISION order */
proc sort data=uscb out=divstate;
   by division;
run;

    /* remove interior boundaries within divisions */
proc gremove data=divstate out=remstate;
   by division;
   id state;
run;
```

```
    /* define title and footnote for map */
title 'U.S. State Map';
footnote j=r 'GR35N01(a)  ';

    /* define pattern characteristics */
pattern value=mempty repeat=48 color=blue;

    /* show the original map */
proc gmap map=maps.us data=maps.us all;
   id state;
   choro state / nolegend;
run;

    /* define new title and footnote for map */
title 'U.S. Census Division Map';
footnote j=r 'GR35N01(b)  ';

    /* show the regional map */
proc gmap map=remstate data=remstate all;
   id division;
   choro division / nolegend;
run;
quit;
```

Output 35.1 at the beginning of this chapter shows the map before processing. Output 35.2 at the beginning of this chapter shows the new map after PROC GREMOVE has removed interior state boundaries. This example illustrates the following features:

□ The PROC GREMOVE statement specifies the input and output data sets, DIVSTATE and REMSTATE, respectively.

□ The BY statement in the GREMOVE procedure step specifies the variable, DIVISION, in the input data set that identifies the new unit areas.

□ The ID statement in the GREMOVE procedure step specifies the variable, STATE, in the input data set that identifies the current unit areas.

□ The ID statement in the GMAP procedure step specifies the variable, DIVISION, that identifies the unit areas in the processed data set.

See Also

Chapter 29, "The GMAP Procedure"
for information on map data sets

Chapter 33, "The GPROJECT Procedure"
for information on

□ transforming coordinates stored as longitude and latitude values into horizontal and vertical coordinates on a plane

□ projecting an Annotate data set along with a map data set

Chapter 34, "The GREDUCE Procedure"
for information on reducing the number of points needed to draw a map, thus reducing processing time

CHAPTER *36* **The GREPLAY Procedure**

(continued on next page)

Overview

The GREPLAY procedure replays graphics output stored in SAS catalog entries and manages entries within catalogs. The GREPLAY procedure also creates templates and color maps that you can use while replaying your graphics output.

With the GREPLAY procedure, you can use windows or line mode to

☐ select one or more catalog entries for replay and route them to your display or other devices, such as plotters and printers

☐ design templates and create color maps

☐ manage entries in SAS catalogs by

   ☐ creating logical groupings of catalog entries containing graphics output

   ☐ renaming, deleting, or copying catalog entries containing graphics output, templates, and color maps

   ☐ rearranging catalog entries containing graphics output

☐ use templates to create new graphics output by selecting one or more catalog entries for replay in template panels on a single display.

The GREPLAY procedure stores graphics output, templates, and color maps in SAS catalog entries.

Output 36.1 shows graphics output from four catalog entries replayed on a single display. This output was created using a GREPLAY template.

Output 36.1 *Graphics Output in a Template (GR36N01)*

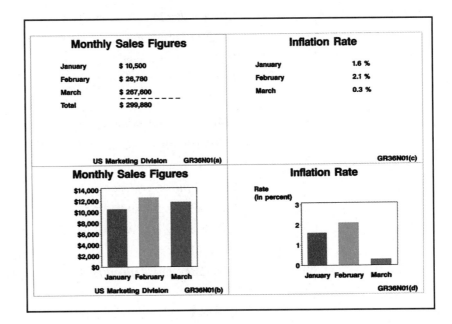

GREPLAY Procedure Syntax

The GREPLAY procedure uses the following statements:

□ The PROC GREPLAY statement is required.

> **PROC GREPLAY** <BYLINE>
> <CC=*color-map-catalog*>
> <CMAP=*color-map-name*>
> <FS>
> <GOUT=*output-catalog*>
> <IGOUT=*input-catalog*>
> <NOBYLINE>
> <NOFS>
> <PRESENTATION>
> <TC=*template-catalog*>
> <TEMPLATE=*template-name*>;

□ If you use the NOFS option in the PROC GREPLAY statement or if you are running the GREPLAY procedure in a non-full-screen or batch environment, you can use the following line-mode statements. You can submit as many of each statement as you want with a single PROC GREPLAY statement.

> **?** *required-argument*;
>
> **BYLINE**;
>
> **CC** *color-map-catalog*;
>
> **CCOPY** <*catalog.*>*color-map-name*<*.CMAP*>;
>
> **CDEF** *color-map-name* <DES='*string*'>
> <*color-number/from-color:to-color*>
> < . . . *color-number/from-color:to-color*>;
>
> **CDELETE** *color-map-entry* < . . . *color-map-entry-n*> | _ALL_;
>
> **CMAP** *color-map-name*;

COPY *entry-id* < . . . *entry-id-n*> | _ALL_;

DELETE *entry-id* < . . . *entry-id-n*> | _ALL_;

DEVICE *device-name*;

END;

FS;

GOUT *output-catalog*;

GROUP *entry-id* < . . . *entry-id-n*>;

IGOUT *input-catalog*;

LIST *required-argument*;

MODIFY *modify-entry* < . . . *modify-entry-n*>;

MOVE *entry-id-1* AFTER | BEFORE *entry-id-2*;

NOBYLINE;

PREVIEW *template-entry* < . . . *template-entry-n*> | _ALL_;

QUIT;

REPLAY *entry-id* < . . . *entry-id-n*> | _FIRST_ | _LAST_ | _ALL_;

STOP;

TC *template-catalog*;

TCOPY <*catalog.*>*template-name*<*.TEMPLATE*>;

TDEF *template-name* <DES= '*description*'>
　　　<*panel-definition*> < . . . *panel-definition-n*>;

TDELETE *template-entry* < . . . *template-entry-n*> | _ALL_;

TEMPLATE *template-name*;

TREPLAY *select-pair* < . . . *select-pair-n*>;

GREPLAY Procedure Description

The following sections address issues that pertain to the GREPLAY procedure as a whole: terminology, methods of use, and a summary of use.

Terminology

The following terms are used in the discussion of the GREPLAY procedure and are defined in the Glossary.

catalog	panel
catalog entry	replay
color map	template

Methods of Using the GREPLAY Procedure

You can replay graphics output and manage catalog entries containing graphics output by using the GREPLAY procedure windows or by submitting line-mode statements. By default, if your device supports full-screen mode, the GREPLAY procedure uses the GREPLAY procedure windows.

To invoke the GREPLAY procedure windows on a full-screen device, submit the PROC GREPLAY statement as follows:

```
proc greplay;
```

SAS/GRAPH software then displays the PROC GREPLAY window.

You can use line-mode statements instead of the GREPLAY procedure windows to replay graphics output and manage catalogs. The GREPLAY procedure uses line mode automatically if you do not have a full-screen device. To use the GREPLAY procedure in line mode on a full-screen device, submit the PROC GREPLAY statement with the NOFS option as follows:

```
proc greplay nofs;
```

Once you submit the PROC GREPLAY statement, you can enter and submit line-mode statements without resubmitting the PROC GREPLAY statement for each line-mode statement. When using the GREPLAY procedure in line mode, you can create templates and color maps using code that can be easily transferred to another operating system.

You can exit the GREPLAY procedure in line mode in these three ways:

□ Submit the END, QUIT, or STOP statement.

□ Submit another PROC statement or a DATA step.

□ Exit your SAS session.

If you are using the GREPLAY procedure in batch mode, use GREPLAY line-mode statements. The syntax for batch mode is the same as the syntax for line mode.

Duplicate Entry Names

When you copy a catalog entry containing graphics output, a template, or a color map to another catalog or within the same catalog, the name of the entry being copied may duplicate the name of an existing entry in the target catalog. If a copy duplicates an existing name, the GREPLAY procedure uses the following naming conventions to prevent duplication of the name.

□ For names that are fewer than 8 characters, the procedure adds a number to the end of the name. For example, if you copy a template named MYTEMP to a catalog that already contains a template by that name, the procedure assigns the name MYTEMP1 to the copied template.

□ For names that are 8 characters long, the procedure drops the last character from the name before adding the suffix. For example, if you copy a color map named COLORMAP to a catalog that already contains a color map by that name, the procedure assigns the name COLORMA1 to the copied color map.

The GREPLAY procedure uses the same technique for the names of entries containing graphics output produced by the template facility.

Specifying Catalogs, Templates, and Color Maps

The GREPLAY procedure can use up to four different catalogs. The catalogs and descriptions follow:

input catalog
: the catalog that contains the graphics output, stored in catalog entries, that you want to replay.

output catalog
: the catalog where graphics output produced by the template facility is stored. The output catalog is also the destination of copied entries containing graphics output.

template catalog
: the catalog where templates created using the GREPLAY procedure are stored. The template catalog also may contain previously created templates that you want to modify or templates to use for replaying your graphics output.

color map catalog
: the catalog where color maps created using the GREPLAY procedure are stored. The color map catalog also may contain previously created color maps that you want to modify or color maps to use when replaying your graphics output.

You can assign a different SAS catalog to each catalog, or you may use the same SAS catalog for all four catalogs. A single SAS catalog may contain graphics output, color maps, and templates.

Table 36.1 shows you the different ways you can assign catalogs to each location.

Table 36.1 *Assigning Catalogs*

Catalog	Ways to Assign
input	IGOUT= option in the PROC GREPLAY statement
	IGOUT line-mode statement
	IGOUT field in the PROC GREPLAY window
output	GOUT= option in the PROC GREPLAY statement
	GOUT line-mode statement
	GOUT field in the PROC GREPLAY window
template	TC= option in the PROC GREPLAY statement
	TC line-mode statement
	TC field in the PROC GREPLAY window
color map	CC= option in the PROC GREPLAY statement
	CC line-mode statement
	CC field in the PROC GREPLAY window

In addition, you can assign a current template, which you can use when replaying graphics output, and a current color map, which you can use to remap colors when replaying graphics output. To assign the current template, use one of the following:

□ the TEMPLATE= option in the PROC GREPLAY statement

□ the TEMPLATE line-mode statement

□ the Template field in the PROC GREPLAY window.

To assign the current color map, use one of the following:

□ the CMAP= option in the PROC GREPLAY statement

□ the CMAP line-mode statement

□ the Cmap field in the PROC GREPLAY window.

Summary of Use

To invoke the GREPLAY procedure, submit a PROC GREPLAY statement in your SAS session. To manage a catalog or replay graphics output, assign an input catalog. You can use either GREPLAY procedure windows or GREPLAY line-mode statements to manage catalogs and replay graphics output.

Once the GREPLAY procedure is active, you can

□ select one or more entries or groups of entries for replay using the PROC GREPLAY or PRESENTATION window.

□ group and rearrange catalog entries containing graphics output.

□ create or modify templates. Templates are used to describe positioning on a single display for the graphics output stored in one or more catalog entries.

□ create or modify color maps. Color maps enable you to change the colors in graphics output by mapping existing colors to new colors.

□ display graphics output from several catalog entries on one display by replaying the graphics output in a template.

Replaying Graphics Output

In order to select catalog entries for replay, you must first assign an input catalog that contains the graphics output to be replayed. Then, using the PROC GREPLAY window or the PRESENTATION window, you can replay the graphics output by placing an S in the window's select field for the entry. When you press ENTER, the graphics output stored in the selected entry is displayed.

Using the GREPLAY procedure in line mode, you can replay graphics output from a catalog entry using the REPLAY statement as shown here:

```
libname mylib SAS-data-library;

proc greplay igout=mylib.graphs nofs;
   replay graph1;
quit;
```

Managing Catalog Entries

Before you can manage catalog entries using the GREPLAY procedure, you need to assign an input catalog and, optionally, an output catalog. You can use the GREPLAY procedure to copy entries from the input catalog to the output catalog, arrange entries in the input catalog into logical groupings, delete entries that are no longer needed from the input catalog, change the names and descriptions of entries in the input catalog, or change the order of entries in the input catalog. Table 36.2 shows how you can accomplish these tasks using either line-mode statements or the GREPLAY procedure windows.

Table 36.2 Managing
Catalogs Using Windows and
Line Mode

Task	Line-mode Statement	PROC GREPLAY Window Command
copy graphics output from the input catalog to the output catalog ★	COPY statement	C selection field command
arrange entries into logical groupings	GROUP statement	GROUP command and group identifiers in the selection field
delete unneeded entries	DELETE statement	DEL selection field command
change entry names and descriptions	MODIFY statement	MODIFY command
reorder the entries	MOVE statement	M, A, and B selection field commands

★You must assign an output catalog before copying graphics output.

Creating Templates and Color Maps

You can use the GREPLAY procedure to create templates and color maps. You can use templates to replay graphics output from several catalog entries on a single display, or to change the shape or size of graphics output. You can use color maps to remap colors when replaying graphics output.

Before creating a template, you must assign a template catalog. Then if you are using the GREPLAY procedure windows, you can use the TEMPLATE DESIGN window to define and preview a template. If you are using the GREPLAY procedure in line-mode, use the TDEF statement to define a template and the PREVIEW statement to preview a template. For example, the following line-mode statements define and preview a template named TEMPLT:

```
tdef templt 1/def;
preview templt;
```

Before creating a color map, you must assign a color map catalog. Then if you are using the GREPLAY procedure windows, you can use the COLOR MAPPING window to define a color map. If you are using the GREPLAY procedure in line mode, use the CDEF statement to define a color map. For example, the following statement defines a color map named CLRMAP:

```
cdef clrmap 1 / cyan : blue;
```

Replaying Graphics Output in a Template

You can use the GREPLAY procedure to create new graphics output by replaying existing graphics output in templates. Before you can replay graphics output in a template, you must assign a template catalog and a current template. If you are using the GREPLAY procedure windows, you can replay graphics output in a template by placing template panel numbers for the current template in the selection field of the catalog entries you want to replay. If you are using the GREPLAY procedure in line mode, you can replay graphics output in a template using the TREPLAY statement to identify the panel number and entry name as follows:

```
treplay 1:graph1 2:graph2;
```

When you replay graphics output in a template, the new graphics output created by the GREPLAY procedure is automatically stored in the output catalog.

PROC GREPLAY Statement

The PROC GREPLAY statement initiates the procedure and, if necessary, does the following:

□ specifies whether windows or line-mode statements are used initially (you can switch back and forth within a session).

□ specifies whether the session is used for catalog management and normal presentation or special *executive* presentation.

□ identifies the input catalog to use (you can change the input catalog during a catalog management session). Any catalog can be used for input. However, the GREPLAY procedure manages only these three types of catalog entries:

  □ graphics output (catalog entries of type GRSEG)

  □ color maps (catalog entries of type CMAP)

  □ templates (catalog entries of type TEMPLATE).

□ identifies the output catalog to use.

□ identifies other catalogs and catalog entries to use for color mapping and templates (you can change the catalog and catalog entries in your session).

You can exit the GREPLAY procedure in line mode by submitting the QUIT, STOP, or END statement or by submitting another DATA or PROC step. You can exit the GREPLAY procedure windows by issuing the END command from the PROC GREPLAY window.

Syntax

The general form of the PROC GREPLAY statement is

PROC GREPLAY <BYLINE>
    <CC=*color-map-catalog*>
    <CMAP=*color-map-name*>
    <FS>
    <GOUT=*output-catalog*>

              <IGOUT=*input-catalog*>
              <NOBYLINE>
              <NOFS>
              <PRESENTATION>
              <TC=*template-catalog*>
              <TEMPLATE=*template-name*>;

PROC GREPLAY statement options are fully described in "Options" later in this section.

Requirements

The GREPLAY procedure has different requirements depending on the tasks you want to perform. You must specify a device driver to invoke the GREPLAY procedure. Depending on the tasks you want to perform, you may also need to do the following:

☐ To assign a current color map or create new color maps, you must assign a color map catalog.

☐ To assign a current template or create new templates, you must assign a template catalog.

☐ To replay graphics output in a template, you must assign a template catalog and a current template.

☐ To replay graphics output using a color map, you must assign a color map catalog and a current color map.

☐ To move, group, or delete catalog entries containing graphics output and to replay graphics output, you must assign an input catalog.

☐ To copy catalog entries containing graphics output, you must assign an input and, optionally, an output catalog.

    Catalog, template, and color map names containing underscore characters cannot be used in the GREPLAY procedure windows.

Options

You can use the following options in the PROC GREPLAY statement.

BYLINE
    specifies that the BY statement information for the SAS catalog entries should be displayed. The BY statement information appears directly beneath the primary description of the entry. By default, the BY statement information is displayed.

CC=*color-map-catalog*
    specifies the name of the color map catalog to use with the GREPLAY procedure. Use the CMAP= option to assign a current color map contained in *color-map-catalog*.

CMAP=*color-map-name*
    assigns a current color map to use when replaying graphics output, where *color-map-name* is the name of an existing color map in the catalog specified in the CC= option. If *color-map-name* is not in the catalog, an error message is written to the SAS log. *Color-map-name* must have a catalog entry type of CMAP.

If you do not specify a color map catalog using the CC= option when using the CMAP= option, a warning message is written to the SAS log.

FS

specifies that the GREPLAY procedure should use windows. By default, if your device supports full-screen mode, the GREPLAY procedure uses windows. If your device does not support full-screen mode, the procedure begins execution in line mode and the FS option has no effect.

GOUT=*output-catalog*

specifies the name of the output catalog in which to save the graphics output produced by the GREPLAY procedure. In addition, catalog entries containing graphics output can be copied to *output-catalog*. By default, graphics output produced by the procedure is stored in the catalog WORK.GSEG, which is erased at the end of your session. *Output-catalog* can be the same catalog specified in the IGOUT= option.

IGOUT=*input-catalog*

specifies the name of the input catalog to use with the GREPLAY procedure. The input catalog that you specify with the IGOUT= option should be a catalog containing the graphics output to be replayed. *Input-catalog* can be the same catalog specified in the GOUT= option.

NOBYLINE

suppresses the BY statement information for the SAS catalog entries. The BY statement information appears directly beneath the primary description of the entry. By default, the BY statement information is displayed.

NOFS

specifies that the GREPLAY procedure should use line mode. By default, if your device supports full-screen mode, the GREPLAY procedure uses windows. If your device does not support full-screen mode, the procedure uses line mode, regardless of whether you used the FS option or the NOFS option.

PRESENTATION

specifies that the GREPLAY procedure should open the PRESENTATION window and use the catalog specified by the IGOUT= option as the input catalog. The PRESENTATION option is often used in applications to prevent the application users from deleting or reordering the catalog entries. You can only replay graphics output from the PRESENTATION window; you cannot manage catalogs or create templates and color maps from this window.

You must use the IGOUT= option when you use the PRESENTATION option. The PRESENTATION option overrides the NOFS option on full-screen devices.

TC=*template-catalog*

specifies the name of the template catalog to use with the GREPLAY procedure. Use the TEMPLATE= option to assign a current template from *template-catalog*.

TEMPLATE=*template-name*
> assigns a current template to use when replaying graphics output where *template-name* is the name of an existing template in the template catalog specified in the TC= option. If *template-name* is not in the catalog, an error message is written to the SAS log. *Template-name* must have a catalog entry type of TEMPLATE.
>
> If you do not specify the name of a template catalog using the TC= option when you use the TEMPLATE= option, a warning message is written to the SAS log.

GREPLAY Line-Mode Statements

If you use the NOFS option in the PROC GREPLAY statement when you invoke the procedure or if you are running the GREPLAY procedure in a non-full-screen or batch environment, you can use line-mode statements to perform tasks with the GREPLAY procedure. The following sections describe the statements you can use with the GREPLAY procedure in the line-mode or batch environment.

?

Prints the current option value or device driver

The ? statement prints the current value of certain PROC GREPLAY options or the current device driver. The output from the ? statement is sent to the SAS log.

Syntax

The general form of the ? statement is

? *required-argument*;

☐ *required-argument* must be one of the following:

CC
CMAP
DEVICE
GOUT
IGOUT
TC
TEMPLATE

Requirements

You must use one (and only one) of the following arguments with the ? statement.

CC
>prints the name of the current color map catalog. If no color map catalog has been assigned, the GREPLAY procedure issues a message indicating that a catalog has not been assigned.

CMAP
>prints the name of the current color map. If no color map has been assigned, the GREPLAY procedure issues a message indicating that a color map has not been assigned.

DEVICE
DEV
>prints the name of the current device driver.

GOUT
>prints the name of the current output catalog. If no output catalog has been assigned, the GREPLAY procedure issues a message indicating that a catalog has not been assigned.

IGOUT
>prints the name of the current input catalog. If no input catalog has been assigned, the GREPLAY procedure issues a message indicating that a catalog has not been assigned.

TC
>prints the name of the current template catalog. If no template catalog has been assigned, the GREPLAY procedure issues a message indicating that a catalog has not been assigned.

TEMPLATE
>prints the name of the current template. If no template has been assigned, the GREPLAY procedure issues a message indicating that a template has not been assigned.

BYLINE

Displays BY statement information

The BYLINE statement specifies that BY statement information should be displayed. BY statement information appears directly beneath the primary description of the catalog entries when you list the contents of the input catalog. By default, the BY statement information is displayed.

Syntax

The general form of the BYLINE statement is

BYLINE;

CC

Specifies a color map catalog

The CC statement specifies a color map catalog for the GREPLAY procedure. You may change the color map catalog without exiting the procedure by using the CC statement.

Syntax

The general form of the CC statement is

CC *color-map-catalog*;

□ *color-map-catalog* is the name of a SAS catalog where color maps should be stored or the name of a SAS catalog containing color maps.

CCOPY

Copies a color map

The CCOPY statement copies color maps from another catalog to the color map catalog or creates a duplicate copy of a color map within the color map catalog.

Syntax

The general form of the CCOPY statement is:

CCOPY <*catalog.*>*color-map-name*<*.CMAP*>;

□ *catalog* is the name of the SAS catalog containing the color map to be copied.

□ *color-map-name* is the name of the color map to be copied.

□ *.CMAP* is the catalog entry type.

If a color map of the same name already exists in the color map catalog, the GREPLAY procedure uses a naming convention to avoid a duplicate name. See "Duplicate Entry Names" earlier in this chapter for more information.

Requirements

You must assign a color map catalog before using the CCOPY statement.

Using the CCOPY Statement

To copy a color map from one catalog to the color map catalog, you must first assign a color map catalog. *Catalog* should be the name of the catalog from which the color map is copied. For example, if you want to copy HP.CMAP from the catalog named ONE.CCAT to the catalog named TARGET.CLRMAP, use the following statements:

```
libname target 'SAS-data-library';
libname one 'SAS-data-library';
```

```
proc greplay nofs;
   cc target.clrmap;
   ccopy one.ccat.hp.cmap;
quit;
```

To create a duplicate copy of a color map, simply omit *catalog* from your CCOPY statement. For example, to create a duplicate copy of the color map named HP.CMAP in the color map catalog, use the following statement:

```
ccopy hp.cmap;
```

SAS/GRAPH software uses a naming convention to avoid duplicating an existing name. See "Duplicate Entry Names" earlier in this chapter for more information.

CDEF

Defines a color map

The CDEF statement defines or modifies a color map in the color map catalog. A color map is a list of up to 256 pairs of colors that enables you to change the colors in graphics output by mapping the original colors to a list of new colors. Color maps are useful for controlling how colors that are not available on the current device are remapped.

When you assign a current color map and replay graphics output stored in a catalog entry, any color in your graphics output that appears in the From column of the color map is mapped to the corresponding color in the To column of the color map. The new colors are not saved with the graphics output and replaying graphics output using a color map does not create new graphics output.

Syntax

The general form of the CDEF statement is

CDEF *color-map-name* <DES='*string*'>
    <*color-number/from-color:to-color*>
    < . . . *color-number-n/from-color:to-color*>;

□ *color-map-name* is the name of an existing or new color map. *Color-map-name* must be a valid SAS name.

□ *color-number* is the number of a color pair.

□ *from-color* is the color to be mapped.

□ *to-color* is the new color that replaces *from-color* in the replayed graphics output.

Requirements

To use the CDEF statement, you must assign a color map catalog. If the color map name you specify with the CDEF statement is not in the color map catalog, then the procedure creates a new color map. If the color map name is already in the color map catalog, then the procedure modifies or adds to that color map.

CDEF

continued

Option

You can use the following option with the CDEF statement.

DES='*string*'
> specifies a descriptive string, up to 40 characters long, that appears in the Description field of the catalog entry for the color map. By default, the GREPLAY procedure assigns a description of
> **** NEW COLOR MAP **** to the color map.

CDELETE

Deletes a color map

The CDELETE statement deletes color maps from the current CC catalog.
> **Note:** The GREPLAY procedure does not prompt you to confirm your request to delete color maps.

Syntax

The general form of the CDELETE statement is

CDELETE *color-map-entry* < . . . *color-map-entry-n*> | _ALL_;

CDEL *color-map-entry* < . . . *color-map-entry-n*> | _ALL_;

□ *color-map-entry* is the name of a color map that you want to delete in the color map catalog. You can submit a single entry or a list of entries in one CDELETE statement.

□ _ALL_ specifies that all color maps should be deleted from the color map catalog.

CMAP

Assigns the current color map

The CMAP statement assigns the current color map to use when replaying graphics output.

Syntax

The general form of the CMAP statement is

CMAP *color-map-name*;

□ *color-map-name* names an existing color map, contained in the color map catalog, to use when replaying your graphics output.

Requirements

You must assign a color map catalog before using the CMAP statement. If the color map you specify in the CMAP statement is not in the current color map catalog, the GREPLAY procedure issues an error message in the SAS log.

COPY

Copies entries containing graphics output

The COPY statement copies catalog entries containing graphics output from the input catalog to the output catalog. You can copy individual entries, groups of entries, or an entire catalog.

Syntax

The general form of the COPY statement is

COPY *entry-id* < . . . *entry-id-n*> | _ALL_;

- □ *entry-id* is the number or name of a SAS catalog entry containing graphics output or the number or name of a group of entries to be copied from the input catalog to the output catalog. You can submit a single entry or a list of entries in one COPY statement. A list of entries can contain both numbers and names. See the REPLAY statement later in this chapter for more information on specifying *entry-id*.

- □ _ALL_ specifies that the graphics output stored in all of the entries in the input catalog should be copied to the output catalog.

Requirements

You must assign an input catalog and an output catalog before using the COPY statement. You cannot use the COPY statement to create a duplicate of an entry containing graphics output in the same catalog. You can have only one copy of an entry containing graphics output in a catalog.

DELETE

Deletes entries containing graphics output

The DELETE statement deletes SAS catalog entries containing graphics output from the current input catalog.

   Note: The GREPLAY procedure does not prompt you to confirm your request to delete an entry containing graphics output.

DELETE

continued

Syntax

The general form of the DELETE statement is

DELETE *entry-id* < . . . *entry-id-n*> | _ALL_;

DEL *entry-id* < . . . *entry-id-n*> | _ALL_;

□ *entry-id* is the number or name of a SAS catalog entry containing graphics output or the number or name of a group that you want to delete from the input catalog. You can submit a single entry or a list of entries in one DELETE statement. A list of entries can contain both numbers and names. See the REPLAY statement later in this chapter for more information on specifying *entry-id*.

□ _ALL_ specifies that all of the entries containing graphics output should be deleted from the input catalog.

DEVICE

Specifies the device driver

The DEVICE statement specifies the device driver to use for replaying graphics output.

Syntax

The general form of the DEVICE statement is

DEVICE *device-name*;

DEV *device-name*;

□ *device-name* is the name of a SAS/GRAPH device driver.

Requirements

You must specify a device driver that your graphics device can support. You must also specify the name of a device driver that is available in your SAS session. The device driver you specify becomes the current device and is used for subsequent replays until you submit another DEVICE statement or change the device driver in another way.

Using the DEVICE Statement

The DEVICE statement is useful during an interactive SAS/GRAPH session in which you are using both a display and a hardcopy device. You can use the DEVICE statement to switch from one device to another. See Chapter 4, "Device Drivers," for more information on specifying device drivers.

END

Terminates the procedure

The END statement terminates the GREPLAY procedure. The END statement performs the same function as the QUIT and STOP statements.

Syntax

The general form of the END statement is

END;

FS

Switches to the GREPLAY procedure windows

The FS statement switches from line mode to the GREPLAY procedure windows.

Syntax

The general form of the FS statement is

FS;

Requirements

Your device must support full-screen mode in order to use the GREPLAY procedure windows. If your device does not support full-screen mode, the GREPLAY procedure issues a message in the SAS log and remains in line mode. If windows are available, the PROC GREPLAY window is displayed. Once you are in the PROC GREPLAY window, you can use the NOFS command to return to line mode.

GOUT

Specifies the output catalog

The GOUT statement assigns the output catalog for the GREPLAY procedure. You may change the output catalog without exiting the procedure by using the GOUT statement.

Syntax

The general form of the GOUT statement is

GOUT *output-catalog*;

□ *output-catalog* is the name of a SAS catalog that you want to use as an output catalog. By default, the output catalog is WORK.GSEG.

GROUP

Creates groups of graphics entries

The GROUP statement creates groups of catalog entries in the current input catalog. You can manage and display groups of entries with the DELETE, COPY, and REPLAY statements the same way you manage single entries.

Syntax

The general form of the GROUP statement is

GROUP *entry-id* < . . . *entry-id-n*>;

☐ *entry-id* is the number or name of a catalog entry containing graphics output. All of the entries specified in the GROUP statement are included in a single group with a group header. You can submit a single entry or a list of entries with a single GROUP statement. A list of entries can contain both entry numbers and entry names. See the REPLAY statement later in this chapter for more information on specifying *entry-id*.

Using the GROUP Statement

Only one group can be created per group statement. The default name for a group header is GROUP. The default description for the group header is *** new group ***. The GREPLAY procedure uses a naming convention to avoid duplicate names. See "Duplicate Entry Names" earlier in this chapter for more information on the naming convention.

To change the name (and description) of a group, use the MODIFY statement.

IGOUT

Specifies the input catalog

The IGOUT statement assigns the input catalog for the GREPLAY procedure. You may change the input catalog without exiting the procedure by using the IGOUT statement.

Syntax

The general form of the IGOUT statement is

IGOUT *input-catalog*;

☐ *input-catalog* is a SAS catalog with entries containing graphics output that you want to replay.

Using the IGOUT Statement

If you do not use the GOUT= option in the PROC statements of SAS/GRAPH procedures used to create graphics output, your graphics output is automatically stored in the WORK.GSEG catalog. You can replay the graphics output stored in this catalog as follows:

```
proc greplay nofs;
   igout work.gseg;
   replay _all_;
```

LIST

Prints catalog entries, template definitions, or color map definitions

The LIST statement prints the entries in the input, template, and color map catalogs and the contents of templates and color maps. The output from the LIST statement is sent to the SAS log.

Syntax

The general form of the LIST statement is

LIST *required-argument*;

□ *required-argument* must be one of the following:

> CC
>
> CMAP
>
> IGOUT
>
> TC
>
> TEMPLATE

Requirements

You must use one (and only one) of the following arguments in the LIST statement:

CC
> prints the color maps in the current color map catalog. If the catalog contains both templates and color maps, only color maps are listed.

CMAP
> prints the *From* and *To* color values in the current color map.

IGOUT
> prints the number, names, and descriptions of the entries in the input catalog containing graphics output. In addition, the type of graphics output (dependent or independent) is shown.

LIST
continued

TC
> prints the templates in the current template catalog. If the catalog contains both templates and color maps, only the templates are listed.

TEMPLATE
> prints the panel definition values of the current template.

MODIFY

Changes the name, description, and BY statement information

The MODIFY statement modifies the name, description, and BY statement information of entries or group headers in the input catalog.

Syntax

The general form of the MODIFY statement is

MODIFY *modify-entry* < . . . *modify-entry-n*>;

□ *modify-entry* has the following format:

> *entry-id/required-arguments*

where

> □ *entry-id* is a name or number for an entry containing graphics output or a name or number for a group header in the input catalog.

> □ *Required-arguments* must be one or more of the following:

>> NAME=*name*

>> DES='*string*'

>> BYLINE='*string*'

Requirements

You must use one or more of the following arguments in each *modify-entry* in the MODIFY statement:

NAME=*name*
> specifies the new *name* for the entry. *Name* can be up to eight characters long and must be a valid SAS name.

DES='*string*'
> specifies a character string that describes the entry. *String* can be up to 40 characters long and must be enclosed in quotes.

BYLINE='*string*'
> specifies a character string that can be used for additional information or for BY statement information. *String* can be up to 40 characters long and must be enclosed in quotes. BY statement information appears directly beneath the primary description of the catalog entry.

MOVE

Rearranges the catalog entries

The MOVE statement changes the order of the catalog entries in the input catalog by moving entries either before or after other entries.

Syntax

The general form of the MOVE statement is

MOVE *entry-id-1* AFTER | BEFORE *entry-id-2*;

□ *entry-id-1* is the name or number of an existing catalog entry or a group header to be moved.

□ *entry-id-2* is the name or number of an existing catalog entry or a group header. *Entry-id-1* can be placed before or after *entry-id-2*.

□ AFTER | BEFORE specifies whether *entry-id-1* should be moved before or after *entry-id-2*.

Using the MOVE Statement

You can use the MOVE statement to change the order of entries in the input catalog. For example, if you specify the following, the entry named GRAPH1 is moved after the entry named GRAPH2:

```
move graph1 after graph2;
```

To move an entire group, use the name of the group for *entry-id-1*. To move an entry into a group, move the entry after a group header or before or after an entry in the group.

NOBYLINE

Suppresses BY statement information

The NOBYLINE statement specifies that BY statement information should be suppressed. BY statement information appears directly beneath the primary description for the entry. By default, the BY statement information is displayed.

Syntax

The general form of the NOBYLINE statement is

NOBYLINE;

PREVIEW

Previews templates

The PREVIEW statement displays the panel outlines for one or more templates using the current device.

Syntax

The general form of the PREVIEW statement is

PREVIEW *template-entry* $<$ . . . *template-entry-n*$>$ | _ALL_;

☐ *template-entry* is the name of a template entry contained in the current template catalog. You can preview one entry or a list of entries with one PREVIEW statement.

☐ _ALL_ previews all templates in the current template catalog.

Requirements

Use the TC statement to specify the template catalog before using the PREVIEW statement. You can preview any template in the current template catalog.

Using the PREVIEW Statement

When you are previewing a list of templates, press END or ENTER to preview the next template in the list.

If you preview a template that contains panels with no defined color, the procedure uses the first color in the colors list to outline the panels.

The graphics output produced when you preview a template is stored in a catalog named WORK.GTEM, which is deleted at the end of your session.

QUIT

Terminates the procedure

The QUIT statement terminates the GREPLAY procedure. The QUIT statement performs the same function as the END and STOP statements.

Syntax

The general form of the QUIT statement is

QUIT;

REPLAY

Replays graphics entries

The REPLAY statement selects one or more entries for replay from the current input catalog.

Syntax

The general form of the REPLAY statement is

REPLAY *entry-id* < . . . *entry-id-n*> | _FIRST_ | _LAST_ | _ALL_;

PLAY *entry-id* < . . . *entry-id-n*> | _FIRST_ | _LAST_ | _ALL_;

□ *entry-id* is a number or name of a catalog entry containing graphics output or the number or name of a group header in the input catalog. You can submit one or more replay items in one REPLAY statement. A list of replay items can contain both entry numbers and entry names.

□ _ALL_ replays the graphics output from all of the entries in the input catalog.

□ _FIRST_ replays the graphics output stored in the first entry in the input catalog.

□ _LAST_ replays the graphics output stored in the last entry in the input catalog.

Requirements

If any entries specified in a REPLAY statement are not found in the input catalog, PROC GREPLAY issues a message in the SAS log. The procedure continues to replay valid entries.

Using the REPLAY Statement

You can specify both entry names and entry numbers in a single REPLAY statement. The following statement selects the entry named GRAPH and the third entry in the catalog for replay:

```
replay graph 3;
```

An entire group can be replayed by specifying the name or number of the group header in the REPLAY statement.

STOP

Terminates the procedure

The STOP statement terminates the GREPLAY procedure. The STOP statement performs the same function as the QUIT and END statements.

Syntax

The general form of the STOP statement is

STOP;

TC

Assigns the template catalog

The TC statement specifies the template catalog for the GREPLAY procedure. You can change the template catalog without exiting the procedure by using the TC statement.

Syntax

The general form of the TC statement is

TC *template-catalog*;

□ *template-catalog* is the name of a SAS catalog where templates are to be stored or the name of a SAS catalog containing templates.

TCOPY

Copies templates

The TCOPY statement copies templates from another catalog to the template catalog or creates a duplicate copy of a template within the template catalog.

Syntax

The general form of the TCOPY statement is

TCOPY <*catalog.*>*template-name*<.TEMPLATE>;

□ *catalog* is the name of the SAS catalog containing the template to be copied.

□ *template-name* is the name of the template to be copied.

□ .TEMPLATE is the catalog entry type.

The procedure uses a naming convention to prevent duplicate names. See "Duplicate Entry Names" earlier in this chapter for more information.

Requirements

You must assign a template catalog before using the TCOPY statement.

Using the TCOPY Statement

To copy a template from another catalog to the template catalog, specify *catalog* as the catalog from which the template should be copied. For example, if you want to copy NEWFOUR.TEMPLATE from the catalog named ONE.TEMPLT to the catalog named TARGET.TEMPLT, use the following statements:

```
libname target 'SAS-data-library';
libname one 'SAS-data-library';
```

```
proc greplay nofs;
   tc target.templt;
   tcopy one.templt.newfour.template;
quit;
```

To create a duplicate copy of a template, just omit *catalog* from your TCOPY statement. For example, to create a duplicate copy of a template named NEWFOUR within the template catalog, you could use the following statement:

```
tcopy newfour.template;
```

SAS/GRAPH software uses a naming convention to avoid duplicate names. See "Duplicate Entry Names" earlier in this chapter for more information.

TDEF

Defines templates

The TDEF statement defines or modifies templates in the current template catalog. Templates are often used to describe positioning for replaying graphics output from several catalog entries on a single display.

Syntax

The general form of the TDEF statement is

TDEF *template-name* <DES='string'>
        <*panel-definition*> < . . . *panel-definition-n*>;

□ *template-name* is the name of an existing or new template. *Template-name* must be a valid SAS name.

□ *panel-definition* has the following format:

   panel-number/<*options*>

   □ *panel-number* is the number of the panel being defined.

   □ *options* may be one or more of the following:

      CLIP

      COLOR=*border-color*

      COPY=*panel-number*

      DEF

      DELETE

      LLX=*x*

      LLY=*y*

      LRX=*x*

      LRY=*y*

      ROTATE=*degrees*

      SCALEX=*factor*

      SCALEY=*factor*

      ULX=*x*

TDEF

continued

ULY=*y*

URX=*x*

URY=*y*

XLATEX=*distance*

XLATEY=*distance*

TDEF statement options are fully described in "Options" later in this section.

Requirements

You must assign a template catalog before using the TDEF statement. If the template name you specify with the TDEF statement is not in the template catalog, the procedure creates the template. If the template name is already in the template catalog, the procedure modifies or makes additions to that template.

The only required portion of this statement is the template name. However, if you use the TDEF statement and specify only the template name without using any other options, no changes are made to an existing template and no new template is created.

Options

You may use one or more of the following options in the TDEF statement.

CLIP

specifies that any panels behind this panel should be clipped. If clipping is in effect for a panel, only the graphics output to be placed in that panel can appear in the space that the panel occupies unless a previous panel occupies all or part of that space.

COLOR=*border-color*

specifies the color of the panel border. If you omit *border-color*, then no border is displayed around the panel when you replay graphics output in the panel. If you preview a template that contains a panel without a border color, the GREPLAY procedure uses the first color in the colors list as the outline for the border.

COPY=*panel-number*

specifies the number of the panel definition to be copied to this panel.

DEF

specifies a default panel. A default panel has the following characteristics:

Panel Corner	Coordinates
lower left	(0,0)
upper left	(0,100)
upper right	(100,100)
lower right	(100,0)

DELETE
DEL
    deletes the panel.

DES='*string*'
    specifies a string, up to 40 characters long, that appears in the
    Description field of the catalog entry for the template. By default, the
    procedure uses *** new template *** for the description.

LLX=x
    specifies the X coordinate of the lower-left corner of the panel. Units
    for x are percentage of the graphics output area.

LLY=y
    specifies the Y coordinate of the lower-left corner of the panel. Units
    for y are percentage of the graphics output area.

LRX=x
    specifies the X coordinate of the lower-right corner of the panel. Units
    for x are percentage of the graphics output area.

LRY=y
    specifies the Y coordinate of the lower-right corner of the panel. Units
    for y are percentage of the graphics output area.

ROTATE=*degrees*
    specifies the rotation angle for the panel. The coordinates of the panel
    corners are automatically adjusted.

SCALEX=*factor*
    specifies the scale factor for the X coordinates in the panel. This scale
    factor can be used to increase or decrease the size of the panel in the
    X direction or to reverse the X coordinates for the panel.

SCALEY=*factor*
    specifies the scale factor for Y coordinates in the panel. This scale
    factor can be used to increase or decrease the size of the panel in the
    Y direction or to reverse the Y coordinates for the panel.

ULX=x
    specifies the X coordinate of the upper-left corner of the panel. Units
    for x are percentage of the graphics output area.

ULY=y
    specifies the Y coordinate of the upper-left corner of the panel. Units
    for y are percentage of the graphics output area.

URX=x
    specifies the X coordinate of the upper-right corner of the panel. Units
    for x are percentage of the graphics output area.

URY=y
    specifies the Y coordinate of the upper-right corner of the panel. Units
    for y are percentage of the graphics output area.

TDEF

continued

XLATEX=*distance*

specifies the distance to move the X coordinates of the panel. Units for *distance* are percentage of the graphics output area.

XLATEY=*distance*

specifies the distance to move the Y coordinates of the panel. Units for *distance* are percentage of the graphics output area.

Using the TDEF Statement

You can use coordinate values less than 0 and greater than 100 for the LLX=, LLY=, LRX=, LRY=, ULX=, ULY=, URX=, and URY= options. By using values less than 0 and greater than 100, you can zoom in on the graphics output. That is, you can see only that part of the replayed graphics output in the range from 0 to 100 percent of the graphics output area.

The values that you supply for the SCALEX= and SCALEY= options are used to change the size and orientation of the panel. The scale factors are used for the corresponding X and Y coordinates of the panel. For example, if you specify

```
scalex=.5
scaley=2
```

the X coordinates are scaled to half the original size, and the Y coordinates are scaled to twice the original size.

If you supply a scale factor of zero, all of the coordinates are set to the same value. If you use a scale factor of 1, nothing happens. If you use a scale factor greater than 1, the values of the coordinates are increased and hence the size of the panel increases. If you use a scale factor less than 1 but greater than zero, the values of the coordinates are decreased and hence the size of the panel decreases. If you use a negative scale factor, the coordinates are reversed and hence the panel (and any graphics output replayed in the panel) is reversed.

TDELETE

Deletes templates

The TDELETE statement deletes templates from the template catalog.

Note: The GREPLAY procedure does not prompt you to confirm your request to delete templates.

Syntax

The general form of the TDELETE statement is

TDELETE *template-entry* < . . . *template-entry-n*> | _ALL_;

TDEL *template-entry* < . . . *template-entry-n*> | _ALL_;

□ *template-entry* is the name of a template to be deleted from the template catalog. You can submit a single entry or a list of entries in a single TDELETE statement.

□ _ALL_ deletes all templates in the template catalog.

TEMPLATE

Specifies a current template

The TEMPLATE statement assigns a current template to use when replaying graphics output.

Syntax

The general form of the TEMPLATE statement is:

TEMPLATE *template-name*;

□ *template-name* is the name of an existing template to use when replaying graphics output. Use the TREPLAY line-mode statement to replay graphics output in the template.

Requirements

You must assign a template catalog before using this statement. If you specify a template that is not in the current template catalog or if you specify a template before you have assigned a template catalog, the GREPLAY procedure issues an error message.

TREPLAY

Selects entries containing graphics output for replay in a template

The TREPLAY statement selects one or more catalog entries for replay in template panels. When you replay existing graphics output in a template, the GREPLAY procedure creates new graphics output that is stored in the output catalog.

Syntax

The general form of the TREPLAY statement is

TREPLAY *select-pair* $<$ . . . *select-pair-n*$>$;

TPLAY *select-pair* $<$ . . . *select-pair-n*$>$;

□ *select-pair* has the following format:

   panel-number:entry-id

TREPLAY

continued

☐ *panel-number* is the number of the panel in the current template in which to replay the graphics output.

☐ *entry-id* is the name or number of a catalog entry containing the graphics output to be replayed in *panel-number*.

Requirements

You must assign a template catalog and a current template before using the TREPLAY statement.

Using the TREPLAY Statement

You can replay as many entries as you want in a single TREPLAY statement as shown here:

```
treplay 1:plot1 2:plot2 3:chart1;
```

PLOT1 will be placed in panel 1 of the current template, PLOT2 will be placed in panel 2, and CHART1 will be placed in panel 3. You can use entry numbers in place of entry names.

Line-Mode Statement Examples

The following examples illustrate major features of the GREPLAY procedure in line mode.

Creating a Template

This example uses the TDEF line-mode statement to define a template containing four panels of equal size.

The following program statements produce the log output shown in Output 36.2:

```
/* set the graphics environment */
goptions reset=global gunit=pct border
        ftext=swissb htitle=6 htext=3;

/* start the GREPLAY procedure */
proc greplay tc=tempcat
        nofs;

/* define a template */
tdef newfour des='Four squares of equal size'

      /* define panel 1 */
    1/llx=0    lly=0
      ulx=0    uly=50
      urx=50   ury=50
      lrx=50   lry=0
      color=blue
```

```
                    /* define panel 2 */
            2/llx=0    lly=50
              ulx=0    uly=100
              urx=50   ury=100
              lrx=50   lry=50
              color=red

                    /* define panel 3 */
            3/llx=50   lly=50
              ulx=50   uly=100
              urx=100  ury=100
              lrx=100  lry=50
              color=green

                    /* define panel 4 */
            4/llx=50   lly=0
              ulx=50   uly=50
              urx=100  ury=50
              lrx=100  lry=0
              color=lib;

            /* assign current template */
        template newfour;

            /* list contents of current template */
        list template;
    quit;
```

Output 36.2 *Defining a Template (GR36N02)*

```
1          /* set the graphics environment */
2     goptions reset=global gunit=pct border
3              ftext=swissb htitle=6 htext=3;
4
5          /* start the GREPLAY procedure */
6     proc greplay tc=tempcat
7              nofs;
NOTE: Enter greplay commands or statements.
8
9          /* define a template */
10    tdef newfour des='Four squares of equal size'
11
12             /* define panel 1 */
13        1/llx=0    lly=0
14          ulx=0    uly=50
15          urx=50   ury=50
16          lrx=50   lry=0
17          color=blue
18
19             /* define panel 2 */
20        2/llx=0    lly=50
21          ulx=0    uly=100
22          urx=50   ury=100
23          lrx=50   lry=50
24          color=red
25
26             /* define panel 3 */
27        3/llx=50   lly=50
28          ulx=50   uly=100
29          urx=100  ury=100
30          lrx=100  lry=50
31          color=green
32
33             /* define panel 4 */
34        4/llx=50   lly=0
35          ulx=50   uly=50
36          urx=100  ury=50
37          lrx=100  lry=0
38          color=lib;
```

(continued on next page)

```
(continued from previous page)

39
40            /* assign current template */
41       template newfour;
42
43            /* list contents of current template */
44       list template;
NEWFOUR         Four squares of equal size
Pan Clp Color       Ll-x  Ll-y  Ul-x   Ul-y   Ur-x   Ur-y  Lr-x   Lr-y
   1     BLUE        0.0   0.0   0.0    50.0   50.0   50.0  50.0    0.0
   2     RED         0.0  50.0   0.0   100.0   50.0  100.0  50.0   50.0
   3     GREEN      50.0  50.0  50.0   100.0  100.0  100.0 100.0   50.0
   4     LIB        50.0   0.0  50.0    50.0  100.0   50.0 100.0    0.0
45   quit;

   .
   .
   .
```

This example illustrates the following features:

☐ The TC= option in the PROC GREPLAY statement assigns TEMPCAT as the template catalog. Because TEMPCAT is a one-level name, it is a temporary catalog that will be deleted at the end of the session.

☐ The TDEF statement defines a template with four panels.

☐ The TEMPLATE statement assigns the newly defined template, NEWFOUR, as the current template.

☐ The LIST statement lists the panel definitions in the current template.

Creating a Color Map

This example uses the CDEF line-mode statement to define a color map.

The following program statements produce the log output shown in Output 36.3:

```
    /* set the graphics environment */
goptions reset=global gunit=pct border
        ftext=swissb htitle=6 htext=3;

    /* start the GREPLAY procedure */
proc greplay cc=clrmap nofs;

    /* define a color map */
cdef mycolor des='Special Color Map'
       1 / pink  : red
       2 / cyan  : blue
       3 / lig   : green;

    /* specify current color map */
cmap mycolor;

    /* list the contents of the color map */
list cmap;
quit;
```

Output 36.3 *Defining a Color Map (GR36N03)*

```
 1          /* set the graphics environment */
 2       goptions reset=global gunit=pct border
 3               ftext=swissb htitle=6 htext=3;
 4
 5          /* start the GREPLAY procedure */
 6       proc greplay cc=clrmap nofs;
NOTE: Enter greplay commands or statements.
 7
 8             /* define a color map */
 9          cdef mycolor des='Special Color Map'
10             1 / pink  : red
11             2 / cyan  : blue
12             3 / lig   : green;
13
14             /* specify current color map */
15          cmap mycolor;
16
17             /* list the contents of the color map */
18          list cmap;
     MYCOLOR        Special Color Map
          FROM         TO
        1  PINK        RED
        2  CYAN        BLUE
        3  LIG         GREEN
19       quit;



          .
          .
          .
```

This example illustrates the following features:

□ The CC= option in the PROC GREPLAY statement assigns CLRMAP as the color map catalog.

□ The CDEF statement defines a color map named MYCOLOR that contains three color pairs.

□ The LIST statement lists the color values in the current color map.

Copying a Catalog Entry Containing Graphics Output

This example uses the COPY line-mode statement to copy a catalog entry containing graphics output from one catalog to another.

The following program statements produce the log output shown in Output 36.4:

```
    /* set the graphics environment */
    /* suppress the graphics output */
goptions reset=global gunit=pct border
        ftext=swissb htitle=6 htext=3
        nodisplay;


    /* create some graphics output */
proc gslide gout=mycat;
    title 'Graph Number 1';
run;
    title 'Graph Number 2';
run;
    title 'Graph Number 3';
run;
```

```
                         /* start the GREPLAY procedure */
              proc greplay igout=mycat
                         gout=outcat
                         nofs;

                  /* list the contents of MYCAT */
              list igout;

                  /* copy a graph to GOUT catalog */
              copy gslide2;

                  /* change IGOUT to OUTCAT */
              igout outcat;

                  /* list the contents of OUTCAT */
              list igout;
          quit;
```

Output 36.4 *Copying Graphics Output (GR36N04)*

```
1        /* set the graphics environment */
2        /* suppress the graphics output */
3    goptions reset=global gunit=pct border
4           ftext=swissb htitle=6 htext=3
5           nodisplay;
6
7        /* create some graphics output */
8    proc gslide gout=mycat;
9        title 'Graph Number 1';
10   run;

11       title 'Graph Number 2';
12   run;

13       title 'Graph Number 3';
14   run;

15
16       /* start the GREPLAY procedure */

  .
  .
  .


17   proc greplay igout=mycat
18              gout=outcat
19              nofs;
NOTE: Building list of graphs from the catalog.

NOTE: Enter greplay commands or statements.
20
21          /* list the contents of MYCAT */
22       list igout;
NOTE: Graphs on WORK.MYCAT
       NAME           DESCRIPTION
   1   GSLIDE    I    OUTPUT FROM PROC GSLIDE
   2   GSLIDE1   I    OUTPUT FROM PROC GSLIDE
   3   GSLIDE2   I    OUTPUT FROM PROC GSLIDE
23
24          /* copy a graph to GOUT catalog */
25       copy gslide2;
26
27          /* change IGOUT to OUTCAT */
28       igout outcat;
NOTE: Building list of graphs from the catalog.

29
30          /* list the contents of OUTCAT */
31       list igout;
NOTE: Graphs on WORK.OUTCAT
       NAME           DESCRIPTION
   1   GSLIDE2   I    OUTPUT FROM PROC GSLIDE
32   quit;


  .
  .
  .
```

This example illustrates the following feature:

□ The COPY statement copies the catalog entry named GSLIDE2 from the input catalog to the output catalog.

Creating Groups of Entries

This example uses the GROUP line-mode statement to create a group of entries containing graphics output.

The following program statements produce the log output shown in Output 36.5:

```
/* set the graphics environment  */
/* suppress the graphics display */
goptions reset=global gunit=pct border
        ftext=swissb htitle=6 htext=3
        nodisplay;

/* create some graphics output */
proc gslide gout=mycat;
   title 'Graph Number 1';
run;
   title 'Graph Number 2';
run;
   title 'Graph Number 3';
run;

/* start the GREPLAY procedure */
proc greplay igout=mycat nofs;

   /* list the contents of MYCAT */
   /* before creating the group  */
   list igout;

   /* create a group of graphs */
   group gslide2 gslide1;

   /* list the contents of MYCAT */
   /* after creating the group   */
   list igout;
quit;
```

Output 36.5 *Grouping GRSEG Entries (GR36N05)*

```
1      /* set the graphics environment  */
2      /* suppress the graphics display */
3    goptions reset=global gunit=pct border
4            ftext=swissb htitle=6 htext=3
5            nodisplay;
6
7      /* create some graphics output */
8    proc gslide gout=mycat;
9       title 'Graph Number 1';
10   run;

11      title 'Graph Number 2';
12   run;

13      title 'Graph Number 3';
14   run;
```

(continued on next page)

```
(continued from previous page)

15
16          /* start the GREPLAY procedure */

  .
  .
  .

17   proc greplay igout=mycat nofs;
NOTE: Building list of graphs from the catalog.

NOTE: Enter greplay commands or statements.
18
19          /* list the contents of MYCAT */
20          /* before creating the group */
21      list igout;
NOTE: Graphs on WORK.MYCAT
      NAME           DESCRIPTION
  1   GSLIDE      I   OUTPUT FROM PROC GSLIDE
  2   GSLIDE1     I   OUTPUT FROM PROC GSLIDE
  3   GSLIDE2     I   OUTPUT FROM PROC GSLIDE
22
23          /* create a group of graphs */
24      group gslide2 gslide1;
NOTE: Building list of graphs from the catalog.

25
26          /* list the contents of MYCAT */
27          /* after creating the group   */
28      list igout;
NOTE: Graphs on WORK.MYCAT
      NAME           DESCRIPTION
  1   GSLIDE      I   OUTPUT FROM PROC GSLIDE
  2   GROUP          *** new group ***
  3   GSLIDE2     I   OUTPUT FROM PROC GSLIDE
  4   GSLIDE1     I   OUTPUT FROM PROC GSLIDE
39   quit;

  .
  .
  .
```

This example illustrates the following feature:

□ The GROUP statement creates a group containing the catalog entries named GSLIDE2 and GSLIDE1. Note the default name and description used for the group header.

Changing an Entry Description

This example uses the MODIFY line-mode statement to change the Description field for a catalog entry.

The following program statements produce the log output shown in Output 36.6:

```
/* set the graphics environment */
/* suppress the graphics output */
goptions reset=global gunit=pct border
        ftext=swissb htitle=6 htext=3
        nodisplay;


/* create some graphics output */
proc gslide gout=mycat;
    title 'Graph Number 1';
run;
    title 'Graph Number 2';
run;
    title 'Graph Number 3';
run;
```

```
            /* start the GREPLAY procedure */
        proc greplay igout=mycat nofs;

            /* list the contents of MYCAT */
          list igout;

            /* modify a graph description */
          modify gslide1 / des='Graph Number 2';

            /* list the contents of IGOUT catalog */
          list igout;
        quit;
```

Output 36.6 *Modifying an Entry Description (GR36N06)*

```
1        /* set the graphics environment */
2        /* suppress the graphics output */
3     goptions reset=global gunit=pct border
4            ftext=swissb htitle=6 htext=3
5            nodisplay;
6
7        /* create some graphics output */
8     proc gslide gout=mycat;
9        title 'Graph Number 1';
10    run;

11       title 'Graph Number 2';
12    run;

13       title 'Graph Number 3';
14    run;

15
16       /* start the GREPLAY procedure */

   .
   .
   .

17    proc greplay igout=mycat nofs;
NOTE: Building list of graphs from the catalog.

NOTE: Enter greplay commands or statements.
18
19           /* list the contents of MYCAT */
20        list igout;
NOTE: Graphs on WORK.MYCAT
      NAME            DESCRIPTION
   1  GSLIDE     I    OUTPUT FROM PROC GSLIDE
   2  GSLIDE1    I    OUTPUT FROM PROC GSLIDE
   3  GSLIDE2    I    OUTPUT FROM PROC GSLIDE
21
22           /* modify a graph description */
23        modify gslide1 / des='Graph Number 2';
24
25           /* list the contents of IGOUT catalog */
26        list igout;
NOTE: Graphs on WORK.MYCAT
      NAME            DESCRIPTION
   1  GSLIDE     I    OUTPUT FROM PROC GSLIDE
   2  GSLIDE1    I    Graph Number 2
   3  GSLIDE2    I    OUTPUT FROM PROC GSLIDE
27    quit;

   .
   .
   .
```

This example illustrates the following feature:

□ The MODIFY statement changes the Description field for the entry named GSLIDE1.

Replaying Graphics Output in a Template

This example uses the TREPLAY line-mode statement to select three catalog entries containing graphics output for replay in a template.

The following program statements produce the graphics output shown in Output 36.7:

```
                    /* set the graphics environment  */
                    /* suppress the graphics display */
           goptions reset=global gunit=pct border
                    ftext=swissb htitle=8 htext=5
                    nodisplay;

                    /* generate some graphs */
           proc gslide gout=grafcat;
              title 'Graph Number 1';
              footnote j=r 'GR36N07(a)  ';
           run;
              title 'Graph Number 2';
              footnote j=r 'GR36N07(b)  ';
           run;
              title 'Graph Number 3';
              footnote j=r 'GR36N07(c)  ';
           run;

                    /* display the graphics output */
           goptions display;

                    /* start the GREPLAY procedure */
           proc greplay igout=grafcat
                        tc=tempcat
                        nofs;

                 /* define a template */
             tdef newfour des='Four squares of equal size'

                      /* define panel 1 */
                 1/llx=0    lly=0
                   ulx=0    uly=50
                   urx=50   ury=50
                   lrx=50   lry=0
                   color=blue

                      /* define panel 2 */
                 2/llx=0    lly=50
                   ulx=0    uly=100
                   urx=50   ury=100
                   lrx=50   lry=50
                   color=red

                      /* define panel 3 */
                 3/llx=50   lly=50
                   ulx=50   uly=100
                   urx=100  ury=100
                   lrx=100  lry=50
                   color=green
```

```
                              /* define panel 4 */
                    4/llx=50  lly=0
                      ulx=50  uly=50
                      urx=100 ury=50
                      lrx=100 lry=0
                      color=lib;

               /* assign current template */
            template newfour;

               /* replay three graphs into template */
            treplay 1:gslide
                    2:gslide1
                    3:gslide2;
         quit;
```

Output 36.7 *Three Graphs Replayed in a Template (GR36N07)*

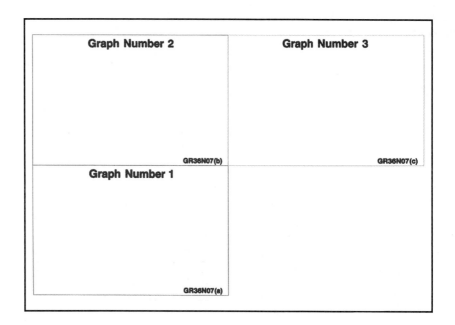

This example illustrates the following features:

□ The IGOUT= option in the PROC GREPLAY statement assigns the catalog named GRAFCAT as the input catalog. The TC= option assigns the catalog named TEMPCAT as the template catalog.

□ The TDEF statement defines a new template, NEWFOUR.

□ The TEMPLATE statement assigns NEWFOUR as the current template.

□ The TREPLAY statement replays three entries using the NEWFOUR template. Since the fourth panel is not listed in the TREPLAY statement, it does not appear in the graphics output.

GREPLAY Procedure Windows

You can use the GREPLAY procedure windows to replay graphics output, manage SAS catalogs, and create new graphics output.

The PROC GREPLAY window is the first window displayed when you invoke the GREPLAY procedure windows and do not use the PRESENTATION option. In addition, you can open these four subsidiary windows:

□ PRESENTATION window

□ DIRECTORY window

□ TEMPLATE DESIGN window

□ COLOR MAPPING window.

Figure 36.1 shows how these windows relate to each other. Each window can be scrolled forward or backward as needed to display additional fields and information. Each of these windows is described in detail following "Window Commands." The windows are discussed in order of appearance.

Figure 36.1 *GREPLAY Procedure Windows*

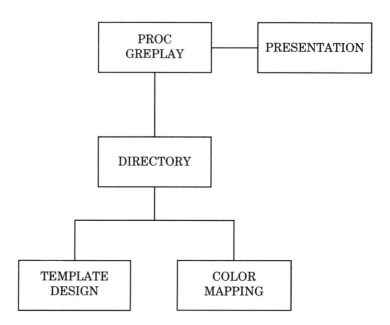

You perform tasks using the GREPLAY procedure windows by entering commands on the command line and entering values in the fields displayed in the windows.

Window Commands

GREPLAY procedure window commands can be entered directly on the command line of a window, selected from the PMENU facility, or programmed as functions keys using the KEYS window of the SAS Display Manager System. (Many function keys are predefined for use in the PROC GREPLAY window.) Table 36.3 describes the commands for the GREPLAY procedure windows. The table names the command, describes the syntax of the command, indicates in which windows the command can be used, and describes the action performed by the command. Many other display manager commands can be used in the window as well.

Table 36.3 *GREPLAY*
Procedure Window Commands

Command	Used in	Description
BACKWARD	all windows	scrolls backward (up) through the information in the current window.
BROWSE *color-map-name*.CMAP	PROC GREPLAY	opens the COLOR MAPPING window to browse color map *color-map-name* in the color map catalog. You must define a color map catalog before using this command.
BROWSE *template-name*.TEMPLATE	PROC GREPLAY	opens the TEMPLATE DESIGN window to browse template *template-name* in the template catalog. You must define a template catalog before using this command.
BROWSE	DIRECTORY	opens the COLOR MAPPING or TEMPLATE DESIGN window to browse a catalog entry in the current (displayed) catalog. See "BROWSE Command" later in this section for additional information and command syntax.
BYLINE	PROC GREPLAY	displays the BY statement information for catalog entries. The BY statement information appears directly beneath the primary description for each entry. The BY statement information is displayed by default.
NOBYLINE	PROC GREPLAY	suppresses the BY statement information for catalog entries. The BY statement information appears directly beneath the primary description for each entry. The BY statement information is displayed by default.
CANCEL	all windows	closes the current window and ignores the changes that were made while the window was open. If you used the SAVE command while the window was open, the CANCEL command closes the current window and ignores changes that were made since the window was last saved.
CC	PROC GREPLAY	opens the DIRECTORY window and displays the entries in the color map catalog. You must assign a color map catalog before using this command.
CLEAR	TEMPLATE DESIGN, COLOR MAPPING	clears all the fields displayed in the current window.
COPY	DIRECTORY	copies a template or color map. See "COPY Command" later in this section for additional information and command syntax.
DOWN	all windows	scrolls forward (down) through the information in the current window
EDIT *color-map-name*.CMAP	PROC GREPLAY	opens the COLOR MAPPING window to edit color map *color-map-name* in the current color map catalog. If *color-map-name* does not exist, the GREPLAY procedure creates the color map. You must assign a color map catalog before using this command.

(*continued*)

Table 36.3 (continued)

Command	Used in	Description
EDIT *template-name*.TEMPLATE	PROC GREPLAY	opens the TEMPLATE DESIGN window to edit template *template-name* in the current template catalog. If *template-name* does not exist, the GREPLAY procedure creates the template. You must assign a template catalog before using this command.
EDIT	DIRECTORY	opens the COLOR MAPPING or TEMPLATE DESIGN window to edit a catalog entry in the current (displayed) catalog. See "EDIT Command" later in this section for additional information and command syntax.
END	all windows	closes the current window and saves all changes made in that window.
END	during graphics output replay	replays the graphics output from the next entry if there are additional entries to replay. Returns to the PROC GREPLAY or PRESENTATION window if there are no additional entries to replay.
FORWARD	all windows	scrolls forward (down) through the information in the current window.
GROUP	PROC GREPLAY	creates groups of entries based on the group identifiers in the SEL field. See "Creating Groups within the List of Entries" later in this chapter for more information.
MODIFY	PROC GREPLAY	enables you to change the contents of the Name and Description fields for an entry. You can also change the BY statement information, if it is displayed for an entry. Change the contents of the fields by typing over the current information.
NOFS	PROC GREPLAY	switches to the GREPLAY procedure in line mode. This enables you to submit additional GOPTIONS, OPTIONS, LIBNAME, and FILENAME statements without exiting the GREPLAY procedure. Once you are in line mode, use the FS line mode statement to return to the PROC GREPLAY window.
PRESENTATION | PRES	PROC GREPLAY	opens the PRESENTATION window. You must assign an input catalog before you can open the PRESENTATION window. See "PRESENTATION Window" later in this chapter for more information on the PRESENTATION window.
PREVIEW	PROC GREPLAY	displays outlines of the panels in the current template assigned in the Template field.
PREVIEW	TEMPLATE DESIGN	displays outlines of the panels in the template defined in the TEMPLATE DESIGN window.
SAVE	TEMPLATE DESIGN, COLOR MAPPING	saves the values in the current window but does not close the current window.
TC	PROC GREPLAY	opens the DIRECTORY window and displays the entries in the template catalog. You must assign a template catalog before using this command.
UP	all windows	scrolls backward (up) through the information in the current window.

BROWSE Command

You can use the BROWSE command in the DIRECTORY window to browse a color map or template. The general form of the BROWSE command used in the DIRECTORY window is

BROWSE *entry-name*<.CMAP | .TEMPLATE>

□ *entry-name* is the name of the color map or template to be browsed.

□ .CMAP | .TEMPLATE is the catalog entry type.

If you open the DIRECTORY window using the CC command in the PROC GREPLAY window and you omit the catalog entry type in the BROWSE command, the catalog entry type defaults to CMAP.

If you open the DIRECTORY window using the TC command in the PROC GREPLAY window and you omit the catalog entry type in the BROWSE command, the catalog entry type defaults to TEMPLATE.

EDIT Command

You can use the EDIT command in the DIRECTORY window to update or create a color map or template. The general form of the EDIT command used in the DIRECTORY window is

EDIT *entry-name*<.CMAP | .TEMPLATE>

□ *entry-name* is the name of the color map or template to be updated or created.

□ .CMAP | .TEMPLATE is the catalog entry type.

If you open the DIRECTORY window using the CC command in the PROC GREPLAY window and you omit the catalog entry type in the EDIT command, the catalog entry type defaults to CMAP.

If you open the DIRECTORY window using the TC command in the PROC GREPLAY window and you omit the catalog entry type, the catalog entry type defaults to TEMPLATE.

COPY Command

You can use the COPY command in the DIRECTORY window to copy a color map or template from one catalog to another. The general form of the COPY command used in the DIRECTORY window is

COPY <*catalog-1.*>*entry-name-1*<.CMAP | .TEMPLATE>
      <<*catalog-2.*>*entry-name-2*<.CMAP | .TEMPLATE>>

□ *catalog-1* is the name of the catalog to be copied from.

□ *catalog-2* is the name of the catalog to be copied to. It must be the current (displayed) catalog.

□ *entry-name-1* is the name of the entry to be copied.

□ *entry-name-2* is the name of the entry to be copied to.

□ .CMAP | .TEMPLATE is the catalog entry type. *Entry-name-1* and *entry-name-2* must have the same catalog entry type. If you opened the DIRECTORY window using the CC command, the catalog entry type defaults to CMAP. If you opened the DIRECTORY window using the TC command, the catalog entry type defaults to TEMPLATE.

The COPY command copies *entry-name-1* to *entry-name-2*. If you omit *catalog-1*, you must omit *catalog-2*, and *entry-name-1* is copied into *entry-name-2* in the current (displayed) catalog. If you omit *entry-name-2*, you must specify *catalog-1*, and *catalog-1* cannot be the current catalog.

PROC GREPLAY Window

The PROC GREPLAY window is the first window to appear when you submit the PROC GREPLAY statement on a full-screen device without the PRESENTATION or NOFS option. This window can be used for both replaying graphics output and managing catalog entries containing graphics output. You can perform the following replay tasks using the PROC GREPLAY window:

□ select single catalog entries for replay

□ select one or more entries for replay in a template

□ select a group of entries for replay

□ select several entries to replay in sequence.

In addition, you can perform the following catalog management tasks using the PROC GREPLAY window:

□ copy catalog entries from the input catalog to the output catalog

□ change the order of the catalog entries in the input catalog

□ delete unneeded catalog entries from the input catalog

□ modify the names and descriptions of catalog entries in the input catalog

□ create groups of related catalog entries.

Display 36.1 shows the PROC GREPLAY window.

Display 36.1 PROC GREPLAY *Window*

```
┌PROC GREPLAY─────────────────────────────────────────────────────┐
│ Command ===>                                                     │
│                                                                  │
│  IGOUT: SCREEN.GRAPHS      GOUT: _____   Device: IBM3179 │
│  TC:    _____      Template: _____     Scroll: PAGE    │
│  CC:    _____      Cmap: _____                         │
│                                                                  │
│                                                                  │
│  Sel  Name      Type  Description                   Created      │
│                                                                  │
│  ____  GCHART    I    VBAR CHART OF BRANCH           11/30/89     │
│  ____  GCHART1   I    VBAR CHART OF AGENT            11/30/89     │
│  ____  GCHART2   I    VBAR CHART OF SALES            11/30/89     │
│  ____  GCHART3   I    VBAR CHART OF COST             11/30/89     │
│  ____  GCHART4   I    VBAR CHART OF RETURN           11/30/89     │
│  ____  GCHART5   I    VBAR CHART OF QUAN             11/30/89     │
│  ____  GCHART6   I    VBAR CHART OF STATE            11/30/89     │
│  ____  GCHART7   I    VBAR CHART OF STATENM          11/30/89     │
│  ____  GPLOT     I    PLOT OF HEIGHT * WEIGHT        11/30/89     │
│  ____  GPLOT1    I    PLOT OF SALES * COST           11/30/89     │
│  ____  GPLOT2    I    PLOT OF SALES * QUAN           11/30/89     │
│  ____  GPLOT3    I    PLOT OF COST * RETURN          11/30/89     │
│                                                                  │
└──────────────────────────────────────────────────────────R──────┘
```

Table 36.4 lists the definitions of the fields in the PROC GREPLAY window.

Table 36.4 *PROC GREPLAY*
Window Fields

Field	Equivalent Line-Mode Statement	Valid Values	Description
IGOUT	IGOUT	SAS catalog	name of the input catalog containing graphics output to be replayed.
GOUT	GOUT	SAS catalog	name of the output catalog to which entries from the input catalog can be copied or in which new graphics output produced by the GREPLAY procedure is stored. If you do not assign an output catalog, graphics output is automatically written to the temporary catalog, WORK.GSEG.
TC	TC	SAS catalog	name of the template catalog. When this field is completed, you can use the TC command to open the DIRECTORY window and display the contents of the template catalog.
Template	TEMPLATE	template entry in template catalog	name of the current template. The current template must be a template contained in the template catalog. You can replay graphics output into the current template.
CC	CC	SAS catalog	name of the color map catalog. When this field is completed, you can use the CC command to open the DIRECTORY window and display the contents of the color map catalog.
Cmap	CMAP	color map entry in color map catalog	name of the current color map. The current color map must be a color map contained in the color map catalog. The current color map is used to remap colors when you replay graphics output.
Device	DEVICE	SAS/GRAPH device entry	name of the device driver used to replay the graphics output.
Scroll	none	PAGE, MAX, HALF, *n*	current scroll value. *n* specifies the number of lines to scroll. The default scroll value is PAGE.
Sel	none	selection field commands	selection field command or letters and numbers for grouping the entries in a catalog. See "Selection Field Commands" later in this chapter for additional information on selection field commands. See "Creating Groups within the List of Entries" later in this chapter for additional information on grouping entries in a catalog.
Name	none		eight-character name for an entry. The name displayed can be □ the one specified with the NAME= option in the PROC step that created the graphics output □ the default name provided by the procedure that produced the graphics output □ a name that has been changed with the MODIFY command or the MODIFY line-mode statement. Use the MODIFY command to change the value of the Name field.
Type	none	protected	type of graphics output, either dependent (D) or independent (I). Although either type of graphics output can be replayed with PROC GREPLAY, only independent graphics output can be replayed using the template facility. For more information on dependent and independent graphics output, see Chapter 3, "Graphics Output."

(continued)

Table 36.4 (continued)

Field	Equivalent Line-Mode Statement	Valid Values	Description
Description	none		forty-character description of the entry. The description displayed can be □ the one specified with the DESCRIPTION= option in the PROC step that created the graphics output □ the default description provided by the procedure that produced the graphics output □ a description that has been changed with the MODIFY command or the MODIFY line-mode statement. Use the MODIFY command to change the value of the Description field. If present, BY statement information is displayed directly beneath the primary description for each entry.
Updated	none	protected	date when the graphics output was created.

You do not need to complete all of the PROC GREPLAY window fields in order to replay graphics output. See "Using the PROC GREPLAY Window" later in this chapter for information on using the PROC GREPLAY window.

Selection Field Commands

The commands in Table 36.5 can be used in the Sel field of the PROC GREPLAY window. You can place commands in the Sel fields for several entries at the same time.

Table 36.5 Selection Field Commands in the PROC GREPLAY Window

Command	Description
A	places the entry marked with the M selection field command after the selected entry.
B	places the entry marked with the M selection field command before the selected entry.
C	copies an entry to the output catalog.
DEL	deletes the selected entry from the input catalog. **Note:** There is no way to restore a catalog entry once it has been deleted.
M	moves the selected entry to the location specified by the A or B selection field command.
n	replays the entry in template panel n in the current template. You must assign a current template before specifying a panel number.
S	selects the entry for replay.
Sn	selects an entry or entries for replay. n specifies the sequence of replay, where the lowest value of n is replayed first, the second lowest value is replayed second, and so on.

PRESENTATION Window

Once you have created and organized your catalog, you may want to use the PRESENTATION window in an application for replaying graphics output. The PRESENTATION window enables you to replay graphics output while preventing you from deleting entries or changing templates and color maps. The PRESENTATION window is a modified version of the PROC GREPLAY window and contains only the Select, Description, and Scroll fields. To open the PRESENTATION window, do one of the following:

□ Enter the name of a catalog in the IGOUT field in the PROC GREPLAY window, and issue the PRES command.

□ Include the PRESENTATION option and the IGOUT= option in the PROC GREPLAY statement when you invoke the procedure.

Display 36.2 shows an example of a PRESENTATION window.

Display 36.2 PRESENTATION
Window

```
┌PROC GREPLAY──────────────────────────────────────────────────────┐
┌PROC GREPLAY: PRESENTATION────────────────────────────────────────┐
│ Command ===>                                                      │
│                                                                   │
│                                                                   │
│    Select        Description                       Scroll: PAGE   │
│                                                                   │
│     ────         VBAR CHART OF BRANCH                             │
│     ────         VBAR CHART OF AGENT                              │
│     ────         VBAR CHART OF SALES                              │
│     ────         VBAR CHART OF COST                               │
│     ────         VBAR CHART OF RETURN                             │
│     ────         VBAR CHART OF QUAN                               │
│     ────         VBAR CHART OF STATE                              │
│     ────         VBAR CHART OF STATENM                            │
│     ────         PLOT OF HEIGHT * WEIGHT                          │
│     ────         PLOT OF SALES * COST                             │
│     ────         PLOT OF SALES * QUAN                             │
│     ────         PLOT OF COST * RETURN                            │
│                                                                   │
│                                                                   │
│                                                                   │
│                                                                 R─┘
```

Table 36.6 lists the definitions of the fields in the PRESENTATION window.

Table 36.6 *PRESENTATION*
Window Fields

Field	Valid Values	Description
Select	S	selects a catalog entry for replay.
	S*n*	selects an entry or entries for replay. *n* specifies the sequence of replay, where the lowest value of *n* is replayed first, the second lowest value is replayed second, and so on.
Description	protected	is a 40-character description of the entry. The description displayed can be □ the one specified with the DESCRIPTION= option in the PROC step that created the graphics output □ the default description provided by the procedure that produced the graphics output □ a description that has been edited with the MODIFY command in the PROC GREPLAY window.
Scroll	PAGE, MAX, HALF, *n*	displays the current scroll value. *n* is a number that specifies the number of lines to scroll. The default scroll value is PAGE. You can change the current value in the Scroll field by typing over it.

DIRECTORY Window

The DIRECTORY window lists the entries, including templates and color maps, in a SAS catalog. This can be either the template or color map catalog that you assigned. A SAS catalog can contain entries of any catalog entry type, including TEMPLATE (templates), CMAP (color maps), and GRSEG (graphics output).

To open the DIRECTORY window, specify a template catalog and issue the TC command in the PROC GREPLAY window or specify a color map catalog and issue the CC command in the PROC GREPLAY window.

Display 36.3 shows an example of the DIRECTORY window.

Display 36.3 *DIRECTORY*
Window

```
┌GREPLAY: DIRECTORY SASHELP.TEMPLT (B)──────────────────────────┐
│ Command ===>                                                  │
│                                                               │
│     Name    Type      Description                    Updated  │
│                                                               │
│  _  H2      TEMPLATE 1 BOX LEFT, 1 BOX RIGHT           11/27/89│
│  _  H2S     TEMPLATE 1 BOX LEFT, 1 BOX RIGHT (WITH SPACE) 11/27/89│
│  _  H3      TEMPLATE 3 BOXES ACROSS (HORIZONTALLY)     11/27/89│
│  _  H3S     TEMPLATE 3 BOXES ACROSS (WITH SPACE)       11/27/89│
│  _  H4      TEMPLATE 4 BOXES ACROSS (HORIZONTALLY)     11/27/89│
│  _  H4S     TEMPLATE 4 BOXES ACROSS (WITH SPACE)       11/27/89│
│  _  L1R2    TEMPLATE 1 BOX LEFT, 2 BOXES RIGHT         11/27/89│
│  _  L1R2S   TEMPLATE 1 BOX LEFT, 2 BOXES RIGHT (WITH SPACE) 11/27/89│
│  _  L2R1    TEMPLATE 2 BOXES LEFT, 1 BOX RIGHT         11/27/89│
│  _  L2R1S   TEMPLATE 2 BOXES LEFT, 1 BOX RIGHT (WITH SPACE) 11/27/89│
│  _  L2R2    TEMPLATE 2 BOXES LEFT, 2 BOXES RIGHT       11/27/89│
│  _  L2R2S   TEMPLATE 2 BOXES LEFT, 2 BOXES RIGHT (WITH SPACE) 11/27/89│
│  _  U1D2    TEMPLATE 1 BOX UP, 2 BOXES DOWN            11/27/89│
│  _  U1D2S   TEMPLATE 1 BOX UP, 2 BOXES DOWN (WITH SPACE) 11/27/89│
│  _  U2D1    TEMPLATE 2 BOXES UP, 1 BOX DOWN            11/27/89│
│  _  U2D1S   TEMPLATE 2 BOXES UP, 1 BOX DOWN (WITH SPACE) 11/27/89│
│  _  V2      TEMPLATE 1 BOX UP, 1 BOX DOWN              11/27/89│
│  _  V2S     TEMPLATE 1 BOX UP, 1 BOX DOWN (WITH SPACE) 11/27/89│
└────────────────────────────────────────────────────────────R─┘
```

The DIRECTORY window lists the names (up to eight characters long) of the catalog entries, gives a brief description (up to 40 characters long) of each, and indicates the date on which each entry was created or last changed. Although all catalog entry types are displayed in the DIRECTORY window, you can manage only entries of type CMAP or TEMPLATE from this window.

Table 36.7 lists the definitions of the fields in the DIRECTORY window.

Table 36.7 *DIRECTORY Window Fields*

Field	Description
Name	eight-character name for a template or color map. Use the R selection field command to change the value of the Name field.
Type	type of catalog entry.
Description	forty-character description of the catalog entry. The description displayed can be □ the default description provided by the procedure that created the entry □ a description that has been edited with the MODIFY command in the PROC GREPLAY window or entered in the TEMPLATE DESIGN or COLOR MAP window. Use the R selection field command to change the value of the Description field.
Updated	date when the entry was created or last modified. An entry is modified any time you make and save changes to the entry. You cannot change the value of this field.

Selection Field Commands

The commands in Table 36.8 can be used in the single-character selection field of the DIRECTORY window.

Table 36.8 *Selection Field Commands in the DIRECTORY Window*

Command	Description
X, E, S	edits the template or color map stored in the catalog entry
B	browses the template or color map stored in the catalog entry
R	enables you to change the name and description of an entry
D	deletes the catalog entry containing a template or color map. The procedure prompts you to verify the delete before deleting the entry.

TEMPLATE DESIGN Window

The TEMPLATE DESIGN window lets you design templates for presenting graphics output. A template consists of one or more panels. You design a template by

□ specifying the coordinates of its panels

□ determining the order in which panels are filled.

Once you enter coordinates for a panel, you can alter them easily by using the Scale, Xlate (translate), and Rotate utility fields. These utility fields recalculate coordinate values automatically.

To open the TEMPLATE DESIGN window, place an S beside the name of an existing template in the DIRECTORY window, or enter the following command on the command line of the DIRECTORY window:

edit *template-name*.template

When you press ENTER, the TEMPLATE DESIGN window is displayed as shown in Display 36.4.

You also can open the TEMPLATE DESIGN window from the PROC GREPLAY window by entering the name of the template catalog in the TC field and entering the following command on the command line of the PROC GREPLAY window:

edit *template-name*.template

Display 36.4 shows an example of the TEMPLATE DESIGN window.

Display 36.4 *TEMPLATE DESIGN Window*

```
┌GREPLAY: DIRECTORY SASHELP.TEMPLT (B)────────────────────────────
 Command ===>

    Name      Type     Description                          Updated

┌PROC GREPLAY: TEMPLATE DESIGN──────────────────────────────────
 Command ===>

   TEMPLATE: H4                                TC: SASHELP.TEMPLT
   DESC: 4 BOXES ACROSS (HORIZONTALLY)         Scroll: PAGE
                                               Device: IBM3179
 Panel Clp Color      L-left U-left U-right L-right  Scale  Xlate  Rotat

    1   _  WHITE   X:   0.0    0.0   25.0   25.0   X: _____ _____  ___
                   Y:   0.0  100.0  100.0    0.0   Y: _____ _____

    2   _  WHITE   X:  25.0   25.0   50.0   50.0   X: _____ _____  ___
                   Y:   0.0  100.0  100.0    0.0   Y: _____ _____

    3   _  WHITE   X:  50.0   50.0   75.0   75.0   X: _____ _____  ___
                   Y:   0.0  100.0  100.0    0.0   Y: _____ _____

                                                                      ─R
```

Table 36.9 defines the fields in the TEMPLATE DESIGN window.

Table 36.9 *TEMPLATE DESIGN Window Fields*

Field	Equivalent Line-Mode Statement and Options	Description
TEMPLATE	none	names the template being created or modified in the TEMPLATE DESIGN window. This field cannot be modified in this window.
DESC	TDEF DES= option	describes the template. This field can contain up to 40 characters, including blank spaces.
TC	TC	gives the name of the catalog in which the displayed template is stored. This field cannot be modified from this window.
Scroll	none	displays the scroll value. Valid values are PAGE, MAX, HALF, or a number specifying the number of lines to scroll. The default value is PAGE.

(continued)

Table 36.9 (continued)

Field	Equivalent Line-Mode Statement and Options	Description
Device	DEVICE	displays the name of the current device driver. You can change the current device driver by typing over this field.
Panel	TDEF *panel-number*	specifies the number of the panel being defined. Possible values are 0 through 999. Panels are drawn in order according to the number you specify in the Panel field.
Clp	TDEF CLIP option	specifies whether or not clipping is in effect for a panel. For more information on clipping, see "Designing Your Template" later in this chapter.
Color	TDEF COLOR= option	specifies the color used to draw the border around the panel. You can specify any valid SAS color in this field. If you leave this field blank, a border is not drawn around the graphics output you replay in the template. If you preview a template that contains a panel without a border color, the procedure uses the first color in the colors list for the panel outline.
L-left	TDEF LLX= and LLY= options	specifies the X and Y coordinates for the lower-left corner of the panel. Units are percentage of the graphics output area.
U-left	TDEF ULX= and ULY= options	specifies the X and Y coordinates for the upper-left corner of the panel. Units are percentage of the graphics output area.
U-right	TDEF URX= and URY= options	specifies the X and Y coordinates for the upper-right corner of the panel. Units are percentage of the graphics output area.
L-right	TDEF LRX= and LRY= options	specifies the X and Y coordinates for the lower-right corner of the panel. Units are percentage of the graphics output area.
Scale	TDEF SCALEX= and SCALEY= options	specifies a factor used to scale the length of the panel's edges. See "Scaling Your Template Panels" later in this chapter for additional information. You do not have to specify the same Scale value for X and Y.
Xlate	TDEF XLATEX= and XLATEY= options	specifies a distance to move the panel up, down, left, or right in the window. The values you specify for X and Y are added to the values that define the X and Y coordinates for the panel. See "Moving Your Template Panels" later in this chapter for more information You do not have to specify the same Xlate value for X and Y.
Rotate	TDEF ROTATE= option	specifies the angle, in degrees, at which the panel should be rotated. If you enter a value for the Rotate field and press ENTER, the coordinates are recalculated. Rotating a panel causes the graphics output displayed in it to be rotated. Valid values for the Rotate field are −99 to 999.

Panel Field Commands

The commands in Table 36.10 can be used in the panel field in the TEMPLATE DESIGN window.

Table 36.10 *Panel Field Commands in the TEMPLATE DESIGN Window*

Command	Description
C	copies a panel definition to the position indicated by the O panel field command.
D	deletes the panel from the template.
INI	initializes a panel to the size of the window. An initialized window has the following panel coordinates: lower-left corner at (0,0) upper-left corner at (0,100) upper-right corner at (100,100) lower-right corner at (100,0) You can change the size and location of the initialized panel using the Scale and Xlate fields.
O	marks the destination of a panel being copied using the C panel field command.

Sample Templates

Several sample templates are provided with SAS/GRAPH software for use with the template facility of PROC GREPLAY. To view the templates, assign SASHELP.TEMPLT as the template catalog and use the TC window command to open the DIRECTORY window for the catalog.

You can use the sample templates for replaying graphics output by assigning one as the current template.

COLOR MAPPING Window

A color map is a list that contains up to 256 pairs of colors used to map colors in existing graphics output to new colors when replaying the graphics output. The From color indicates the color that should be changed, and the To color indicates to which color the old color should be changed. When you replay graphics output contained in a catalog entry and assign a current color map, any color in the graphics output that appears in the From column of the color map is mapped to the corresponding color in the To column of the color map. Using a color map does not change the contents of the replayed graphics output and does not produce new graphics output unless a template is also used.

To open the COLOR MAPPING window, place an S beside the name of an existing color map in the DIRECTORY window, or enter the following command on the command line of the DIRECTORY window:

    edit *color-map-name*.cmap

When you press ENTER, the COLOR MAPPING window is displayed as shown in Display 36.5.

You also can open the COLOR MAPPING window from the PROC GREPLAY window by entering the name of the color map catalog in the CC field and entering the following command on the command line of the PROC GREPLAY window:

    edit *color-map-name*.CMAP

Display 36.5 shows an example of the COLOR MAPPING window.

Display 36.5 COLOR
MAPPING Window

```
┌GREPLAY: DIRECTORY SCREEN.COLORS (E)────────────────────────────────┐
│ Command ===>                                                        │
│                                                                     │
│     Name     Type    Description                       Updated      │
│                                                                     │
┌PROC GREPLAY: COLOR MAPPING─────────────────────────────────────────┐
│  Command ===>                                                       │
│                                                                     │
│    CMAP: HP                                 CC: SCREEN.COLORS        │
│    DESC: COLOR MAP FOR C57 PRINTER          Scroll: PAGE            │
│                                                                     │
│                        From            To                           │
│                                                                     │
│                        BLUE            BLACK                         │
│                        RED             BLACK                         │
│                        GREEN           BLACK                         │
│                        WHITE           BLACK                         │
│                        ─────           ─────                         │
│                        ─────           ─────                         │
│                        ─────           ─────                         │
│                        ─────           ─────                         │
│                        ─────           ─────                         │
│                        ─────           ─────                       R─┘
└─────────────────────────────────────────────────────────────────────┘
```

Table 36.11 defines the fields in the COLOR MAPPING window.

Table 36.11 COLOR
MAPPING Window Fields

Field	Equivalent Line-Mode Statement	Description
CMAP	none	names the color map being created or modified. This field cannot be modified from this window.
DESC	CDEF DES= option	describes the template. This field can contain up to forty characters, including blank spaces.
CC	CC	gives the name of the color map catalog in which this color map is stored. This field cannot be modified from this window.
Scroll	none	displays the scroll value. Valid values are PAGE, MAX, HALF, or a number specifying the number of lines to scroll. The default value is PAGE.
From	CDEF *from-color*	identifies the color in the replayed graphics output that should be changed.
To	CDEF *to-color*	identifies the color that the From color should be changed to during replay.

Using the GREPLAY Procedure Windows

The following sections discuss how to use the GREPLAY procedure windows.

Using the PROC GREPLAY Window

The GREPLAY procedure provides an easy way to replay graphics output from a catalog and manage catalogs. You can perform the following tasks from the PROC GREPLAY window:

□ list the entries in the input catalog that contain graphics output

□ select entries containing graphics output for replay

□ modify catalog entries by editing the Name and Description fields, as well as BY statement information

□ group catalog entries in the input catalog

□ reorder the list of entries in the input catalog

□ copy entries from the input catalog to the output catalog

□ delete entries in the input catalog

□ suppress or display BY statement information

□ open other GREPLAY procedure windows.

These tasks are described in more detail in the following sections.

Listing the Catalog Entries Containing Graphics Output

To display a list of the entries in a SAS catalog that contain graphics output using the GREPLAY procedure, you must assign an input catalog. You can assign an input catalog by doing either of the following:

□ Use the IGOUT= option in the PROC GREPLAY statement to name the SAS catalog containing entries with graphics output. When you submit the PROC GREPLAY statement, the PROC GREPLAY window displays the list of entries in the input catalog.

□ If the PROC GREPLAY window is already open, use the IGOUT field to name the input catalog containing your graphics output. When you press ENTER, the PROC GREPLAY window displays a list of the entries in the input catalog that contain graphics output.

If your list of entries is too long to fit in one window, use the FORWARD or DOWN command or use the FORWARD key to scroll the list forward. To scroll backward toward the beginning of the list of entries, use the BACKWARD or UP command or use the BACKWARD key.

You can change the input catalog without exiting the GREPLAY procedure by typing over the IGOUT field in the PROC GREPLAY window.

Replaying the Entries in the List

To replay any of the entries in the input catalog that contain graphics output, place an S in the Sel field next to the entry containing the graphics output you want to replay. When you press ENTER, the graphics output in the entry you selected is displayed using the current device driver. If you want to replay more than one entry, place an S beside each entry you want to replay.

To select the order of replay for several entries, you can enter S*n* in the Sel field next to the entries, where *n* is a one- or two-digit number that indicates the order of replay. When you press ENTER, the graphics output stored in the first entry is shown. You can cycle through the remaining entries and return to the PROC GREPLAY window. Display 36.6 illustrates the use. of the S*n* selection field command. The entries are replayed in the following order:

1. GCHART2

2. GCHART3

3. GCHART1

Display 36.6 *Specifying a Replay Order*

```
┌PROC GREPLAY─────────────────────────────────────────────────────┐
│ Command ===>                                                     │
│                                                                  │
│ IGOUT: SCREEN.GRAPHS      GOUT: _____   Device: IBM3179│
│ TC:     _____   Template: _____      Scroll: PAGE   │
│ CC:     _____   Cmap: _____                         │
│                                                                  │
│                                                                  │
│ Sel   Name     Type   Description                       Updated  │
│                                                                  │
│ ___   GCHART    I     VBAR CHART OF BRANCH              11/30/89  │
│ s3_   GCHART1   I     VBAR CHART OF AGENT               11/30/89  │
│ s1_   GCHART2   I     VBAR CHART OF SALES               11/30/89  │
│ s2_   GCHART3   I     VBAR CHART OF COST                11/30/89  │
│ ___   GCHART4   I     VBAR CHART OF RETURN              11/30/89  │
│ ___   GCHART5   I     VBAR CHART OF QUAN                11/30/89  │
│ ___   GCHART6   I     VBAR CHART OF STATE               11/30/89  │
│ ___   GCHART7   I     VBAR CHART OF STATENM             11/30/89  │
│ ___   GPLOT     I     PLOT OF HEIGHT * WEIGHT           11/30/89  │
│ ___   GPLOT1    I     PLOT OF SALES * COST              11/30/89  │
│ ___   GPLOT2    I     PLOT OF SALES * QUAN              11/30/89  │
│ ___   GPLOT3    I     PLOT OF COST * RETURN             11/30/89  │
│                                                                  │
│                                                                  │
└────────────────────────────────────────────────────────────R────┘
```

You can use the GWAIT= graphics option to display graphics output in a series without pressing ENTER between graphs. See Chapter 5, "Graphics Options and Device Parameters Dictionary," for more information on the GWAIT= graphics option.

You can select a group of entries for replay by entering an S in the Sel field beside the group name. When you press ENTER, the graphics output from the first entry in the group you selected is displayed. You can cycle through the rest of the entries in the group and return to the PROC GREPLAY window.

Modifying the List of Entries

To change the names, descriptions, and BY statement information of entries or group headers, issue the MODIFY command on the command line in the PROC GREPLAY window. The Values in the Name and Description fields and the BY statement information are highlighted and you can modify these fields by typing new information directly over the current information. When you have entered all your changes, issue the MODIFY command again. You also can replay, group, and delete entries while you are in modify mode.

Creating Groups within the List of Entries

You may find it useful to arrange the entries in your catalog in groups that can be replayed later. To create groups of entries, issue the GROUP command on the command line. The following prompt appears:

PRESS ENTER TO PROCESS SELECTIONS OR RESUBMIT GROUP TO CANCEL

To define the groups, enter letters, numbers, or a combination of both in the Sel field beside the entries you would like to group.

For example, to create one group that contains the entries named GPLOT1, GCHART1, and GCHART5 and another group that contains the entries named GPLOT2, GPLOT3, and GCHART6, you can use the letter A to denote the first group and the letter B to denote the second group. Leave the Sel field blank beside the entries you do not want to include in the group.

Display 36.7 shows the PROC GREPLAY window after issuing the GROUP command with the grouping designations in the Sel fields. Display 36.8 shows the entries placed in their new groups.

Display 36.7 *Creating a Group of Entries*

```
┌PROC GREPLAY──────────────────────────────────────────────────────────┐
│ Command ===>                                                          │
│                                                                       │
│ IGOUT: SCREEN.GRAPHS        GOUT: _____    Device: IBM3179 │
│ TC:    _____     Template: _____        Scroll: PAGE    │
│ CC:    _____     Cmap:   _____                          │
│                                                                       │
│ PRESS ENTER TO PROCESS SELECTIONS OR RESUBMIT GROUP TO CANCEL.        │
│ Sel  Name      Type   Description                       Updated       │
│                                                                       │
│ ____ GCHART    I     VBAR CHART OF BRANCH              11/30/89       │
│ a___ GCHART1   I     VBAR CHART OF AGENT               11/30/89       │
│ a___ GCHART5   I     VBAR CHART OF QUAN                11/30/89       │
│ b___ GCHART6   I     VBAR CHART OF STATE               11/30/89       │
│ ____ GPLOT     I     PLOT OF HEIGHT * WEIGHT           11/30/89       │
│ a___ GPLOT1    I     PLOT OF SALES * COST              11/30/89       │
│ b___ GPLOT2    I     PLOT OF SALES * QUAN              11/30/89       │
│ b___ GPLOT3    I     PLOT OF COST * RETURN             11/30/89       │
│                                                                       │
│                                                                       │
│                                                                       │
│                                                                     R─┘
```

Display 36.8 *PROC GREPLAY Window after Creating Groups*

```
┌PROC GREPLAY──────────────────────────────────────────────────────────┐
│ Command ===>                                                          │
│                                                                       │
│ IGOUT: SCREEN.GRAPHS        GOUT: _____    Device: IBM3179 │
│ TC:    _____     Template: _____        Scroll: PAGE    │
│ CC:    _____     Cmap:   _____                          │
│                                                                       │
│                                                                       │
│ Sel  Name      Type   Description                       Updated       │
│                                                                       │
│ ____ GCHART    I     VBAR CHART OF BRANCH              11/30/89       │
│ ____ GPLOT     I     PLOT OF HEIGHT * WEIGHT           11/30/89       │
│ ...                                                                   │
│ ____ GROUP           *** new group ***                11/30/89       │
│ ____ GCHART1   I     VBAR CHART OF AGENT               11/30/89       │
│ ____ GCHART5   I     VBAR CHART OF QUAN                11/30/89       │
│ ____ GPLOT1    I     PLOT OF SALES * COST              11/30/89       │
│ ...                                                                   │
│ ____ GROUP1          *** new group ***                11/30/89       │
│ ____ GCHART6   I     VBAR CHART OF STATE               11/30/89       │
│ ____ GPLOT2    I     PLOT OF SALES * QUAN              11/30/89       │
│ ____ GPLOT3    I     PLOT OF COST * RETURN             11/30/89       │
│                                                                     R─┘
```

Note that the groups use the default group header name and description. You can change the default name and description of a group by using the MODIFY command. See "Modifying the List of Entries" earlier in this section.

Moving Individual Entries

To move an entry, type M in the Sel field of the entry to be moved. Type A in the Sel field of the entry or group header the moved entry should be placed after or type B in the Sel field of the entry or group header the moved entry should be placed before. If an individual entry is placed before or after an entry that is in a group or after a group header, then the moved entry is added to that group. If an individual entry is placed before a group header, the entry is not included in the group.

Display 36.9 shows how you could move the entry named GCHART5 after the entry named GPLOT1.

Display 36.9 *Moving an Entry*

```
┌PROC GREPLAY────────────────────────────────────────────────────────┐
│  Command ===>                                                        │
│                                                                      │
│    IGOUT: SCREEN.GRAPHS         GOUT: _____      Device: IBM3179 │
│    TC:    _____        Template: _____      Scroll: PAGE  │
│    CC:    _____        Cmap: _____                        │
│                                                                      │
│                                                                      │
│    Sel   Name      Type   Description                    Updated     │
│                                                                      │
│    ___   GCHART     I     VBAR CHART OF BRANCH           11/30/89    │
│    ___   GCHART1    I     VBAR CHART OF AGENT            11/30/89    │
│    m__   GCHART5    I     VBAR CHART OF QUAN             11/30/89    │
│    ___   GCHART6    I     VBAR CHART OF STATE            11/30/89    │
│    ___   GPLOT      I     PLOT OF HEIGHT * WEIGHT        11/30/89    │
│    a__   GPLOT1     I     PLOT OF SALES * COST           11/30/89    │
│    ___   GPLOT2     I     PLOT OF SALES * QUAN           11/30/89    │
│    ___   GPLOT3     I     PLOT OF COST * RETURN          11/30/89    │
│                                                                      │
│                                                                      │
│                                                                      │
│                                                                      │
│                                                                    R─┘
```

Moving Groups of Entries

To move a group of entries, type M in the Sel field of the group header. Type A in the Sel field of the entry or group header the moved group should be placed after or type B in the Sel field of the entry or group header the moved group should be placed before. If a group header is placed before or after an individual entry, the whole group moves to that position. If a group header is placed before or after an entry in another group or after another group header, the entries in the moved group are added to the other group and the group header for the moved group is deleted.

Copying Entries between SAS Catalogs

To copy an entry or group of entries from the input catalog to the output catalog, place a C in the Sel field next to the entry, entries, or group of entries you want to copy, and press ENTER. When you copy a group, all of the entries within that group are copied to the new catalog. This process also copies the group header so that the group retains its integrity in the new catalog.

Note: You cannot use the C selection field command to create a duplicate of an entry containing graphics output in the same catalog. You can have only one copy of an entry containing graphics output in a catalog.

Deleting Entries from a Catalog

To delete an entry or group of entries from the input catalog, type DEL in the Sel field next to the entry or group you want to delete. Deleting all of the entries in a group deletes the group header.

Note: You are not prompted to confirm your request to delete an entry or group of entries. Be careful when deleting entries.

Suppressing or Displaying BY Statement Information

To suppress the BY statement information, issue the NOBYLINE command on the command line in the PROC GREPLAY window. To display the BY statement information again, issue the BYLINE command on the command line in the PROC GREPLAY window. BY statement information appears directly beneath the main description of the catalog entry.

Entering the GREPLAY Procedure in Line Mode

To go from the GREPLAY procedure windows to the GREPLAY procedure in line mode without exiting the procedure, issue the NOFS command on the command line in the PROC GREPLAY window. Once you are in line mode, you can submit GREPLAY line-mode statements. You may find the GREPLAY procedure in line mode particularly helpful because it allows you to submit additional LIBNAME, GOPTIONS, OPTIONS, and FILENAME statements without exiting the GREPLAY procedure.

To return to the GREPLAY procedure windows from line mode, use the FS line-mode statement.

Exiting the GREPLAY Procedure

When you are done using the GREPLAY procedure, you can exit the procedure by issuing the END command in the PROC GREPLAY window.

Using the PRESENTATION Window

In the PRESENTATION window, you can replay graphics output from the list of entries in the input catalog. To replay any of the entries in the list, place an S in the Select field next to the entry you want to replay. When you press ENTER, the entry you selected is displayed. If you want to replay the graphics output stored in more than one entry, place an S beside each entry you want to replay.

To select the order of replay for several entries, you can enter S*n* in the Select field next to the entries, where *n* is a one- or two-digit number that indicates the order of replay.

Using the DIRECTORY Window

You can store templates and color maps in SAS catalogs. You can use the DIRECTORY window commands and selection field commands to edit, browse, copy, or delete templates or color maps stored in a catalog.

Copying Templates and Color Maps

If you want to copy a template or color map from another catalog to the current (displayed) catalog, use the COPY command in the DIRECTORY window. For example, if you want to copy TEST.TEMPLATE from the catalog named PUBLIC.TEMPLT to the catalog named PRIVATE.TEMPLT, go to the DIRECTORY window for the PRIVATE.TEMPLT catalog and issue the following command:

```
copy public.templt.test.template
```

If you want to create a duplicate copy of a template or color map within the catalog displayed in the DIRECTORY window, use the COPY command to create a duplicate copy. For example, if you want to copy TEST.TEMPLATE to FINAL.TEMPLATE, issue the following command:

```
copy test.template final.template
```

Using the TEMPLATE DESIGN Window

You can create or modify a template by entering values in the fields in the TEMPLATE DESIGN window.

Editing a Template

To create a new template or to change an existing one, first assign a template catalog. Then enter the following command on the command line in the PROC GREPLAY or DIRECTORY window and press ENTER:

```
edit template-name.template
```

Template-name is the name of the template you want to create or change. If *template-name* already exists in the template catalog, you can modify the template definition. If *template-name* is not in the template catalog, a new template is created in the catalog.

As an alternative to the EDIT command, you can place an S in the selection field for the template entry in the DIRECTORY window.

When you edit a template, the GREPLAY procedure opens the TEMPLATE DESIGN window, which lets you design or change templates.

Designing Your Template

Each template can be composed of multiple panels numbered from 0 through 999. For each panel within the template you design, designate the position of the template corners as an X,Y coordinate pair. The window coordinates are based on percentage of the graphics output area. The origin of the window is located in the lower-left corner of the display. Figure 36.2 shows the coordinate system for the graphics output area.

Figure 36.2 *Template Coordinate System*

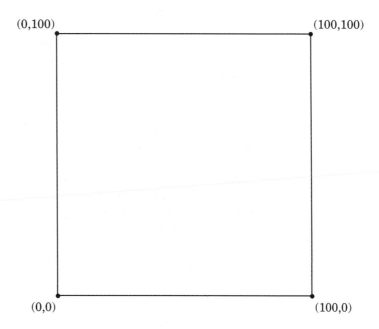

You can specify the size and shape of each panel by entering the X and Y coordinates for the corners of each panel. The coordinates do not need to form a rectangle and the panel does not need four distinct corners. If you use coordinates greater than 100 or less than 0, only those parts of the replayed graphics output that fall between 0 and 100 are visible. You can use coordinate values greater than 100 or less than 0 to zoom in on graphics output.

The GREPLAY procedure fills in any coordinate fields that were left blank with the default value for the coordinate. The following table lists the default values:

Panel Corner	Coordinates
lower left	(0,0)
upper left	(0,100)
upper right	(100,100)
lower right	(100,0)

If you define the coordinates of the right corners to be less than the left corners, the panel, and any graphics output replayed in the panel, are reversed from right to left. If you define the coordinates of the lower edge of the panel to be greater than the upper edge, the panel, and any graphics output replayed in the panel, are reversed from top to bottom.

You can place any character in the Clp field for a panel to activate clipping for that panel. If clipping is in effect for a panel, only the graphics output to be placed in that panel can appear in the space that the panel occupies in the window unless a previous panel occupies all or part of that space. Note that using the Clp field when it is not needed uses a great deal of unnecessary processing time.

Any subsequent panels are clipped if they overlap the clipping panel's area. Panels drawn before the clipping panel are *not* clipped. For example, if a template has four panels and you have specified clipping for panels 2 and 3, then panel 2 clips panels 3 and 4. Panel 3 clips panel 4. However, neither panel 2 nor panel 3 clips panel 1.

Scaling Your Template Panels

Without recalculating any coordinates yourself, you can change the size of a panel in your template or reverse (flip) the panel. To do this, enter scale factors in the Scale field. The GREPLAY procedure uses the scale factor to change the coordinates of the panel.

A scale value of 0 sets the values of the panel coordinates for that direction to a single point. Scale values less than 1 but greater than 0 decrease the panel size. Scale values that are greater than 1 increase the panel size. Scale values of 1 have no effect. Scale values less than 0 reverse the panel coordinates. You can use different scale values for the X and Y coordinates.

For example, to create a panel one-half the size of the original panel, specify .5 for the X and Y values in the Scale field.

If scaling, moving, or rotating is specified for a new panel without entering any coordinates, the GREPLAY procedure initializes the coordinates to their default values and then applies the specified changes.

Moving Your Template Panels

To move a panel up, down, left, or right in the template, use the Xlate field in the TEMPLATE DESIGN window. The Xlate values must be specified in percentage of the graphics output area. When you enter a value in an Xlate field and press ENTER, the panel is moved in the X or Y direction.

A negative Xlate value moves a panel down when specified for Y or to the left when specified for X. A positive Xlate value moves a panel up when specified for Y or to the right when specified for X. You can use different values for X and Y Xlate values.

Rotating Your Template Panels

To rotate a panel, use the Rotate field in the TEMPLATE DESIGN window. The Rotate values must be in degrees and can be positive or negative. When you enter a value in a Rotate field and press ENTER, the coordinates for the panel are recalculated based on the Rotate value. Note that if you rotate a panel, any graphics output replayed in the panel is rotated too.

The Device field is important for rotations because the device's aspect ratio is used in the calculation to preserve the original shape of a template after rotation. Make sure you are using the device driver for your final output device when you use the Rotate field.

Previewing Your Template

You can preview the template you created by issuing the PREVIEW command in the TEMPLATE DESIGN window. The template is displayed on your current device. The graphics output created by previewing the template is stored in a catalog named WORK.GTEM, which is deleted at the end of your session.

Note: You can preview the current template by issuing the PREVIEW command on the command line of the PROC GREPLAY window.

Using the COLOR MAPPING Window

You can create or modify a color map by entering values in the fields provided in the COLOR MAPPING window.

Editing Your Color Map

You can open the COLOR MAPPING window by entering the following command on the command line of the DIRECTORY window:

```
edit color-map-name.CMAP
```

Color-map-name is the name of the color map you want to edit. You also can use the EDIT command from the PROC GREPLAY window. If you want to use the EDIT command from the PROC GREPLAY window, you must first assign a color map catalog.

As an alternative to the EDIT command, you can enter an S in the selection field beside the name of a color map and press ENTER. You can create or modify a color map by entering pairs of colors in the From and To fields in the COLOR MAPPING window.

Designing Your Color Map

Each color map can contain up to 256 color pairs. You can change the value of an existing color pair by typing new values over the current values. To add a color pair to the color map, type the new values in the From and To fields. To save the color map, issue the END or SAVE command on the command line of the COLOR MAPPING window.

Presenting Your Graphics Output

The following are some of the ways you can present your graphics output using the GREPLAY procedure:

□ display graphics output from one or more catalog entries on a single page using a template

□ display graphics output from a single procedure or different procedures on the same display

□ store new graphics output, created using the template facility, in a SAS catalog

□ remap unsupported colors on a device to colors that are supported by that device.

To accomplish these tasks, you must use the PROC GREPLAY, DIRECTORY, TEMPLATE DESIGN, and COLOR MAPPING windows.

Replaying Your Entries in a Template

To replay graphics output in a template, you must assign a template catalog and a current template that will be used for replay.

Once you have assigned a current template, you can use the PROC GREPLAY window to select entries for replay in the template by entering template panel numbers in the Sel field next to the names of the entries to be presented. Display 36.10 shows an example of replaying graphics output in a template. The numbers shown in the Sel field correspond to panels in the current template, shown in the Template field.

Display 36.10 *Replaying Graphics Output in a Template*

```
┌PROC GREPLAY─────────────────────────────────────────────┐
│ Command ===>                                            │
│                                                         │
│ IGOUT: SCREEN.GRAPHS      GOUT: _____      Device: IBM3179 │
│ TC:    SASHELP.TEMPLT     Template: H4          Scroll: PAGE    │
│ CC:    _____       Cmap: _____                 │
│                                                         │
│                                                         │
│ Sel  Name     Type   Description              Updated   │
│                                                         │
│ 1__  GCHART   I     VBAR CHART OF BRANCH      11/30/89  │
│ 2__  GCHART1  I     VBAR CHART OF AGENT       11/30/89  │
│ ___  GCHART5  I     VBAR CHART OF QUAN        11/30/89  │
│ ___  GCHART6  I     VBAR CHART OF STATE       11/30/89  │
│ ___  GPLOT    I     PLOT OF HEIGHT * WEIGHT   11/30/89  │
│ 3__  GPLOT1   I     PLOT OF SALES * COST      11/30/89  │
│ 4__  GPLOT2   I     PLOT OF SALES * QUAN      11/30/89  │
│ ___  GPLOT3   I     PLOT OF COST * RETURN     11/30/89  │
│                                                         │
│                                                         │
│                                                         │
│                                                         │
│                                                       R │
└─────────────────────────────────────────────────────────┘
```

When you press ENTER, you see your graphics output displayed in the specified panel. You can replay graphics output from more than one entry in a single panel. That is, you can use the same panel number for more than one entry. Replaying graphics output in a template creates a new entry containing graphics output. This new entry is placed in the output catalog. If you have not assigned an output catalog, the graphics output is stored in the catalog named WORK.GSEG.

You do not need to select an entry for every panel of the template. Unused panels in the template are left empty.

Replaying Your Entries Using a Color Map

To replay your graphics output using a color map, you must assign a CC catalog and a current color map.

Once you have assigned a current color map, the color map is used for any entries that you replay.

Note: The remapped colors are not saved with the graphics output in the catalog entry and no new graphics output is produced.

If you want to stop using a color map, erase the name in the Cmap field.

Window Example

The following example illustrates major features of the GREPLAY procedure windows.

Using Windows to Create a Template and Display Graphics Output

The following example creates a template containing three panels. This example also creates a permanent catalog called MYLIB.TEMPCAT that is used to store the template.

Note: In order to select one or more entries for replay in the template in this example, you must have some graphics output stored in the catalog named WORK.GSEG.

Here are the steps to create a new template, preview it, and display graphics output in the template:

1. Open the PROC GREPLAY window, specifying an input catalog and a template catalog as follows:

```
libname mylib 'SAS-data-library';

proc greplay igout=work.gseg
             tc=mylib.tempcat;
```

When the PROC GREPLAY window appears, issue the TC command on the command line. The DIRECTORY window for the new catalog, MYLIB.TEMPCAT, is displayed.

2. To create a new template called NEWTHREE, enter the following command on the command line of the PROC GREPLAY window:

```
edit newthree.template
```

When you press ENTER, the TEMPLATE DESIGN window for the template NEWTHREE is displayed. Fill in the fields as shown in Display 36.11.

Display 36.11 *Defining a Template*

```
┌PROC GREPLAY───────────────────────────────────────────────────────┐
│ Command ===>                                                        │
│                                                                     │
│ IGOUT: WORK.GSEG          GOUT: _____   Device: IBM3179    │
│ TC:    SCREEN.TEMPLT      Template: _____      Scroll: PAGE       │
│┌PROC GREPLAY: TEMPLATE DESIGN──────────────────────────────────────┐│
││ Command ===>                                                       ││
││                                                                    ││
││   TEMPLATE: NEWTHREE                         TC: SCREEN.TEMPLT     ││
││   DESC: THREE PANELS                         Scroll: PAGE          ││
││                                              Device: IBM3179       ││
││  Panel Clp Color     L-left U-left U-right L-right  Scale Xlate Rotat ││
││                                                                    ││
││    1   _  BLUE    X:  0.0    0.0   50.0   50.0   X: ____ ____  ___ ││
││                   Y:  0.0   50.0   50.0    0.0   Y: ____ ____      ││
││                                                                    ││
││    2   _  RED     X:  0.0    0.0   50.0   50.0   X: ____ ____  ___ ││
││                   Y: 50.0  100.0  100.0   50.0   Y: ____ ____      ││
││                                                                    ││
││    3   _  GREEN   X: 50.0   50.0  100.0  100.0   X: ____ ____  ___ ││
││                   Y:  0.0  100.0  100.0    0.0   Y: ____ ____      ││
││                                                                 R──┘│
└────────────────────────────────────────────────────────────────────┘
```

The template you have defined contains three rectangular panels. The panels are colored blue, red, and green.

3. When you have entered the values necessary to create the template, you can preview the template to see how it looks. Issue the PREVIEW command on the command line of the TEMPLATE DESIGN window to view the template NEWTHREE. When you have finished viewing the template, press ENTER or END to return to the TEMPLATE DESIGN window.

Return to the DIRECTORY window by issuing the END command. The template is automatically saved.

4. Now you are ready to replay the graphics output stored in the WORK.GSEG catalog using the template. Return to the PROC GREPLAY window by issuing the END command. Next, define

NEWTHREE as the current template by typing its name in the
Template field. To replay your graphics output in the template, type the
panel numbers 1 through 3 in the Sel field next to the entries that you
want to replay. For example, your window might look something like
Display 36.12.

Display 36.12 *Displaying*
Graphics Output in a Template

```
┌PROC GREPLAY─────────────────────────────────────────────────────┐
│ Command ===>                                                     │
│                                                                  │
│  IGOUT: SCREEN.GRAPHS      GOUT: _____    Device: IBM3179  │
│  TC:    SCREEN.TEMPLT      Template: NEWTHREE    Scroll: PAGE     │
│  CC:    _____      Cmap: _____                         │
│                                                                  │
│                                                                  │
│  Sel  Name      Type   Description                     Updated   │
│                                                                  │
│  ___  GCHART    I      VBAR CHART OF BRANCH            11/30/89   │
│  1__  GCHART1   I      VBAR CHART OF AGENT             11/30/89   │
│  2__  GCHART5   I      VBAR CHART OF QUAN              11/30/89   │
│  3__  GCHART6   I      VBAR CHART OF STATE             11/30/89   │
│  ___  GPLOT     I      PLOT OF HEIGHT * WEIGHT         11/30/89   │
│  ___  GPLOT1    I      PLOT OF SALES * COST            11/30/89   │
│  ___  GPLOT2    I      PLOT OF SALES * QUAN            11/30/89   │
│  ___  GPLOT3    I      PLOT OF COST * RETURN           11/30/89   │
│                                                                  │
│                                                                  │
│                                                                  │
│                                                                  │
│                                                               ─R─│
└──────────────────────────────────────────────────────────────────┘
```

By displaying graphics output in a template, you create new graphics
output. The graphics output is stored in a catalog entry in the output
catalog. In this example, because you have not assigned an output
catalog, the output is stored in the default output catalog,
WORK.GSEG. As a result, the list of entries in the WORK.GSEG
catalog is updated to show the new entry that was created by the
template facility.

See Also

Chapter 2, "Running SAS/GRAPH Programs"
for more information on

☐ the GRAPH windows. The GRAPH windows can be used to display
catalog entries containing graphics output

☐ SAS/GRAPH catalog entries

Chapter 3, "Graphics Output"
for more information on

☐ device-independent and device-dependent catalog entries

☐ storing your graphics output in catalogs

CHAPTER *37* The GSLIDE Procedure

Overview

The GSLIDE procedure displays graphics output consisting of text and straight lines generated by TITLE, FOOTNOTE, and NOTE statements. In addition, the procedure can display graphics output generated by an Annotate data set.

Use the GSLIDE procedure to display output from Annotate data sets when you want to include currently defined titles and footnotes on the output and use certain graphics options such as BORDER. To display Annotate graphics without these, use the GANNO procedure.

The GSLIDE procedure displays text and graphics generated by SAS/GRAPH software. To display an external text file as graphics output, use the GPRINT procedure.

Output 37.1 shows a text slide produced with TITLE, FOOTNOTE, and NOTE statements. The procedure uses the FRAME and BORDER options. Output 37.2 shows output from an Annotate data set displayed with titles and footnotes generated by TITLE and FOOTNOTE statements.

Output 37.1 *Text Slide Produced by the GSLIDE Procedure (GR37N01)*

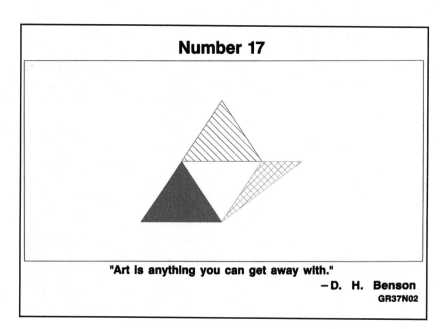

Output 37.2 *Output from an Annotate Data Set Displayed with the GSLIDE Procedure (GR37N02)*

GSLIDE Procedure Syntax

The GSLIDE procedure uses the following statements:

☐ The PROC GSLIDE statement is required.

PROC GSLIDE <ANNOTATE=*Annotate-data-set*>
<GOUT=*output-catalog*>
<*appearance-options*>
<*description-options*>;

□ *appearance-options* can be one or more of the following:

BORDER

CFRAME=*frame-color*

FRAME

LFRAME=*line-type*

WFRAME=*n*

where *n* is the thickness of the frame

□ *description-options* can be one or more of the following:

NAME='*string*'

DESCRIPTION='*string*'

□ The following statement is optional and local:

NOTE <*options*> <'*text*'>;

□ The following statements are optional and global:

FOOTNOTE<1 . . . 10> <*options*> <'*text*'>;

TITLE<1 . . . 10> <*options*> <'*text*'>;

Options are fully described in "Options" later in this chapter.

Statement Descriptions

The purpose of each statement is described here.

FOOTNOTE	defines the text and appearance of footnotes. (See Chapter 11, "The FOOTNOTE Statement.")
NOTE	defines the text and appearance of the notes that appear in the procedure output area. (See Chapter 14, "The NOTE Statement.")
PROC GSLIDE	starts the procedure. It optionally specifies the name of an Annotate data set as well as additional output options.
TITLE	defines the text and appearance of titles. (See Chapter 17, "The TITLE Statement.")

GSLIDE Procedure Description

The GSLIDE procedure is intended to produce text slides. It also provides an easy way to put titles, notes, and footnotes on output produced entirely with an Annotate data set.

If you use the GSLIDE procedure with Annotate data sets that contain data-dependent coordinates, the resulting coordinate values may exceed the range of 0 to 100 used by the graphics output area, and some of the output may not be displayed. In this case, use the GANNO procedure, which can scale the output to fit the available space. See Chapter 22, "The GANNO Procedure," for details.

Terminology

The following terms are used in the discussion of the GSLIDE procedure and are defined in the Glossary:

border   graphics output area
frame   procedure output area
graphics output   string

Several of these terms are illustrated in Figure 2.3 in Chapter 2, "Running SAS/GRAPH Programs."

RUN Groups

The GSLIDE procedure supports RUN-group processing. It does not have any action statements, but all currently defined titles, footnotes, and notes, as well as any annotation, are displayed each time a RUN statement is submitted. TITLE and FOOTNOTE definitions can be canceled or redefined while the GSLIDE procedure is active, and they remain in effect after procedure execution is terminated. NOTE definitions remain in effect until the GSLIDE procedure is terminated, at which time they are canceled. To cancel NOTE definitions while the procedure is active, specify RESET=NOTE in a GOPTIONS statement. GSLIDE procedure execution terminates when a QUIT statement, another PROC statement, or a DATA step is encountered.

For more information on RUN-group processing, see "Using RUN Groups" in Chapter 2. See also Chapter 11, Chapter 14, and Chapter 17 for complete descriptions of the FOOTNOTE, NOTE, and TITLE statements, respectively.

Global Statements

All currently defined titles and footnotes are displayed in every picture generated by the procedure or by a RUN group. To display different titles or footnotes on your output, define the titles or footnotes at the beginning of a RUN group. Any TITLE or FOOTNOTE definitions of a higher level (that is, lower number) remain in effect and are displayed on the output. See Chapter 17 and Chapter 11 for details.

PROC GSLIDE Statement

The PROC GSLIDE statement initiates the GSLIDE procedure and provides options to enhance the appearance of the graphics output as well as to save, name, and describe output. The GSLIDE procedure can optionally specify a data set to be used for annotation.

Requirements

At least one of the following must be used with the PROC GSLIDE statement:

□ a TITLE, FOOTNOTE, or NOTE statement

□ the ANNOTATE= option

□ the BORDER, FRAME, CFRAME=, LFRAME=, or WFRAME= option

□ the BORDER graphics option.

Options

You can use the following options with the PROC GSLIDE statement:

ANNOTATE=*Annotate-data-set*
ANNO=*Annotate-data-set*
    specifies a data set to be used for annotation. *Annotate-data-set* must contain the appropriate Annotate variables. See Chapter 18, "The Annotate Data Set," for details.

BORDER
    draws a border around the graphics output area, which includes the title area, the footnote area, and the procedure output area.

    A color specification for the border is searched for in the following order:

    1. the CTITLE= option in a GOPTIONS statement

    2. the CTEXT= option in a GOPTIONS statement

    3. the default, the first color in the colors list.

    See also "Drawing Frames and Borders" later in this chapter.

CFRAME=*frame-color*
    draws a frame around the procedure output area in the specified color. If you use both the CFRAME= and FRAME options, FRAME is ignored.
    Note: The CFRAME= option does not color the background of the slide. See also "Drawing Frames and Borders" later in this chapter.

DESCRIPTION=*'string'*
DES=*'string'*
    specifies a descriptive string, up to 40 characters long, that appears in the Description field of the catalog entry for the picture. The description does not appear on the picture. By default, the GSLIDE procedure assigns the description OUTPUT FROM PROC GSLIDE.

FRAME
    draws a frame around the procedure output area. By default, the frame color is the first color in the colors list. If you want to specify a different color for the frame, use the CFRAME= option instead. If you use the CFRAME=, LFRAME=, or WFRAME= option with the FRAME option, the FRAME option is ignored.
    See also "Drawing Frames and Borders" later in this chapter.

GOUT=*output-catalog*
    specifies the SAS catalog in which to save the output produced by PROC GSLIDE for later replay. If you do not use the GOUT= option, catalog entries are written to the default graphics catalog WORK.GSEG, which is erased at the end of your session. See Chapter 3, "Graphics Output," for more details.

LFRAME=*line-type*
    specifies the line type for a frame and draws a frame around the procedure output area. Valid values for *line-type* are 1 through 46. Line types are shown in Table 16.5 in Chapter 16, "The SYMBOL Statement." By default, LFRAME=1, which produces a solid line. If you use both the LFRAME= and FRAME options, FRAME is ignored.

NAME=*'string'*

specifies a string of up to eight characters that appears in the Name field of the catalog entry for the output. By default, the name assigned is GSLIDE. If either the name specified or the default name duplicates an existing name in the catalog, then SAS/GRAPH software adds a number to the duplicate name to create a unique name, for example, GSLIDE2.

WFRAME=*n*

specifies the width of the frame where *n* is a number. The thickness of the frame increases directly with *n*, but the thickness of the line may vary from device to device. By default, WFRAME=1, which is the thinnest line. The WFRAME= option also draws the frame. If you use both the WFRAME= and FRAME options, FRAME is ignored.

Using the GSLIDE Procedure

The following section explains the differences between options that generate borders and frames.

Drawing Frames and Borders

Like the BORDER option in a GOPTIONS statement, the BORDER option in the PROC GSLIDE statement draws a box around the graphics output area. However, the border generated by the GSLIDE procedure remains in effect only for the duration of the procedure.

Both BORDER options use the color specified by the CTITLE= or CTEXT= graphics option if either of these options is used; otherwise, the border color is the first color in the colors list.

While the BORDER option draws a box around the graphics output area, the FRAME option draws a box or frame around the procedure output area. Use the FRAME option to draw a frame in the default color, line type, and width. Otherwise, use one or more of the CFRAME=, LFRAME=, or WFRAME= options.

You can specify a colored frame with the CFRAME= option. Note that CFRAME= does not fill the procedure output area with color. However, the CBACK= graphics option can be used to provide a background color for the graphics output area. You can specify the type of line for the frame with the LFRAME= option and the width of the frame with the WFRAME= option.

Examples

The following examples illustrate some of the features of the GSLIDE procedure.

Producing Text Slides

This example illustrates how to use some of the PROC GSLIDE statement options along with FOOTNOTE, NOTE, and TITLE statements to produce text slides. For this example, the NOTE statement uses the MOVE= option to position the text. Using PCT (percentage) as the unit ensures that the positioning of the text is consistent from device to device.

The following program statements produce Output 37.3:

```
   /* set graphics environment */
goptions reset=global gunit=pct
        ftext=swissb htitle=6 htext=3;

   /* specify a color for text and border */
goptions ctitle=red;

   /* define titles and footnotes */
title1 'Byte Computer Company';
title2 h=5 '123 Main Street';
title3 h=5 'Cary, North Carolina';
footnote1 h=4 j=1 ' Phone: (919) 555-3011'
        j=r 'Fax: (919) 555-4233 ';
footnote2 j=r 'GR37N03 ';

   /* generate slide */
proc gslide border lframe=22 wframe=5;
   note h=5
        move=(20,60) 'Your dependable supplier of'
        move=(30,50) f=special 'K' f=swissb ' hardware'
        move=(30,43) f=special 'K' f=swissb ' software'
        move=(30,36) f=special 'K' f=swissb ' documentation';
run;
quit;
```

Output 37.3 *Displaying TITLE, NOTE, and FOOTNOTE Statements with the GSLIDE Procedure (GR37N03)*

This example illustrates the following features:

□ The BORDER option in the PROC GSLIDE statement generates a border around the entire graphics output area.

□ The LFRAME= option selects the line type and draws the frame around the procedure output area.

□ The WFRAME= option controls the width of the line used for the frame.

□ TITLE, FOOTNOTE, and NOTE statements generate the text displayed by the GSLIDE procedure.

Displaying Annotate Graphics

In this example the GSLIDE procedure displays a vertical bar chart that is generated by the Annotate facility. The data set, SALES89, contains the name of the site, SITENAME, and the average number of sales for that site, MEAN. The Annotate data set ANNO uses the data from SALES89 to determine

□ the value of the label below each bar

□ the height of each bar

□ the value of the label within each bar

□ the position of the label within each bar.

The following program statements produce Output 37.4.

```
    /* set graphics environment */
goptions reset=global gunit=pct border
        ftext=swissb htitle=6 htext=3;

    /* create data set of sales information */
data sales89;
    length sitename $ 10;
    input sitename $ 1-10 mean 12-14;
    cards;
Paris      347
Washington 398
London     375
Sidney     413
Tokyo      317
;
run;

    /* create Annotate data set */
data anno;
    length function color $ 8;
    retain line 0 xsys ysys hsys '3' x 16 color 'blue';
    set sales89 end=end;

    /* move to the beginning point */
function='move'; x=x+8; y=20; output;

    /* draw bar representing number of sales */
function='bar'; y=y+(mean/10); x=x+7;
style='solid'; color='green'; output;
```

```
      /* label the bar with name of site */
   function='label'; y=15; x=x-3; size=3;
   position='5'; style='swissb';
   color='blue'; text=sitename; output;

      /* move to point where number begins */
      /* and label the bar                 */
   function='label'; y=y+(mean/10)-2; x=x-1;
   text=left(put(mean,3.)); position='5'; style='swissb';
   size=3; color='blue'; output;

      /* at end of data set, draw an axis line */
   if end then do;
      function='move'; x=17; y=20; output;
      function='draw'; x=82; y=20; line=1;
      size=1; color='red'; output;
   end;
run;

   /* define title and footnote */
title 'Projected Sales for First Quarter 1989';
footnote j=r 'GR37N04  ';

   /* display the annotation */
proc gslide annotate=anno;
run;
quit;
```

Output 37.4 Displaying Annotate Graphics with the GSLIDE Procedure (GR37N04)

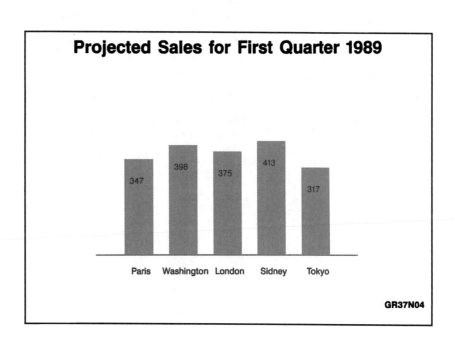

This example illustrates the following features:

□ The GSLIDE procedure displays the graphics elements drawn by the commands in the Annotate data set specified by the ANNOTATE= option.

□ In addition to displaying the output generated by the Annotate data set, the GSLIDE procedure displays the TITLE and FOOTNOTE definitions as well as the border specified in the GOPTIONS statement.

See Also

Chapter 2, "Running SAS/GRAPH Programs"
for additional information on the graphics output area and the procedure output area

Chapter 3, "Graphics Output"
for additional information on catalog entries

Chapter 5, "Graphics Options and Device Parameters Dictionary"
for additional information on the BORDER and CBACK= graphics options

Chapter 7, "SAS/GRAPH Colors"
for information on the selection and use of colors

Chapter 11, "The FOOTNOTE Statement"
for details on putting footnotes on output

Chapter 14, "The NOTE Statement"
for details on putting other text on output

Chapter 16, "The SYMBOL Statement"
for a table of line types

Chapter 17, "The TITLE Statement"
for details on putting titles on output

Chapter 18, "The Annotate Data Set"
for information on constructing Annotate data sets

Chapter 32, "The GPRINT Procedure"
for information on creating graphic slides from regular SAS output

CHAPTER 38 THE GTESTIT Procedure

Overview

The GTESTIT procedure is a diagnostic tool for testing the installation of SAS/GRAPH software and the configuration of your device. Use the GTESTIT procedure when you want to

□ test a new device

□ test the settings of a device driver you are developing

□ identify the colors and some of the SAS/GRAPH lines and fills for your device

□ review some of your current settings of device parameters and graphics options

□ test changes in settings of device parameters and graphics options.

Refer to "Pictures Displayed by the GTESTIT Procedure" later in this chapter for examples of the pictures displayed by the GTESTIT procedure.

GTESTIT Procedure Syntax

The GTESTIT procedure uses the following statement:

PROC GTESTIT <PICTURE=1 | 2 | 3>
       <GOUT=*output-catalog*>;

GTESTIT Procedure Description

The GTESTIT procedure can produce three pictures that provide information to help you determine if your device is configured correctly. Although it does not show and test the settings of all device parameters and graphics options, the GTESTIT procedure does show and test some of the most commonly used ones.

Terminology

The following terms are used in the discussion of the GTESTIT procedure and are defined in the Glossary:

aspect ratio	device parameter
colors list	graphics option
device entry	graphics output area

Global Statements

With the exception of the GOPTIONS statement, the GTESTIT procedure ignores all global statements.

PROC GTESTIT Statement

The PROC GTESTIT statement starts the GTESTIT procedure and, optionally, specifies the picture or pictures to be displayed and the catalog in which to store the output. By default, if you submit the PROC GTESTIT statement without any options, the GTESTIT procedure displays all three pictures in sequence and stores them in the default catalog, WORK.GSEG.

Options

You can use the following options with the PROC GTESTIT statement:

GOUT=*output-catalog*
    specifies the SAS catalog in which to save the output produced by the GTESTIT procedure for later replay. If you do not use the GOUT= option, catalog entries are written to the default catalog, WORK.GSEG, which is erased at the end of your session. See Chapter 3, "Graphics Output," for details.

PICTURE=1 | 2 | 3
PIC=1 | 2 | 3
    indicates the number of the test pattern to display. By default, all three display. If you specify PICTURE−1, the test pattern displaying the available colors and patterns is shown. Specify PICTURE=1 when you want to see examples of the colors, line types, and fills. If you specify PICTURE=2, the test pattern for continuous drawing ability is shown. If you specify PICTURE=3, the test pattern for drawing polygons, ellipses, and justified text is shown. If you include more than one PICTURE= option, the GTESTIT procedure displays only the last picture you specify.

Using the GTESTIT Procedure

The GTESTIT procedure can display three different pictures, each showing different features of your device.

Pictures Displayed by the GTESTIT Procedure

Picture 1 shows a test pattern and gives the values of some of the device settings in effect. When picture 1 is displayed, the values of the displayed settings, plus some others also, are listed in the LOG window for the procedure. The values of most of these settings are determined by device parameters specified in the catalog entry for the current device or by graphics options specified in a GOPTIONS statement.

For most devices, picture 1 appears in the lower-left corner of the plot or screen, as shown in Output 38.1.

Output 38.1 *Picture 1 of the GTESTIT Procedure (GR38N01)*

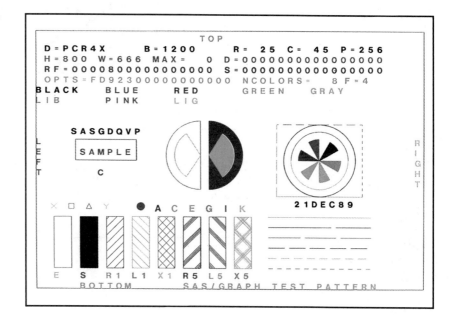

Picture 2 tests your device's ability to draw lines. Picture 2 always displays in the first color of the current colors list. Output 38.2 shows picture 2 of the GTESTIT procedure.

Output 38.2 *Picture 2 of the GTESTIT Procedure (GR38N02)*

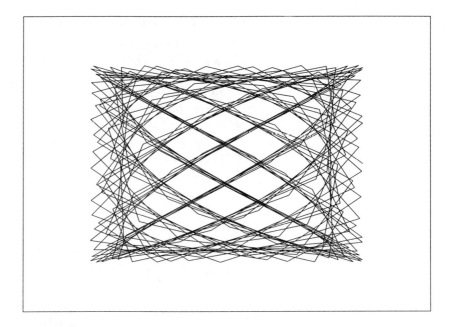

Picture 3 tests your device's ability to draw simple polygons, polygons with multiple boundaries (also known as *holes*), ellipses, and justified text. Output 38.3 shows picture 3 of the GTESTIT procedure.

Output 38.3 *Picture 3 of the GTESTIT Procedure (GR38N03)*

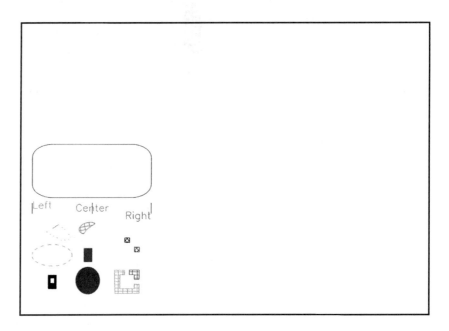

Values Displayed in Picture 1 and the LOG Window

Table 38.1 provides an explanation of the values displayed in picture 1 of the GTESTIT procedure. It also provides the equivalent graphics option or device parameter. A complete description of the graphics options and device parameters is included in Chapter 5, "Graphics Options and Device Parameters Dictionary."

Table 38.1 *GTESTIT Values Displayed in Picture 1*

GTESTIT Value	Equivalent Graphics Option or Device Parameter	Description
D=	DEVICE=	shows the device driver you are using.
B=	BAUD=	shows the value of the BAUD= graphics option.
R=	VPOS=	shows the number of rows.
C=	HPOS=	shows the number of columns.
P=	MAXCOLORS=	shows the total number of colors (foreground and background) that your device can display. If your device can display more than 15 colors, picture 1 shows only 15 colors, but the LOG window lists all of the available colors.
H=		shows the height of character cells in pixels.
W=		shows the width of character cells in pixels.
MAX=	MAXPOLY=	shows the maximum number of vertices that can be processed by a hardware polygon command. If MAX=0, then the number of vertices is unbounded.
D= ★	DASHLINE=	shows the hardware dashed-line patterns available. The value displayed is a hexadecimal string.
RF= ★	RECTFILL=	shows the hardware rectangle-fill patterns available. The value displayed is a hexadecimal string.
S= ★	SYMBOLS=	shows the hardware symbols available. The value displayed is a hexadecimal string.
OPTS= ★	DEVOPTS=	shows the other hardware options available. The value displayed is a hexadecimal string.
NCOLORS=	COLORS=	shows the number of colors in the colors list or the number of foreground colors.
F=	FILLINC=	shows the solid fill increment (the number of pixels between strokes when doing a solid fill).

★In the device entry, this field is blank. The value displayed by the GTESTIT procedure comes from an internal default in the device driver.

Table 38.2 lists the GTESTIT values that appear only in the LOG window. It also provides the equivalent graphics option or device parameter. Complete information about the graphics options and device parameters can be found in Chapter 5.

Table 38.2 *GTESTIT Values Shown in the LOG Window*

GTESTIT Value	Equivalent Graphics Option or Device Parameter	Description
Background color=	CBACK=	tells the background color used.
Color1= ... Colorn=	COLORS=	lists the default colors list for the device. N is equal to the NCOLORS= value.
Ratio=	ASPECT=	shows the aspect ratio of the device, which is the ratio of width to height of character cells.
Hsize=	HSIZE=	shows the horizontal size of the area used on the device for the graphics display. The default unit is inches.
Vsize=	VSIZE=	shows the vertical size of the area used on the device for the graphics display. The default unit is inches.

The GTESTIT procedure does not display the settings of all device parameters and graphics options. Use the GOPTIONS procedure to obtain a list of graphics options settings for your current SAS session. Use the GDEVICE procedure to inspect or change the settings of all device parameters for your device. See "Testing a GOPTIONS Statement" later in this chapter for an illustration of how changing graphics options affects the GTESTIT procedure output.

Output 38.4 shows a sample of the information that appears in the LOG window after running picture 1 in the GTESTIT procedure. An asterisk (*) after the P= or F= option indicates that the value for that option is greater than 999.

Output 38.4 Sample Log
from GTESTIT Procedure

```
2        /* set the graphics environment */
3     goptions hpos=45 vpos=25 ftext=;
4
5        /* display the first picture */
6        /* of the GTESTIT procedure  */


7     proc gtestit picture=1;
8     run;

D=IBM3179  B=1200     R= 25 C= 45 P=256
H= 13 W= 15 MAX=   0 D=C000000000000000
RF=8000800000000000 S=0000000000000000
OPTS=D592644000000000 NCOLORS=  7
Background color = BLACK
Color 1 = BLUE
Color 2 = RED
Color 3 = PINK
Color 4 = GREEN
Color 5 = CYAN
Color 6 = YELLOW
Color 7 = WHITE
Ratio = 0.65497
Hsize = 8.97638
Vsize = 5.87927
F=1
```

Effect of Device Parameters and Graphics Options on GTESTIT Pictures

Many of the settings displayed in GTESTIT pictures can be permanently changed by modifying the parameters for the device entry using the GDEVICE procedure or temporarily overridden by specifying a new value in a GOPTIONS statement. For more information on setting graphics options and device parameters, see Chapter 12, "The GOPTIONS Statement"; Chapter 25, "The GDEVICE Procedure"; and Chapter 4, "Device Drivers."

When you change one of these graphics options or device parameters, you can test the results by running the GTESTIT procedure. Any of the device parameters or graphics options that are shown in the picture will reflect the changes. For example, if you specify FTEXT=SWISSB, the text appears in the SWISSB font. If you specify COLORS=(RED GREEN), the output displays in only red and green.

Example

Testing a GOPTIONS Statement

This example illustrates how a GOPTIONS statement can affect the graphics output produced by the GTESTIT procedure. The GOPTIONS statement in this example resets the font to the default, specifies a limited colors list, and enlarges the size of the elements in the graphics output by decreasing the number of rows and columns from the default number of rows and columns.

Output 38.5 shows picture 1 of the GTESTIT procedure when the COLORS= option is used in a GOPTIONS statement. Note how the colors displayed in Output 38.5 and listed in Output 38.6 differ from the colors in Output 38.1 and Output 38.4 earlier in this chapter.

```
        /* set the graphics environment */
goptions ftext=
          colors=(blue red green)
          hpos=45 vpos=25;


    /* display the first picture */
    /* of the GTESTIT procedure  */
proc gtestit picture=1;
run;
```

Output 38.5 *Picture 1 of the GTESTIT Procedure Using a Limited Colors List (GR38N04)*

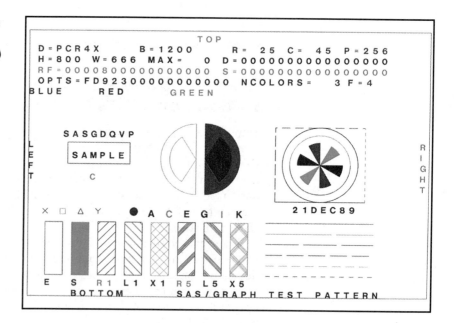

Output 38.6 shows the values displayed in the LOG window when the GTESTIT procedure uses COLORS=(BLUE RED GREEN).

Output 38.6 *Log Produced when Using a Limited Colors List*

```
1          /* set the graphics environment */
2    goptions ftext=
3             colors=(blue red green)
4             hpos=45 vpos=25;
5
6          /* display the first picture */
7          /* of the GTESTIT procedure  */
8    proc gtestit picture=1;
9    run;

D=IBM3179  B=1200    R= 25 C= 45 P=256
H= 13 W= 15 MAX=  0 D=C000000000000000
RF=8000800000000000 S=0000000000000000
OPTS=D592644000000000 NCOLORS=  3
Background color = BLACK
Color 1 = BLUE
Color 2 = RED
Color 3 = GREEN
Ratio = 0.65497
Hsize = 8.97638
Vsize = 5.87927
F=1
```

This example illustrates the following features:

□ The FTEXT= graphics option resets the font to the default font.

□ The COLORS= graphics option can determine the colors displayed in picture 1 and listed in the LOG window. COLORS= also can determine the value of NCOLORS=.

□ The HPOS= graphics option selects 45 columns for the graphics output.

□ The VPOS= graphics option selects 25 rows for the graphics output.

See Also

Chapter 5, "Graphics Options and Device Parameters Dictionary"
for more information on the values of graphics options and device parameters displayed in picture 1

Chapter 12, "The GOPTIONS Statement"
for more information on how to set graphics options

Chapter 25, "The GDEVICE Procedure"
for more information on how to set device parameters

Chapter 30, "The GOPTIONS Procedure"
for details of how to display the current graphics options settings

SAS/GRAPH Software: Using Graphics Devices for your host environment
for information on how your device should be configured and information about default device parameters and device capabilities

CHAPTER 39 The G3D Procedure

Overview

The G3D procedure produces three-dimensional graphs that plot one vertical variable (z) for a position on a plane specified by two horizontal variables (x and y). The coordinates of each point correspond to the values of three numeric variable values in an observation of the input data set. The observation may contain values in the form $z=f(x,y)$ or independent values such as the altitude at a given longitude and latitude.

Using the G3D procedure, you can

□ produce surface plots, needle plots, or scatter plots

□ examine the shape of your data

□ observe data trends in a scatter or needle plot without having a complete grid of *x* and *y* variable values.

□ produce scatter or needle plots in which size, shape, or color is used to represent a data class or the value of a fourth variable.

The following output illustrates the types of graphs the G3D procedure can produce. The same input data set is used for each graph.

Output 39.1 illustrates a surface plot. Surface plots let you examine the three-dimensional shape of your data.

Output 39.1 *Sample G3D Surface Plot (GR39N01(a))*

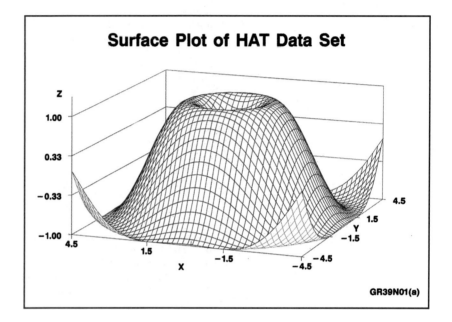

Output 39.2 and Output 39.3 illustrate needle and scatter plots. Needle and scatter plots let you examine three-dimensional data points instead of surfaces. They also let you classify your data using size, color, shape, or a combination of these features.

Output 39.2 *Sample G3D Needle Plot (GR39N01(b))*

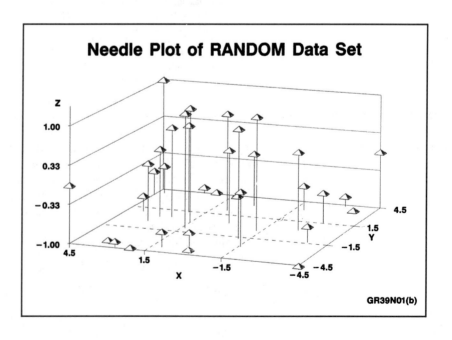

Output 39.3 *Sample G3D Scatter Plot (GR39N01(c))*

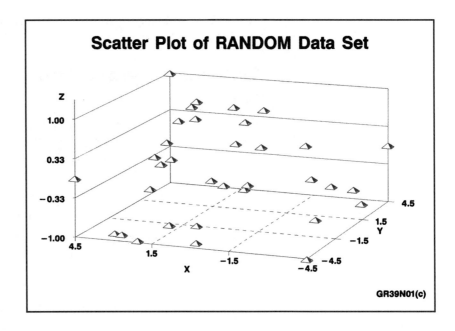

G3D Procedure Syntax

The G3D procedure uses the following statements:

□ The G3D procedure statement is required.

PROC G3D <DATA=*SAS-data-set*>
    < ANNOTATE=*Annotate-data-set*>
    <GOUT=*output-catalog*>;

□ At least one of the following statements is required:

PLOT *y*x=z*
    </ < ANNOTATE=*Annotate-data-set*>
    <*appearance-options*>
    <*axes-options*>
    <*description-options*>>;

SCATTER *y*x=z*
    </ < ANNOTATE=*Annotate-data-set*>
    <*appearance-options*>
    <*axes-options*>
    <*description-options*>>;

□ The following statements are optional and local:

BY <*options*> *variable*;

NOTE <*options*> <'*text*'>;

□ The following statements are optional and global:

FOOTNOTE<1 . . . 10> < *options*> <'*text*'>;

TITLE<1 . . . 10> < *options*> <'*text*'>;

For complete statement syntax, see the section on the appropriate statement.

Statement Descriptions

The purpose of each statement is described here:

BY | specifies the variable or variables by which the data are grouped for processing. A separate graph is produced for each value of the BY variable. See Chapter 10, "The BY Statement."

FOOTNOTE | defines the text and appearance of footnotes. See Chapter 11, "The FOOTNOTE Statement."

NOTE | defines the text and appearance of notes that appear in the procedure output area. See Chapter 14, "The NOTE Statement."

PLOT | creates surface plots using input data set variables as the source of three-dimensional coordinates.

PROC G3D | starts the procedure and specifies the name of the input data set to be used, as well as any additional input or output options.

SCATTER | creates scatter or needle plots using input data set variables as the source of three-dimensional coordinates.

TITLE | defines the text and appearance of titles. See Chapter 17, "The TITLE Statement."

G3D Procedure Description

The following sections address issues that pertain to the G3D procedure as a whole: terminology, special data considerations and the use of global statements.

Terminology

The following terms are used in the discussion of the G3D procedure and are defined in the Glossary. Some of these terms and some additional terms are illustrated in Figure 39.1.

axis
graph
label
major tick mark

needle plot
scatter plot
surface plot

Figure 39.1 *G3D Procedure Terms*

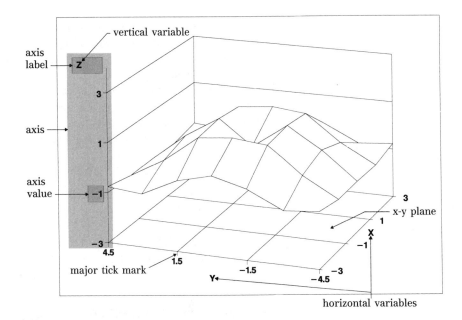

Data Considerations

The G3D procedure requires data sets that include three numeric variables: two horizontal variables plotted on the *x* and *y* axes that define an *x-y* plane, and a vertical variable plotted on the *z* axis rising from the *x-y* plane.

Scatter and Needle Plots

An input data set for scatter plots must include at least two observations containing different values for each of the three variables specified in the plot request so that the G3D procedure can scale the axes. If the data set does not meet these requirements, SAS/GRAPH software issues an error message and no graph is produced.

For scatter and needle plots, only one *z* value is plotted for a combination of *x* and *y*. For example, you cannot draw a sphere using the SCATTER statement. If there is more than one observation for a combination of *x* and *y* in the data set, only the last such point is used. See "Simulating an Overlaid Scatter or Needle Plot" later in this chapter for information on producing scatter and needle plots with more than one vertical value for each X-Y combination.

Surface Plots

For surface plots, the observations in the input data set should form an evenly spaced grid of horizontal (*x* and *y*) values and exactly one vertical *z* value for each of these combinations. For example, data containing 5 distinct values for *x* and 10 distinct values for *y* should be part of a data set that contains 50 observations with values for *x*, *y*, and *z*.

The data set must contain nonmissing *z* values for at least 50 percent of the grid cells in order for the G3D procedure to produce a satisfactory plot. When the G3D procedure cannot produce a satisfactory surface plot because of missing *z* values, SAS/GRAPH software issues a warning message and a graph may not be produced. To correct this problem, you should process the data set with the G3GRID procedure and use the processed data set as the input data set for the G3D procedure. The G3GRID procedure interpolates the necessary values to produce a data set with nonmissing *z* values for every combination of *x* and *y*. The G3GRID procedure can also smooth data for use with the G3D procedure. You use the output data set from the G3GRID procedure as the input data set for the G3D procedure.

For surface plots, only one *z* point is plotted for each combination of *x* and *y*. For example, you cannot draw a sphere using the PLOT statement. If there is more than one observation for a combination of *x* and *y* in the data set, only the last such point is used.

Changing Data Ranges

By default, the range of the *z* axis is defined by the minimum and maximum *z* values in the input data set. You can restrict or expand the range of the *z* axis by using the ZMIN= and ZMAX= options in the PLOT or SCATTER statement. To restrict the range of an *x* or *y* axis, you can use a WHERE statement in the PROC step or a WHERE or IF statement in a DATA step to create a subset of the data set.

Global Statements

All currently defined titles and footnotes are displayed in every graph generated by the procedure.

Note: AXIS and LEGEND definitions are not supported by the G3D procedure. You can use the Annotate facility or TITLE, FOOTNOTE, and NOTE statements to produce legends, tick mark values, and axis labels. See "Controlling the Axes" in "PLOT Statement" and "SCATTER Statement" for information on controlling axis labels and tick mark values with PLOT statement and SCATTER statement options.

PROC G3D Statement

The PROC G3D statement initiates the procedure and, if necessary, specifies the input data set. In addition, it can specify a data set for annotation and a destination catalog for graphics output.

Syntax

The general form of the PROC G3D statement is

PROC G3D <DATA=*SAS-data-set*>
        <ANNOTATE=*Annotate-data-set*>
        <GOUT=*output-catalog*>;

Requirements

The G3D procedure must have an input data set. By default, the procedure uses the most recently created data set as its input data set. You can use the DATA= option to select a specific data set. If no data set has been created in the current SAS session and the DATA= option is not supplied, an error occurs and the procedure stops.

You must specify at least one PLOT or SCATTER statement with the procedure.

Options

You can use the following options in the PROC G3D statement. Options used in a PROC G3D statement affect all the graphs produced by the procedure.

ANNOTATE=*Annotate-data-set*
ANNO=*Annotate-data-set*

> specifies a data set to provide annotation for all plots produced by the G3D procedure. (To annotate individual graphs, use the ANNOTATE= option in a PLOT or SCATTER statement.) *Annotate-data-set* must contain the appropriate Annotate variables. See Chapter 18, "The Annotate Data Set" for details.

DATA=*SAS-data-set*

> specifies the data set that contains the numeric data values to be represented on a surface, needle, or scatter plot. By default, the procedure uses the most recently created data set.

GOUT=*output-catalog*

> specifies the SAS catalog in which to save the graphics output produced by the G3D procedure for later replay. You can use the GREPLAY procedure to view the graphs stored in the catalog. By default, catalog entries are written to the default catalog WORK.GSEG, which is erased at the end of your session.

PLOT Statement

The PLOT statement produces three-dimensional surface plots of the values of the three-variable combination specified in the statement.

The plots represent the shape of the surface described by the values of the horizontal variables (*x* and *y*) and the vertical variable (*z*). The values of the vertical variable are plotted on a *z* axis. The values of the horizontal variables are plotted on the *x* and *y* axes.

Syntax

The general form of the PLOT statement is

PLOT *y**x=*z*
> </ <ANNOTATE=*Annotate-data-set*>
> <*appearance-options*>
> <*axes-options*>
> <*descriptive-options*>>;

□ PLOT variables are as follows:

y   is a horizontal variable whose values are plotted on the *y* axis

x   is a horizontal variable whose values are plotted on the *x* axis

z   is a vertical variable whose values are plotted on the *z* axis.

□ *appearance-options* can affect one or more of the following:

□ color selection

CBOTTOM=*bottom-surface-color*

CTOP=*top-surface-color*

□ surface appearance

SIDE

XYTYPE=1 | 2 | 3

where 1 | 2 | 3 specifies the direction of lines representing the surface

□ rotating and tilting

ROTATE=*angle-list*

where *angle-list* specifies angles at which to rotate the *x-y* plane about the *z* axis

TILT=*angle-list*

where *angle-list* specifies angles at which to tilt the graph toward you

□ *axes-options* can affect one or more of the following:

□ color selection

CAXIS=*axis-color*

CTEXT=*text-color*

□ axis characteristics

GRID

NOAXIS

NOLABEL

XTICKNUM=*n*

where *n* is the number of major tick marks on the *x* axis

YTICKNUM=*n*

where *n* is the number of major tick marks on the *y* axis

ZMAX=*value*

where *value* specifies the maximum value displayed on a plot's *z* axis

ZMIN=*value*

where *value* specifies the minimum value displayed on a plot's *z* axis

ZTICKNUM=*n*

where *n* is the number of major tick marks on the *z* axis

□ *description-options* can be one or both of the following:

DESCRIPTION='*string*'

NAME='*string*'

Plot statement options are fully described in "Options" later in this section.

Requirements

A PLOT statement must specify exactly one plot request. The plot request specifies a combination of three variables from the input data set. Variables specified in PLOT statements must be numeric variables.

Options

You can use the following options in the PLOT statement. Options used in a PLOT statement affect all graphs produced by that statement. If you use any of the following options, separate them from the plot request with a slash (/). If you do not use any options, omit the slash.

ANNOTATE=*Annotate-data-set*
ANNO=*Annotate-data-set*
> specifies a data set to be used for annotation of graphs produced by the statement. *Annotate-data-set* must contain the appropriate Annotate variables. See Chapter 18 for details.
>
> If the ANNOTATE= option is also used with the PROC G3D statement, both sets of annotation are applied. If you specify BY-group processing, the Annotate data set must contain the BY variable. For details, see "Using BY-Group Processing with the Annotate Facility" in Chapter 18 and "Details of BY-Group Processing" in Chapter 10.

CAXIS=*axis-color*
> specifies a color for axis lines and tick marks. By default, axes are displayed in the second color in the current colors list.

CBOTTOM=*bottom-surface-color*
> specifies a color for the bottom of the plot surface. By default, the bottom surface is displayed in the fourth color in the current colors list.

CTEXT=*text-color*
> specifies a color for all text on the axes, including tick mark values and axis labels. If you do not use the CTEXT= option, a color specification is searched for in the following order:
>
> 1. the CTEXT= option in a GOPTIONS statement
>
> 2. the default, the first color in the colors list.

CTOP=*top-surface-color*
> specifies a color for the top of the plot surface. By default, the top surface is displayed in the third color in the current colors list.

DESCRIPTION='*string*'
DES='*string*'
> specifies a descriptive string, up to 40 characters long, that appears in the Description field of the catalog entry for the graph. The description does not appear on the graph. By default, the procedure assigns a description of the form PLOT OF $y*x=z$, where $y*x=z$ is the request specified in the PLOT statement.

GRID
> draws reference lines at the major tick marks on all axes. Output 39.5 in "PLOT Statement Examples" later in this chapter illustrates the use of the GRID option.

NAME='*string*'

specifies a string, up to eight characters long, that appears in the Name field of the catalog entry for the graph. *String* must be a valid SAS name. By default, the name assigned is G3D. If either the name specified or the default name duplicates an existing name in the catalog, SAS/GRAPH software adds a number to the duplicate name to create a unique name, for example, G3D2.

NOAXIS
NOAXES

specifies that a plot have no axes, axis labels, or tick mark values.

NOLABEL

specifies that a plot have no axis labels or tick mark values. Use this option if you want to generate axis labels and tick mark values with an Annotate data set.

ROTATE=*angle-list*

specifies one or more angles at which to rotate the *x-y* plane about the perpendicular *z* axis. The units for *angle-list* are degrees. By default, ROTATE=70.

Angle-list can be specified in the following ways:

n n . . . n

n,n, . . . ,n

n TO *n* <BY *increment*> <*n . . . n*> <*n, . . . ,n*>

n n . . . n TO *n* <BY *increment*> <*n . . . n*>

n,n, . . . ,n TO *n* <BY *increment*> <*n, . . . ,n*>

The values specified in *angle-list* can be negative or positive and can be larger than 360° . For example, a rotation angle of 45° can also be expressed as follows:

```
rotate=405
rotate=-315
```

Specifying a sequence of angles produces separate graphs for each angle. The angles specified in the ROTATE= option are paired with any angles specified with the TILT= option. If one option contains fewer values than the other, the last value in the shorter list is paired with the remaining values in the longer list. (See the TILT= option later in this section.)

SIDE

produces a surface graph with a side wall. Output 39.6 in "PLOT Statement Examples" later in this chapter illustrates the use of the SIDE option.

TILT=*angle-list*

specifies one or more angles at which to tilt the graph toward you. The units for *angle-list* are degrees. By default, TILT=70.

Angle-list can be specified in the following ways:

n n . . . n

n,n, . . . ,n

n TO *n* <BY *increment*> <*n . . . n*> <*n, . . . ,n*>

n n . . . n TO *n* <BY *increment*> <*n . . . n*>

n,n, . . . ,n TO *n* <BY *increment*> <*n, . . . ,n*>

The values specified in *angle-list* must be 0 through 90.

Specifying a sequence of angles produces separate graphs for each angle. The angles specified in the TILT= option are paired with any angles specified with the ROTATE= option. If one option contains fewer values than the other, the last value in the shorter list is paired with the remaining values in the longer list. (See the ROTATE= option earlier in this section.)

XTICKNUM=*n*
YTICKNUM=*n*
ZTICKNUM=*n*

specify the number of major tick marks located on a plot's *x*, *y*, or *z* axis, respectively. The value for *n* must be 2 or greater. By default, XTICKNUM=4, YTICKNUM=4, and ZTICKNUM=4.

XYTYPE=1 | 2 | 3

specifies the direction of lines used to represent the surface. XYTYPE=1 displays the surface using lines representing *y* axis values. That is, it only draws lines parallel to the *x* axis. XYTYPE=2 displays the surface using lines representing *x* axis values. That is, it only draws lines parallel to the *y* axis. XYTYPE=3 displays the surface using lines representing values for both the *x* and *y* axes, creating a fishnet-like surface. By default, XYTYPE=3. See Figure 39.3 in "Changing the Surface Appearance" later in this chapter for an example of the effect of the XYTYPE= option on the appearance of the surface.

ZMAX=*value*
ZMIN=*value*

specify the maximum and minimum values displayed on a plot's *z* axis. By default, the *z* axis is defined by the minimum and maximum *z* values in the data set. You can use the ZMIN= and ZMAX= options to extend the *z* axis beyond this range. The value specified by the ZMAX= option must be greater than that specified by the ZMIN= option.

If you specify a ZMAX= or ZMIN= value within the actual range of the *z* variable values, the plot's data values are clipped at the specified level. For example, if the minimum *z* value in the data set is 0 and you specify ZMIN=1, the values of *z* that are less than 1 will be plotted as if they are 1.

Using the PLOT Statement

You can include any number of PLOT statements within the procedure. For example, the following statements produce two surface plots:

```
plot y*x=z;
plot b*a=c;
```

You can also use PLOT statement options to specify

□ an Annotate data set for graphic enhancement

□ appearance characteristics

□ axes characteristics

□ descriptive characteristics.

Rotating and Tilting the Plot

Since plot information on surface plots can be hidden by peaks and valleys, the TILT= and ROTATE= options can change the viewing angle and display plot areas that are hidden from view. Figure 39.2 shows how the ROTATE= and TILT= options can change the viewing angle of the graph.

The ROTATE= option enables you to view data from any angle around the three-dimensional surface. It rotates the horizontal (*x-y*) plane about the *z* axis. This option is useful for bringing into view peaks and valleys previously hidden by other parts of a plot's surface.

The TILT= option enables you to accentuate the peaks and valleys of the surface by tilting the surface toward or away from you.

At certain combinations of TILT= and ROTATE= angles, the tick mark values may overlap.

Figure 39.2 *Rotating and Tilting a Graph*

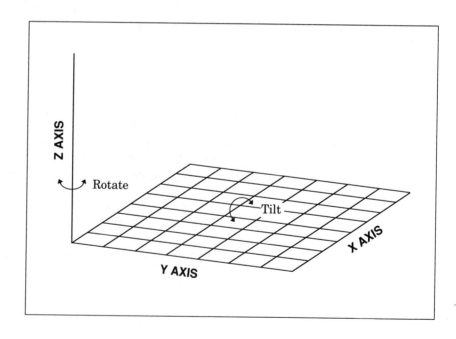

Controlling the Axes

PLOT statement options enable you to specify characteristics for all three plot axes. You can also specify characteristics for reference lines.

Note: The G3D procedure does not support AXIS definitions.

You can specify axis color using the CAXIS= option or specify that plots display no axes, no axis labels, or no tick mark values. You can also specify the number of tick marks, minimum and maximum values for the z axis, and whether grid lines connect axis tick marks. Because the relationship between a plot's surface and the actual data values can be difficult to interpret, PLOT statement options can improve a graph by changing the number of tick marks on the axes or restricting the range of the vertical (z) variable. You can use the XTICKNUM=, YTICKNUM=, and ZTICKNUM= options to control the number of major tick marks on the x, y, and z axes, respectively. In addition, you can use the ZMIN= and ZMAX= options to control the range of values plotted on the z axis.

You can change the font and height of axis labels and axis values by specifying the desired font and height with the FTEXT= and HTEXT= graphics options.

Changing the Surface Appearance

You can use the XYTYPE= option to change the appearance of the surface of the plot. This option lets you select the direction of the lines that form the surface plot. Figure 39.3 shows examples of each type of plot surface.

Figure 39.3 *Surface Appearance for Different XYTYPE= Values*

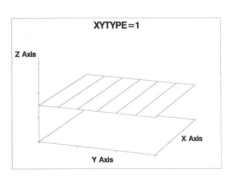
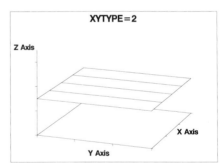
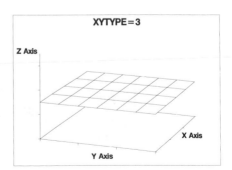

PLOT Statement Examples

The following examples illustrate major features of the PLOT statement within the G3D procedure.

Default Surface Plot

This example uses the PLOT statement to produce a surface plot of a function. The following program statements produce Output 39.4:

```
   /* set the graphics environment */
goptions reset=global gunit=pct border
        ftext=swissb htitle=6 htext=3;

   /* create the data set HAT */
data hat;
   do x=-5 to 5 by 0.25;
      do y=-5 to 5 by 0.25;
         z=sin(sqrt(x*x+y*y));
         output;
      end;
   end;
run;

   /* define title and footnote for plot */
title 'Surface Plot of HAT Data Set';
footnote j=r 'GR39N02  ';

   /* show the plot */
proc g3d data=hat;
   plot y*x=z;
run;
```

Output 39.4 Surface Plot
(GR39N02)

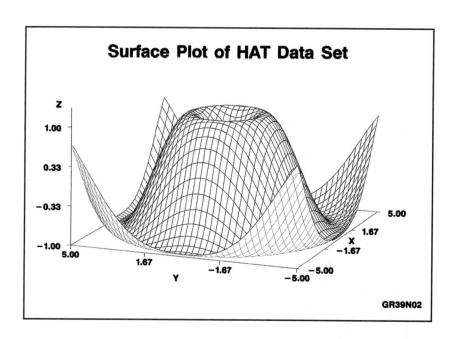

This example illustrates the following features:

□ The PLOT statement specifies the plot request, Y*X=Z.

□ Default values are used for the *x*, *y*, and *z* axes.

□ The default rotation of 70° is used.

Rotated Surface Plot with Reference Lines

This example uses the PLOT statement to produce a surface plot of a function. The surface plot is rotated 45° . The following program statements produce Output 39.5:

```
/* set the graphics environment */
goptions reset=global gunit=pct border
         ftext=swissb htitle=6 htext=3;

/* create the data set HAT */
data hat;
   do x=-5 to 5 by .25;
      do y=-5 to 5 by .25;
         z=sin(sqrt(x*x+y*y));
         output;
      end;
   end;
run;

/* define title and footnote for plot */
title 'Surface Plot of HAT Data Set';
footnote j=r 'GR39N03  ';

/* show the plot */
proc g3d;
   plot y*x=z
        / grid
          rotate=45
          ctop=green
          cbottom=blue
          yticknum=5
          zticknum=5
          zmin=-3
          zmax=1;
run;
```

Output 39.5 Rotated Surface
Plot (GR39N03)

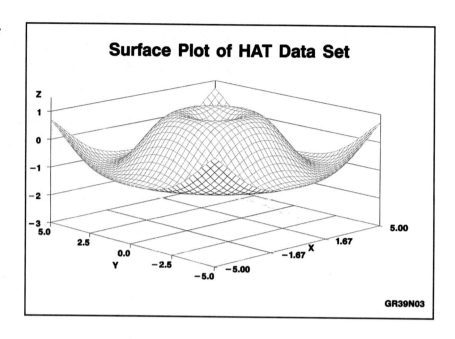

This example illustrates the following features:

□ The GRID option draws reference lines for all *x*, *y*, and *z* axis tick marks.

□ The ROTATE= option specifies a rotation angle of 45° for the plot.

□ The YTICKNUM= and ZTICKNUM= options specify the number of tick marks for the *y* and *z* axes.

□ The ZMIN= and ZMAX= options specify the minimum and maximum values for the *z* axis.

Tilted Surface Plot with Side Walls

This example uses the PLOT statement to produce a surface plot of a function. The surface plot is tilted 15°. The following program statements produce Output 39.6:

```
    /* set the graphics environment */
goptions reset=global gunit=pct border
        ftext=swissb htitle=6 htext=3;

    /* create the data set HAT */
data hat;
   do x=-5 to 5 by .25;
      do y=-5 to 5 by .25;
         z=sin(sqrt(x*x+y*y));
         output;
      end;
   end;
run;
```

```
          /* define title and footnote for plot */
     title 'Surface Plot of HAT Data Set';
     footnote j=r 'GR39N04  ';

          /* show the plot */
     proc g3d;
        plot y*x=z
               / side
                  tilt=15;
     run;
```

Output 39.6 *Tilted Surface Plot (GR39N04)*

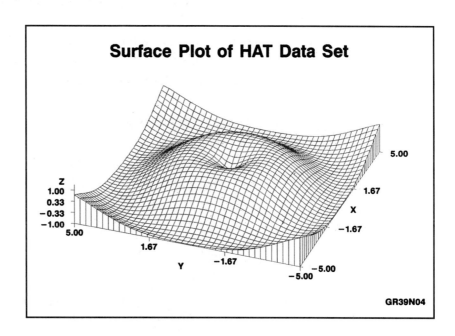

This example illustrates the following features:

□ The SIDE option draws a side wall for the graph.

□ The TILT= option specifies a tilt angle of 15° for the plot.

□ The default rotation of 70° is used.

SCATTER Statement

The SCATTER statement produces three-dimensional needle or scatter plots of the values of the three-variable combinations specified in the statement. Because a scatter graph displays a symbol for each data point, it is not sensitive to missing values like a surface graph produced by a PLOT statement. The G3D procedure can include any number of SCATTER statements.

SCATTER statement options can assign names and descriptions to graphics catalog entries generated by the procedure, manipulate plot axes, and modify the appearance of a graph.

By default, the SCATTER statement produces a needle plot. When the lines drawn from the data points to the base plane complicate a graph, you can use the NONEEDLE option to produce a scatter plot.

Syntax

The general form of the SCATTER statement is

SCATTER *y*x=z*
       </ <ANNOTATE=Annotate-data-set>
        <appearance-options>
        <axes-options>
        <description-options>>;

□ SCATTER variables are as follows:

  y   specifies a horizontal variable whose values are plotted on the *y* axis

  x   specifies a horizontal variable whose values are plotted on the *x* axis

  z   specifies a vertical variable whose values are plotted on the *z* axis.

□ *appearance-options* can affect one or more of the following:

  □ point appearance

    COLOR=*'data-point-color'* | *data-point-color-variable*

    NONEEDLE

    SHAPE= *'symbol-name'* | *shape-variable*

    SIZE=*value* | *size-variable*

  □ rotating and tilting

    ROTATE=*angle-list*

       where *angle-list* specifies angles at which to rotate the *x* and *y* axes about the *z* axis

    TILT=*angle-list*

       where *angle-list* specifies angles at which to tilt the graph toward you

□ *axes-options* can affect one or more of the following:

  □ color selection

    CAXIS=*axis-color*

    CTEXT=*text-color*

  □ axis characteristics

    GRID

    NOAXIS

    NOLABEL

    XTICKNUM=*n*

       where *n* is the number of major tick marks on the *x* axis

    YTICKNUM=*n*

       where *n* is the number of major tick marks on the *y* axis

ZMAX=*value*

> where *value* specifies the maximum value displayed on a plot's z axis

ZMIN=*value*

> where *value* specifies the minimum value displayed on a plot's z axis

ZTICKNUM=*n*

> where *n* is the number of major tick marks on the z axis

□ *description-options* can be one or more of the following:

DESCRIPTION='*string*'

NAME='*string*'

Scatter statement options are fully described in "Options" later in this section.

Requirements

A SCATTER statement must specify exactly one plot request. The plot request specifies a combination of three variables from the input data set. Variables specified in SCATTER statements must be numeric variables. The SCATTER statement does not require a full grid of observations for the horizontal variable.

The keyword SCATTER can be abbreviated SCAT.

Options

You can use the following options in the SCATTER statement. Options used in a SCATTER statement affect all graphs produced by that statement. If you use any of the following options, separate them from the scatter request with a slash (/). If you do not use any options, omit the slash.

ANNOTATE=*Annotate-data-set*
ANNO=*Annotate-data-set*
> specifies a data set to be used for annotation of graphs produced by the statement. *Annotate-data-set* must contain the appropriate Annotate variables. See Chapter 18 for details.
>
> If the ANNOTATE= option is also used with the PROC G3D statement, both sets of annotation are applied. If you specify BY-group processing, the Annotate data set must contain the BY variable. For details, see "Using BY-Group Processing with the Annotate Facility" in Chapter 18 and "Details of BY-Group Processing" in Chapter 10.

CAXIS=*axis-color*
> specifies a color for axis lines and tick marks. By default, axes are displayed in the second color in the colors list.

COLOR='*data-point-color*' | *data-point-color-variable*

specifies a color name or a character variable in the input data set whose values are color names. These color values determine the color or colors of the shapes that represent a plot's data points. Color values must be valid color names for the device used. By default, plot shapes are displayed in the third color in the current colors list.

If you specify COLOR='*data-point-color*', all shapes are drawn in that color. For example, the procedure uses YELLOW for all graph shapes when you specify

```
color='yellow'
```

If you specify COLOR=*data-point-color-variable*, the color of the symbol is determined by the value of the color variable for that observation. For example, the procedure uses the value of the variable CLASS as the color for each data point shape when you specify

```
color=class
```

Using COLOR=*data-point-color-variable* enables you to assign different colors to the shapes to classify data.

CTEXT=*text-color*

specifies a color for all text on the axes, including tick mark values and axis labels. If you do not use the CTEXT= option, a color specification is searched for in the following order:

1. the CTEXT= option in a GOPTIONS statement

2. the default, the first color in the colors list.

DESCRIPTION='*string*'
DES='*string*'

specifies a descriptive string, up to 40 characters long, that appears in the Description field of the catalog entry for the graph. The description does not appear on the graph. By default, the procedure assigns a description of the form SCATTER OF $y^*x=z$, where $y^*x=z$ is the request specified in the SCATTER statement.

GRID

draws reference lines at the major tick marks on all axes. Output 39.8 in "SCATTER Statement Examples" later in this chapter illustrates the use of the GRID option.

NAME='*string*'

specifies a string, up to eight characters long, that appears in the Name field of the catalog entry for the graph. *String* must be a valid SAS name. By default, the name assigned is G3D. If either the name specified or the default name duplicates an existing name in the catalog, SAS/GRAPH software adds a number to the duplicate name to create a unique name, for example, G3D2.

NOAXIS
NOAXES

specifies that a plot have no axes, axis labels, or tick mark values.

NOLABEL

specifies that a plot have no axis labels or tick mark values. Use this option if you want to generate axis labels and tick mark values with an Annotate data set.

NONEEDLE

specifies that a plot have no lines connecting the shapes representing data points to the *x-y* plane. The NONEEDLE option produces a scatter plot. The NONEEDLE option has no effect when SHAPE='PILLAR' or SHAPE='PRISM'.

ROTATE=*angle-list*

specifies one or more angles at which to rotate the *x-y* plane about the perpendicular *z* axis. The units for angle-list are degrees. By default, ROTATE=70.

Angle-list can be specified in the following ways:

n n . . . n

n,n, . . . ,n

n TO *n* <BY *increment*> <*n . . . n*> <*n, . . . ,n*>

n n . . . n TO *n* <BY *increment*> <*n . . . n*>

n,n, . . . ,n TO *n* <BY *increment*> <*n, . . . ,n*>

The values specified in *angle-list* can be negative or positive and can be larger than 360°. For example, a rotation angle of 45° can also be expressed in the following ways:

```
rotate=405
rotate=-315
```

Specifying a sequence of angles produces separate graphs for each angle. The angles specified in the ROTATE= option are paired with any angles specified with the TILT= option. If one option contains fewer values than the other, the last value in the shorter list is paired with the remaining values in the longer list. See the TILT= option later in this section.

SHAPE= '*symbol-name*' | *shape-variable*

specifies a symbol name or a character variable whose values are valid symbol names. Symbols represent a scatter plot's data points. By default, SHAPE='PYRAMID'.

Valid values for *symbol-name* are

BALLOON	DIAMOND	PRISM
CLUB	FLAG	PYRAMID
CROSS	HEART	SPADE
CUBE	PILLAR	SQUARE
CYLINDER	POINT	STAR.

Figure 39.4 illustrates these symbol types with needles.

(SHAPE= continued)

Figure 39.4 *Scatter Plot Symbols*

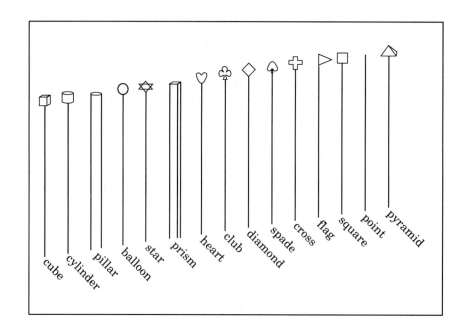

If you specify SHAPE='*symbol-name*', all data points are drawn in that shape. For example, the procedure draws all data points as balloons when you specify

```
shape='balloon'
```

If you specify SHAPE=*shape-variable*, the shape of the data point is determined by the value of the shape variable for that observation. For example, the procedure uses the value of the variable CLASS for a particular observation as the shape for that data point when you specify

```
shape=class
```

Using SHAPE=*shape-variable* enables you to assign different shapes to the data points to classify data.

SIZE=*value* | *size-variable*
specifies either a constant or a numeric variable, the values of which determine the size of symbol shapes on the scatter or needle plot.

If you specify SIZE=*value*, all data points are drawn in that size. For example, if you specify SIZE=3, the procedure draws all symbol shapes three times the normal size. By default, SIZE=1.0. The units are in default symbol size.

If you specify SIZE=*size-variable*, the size of the data point is determined by the value of the size variable for that observation. For example, when you specify SIZE=CLASS, the procedure uses the value of the variable CLASS for each observation as the size of that data point. Using SIZE=*size-variable* enables you to assign different sizes to the data points to classify data.

TILT=*angle-list*
specifies one or more angles at which to tilt the graph toward you. The units for *angle-list* are degrees. By default, TILT=70.

Angle-list can be specified in the following ways:

n n . . . n

n,n, . . . ,n

n TO *n* <BY *increment*> <*n . . . n*> <*n, . . . ,n*>

n n . . . n TO *n* <BY *increment*> <*n . . . n*>

n,n, . . . ,n TO *n* <BY *increment*> <*n, . . . ,n*>

The values specified in *angle-list* must be 0 through 90.

Specifying a sequence of angles produces separate graphs for each angle. The angles specified in the TILT= option are paired with any angles specified with the ROTATE= option. If one option contains fewer values than the other, the last value in the shorter list is paired with the remaining values in the longer list. (See the ROTATE= option earlier in this section.)

XTICKNUM=*n*
YTICKNUM=*n*
ZTICKNUM=*n*

specify the number of major tick marks located on a plot's *x*, *y*, or *z* axis, respectively. The value for *n* must be 2 or greater. By default, XTICKNUM=4, YTICKNUM=4, and ZTICKNUM=4.

ZMAX=*value*
ZMIN=*value*

specify the maximum and minimum values displayed on a plot's *z* axis. By default, the *z* axis is defined by the minimum and maximum *z* values in the data. You can use the ZMIN= and ZMAX= options to extend the *z* axis beyond this range. The value specified by the ZMAX= option must be greater than that specified by the ZMIN= option. If you specify a ZMAX= or ZMIN= value within the actual range of the *z* variable values, the plot's data values are clipped at the specified level.

Using the SCATTER Statement

You can include any number of SCATTER statements within the procedure. For example, the following statements produce two scatter plots:

```
scatter y*x=z;
scatter b*a=c;
```

You can use SCATTER statement options to specify

□ an Annotate data set for graph enhancement and drawing solid plot symbols

□ appearance characteristics

□ axes characteristics

□ descriptive characteristics.

Rotating and Tilting the Plot

Since plot information on scatter and needle plots can be hidden by uneven data, the TILT= and ROTATE= options can change the viewing angle and display plot areas that are hidden from view. Figure 39.2 in "Using the PLOT Statement" earlier in this chapter shows how the ROTATE= and TILT= options can change the viewing angle of the graph.

The ROTATE= option enables you to view data from any angle around the three-dimensional graph. It rotates the horizontal X-Y plane about the z axis. This option is useful for bringing into view data points previously hidden by other data points on a plot.

The TILT= option enables you to accentuate the location of data points by tilting the surface toward or away from you.

At certain combinations of TILT= and ROTATE= angles, the tick mark values may overlap.

Controlling the Axes

SCATTER statement options enable you to specify characteristics for all three plot axes. You can also specify characteristics for reference lines.

Note: The G3D procedure does not support AXIS definitions.

You can specify axis color using the CAXIS= option or specify that plots display no axes, no axis labels, or no tick mark values. You can also specify the number of tick marks, minimum and maximum values for the z axis, and whether grid lines connect axis tick marks. Because the relationship between a plot's data points and the actual data values can be difficult to interpret, SCATTER statement options can improve a graph by changing the number of tick marks on the axes or restricting the range of the vertical (z) variable. You can use the XTICKNUM=, YTICKNUM=, and ZTICKNUM= options to specify the number of major tick marks on the x, y, and z axes, respectively. You can use the ZMIN= and ZMAX= options to control the range of values plotted on the z axis.

You can change the font and height of axis labels and axis values by specifying the desired font and height with the FTEXT= and HTEXT= graphics options.

Changing the Appearance of the Points

You can use the COLOR=, SHAPE=, and SIZE= options to change the appearance of your scatter or needle plot or to classify data using color, shape, size, or any combination of these features. Figure 39.4 in "SCATTER Statement Options" illustrates the shape names you can specify in the SHAPE= option.

For example, to make all of the data points red balloons at twice the normal size, use

```
scatter y*x=z / color='red' shape='balloon' size=2;
```

To size your points according to the values of the variable TYPE in your input data set, use

```
scatter y*x=z / size=type;
```

Simulating an Overlaid Scatter or Needle Plot

You can approximate an overlaid scatter or needle plot by graphing multiple values for the vertical (z) variables for a single (x, y) position in a single scatter or needle plot. To do this, you can add a small value to the value of one of the horizontal variables (x or y) to give the observation a slightly different (x, y) position, thus enabling the procedure to plot both values of the vertical (z) variable. You can represent each different vertical (z) variable with a different symbol, size, or color. The resulting plot appears to be multiple plots overlaid on the same axes.

For example, suppose you want to graph a data set that contains two values for the vertical variable Z for each combination of variables X and Y. You could produce the original data set with a DATA step like the following:

```
data planes;
   input x y z shape $;
   cards;
1 1 1 PRISM
1 2 1 PRISM
1 3 1 PRISM
2 1 1 PRISM
2 2 1 PRISM
2 3 1 PRISM
3 1 1 PRISM
3 2 1 PRISM
3 3 1 PRISM
1 1 2 BALLOON
1 2 2 BALLOON
1 3 2 BALLOON
2 1 2 BALLOON
2 2 2 BALLOON
2 3 2 BALLOON
3 1 2 BALLOON
3 2 2 BALLOON
3 3 2 BALLOON
;
run;
```

Note that the SHAPE variable is assigned a different value for each different Z value for a single combination of X and Y values.

Ordinarily, the SCATTER statement would only plot the Z value for the last observation for a single combination of X and Y. However, you can use a DATA step like the following to assign a slightly different (x, y) position to all observations where the value of Z is greater than 1:

```
data planes2;
   set planes;
   if z > 1 then x = x + .000001;
run;
```

Then you can use a SCATTER statement to produce a plot like the one in Figure 39.5:

```
proc g3d data=planes2;
   scatter x*y=z / zmin=0 shape=shape;
run;
```

Figure 39.5 *Simulated Overlaid Needle Plot*

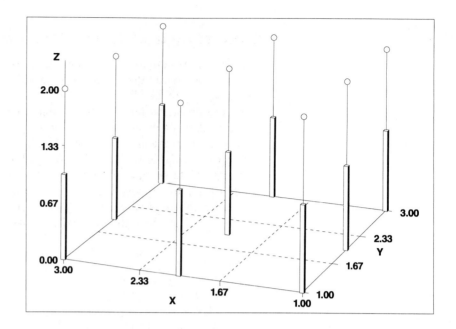

SCATTER Statement Examples

The following examples illustrate major features of the SCATTER statement.

Needle and Scatter Plots with Shape Symbols and Color

This example uses the SCATTER statement to produce a needle plot and a scatter plot of iris flower characteristics. It uses shape symbols and color to distinguish among information for various iris species. The following program statements produce Output 39.7 and 39.8:

```
/* set the graphics environment */
goptions reset=global gunit=pct border
         ftext=swissb htitle=6 htext=3;

/* create data set IRIS */
data iris;
   length species $12. colorval $8. shapeval $8.;
   input sepallen sepalwid petallen petalwid spec_no;
   if spec_no=1 then do;
      species='setosa';
      shapeval='club';
      colorval='blue';
   end;
   if spec_no=2 then do;
      species='versicolor';
      shapeval='diamond';
      colorval='red';
   end;
   if spec_no=3 then do;
      species='virginica';
      shapeval='spade';
      colorval='green'   ;
   end;
```

```
   sizeval=sepalwid/30;
   cards;
50 33 14 02 1
64 28 56 22 3
more data lines
63 33 60 25 3
53 37 15 02 1
;
run;

   /* define titles and footnotes for graph */
title1 'Iris Species Classification';
title2 'Physical Measurement';
title3 'Source: Fisher (1936) Iris Data';
footnote1 j=l '  Petallen: Petal Length in mm.'
          j=r 'Petalwid: Petal Width in mm.  ';
footnote2 j=l '  Sepallen: Sepal Length in mm.'
          j=r 'Sepal Width not shown          ';
footnote3 j=r 'GR39N05(a)  ';

   /* show the graph using NOTE statement for legend */
proc g3d data=iris;
   scatter petallen*petalwid=sepallen
          / color=colorval
            shape=shapeval;

      /* create a legend using NOTE statements */
   note;
   note j=r 'Species:   ' c=green 'Virginica        '
        j=r c=red 'Versicolor      '
        j=r c=blue 'Setosa          ';
run;

   /* define new title and footnotes */
title3;
footnote1 j=l '  Source: Fisher (1936) Iris Data';
footnote2 j=r 'GR39N05(b)  ';

   /* show the graph using LABEL statements to     */
   /* label the axes                               */
proc g3d data=iris;
   scatter petallen*petalwid=sepallen
          / noneedle
            grid
            color=colorval
            shape=shapeval;

      /* change the axes labels */
   label petallen='Petal Length'
         petalwid='Petal Width'
         sepallen='Sepal Length';
run;
```

Output 39.7 *Needle Plot of Iris Data (GR39N05(a))*

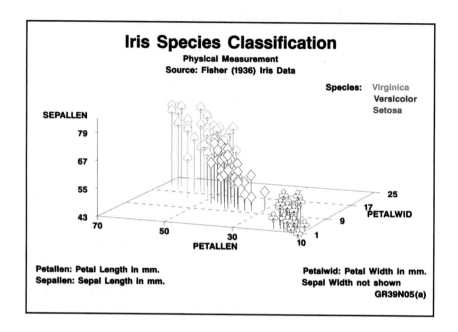

Output 39.8 *Scatter Plot of Iris Data (GR39N05(b))*

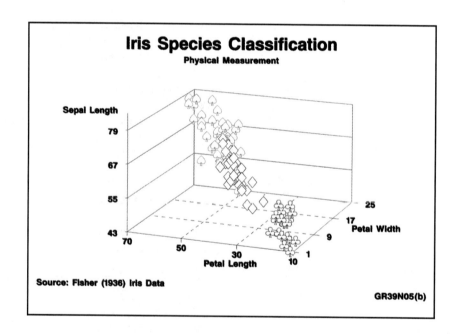

This example illustrates the following features:

□ The SCATTER statements specify the plot request PETALLEN*PETALWID=SEPALLEN.

□ For the first invocation of the G3D procedure, which produces Output 39.7,

　□ the COLOR= option specifies the character variable in the input data set that contains color information for the plot

　□ the SHAPE= option specifies the character variable in the input data set that contains shape information for the plot

　□ the NOTE statements use color as a key to different iris species

　□ the FOOTNOTE statements explain the default axis labels.

□ For the second invocation of the procedure, which produces
Output 39.8,

□ the NONEEDLE option suppresses the line drawn from the *x-y* plane
to the plot point

□ the GRID option draws reference lines for *x*, *y*, and *z* axis tick
marks

□ the LABEL statement associates labels with variable names,
resulting in improved axis labels.

The two graphs were produced by two separate invocations of the
procedure so that the output from the NOTE statement would not
appear in Output 39.8.

Rotated Scatter Plot

This example uses the SCATTER statement to produce a scatter plot of
humidity data. It uses color to distinguish air temperature ranges. The
plot is rotated −15°. The following program statements produce Output
39.9:

```
      /* set the graphics environment */
goptions reset=global gunit=pct border
         ftext=swissb htitle=6 htext=3;


      /* generate the data set HUMID */
data humid;
    length colorval $ 8.;
    label wtemp='Wet-Bulb Temp';
    label relhum='Rel. Humidity';
    label atemp='   Air Temp.';
    input atemp wtemp relhum;
    if atemp<26 then colorval="blue";
    else if atemp>=26 and atemp<+52 then colorval="red";
    else if atemp>=52 and atemp<78 then colorval="green";
    else if atemp>=78 and atemp<+104 then colorval="lib";
    else if atemp>104 then colorval="pink  ";
    cards;
0    1    67
0    2    33
more data lines
130  34   29
130  35   28
;
run;


      /* define title and footnotes for graph */
title 'Relative Humidity in Percent';
footnote1 j=l '  Source: William L. Donn, Meteorology, Fourth Edition';
footnote2 j=r 'GR39N06  ';
```

```
                    /* show the graph */
                proc g3d data=humid;
                    scatter atemp*wtemp=relhum
                            / shape='pillar'
                              color=colorval
                              caxis=blue
                              rotate=-15
                              size=.5
                              yticknum=5
                              xticknum=2
                              zticknum=4
                              zmin=0
                              zmax=100;
                run;
```

Output 39.9 *Scatter Plot of Humidity Data (GR39N06)*

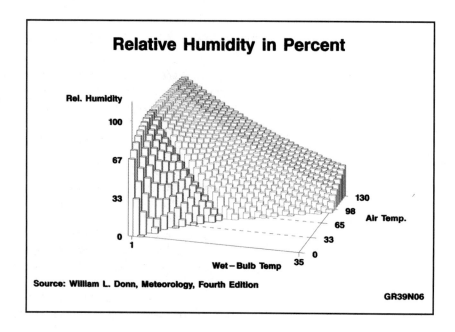

This example illustrates the following features:

□ The SHAPE= option specifies the shape PILLAR for the data symbol.

□ The ROTATE= option specifies a rotation angle of −15° for the plot.

□ The SIZE= option specifies the size of the symbols in the graph.

□ The XTICKNUM=, YTICKNUM=, and ZTICKNUM= options specify the number of tick marks for the x, y, and z axes, respectively.

□ The ZMIN= and ZMAX= options specify the minimum and maximum values for the z axis.

See Also

Chapter 18, "The Annotate Data Set"
> for information on using the Annotate facility with the G3D procedure

Chapter 24, "The GCONTOUR Procedure"
> for information on contour plots

Chapter 40, "The G3GRID Procedure"
> for information on interpolating or smoothing input data sets for the G3D procedure

SAS Language: Reference
> for information on the WHERE and IF statements

References

Fisher, R.A. (1936), "The Use of Multiple Measurements in Taxonomic Problems," *Annals of Eugenics*, 7, 179–188.

Watkins, S.L. (1974), "Algorithm 483, Masked Three-Dimensional Plot Program with Rotations (J6)," in *Collected Algorithms from ACM*, New York: Association for Computing Machinery.

CHAPTER *40* # The G3GRID Procedure

Overview

The G3GRID procedure creates data sets that the G3D or GCONTOUR procedure can use to produce three-dimensional surface or contour plots. Using the G3GRID procedure you can

☐ create a rectangular grid of interpolated or smoothed values from irregularly spaced observations for use in a three-dimensional surface or contour plot

☐ complete a rectangular grid of interpolated or smoothed values for an input data set with an insufficient number of observations to produce a three-dimensional surface or contour plot

☐ interpolate or smooth noisy data for a three-dimensional graph.

Note: The G3GRID procedure does not produce any graphics output. Instead, the output data set generated by the G3GRID procedure is normally used as input to the G3D or GCONTOUR procedure.

Output 40.1 shows a collection of data points, where $z=f(x, y)$. These points are randomly distributed and cannot be displayed with a G3D surface plot but can be displayed with a scatter or needle plot.

Output 40.1 *Scatter Plot of Data Set before G3GRID Processing (GR40N01(a))*

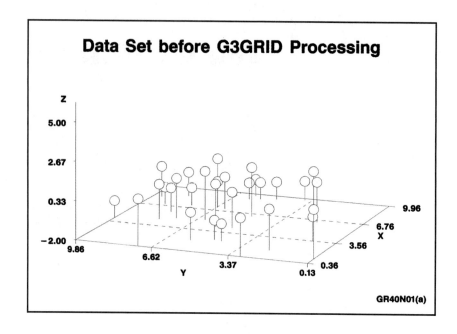

Output 40.2 shows a surface plot of the data set created by a G3GRID interpolation of the original data set shown in Output 40.1.

Output 40.2 *Surface Plot of Data Set after G3GRID Processing (GR40N01(b))*

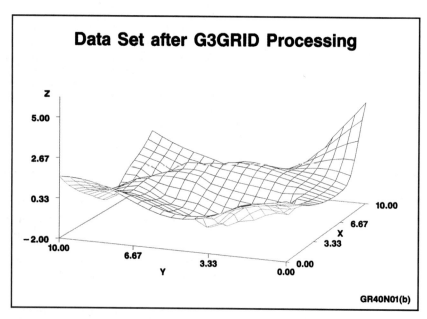

Note: The evenly distributed horizontal (x, y) data points form a grid for the three-dimensional graph.

G3GRID Procedure Syntax

The G3GRID procedure uses the following statements:

□ The G3GRID statement is required.

PROC G3GRID <DATA=*SAS-data-set*>
　　　　<OUT=*SAS-data-set*>
　　　　<OUTTRI=*SAS-data-set*>;

□ The GRID statement is required. You can use only one GRID statement with the procedure.

> **GRID** *y*x=z< . . . z-n>*
> </ <grid-options>*
> *<interpolation-options>>;*

□ The BY statement is optional and local.

> **BY** <options> *variable*;

For complete statement syntax, see the section on the appropriate statement.

Statement Descriptions

The purpose of each statement is described here.

BY	specifies the variable or variables by which the data are grouped for processing. A separate grid is produced for each value of the BY variable. See Chapter 10, "The BY Statement."
GRID	creates a data set whose *x* and *y* (horizontal) variable values form a complete grid and interpolates the value of the vertical (*z*) variables for each point on the *x-y* plane. You can specify multiple vertical variables for the two horizontal variables specified.
PROC G3GRID	starts the procedure and specifies the name of the data set to be used and any additional output options.

G3GRID Procedure Description

The following sections address issues that pertain to the G3GRID procedure as a whole: terminology and special data considerations.

Terminology

The following terms are used in the discussion of the G3GRID procedure and are defined in the Glossary.

coordinates	interpolate
function	spline
grid request	surface plot

Data Considerations

Each data set processed by the G3GRID procedure must contain at least three numeric variables:

□ two numeric horizontal variables, (*x*, *y*)

□ one or more numeric vertical variables, *z* through *z-n*.

If you specify more than one vertical variable, the G3GRID procedure performs a separate analysis and produces interpolated or smoothed values for each vertical variable. If more than one observation in the input data set has the same values for both horizontal variables, *x* and *y*, a warning message is printed, and only the first such point is used in the interpolation.

By default, the interpolation is performed after both variables are similarly scaled because the interpolation methods assume that the scales of *x* and *y* are comparable.

Multiple Vertical Variables

By naming multiple vertical (*z* through *z-n*) variables in your GRID statement, you can produce a data set that contains two horizontal variables and multiple vertical variables. You can use the resulting data set to produce plots of the relationships of the two horizontal variables to different vertical variables.

Horizontal Variables along a Nonlinear Curve

If the points generated by the horizontal variables tend to lie along a curve, a poor interpolation or spline may result. In such cases, both the vertical variable or variables and one of the horizontal variables should be modeled as a function of the remaining horizontal variable. You can use a scatter plot of the two horizontal variables to help you determine the appropriate function.

If the horizontal variable points are collinear, the procedure interpolates the function as constant along lines perpendicular to the line in the plane generated by the input data points.

PROC G3GRID Statement

The PROC G3GRID statement initiates the procedure and, if necessary, specifies the input data set. In addition, it can optionally specify one or two output data sets.

Syntax

The general form of the G3GRID statement is

PROC G3GRID <DATA=*SAS-data-set*>
       <OUT=*SAS-data-set*>
       <OUTTRI=*SAS-data-set*>;

Requirements

The G3GRID procedure must have an input data set. By default, the procedure uses the most recently created data set as its input data set. You can use the DATA= option to select a specific data set. If no data set has been created in the current SAS session and the DATA= option is not supplied, an error occurs and the procedure stops.

The input data set must contain at least three numeric variables, as described in "Data Considerations" earlier in this chapter, and must contain the numeric variables specified in the GRID statement used with the PROC G3GRID statement.

Options

You can use the following options in the PROC G3GRID statement:

DATA=*SAS-data-set*
> specifies the data set to be used by the G3GRID procedure. By default, the procedure uses the most recently created data set.

OUT=*SAS-data-set*
> specifies the output data set. The data set will contain any BY variables specified, the interpolated or smoothed values of the vertical variables (z through z-n), and the coordinates for all grid positions on the horizontal (x-y) plane. If smoothing is specified, the output data set also contains a variable named _SMTH_, whose value is a smoothing parameter. The observations in this data set are ordered by any variables specified with a BY statement. By default, the output of PROC G3GRID replaces the contents of the input data set.
>
> Depending on the shape of the original data and the options used, the output data set may contain values for the vertical (z through z-n) values that are outside the range of the original values in the data set.

OUTTRI=*SAS-data-set*
> specifies an additional output data set containing triangular coordinates. The data set will contain any BY variables specified, the two horizontal variables giving the horizontal (x-y) plane coordinates of the input points, and a variable named TRIANGLE that uses integer values to label the triangles. The observations in this data set are ordered by any variables specified with a BY statement. The OUTTRI= option is not valid when you use the SPLINE option in the GRID statement used with the PROC G3GRID statement.
>
> The data set contains three observations for each value of the variable TRIANGLE. The three observations give the coordinates of the three vertices of the triangle. Points on the convex hull of the input data set of points are also assumed to lie in degenerate triangles whose other vertices are at infinity. The points in the convex hull can be recovered by keeping only those triangles with exactly two missing vertices.
>
> By default, no OUTTRI= data set is produced.

GRID Statement

The GRID statement specifies the variables for interpolation or smoothing. These variables include two horizontal variables (x,y) and one or more vertical variables (z through z-n) that will be interpolated or smoothed as if it were a function of the two horizontal variables. GRID statement options can specify the number of observations in the output data set, output values for the two horizontal variables, and the type of interpolation used to determine values for the vertical variables.

Syntax

The general form of the GRID statement is

GRID *y*x=z< . . . z-n>*
    </ <grid-options>
        <interpolation-options>>;

□ GRID variables are defined as follows:

y*x   names the two horizontal variables that form the
                horizontal (*x-y*) plane

z through *z-n*   names one or more vertical variables for the
                interpolation.

□ *grid-options* can be one or more of the following:

AXIS1=*ascending-value-list*

   where *ascending-value-list* gives numeric values for the first (*y*)
   variable in the output data set

AXIS2=*ascending-value-list*

   where *ascending-value-list* gives numeric values for the second (*x*)
   variable in the output data set

NAXIS1=*n*

   where *n* specifies the number of values for the first (*y*) variable in
   the output data set

NAXIS2=*n*

   where *n* specifies the number of values for the second (*x*) variable
   in the output data set

□ *interpolation-options* can be one or more of the following:

JOIN

NEAR=*n*

   where *n* specifies the number of nearby data points to use when
   estimates are computed

NOSCALE

PARTIAL

SMOOTH=*ascending-value-list*

   where *ascending-value-list* specifies numbers to be used as
   smoothing parameters

SPLINE

Grid statement options are fully described in "Options" later in this
section.

Requirements

The GRID statement creates a data set using variables from the input data set.

It must specify numeric variables from the input data set. Although the GRID statement can specify only two horizontal variables, it can include multiple vertical variables. Names of multiple vertical variables must be separated by at least one blank, as in this example:

```
grid x*y=z w u v;
```

Options

You can use the following options in the GRID statement. Options used in a GRID statement affect all output produced by that statement. If you use any of the following options, separate them from the grid request with a slash (/). If you do not use any options, omit the slash.

AXIS1=*ascending-value-list*
> specifies a list of numeric values to assign to the first (y) variable in the grid request for the output data set. Numbers specified with this option determine the number of values for y and override a value specified with the NAXIS1= option.
>
> *Ascending-value-list* must be in ascending order. It can be specified in the following ways:
>
> *n n . . . n*
>
> *n,n, . . . ,n*
>
> *n* TO *n* <BY *increment*> <*n . . . n*> <*n, . . . ,n*>
>
> *n n . . . n* TO *n* <BY *increment*> <*n . . . n*>
>
> *n,n, . . . ,n* TO *n* <BY *increment*> <*n, . . . ,n*>

AXIS2=*ascending-value-list*
> specifies a list of numeric values to assign to the second (x) variable in the grid request for the output data set. Numbers specified with this option determine the number of values for x and override a value specified with the NAXIS2= option.
>
> *Ascending-value-list* must be in ascending order. It can be specified in the following ways:
>
> *n n . . . n*
>
> *n,n, . . . ,n*
>
> *n* TO *n* <BY *increment*> <*n . . . n*> <*n, . . . ,n*>
>
> *n n . . . n* TO *n* <BY *increment*> <*n . . . n*>
>
> *n,n, . . . ,n* TO *n* <BY *increment*> <*n, . . . ,n*>

JOIN
> uses a linear interpolation within a set of triangular regions formed from the input data set. This interpolation method creates values in the range of the initial values of the vertical variable, but the resulting interpolated surface may not be smooth.

NAXIS1=*n*

> specifies the number of values for the first (*y*) variable in the grid request for the output data set. The actual values used for *y* are determined by taking the minimum and maximum values of *y* and dividing the range into *n*−1 equal sections. By default, NAXIS1=11.
>
> A value specified with the NAXIS1= option is ignored if values are also specified with the AXIS1= option.

NAXIS2=*n*

> specifies the number of values for the second (*x*) variable in the grid request for the output data set. The actual values used for *x* are determined by taking the minimum and maximum values of *x* and dividing the range into *n*−1 equal sections. By default, NAXIS2=11.
>
> A value specified with the NAXIS2= option is ignored if values are also specified with the AXIS2= option.

NEAR=*n*

> specifies the number of nearest data points to use for computing the estimates of the first and second derivatives. As NEAR= values become larger, time and computation costs increase significantly. The NEAR= option is ignored if the SPLINE option is specified. The value of *n* must be greater than or equal to 3. By default, NEAR=3.
>
> If the number of input data points is insufficient for the number specified with the NEAR= option, a smaller number of data points is used.

NOSCALE

> specifies that the *x* and *y* variables not be scaled to the same range before interpolation. By default, the interpolation is performed after both variables are similarly scaled because the interpolation methods assume that the scales of *x* and *y* are comparable.

PARTIAL

> specifies that a spline be used to estimate the derivatives for the biquintic polynomial interpolation. A bivariate spline is fit to the nearest neighbors and used to estimate the needed derivatives. This option produces results that are less smooth than those produced by the SPLINE option and uses fewer computer resources. However, the results produced by the PARTIAL option are smoother than those produced by the default. The PARTIAL option is ignored if both the PARTIAL and SPLINE options are used.

▶ *Caution: Use this option only when you also use the SPLINE option.*

SMOOTH=*ascending-value-list*

> specifies a list of numbers for smoothing parameters.
>
> For each value λ of the smoothing parameter, a function $\mathbf{u}(x, y)$ is formed that minimizes

$$\frac{1}{n} \Sigma_{j=1}^{n} \left(\mathbf{u}(x_j, y_j) - z_j\right)^2 + \lambda \Sigma_{j=0}^{2} \int_{-\infty}^{\infty} \int_{-\infty}^{\infty} \binom{2}{j} \left(\frac{\partial^2 \mathbf{u}}{\partial x^j \partial y^{2-j}}\right)^2 dx dy$$

> where *n* is the number of data points and the pairs (x_j, y_j) are the available points, with corresponding function values z_j (Wahba 1979).

The higher the value of the smoothing parameter, the smoother the resulting interpolation. The lower the smoothing parameter, the closer the resulting surface is to the original data points. A smoothing parameter of 0 will produce the same results as the SPLINE option without the SMOOTH= option.

This procedure is repeated for each value of the smoothing parameter. The output data set specified in the OUT= option contains the interpolated values, the values of the grid points, and the values of the smoothing parameter in the variable _SMTH_. The output data set contains a separate grid for each value of the smoothing parameter.

Ascending-value-list must be in ascending order. It can be specified in the following ways:

n n . . . n

n,n, . . . ,n

n TO *n* <BY *increment*> <*n . . . n*> <*n, . . . ,n*>

n n . . . n TO *n* <BY *increment*> <*n . . . n*>

n,n, . . . ,n TO *n* <BY *increment*> <*n, . . . ,n*>

SPLINE

specifies the use of a bivariate spline (Harder and Desmarais 1972, Meinguet 1979) to interpolate or to form a smoothed estimate if the SMOOTH= option is also used. This option results in the use of an order n^3 algorithm, where n is the number of input data points. Consequently, this method can be time-consuming. If you use more than 100 input points, the procedure may use excessive time.

Using the GRID Statement

The GRID statement specifies the grid request for the G3GRID procedure. You can use GRID statement options to specify

□ the number of *x* and *y* values in the output data set

□ the values of *x* and *y* in the output data set

□ the interpolation method and characteristics for the output data set.

The OUT= Data Set

The output data set identified with the OUT= option in the PROC G3GRID statement contains the two horizontal variables, the interpolated or smoothed vertical variables, and the BY variables, if any. If the GRID statement's SMOOTH= option is used, the output data set also contains a variable named _SMTH_, with a value equal to that of the smoothing parameter.

By default, the G3GRID procedure produces a data set with 121 observations for combinations of eleven values for each of the horizontal variables, *x* and *y*. To create a data set with a different number of observations, you can use the NAXIS1= or NAXIS2= options with the GRID statement to specify the number of the values of *y* or *x*, respectively. Or, you can use the GRID statement's AXIS1= or AXIS2= options to specify the actual values for *y* or *x*, respectively.

Table 40.1 shows the number of observations that will be in the output data set if any of these options are used.

Table 40.1 *Number of Observations Contained in the Output Data Set*

Options Specified	Number of Observations in Output Data Set
None	121
AXIS1=	(number of values for AXIS1=) * 11
AXIS2=	(number of values for AXIS2=) * 11
NAXIS1=	(value of NAXIS1=) * 11
NAXIS2=	(value of NAXIS2=) * 11
AXIS1=, AXIS2=	(number of values for AXIS1=) * (number of values for AXIS2=)
AXIS1=, NAXIS1=	(number of values for AXIS1=) * 11
AXIS1=, NAXIS2=	(number of values for AXIS1=) * (value of NAXIS2=)
AXIS2=, NAXIS1=	(number of values for AXIS2=) * (value of NAXIS1=)
AXIS2=, NAXIS2=	(number of values for AXIS2=) * 11
NAXIS1=, NAXIS2=	(value of NAXIS1=) * (value of NAXIS2=)

If you specified multiple smoothing parameters, the number of observations in the output data set will be the number shown in Table 40.1 multiplied by the number of smoothing values specified in the SMOOTH= option. If you use BY-group processing, multiply the number in the table by the number of BY groups.

Depending on the shape of the original data and the options specified, the output data set may contain values for the vertical (z) values that are outside the range of the original values in the data set.

Default Bivariate Interpolation

Unless you specify the SPLINE option, the G3GRID procedure is an interpolation procedure. That is, it calculates z values for (x, y) points that are missing from the input grid. The surface formed by the interpolated data passes precisely through the data points in the input data set.

This default method of interpolation will work best for fairly smooth functions with values given at uniformly distributed points in the plane. If the data points in the input data set are erratic, the default interpolated surface can be erratic.

This default method is a modification of that described by Akima (1978). This method consists of

1. dividing the plane into nonoverlapping triangles using the positions of the available points

2. fitting a bivariate fifth degree polynomial within each triangle

3. calculating the interpolated values by evaluating the polynomial at each grid point that falls in the triangle.

The coefficients for the polynomial are computed based on

□ the values of the function at the vertices of the triangle

□ the estimated values for the first and second derivatives of the function at the vertices.

The estimates of the first and second derivatives are computed using the n nearest neighbors of the point, where n is the number specified in the GRID statement's NEAR= option. A Delauney triangulation (Ripley 1981, p. 38) is used for the default method. The coordinates of the triangles are available in an output data set if requested by the OUTTRI= option in the PROC G3GRID statement.

Spline Interpolation

If the SPLINE option is specified, a method is used that produces an interpolation or smoothing that is optimally smooth in a certain sense (Harder and Desmarais 1972, Meinguet 1979). The surface generated can be thought of as one that would be formed if a stiff, thin metal plate were forced through or near the given data points. For large data sets, this method is substantially more expensive than the default method.

The function **u**, formed when you specify the SPLINE option, is determined as follows. Letting

$$t_j = (x_j, y_j)$$

$$t = (x, y)$$

and

$$|t - t_j| = ((x - x_j)^2 + (y - y_j)^2)^{1/2}$$

$$\mathbf{u}(x, y) = \Sigma_{j=1}^n c_j E(t, t_j) + d_0 + d_1 x + d_2 y$$

where

$$E(s, t) = |s - t| \log(|s - t|) \quad .$$

The coefficients $c_1, c_2, \ldots, c_n$ and d_1, d_2, d_3 of this polynomial are determined by the following equations:

$$(\mathbf{E} + n\lambda\mathbf{I})\,\mathbf{c} + \mathbf{T}\,\mathbf{d} = \mathbf{z}$$

and

$$\mathbf{T}'\,\mathbf{c} = \mathbf{0}$$

where

E	is the $n \times n$ matrix $E(t_i, t_j)$
I	is the $n \times n$ identity matrix
λ	is the smoothing parameter specified in the SMOOTH= option
c	is $(c_1, \ldots, c_n)'$
z	is $(z_1, \ldots, z_n)'$
d	is $(d_1, d_2, d_3)'$
T	is the $n \times 3$ matrix whose ith row is $(1, x_i, y_i)$.

See Wahba (1979) for more detail.

Spline Smoothing

You can use the GRID statement's SMOOTH= option with the SPLINE option to produce a smoothed spline. The value or values specified in the SMOOTH= option are substituted for λ in the equation described in "Spline Interpolation" earlier in this section. A smoothed spline trades closeness to the original data points for smoothness. You might want to try several values for the SMOOTH= option to find a value that produces the best balance between smoothness and fit to the original data.

GRID Statement Examples

The following examples illustrate major features of the GRID statement within the G3GRID procedure. First, however, a scatter plot of the original data set used with the GRID statement is given.

Scatter Plot of Original Random Data

This example draws a scatter plot of the original data used in these examples. It should be compared with the other examples in the chapter that use data sets derived by means of the G3GRID procedure from this original data.

The following program statements produce Output 40.3:

```
/* set the graphics environment */
goptions reset=global gunit=pct border
        ftext=swissb htitle=6 htext=3;

/* create data set NUMS using a set of */
/* randomly sampled points            */
data nums;
   keep x y z;
   do i=1 to 30;
      x=10*ranuni(33)-5;
      y=10*ranuni(35)-5;
      z=sin(sqrt(x*x+y*y));
      output;
   end;
run;

/* define title and footnote for graph */
title 'Scatter Plot of NUMS Data Set';
footnote j=r 'GR40N02   ';

/* show the needle graph */
proc g3d data=nums;
   scatter y*x=z;
run;
```

Output 40.3 *Scatter Plot of Original Data (GR40N02)*

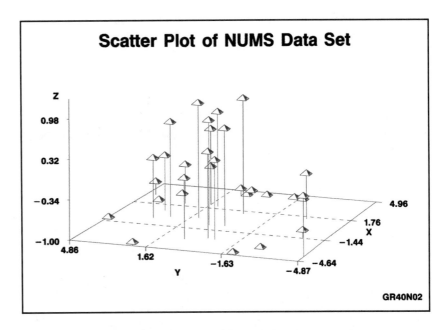

Surface Plot after Default Interpolation

This example demonstrates the default interpolation method used by the GRID statement. The G3D procedure is used to display the data set created by the G3GRID procedure.

The following program statements produce Output 40.4:

```
    /* set the graphics environment */
goptions reset=global gunit=pct border
         ftext=swissb htitle=6 htext=3;

    /* create data set NUMS using a set of */
    /* randomly sampled points            */
data nums;
   keep x y z;
   do i=1 to 30;
      x=10*ranuni(33)-5;
      y=10*ranuni(35)-5;
      z=sin(sqrt(x*x+y*y));
      output;
   end;
run;

    /* process points with PROC G3GRID */
proc g3grid data=nums out=gridnums;
   grid y*x=z
        / axis1=-5 to 5 by .5
          axis2=-5 to 5 by .5;
run;

    /* define title and footnote for graph */
title 'Surface Plot of NUMS Data Set';
footnote j=r 'GR40N03  ';
```

```
/* show the surface graph */
proc g3d data=gridnums;
   plot y*x=z;
run;
```

Output 40.4 *Surface Plot of Data after Default Interpolation (GR40N03)*

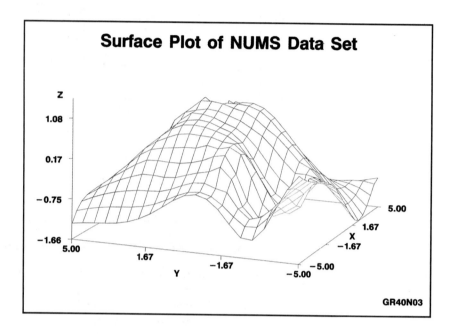

This example illustrates the following features:

□ The GRID statement specifies the variables for the output data set, Y*X=Z.

□ The AXIS1= option lists the values to assign to the first variable, Y.

□ The AXIS2= option lists the values to assign to the second variable, X.

Surface Plot Showing Data after Spline Interpolation

This example demonstrates the spline interpolation method used by the GRID statement. The G3D procedure is used to display the data set created by the G3GRID procedure.

The following program statements produce Output 40.5:

```
/* set the graphics environment */
goptions reset=global gunit=pct border
      ftext=swissb htitle=6 htext=3;

/* create data set NUMS using a set of */
/* randomly sampled points             */
data nums;
   keep x y z;
   do i=1 to 30;
      x=10*ranuni(33)-5;
      y=10*ranuni(35)-5;
      z=sin(sqrt(x*x+y*y));
      output;
   end;
run;
```

```
    /* process points with PROC G3GRID */
proc g3grid data=nums out=gridnums;
   grid y*x=z
        / spline
          axis1=-5 to 5 by .5
          axis2=-5 to 5 by .5;
run;

    /* define title and footnote for graph */
title 'Surface Plot of NUMS Data Set';
footnote j=r 'GR40N04  ';

    /* show the surface graph */
proc g3d data=gridnums;
   plot y*x=z ;
run;
```

Output 40.5 *Surface Plot of Data after Spline Interpolation (GR40N04)*

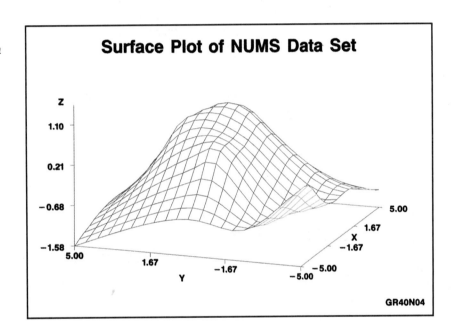

This example illustrates the following feature:

□ The SPLINE option specifies the use of a bivariate spline for the data set interpolation.

Surface Plot of Data after Smoothed Spline Interpolation

This example demonstrates the smoothed spline interpolation method used by the GRID statement. The G3D procedure is used to display the data set created by the G3GRID procedure.

The following program statements produce Output 40.6:

```
    /* set the graphics environment */
goptions reset=global gunit=pct border
         ftext=swissb htitle=6 htext=3;
```

```
    /* create data set NUMS using a set of */
    /* randomly sampled points             */
data nums;
   keep x y z;
   do i=1 to 30;
      x=10*ranuni(33)-5;
      y=10*ranuni(35)-5;
      z=sin(sqrt(x*x+y*y));
      output;
   end;
run;

    /* process points with PROC G3GRID */
proc g3grid data=nums out=gridnums;
   grid y*x=z
        / spline
          smooth=.05
          axis1=-5 to 5 by .5
          axis2=-5 to 5 by .5;
run;

    /* define title and footnote for graph */
title 'Surface Plot of NUMS Data Set';
footnote j=r 'GR40N05  ';

    /* show the surface graph */
proc g3d data=gridnums;
   plot y*x=z;
run;
```

Output 40.6 Surface Plot after Smoothed Spline Estimation (GR40N05)

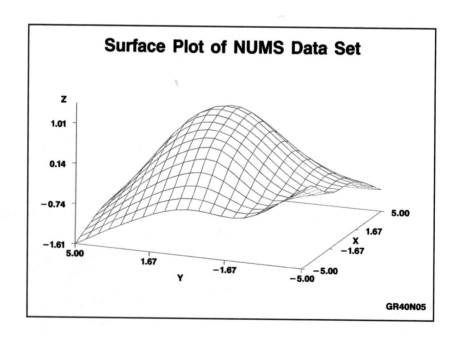

This example illustrates the following feature:

□ The SMOOTH= option specifies a number used for the smoothing parameter during spline interpolation.

Surface Plot of Data after Partial Spline Interpolation

This example demonstrates the partial spline interpolation method used by
the GRID statement. The G3D procedure is used to display the data set
created by the G3GRID procedure.

The following program statements produce Output 40.7:

```
/* set the graphics environment */
goptions reset=global gunit=pct border
         ftext=swissb htitle=6 htext=3;

/* create data set NUMS using a set of */
/* randomly sampled points             */
data nums;
   keep x y z;
   do i=1 to 30;
      x=10*ranuni(33)-5;
      y=10*ranuni(35)-5;
      z=sin(sqrt(x*x+y*y));
      output;
   end;
run;

/* process points with PROC G3GRID */
proc g3grid data=nums out=gridnums;
   grid y*x=z
        / partial
          near=8
          axis1=-5 to 5 by .5
          axis2=-5 to 5 by .5;
run;

/* define title and footnote for graph */
title 'Surface Plot of NUMS Data Set';
footnote j=r 'GR40N06  ';

/* show the surface */
proc g3d data=gridnums;
   plot y*x=z;
run;
```

Output 40.7 *Surface Plot after Partial Spline Interpolation Using Eight Nearest Neighbors (GR40N06)*

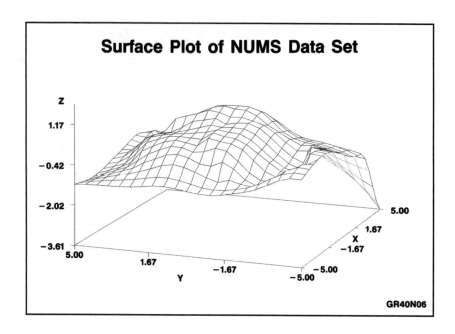

This example illustrates the following features:

□ The PARTIAL option specifies that a spline be used to estimate the derivatives for the biquintic polynomial interpolation.

□ The NEAR= option specifies the number of nearest neighbors to be used for computing the estimates of the first and second derivatives.

Contour Plot of Data after Default Interpolation and Spline Interpolation

This example demonstrates the default and spline interpolation methods used by the GRID statement. The GCONTOUR procedure is used to display the data set created by the G3GRID procedure.

The following program statements produce Output 40.8 and 40.9:

```
    /* set the graphics environment */
goptions reset=global gunit=pct border
         ftext=swissb htitle=6 htext=3;

    /* create data set NUMS using a set of */
    /* randomly sampled points             */
data nums;
   keep x y z;
   do i=1 to 30;
      x=10*ranuni(33)-5;
      y=10*ranuni(35)-5;
      z=sin(sqrt(x*x+y*y));
      output;
   end;
run;

    /* define title and footnote for graph */
title 'Contour Plot of NUMS Data Set';
footnote j=r 'GR40N07(a)  ';
```

```
                        /* define axis characteristics */
                    axis width=3;

                        /* process points with PROC G3GRID */
                    proc g3grid data=nums out=gridnums;
                       grid y*x=z
                            / axis1=-5 to 5 by .5
                              axis2=-5 to 5 by .5;
                    run;

                        /* show the contour after default interpolation */
                    proc gcontour data=gridnums;
                       plot y*x=z / haxis=axis1 vaxis=axis1;
                    run;

                        /* define new footnote for graph */
                    footnote j=r 'GR40N07(b)  ';

                        /* process points with PROC G3GRID */
                    proc g3grid data=nums out=spline;
                       grid y*x=z
                            / spline
                              axis1=-5 to 5 by .5
                              axis2=-5 to 5 by .5;
                    run;

                        /* show the contour after spline interpolation */
                    proc gcontour data=spline;
                       plot y*x=z / haxis=axis1 vaxis=axis1;
                    run;
```

Output 40.8 *Contour Plot after Default Interpolation (GR40N07(a))*

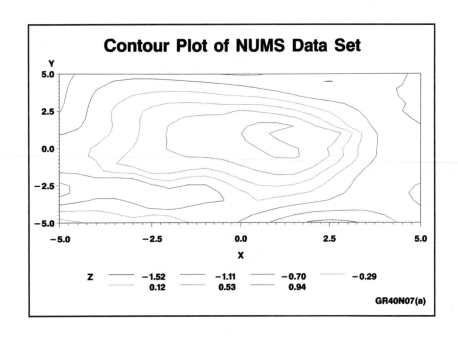

Output 40.9 Contour Plot
after Spline Interpolation
(GR40N07(b))

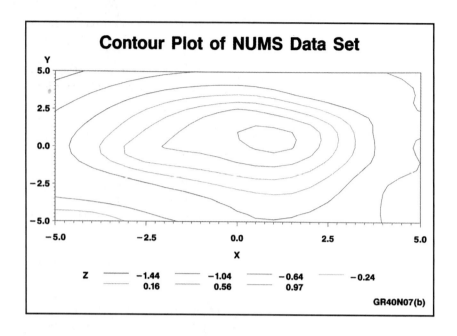

This example illustrates the following features:

□ The AXIS1= option lists the values to assign to the first variable, Y.

□ The AXIS2= option lists the values to assign to the second variable, X.

□ The SPLINE option specifies the use of a bivariate spline for the second
data set interpolation.

See Also

Chapter 10, "The BY Statement"
  for more information on using BY variables

Chapter 24, "The GCONTOUR Procedure"
  for more information on contour plots

Chapter 39, "The G3D Procedure"
  for more information on three-dimensional surface, scatter, and needle
  plots

References

Akima, Hiroshi (1978), "A Method of Bivariate Interpolation and Smooth
  Surface Fitting for Irregularly Distributed Data Points," *ACM
  Transaction on Mathematical Software*, 4, 148–159.

Harder, R.L. and Desmarais, R.N. (1972), "Interpolation Using Surface
  Splines," *Journal of Aircraft*, 9, 189–191.

Meinguet, Jean (1979), "Multivariate Interpolation at Arbitrary Points
  Made Simple," *Journal of Applied Mathematics and Physics*, 30,
  292–304.

Ripley, B.D. (1981), *Spatial Statistics*, New York: John Wiley & Sons, Inc.

Wahba, Grace (1979), "How to Smooth Curves and Surfaces with Splines
  and Cross-validation," in U.S. Army Research Office Report 79–2,
  Proceedings of the 24th Conference on the Design of Experiments.

Glossary

absolute coordinates
coordinates measured from the origin (0,0) of the coordinate system. See also the entry for relative coordinates.

aspect ratio
the ratio of the width of the display to its height. In SAS/GRAPH software, the ASPECT= graphics option simulates a change in the aspect ratio of the display, causing fonts and circles to be compressed horizontally or vertically, or both.

attribute
a characteristic of a graphics element. Examples of an attribute include color, line type, text font, text justification, and fill pattern.

axis
the scale on which the values of the *x*, *y*, or *z* coordinate are represented. In SAS/GRAPH documentation, the term *axis* may also refer collectively to the axis line, the major and minor tick marks, the major tick mark values, and the axis label.

axis area
an area bound by axes; this area may be enclosed by an axis frame. See also the entry for frame.

baseline
in a font, the line upon which the characters rest. See Figure 26.1.

block map
a three-dimensional map that uses blocks of varying heights to indicate the ordinal magnitude of a response variable for a unit area.

border
the line drawn around the entire graphics output area. The area enclosed by a border includes the title and footnote areas as well as the procedure output area. See also the entry for frame.

boundary
in the GMAP procedure, a separating line or point that distinguishes between two or more unit areas or segments.

BY variable
a variable, identified in a BY statement, whose values define groups of observations to be processed.

capline
the highest point of a normal uppercase letter. See Figure 26.1.

catalog
See the entry for SAS catalog.

cell
a unit of measure defined by the number of rows and the number of columns in the graphics output area. See also the entry for aspect ratio.

CGM
See the entry for computer graphics metafile (CGM).

character up vector
> the angle at which a character is positioned. The character up vector has two components, **x** and **y**, which determine the angle. See Figure 21.8.

chart
> a graph in which graphics elements (bars, pie slices, and so on) show the magnitude of a statistic. The graphics elements can represent one value (discrete variables) or a range (continuous variables).

chart statistic
> the statistical value calculated for the chart variable: frequency, cumulative frequency, percentage, cumulative percentage, sum, mean, or any combination of these values.

chart variable
> a variable in the input data set used to categorize the data represented on the chart.

choropleth map
> a two-dimensional map that uses color and fill pattern combinations to represent levels of magnitude or categories.

color, predefined
> one of the set of colors for which SAS/GRAPH software provides predefined names, for example, VIGB, BLUE, and CYAN.

color, user-defined
> a color expressed in RGB, HLS, or gray-scale format. See also the entries for RGB, HLS, and gray scale.

color map
> a table used to translate colors when replaying graphics output using the GREPLAY procedure. The table is contained in a catalog entry.

colors list
> the list of foreground colors available for the graphics output. The colors list is either the default list established from the device entry or the list specified by the COLORS= graphics option and the COLOR= options in other statements. The colors specified in COLOR= options in any statement must be valid for the device.

computer graphics metafile (CGM)
> a graphics output file written according to the ANSI X3.122-1986 standard so that it can be read by different applications programs or used on different machines. SAS/GRAPH software enables you to use CGMs to export graphics output to other software products. SAS/GRAPH software can also import CGMs created by other software products or by SAS/GRAPH software.

confidence limits
> the upper and lower limits of a confidence band for a regression line. That is, there is a percentage of confidence (typically 95%) that the true regression line lies within the band.

contour plot
> a plot that displays curving lines, rectangles, or patterns to represent levels of magnitude (z) corresponding to a location (x,y).

convert
>   to change a SAS file from its original format to a format appropriate to another version of the SAS System under the same operating system. Use the V5TOV6 procedure to convert SAS/GRAPH files from Version 5 to Release 6.06.

coordinate system
>   the context within which to interpret coordinates. In the Annotate facility, coordinate systems vary according to their origin, limits, and units.

coordinates
>   values representing the position of a data point or a graphics element. A point on a graph has a unique location specified by its coordinates: (x, y, z). Each coordinate represents a distance along an axis, which is measured from the origin of the coordinate system.

data area
>   the area in the graphics output area in which data values are positioned. The area can be enclosed by axes (for example, the axes of a plot of two variables), by a map (for example, a map produced with the GMAP procedure), or by a pie chart (for example, a pie chart produced with the GCHART procedure).

density
>   in the GREDUCE procedure, the density determines the number of points, and consequently the amount of detail, in a map.

dependent variable
>   1) a variable whose value depends on the value of another variable or variables. 2) a variable that is a function of one or more independent variables. In a two-dimensional plot, the dependent variable is plotted on the y (vertical) axis. In a three-dimensional plot, the dependent variable is plotted on the z axis.

device-dependent catalog entry
>   a SAS catalog entry that can be replayed only on the device for which it was created. The entry contains graphics output in a device-specific format. See also the entry for device-independent catalog entry.

device driver
>   a set of routines that generate specific commands needed to display a graph on a particular device.

device entry
>   a SAS catalog entry that stores the parameter values that are used with a particular output device.

device-independent catalog entry
>   a SAS catalog entry that can be replayed on any device supported by SAS/GRAPH software. Graphics output is stored in the entry in device-independent format, that is, in a common format not tailored to any specific device.

device map
>   a SAS catalog entry used to translate characters from their SAS/GRAPH internal character encoding to a device-specific encoding for display using the device's hardware character set.

device parameter

a value in a device entry that defines a default behavior of a device driver. Some device parameters can be overridden by graphics options. See also the entry for graphics option.

display

the area of the monitor that displays what the software presents to you.

export

1) to put a SAS data library, a SAS catalog, or a SAS data set into transport format and store it in a SAS transport file. Use the CPORT procedure to export catalogs and data sets, either individually or as a SAS data library. 2) to put a SAS catalog entry containing graphics output into a format that can be moved to another software product. When exporting graphics output to another software product, use a computer graphics metafile (CGM) or another graphics stream file, depending on the requirements of the software.

fill pattern

the pattern (lines, cross-hatching, and so on) or solid color used to fill an area in a graph. A fill pattern with no color or pattern is an empty pattern. See also the entry for pattern type.

font

a complete set of all the characters of the same design and style. In SAS/GRAPH software, size is specified separately. The characters in a font can be figures or symbols as well as alphanumeric characters. See also the entry for type style.

font, hardware

a font stored in an output device. See also the entry for font, software.

font, software

a font in which the characters are drawn by graphics software. See also the entry for font, hardware.

font maximum

the highest vertical coordinate in a font. See Figure 26.1.

font minimum

the lowest vertical coordinate in a font. See Figure 26.1.

font units

units defined by the range of coordinates specified in the font data set. For example, a font in which the vertical coordinates range from 10 to 100 has 90 font units.

frame

1) in the GSLIDE procedure, the line drawn around the procedure output area. 2) in other procedures, a line that encloses the axis area. 3) in a legend, a line enclosing the entire legend. See also the entry for border.

function

1) a SAS function, that is, a routine that returns a value resulting from zero or more arguments. 2) a mathematical relationship between independent and dependent variables that assigns exactly one value of the dependent variable to each combination of independent variables.

graph
> 1) a visual representation of data showing the variation of a variable in comparison to one or more other variables. 2) graphics output.

graphics device
> any terminal, printer, or other output device capable of displaying or producing a hardcopy of graphics output.

graphics element
> a visual element of a picture. For example, a bar is a graphics element that can be used to construct a graph.

graphics option
> a value specified in a GOPTIONS statement that controls some attribute of the graphics output. The values specified remain in effect only for the duration of the SAS session. Some graphics options override device parameters.

graphics output
> output from a graphics program. It can be stored, displayed, or printed. Device-dependent output can be sent directly to a device. Device-independent output must be processed by a device driver before being sent to a graphics device.

graphics output area
> the area where a picture is drawn. Typically, the full drawing area of the device is used, but you can control the dimensions of the drawing area with graphics options or device parameters.

graphics primitive
> a function that draws a graphics element.

graphics stream file (GSF)
> a file containing device-dependent graphics commands from a SAS/GRAPH device driver. This file can be sent to a graphics device or to other software packages.

gray scale
> a color-coding scheme that specifies a color in terms of gray components. Gray-scale color codes are commonly used on some laser printers and PostScript devices.

grid request
> the request specified in a GRID statement in the G3GRID procedure that identifies the horizontal variables that identify the x-y plane and one or more z variables for the interpolation.

group variable
> a variable in the input data set used to categorize chart variable values into groups that are separately represented on the graph.

GSF
> See the entry for graphics stream file (GSF).

HLS
> a color-coding scheme that specifies a color in terms of its hue, lightness, and saturation components. See also the entry for RGB.

import

1) to restore a SAS transport file to its original form (a SAS data library, a SAS catalog, or a SAS data set) in the format appropriate to the host operating system. Use the CIMPORT procedure to import a SAS transport file created by the CPORT procedure. 2) to read a computer graphics metafile (CGM) and store the graphics output in a SAS catalog. Use the GIMPORT procedure to import the CGM.

independent variable

a variable that does not depend on the value of another variable; in a two-dimensional plot, the independent variable is usually plotted on the x (horizontal) axis.

interpolate

to estimate values between two or more known values.

justify

to position text in relation to the left or right margin or the center of the line. Text that is left- or right-justified is positioned so that all lines start at the left margin or end at the right margin, respectively. Text that is center-justified is positioned so that the middle of each line of text is halfway between the left and right margins.

key map

a SAS catalog entry used to translate the values generated by the keyboard to their corresponding SAS/GRAPH internal character encoding.

label

1) the text that names the variable associated with an axis, a legend, or a bubble in a bubble plot. By default, this text is the name of a variable or of a label previously assigned with a LABEL statement. The text of a label also can be specified with the LABEL= option. 2) in pie and star charts, the midpoint value and the value of the chart statistic for a slice or spine. 3) in the Annotate facility, the text displayed by the LABEL function or macro.

latitude

the angular measure between the equator and the circle of parallel on which a point lies.

legend

a visual key to graphic elements in a graph. For example, different areas of a map may be keyed by color, or the plots of two variables may be keyed by the symbols used to mark the data points or the fill patterns in areas. In SAS/GRAPH software, the term *legend* may refer collectively to the legend value, the legend value description, the legend label, and the legend frame. See Figure 13.1.

longitude

the angular measure between the reference meridian and the plane intersecting both poles and a point. The reference meridian, called the prime meridian, is assigned a longitude of zero and other longitude values are measured from there in appropriate angular units (degrees or radians, for example).

major tick mark

    a primary element on the scale of an axis. In SAS/GRAPH software, major tick mark locations are chosen automatically but can be specified explicitly. The value displayed at each major tick mark can be explicitly assigned or suppressed. See also the entry for minor tick mark.

map

    a graphic representation of an area, often a geographic area, but also any other area of any size.

meridian

    an imaginary circle of constant longitude around the surface of the Earth perpendicular to the equator. See also the entry for parallel.

midpoint

    a value that identifies categories of chart variable data represented on a graph. A midpoint value represents a range of values or a single value.

minor tick mark

    a tick mark between major tick marks. Minor tick marks do not display values. The number of minor tick marks displayed is determined either by default by the procedure or explicitly with options. See also the entry for major tick mark.

needle plot

    1) in the G3D procedure, a plot that displays a symbol at each data point that is connected by a line to the x-y plane. 2) in the GPLOT procedure, a plot in which a vertical line connects each data point to a horizontal line drawn at 0 on the vertical axis.

offset

    1) on an axis, the distance from the axis origin to the first major tick mark or to the middle of the first bar, or the distance from the last major tick mark or from the middle of the last bar to the end of the axis line. 2) in a legend, the distance between the edge of the legend or legend frame and the axis frame or the border surrounding the graphics output area.

origin

    1) in a coordinate system, the location of (0,0). 2) the intersection of coordinate axes. 3) in the AXIS statement, the point at which the axis line begins (the left end of the horizontal axis or the bottom of the vertical axis). 4) in the LEGEND statement, the location of the lower-left corner of the legend.

palette

    the set of all color selections possible on a graphics device. See also the entry for colors list.

panel

    in the GREPLAY procedure, a part of the template in which one or more pictures can be displayed. A template can contain one or more panels.

parallel

    an imaginary circle of constant latitude around the surface of the Earth parallel to the equator. See also the entry for meridian.

pattern type

the set of fill patterns that are valid for a particular type of graph. The PATTERN statement supports three pattern types: bar and block patterns, map and plot patterns, and pie and star patterns. See also the entry for fill pattern.

pen mounts

on a pen plotter, the holders for the drawing pens.

picture

graphics output that is visible, for example, displayed, printed, or plotted.

pie chart

a chart made up of a circle divided by radial lines, used to display the relative contribution of each part to the whole. Each value is shown as a solid segment of arc, or pie slice.

plot

a graph consisting of data points placed by coordinates. Each coordinate represents the value of a variable. See also the entry for coordinates.

plot line

the line joining the data points in a plot.

polygon

a closed figure bounded by lines.

polygon font

a font in which the characters are drawn with polygons. The enclosed area can be filled or empty. See Figure 26.3. See also the entry for stroked font.

prism map

a three-dimensional map that uses prisms (polyhedrons with two parallel surfaces) of varying height to indicate the ordinal magnitude of a response variable.

procedure output area

the portion of the graphics output area remaining after the title and footnote areas are allocated. Legends can also reduce the size of the procedure output area.

projection

a two-dimensional map representation of unit areas on the surface of a sphere, for example, geographic regions on the surface of the Earth.

RGB

a color-coding scheme that specifies a color in terms of its red, green, and blue components. See also the entry for HLS.

regression analysis

an analysis of the relationship between two variables, expressed as a mathematical function. On a scatter plot, this relationship is diagrammed as a line drawn through data points, either a straight line (simple regression) or a curve (higher-order regression).

relative coordinates
>coordinates measured from a point other than the origin, usually from the endpoint of the last object drawn. See also the entry for absolute coordinates.

replay
>to display graphics output that has been stored in a catalog entry.

response variable
>in the GMAP procedure, a SAS data set variable containing a value to be represented in conjunction with a map unit area (for example by filling the area with a particular pattern or by drawing a block of representative height in the area).

SAS catalog
>a SAS file that is a member of a SAS data library and that stores many different kinds of information in smaller units called catalog entries. SAS/GRAPH software uses device, template, font, color map, key map, and device map entries, as well as entries that contain graphics output.

SAS transport file
>a sequential file containing a SAS data library, a SAS catalog, or a SAS data set in transport format. The transport format written by the CPORT procedure is the same for all operating systems and many releases of the SAS System. Thus, the CIMPORT procedure in Release 6.06 running under any operating system can read a transport file created by the CPORT procedure in Release 6.06 under any operating system.
>
>Only PROC CIMPORT can read a transport file created by PROC CPORT. PROC CIMPORT can read only transport files created by PROC CPORT.

■ **Host Information** . . . .
>On some operating systems, a transport file must have special characteristics. See your operating system specific documentation for details.
>
>. . . . . ■

scatter plot
>a two- or three-dimensional plot that displays a symbol at each data point.

segment
>1) in the GMAP procedure, a polygon that is a part of a unit area consisting of more than one polygon. For example, consider a map of Hawaii; the representation of the single unit area (the state) consists of a group of individual segments (the islands), each of which is a separate polygon. 2) in the GFONT procedure, a single continuous line that forms part or all of a character or symbol. 3) a collection of graphics primitives that can be manipulated as a unit.

spine
>a line in a star chart used to represent the relative value of the chart statistic for a midpoint. Spines are drawn outward from the center of the chart.

spline
: a method of interpolation in which a smooth line or surface connects data points.

standard deviation
: a statistical measure of the variability of data values, calculated as the positive square root of the variance.

string
: a sequence of alphanumeric characters.

stroked font
: a font in which the characters are drawn with discrete line segments or circular arcs. See Figure 26.2. See also the entry for polygon font.

subgroup variable
: the variable in the input data set for a chart that is used to create segments of the bars on the chart.

surface map
: a three-dimensional map that uses spikes of varying heights to indicate levels of magnitude.

surface plot
: a plot that displays a fishnet-like surface formed by the values of the plot's response (z) variables.

template
: in the GREPLAY procedure, a framework that enables you to display one or more pictures on a page.

text string
: See the entry for string.

transformation
: in the DATA Step Graphics Interface (DSGI), a mapping of the window coordinates to the viewport coordinates.

type style
: a typeface design and its variations, for example, Swiss, Swiss Bold, and Swiss Italic. See also the entry for font.

unit area
: a polygon or group of polygons on a map, for example, a state, province, or country. In a map data set, a unit area consists of all the observations with the same values for the unit area identification variables. (The ID statement specifies which variable or variables in the map data set are unit area identification variables.)

value
: 1) on an axis, the text that labels a major tick mark. 2) in a legend, the lines, bars, and shapes that the legend explains. 3) the value of a variable.

viewport
: in the DATA Step Graphics Interface (DSGI), a section of the display into which you place graphics elements or graphics output.

window
> 1) a sizable, movable object on the display in which a user interacts with a program. 2) in the DATA Step Graphics Interface (DSGI), a coordinate system that is used with a viewport and that can be defined by the user.

Index

A

P

PATTERN window (*continued*)
  canceling changes 384
  clearing definitions 383
  closing 384
  commands 381–382
  defining 35
  description 381
  Information window 382–383
  locating definitions 383
  opening 383
  saving definitions 384
  using 383–384
PATTERNID= option
  BLOCK statement (GCHART) 773–774
  effect on block patterns (GCHART) 778
  example in BLOCK statement (GCHART) 780
  example in HBAR statement (GCHART) 801
  example with AXIS definitions 255
  examples in VBAR statement (GCHART) 862, 864
  HBAR statement (GCHART) 792
  overriding LEGEND= option (GCHART) 771, 789, 849
  selecting patterns for bars 386
  selecting patterns for bars (GCHART) 799, 859–860
  suppressing subgroup legends (GCHART) 774, 794, 798, 854, 858
  VBAR statement (GCHART) 852
  with LEGEND definitions, in GCHART procedure 337
PCOLS device parameter 132
  See also LCOLS device parameter
  See also PROWS device parameter
  See also ROTATE device parameter
  adjusting graphics output size 1137
  changing aspect ratio of cells 1139
  effect on graphics output 1137
  effect on software fonts 1139
  overridden by HPOS= graphics option 123–124, 127, 132
  setting number of columns 1137
pen plotters
  See also FILLINC= graphics option
  See also PAPERFEED= graphics option
  See also PAPERLIMIT= graphics option
  See also PENMOUNTS= graphics option
  See also REPAINT= graphics option
  controlling aspect ratio 86–87
  controlling plotting speed 144
PENMOUNTS= graphics option 132
  overriding of MAXCOLORS device parameter 132
  specifying number of pen holders 196
PERCENT option
  HBAR statement (GCHART) 792
  overridden by CFREQ option (GCHART) 852
  overridden by FREQ option (GCHART) 848, 852
  overriding MEAN option (GCHART) 850
  overriding SUM option (GCHART) 854
  VBAR statement (GCHART) 852
PERCENT= option
  example in PIE statement (GCHART) 822
  PIE statement (GCHART) 816
  STAR statement (GCHART) 833
percentage statistic
  calculating with FREQ= option (GCHART) 788, 813–814, 830, 831, 848, 855
  calculating with the G100 option 788
  GCHART procedure 764

PICTURE= option
  PROC GTESTIT statement 1270
pie and star patterns
  See also PATTERN statement
  See also VALUE= option
  default fill patterns 380
  illustrations 367, 381
  used with Annotate facility 386
  used with GCHART procedure 379, 386–387
pie charts
  example of exploded pie chart (DSGI) 601
  example with Annotate facility 501
  examples 395, 755
  patterns for 379–381
PIE function, Annotate facility
  example with custom pie chart 503
  patterns used with 386
  syntax and description 552–553
  variables with 553–555
PIE operator, GDRAW function
  attributes used with 615
  syntax and description 694–695
PIE statement, GCHART procedure 809–827
  BY-group processing 264
  chart variable and midpoint values 817–818
  description 809
  example with PATTERN statement 394
  examples 821–827
  group variable and pie groups 818
  labels and headings 818–819
  options 811–817
  patterns for pie charts 819
  requirements 811
  slice labeling options 819–821
  syntax 809–811
  using 817–821
PIECNTR function, Annotate facility
  syntax and description 556
  variables with 556–557
PIEFILL device parameter 133
PIEFILL graphics option 133
PIEXY function, Annotate facility
  example with pie chart 503
  syntax and description 557–558
  variables with 558–559
PIEXY macro, Annotate facility
  syntax and description 577–578
PLACEMENT command
  AXIS window 234
  LEGEND window 320
Placement window
  AXIS window 236–237
  LEGEND window 322–323
PLOT statement, GCONTOUR procedure
  appearance characteristics 882
  axis order selection 881
  contour level selection 879–880
  examples 883–887
  global statements with 882
  options 874–878
  overview 872
  requirements 874
  syntax 872–874
  using 879–882

U

UCC device parameter 149
ULX= option
  TDEF statement (GREPLAY) 1219
ULY= option
  TDEF statement (GREPLAY) 1219
UNDERLIN= option
  example in FOOTNOTE statement 288
  examples in TITLE statement 459, 461
  FOOTNOTE statement 282–283
  NOTE statement 358
  reset by other options 283, 285, 358, 360, 453, 455
  TITLE statement 453
uniform fonts
  definition 937
  dependent on regular fonts 167
  effect of MWIDTH= option 947
  specifying with CHARSPACETYPE= option 946
  specifying with UNIFORM option 949
UNIFORM option
  See also CHARSPACETYPE= option
  See also MWIDTH= option
  PROC GFONT statement 949
  PROC GPLOT statement 1082–1083
units of measurement
  See GUNIT= graphics option
UP command
  GDEVICE procedure windows 909
  GRAPH windows 55
  GREPLAY procedure windows 1234
UPDATE operator, GRAPH function
  changing operating states 616
  closing graphic segments 613
  example with DSGI 631
  syntax and description 699
URX= option
  TDEF statement (GREPLAY) 1219
URY= option
  TDEF statement (GREPLAY) 1219
user-defined colors
  devices not supporting 194
  devices supporting 194–195
user-generated fonts
  See also fonts
  See also GFONT procedure
  See also software fonts
  displaying 933, 938
  libref GFONT0 required 940
  specifying 938

V

VALUE command
  AXIS window 234
  LEGEND window 320
VALUE= option
  AXIS statement 227–228
  AXIS window 241, 243, 245
  bar and block patterns 376–377
  compared to ORDER= option (AXIS) 227
  default fill patterns for bars and blocks 377
  default fill patterns for maps and plots 378

default fill patterns for pie and star slices 380
effect of invalid values (PATTERN) 384
effect on pattern sequences 370–373
example in LEGEND statement 340
example in STAR statement (GCHART) 842
example with plot (GPLOT) 1117
examples in AXIS statement 256, 258
examples in PATTERN statement 390, 391, 393, 395
examples in PIE statement (GCHART) 822, 824
examples in SYMBOL statement 431, 435, 437, 440
LEGEND statement 313–314
LEGEND window 329, 331
map and plot patterns 377–379
modifying major tick mark values (AXIS) 219–220
omitting, effect of (PATTERN) 384
overriding of CTEXT= option (GCHART) 847
PATTERN statement 376–381
PATTERN window 383
pie and star patterns 379–381
PIE statement (GCHART) 817
positioning pie slice labels (GCHART) 818–819
positioning star labels (GCHART) 837
special symbol table 421
specifying plot symbols 427
STAR statement (GCHART) 834
SYMBOL statement 420–422
SYMBOL window 424
text description parameters with 228–231, 314–318
valid values with GCHART procedure 376
valid values with GCONTOUR procedure 377–378
valid values with GMAP procedure 376, 377–378
valid values with GPLOT procedure 377–378
with COUTLINE= option (GCONTOUR) 875
with FONT= option (SYMBOL) 409–410, 420–422, 427
with GCHART procedure 249
Value window
  AXIS window 241–243
  LEGEND window 327–329
values for chart variables
  See chart variables
VAXIS= option
  BUBBLE statement (GPLOT) 1089
  BUBBLE2 statement (GPLOT) 1094
  effect on INTERPOL= option (SYMBOL) 411, 412, 417
  effect on MODE= option (SYMBOL) 419
  example in BUBBLE statement (GPLOT) 1092
  example in BUBBLE2 statement (GPLOT) 1099
  example in PLOT statement (GCONTOUR) 884
  example in PLOT2 statement (GPLOT) 1129
  examples in PLOT statement (GPLOT) 1114, 1115, 1119
  examples with AXIS definitions 251, 253, 257
  PLOT statement (GCONTOUR) 878
  PLOT statement (GPLOT) 1107
  PLOT2 statement (GPLOT) 1121
  preventing clipping in bubble plots (GPLOT) 1090
  specifying values for right vertical axis (GPLOT) 1095
  with AXIS definitions, in GCONTOUR procedure 249
  with AXIS definitions, in GPLOT procedure 249
VBAR statement, GCHART procedure 842–865
  BY-group processing 264
  chart statistics and response axes 857
  chart variables and midpoint axes 856
  description 842
  displaying statistics 858–859

W

WFRAME= option
  drawing frames 1264
  example in PROC GSLIDE statement 1266
  overriding FRAME option 1263, 1264
  PROC GSLIDE statement 1264
WHEN variable, Annotate facility
  BAR function 539
  controlling processing of observations 493–494
  DRAW function 543
  DRAW2TXT function 545
  example with LABEL function 498
  example with POLY function 493
  FRAME function 546
  LABEL function 550
  MOVE function 552
  overlaying of Annotate graphics elements 493–494
  PIE function 555
  PIECNTR function 557
  PIEXY function 558
  POINT function 560
  POLY function 562
  POLYCONT function 564
  SYMBOL function 569
  syntax and description 528
WHERE= data set option
  example with reduced map (GREDUCE) 1180
  with map data sets 1060
  with map data sets (GREDUCE) 1177
WHERE statement
  effect on RUN-group processing 40
  restricting range of chart variables (GCHART) 763
  with map data sets 1060
width of display area
  See XMAX device parameter
  See XPIXELS device parameter
width of graphics output area
  See VSIZE= graphics option
  See XMAX device parameter
WIDTH= option
  See also WIDTH= tick mark description parameter
  AXIS statement 228
  AXIS window 235
  changes and enhancements xlvii
  displaying statistics (GCHART) 858–859
  example in VBAR statement (GCHART) 864
  examples in AXIS statement 251, 253
  examples in SYMBOL statement 431, 437
  HBAR statement (GCHART) 795
  SYMBOL statement 422
  SYMBOL window 425
  VBAR statement (GCHART) 855
WIDTH= tick mark description parameter
  See also WIDTH= option
  AXIS statement 232
  AXIS window 238, 239
  example in AXIS statement 253
window commands
  See commands
WINDOW operator, GASK routine
  syntax and description 684

WINDOW operator, GSET function
  defining windows 624–625
  example of enlarging area of graphs 642
  example of scaling graphs using windows 639
  example with viewport 636
  syntax and description 733
windows
  See names of specific windows
windows, DSGI
  See viewports and windows, DSGI
WORK.GSEG default catalog 30
WORK libref 32
WSAC operating state, DSGI 606
WSACTIVE operator, GASK routine
  syntax and description 685
WSOP operating state, DSGI 606
WSOPEN operator, GASK routine
  syntax and description 685

X

X= argument
  SCALE statement (GIMPORT) 979
  TRANSLATE statement (GIMPORT) 979
X variable, Annotate facility
  BAR function 539
  DRAW function 543
  effect of XSYS variable 475
  example with DRAW function 483
  example with LABEL function 482
  example with MOVE function 483
  LABEL function 550
  MOVE function 552
  PIE function 555
  PIECNTR function 557
  POINT function 560
  POLY function 562
  POLYCONT function 564
  specifying coordinates 475
  SYMBOL function 569
  syntax and description 529
X variable, GFONT procedure
  example 961
  font data set 950, 956
XADJ variable, GFONT procedure
  example 966
  kern data set 957
XC variable, Annotate facility
  BAR function 539
  DRAW function 543
  effect of XSYS variable 475
  LABEL function 550
  MOVE function 552
  PIE function 555
  PIECNTR function 557
  POINT function 560
  POLY function 562
  POLYCONT function 564
  specifying coordinates 475
  SYMBOL function 569
  syntax and description 529–530

Z

our Turn

n you spare five minutes? We want to know what you think about
S/GRAPH Software: Reference, Version 6, First Edition, Volume 1 and
lume 2. Because we are constantly revising the documentation, we would
e your comments on how to improve it. Please respond to the questions
low by filling in the blanks or checking (✔) the boxes (as many as are
eded to answer each question). We also welcome comments on additional
ges; just fold them inside of this postage-paid form and mail them to
S Institute.

ho Are You?

. Which of the categories below best describe your industry?
- ☐ academic
- ☐ communications
- ☐ computers (hardware/software)
- ☐ finance/banking
- ☐ government
- ☐ health care
- ☐ insurance
- ☐ manufacturing
- ☐ pharmaceutical
- ☐ utilities
- ☐ other: _____

. Which of the categories below best describe your job?
- ☐ computer programmer
- ☐ computer user, but not a programmer
- ☐ supervisor/manager
- ☐ student
- ☐ other: _____

. How long have you been using SAS/GRAPH software?
- ☐ fewer than six months
- ☐ six months to one year
- ☐ one to three years
- ☐ three or more years

. What is your level of expertise with SAS/GRAPH software?
(circle the number that applies)

Beginner		Intermediate User		Expert
1	2	3	4	5

. List the SAS software you have used other than SAS/GRAPH software
(for example, base SAS, SAS/AF, SAS/FSP, and so on). If you have not
used any other SAS software, write "None." _____

6. How long have you used other SAS software products (not including
SAS/GRAPH software)?
- ☐ no previous use
- ☐ fewer than six months
- ☐ six months to one year
- ☐ one to three years
- ☐ three or more years

7. How long have you used software *other* than SAS software?
- ☐ no previous use
- ☐ fewer than six months
- ☐ six months to one year
- ☐ one to three years
- ☐ three or more years

What Kind of Computer System Do You Have?

1. Under what operating system(s) are you running SAS/GRAPH
software?

_____

2. Which method(s) do you use to run SAS/GRAPH software?
- ☐ batch mode
- ☐ SAS Display Manager System
- ☐ interactive line mode
- ☐ noninteractive line mode

3. What kind of graphics output device(s) do you have available?
- ☐ graphics terminal
- ☐ plotter
- ☐ none
- ☐ printer
- ☐ camera
- ☐ other(s): _____

How and When Do You Use This Manual?

1. Approximately what percentage of your work time is spent using
SAS/GRAPH software?
- ☐ 1–10%
- ☐ 11–25%
- ☐ 26–50%
- ☐ 51–75%
- ☐ 76–100%

2. Number the following steps in the order you take them when you need
to learn something about SAS/GRAPH software.
- ____ use this manual
- ____ ask an experienced user
- ____ take an Institute training course
- ____ other: _____
- ____ use the SAS help facility
- ____ call the Institute's Technical Support Division
- ____ call your local SAS Software Consultant

3. When you use this manual, what is your preferred method for
finding the information you are looking for?
- ☐ using the table of contents
- ☐ using the index
- ☐ using the list of illustrations
- ☐ thumbing through the manual

4. Which of the chapters below have you read?
- ☐ "Changes and Enhancements"
- ☐ "Using This Book"
- ☐ 1, "Introduction to SAS/GRAPH Software"
- ☐ 2, "Running SAS/GRAPH Programs"

5. How did you acquire this copy of *SAS/GRAPH Software: Reference*?
- ☐ you bought it personally
- ☐ your company owns it, but this is your personal copy
- ☐ your company owns it, and you share it with several people
- ☐ this is your company's only copy
- ☐ you borrowed it
- ☐ other: _____

How Easy Is This Manual To Use?

1. List the chapters that were especially useful to you:

_____ _____ _____

_____ _____ _____

2. List the chapters that gave you too little information:

_____ _____ _____

_____ _____ _____

3. List key information that you think was missing:

_____

4. List topics that you had trouble finding:

_____

_____

5. List topics that you found confusing:

_____

_____

6. a. Did you find the examples in this book helpful?
- ☐ they helped you use SAS/GRAPH software in your job
- ☐ they were not relevant to your use of SAS/GRAPH software

b. If they were not relevant, what types of examples do you need?

_____

_____

7. List any chapters that need more examples:

——————————— ——————————— ———————————

——————————— ——————————— ———————————

8. Other comments:

——————————————————————————————————————

——————————————————————————————————————

How Easy Is SAS/GRAPH Software to Use?

1. List the areas of SAS/GRAPH software that you had particular difficulty in using or understanding:

——————————— ——————————— ———————————

——————————— ——————————— ———————————

2. How often did this manual help you solve these difficulties?

☐ always ☐ rarely
☐ often ☐ never
☐ occasionally ☐ did not consult the manual

Thank you for your time and effort. If you or your company would like copy of the *Publications Catalog*, which lists available documentation from SAS Institute, please enter the following information:

Name ——————————————————— Date ——————

Organization ——————————————————————————

Telephone ——————————————————————————

Address ——————————————————————————

City ——————————— State ——— ZIP Code ————

FOLD THIS PORTION BACK FIRST
